'In this collection of essays, suggestively titled *Becoming Marxist*, Ted Stolze gives us a privileged view of the development of the conceptual machine of his philosophy, above all, around the virtuous circle of Marx-Spinoza, but also, at the same time, in relation to the gesture that most clearly characterizes his originality in the panorama of contemporary critical thought, which consists in thinking one into the other, and together, Deleuze, Negri and Althusser.'
—*Vittorio Morfino, Senior Researcher in the History of Philosophy at the University of Milan-Bicocca*

'Ted Stolze's *Becoming Marxist* reveals at its core not only that Becoming Marxist is an ongoing process of transformation, a continual process of engaging with the conjunctures of history and philosophy – but that it is inseparable from other becomings that are both theoretical and political. In terms of the former, Stolze's book engages with the thought of Deleuze, Spinoza, Negri, and Habermas, situating itself with respect to the major philosophical debates within Marxism, but it is with respect to the latter that Stolze's book stands out. The book engages with some of the major practical challenges to Marxist politics, climate change and religious conflict and intolerance. The book is exemplary in its militant commitment to theoretical rigor and practical engagement, demonstrating that Marxism is less a totalizing theory than a continuing process of militant transformation.'
—*Jason Read, Associate Professor of Philosophy, University of Southern Maine*

'From Spinoza to Althusser and Deleuze with Paul of Tarsus as a constant interlocutor, Ted Stolze retraces the "underground current" of materialism as a philosophical tendency, offering invaluable insights on the political significance of materialist philosophical interventions and reminding us of the many associations of materialism with resistance and the struggle for social justice and human emancipation.'
—*Panagiotis Sotiris, writer and activist in Greece*

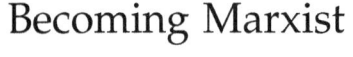

Historical Materialism Book Series

The Historical Materialism Book Series is a major publishing initiative of the radical left. The capitalist crisis of the twenty-first century has been met by a resurgence of interest in critical Marxist theory. At the same time, the publishing institutions committed to Marxism have contracted markedly since the high point of the 1970s. The Historical Materialism Book Series is dedicated to addressing this situation by making available important works of Marxist theory. The aim of the series is to publish important theoretical contributions as the basis for vigorous intellectual debate and exchange on the left.

The peer-reviewed series publishes original monographs, translated texts, and reprints of classics across the bounds of academic disciplinary agendas and across the divisions of the left. The series is particularly concerned to encourage the internationalization of Marxist debate and aims to translate significant studies from beyond the English-speaking world.

For a full list of titles in the Historical Materialism Book Series available in paperback from Haymarket Books, visit:
https://www.haymarketbooks.org/series_collections/1-historical-materialism

Becoming Marxist

*Studies in Philosophy,
Struggle, and Endurance*

Ted Stolze

Haymarket Books
Chicago, IL

First published in 2018 by Brill Academic Publishers, The Netherlands
© 2018 Koninklijke Brill NV, Leiden, The Netherlands

Published in paperback in 2020 by
Haymarket Books
P.O. Box 180165
Chicago, IL 60618
773-583-7884
www.haymarketbooks.org

ISBN: 978-1-64259-189-7

Distributed to the trade in the US through Consortium Book Sales and Distribution (www.cbsd.com) and internationally through Ingram Publisher Services International (www.ingramcontent.com).

This book was published with the generous support of Lannan Foundation and Wallace Action Fund.

Special discounts are available for bulk purchases by organizations and institutions. Please call 773-583-7884 or email info@haymarketbooks.org for more information.

Cover design by Jamie Kerry and Ragina Johnson.

Printed in the United States.

10 9 8 7 6 5 4 3 2 1

Library of Congress Cataloging-in-Publication data is available.

In memory of my father, mother, and brother

Nightmare, nightmare, struggle, despair and dream ...
– THOMAS MCGRATH, *Letter to an Imaginary Friend*

Contents

Preface XI
Acknowledgements XV
Abbreviations XX

PART 1
Marxism and the History of Philosophy

1 What is a Philosophical Tendency? 3

2 Paul of Tarsus, Thinker of the Conjuncture 36

3 Paul's Gift Economy: Wages, Debt, and Debt Cancellation 60

4 Althusser and the Problem of Historical Individuality 75

5 'The Roaring of the Sea': Hobbes on the Madness of the Multitude 93

6 Spinoza's Three Modes of Rebellion: Indignant, Glorious, and Serene 112

7 Alexandre Matheron on Militant Reason and the Intellectual Love of God 139

Interlude. An Ethics for Marxism: Spinoza on Fortitude 153

PART 2
Marxism and Contemporary Philosophy

8 Death and Life in Marx's *Capital*: an Ethical Investigation 177

9 Hegel or Spinoza: Substance, Subject, and Critical Marxism 187

10 Contradictions of Hyperreality: Baudrillard, Žižek, and Virtual Dialectics 199

11 A Marxist Encounter with the Philosophy of Gilles Deleuze   211

12 Deleuze and Althusser: Flirting with Structuralism   221

13 Marxist Wisdom: Antonio Negri on the Book of Job   235

14 A Displaced Transition: Habermas on the Public Sphere   248

PART 3
Self-Emancipation, Then and Now

15 Self-Emancipation and Political Marxism   263

16 Islamophobia and Self-Emancipation   293

17 Climate Crisis, Ideology, and Collective Action   304

Coda. Beatitude: Marx, Aristotle, Averroes, Spinoza   322

Bibliography   353
Index   400

Preface

The question explored in this book of 'becoming Marxist' has little to do with how Karl Marx himself 'became a Marxist' – although this is doubtless an important biographical and historical question.[1] Rather, herein lies a *philosophical* question: how to do philosophy as a Marxist and, at the same time, keep this emancipatory tradition alive by borrowing concepts that arise outside of Marxism itself. How to 'become Marxist' is a question that I have personally pondered ever since I encountered the writings of Gilles Deleuze in the 1980s. In 1991 I sent Deleuze a copy of my first serious publication, 'A Marxist Encounter with the Philosophy of Gilles Deleuze', and he kindly replied with a brief note (which I have transcribed from the following page):[2]

Cher Ted Stolze,

Merci de m'avoir envoyé votre texte. Je l'ai trouvé trés interessant, allant à l'éssentiel, donnant toute sa porteé au theme du dévenir. Je suis comme vous, et je me suis jamais senti autant 'marxiste' que dans le triomphe actuel du capitalisme – triomphe, il est vrai, fondé sur la froid exclusion de ¾ de l'humanité.

Bien à vous,

Gilles Deleuze

---

1 The unsurpassed account of Marx's intellectual and political development remains Hal Draper's multivolume series (Draper 1977–1990). Although Marx famously rejected the appellation 'Marxist', his point was to insist on the open-ended, non-dogmatic nature of his analysis of capitalism, not to reject the analysis itself.
2 'Thank you for having sent me your text. I have found it very interesting, going to the essential, giving all its stress to the theme of becoming. I am like you, and I have never sensed myself as much 'marxist' as in the current triumph of capitalism – a triumph, it is true, based on the cold exclusion of ¾ of humanity'.

I had once hoped to write a book devoted exclusively to Deleuze and Marx, and bearing the title *Becoming Marxist*. However, I have not worked on Deleuze's philosophy for many years. This has been largely because after my dissertation proposal in the mid-nineties on Deleuze and Guattari's theory of desire was rejected, I turned instead to reading Spinoza in earnest. So this is not the book I had hoped to write, but its title indicates my continued love for Deleuze's philosophy. It has especially been through, and because of, *Anti-Oedipus*,[3] Deleuze's great work with Félix Guattari, that I became interested in the potent combination of Spinoza and Marx – but not only of Spinoza and Marx. Through its

---

3   Deleuze and Guattari 2009, which was originally published in French as Deleuze and Guattari 1972.

PREFACE   XIII

proliferation of references to authors and texts I had not yet read, *Anti-Oedipus* became a kind of militant philosophical manual to me for many years to come.

I should say a word about the essays comprising this collection. Because they reflect the peculiarities and 'aberrant movements'[4] of my political and philosophical development over the last thirty years, I have resisted the temptation to add much to them (especially the two early pieces on Deleuze). Rather, I have altered them primarily by embroidering along their edges and by updating bibliographical references.

If these studies have a common theme, or guiding thread, it is the question of how to persist, how to keep faith as a critically engaged Marxist through hard economic, political, and intellectual times. What haunts this book is an image of philosophers as mediators between the pursuit of general claims regarding the nature of reality and the concrete needs of humanity and other species on our planet during this historical conjuncture.[5] Another way of putting this would be to add a seventh 'type' of philosopher to Justin Smith's recent sixfold classification[6] of the 'curiosa', or inquirer into the natural world, the 'sage', the 'gadfly', the 'ascetic', the 'mandarin', and the 'courtier': what we could call the *militant* philosopher.

A 'militant', in my view, is not someone who is especially 'angry' or 'impatient' but instead someone who pursues a course similar to the one identified by Paul of Tarsus, who movingly wrote in his letter to the assembly of Jesus loyalists in the Roman colony of Philippi in northern Greece that 'this one thing I do: forgetting what lies behind and straining forward to what lies ahead, I press on toward the goal for the prize'.[7] Not surprisingly, the Black Freedom Struggle of the 1950s and 1960s in the United States reclaimed this image of keeping your 'eyes on the prize' of social justice.[8]

Although during my youth there were many compelling militant figures – among whom I would like to pay personal tribute to Jean-Paul Sartre, Hal Draper, Herbert Marcuse, Rudi Dutschke, Martin Luther King, Jr., Malcolm x

---

4 See Lapoujade 2017.
5 Or – to use Jürgen Habermas's expression – one could say that philosophy serves as a 'stand-in' (*Platzhalter*) and 'interpreter' as opposed to its historically 'problematic roles' of 'usher' (*Platzanweiser*) and 'judge' (Habermas 1990, p. 4).
6 See Smith 2016.
7 Phil 3.13–14. By 'prize' and 'goal' Paul alludes to Greek popular sports competitions (especially in Philippi), namely, foot races, their finishing posts, and their awarded prizes. For all of its shortcomings (some of which I discuss in Chapter 2 below), this is the merit of Alain Badiou's book on Paul, namely, to reclaim Paul as a model for what he calls a 'new militant figure' (Badiou 2003, p. 2).
8 Indeed, 'Keep Your Eyes on the Prize' was the title of a popular 'movement song' of that era.

(Malik el-Shabazz), James Baldwin, Ella Baker, Robert Moses, Fanny Lou Hamer, Stokely Carmichael (Kwame Ture), Mario Savio, and Roxanne Dunbar-Ortiz – the one who especially speaks to me in middle age is Daniel Berrigan, who gave a talk at my college in the mid-1970s, not long after he had been released from prison for his participation in draft resistance.[9] I shall never forget Berrigan's soft-spokenness and calm demeanour on the stage, for he was utterly different from other speakers at campus events I had attended. Before us stood a Jesuit priest, and a convicted felon, now wearing a plaid shirt and corduroy trousers with a very large grease stain on the front leg. I suddenly realised that what 'lies beyond ... lies within', as Berrigan succinctly expresses in a poem.[10] Again, if there is a common theme running through these studies, it is surely Berrigan's dialectic between inner and outer struggles for a more just world.

Finally, I should note that in this book – in the spirit of militant philosophy – there are no formulae, recipes, or advice for all those movement and party organisers who continue to do the hard work of building alternatives to global capitalist exploitation, alienation, and ecological devastation. I only hope to provide such organisers with a few concepts and arguments that may be useful as 'weapons' in the class struggle.[11] This is the task of philosophers in the service of radical social transformation.

---

9   On Berrigan's involvement with the actions of the 'Catonsville Nine', see the stirring work by Shawn Francis Peters (Peters 2012).
10 The poem is 'Beyond' and may be found in Berrigan 1998, p. 397.
11 On 'philosophy as a revolutionary weapon', see Althusser 2001, pp. 1–11.

Acknowledgements

Since it has taken so long to complete this book, my acknowledgements should be as thorough as possible. First and foremost, I am grateful to my mother, Charlotte, and my father, Craig, who lived through the Great Depression and conveyed to me an abiding sense of social justice and a biblically grounded faith. They have not lived to see this book, but anything of value in what I have written over the years may be traced back one way or another to how I was raised by them. I miss them both every day of my life.

For my brother, Craig Leigh (no longer with us, either) and my sisters, Tina and Kristen, I also give thanks. Our family has always been supportive of one another, but I suspect they have wondered at times about the wisdom of my academic and political decisions. My brother once asked me from his hospital bed why I was able to be so bold in what I taught and wrote (he worked for Boeing), and I responded that I was fortunate to have the support of academic freedom and a strong faculty union (of which I was president for five years). I still have both, and for that I remain grateful.

I must thank my only philosophical and political mentor, Warren Montag. Warren's generosity has been inexhaustible ever since I foolishly criticised him when he gave a guest lecture in a graduate seminar on Marx and Ideology for not being radical enough – a false alternative of 'his' Althusser and 'my' Deleuze/Negri if ever there were one!

My dear friend Richard Hunt has been gone for many years, but I think about him often. We spent innumerable hours working together in a post room at Claremont School of Theology, having lunch, seeing movies, discussing what we were reading, haunting Southern California's independent bookstores (of which there used to be many). I know he would have read this book, and I'd like to think that he would have approved of its style.

How does one become a socialist? Only through the close collaboration of friends and comrades. I met Darrel Moellendorf and Joe Lynch in the Philosophy Department at Claremont Graduate University, and the three of us formed an informal collective, as we worked together in the anti-Apartheid and Central America solidarity movements. We read Marxist classics together. We also ran together. What is more, Darrel and Joe have been, and will forever remain, my non-biological brothers.

In Claremont I also befriended Wonil Kim and Il-bung Choi, whose passion for democracy and workers' rights in South Korea offered me my first concrete example of internationalism.

While living in Claremont and then Riverside during the 1980s, I participated in helping to establish and build Southern Californian branches of Solidarity, an admirable socialist organisation whose work provided me with my first real political education and experiences of organising. I am grateful for my work with comrades in Solidarity, in particular, Walt Sheasby and Gene Warren, both of whom conveyed to me the urgency for Marxists to pursue a vigorous ecological critique of capitalism. I also remain the political student of Bob Brenner, whose regularly updated 'nature of the period' internal documents for Solidarity unfailingly stressed the possibility of self-emancipatory struggles to change the world.

When I moved from Southern California to the San Francisco Bay Area, I accompanied Carol Stanton, my companion of more than a decade, and my first wife. My debt to her is immeasurable. I am grateful to have met Carol and grateful to have spent so many good years together.

While living, teaching, and engaging in politics in the Bay Area, I was fortunate to meet Ken and Fidel, who kept up my spirits during some extremely difficult periods, helped move me more times than I care to recall, and shared with me their passion for dialectical biology.

I am grateful to all my Muslim students and friends at CSU, Hayward (now East Bay), who in the anxiety-inducing aftermath of 9/11 taught me a great deal about how to maintain critical fidelity to a cause. I pledged to them then, and I again pledge to my Muslim students at Cerritos College, to do everything in my power to challenge Islamophobia wherever I encounter it.

To Mark, my comrade of many years, I owe much for his uncanny ability to combine a deep knowledge of Althusser with equally insightful activism. The study group we once organised on Marx's *Capital* that met at Berkeley's Au Coquelet restaurant was as memorable as our road trip to New Mexico. Our study group on Althusser – with younger comrades like Joseph, Tatiana, and Oscar – that met at Harry's Place (a restaurant) in Santa Barbara made me feel a bit less theoretically isolated.

To my colleagues in the Cerritos College Department of Philosophy I owe a huge debt of gratitude for their personal support over the last decade and for their devotion to the cause of teaching philosophy to first-generation college students. I would like to single out for praise my former department chair, Ana Torres-Bower, and my wonderful friends over the years: Joseph Van de Mortel, Leslie Stapp, Bob Sliff, Clayton Kradjian, J.P. Pereira, and Corine Sutherland. Also, many thanks to Andrew Rehfeld and Tim Chatman, who served as my 'interns' for a year, and who helped me to provide a genuinely collaborative teaching environment. Thanks to all my colleagues for making our department a dynamic and caring place for our students to cultivate a love for all things philosophical.

ACKNOWLEDGEMENTS

To Ched Myers I owe an understanding of how to conduct Biblical scholarship in the service of radical discipleship and social transformation.

To Solomon Namala, all my colleagues and brothers and sisters in the Cerritos College Faculty Federation, and Jeff Boxer (the only labour attorney I have known well), I owe many practical lessons in building a democratic and effective union local.

To John Marot I owe a renewed interest in reading Lenin carefully and critically. John and I met in Solidarity, lost touch for many years, but then reestablished our friendship when we both found ourselves teaching at Cerritos College. I've read John's elegant book, and I wish mine were written as precisely.

To the editors at *Rethinking Marxism* I owe much for their vital journal and conferences, all of which I have faithfully attended.

To Sebastian Budgen I owe frequent injunctions to 'get back to work!' Sebastian knows as well as anyone why I have taken so long to complete this book. But if not for *Historical Materialism*, and especially HM London conferences, I would have had no reason to continue my research and writing.

To Danny Hayward I am in debt for his expertise in cleaning up a very untidy manuscript.

To Hasana Sharp, Jason Read, David McInerney, Sue Ruddick, Tom Carmichael, Bill Lewis, and Geoff Pfeifer I owe their collaboration on various panels at *Rethinking Marxism* and *Historical Materialism* conferences, without which I would not have been able to test some of the arguments that gave rise to several chapters in this book.

To Vittorio Morfino and Filippo Del Lucchese, my Italian comrades in arms, I owe their trust in, and publication of, my work on Spinoza. To Filippo I also owe the great honour of having been invited to participate in a remarkably stimulating Spinoza conference in Bologna in 2005.

To Panagiotis Sotiris, my Greek comrade, I am endebted for his remarkable example of the fusion of theory and practice.

To Agon Hamza, my geographically far-removed friend in Prishtina, Kosovo, I owe a comradeship that enabled me to find a new readership for my work. Without his (and Frank Ruda's) brilliant editorship of *Crisis & Critique* several of these chapters would not yet have seen the light of day.

To Cindy Zeiher, editor of *Continental Thought and Theory*, I am especially grateful for her encouragement of my work on 'Pauline Marxism'.

To Robb Johnson, whose unique musical voice has kept intact my faith in socialism for twenty years, I give thanks: in Robb's words, winter forever turns to spring.

Finally, my life began anew when I met Launa Nelson a decade ago. We met through our AFT local, she took a huge chance on me, and I cannot imagine my life without her. Every day Launa makes my life worth living.

Thomas, my favourite young socialist – now you know why your dad disappeared so often into his study. I'm finally coming out into the real world again to play with you, as my dad played catch in the backyard so many times with me. Let's head to Mother's Beach!

∴

Most of the chapters in this collection have appeared in previous form:

Chapter 1: 'What is a Philosophical Tendency?', *Historical Materialism* 23.4, pp. 3–38.

Chapter 2: 'Paul of Tarus, Thinker of the Conjuncture', in *Althusser and Theology*, edited by Agon Hamza, pp. 129–51, Leiden: Brill, 2016.

Chapter 3: 'Paul's Gift Economy: Wages, Debt, and Debt Cancellation', *Continental Thought & Theory* 2, pp. 452–72.

Chapter 4: 'Althusser and the Problem of Historical Individuality', *Crisis & Critique* 2.2 2015, pp. 195–214.

Chapter 5: '"Il mugghiare del mare": Hobbes e la follia della moltitudine' [translation], *Quaderni Materialisti* Vol. 3–4, 2005, pp. 127–46.

Chapter 6: 'Le tre forme della ribellione secondo Spinoza: indignata, gloriosa et soddisfatta' [translation], *Storia politica della moltitudine: Spinoza et la modernità*, edited by Flippo Del Lucchese, pp. 150–69, Roma: Derive Approdi, 2009; and 'Spinoza on the Glory of Politics', in *Spinoza: individuo e moltitudine*, pp. 327–39, Cesena: Società Editrice 'Il Ponte Vecchio', 2007.

Chapter 7: 'Alexandre Matheron on Militant Reason and the Intellectual Love of God', *Crisis and Critique* 2.1, 2015, pp. 153–69.

Interlude: 'An Ethics for Marxism: Spinoza on Fortitude', *Rethinking MARXISM* 26.4, 2014, pp. 561–80.

Chapter 9: 'Hegel or Spinoza: Substance, Subject, and Critical Marxism', *Crisis & Critique* 1.3, 2014, pp. 355–69.

ACKNOWLEDGEMENTS   XIX

Chapter 10: 'Contradictions of Hyperreality: Baudrillard, Žižek, and Virtual Dialectics', *The International Journal of Žižek Studies* 10.1, 2016, pp. 88–100.

Chapter 11: 'A Marxist Encounter with the Philosophy of Gilles Deleuze', *Rethinking MARXISM* 3.3–4, 1990, pp. 287–96.

Chapter 12: 'Deleuze and Althusser: Flirting with Structuralism', *Rethinking MARXISM* 10.3, 1998, pp. 51–63.

Chapter 13: 'Marxist Wisdom: Antonio Negri on the Book of Job', *The Philosophy of Antonio Negri, Volume 2: Revolution in Theory*, edited by Timothy S. Murphy and Abdul-Karim Mustapha, pp. 129–40, Ann Arbor, MI: Pluto Press, 2007.

Chapter 14: 'A Displaced Transition: Habermas on the Public Sphere', in *Masses, Classes, and Ideas*, edited by Mike Hill and Warren Montag, pp. 146–57, New York, NY: Verso Books, 2000.

Chapter 17: 'Climate Crisis, Ideology, and Collective Action', *Crisis & Critique* 1.1, 2014, pp. 137–52.

Coda: 'Beatitude: Marx, Aristotle, Averroes, Spinoza', *Continental Thought & Theory* 4, 2017, pp. 527–65.

Abbreviations

References to Spinoza's *Ethics* are based on Spinoza 1996. However, I have generally retranslated from Spinoza's Latin text, the standard edition of which may be found in Spinoza 1925. I have adopted the following abbreviation scheme: 'p' indicates a proposition, 'c' indicates a corollary, 'd' indicates definition, 's' indicates a scholium, and 'def aff' indicates the definitions of the affects to be found at the end of Part Three. For example, E3p59s refers to *Ethics*, Part three, Proposition 59, scholium.

References to Spinoza's *Tractatus Politicus* (TP) are based on Spinoza 2001. However, I have frequently retranslated passages from Spinoza's Latin text, the standard edition of which may be found in Spinoza 2005. I have adopted the following abbreviation scheme: 'TP 2.13' indicates Chapter Two, Section Thirteen.

References to Spinoza's *Tractatus Theologico-Politicus* (TTP) are based on Spinoza 2007. However, I have frequently retranslated passages from Spinoza's Latin text, the standard edition of which may be found in Spinoza 1999. I have adopted the following abbreviation scheme: 'TTP 18.5' indicates Chapter Eighteen, Section Five.

References to Spinoza's *Epistolae* or Letters are based on Spinoza 1995. I have adopted the following abbreviation scheme: 'Ep 76' indicates Letter 76 (to Albert Burgh).

References to Hobbes's *Leviathan* are to the chapter and section as indicated in Edwin Curley's edition in Hobbes 1994. For example, 'L 13.5' indicates *Leviathan*, Chapter Thirteen, Section Five.

PART 1

Marxism and the History of Philosophy

∴

CHAPTER 1

What is a Philosophical Tendency?*

Despite serious lapses to the contrary in the past, Marxism is not, nor should it aspire to become, a 'theory of everything'.[1] Accordingly, there is no such thing as a comprehensive and exhaustive Marxist philosophy. At most there are – and can only be – Marxist *interventions* within a complex philosophical field.[2] Such interventions are unending yet always incomplete; indeed, as Pierre Macherey once contended, Marxism is not a 'finished theory, with its system of prepared responses and fossilized concepts' but is instead a 'knot of simple and concrete problems'.[3] So let us loosen that knot, investigate a concrete – but perhaps not so simple – problem, and engage in doing philosophy 'in a materialist way'.[4]

No doubt, as Slavoj Žižek has compellingly argued, philosophers periodically have to rethink the meaning of materialism in light of new scientific, cultural, and political events – such 'breakthroughs' as relativity theory, quantum physics, Freudian psychoanalysis, and 'the failures of twentieth-century communism'.[5] In that spirit, then, let us return to, clarify, and defend what remains valuable in the materialist philosophical project initiated some fifty years ago by Louis Althusser.[6] In order better to situate Althusser's project, we must consider not only such predecessors as V.I. Lenin and Jean-Toussaint Desanti but also such successors as Pierre Macherey and Pierre Raymond.[7]

---

* This chapter has been previously published in *Historical Materialism* 23.4, pp. 3–38.
1 Marxists, of course, are not the only ones tempted to pursue an all-encompassing worldview. For example, certain researchers have increasingly claimed to see evidence of evolution by means of natural selection at work here, there, and everywhere – from neuroscience to politics, economics, and culture – to the point of envisioning Darwin's legacy to be what Daniel Dennett has called a 'universal acid ... [that] eats through just about every traditional concept and leaves in its wake a revolutionized world-view, with most of the old landmarks still recognizable, but transformed in fundamental ways' (Dennett 1996, p. 63). For the case against such 'ultra-Darwinism', see Rose 2005b, pp. 209–49.
2 In his recent introduction to Marxist philosophy, John Molyneux has provided activists with a valuable intervention, but he proceeds as if the terms 'Marxism' and 'philosophy' were unproblematic. See Molyneux 2012.
3 Macherey 1998, p. 18. All translations from French are mine.
4 Macherey 1983.
5 Žižek 2014a.
6 See especially the essays collected in Althusser 1976; 2011 in which Althusser characterises philosophical practice as unfolding on a 'battlefield' of competing materialist and idealist tendencies.
7 See, for example, Lenin 1972a; 1972b; Desanti 2006; 2008, Raymond 1973; 1977; 1982, and Macherey 1999.

However, as we shall quickly discover, this ongoing project to establish a philosophical practice that would be appropriate for Marxism does not simply consist of identifying and defending a 'materialist' position in philosophy against external 'idealist' challenges or threats. On the contrary, it recognises that there exists an interminable struggle between inextricably linked but ever-shifting materialist and idealist tendencies – a struggle that operates as a defining feature in the history of philosophy.[8] As a result, the problem to be explored in this chapter concerns how best to conceptualise this struggle and to determine whether or not the term 'tendency' holds analytical value and can serve as an important conceptual resource for Marxists working within the field of philosophy.[9]

1 Lenin on Philosophical Partisanship and Realism

Let us begin with Chapter Six of Lenin's book *Materialism and Empirio-Criticism*, first published in 1908, in which he addresses the question of 'parties in philosophy and philosophical blockheads' and argues that there exist

> *two* principal alignments, two fundamental trends in the solution of philosophical problems. Whether nature, matter, the physical, the external world should be taken as primary, and consciousness, mind, sensation (experience – as the *widespread* terminology of our time has it), the psychical, etc., should be regarded as secondary – that is the root question which *in fact* continues to divide the philosophers into *two great camps*. The source of thousands upon thousands of errors and of the confusion reigning in this sphere is the fact that beneath the envelope of terms, definitions, scholastic devices and verbal artifices, these two fundamental trends are *overlooked*.[10]

---

8   However, the unremitting struggle of tendencies that traverses the history of philosophy is precisely what Žižek has often failed to appreciate, especially when he has too starkly pitted Hegel against Spinoza. See Chapter 9 below.
9   My attempt to clarify and defend the writings of Althusser and Macherey on materialism and idealism is analogous to how Alberto Toscano has explored the unavoidability of 'partisan thought' by linking the recent work of Alain Badiou to Lenin via Carl Schmitt and Michel Foucault. See Toscano 2009.
10 Lenin 1972, p. 348. For a careful reconstruction of Lenin's intervention over, and argument in favour of, philosophical partisanship, see Lecourt 1973.

WHAT IS A PHILOSOPHICAL TENDENCY?

In this passage Lenin draws a sharp line between the two philosophical camps, between which there can be no common ground. He invokes Marx and Engels in this regard, who he insists

> were partisans in philosophy from start to finish ... [and] able to detect the deviations from materialism and concessions to idealism and fideism in each and every 'new' tendency.[11]

As commentators have noted, Lenin uses the term 'materialism' in a way that would today be called *realism*, the philosophical position that the external physical world exists prior to, and independent of, human consciousness but remains knowable.[12]

A decade later, without disavowing his previous commitment to realism, in the midst of the compelling 'philosophical moment'[13] occasioned by the First World War, Lenin acknowledges in his private notebooks that 'intelligent idealism is closer to intelligent materialism than stupid materialism'.[14] Elaborating on this distinction, he suggests that 'intelligent' idealism is 'dialectical' and 'stupid' materialism is 'metaphysical, undeveloped, dead, crude, [and] rigid'.[15] To be sure, Lenin's point is that one should not draw a *permanent* line of demarcation between all forms of materialism and all forms of idealism, for he observes that

> philosophical idealism is *only* nonsense from the standpoint of simple, metaphysical materialism. From the standpoint of *dialectical* materialism, on the other hand, philosophical idealism is a *one-sided*, exaggerated ... development ... of one of the features, aspects, facets of knowledge into an absolute, *divorced* from matter, from nature, apotheosised.

However, Lenin rejects the line metaphor as misleading. In his view,

> human knowledge is not (or does not follow) a straight line, but a curve, which endlessly approximates a series of circles, a spiral. Any fragment, segment, section of this curve can be transformed (transformed one-sidedly) into an independent, complete, straight line, which then (if one

---

11 Lenin 1972, p. 352.
12 See Ruben 1979, pp. 165–99; and Marot 2012, p. 224.
13 Balibar 2007.
14 Lenin 1972, p. 276.
15 Lenin 1972, p. 276.

does not see the wood for the trees) leads into the quagmire, into clerical obscurantism (where it is *anchored* by the class interests of the ruling classes).[16]

Much debate has arisen over whether or not Lenin's emphasis on dialectics in his *Philosophical Notebooks* should be read as a critique – even the repudiation and surpassing – of the earlier 'reflection theory' expressed in *Materialism and Empirio-Criticism*. However, the two works are philosophically compatible.[17] It may be the case, as David-Hillel Ruben has noted, that there are 'changes in emphasis, shifts in focus, but none of this is strong enough to bifurcate Lenin into a philosophically "early" and "late" Lenin'.[18] Lenin's point in his 1908 book (which was reprinted in Russian 1920)[19] is a scientific one. It is not a narrowly partisan work but one in which Lenin seeks to show that the perspective of those Russian Marxists who were influenced by the idealist turn in physics led by Ernst Mach was an intellectual dead end.[20] It is quite possible – and even desirable – to maintain a robust ontological commitment to realism, as Lenin does in *Materialism and Empirio-Criticism*, with an equally robust epistemological commitment to nonreductive materialism regarding the process of intellectual production and practical commitment to the priority of practice over theory. Antonio Negri has argued that Lenin's encounter with Hegel adds

> a new and more valuable aspect to the most appropriate Marxist interpretation of Hegel (which is Marx's). This is an awareness of the ontologically dominant role of collective praxis, of workers' and revolutionary praxis. At this stage, we can definitively see materialism as a working-class science of revolution, free from the mechanistic tradition, and as the embodiment of a revolutionary and operative realism. Dialectics becomes the *weapon of the proletariat*, finally equipped to sustain its experiences.[21]

Negri's point about the 'ontologically dominant role of praxis' should not be overstated, however; Lenin highlights his epistemological and practical commitments without repudiating his earlier ontological commitment in *Materi-*

---

16   Lenin 1972, p. 363.
17   See Lecourt 1973, pp. 49–69 and Ruben 1979, pp. 165–9.
18   Ruben 1979, pp. 168–9.
19   Marot 2012, p. 234.
20   Marot 2012, pp. 220–37.
21   Negri 2014, pp. 184.

alism and Empirio-Criticism. Indeed, he is philosophically justified in doing so: thinking about the world and acting within it presuppose that there exists an external world prior to, and independent of, such thinking and acting. Otherwise, recalling Marx's 'Eleventh Thesis on Feuerbach', there would be nothing to interpret or to change.[22]

But let us return to our main concern, namely, how to understand philosophical tendencies. Following Engels,[23] Lenin emphasises the *relative priority* of materialism over idealism but not the possibility of the former eliminating the latter. The interminable struggle between inextricably linked materialist and idealist tendencies operates as a defining feature of philosophical development. Along this spectrum would range a wide variety of materialisms and idealisms, some of which could be termed 'stupid', and some of which could be termed 'intelligent'.

2   Desanti's Intervention

In 1956, just prior to the Soviet invasion of Hungary that in large part prompted him – after a sustained period of dissidence – to leave the French Communist Party in 1960,[24] the *résistant* and philosopher Jean-Toussaint Desanti published his *Introduction à l'histoire de la philosophie*, a short book that Alexandre Matheron has characterised as one of the best Marxist works concerning the history of philosophy.[25] Desanti deepened and enriched Lenin's brief remarks on the struggle between idealism and materialism as he sketched a Marxist method to the history of philosophy and applied this method to the social background of

---

22   Marx famously wrote that 'the philosophers have only interpreted the world, in various ways; the point is to change it' (Marx 2000, p. 4). However, in no way does he thereby overlook in this thesis the importance of (a) interpreting what we might call (b) an 'interpretable' world; he is simply stressing that equal weight should be given to (c) the process of social transformation. In Kantian language, we could say that for Marx interpretation without practice is empty, but practice without interpretation is blind. Here I take strong exception to Frank Ruda's (2014, p. 96) contention that what is needed is not social *transformation* but social *affirmation*.
23   Engels (1990, p. 366) had argued that 'the question of the relation of thinking to being ... split the philosophers into two great camps. Those who asserted the primacy of the mind over nature and, therefore, in the last instance, assumed world creation in some form or other – and among the philosophers, e.g., Hegel, this creation often becomes still more intricate and impossible than in Christianity – comprised the camp of idealism. The others, who regarded nature as primary, belong to the various schools of materialism'.
24   Desanti 1994, p. 10.
25   Matheron 2000, p. 174.

Spinoza.[26] In addition, Desanti's book provides for the Cold War era a philosophical broadside against both 'bourgeois historiography' and attempts by such philosophers as Bertrand Russell to discredit the value of Marxism for the philosophical enterprise.[27]

Although he doesn't use the concept of 'tendency', Desanti argues that 'the question "materialism or idealism?"' necessarily 'dominates every philosophy, even if this question is not clearly perceived and is not explicitly formulated by the thinker'.[28] Indeed, he maintains that the struggle between idealism and materialism has been 'the centre of the entire history of philosophy'. Such struggle, he adds, is neither a merely 'empirical observation nor an arbitrary reconstruction based on suitably chosen examples' but is 'the very essence of philosophy: it is the expression of the process of knowledge by concepts at the heart of society'.[29] Desanti explains that historians of philosophy, and of ideology in general,

> strive to determine what is the nature of the relationship between the elements of culture inherited from the past and the new requirements unfolding at the heart of the superstructure, between the objective categories stemming from practice and scientific activity and the ideological requirements proper to society.[30]

Yet trying to apply this methodology to understanding specific philosophers in their objective historical contexts, however, would prove to be exceedingly difficult for Desanti. For example, in his 1956 book Desanti falters when it comes not just to identifying the broad 'internal contradictions of Spinoza's doctrine' and of the latter's historical situation in seventeenth-century Holland; he fails to engage in a fine-grained analysis of the argumentative nuances of such works as the *Ethics*. Desanti never completed or published a promised second volume that would have achieved his ultimate goal.[31]

---

26   Between 1949 and 1954 Desanti also published several substantive articles on the history of philosophy in the Communist journal *La Nouvelle Critique* in which he examined Lenin as a 'new philosopher' and the relationship among Kant, Hegel, and existentialism. See Desanti 2008, pp. 229–332.
27   Desanti 2006, p. 46.
28   Desanti 2006, p. 58.
29   Desanti 2006, p. 80.
30   Desanti 2006, p. 121 n. 1.
31   As Matheron (2000, p. 174) has noted, many years later Desanti's unfulfilled project of a Marxist reconstruction of Spinoza's objective context and philosophical system would be resumed by Antonio Negri (1991).

Although some pages of *Introduction à l'histoire de la philosophie* resemble an orthodox, even vulgar, Marxist manual on historical and dialectical materialism, nonetheless Desanti's great contribution was to redirect questions of materialism and idealism away from global assessments of the value of such prominent figures as Spinoza or Hegel – or even Russell, for that matter – and toward careful reconstructions of their socio-economic backgrounds and attentive readings of their texts.

Louis Althusser disavowed any influence of Desanti over his own thought; indeed, he indicted the latter for both his phenomenological leanings and his – during the late 40s and early 50s, at any rate – Stalinist politics.[32] Yet it was this 'Husserlian Marxist'[33] who not only introduced Althusser to Spinoza's philosophy[34] but also offered him a compelling way to conceive of the antagonism between idealism and materialism in the history of philosophy.[35]

3 Althusser's Contribution

Let us turn, then, to Louis Althusser, who addresses the concept of 'tendency' for the first time in a 1960 review essay 'On the Young Marx', when he criticises an attempt by the Soviet philosopher Nikolai Lapine to distinguish between Marx's Feuerbachian 'self-consciousness' and the underlying *materialist* tendency that was 'objectively in contradiction' with that self-consciousness.[36] Althusser argues that Lapine's approach suffered from Hegelian teleological presuppositions. In a word, Althusser quips, 'we are given *an abstraction from the problem itself as if it were the solution*'.[37] One could envision a different methodology, but, he adds, 'the very concept of "tendency" must be renounced'. In short, Lapine's Hegelian 'systematics' should be abandoned.

---

32 See, for example Althusser's disdainful 1976 recollections of his youthful philosophical and political encounter with Desanti (Althusser 1993, esp. pp. 161, 178–9, 328, 340–1).
33 See Althusser 1993, p. 176.
34 Peden 2014, pp. 98–103.
35 Here I disagree with Knox Peden when he argues that the 'philosophical essentials' of Althusser's project – and debt to Desanti – had 'nothing to do with Marx and almost everything to do with Spinoza' (Peden 2014, p. 148). On the contrary, how to conceptualise the antagonism between materialism and idealism owes nothing to Spinoza and long before Althusser was already one of the defining features of Marxist philosophical reflection and intervention. Such investigations continued under the influence of Althusser in the writings of Pierre Raymond (1973), Pierre Macherey (1999), and Dominique Lecourt (1973; 1981).
36 Althusser 2005, pp. 61–2.
37 Althusser 2005, p. 62.

As is well known, by 1967 Althusser had begun to reassess his earlier work and to criticise what he called his 'theoreticist' tendency. It is noteworthy that in his lectures on *Philosophy and the Spontaneous Philosophy of the Scientists* (later revised and published in French in 1974), Althusser distinguishes between what he called two 'elements' in any science: Element 1 and Element 2.[38]

Element 1 arises spontaneously from within scientific practice itself and can take the form of Theses that have a 'materialist and objectivist character'.[39] By contrast, Element 2 just as spontaneously originates from outside of science and is 'a reflection *on* scientific practice by means of philosophical Theses elaborated *outside* this practice by the religious, spiritualist or idealist-critical "philosophies of science" manufactured by philosophers or scientists'.[40] Althusser distinguishes Element 1 as the 'materialist' and Element 2 as the 'idealist' element at stake in debates about science that especially occur during periods of scientific 'crisis'. Unfortunately, in the 'spontaneous philosophy' in which scientists live and work, the idealist element typically dominates the materialist element. For Althusser the whole point of Marxist philosophical interventions into science is not to tell scientists how to carry out their research but to upset the domination of scientific practice by idealist Element 2 to the benefit of materialist Element 1.

In this regard, perhaps the key conceptual distinction made by Althusser in his 1967 lectures is between, on the one hand, 'true' or 'false' (terms that designate scientific propositions) and, on the other hand, 'correct' or 'incorrect' (terms that designate philosophical propositions). What is 'true' (or 'false') has to do with knowledge, whereas what is 'correct' (or 'incorrect') has to do with practice. In one of his typically bold formulations, Althusser declares that '*Correct* is the password that will permit us to enter into philosophy'.[41]

However, the 'correctness' of a philosophical position is not 'pre-established'; it requires continual *adjustment*. As a result, philosophers must modify their theses and positions

> by taking account of all the elements that make up the existing political, ideological and theoretical conjuncture, by taking account of what it calls the 'Whole' ... We know that, and we can show that it is so: every great philosophy (Plato, Descartes, Kant, Hegel, etc.) has always taken into account the political conjuncture (the great events of the class struggle),

---

38 Althusser 2011, pp. 132–44.
39 Althusser 2011, pp. 132–3.
40 Althusser 2011, p. 133.
41 Althusser 2011, p. 102.

the ideological conjuncture (the great conflicts between and within practical ideologies), *and* the theoretical conjuncture.[42]

⁂

In his 1968 lecture on 'Lenin and Philosophy', Althusser pursues this line of reasoning and contended that 'philosophy is nothing but a tendency struggle, the *Kampfplatz* that Kant discussed';[43] and in his 1974 essay 'Elements of Self-Criticism' he evokes again the Kantian metaphor of a theoretical 'battlefield' on which philosophical tendencies 'group themselves in the last instance around the antagonism between idealism and materialism'.[44] Althusser again argues that tendencies are neither true nor false but must be evaluated by criteria appropriate to *practice*: hence, they are either 'correct' or 'deviant'. Moreover, he insists, 'correctness does not fall from the sky: it has to be worked for, and may involve considerable effort, and it must be continually reworked: there must be *adjustment*'.[45] Idealist and materialist tendencies are invariably 'mixed-up', and so in every philosophy 'there exist manifest or latent elements of the *other* tendency'.[46] As a result, there is no guarantee of success in defending materialism, since a Marxist philosopher must fight

> if not everywhere at the same time, at least on several fronts, taking account both of the principal tendency and of the secondary tendencies, both of the principal stake and of the secondary stakes, while all the time 'working' to occupy correct positions. All this will obviously not come about through the miracle of a consciousness capable of dealing with all problems with perfect clarity. There is no miracle.[47]

There are no miracles: the Spinozist allusion[48] could not be starker and more pertinent.[49] Yet something miraculous did appear in Althusser's final writings: the prospect of an 'aleatory' materialism that could escape altogether the

---

42 Althusser 2011, p. 103.
43 Althusser 2011, p. 193.
44 Althusser 1976, p. 142.
45 Althusser 1976, p. 143.
46 Althusser 1976, p. 145.
47 Althusser 1976, p. 144.
48 For Spinoza's fullest account of miracles as unusual but misconceived natural phenomena, see his *Theological-Political Treatise*, Chapter Six (Spinoza 1996, pp. 81–96).
49 Although Althusser explicitly devotes only a few published pages to Spinoza, the latter's concepts are scattered implicitly throughout his writings. See Matheron 2012.

'trap' between idealist and materialist tendencies in the history of philosophy. Or, at least this is the possibility about which Althusser muses – indeed, he calls it 'raving' – in a letter to Fernanda Navarro, in which he listed Epicurus, Spinoza, Marx ('when he is properly understood'), and Nietzsche as producing philosophies 'that express the exigency to abandon idealism and move towards what may be called (if you like) materialism'.[50] However, Pierre Raymond persuasively argues that such escape is impossible and risks introducing an insupportable dualism between 'bad' idealisms and materialisms, on the one hand, and a 'good' materialism on the other. Instead, Raymond maintains, the idealism/materialism divide remains internal to any 'aleatory' conception of materialism.[51]

Of course, one could respond to Raymond's objection that what Althusser means by 'aleatory' is simply a recapitulation and conceptual refinement of certain themes already present in his mature writings, for example, 'overdetermination' (redirected in a non-psychologist direction) and 'conjuncture' (with a renewed emphasis on the singularity of what is historically unforeseeable).[52] However, in order to do so, and in order to prolong and sustain the materialist tendency, an idealist counter-tendency must be identified and overcome ('encroached upon', to use Althusser's terminology, or 'reversed' to use Raymond's).[53] Otherwise, the risk of the 'aleatory' opening up the way for a miraculous 'idealism of the encounter' remains in force. If we are willing to acknowledge 'the contradictions that haunt Althusser's texts',[54] we must also be prepared to draw a line of demarcation *within* the late Althusser's own philosophical project. Marxists must remain vigilant partisans in what Warren Montag has called philosophy's 'perpetual war of tendencies'.[55]

∴

Another, more substantial, work by Althusser was completed just prior to his fragmentary musings about aleatory materialism and has been published posthumously: *Initiation à la philosophie aux les non-philosophes*, which was

---

50 Althusser 2006, p. 218.
51 Raymond 2015. André Tosel has suggested that the late Althusser's conception of the 'aleatory' implicitly breaks with Spinoza's critique of supernaturalism and is indebted to Blaise Pascal's defence of miracles; see Tosel 2013, pp. 32–40.
52 Montag 2013, pp. 9–10.
53 On what is at stake is the distinction between philosophical 'encroachment' and 'reversal', see Althusser 2006, pp. 222–5 and Raymond 2015, p. 185.
54 Montag 2013, p. 12.
55 Montag 2013, p. 5.

intended to serve as an introduction to philosophy for 'non-philosophers'.[56] Even if this philosophical 'manual'[57] is not definitive, nonetheless it marks one of the highpoints of Althusser's philosophical project. In it Althusser extends and refines his re-conceptualisation of philosophy as class struggle in theory but without quixotically seeking a definitive form of materialism that once and for all would be purged of idealist distortion. For example, he reiterates that

> every idealist philosophy necessarily includes materialist arguments in itself, and the other way around. There is no pure philosophy in the world: read, there is no wholly idealist or materialist philosophy. Even what is called Marxist materialist philosophy will never be able to lay claim to being wholly materialist, for to do so it would be to abandon the fight by renouncing the idea of preventatively occupying positions held by idealism.[58]

Let us consider a key issue addressed in *Initiation à la philosophie aux les non-philosophes* that especially highlights the struggle between idealist and materialist tendencies in the history of philosophy. Althusser contends that idealists have regularly conceived of the *origin* of the world out of nothingness – whether or not in the religious sense of God's creative act – whereas materialists (Epicurus and Lucretius are his examples) have been interested in the *beginning* of the world, which arises from

> pre-existent matter, which becomes a world thanks to the (contingent, arbitrary) *encounter* of its elements. And this encounter which commands everything is the figure of contingency and chance, yet it produces the necessity of the World. Thus chance produces necessity by itself, with no intervention by God. This is tantamount to saying that the World produces itself, and that by substituting the materialist of the beginning (or the event, the advent) for the idealist question of the Origin, *we eliminate meaningless questions*: not just the question of the Origin of the World, but also everything connected with it – the question of God, of his omnipotence, of his incomprehensibility, of time and eternity, and so on.[59]

---

56 Althusser 2014a; translated into English as Althusser 2017.
57 See G.M. Goshgarian's editorial note in Althusser 2017, pp. 15–17.
58 Althusser 2014a, p. 162.
59 Althusser 2017, pp. 29–30.

One could object that the distinction made by Althusser between origin and beginning is analytically imprecise, for the biblical creation stories arguably lend themselves to a materialist interpretation.[60] Indeed, the subsequent development of the monotheistic doctrine of *creatio ex nihilo* suggests an idealist encroachment or reversal. Consequently, a philosophical line of demarcation between origin and beginning should not be drawn in such a way that religious creation narratives are aligned wholly with idealism; a materialist element continues to haunt these narratives.

At any rate, a variation on the search for origins, Althusser suggests, was the 'myth of the state of nature'.[61] Idealists have tended to search for a pre-social *origin* to human beings, if only as a thought experiment. The so-called 'State of Nature' that figures so prominently in early modern political thought is

> a mythic state in which idealist philosophers imagine that people lived before entering the state of society: Robinson Crusoe's solitude, for example, or a community without the 'drawbacks of society' as we know it.[62]

What Althusser finds instructive about this myth is that it

> nevertheless contained ... in a way that might be called *inverted*, or, rather, *displaced*, recognition of the material reality of the conditions of existence of human (sexual) reproduction, production, and knowledge. Of course, to arrive at that conclusion, we have to be able to 'interpret' these myths and philosophies. But our interpretation is not arbitrary. On the

---

60   For example, Levenson 1994 has persuasively argued that Genesis 1.1–2:3 presents the creation of the world out of unformed – but still material – chaos as opposed to the creation of matter itself from nothingness. Moreover, there has arisen a lively debate among biblical scholars regarding the meaning of the key Hebrew verb ברא (*bara'*) used in this narrative, which Ellen van Wolde (2009) argues has the connotation of 'to separate' instead of 'to create' the primal material stuff. Van Wolde's interpretive position has been contested in Becking and Korpel 2010, to which she has replied in van Wolde and Rezetko 2011.

61   Althusser 2017, pp. 72–7. See also Boer and Petterson 2014 for a fascinating account of how early modern political theorists like Grotius, Locke, Smith, and Malthus envisioned the 'state of nature' as a way to come to terms with the biblical story of the Garden of Eden and so appropriated a myth of the 'Fall' as an ideological justification for nascent capitalist social relations. For an exhaustive scholarly reconstruction of the Eden narrative within its original Israelite and ancient Near Eastern setting, see Zevit 2013.

62   Althusser 2017, p. 72.

contrary, it is based on elements that well and truly figure *in these myths* and philosophies, and doubtless do so not by accident, but by a profound necessity.[63]

In particular,

> philosophical myths of the state of nature ... sprang up in the formative period of the rising bourgeoisie ... [and] they expressed its aspirations, reflected its problems, and held out its solutions – that they were intended, accordingly, to *cement its unity*, rallying round it all those who had a stake in its social and political triumph.[64]

But how did such myths appeal to 'the reality of these masses's living conditions, of their experience and needs' and thereby 'win them over'? By breaking their 'resistance ... in advance' and by 'anticipat[ing] and forestall[ing] their "opposition"'

> ... to the conception of the world presented to them, which serves not their interests, but those of very different human groups: a priestly caste, the Church, the social class in power and so on.[65]

According to Althusser, such critical inquiry enables us to grasp that philosophy

> does not just content itself with stating propositions (or 'Theses') about all existing beings, or all possible and therefore nonexistent beings; it states these propositions in a way *that has to do less with the knowledge of these beings than with the conflicts of which they may be the stakes*. That is why every philosophy (let us not hesitate to go that far) is haunted by its opposite. That is why idealism is haunted by materialism, just as materialism is haunted by idealism; for every philosophy reproduces within itself, in some sort, the conflict in which it finds itself engaged outside itself.[66]

---

63 Althusser 2017, p. 75.
64 Althusser 2017, p. 76.
65 Althusser 2017, p. 76.
66 Althusser 2017, p. 76.

Moreover, we can appreciate better the distinctive nature of philosophical *abstraction* and how it differs from scientific and ideological forms of abstraction:

> [Philosophy] is a very strange abstraction indeed, for it aims not to produce knowledge of things that exist in the world, as science does, but, rather, to speak about all that exists (and even all that does not), in a mode that implies *a previous conflict*, still present, involving the place, meaning and function of these beings, a conflict which commands philosophy *from without* and which philosophy has to bring *within itself* in order to exist as philosophy. It is, then, an *active*, and, as it were, *polemical abstraction*, divided against itself, which concerns not just its ostensible 'objects', inasmuch as these can exist or not, but also its own positions, its own 'theses'. For these theses can be affirmed only on the paradoxical condition that they are simultaneously negated by contradictory theses which, to be sure, are relegated to the margins of the philosophy in question, yet are present in it nonetheless.[67]

The upshot is that philosophy cannot overcome its internal struggle between materialist and idealist tendencies, because it exists and operates only by reproducing actually existing external social conflicts and scientific disputes that continually reemerge in mediated forms.

4   Macherey on the Struggle of Philosophical Tendencies

In an essay published in 1976, Pierre Macherey refined Althusser's insights and explored the history of philosophy as a 'struggle of tendencies' between materialism and idealism.[68] What is at stake for Macherey in this essay is not to defend a Marxist philosophy but to explore an alternative way to do philosophy as a Marxist.

Macherey's essay originated in a 1973 book-length manuscript devoted to 'Three Remarks on Marxist Philosophy'; in particular, it recapitulated the second remark devoted to the 'philosophical category of experience'.[69] However, when the essay was finally published in the French Communist Party's theor-

---

67   Althusser 2017, pp. 76–7.
68   'L'Histoire de la philosophie considérée comme une lutte de tendances', reprinted in Macherey 1999, pp. 35–64.
69   A detailed outline of whose contents Macherey has provided (1999, pp. 77–8).

etical journal *La Pensée*, in order to shorten an already lengthy piece Macherey decided to cut an opening section on dialectics. This section eventually appeared in translation in a 1988 issue of a German journal as Macherey's personal tribute to the influence of Althusser.[70]

Macherey's purpose is to argue that the history of philosophy is an objective process determined by 'historical, material conditions that don't depend on the coherence of a system or the intention of an author'.[71] Moreover, the history of philosophy is a dialectical, and so contradictory, development between idealist and materialist tendencies whose interrelationship is continually shifting. The key question Macherey seeks to address is how such a dialectical materialist understanding of the history of philosophy contributes to enriching our concrete knowledge of philosophy in its historical development.[72]

Especially striking is Macherey's argument that no philosophical category is ever fixed once and for all but is continually up for grabs, depending on the objective historical conditions and the outcome of the struggle between idealist and materialist tendencies. For example, Macherey insists that materialism is not realism but instead that realism is an 'inconsequent materialism'. His point is that various forms of idealism have regularly exploited the category of the 'real' and substituted thought for objective material reality that in fact exists prior to and independent of thought. At the same time, he notes, idealism 'dissimulates the true nature of philosophy as a struggle of tendencies', claims to be 'beyond' such tendencies, and refuses to admit their existence.[73]

The upshot is that materialism can effectively challenge idealism 'on the terrain of philosophical struggle only by developing it, that is, by transforming it into a consequent, dialectical materialism'.[74] The struggle of philosophical tendencies, then, is not 'an abstract confrontation, a debate of ideas, or the fortuitous encounter of two assailants' who square off in order to resolve a dispute. Rather, it is, Macherey proposes, a contradiction in the precise sense of a 'unity of contraries' or a 'one that divides into two'.[75]

---

70   'Un se divise en deux', reprinted in Macherey 1999, pp. 64–73.
71   Macherey 1999, p. 35.
72   Macherey 1999, pp. 35–6.
73   Macherey 1999, p. 36.
74   Macherey flirts here with the idea that such a 'consequent materialism' could entirely suppress the idealist counter-tendency. I again concur with Raymond that such a pure, self-standing materialism is neither attainable nor desirable. Indeed, it would be lifeless, inert.
75   Macherey 1999, pp. 37–8.

5   Tendencies, Lines, and Positions

So what exactly is a philosophical tendency? To use Kantian language, it concerns how one 'orients oneself' within theory and practice.[76] Furthermore, there exist idealist orientations and materialist orientations, which should be regarded as 'lines' in the sense of regulative principles or procedures.

Following Lenin,[77] Wal Suchting once proposed that philosophical lines are similar to political lines, because they 'induce opposed effects, cognitively and socially'.[78] Materialist and idealist tendencies, then, serve as 'principle' or 'fundamental' lines to provide 'guide-lines for informed action to bring about certain changes' – for example, in the form of 'programmes, stances, attitudes, orientations, strategies'[79] – and can be 'rationally assessed (in general terms) by considering the effects on the political situation induced by following that line'.[80] Suchting argued that

> since these effects relate to specific objective social forces, materialism and idealism are also 'lines' in the yet further sense of *military* lines: they divide groups into warring camps. Hence the thesis that the history of philosophy is the history of the struggle between the two.[81]

But we should add to Suchting's perspective a note of caution: to say that idealism and materialism are 'principal lines' does not mean that they are the *only* philosophical tendencies imaginable or identifiable. Paul Ricoeur once objected to 'the common opposition in orthodox Marxism between idealism and materialism, as if we can choose only between two colors in order to paint reality'.[82] Macherey responds to Ricoeur's objection by noting that his own project is to rethink the struggle between opposing philosophical tendencies 'in light of the dialectical unity of opposites'. In other words, idealist and materialist tendencies are really only one, because of the 'non-reciprocity of the positions to which they correspond'.[83] This means that for Macherey 'if idealism is the negation of materialism, the opposite is not true: materialism, which is prior to idealism, is not the negation of idealism'.[84]

---

76   See Kant 1996, pp. 7–18.
77   Lenin 1972b, p. 17.
78   Suchting 1986, p. 69.
79   Suchting 1986, p. 63.
80   Suchting 1986, p. 66.
81   Suchting 1986, pp. 69–70.
82   Ricoeur 1986, p. 104.
83   Macherey 1999, p. 81.
84   Macherey 1999, pp. 81–2.

Another way to respond to Ricoeur, however, would be to insist that a finer-grained analysis is both necessary and possible. Althusser's criticism of Lapine's use of the concept 'tendency' as 'too broad and abstract' applies with force here.[85] The struggle between idealism and materialism as principal lines or tendencies does not exhaustively describe the philosophical field of opposing forces: struggles between secondary or subsidiary philosophical tendencies can and do exist, too. There exists a broad array of materialisms as well as idealisms; *in the last instance*, however, each distinctive variety of materialism or idealism belongs to just that philosophical kind and not the other.[86] Moreover, although other secondary tendencies exist and cut across the primary materialist/idealist division, they do not thereby erase it.

For instance, consider one of Macherey's least known but most compelling decades-long areas of research: an investigation of what he has called 'philosophy *à la française*'[87] as distinct from 'French philosophy' in the sense that the latter would describe an activity 'completely determined by belonging to the land and by the filiation of the people or the race'.[88] Macherey has instead sought to trace – and demarcate the internal divisions within – the distinctive institutional forms and practices of philosophy in the wake of the French Revolution. To be precise, he has undertaken a history of philosophical tendencies in France since the late eighteenth century 'in relation to the transformations of society considered in the totality of its economic, political and ideological structures'.[89]

Another example of the struggle between secondary philosophical tendencies is the key pair of tendencies in political philosophy to the study of which Macherey has recently devoted his attention: the 'quotidian' (or 'realist') and the 'utopian'.[90] As Warren Montag has argued, although these 'constitute antithetical ways of grasping reality and imply very different strategies for its trans-

---

85   Althusser 2005, p. 77 n. 39.
86   On the historical variants of materialism, see Bloch 1995; on idealism, see Rockmore 2007 and Dunham, Grant, and Watson 2011.
87   In his 1991 Thesis Defense or *Soutenance* Macherey identifies three broad 'series of questions' with which he has largely been 'preoccupied': Spinozism, the relations of literature and philosophy, and the history of philosophy in France (Macherey 1998, pp. 18–19). It is perhaps not surprising that his reputation in the Anglophone world has largely been based on his publications in the first two areas.
88   Macherey 1998, p. 19.
89   Macherey 1998, p. 19. For a comprehensive collection of Macherey's articles on philosophy *à la française*, see Macherey 2013.
90   See Macherey 2009; 2011.

formation', in the last instance they serve as 'explorations of the same thing from two different perspectives'. Indeed, if utopia is

> strictly speaking to be found nowhere, this is surely because it is everywhere, as immanent as it is transcendent ... a critique of the present already actualized, prevented by nothing but a fragile balance of forces from possessing, that is, inundating and transforming the real.[91]

One could add to Montag's observation that we find here a striking convergence between Macherey and Ernst Bloch, who rejected 'abstract' utopian conceptions and embraced what he called 'concrete utopia'.[92]

Indeed, in an appendix to his book on the history of utopian thought Macherey contends that what distinguished Bloch's philosophy was his attempt to restore to utopia its real or material basis by developing 'an ontology of the possible that incorporates into being the dimension of the ought-to-be'.[93] Bloch thereby sought to overcome the contradiction of the real and the possible 'by positing that being is never anything except what it can be, as a function of its conditions of possibility'. Anticipating Gilles Deleuze's perspective, Bloch demonstrated that 'the possible, in this sense, is therefore the virtual, which, being not yet realized, nonetheless tends toward its realization, in the form of a tendency or an *élan* that propels it beyond, in negation of the given state of affairs'.[94]

∴

In the compelling foreword to a new collection of his articles on the French philosophical reception of Descartes's philosophy, Macherey has returned to the general theme of what constitute distinctively philosophical 'quarrels' and what role they play as a driving force in the history of philosophy.[95] After noting the failure of Kant to find lasting terms of peace for the *Kampfplatz* that is

---

91 Montag 2012.
92 See Bloch 1986b, *passim*.
93 Macherey 2011a, p. 507.
94 Macherey 2011a, p. 510. Macherey especially notes the affinity between Bloch's concept of 'real possibility' and Deleuze's 'transcendental empiricism' (pp. 508–9). Deleuze and Guattari themselves once acknowledged Bloch for having distinguished between 'authoritarian utopias, or utopias of transcendence, and immanent, revolutionary, libertarian utopias' (Deleuze and Guattari 1994, p. 100, 224 n. 12).
95 Macherey 2014a, pp. 9–11.

the history of philosophy, Macherey identifies a number of key philosophical controversies:

> the quarrel of the friends of the forms and the friends of matter during Plato's time; the quarrel over universals during the Middle Ages; the quarrel of the Ancients and the Moderns during the classical age; the *Pantheismusstreit* launched in Germany at the end of the 18th century that had an echo in France after a gap of decades under the name of the quarrel over pantheism; the quarrel over Christian philosophy in the 20th century.[96]

Not one of these fierce disputes was – or ever will be – resolved once and for all. Indeed,

> this permanent atmosphere of controversy casts suspicion on the rational, indeed even the reasonable, character of philosophical activity, and naturally tends to transform its debates into confrontations whose appearance seems more political than scientific and privileges violence, therefore, in the last instance, the conflict of wills over intellectual persuasion by formal arguments and demonstrations in order to assert – that is, to make prevail – theses that seem capable of being asserted only by reciprocally opposing one another and seeking to destroy one another.[97]

Even if the history of philosophy does not quite reduce to Hegel's grisly 'slaughter-bench' (*Schlachtbank*),[98] it nonetheless remains a site of 'bellicose quarrels' that are not more than personal disagreements between philosophers but broaden to become true pitched conceptual battles in which opposing camps do not 'hesitate on occasion to take up arms to the death'.[99]

---

96 Macherey 2014a, p. 9.
97 Macherey, p. 9.
98 Hegel 1986, p. 35. With his graphic image – evoking a religious altar on which animal sacrifice is performed, a butcher's block, and a battlefield – Hegel sought to conceive of history as a process whose underlying intelligible order emerges despite its chaotic surface appearance. Brown and Hodgson's translation of *Schlachtbank* more simply as 'slaughterhouse' (in Hegel 2011, p. 90) fails to capture the nuances of Hegel's polyvalent expression.
99 Macherey 2014a, p. 10.

Lest one be disturbed by this acknowledgement of philosophical 'combativeness',[100] it is worth making two points: first of all, worse than the possible eruption of conceptual violence would be 'indifference' or even the attempted 'neutralisation' of philosophical conflict. Indeed, such an attempt to avoid or eliminate conflict would undermine the very philosophical enterprise. This is because, secondly, the very nature of philosophical activity as a kind of sustained process of argumentation necessitates that every philosophical system engage in debate with a 'more or less fictitious or real adversary' in order for its specific theses to emerge, be identified, and defended.[101]

This is the reason, too, that for Macherey, there can be no decisive interpretation of even a single philosopher's *oeuvre*; on the contrary, the latter remains continually open to reassessment, challenge, and controversy. Consider the mid-twentieth-century reception of Descartes's philosophy in France. Macherey has identified and discussed at length two major twentieth-century 'Cartesian quarrels': the one that arose in the 1950s between Ferdinand Alquié and Martial Gueroult and the one that arose in the 1960s between Michel Foucault and Jacques Derrida. The first quarrel concerned

> the question of knowing whether reading a philosopher presupposes examining the personal genesis of his thought that makes it a singular mental experience, or else seeks only to reconstruct an impersonal and essential argumentative and demonstrative structure taking place within a global typology of systems.

The second quarrel 'brought to light much larger stakes concerning the nature of philosophical discourse and the events of thought for which the latter is the place or occasion'.[102]

The upshot of Macherey's discussion is that 'we have never finished reading and rereading the "classics," inasmuch as the latter carry the stakes of thought that go beyond the age for which they have been written'.[103] Any great philosophical work – whether Descartes's, Spinoza's, or Hegel's – is

> not a catalogue in which would be recorded a certain number of ready-made ideas that would be set down and somehow frozen pending their

---

100   Macherey positively references here Althusser's conception of philosophy as the representation of 'class struggle in theory'.
101   Macherey 2014a, p. 10.
102   Macherey 2014a, pp. 10–11.
103   Macherey 2014a, p. 11.

reactivation; but it is a machine to forge ideas and arguments in the form of an active and living reflection of which dispute or quarrel is one of the most vibrant forms, which does not prevent it from being meaningful in its own way, at its own level.[104]

∴

In this light, Marxist philosophers would do well to follow Althusser's advice, return to the beginning of Western philosophy, and study carefully – if only to *reverse* the outcome of[105] – Plato's *Gigantomachia*, his tale in the *Sophist* of an imaginary 'Battle of Gods and Giants', in which the 'gods' signify middle-period Platonic 'friends of the forms' and the 'giants' signify materialist 'friends of the earth (or bodies)'.[106] At the heart of this battle is an ontological dispute between two philosophical tendencies over the nature of Being (*ousia*). For our purposes here it is instructive that Plato envisioned not the eradication of either tendency but the preservation of both in a perpetual state of mutual tension. In other words, dialectical resolution of the conflict can occur just in case that a true philosopher – as opposed to a mere sophist – decides to reject the one-sidedness of either extreme and strives to 'be like a child "begging for both"' tendencies!'[107] In a commentary on the *Sophist*, Martin Heidegger once pointed out that the philosophical battlefield depicted by Plato between those who conceive of Being in terms of forms and those who conceive of Being in terms of bodies is equally the

> place of a decision ... for the solution of the question resides for Plato precisely in resolving the unilaterality of each position and acquiring a perspective for a concept of Being on the basis of which both positions may become intelligible.[108]

What Heidegger failed to note, however, and what Plato's dialectic preserved, in the last instance, was the dominance of the forms, whereas a reversed *materialist* dialectic would preserve, in the last instance, the dominance of the earth

---

104　Macherey 2014a, p. 11.
105　See Althusser 2014a, pp. 93–6; 333–4. Deleuze (1990, pp. 253–79) envisioned a comparable materialist project of 'reversing' Plato's idealism.
106　*Sophist* 245e–249d (Plato 1993, pp. 36–41). For an outstanding recent commentary, see Brown 1998.
107　*Sophist* 249d (Plato 1998, p. 41). For a classic account of the materialist/idealist divide in ancient Greek philosophy, see Thomson 1977, esp. pp. 302–35.
108　Heidegger 2003, p. 304.

and bodies. Such a project of reversal remains open for Marxists who intervene within the history of philosophy.

6 Addressing Carnap's Objection

In 1928 the Vienna Circle philosopher Rudolf Carnap published an article in which he exposed and repudiated what he considered to be 'pseudo-problems in philosophy'. In particular, he sharply challenged the very distinction that has been operative in our foregoing account of the struggle between materialist and idealist tendencies.[109] For Carnap the epistemological 'theses' of realism and idealism are not true or false – they are *meaningless* and hence not worthy of serious philosophical inquiry. At this juncture, it is worth grappling with Carnap's argument before proceeding further. Let us imagine that there are

> two geographers, a realist and an idealist, who are sent out in order to find out if a mountain that is supposed to be somewhere in Africa is only legendary or if it really exists.[110]

Each geographer, Carnap contends, would arrive at exactly the same empirical result, namely, they would mutually agree that the mountain either exists or does not. Neither the realist nor the idealist thesis would enable – or hinder – the geographers in their investigation. In other words, science has utterly no need of the realist/idealist distinction in order to gain new and accurate knowledge about the external world. It may be true, he allows, that there is a certain 'emotional accompaniment' to the realist thesis, 'for example, the feeling of unfamiliarity with the mountain, the feeling that in many ways it is not subject to, or even resists, my will, and similar feelings'.[111] But such sentiments contribute nothing to science, and philosophers should exclude them from a serious theory of knowledge.

How to respond to Carnap's objection? In a way, he is quite right to insist that science can and does proceed without any special philosophical contribution, whether realist or idealist. And yet he failed to note that idealism invariably tends to distort, to manipulate, in short, to *exploit* scientific knowledge for its own purposes.[112] Philosophical exploitation of science means that

---

109 Reprinted in Carnap 2003, pp. 301–43.
110 Carnap 2003, p. 333.
111 Carnap 2003, p. 334.
112 Here I follow Raymond 1977, pp. 158–75.

the sciences are never seen for what they really are; their existence, their limits, their growing pains (baptized 'crises') or their mechanisms, as interpreted by the idealist categories of the most well-informed philosophies, are *used* from outside; they may be used crudely or subtly, but they are used to furnish arguments or guarantees for extra-scientific values that the philosophies in question objectively serve through their own practice, their 'questions' and their 'theories'. These 'values' pertain to *practical ideologies*, which play their own role in the social cohesion and social conflicts of class societies.[113]

To defend philosophical realism, then, is not to *instruct* scientists or revise scientific method; on the contrary, it serves both to *defend* the relative autonomy of the sciences and to caution scientists themselves from sliding into spontaneous idealist philosophies that misrecognise the results and implications of their own research. Philosophy, Althusser insists, 'does not substitute itself for science: it intervenes, in order to clear a path, to open the space in which a correct line may then be drawn'.[114]

If we think about the relationship between political practice and theory, Althusser's point is further supported. No doubt it is activists – and not philosophers – who continually build movements, organise groups and parties, and make history (within the limits presented by the balance of class forces in a given conjuncture). In this respect, political practice maintains a priority over political theory. As a result, realists from Machiavelli, Spinoza, and Hegel, to Marx, Engels, and Lenin have sought not to give marching orders to activists from the side-lines but to contribute a sober assessment of the objective material forces that activists and movements must confront, and defeat, in order to achieve their political objectives.[115] Carnap himself briefly speculates – but did not follow through on the implications – that 'the pseudo theses of realism and idealism express, not the theoretical content of a scientifically permissible statement, but only ... a certain practical orientation toward life'.[116]

In sum, the struggle of opposing materialist and idealist tendencies is, contrary to Carnap's assertions, hardly 'meaningless' in a practical sense. Indeed, this distinction offers a constructive analytical tool by means of which Marxists can take 'correct' (not 'true') positions within the history of philosophy and

---

113   Althusser 2011, p. 129.
114   Althusser 2011, p. 88.
115   For superb defences of philosophy in the service of political realism, see Geuss 2008 and Finlayson 2015.
116   Carnap 2003, p. 340.

seek to diagnose individual philosophers and their writings. Such tasks require them not crudely to categorise warring camps – Materialists vs. Idealists – but (as we shall see in the next section) carefully to distinguish three levels of philosophical struggle: the ontological, epistemological, and the practical. Moreover, the whole point is not, as Desanti cautions in a moment of self-criticism,

> to criticise a philosophy *from outside*, by merely asserting how the doctrines professed in it were incompatible with the 'principles' of Marxism-Leninism, presumed to be true.[117]

By contrast, non-exploitative Marxist philosophical interventions must occur *from within* texts and traditions themselves, by identifying the concrete ways in which materialist and idealist tendencies arise, clash, and encroach upon one another's conceptual space.

7 Three Levels of Philosophical Struggle

A question remains, though: Why *are* there tendencies in philosophy, indeed, why is there such an operation as philosophy at all?[118] In the opening chapter of his posthumously published book *On the Reproduction of Capitalism* Althusser insists that 'philosophy has not always existed' but requires two conditions: the existence of social classes and the existence of science.[119] Philosophy arises and

---

117 Desanti 1994, p. 9. My emphasis.
118 Thanks to Panagiotis Sotiris for raising this important point after a presentation of an earlier version of this article at the 2013 Historical Materialism conference in London. On philosophy as *operation*, see Macherey 1998, pp. 28–41.
119 Althusser 2014b, p. 13. I leave aside the question of whether science began with Thales, as Althusser maintains, or with Anaximander, as physicist Carlo Rovelli (2011) has compellingly argued. It is also beyond the scope of this chapter to investigate whether or not Althusser was correct to conclude (p. 17) that philosophy originated in ancient Greece and not in ancient India or China, because the first condition (class-divided societies) obtained but not the second condition (the emergence of a science comparable to mathematics). For a compelling argument that the diverse historical practices of philosophy were, and continue to be, irreducibly global, see Van Norden 2017. However, Van Norden is not interested in whether or not distinct *tendencies* existed, for example, in classical Indian and Chinese thought. Consider Buddhist thought, which traverses both geographical and linguistic terrains. David Kalupahana has persuasively argued that a struggle between what he calls 'absolutist' and 'non-absolutist' tendencies underlies the history of Buddhist philosophy. Indeed, as Kalupahana richly illustrates, the Buddha's own 'radical empiricism', i.e. 'the recognition that experience is not atomic but a flux whose content

operates as the way in which the class struggle is represented in theory and, barring the final resolution of that struggle, there can be no end to the conflict of materialist and idealist tendencies.[120] Just as Marxists have not created class struggle but only take sides within it, so too they must defend positions within an already-existing struggle of philosophical tendencies.

Following Roy Bhaskar,[121] we may identify three levels of the philosophical struggle between materialism and idealism: ontological, epistemological, and practical. The ontological struggle concerns whether or not the external physical world exists independent of human consciousness.[122] It would seem

---

is invariably associated with the past' (Kalupahana 1992, pp. 108–9), his 'renunciation of mystery' (Kalupahana 2001), his focus on knowing the world as it really is, and his insistence on the primacy of ethical and meditative practice has regularly been reabsorbed over the centuries into one form after another of absolutist discourse about the transcendent nature of the self, human knowledge, and ultimate reality. However, Kalupahana also reveals how Buddhist thinkers and practitioners have continually sought to recover the Buddha's own non-absolutist insights.

120 With Richard Seaford (2004) we could add that the historical invention of philosophy – which conceives of the universe 'as an *intelligible order* subject to the *uniformity of impersonal* power' (p. 175) – in ancient Greek city-states had as its crucial factor not just the class struggle but the emergence of coinage in the first 'monetarised' societies dominated by the equally abstract, impersonal, and rule-governed power of money. That is to say, 'presocratic metaphysics involves (without *consisting of*) unconscious cosmological projection of the universal power and universal exchangeability of the abstract substance of money' (p. 11). Seaford has also recently initiated an important research project into a comparable philosophical commencement in ancient India (see Seaford 2017). As he explains in an interview, the basis for such a project is not that there was Indian influence on Greek culture (or vice versa) but that 'the same kind of socio-economic development may produce the same kind of metaphysics' (Seaford 2013, p. 5). It should be noted that, as he acknowledges in several footnotes (p. 230 n. 67, p. 238 n. 49, p. 256 n. 118, p. 275 n. 44, p. 293 n. 3, p. 296 n. 11), Seaford has proposed a thesis that expands on Alfred Sohn-Rethel's earlier insight regarding the commencement of pre-socratic philosophy, namely, 'the social upheavals and class struggles ensuing from the development of this [monetary] economy in the various city-states of ancient Greece' that provided the conditions of possibility for 'the beginning of the conceptual mode of thinking [in terms of abstract universals] which is ours to this day and which carries the division of intellectual from manual labour that permeates all class societies based upon commodity production' (Sohn-Rethel 1978, pp. 60, 65). For a similar argument to Seaford's, but one that specifically locates the emergence of philosophical practice in an unfolding crisis of the previously open, substantively egalitarian system of *isonomia* that existed in the Greek colonies of Ionia, see Karatani 2017.

121 Bhaskar 1991a.

122 I take exception, then, to Charles T. Wolfe's reductive definition of materialism as 'the philosophical doctrine that "Everything that exists is material", including human beings, who cannot then have an immortal soul' (Wolfe 2016, p. 1). If, at the ontological level, 'materialism' properly designates 'realism', then there is no further requirement to pos-

that adherence to the materialist position at this level is philosophically non-negotiable for Marxists: one simply cannot envision changing the world without having to identify, confront, and dismantle actually existing structures of domination, oppression, and exploitation. This is why critical realist philosophers like Roy Bhaskar and Andrew Collier have preferred the term 'emancipation' to 'liberation' in order to stress that the goal of socio-political transformation is not the attainment of a blissful psychological state or even an 'amelioration of states of affairs' but the hard-fought transformation of structures.[123] No doubt liberation is good, but emancipation is better. Idealism, by contrast, is

> on the one hand, theoretically, unable to explain the constraints which make emancipation necessary, and, on the other, practically, destined to preserve real constraints from which we could have emancipated ourselves, by proclaiming an emancipation entirely internal to 'the mind' or 'discourse'.[124]

Yet during the spirited discussion that ensued following Althusser's lecture on 'Lenin and Philosophy', Paul Ricoeur complained that Althusser had imposed an alternative of materialism and idealism that was 'completely metaphysical and fictive'.[125] Perhaps. How to respond? If by materialism one means, as Lenin did, a robust commitment to realism, then Ricoeur's objection is beside the point. Either the external physical world exists independent of knowing subjects – or it does not. There can be no third possibility. A realist perspective is indeed metaphysical, but it need not be imposed, let alone fictive.

---

tulate that 'everything that exists is material'. This statement might be true, but one could remain a materialist even if it were false. For example, 'mind', 'consciousness', 'spirit', or 'soul' need not be reducible to 'matter' but, along Aristotelian lines, they could also be understood as the 'form' taken by 'embodied matter'. If so, then an 'Averroist' materialist could, firstly, distinguish between the 'imaginative intellect' (located in each corporeally distinct human being) and the 'receptive intellect' and the 'agent intellect' (both of which are collectively shared by all human beings) and, secondly, argue that although the former is 'corruptible', the latter two are, if not exactly 'immortal', then at least 'eternal' (in Spinoza's sense of the word). For Averroes's debt to, and reworking of, Aristotle's conception of the intellect in *De Anima* III.4–6 (Aristotle 1987, pp. 201–7), see Averroes 2009, pp. 292–363 and, in commentary, see Davidson 1992, pp. 220–356; Libera 2014, pp. 170–81. A fascinating discussion of *De Anima* as a source for the early Marx's conception of universal human 'species being' may be found in Depew 1981–2.

123 See Bhaskar 1991b, pp. 75–6; Collier 1994, pp. 194–200.
124 Collier 1994, p. 200.
125 Althusser 1998, p. 141.

Moreover, realism need not imply *direct* access to the world but is compatible with extensive conceptual mediation and multiple interpretative and evaluative stances.[126]

Indeed, the very reason that philosophy has always, and will always continue to be, the site for a struggle of materialist and idealist tendencies arises precisely at the level of ontology. Since, as Roberto Unger and Lee Smolin have compellingly argued, the passage of time is not illusory but *real*,[127] all forms of human knowledge about the external world will always remain unfinished and incomplete.[128] This is because there are no fixed and unchanging laws of nature that science can hope exhaustively to identify; at most science approximates a complete understanding of the deep structures of the world. To borrow Ilya Prigogine's deepening of a famous Sartrean formula, 'Time precedes existence'.[129]

Likewise, critical Marxists who embrace a 'materialism of time' (or a 'temporality of matter')[130] should concur that, at the historically mediated level of modes of production and concrete social formations, the human sciences (e.g. psychology, sociology, and economics) can achieve at most an approximate understanding of complex and varied human beliefs, motivations, actions, and institutions.[131] As a result, philosophy, which (a) directly emerges from the confluence of the sciences and the class struggle but (b) only indirectly and obliquely represents the class struggle in theory, must itself remain unfinished and incomplete. So too must philosophical texts and traditions embody and

---

126 See Collier 1994.
127 See Unger 2007, pp. 81–110, Smolin 2014, and Unger and Smolin 2015.
128 Marcelo Gleiser has added a striking metaphor: even as scientific knowledge of the world expands, so does its frontiers – analogous to the boundaries of an island – grow (Gleiser 2014). Or, as Althusser argued in the discussion with Paul Ricoeur following his lecture on 'Lenin and Philosophy', the various 'continents' discovered by the sciences remain autonomous, lack 'common borders', and cannot somehow be reassembled – by philosophy or any other means – into a kind of Pangaean supercontinent (Althusser 1998, pp. 141–2).
129 Prigogine 1997, pp. 163–82. The formula used by Jean-Paul Sartre in his 1945 lecture 'Existentialism is a Humanism' was, of course, 'Existence precedes essence'; see Sartre 2007, pp. 20–2. Given that Sartre's objective in this lecture is to establish subjectivity as a philosophical 'point of departure' (p. 20), one could insist that even human subjectivity exhibits conflicting tendencies rooted in the objective nature of the physical world that exists temporally prior to, and independent of, consciousness.
130 Negri 2003, p. 177.
131 In his critical assessment of 'speculative realism', Peter Gratton has also stressed the need for materialist philosophers to embrace Smolin's scientific defence of the realism of time. See Gratton 2014, pp. 201–16.

express an ongoing *real* struggle of materialist and idealist tendencies.[132] Why precisely *these two* tendencies, though?

The answer hinges on the very distinction to be made between materialism and idealism. Materialist tendencies signify the ways in which philosophies embody the recognition that the external world exists prior to, and independent of, the knowing subject and possesses an expanse and temporal evolution such that it can never be fully comprehended. By contrast, idealist tendencies signify the ways in which philosophies embody the relentless desire to know even in excess of what can be known and, as Smolin puts it, are 'just making stuff up'.[133]

Yet epistemologically Lenin was doubtless correct to favour what he called 'intelligent' idealism in comparison with 'stupid', or what we might call *reductionist*, materialism that leaves little room for such *emergent* properties as the free play of creative imagination and the autonomy of critical reason.[134] To his credit, Macherey has never regarded science as providing the only, or even the primary, model for philosophy to emulate. Indeed, literature is an equally appropriate medium for encountering 'philosophy without philosophers'.[135] Moreover, idealist and materialist tendencies traverse literature as thoroughly and diversely as they do philosophical texts. This is why Macherey sought to explain Lenin's materialist conception of representation as a 'broken mirror' of the external world through the latter's articles on Leo Tolstoy.[136]

Materialism at the epistemological level asserts not the primacy of 'matter in motion' (to use Lenin's term)[137] – let alone atoms, quarks, or strings – over consciousness but the productive activity of the knowing subject.[138] Moreover, as Raymond argued,[139] intelligent idealism may offer important insights that serve emancipatory political projects in ways that unintelligent materialism

---

132 A *real* struggle of tendencies means that these tendencies are prior to, and exist independent of, any conceptual analysis that is intended to demarcate them.
133 Smolin 2014, p. 11.
134 Lenin 1972a, p. 276. For the distinction between reductionist and emergentist tendencies in the history of materialism, see Noonan 2012, pp. 17–45.
135 Macherey 1995, p. 229. See also Macherey 2013b.
136 Macherey 2006 [1978], pp. 117–51.
137 See, for example, 'Engels was right when he said that it is not important to which of the numerous schools of materialism or idealism a particular philosopher belongs, but rather whether he takes nature, the external world, *matter in motion*, or spirit, reason, consciousness, etc., as primary' (Lenin 1927b, p. 166; my emphasis).
138 Slavoj Žižek (2014a, pp. 51–89) has rightly stressed the need to defend a 'materialist theory of subjectivity', but he offers no good reason to think that Hegel (as opposed to Spinoza) provides the privileged basis for such a defence. See my discussion in Chapter 9 below.
139 Raymond 1997.

cannot. For example, Marx's sustained effort to extract the 'rational kernel'[140] of Hegel's absolute idealism would not have been possible, let alone necessary, if the latter had operated simply as an elaborate philosophical diversion from real-world struggles. Antonio Negri has more recently shown that within Descartes's writings lie both the radical opening of Renaissance humanism and its eventual closure, reduction, and 'internal erosion' into the 'solitude of the I'.[141]

Yet a note of caution regarding epistemological materialism is in order. Michel Pêcheux once compellingly argued that ideology 'designates the space' of the struggle between idealist and materialist tendencies in philosophy. As a result, forms of idealism tend to identify the process of knowledge without a subject with a centred Subject; whereas forms of materialism tend, on the contrary, 'to dissolve the unity of this identification, revealing the Subject as an effect of the process without a subject'.[142] Indeed, the materialist tendency posits 'the real (including thought which, in a specific form, is determined by it) as a non-unified process, traversed by unevenness and contradictions'.[143] Pêcheux concluded that the two philosophical tendencies

> are not symmetrical: idealism *never* meets anything other than itself, even when it is 'opposing' materialism; the latter, on the contrary, *always* recognizes the existence of idealism, because it is for ever dissociating itself from it.[144]

Finally, then, practical materialism serves as a constraint, preventing both imagination and reason from overreaching their theoretical bounds. Indeed, Andrew Collier has suggested that perhaps the main reason that Marx rejected idealism was

> due to his emphasis on *practice* rather than purely contemplative knowledge, as the main way in which we encounter reality. In practice, we do not just form ideas about the world, we bang our heads against it, and are forced to move beyond the constructs of our own minds.[145]

---

140 See Althusser 2005 for a now-classic formulation of Marx's materialist inversion and repositioning of Hegel's idealist dialectic.
141 Negri 2007, p. 162. On Spinoza's effort to reconstitute the Renaissance humanist project, see Negri 1997.
142 Pêcheux 1982, pp. 197–8.
143 Pêcheux 1982, pp. 199–200.
144 Pêcheux 1982, p. 200.
145 Collier 2008, pp. 142–3.

The most important question for Marxists, then, is not 'What exists?' or 'How can one know it?' but 'How should one act?' Answering the third question well doubtless presumes that one also has good answers to the first two questions; yet, as Macherey has stressed, materialism is ultimately

> not a doctrine, not a theory, not a body of knowledge, but rather a manner of intervention, a philosophical 'position' ... A position is not the theory of an object, the discourse within which the latter is at once represented and constituted; it is the manifestation, the affirmation of an orientation, of a tendency, of a way of moving though, not 'reality', which is not an object of philosophy, but the philosophical field itself, grasped in the concrete complexity of its internal conflicts as the specific site of this intervention.[146]

Or, in Max Horkheimer's moving words,

> materialism is not interested in a world view or in the souls of men. It is concerned with changing the concrete conditions under which men suffer and in which, of course, their souls must become stunted.[147]

Indeed, maintaining the priority of practice over theory is at the heart of what we might call the cultivation of *Marxist practical reason* in the service of working-class self-emancipation.

8   For a Marxist Theory of Action

What might be the conceptual framework for elaborating a Marxist account of practical reason? Here we shall briefly examine the efforts of André Tosel, who has reaffirmed Althusser's and Macherey's emphasis on the priority of practice over theory, insisted that the relationship between production and action must be reformulated, and sought to develop a theory of what he calls 'produ-action'.[148]

Tosel argues that Marx never ignored action in favour of production alone or thought of production as 'separate from the system of actions that realize it'. As Tosel observes,

---

146   Macherey 1983, p. 137.
147   Horkheimer 1986, p. 32.
148   Tosel 1993; 1996.

> [Marx] showed that the capitalist mode of production, the labor process as a teleological activity satisfying human needs in organic exchange with nature is determined as a process of reproduction governed by the principle of valorization that implies production for its own sake ... [but] this process requires the constitution of a system of actions responsible for regulating and directing it in the maintenance of its submission to the principle of valorization.[149]

However, Tosel continues,

> the process of reproduction and the system of actions ... produced contradictions opening onto possibilities of transformation. The constraint exercised over living labor by the principle of valorization (relative surplus value and real submission under capital) simultaneously stimulate the productive energies under the dictatorship of productivity and provoke the resistance of workers expropriated of the means of production, by revealing the possibility of an appropriation of the conditions of production according to relations freed from exploitation.[150]

In sum, there is 'no production without action in production', since the capitalist production process is always internally confronted with the question of whether it can be transformed in more democratic ways, with the limit case being a society of freely associated producers. Likewise, though, there can be 'no action without production', since capitalist production

> displaces its center of gravity from productive actions ... toward non-productive activities, whether they be political, ethical, or aesthetic. In opposition to the vertical logic of the real valorization-subsumption that reduces the possibilities of cooperation to a constrained placement of individuals in the economic-political system is the germ of a horizontal logic of exchange regarding the ends of being-in-common, resting on the practices of a really political 'agon'.[151]

Tosel concludes that 'it is impossible to eliminate the pole of production ... just as it is unjustifiable to reduce the pole of action ... The problem would instead be that of their mediation'.[152]

---

149   Tosel 1993, p. 32.
150   Tosel 1993, p. 32.
151   Tosel 1996, p. 136.
152   Tosel 1992, p. 24.

A normative theory of democratic action requires both (a) a 'logic of collective action' to consider macro-subjects like classes, nations, states, and modes of production which go beyond individual choices and (b) a logic of individual prudential action. Tosel is aware that there is a risk involved in weakening the separation between production and action, but

> The moralistic inflation to which an insistence on the exclusive value of practical rationality proper to individual choices can give rise winds up making utterly irrational the logic of collective action by confusing the logics of domination that recover it with the possibilities of communicative interaction that the process of modern labor itself contains.[153]

As a result, Tosel favours an explicitly 'mixed' or 'impure' logic of action that would be simultaneously dialogical and polemical, communicative and strategic.

Finally, it is worth noting that for Tosel the concept of produ-action has more than methodological implications, since a system of constraints can also be a 'system of alternative possibilities'.[154] Indeed, the 'standpoint of communism thus appears as the production and action of the double mediation of production by action and of action by production'.[155] This would, however, be a 'communism of finitude', one that has been 'reinterpreted within the element of finitude, of a rationalism having become reasonable'.[156]

∵

Let us conclude by reiterating the theme of this chapter: that Marxists ought to understand philosophy as an unending, always incomplete struggle of materialist and idealist tendencies. Yet a question remains. Given Althusser's argument that philosophy only exists in class-divided societies in which science is present, would philosophy continue to exist in a post-class society in which science persisted? Although Tosel does not indicate as much, one should presume that the establishment of a communism of finitude would not exclude philosophy, render philosophy superfluous, or definitively realise philosophy as a comprehensive 'consequent materialism' purged of any and all idealist elements. Indeed, one should presume that philosophy would persist as a dis-

---

153   Tosel 1992, p. 25.
154   Tosel 1996, p. 137.
155   Tosel 1993, p. 33.
156   Tosel 1993, p. 34.

tinctive activity – but an activity that more people would be able to pursue, alongside science, religion, art, poetry, music, sports, and other worthy endeavours.[157] In the spirit of Aristotle,[158] Marxists should expect that a maximal reduction of alienated labour and a maximal increase of free time would in no way diminish the human desire to know but would even enhance our capacity to wonder at, explore, and flourish within the marvellous world we inhabit.[159]

---

157   I am deliberately echoing here Marx and Engels's own well-known – and in the eyes of some critics *absurdly and pastorally utopian* – sketch in the *German Ideology* of daily life under communism: 'to hunt in the morning, fish in the afternoon, rear cattle in the evening, criticize after dinner' (Marx 2000, p. 185). However, this list of activities, and their temporal sequence, should hardly be regarded as definitive or mandatory. The whole point is rather to challenge the rigid social division of labour under capitalism in the name of a dramatically expanded scope of human freedom and opportunity for creative pursuits.
158   See Aristotle's famous twofold requirement in *Metaphysics* 982b for the study of philosophy: intellectual curiosity and sufficient leisure time (Aristotle 2016b, pp. 5–6).
159   See Noonan 2012, pp. 78–84 for a compelling discussion of the struggle within capitalism over 'surplus time' as providing the basis for an anti-capitalist project of realising greater free time as an 'open matrix of possibilities' within which persons can flourish by autonomously shaping their own lives.

CHAPTER 2

Paul of Tarsus, Thinker of the Conjuncture*

> As St Paul admirably put it, it is in the 'Logos', meaning in ideology, that we live, move and have our being.
> – LOUIS ALTHUSSER[1]

∴

> To the present hour we are hungry and thirsty, we are poorly clothed and beaten and homeless, and we grow weary from the work of our own hands.
> – 1 Cor 4.11–12

∴

What is a 'conjuncture', and what might it mean to be a 'thinker of' a conjuncture or to 'think in' a conjuncture – let alone to envision a way out of a conjuncture?

'Conjuncture' was Louis Althusser's name for one of the central concepts of Marxist political theory, or what Lenin simply called the 'current situation'.[2] The word denotes the need in politics, for organisers especially, to ascertain the balance of contending forces, to identify the uneven and combined state of the social contradictions arising at any given moment and to which political strategy and tactics must respond. In *For Marx*, for example, Althusser argues that 'what is irreplaceable in Lenin's texts' is

> the analysis of the structure of a *conjuncture*, the displacements and condensations of its contradictions and their paradoxical unity, all of which

---

* This chapter has been previously published in *Althusser and Theology*, edited by Agon Hamza, pp. 129–51, Leiden: Brill, 2016.
1 Althusser 2014b, p. 262. Althusser misquotes from Acts 17.28, when Paul reputedly debated 'the philosophers' before the Areopagus in Athens. In fact, Paul is said to have argued that we 'live, move, and have our being' not in the 'Logos' but in 'God'.
2 For a 'genealogy' of the concept as it has been used in the history of Marxism, see Thao 1999.

are the very existence of that 'current situation' which political action was to transform, in the strongest sense of the word, between February and October, 1917.³

Althusser later refines this concept in terms of how politically to 'think in the conjuncture' and identifies Niccolò Machiavelli as

> the first theorist of the conjuncture or the first thinker consciously, if not to think the concept of conjuncture, if not to make it the object of an abstract and systematic reflection, then at least consistently – in an insistent, extremely profound way – to think in the conjuncture: that is to say, in its concept of an aleatory, singular case.⁴

But Althusser immediately poses a question:

> What does it mean to think in the conjuncture? To think about a political problem under the category of conjuncture? It means, first of all, taking account of all the determinations, all the existing concrete circumstances, making an inventory, a detailed breakdown and comparison of them ... This inventory of elements and circumstances, however, is insufficient. To think in terms of the category of conjuncture is not to think on the conjuncture, as one would reflect on a set of concrete data. To think under the conjuncture is quite literally to submit to the problem induced and imposed by its case.⁵

By this measure, the apostle Paul of Tarsus was a thinker of the conjuncture. However, Paul's project was assuredly not 'Italian national unity', as envisioned by Machiavelli, but instead the establishment of a vast network of inclusive and egalitarian urban assemblies in opposition to Roman imperial order.⁶

To appreciate Paul in this way is, of course, to set aside the long history of interpretations of Paul's letters as implicitly containing later Christian doctrines about incarnation, sin, grace, atonement, justification, and so forth. Yet this interpretative approach understands Paul's life and organising activities

---

3   Althusser 2010, p. 179.
4   Althusser 2000, p. 18.
5   Althusser 2000, p. 18.
6   Philosophical reflection on the apostle Paul as posing an alternative to Roman imperial institutions and values must begin with Crossan and Reed 2004, and the three groundbreaking volumes edited by Horsley 1997; 2000; 2004.

backwards; it stresses his theory over – indeed at the expense of – his practice. Reta Halteman Finger has suggested that when we approach the New Testament from a 'doctrinal model, we tend to read it "on the flat", without taking much time to understand the actual historical and social situation out of which a text was written'.[7] Moreover, as Jerome Murphy-O'Connor remarked in his biography of Paul, 'theological thought actually develops … by historically conditioned insights rather than by logical deduction from a deposit of faith'.[8]

1 Paul's Conjuncture

In order to test the thesis, to be defended below, that Paul can be understood as a thinker of the conjuncture, let us investigate what constituted his own historical conjuncture by considering two episodes from the Acts of the Apostles (henceforth 'Acts')[9] and one passage from Paul's first letter, written to the assembly of Jesus followers in Thessalonica.[10] Call these three aspects or *elements* of Paul's conjuncture. Let us begin with a miraculous healing episode in the Roman colony of Lystra[11] recounted in Chapter 14 of Acts:

> In Lystra there was a man sitting who could not use his feet and had never walked, for he had been crippled from birth. He listened to Paul as he was speaking. And Paul, looking at him intently and seeing that he had faith to

---

7 Finger 2007, p. 8.
8 Murphy-O'Connor 1997, p. v.
9 Of course, one could object that using Acts in this way reconstructs not Paul's but Luke's later conjuncture ('Luke' here signifying the author of a two-part work, probably compiled in the late first or early second century – at least a generation after the death of Paul). This question is methodologically much too complicated for me to address – let alone resolve – here, but see Phillips 2009. Suffice it to say that I agree with those contemporary New Testament scholars who contend that Acts itself is not so much history 'as it happened' but is only the Second Part of an 'epic' narrative largely driven by Luke's own theological-political agenda (see Smith and Tyson 2013, pp. 1–19). Yet there remain incidents recounted by Luke that have the ring of historical truth quite apart from Luke's sophisticated literary construction. As a result, when one sees a convergence between how Paul in his seven 'undisputed' letters (1 Thessalonians, Galatians, 1 and 2 Corinthians, Philippians, Philemon, and Romans) recalls an event or considers a topic and how Luke portrays 'Paul' as a character in Acts, one finds oneself on reasonably solid historical ground. I propose that this is indeed the case for those episodes depicted in Chapters 14 and 19 regarding the ideological, political, and economic stakes of the struggle between Greco-Roman polytheism and Jewish monotheism.
10 Located in the northeastern Greek region of Macedonia.
11 Located in the south of modern Turkey.

be healed, said in a loud voice, 'Stand upright on your feet'. And the man sprang up and began to walk. When the crowds saw what Paul had done, they shouted in the Lycaonian language, 'The gods have come down to us in human form!' Barnabas they called Zeus, and Paul they called Hermes, because he was the chief speaker. The priest of Zeus, whose temple was just outside the city, brought oxen and garlands to the gates; he and the crowds wanted to offer sacrifice. When the apostles Barnabas and Paul heard of it, they tore their clothes and rushed out into the crowd, shouting, 'Friends, why are you doing this? We are mortals just like you, and we bring you good news, that you should turn from these worthless things to the living God, who made the heaven and the earth and the sea and all that is in them. In past generations he allowed all the nations to follow their own ways; yet he has not left himself without a witness in doing good – giving you rains from heaven and fruitful seasons, and filling you with food and your hearts with joy'. Even with these words, they scarcely restrained the crowds from offering sacrifice to them.

But Jews came there from Antioch and Iconium and won over the crowds. Then they stoned Paul and dragged him out of the city, supposing that he was dead. But when the disciples surrounded him, he got up and went into the city. The next day he went on with Barnabas to Derbe.[12]

Although many scholars have written off this episode as an instance of Lukan fabulation, Barbara Graziosi has maintained that it marks a crucial moment in the decline of Greco-Roman polytheism.[13] The narrative not only concerns the difficulty of 'translation' from one language to another (from Lycaonian to Greek), but also, more importantly, the collision of popular polytheism with the novelty of monotheism. As Graziosi observes,

---

12   Acts 14.8–20. All biblical translations are taken from the New Revised Standard Version ('NRSV') in Coogan 2010.
13   Moreover, it parallels Paul's recommendation to serve 'the living and true God' instead of 'idols' (1 Thess 1.9) and his inquiry into the efficacy, and moral consequences, of eating meat that was customarily sacrificed to 'so-called gods' that do not really exist (1 Cor 8.1–13). Elsewhere, Paul criticised what he considered to be the polytheistic failure – through an inversion and undermining of natural reason – to realise that God's 'eternal power and divine nature, invisible though they are, have been understood and seen through the things he has made. So they are without excuse; for though they knew God, they did not honor him as God or give thanks to him, but they became futile in their thinking, and their senseless minds were darkened. Claiming to be wise, they became fools; and they exchanged the glory of the immortal God for images resembling a mortal human being or birds or four-footed animals or reptiles' (Rom 1.18–23).

the author of the Acts offered a scene of stunned confusion and rapid – even instant – translation. Confronted with a miracle, local people reached out for what they thought they knew about the gods, assuming their universality, anthropomorphism, ability to manifest themselves as ordinary mortals, and need of sacrifices.[14]

Or, to borrow from Louis Althusser's theory of ideology,[15] we could note that the entire episode pivots on a popular reception of Barnabas and Paul as 'Zeus' and 'Hermes' in human form, to which Barnabas and Paul react in a dramatic prophetic manner by 'tearing their clothes' as a 'sign of protest' and 'thus seek to stop this response to healing'.[16] Following Althusser, we could say that the crowd's *recognition* of Barnabas and Paul as Greek deities is at the same time the very source of their *misrecognition* of them as apostles of 'the living God'.[17] There remains in this episode and throughout Acts a fierce ideological struggle between monotheism(s)[18] and polytheism(s), which the latter was decisively, but not utterly, to lose.[19]

∴

Let us now examine a second element of Paul's conjuncture: the conflict that arose in Ephesus[20] when an artisan named Demetrius strongly objected to Paul's missionary activities and set off a citywide riot.[21] The episode in Ephesus

---

14 Graziosi 2014, p. 167.
15 See Althusser 2014b.
16 Malina and Pilch 2008, p. 103. Graziosi 2014, p. 168 misconstrues this symbolic 'rending of garments' as disrobing.
17 On the dialectical interplay between ideological 'recognition' and 'misrecognition', see Althusser 2014b, pp. 189–99.
18 The episode also indicates Luke's later perspective on the rift between those Jews who accepted Paul's (and Barnabas's) mission to 'the nations' (*ta ethnē*) and those who did not.
19 See Graziosi 2014, pp. 171–84 on the survival of polytheistic deities as 'demons' but consigned to a Christian negative pantheon. For an intriguing philosophical investigation into how thoroughly or permanently monotheistic attempts to suppress polytheism have succeeded, see DuBois 2014.
20 Located along the Ionian coast of Asia Minor (western Turkey).
21 Robert Stoops, Jr. (1989) has provided a useful survey of scholarship on this incident. Stoops argues that the passage – in keeping with a recurrent theme in the Book of Acts – is Luke's 'apologetic' to bolster the self-image of Jesus followers and to provide them with arguments that their assemblies are 'entitled to the privileges long enjoyed by communities of diaspora Jews' (p. 73). Stoops, however fails to address not only the clash of economic interests but also the challenge that the Jesus movement actually posed to Roman imper-

described in Chapter 19 of Acts offers perhaps 'the most dramatic evocation of any pagan cult in the entire New Testament'.[22]

> ... Paul resolved in the Spirit to go through Macedonia and Achaia, and then to go on to Jerusalem. He said, 'After I have gone there, I must also see Rome'. So he sent two of his helpers, Timothy and Erastus, to Macedonia, while he himself stayed for some time longer in Asia.
>
> About that time no little disturbance broke out concerning the Way. A man named Demetrius, a silversmith who made silver shrines of Artemis, brought no little business to the artisans. These he gathered together, with the workers of the same trade, and said, 'Men, you know that we get our wealth from this business. You also see and hear that not only in Ephesus but in almost the whole of Asia this Paul has persuaded and drawn away a considerable number of people by saying that gods made with hands are not gods. And there is danger not only that this trade of ours may come into disrepute but also that the temple of the great goddess Artemis will be scorned, and she will be deprived of her majesty that brought all Asia and the world to worship her'.
>
> When they heard this, they were enraged and shouted, 'Great is Artemis of the Ephesians!' The city was filled with the confusion; and people rushed together to the theatre, dragging with them Gaius and Aristarchus, Macedonians who were Paul's travelling-companions. Paul wished to go into the crowd, but the disciples would not let him; even some officials of the province of Asia, who were friendly to him, sent him a message urging him not to venture into the theatre. Meanwhile, some were shouting one thing, some another; for the assembly was in confusion, and most of them did not know why they had come together. Some of the crowd gave instructions to Alexander, whom the Jews had pushed forward. And Alexander motioned for silence and tried to make a defense before the people. But when they recognized that he was a Jew, for about two hours all of them shouted in unison, 'Great is Artemis of the Ephesians!' But when the town clerk had quieted the crowd, he said, 'Citizens of Ephesus, who

---

ial order, whether or not Luke himself wanted openly to admit it. After all, he was likely writing from the perspective of a new (late First-Century or early Second-Century) conjuncture that followed the Roman military suppression of the 'Jewish Revolt' triggered in 66 C.E., the sacking of Jerusalem, the destruction of its own temple in 70 C.E., and the reassertion of imperial hegemony.

22 Hall 2014, p. 257. I am indebted to Peter Thomas for pointing out the importance of this episode for reconstructing Paul's historical conjuncture.

is there that does not know that the city of the Ephesians is the temple-keeper of the great Artemis and of the statue that fell from heaven? Since these things cannot be denied, you ought to be quiet and do nothing rash. You have brought these men here who are neither temple-robbers nor blasphemers of our goddess. If therefore Demetrius and the artisans with him have a complaint against anyone, the courts are open, and there are proconsuls; let them bring charges there against one another. If there is anything further you want to know, it must be settled in the regular assembly. For we are in danger of being charged with rioting today, since there is no cause that we can give to justify this commotion'. When he had said this, he dismissed the assembly.[23]

Although there is no reason to believe that this incident occurred exactly as described by Luke, it does have a core of historical reliability.[24] Whether Demetrius was a pious devotee of the cult of the fertility goddess Artemis or simply concerned about decline in his income, attachment to the 'alluring but ferocious goddess'[25] was a powerful influence in Ephesus during this period. The episode has four key features. First of all, it continues the theme of the monotheistic threat posed to longstanding polytheistic practices and beliefs, in this case, those attached to the Temple of Artemis.

Secondly, though, the riot against Paul was not primarily a theological issue. We should distinguish between Demetrius's own motivations and those of the people he was able to stir up. As Robert Knapp has suggested, the popular tumult resulted from 'a simple affirmation by the people that their goddess not only existed, but it was powerful. Anyone threatening that reality was an enemy'. In particular, popular polytheism was

> based upon efficacious supernatural powers who could, with the proper approach, be enlisted in solving the practical problems of the day such as illness, frustration in love, and vengeance against one's enemies and rivals. To attack the existence of, as here, a goddess, undercut a central tool ordinary people used to address their everyday problems.[26]

---

23 Acts 19.23–41.
24 Trebilco 2004, pp. 155–70 offers an extremely persuasive argument to this conclusion in an exhaustive history of ancient Ephesus.
25 Hall 2014, p. 258. For a comprehensive introduction to the cult of Artemis in its Greco-Roman cultural, political, and religious setting, see Rogers 2012.
26 Knapp 2011, p. 18.

Thirdly, Demetrius's vehement opposition to Paul's message is depicted by Luke as an expression of non-Jewish opposition to the early Jesus movement 'motivated by the threat to financial interests' and a kind of 'idolatry' rooted in greed.[27]

Yet, finally, Demetrius's hostility was hardly Luke's imaginary projection but was grounded in reality: temples functioned as vital economic centres of activity during the Greco-Roman period. Hans-Josef Klauck has noted that

> the temple treasury ... consisted of votive gifts, financial contributions and dues that were levied, and amounted to a considerable value (one of the functions of temples was as banks in which money could be deposited for safe keeping or loans could be made against a payment of interest).[28]

Moreover, as Dieter Georgi compellingly argues regarding the corrosive socio-religious impact of money,

> for ancient culture and society ... debts and contracts called for witnesses and sanctions, all divine prerogatives. Temples became involved rather early as trusted institutions. Their trust became quite real in terms of testifying, depositing, crediting, and collecting interest. The priests witnessed and certified the contracting and trading of debts; they wrote and executed obligations against fees and interest. These obligations were traded beyond the original parties and provided profit to the temple and further traders involved. Thus the temple became a bank, and money became an abstraction, depersonalized and dematerialized.[29]

In this light, it is hardly surprising that the Roman writer Pliny the Younger complained to Emperor Trajan in 112 CE about the negative impact of so-called 'Christians' on temple life:

---

27   See Rosner 2007, pp. 152–3. Indeed, as Rosner notes, this passage reiterates Luke's previous critique of non-Jewish polytheistic greed: in Acts 16.16–24 we read that Paul had exorcised a possessed slave girl in Philippi only to have her owners realise that 'their expectation of income had also left', and so they haul Paul and his associate Silas before the local authorities, who, encouraged by an angry crowd, have them flogged and jailed.
28   Klauck 2003, p. 24.
29   Georgi 2005, p. 290. For a comparative study of the 'monumentalisation' of Greco-Roman temples and Jesus's prophetic action against the Jerusalem Temple as a 'den of robbers', see Betz 1997.

> For the contagion of this superstition has spread not only to the cities but also to the villages and farms. But it seems possible to check and cure it. It is certainly quite clear that the temples, which had been almost deserted, have begun to be frequented, that the established religious rites, long neglected, are being resumed, and that from everywhere sacrificial animals are coming, for which until now very few purchasers could be found. Hence it is easy to imagine what a multitude of people can be reformed if an opportunity for repentance is afforded.[30]

Although Pliny wrote a number of decades after the incident in Ephesus as reported by Luke, his worry was that the presence of Christians would adversely affect the availability of 'sacrificial animals' for 'established religious rites'. Likewise, Demetrius would have had reason to feel economically threatened regarding his own manufacture and sale of souvenir 'silver shrines'. Consequently, this episode depicts a violent encounter between two artisans – polytheistic Demetrius and monotheistic Paul – over the future economic wellbeing of the residents of Ephesus and the surrounding area. Not only was Demetrius just as much a product of his conjuncture as Paul, he was determined to protect his material self-interest. By comparison with the shrewd town clerk who was able to calm the enraged crowd but

> does nothing whatever to address Demetrius' business worries; it merely points to his skill with a mob as a spokesman for Roman order and the status quo ... Demetrius, indeed, is the more honest economist and, if we may so put it, theologian.[31]

∴

Finally, let us consider a third and crucial element of Paul's conjuncture, one that served as the historical counterpoint to what Alain Badiou has characterised as the apostle's evocation of the resurrection as a decisive 'Event' to which he strove to remain faithful.[32] For Paul equally evoked the not-yet Event of *par-*

---

30   Translated in Elliott and Reasoner 2011, p. 286.
31   Rowe 2009, p. 49.
32   Badiou 2003. However, it is important, as Neil Elliott has insisted, not to see Paul as an anomaly within First-Century Judaism (as Badiou has a tendency to do) but 'to understand central elements in Paul's story – including his persecution of the Jesus assemblies, his vision of a crucified messiah in heaven, and the resulting apostolic work among "the nations" – in terms that render these elements intelligible within Judaism and continu-

ousia: the triumphant 'return' of Jesus and the eschatological fulfilment of the Reign of God. But what is the meaning of this concept? John Dominic Crossan and Jonathan Reed have provided a Roman template for the experience of *parousia*:

> In its ancient context *parousia* meant the arrival at a city of a conquering general, an important official, an imperial emissary, or, above all, the emperor himself. Whether that advent was good or bad news for the citizens depended absolutely on their prior relationship with the arriving one. It is probably necessary in those cases to translate *parousia* not just as 'visit' but as 'visitation'.[33]

In other words, *parousia* designated an imperial Event. In stark contrast, however, Paul identified, anticipated, and sought to restore hope in a *counter-imperial* Event among the distraught Thessalonian assembly members who were grieving on account of the recent deaths of loved ones. At the end of the letter, Paul quotes a Roman imperial motto only to discredit it: 'When they say, "There is peace and security", then sudden destruction will come upon them, as labor pains come upon a pregnant woman, and there will be no escape!'[34]

To reinforce the image of a moment in time that is unforeseeable and cannot be dated by a calendar, Paul adds that this Counter-Event will 'come like a thief in the night'.[35] In other words, it will surprise even the most vigilant among the faithful Jesus followers. It will turn out to be the most *aleatory* of future encounters.[36]

As a result, what was required at the present moment – *kairos* or conjuncture – was self-control not only over one's desires or emotions, but also over anxious expectation or lapsing into moral laxity. Paul exhorts[37] the Jesus fol-

---

ous with it' (Elliott 2015, p. 243). For a detailed examination of how Paul's use of 'Christ language' was indebted to various forms of 'Messiah language' in ancient Judaism, see Novenson 2012.

33 Crossan and Reed 2004, p. 167.
34 1 Thess 5.3.
35 1 Thess 5.2.
36 Althusser 2006, pp. 163–207, does not include Paul in the 'underground current of the philosophy of the encounter' and is rightly taken to task by Ward Blanton (2014, pp. 39–66).
37 On Paul's use of moral 'exhortation' (*paraenēsis*) in 1 Thessalonians, see Malherbe 2006, pp. 49–66.

lowers in Thessalonica as follows: 'let us be sober, and put on the breastplate of faith and love, and for a helmet the hope of our deliverance'.[38]

Paul's nonviolent symbolic reversal of such visible marks of Roman military power as armour and helmets could not be more poignant. As Georgi once observed,

> The company of Jesus in its collective life, characterized by the triad of faith, love, and hope, is engaged in battle. This battle creates the world – or better, in the eschatological context, it creates it anew. The critical event for the fate of the universe does not come to pass in heaven with God or among the gods. It does not involve the mighty of this world. It has nothing to do with force or violence. It takes place within and through a community held together by faith, love, and hope.[39]

Precisely because Paul's conjuncture reeked of Roman imperial domination, exploitation, and violence,[40] we must not be content to identify the Event (and Counter-Event) to which Paul remained faithful; it is equally vital to identify his strategy for organising, nurturing,[41] and sustaining a 'Christian Revolution'.[42] This would be the way out of Paul's conjuncture, an 'exit strategy' based on the counter-imperial triadic motto of 'faith, hope, and love'.

Here we should rely again on Althusser's theory of 'ideology as interpellation'.[43] After 'they' have hailed members of the Thessalonian assembly – indeed, subjects throughout the Roman Empire – with a triumphalist phrase, Paul responds with a counter-phrase of his own. We might try to reconstruct this ideological challenge-and-riposte as follows:

Interpellation: 'When they [i.e. the Roman authorities] say, "peace and security"' (*eirēnē kai asphaleia*, Greek for the Latin slogan *pax et securitas*)[44]

=> 'then' (*tote*)

---

38 1 Thess 5.7–8. The Greek word *sōtērias* has been translated here as 'deliverance' rather than 'salvation', as in the NRSV, because its connotation is 'a freeing from real or threatening harm or loss' (see Danker 2009, p. 346).
39 Georgi 2009, pp. 27–8.
40 See Carter 2006 and Morley 2010.
41 On Paul's role as a 'nurturer', see Malherbe 2006, pp. 67–77.
42 Míguez 2012, especially pp. 173–82.
43 See Althusser 2014b, pp. 189–97, 261–70.
44 See Oakes 2005.

Counter-interpellation: 'sudden destruction will come upon them (*aiphnidios autois ephistatai olethros*), as labor pains come upon a pregnant woman, and there will be no escape (*kai ou mē ekphygōsin*)!' [i.e. the unexpected downfall of the Roman imperial system].

As many New Testament scholars have noted, in his interpellation/counter-interpellation formula, Paul was pitting against one another two rival conceptions of peace, namely, the *Pax Romana*, based on the real or implied threat of violence and dispossession, as opposed to the biblical conception of peace based on the presence of justice and equality (*eirēnē* had been used since the Septuagint, composed in the late second century BCE, as a Greek equivalent for the Hebrew concept of *shalōm*).[45] What is more, the end of the present conjuncture, Paul suggests, will give birth to something radically new. Although no one knows when this Counter-Event will occur (except perhaps a 'thief'), Paul issued the stern prophetic warning that 'there will be no escape'!

Yet a danger remained implicit in Paul's counter-interpellation: his 'reversal and rejection' of Roman imperial ideology was caught up in, and may have even helped to reproduce, that to which it was vehemently opposed.[46] In this respect, Warren Carter has identified a central contradiction that emerged as Paul (and other early Jesus followers) sought to 'negotiate' the Roman Empire. For example, Carter has argued that

> the frequent appeal to Paul's apocalyptic thinking and use of Jewish eschatological traditions needs problematizing. Such traditions are anti-imperial, as is frequently recognized, but they are also imitative of imperial strategies, including the universal imposition of power and rule and the often violent exclusion and destruction of opponents. The ambivalency of opposition and imitation is not commonly recognized. A similar examination of Paul's Christology (Lord? Savior? Son of God? Christ?) and apostolic authority in community formation is also needed. Titles such as 'Lord' and 'Savior', as well as claims that Jesus is a counter-emperor or victorious over the Roman order, express an equally imperial framework. That is, while Rome's imperialism must be exposed, so must Paul's.[47]

---

45 The classic study of Roman versus biblical conceptions of peace is Wengst 1987. On Paul's understanding of peace and nonretaliation, see Swartley 2006, pp. 189–221; Zerbe 2012, pp. 141–68; Gabrielson 2013; and Keazirian 2014.
46 See Pêcheux 1982, pp. 164–6 on the inability of what he called 'counter-identification' to go beyond 'reversal and rejection' of a given dominant ideology.
47 Carter 2010, p. 24. See also Schüssler Fiorenza 2000 and Punt 2012 on Paul's tendency to

In sum, Paul's counter-imperial praxis may have provided the 'raw material'[48] for an alternative to the Roman Empire, but it could not realise that alternative by organising effective means to break decisively with the latter's structures of social, economic, ideological, and religious power.

2 Paul's Practice

Slavoj Žižek has defined a 'philosophical Event' as 'a traumatic intrusion of something New which remains unacceptable for the predominant view'. Moreover, an Event in philosophy expresses 'a moment of madness: the madness of being captivated by an Idea (like falling in love, like Socrates under the spell of his daemon)'. Finally, philosophies that follow an Event 'are all attempts to contain/control this excess of madness, to renormalize it, to re-inscribe it into the normal flow of things'.[49]

In the life and thought of Paul of Tarsus there doubtless arose a kind of *madness* associated with the philosophical Event to which he strove to remain faithful.[50] But what was the radical opening of the Pauline Event? As Althusser might have put it, what was Paul's 'emptiness of a distance taken'?[51] What was Paul's madness that would have to be contained and controlled by the emergence of 'official' Christianity?[52] Georgi memorably concludes that

> when Luke turned Paul into a religious hero, this fool for Christ was given a belated state funeral. When the victorious wing of the church allied itself with the Caesar, Paul, the rebel for Christ whom Caesar had slain was consigned to a golden hell. Since that day, has up been up and down been down? Can the gods once again dwell in peace in heaven and the rulers stand secure once more upon the backs of their subjects?[53]

---

reinscribe his anti-imperial message within the ideological framework of Roman imperial discourse itself.

48 Pêcheux 1982, p. 164.
49 Žižek 2014b, p. 70.
50 On Paul as a visionary or mystic, see Borg and Crossan 2009 and Shantz 2009.
51 See Althusser 2012, p. 197. Breton 2016, pp. 9–10 notes that Althusser's own encounter with mysticism and negative theology provided a condition of possibility for his personal break with Catholicism and reorientation to Marxism.
52 See Elliott 2006 on 'the canonical betrayal' and 'mystification' of the apostle Paul.
53 Georgi 2009, p. 104.

In a word: Paul's was the madness of a free, equal, and inclusive collective life against Empire.[54] As Georgi explains, this was the subversive 'praxis of faith' that got Paul – like Jesus before him – killed.[55]

Having agreed with Badiou and Žižek so far, there remains, however, the equally, if not more, important question of Paul's *practice*. In his recent book on Althusser, Warren Montag has argued that 'in its practical existence, philosophy must constantly pose to itself the question of its orientation, of the place it occupies and that which the conjuncture demands it accomplish; it must constantly ask, what is to be done?'[56]

What then did Paul believe that he ought to do in his conjuncture? How did Paul decide to *act*? To be precise: What was his livelihood, his vision, his objective, his strategy, his tactics, his basic message, his *mission*?[57] In other words, how did the Pauline Event arise out of, and unfold within, the uneven and combined elements of his historical conjuncture? Here Badiou's work on Paul is not particularly helpful. As Néstor Míguez has observed, 'Badiou removes Paul from the concrete political situation and throws him into a type of theoretical struggle that, although present in Paul, finds its incarnation ... in a concrete confrontation with the practices and ways of the empire'.[58]

Althusser famously proposed that Marx's philosophy largely existed in 'a practical state' and required a 'theoretical labour ... to work out the specific *concept* or *knowledge* of this practical resolution'.[59] So too should we read Acts and Paul's letters with an eye toward working out the concepts and knowledge associated with Paul's practice. We ought to approach Paul not as a defender of 'orthodox' positions on various matters, but rather as an advocate for the 'orthopraxis' of nonviolent resistance to Roman imperial domination.

∴

It is surprising that radical philosophers who have recently written on Paul have scarcely bothered to consider the question of his missionary strategy, namely, his approach to organising and sustaining counter-imperial *ekklēsiai* or

---

54 On Paul's egalitarian model of assemblies as an alternative to Roman everyday violence and exploitation, see especially Ruden 2010.
55 See especially Georgi 2005.
56 Montag 2013, p. 178.
57 For an introduction to what Paul regarded as his egalitarian 'participatory' mission of *theosis* – 'becoming like God by participating in the life of God' – see Gorman 2015.
58 Míguez 2012, p. 10.
59 Althusser 2010, pp. 165–6.

'assemblies of the saints' that are misleadingly called 'churches'.[60] For example, Stanislas Breton rightly noted that 'Paul was too absorbed by his missionary and administrative tasks to have the time or the desire to reflect on his practice'.[61] Yet Breton's own philosophical reflection on Paul's practice anachronistically restricted the latter to narrowly religious categories as 'communion', 'community' (in a religious sense), 'churches', and 'the Church';[62] whereas the distinction between 'religion' and 'politics' simply did not exist in the ancient world, during the Roman Empire, or for Paul.[63]

Moreover, Badiou has argued that

> Paul mobilizes the new discourse in a constant, subtle strategy of displacement relative to Jewish discourse. We have already remarked that references to the Old Testament are as abundant in Paul's texts as those to the sayings of Christ are absent. The task Paul sets for himself is obviously not that of abolishing Jewish particularity, which he constantly acknowledges as the event's principle of historicity, but that of animating it internally by everything of which it is capable relative to the new discourse, and hence the new subject. For Paul, being Jewish in general, and the Book in particular, can and must be resubjectivated.[64]

But Paul's strategy had less to do with a 'resubjectivation' of 'Judaism' – which no more existed in a homogeneous sense than did 'Christianity' during Paul's lifetime[65] – than with a broad appeal to 'the (conquered) nations' (*ta eth-*

---

60   Horsley and Silberman 1997, pp. 145–62 explain Paul's conception of 'assemblies of the saints', and Trebilco 2012 has provided an invaluable lexicon of different terms applied by Jesus followers to themselves, e.g. 'brothers and sisters', 'the believers', 'the saints', 'the assembly', 'disciples', 'the way', and 'Christian'.
61   Breton 2011, p. 126.
62   See Breton 2011, pp. 126–41. Breton's reference to Paul's 'administrative tasks' suffices to indicate such anachronism, but his identification of *koinōnia* as 'communion' also completely obscures that the 'fellowship' (another standard translation) Paul envisioned and sought to establish and sustain was more akin to a theological-political 'solidarity' with the wretched of the Roman imperial system. On Paul's conception of 'equality' (*isotēs*) as requiring mutual 'partnership', see Zerbe 2012, pp. 75–92.
63   See Horsley 1997, pp. 10–24.
64   Badiou 2003, pp. 102–3.
65   On the diversity among 'Second-Temple' Jewish beliefs and practices, see Murphy 2002 and Goodman 2007. However, Schwartz 2014, p. 14 is doubtless correct when he writes that 'ancient Jews were not ... infinitely diverse, boundariless, always and everywhere radically decentred. They were, to be sure, engaged in the permanent project of self-creation, but since everyone always is, this fact alone tells us nothing about the nature of their

nē);[66] to participate in an egalitarian, counter-imperial movement without economic hierarchy and beyond political, cultural, or religious borders. Badiou is more interested in Paul's 'doctrine'[67] and so fails to grasp the importance of the apostle's mission – his *practice*.

∴

Paul's practice can be characterised in four key ways: (1) his self-understanding as an apostle; (2) his organising strategy; (3) his tactics; and (4) his basic message.[68] Let us examine each of these elements in turn.

Paul's claim to apostleship involved six components. First of all, Paul insisted that he had received his authority and been commissioned by the risen Jesus. Secondly, he considered himself to be a servant of the truth and authority of the gospel. Thirdly, Paul believed that he had primarily been sent by God to 'the (conquered) nations'; but also that this mission served, fourthly, as an extension of Israel's own mission from God. Fifthly, Paul embraced an eschatological apostleship; and, finally, he founded egalitarian counter-imperial assemblies of Jesus followers. Paul's stress on 'equality' (*isotēs*) as a community ideal is crucial, as can be seen in his discussion of care for the poor as a defining feature of discipleship. This ideal is evident in 2 Cor 8:14: 'At the present time (*en tō nyn kairō*) your surplus (*perisseuma*) provides what others lack so that their surplus might furnish what you lack at some future time, so that there might be equality (*isotēs*)'.[69] Paul promoted not just equality among poor people themselves but, more radically, 'the equalization of resources between persons of *different* social classes through voluntary redistribution'.[70] As Laurence Welborn has stressed, the 'audacity' of Paul's proposal arose from, and was possible precisely

---

groupness'. Indeed, the variety of Jewish beliefs was compatible with common normative practices like worshipping one God, having one temple, recognising one Torah – or, for that matter, insisting on male circumcision and *kashrut*.

66   Following Lopez 2008, it is clear that Paul's usage demands that *ta ethnē* be rendered not as 'Gentile' (as opposed to 'Jew') but with reference to the peoples who had been conquered by, and remained subservient to, the Roman Empire.

67   Badiou 2003, p. 16. Badiou asks 'What use is all this? You can consult the books. Let's cut straight to the doctrine'. Unfortunately, Paul's doctrine (if this is even the relevant designation for his epistolary interventions) can hardly be discerned straightaway but only in terms of his mission.

68   See James Dunn's remarkably exhaustive treatment of Paul's mission (Dunn 2009, pp. 519–97).

69   Translation taken from Smith and Tyson 2013. For a close reading of the broader Greco-Roman context that makes sense of this line, see Welborn 2013.

70   Welborn 2013, p. 89.

because of, the 'present time' (*kairos*) 'which is not a mundane present, but the Messianic time, which is charged to the bursting point with hope'.[71]

Paul's strategy consisted of three basic elements: to travel from Jerusalem in an enormous loop to Spain and back;[72] next, to pursue his mission especially among the (conquered) nations; finally, to gather a 'collection' from these assemblies to carry back to the Jerusalem assembly. Badiou completely misses the strategic importance of this 'collection for the poor' when he writes that

> in all the groups affiliated with the Christian declaration, funds destined for the Jerusalem community are collected. What does this contribution signify? Here, we encounter once again the conflict between tendencies refereed by the Jerusalem conference's feeble compromise.
>
> The Judeo-Christians see in this paying of tribute an acknowledgment of the primacy of the historical apostles (Peter and the others), as well as the sign that elects Jerusalem – obvious center, along with the Temple, of the Jewish community – as natural center of the Christian movement. The collection thereby affirms a continuity between Jewish communitarianism and Christian expansionism. Lastly, through the collection, external groups recognize that they amount to a diaspora. Paul gives an interpretation of the collection that is the exact opposite. By accepting their donations, the center ratifies the legitimacy of the Gentile-Christian groups. It demonstrates that neither membership of the Jewish community, nor the marks of that membership, nor being situated on the land of Israel are pertinent criteria for deciding whether a constituted group does or does not belong within the Christian sphere of influence.[73]

Badiou offers a traditional interpretation of the collection as a charitable project of internal unification among 'Gentile-Christians' and 'Jews', whereas increasing numbers of New Testament scholars have proposed that this collection served as a material way to demonstrate concrete commitment to 'solidarity' (*koinōnia*) not only among Jesus followers but also with all those who had been 'humiliated'[74] and 'economically vanquished'[75] by Roman political

---

71 Welborn 2013, p. 90.
72 On the strategic implications of Paul's envisioned missionary loop (what in Rom 15.19 he characterises as his journey 'in a circle' or 'in a circuit' [*kyklō*]), see Knox 1964 and Magda 2008. More generally on Paul's travels within, across, and against empire, see Marquis 2013.
73 Badiou 2003, pp. 28–9.
74 For an eloquent discussion of the significance of such solidarity in Jewish and early Christian traditions, see Wengst 1988.
75 See Kahl 2014.

domination and economic exploitation.[76] For example, Ross and Gloria Kinsler have argued that Paul's collection served as his concrete enactment of the ancient Israelite 'jubilee tradition' – as renewed by the Jesus movement – of debt cancellation and economic redistribution.[77] Moreover, Georgi observes that

> The collection of funds for Jerusalem in Paul's interpretation transforms the idea of an economy geared toward growth of production and profit, as the Hellenistic economy already was. The Hellenistic market economy obviously used interest as a major instrument of growth. Paul instead presupposes the biblical prohibition of interest ... now extended to everyone. The money collected for Jerusalem grows also, but into a universal divine worship. The money involved becomes a social force, a gift from community to community. It is intended to forge the vitality of the community to which it is given as well as the health of the community donating. Here obedience and simple kindness are blended. In the process the subjugation of the universe under the Rich One who had become poor has begun, and the unification of humanity has been initiated.[78]

In a succinct and provocative formulation, Georgi concludes that for Paul 'the collection was meant as the founding of a revolution to come'.[79]

Paul's mission, then, relied on an overall 'structural strategy'[80] of covering the breadth and length of the Roman Empire, carrying the gospel primarily to city dwellers, helping to set up and sustain assemblies of Jesus followers along the way, and all the while gathering a monetary collection for the impoverished community in Jerusalem. His itinerary, though, demonstrated considerable tactical flexibility within the framework of his broader missionary strategy. As Bruce Longenecker and Todd Still have pointed out,

---

76   See Georgi 1992, Friesen 2010, Ogereau 2012, and Welborn 2013. Tragically, as Taubes 2004, pp. 17–21 noted, this collection was regarded by the 'Jewish Christian' leadership as 'tainted' because of its having come from non-Jews, and so it was not accepted. As a result, the 'legitimacy' of Paul's global mission remained uncertain even at his death in Rome in the early 60s CE.
77   Kinsler and Kinsler 1999, pp. 146–9.
78   Georgi 2005, p. 297.
79   Georgi 2005, p. 127.
80   See Welborn's 2012 criticism of a class myopia he detects in the stress on charitable contributions in Longenecker 2010.

> Circumstances and forces, whether malevolent or benevolent, sometimes precluded the apostle's ability to move as he willed … With this being said, it does not appear that Paul traveled willy-nilly throughout the Mediterranean world with a knapsack on his back wherever the winds and his whims might carry him.
>
> The popular notion of Paul, the wild-eyed apocalypticist, racing indiscriminately around the Roman Empire in a 'holy hurry' spouting his missionary message to anyone he could buttonhole does not ring true with the data that we have at hand. According to Acts, Paul spent no less than eighteen months in Corinth (18:11) and some three months in Ephesus (20:31). Moreover, when Paul did have to leave a city prematurely, it was local hostility, not an imminent eschatology, that sent the apostle packing.[81]

Paul's tactics were not only city centred but specifically oriented toward provincial capitals accessible by land and sea; aimed at Jewish synagogues; based on appeals to non-Jews who were nonetheless attracted to Jewish beliefs and practices; self-supporting through his own manual labour; and dependent on a team of 'coworkers' (*synergoi*).

Finally, we can identify the eight features of Paul's basic message that formed the core of his orally transmitted and then written *gospel* or 'good news' (*euangelion*): (1) a radical turn from polytheism to monotheism; (2) a proclamation of Jesus as crucified, but (3) vindicated by being raised by God to become 'lord' (*kyrios*) over all things; with (4) an expectation of his imminent return from heaven to earth to establish justice over all nations; as a result, (5) making a demand of exclusive 'loyalty' (*pistis*) by Jesus followers;[82] (6) to be baptised, receive a gift of 'spirit' (*pneuma*), and experience a new way of life; (7) to participate in an inclusive and egalitarian celebration of a common meal: the 'lord's supper'; and (8) to engage in practices of ethical and moral development.

∴

Consider a philosophically disconcerting fact: Paul of Tarsus was a 'tentmaker' (*skēnopoios*).[83] Yet it is striking – and methodologically revealing – that such a simple and well-supported historical observation should have gone largely

---

81　Longenecker and Still 2014, p. 39.
82　Indeed, Gordon Zerbe has proposed the term 'Jesus loyalist'; see Zerbe 2012, pp. 26–46.
83　Acts 18.3.

unnoticed in the contemporary philosophical attempt to reclaim Paul's ideas.[84] Badiou's peculiar description of how Paul might have set up an assembly of Jesus followers is wide of the mark and fails to grasp that Paul was not just a militant in theory but in practice too. Badiou writes that

> Paul begins his teaching by basing himself on the community's institutions. When he arrives in a town, he first intervenes in the synagogue. Unsurprisingly, things go badly with the orthodox, for reasons of doctrine: the stubborn persistence in affirming that Jesus is the Messiah (remember that 'Christ' is simply the Greek word for 'messiah', so that the only continuity between the Good News according to Paul and prophetic Judaism is the equation Jesus = Christ), an affirmation that, in the eyes of the majority of Jews, and for extremely powerful and legitimate reasons, propounds a fraud. Following incidents that, in the conditions of the time, could be extremely violent, and where, basically, one risks one's life, Paul abandons the synagogue and withdraws to the home of a local sympathizer. There he tries to set up a group comprising Judeo-Christians and Gentile-Christians. It seems that very quickly the Gentile-Christians will constitute the majority among the adherents of the group. In light of the minimal concession Paul makes to the Jewish heritage, particularly so far as rites are concerned, this is not in the least surprising. Once the group has been sufficiently consolidated in his eyes (it will then be called an *ekklesia*, from which *eglise* [church] undoubtedly derives, although the former should be envisioned in terms of a small group of militants), Paul entrusts its running to those whose conviction he holds in high regard, and who will become his lieutenants. Then he continues on his voyage.[85]

Badiou is doubtless correct that Paul regularly presented his message in synagogues in at least some cities, as well as in private living quarters (so-called 'house churches'),[86] but he seems unaware of an important new line of schol-

---

84 To be fair, Badiou notes that 'Paul's father is an artisan-retailer, a tent-maker' (2003, p. 16). However, there is no solid historical evidence for such a claim. Furthermore, Badiou draws neither practical nor theoretical consequence from the question of Paul's (or his father's) material means of livelihood.
85 Badiou 2003, pp. 19–20.
86 See Oakes 2009b for a brilliant study of typical 'craftworker houses' unearthed amid the ruins of Pompeii as a way to model the living spaces in which assemblies of Jesus followers would have met. See also Adams 2016 for a broader – and definitive – challenge to the longstanding scholarly consensus that early Jesus followers met almost exclusively

arly research suggesting that Paul conducted much of his evangelisation within the day-to-day routine of his workshop. As Ronald Hock has summarised his ground-breaking research,

> More than any of us has supposed, Paul was *Paul the Tentmaker*. His trade occupied much of his time – from the years of his apprenticeship through the years of his life as a missionary of Christ, from before daylight through most of the day. Consequently, his trade in large measure determined his daily experiences and his social status. His life was very much that of the workshop – of artisan-friends … of leather, knives, and awls; of wearying toil; of being bent over a workbench like a slave and of working side by side with slaves; of thereby being perceived by others and by himself as slavish and humiliated; of suffering the artisan's lack of status and so being reviled and abused.[87]

As an itinerant artisan, Paul would often have struggled to earn enough money for food. While travelling, he would have had to carry his meagre possessions and tools of his trade, slept by the road in cold, rain, and snow, and regularly faced dangers of robbery on land and sea.[88] By plying his trade, though, Paul largely supported himself and was not financially dependent on the community.[89]

There is yet one more historical item that has largely escaped not only Badiou, but also most contemporary radical philosophers in their turn to Paul: Paul did not think, write, or act alone. As Acts and his letters both clearly indicate, he was not a solitary figure in his missionary work but enlisted the help of a 'cadre of coworkers'[90] like Barnabas, Silas, Timothy, Titus, Phoebe, and Chloe. Paul even worked at the same trade as the couple Prisca/Priscilla and Aquila.[91]

---

in private residences. Adams has provided substantial literary and archeological evidence that such meetings also occurred in other venues like workshops, barns, warehouses, hotels, inns, rented dining rooms, bathhouses, gardens, watersides, urban open spaces, and burial sites.

87 Hock 1987, p. 67. Hock has provided the necessary point of departure for any serious consideration of this fact on Paul's missionary practice, preaching, letter writing, and theological development.
88 For a heart-wrenching inventory of Paul's personal hardships, see 2 Cor 11.23–8.
89 Hock 1987, pp. 29–31.
90 Longenecker and Still 2014, p. 40.
91 They were all 'tentmakers' (*skēnopoioi*); see Acts 18.3.

Paul's collaborative mission can even, or especially, be seen when we read his letters, which Badiou rightly characterises as 'interventions' that are 'possessed of all the political passion proper to such interventions'.[92] But they were, in point of fact, genuinely *collective* productions.[93] Indeed, teamwork was necessary for the composition, transmission, and defraying of the expense of these interventions; and Paul relied on trusted secretaries, messengers, and funding.[94]

3   Paul's Place in the Jesus Movement

Krister Stendahl once proposed that Paul's message was 'unique but not universal' and then provided a historical counterfactual to drive the point home:

> 'If there had been no Paul, would Christianity have made it in the Gentile world?' I think anyone who is brought up in Christian schools is inclined to say that had not Paul come along, Christianity would have dwindled into a little Jewish sect, or something like that. Paul himself is very much inclined to think thus, and many of our textbooks back him up gloriously. But what are the facts? The answer is that Christianity may have made it, and made it very well, and furthermore, in the time when it happened, Paul's activities were actually a tremendously complicating factor rather than an asset for a pragmatically successful missionary program.[95]

Raising a slightly different counterfactual question, Richard Bauckham has asked 'What if Paul had Travelled East Rather than West?'[96] But Bauckham more definitively concludes that

> The historical Paul is not diminished if we conclude that, although without Paul much would have been different about the way the early Chris-

---

92   Badiou 2003, pp. 20–1.
93   Blanton 2007, pp. 105–27 offers a fascinating philosophical reflection on the significance of Tertius, who served as Paul's *amanuensis* or secretary in drafting the Letter to the Romans. However, Paul likely relied on secretaries other than Tertius; and their influence over the *content* of his letters should not be exaggerated.
94   See especially Richards 2004.
95   Stendahl 1976, p. 69.
96   Bauckham 2000.

tian movement would have spread across the Roman Empire, it would still have spread, with much the same long-term effects.[97]

Yet contemporary radical philosophers too often regard Paul as a solitary figure and so view him in isolation from the broader Jesus movement in which he played a leading but hardly exclusive role.[98] In reality, Paul competed for influence with other leaders like Peter and James,[99] to say nothing of Apollos, his evangelistic rival in Corinth.[100] Moreover, he struggled to defend his own mission against the backdrop of *other missions*, both Jewish and Hellenistic (e.g. Stoicism, Epicureanism, Neo-Platonism, mystery cults, and imperial state ideologies like emperor worship).[101] As a result, the 'correctness' of Paul's positions was not fixed once for all but required continual *adjustment*.[102] Finally, and perhaps most importantly, none of his organising activities could have been funded without the vital participation of women like Junia, Phoebe, Chloe, and Lydia.[103]

What eventually became 'Christianity', then, must not be retrospectively projected onto Paul's frequently improvised missionary activities. In fact, in his impassioned letters to diverse assemblies of Jesus followers in Thessalonica, Philippi, Galatia, Corinth, and Rome, Paul played the role of a 'troubleshooter' more than that of a 'theologian' or a 'philosopher' as he responded to, and sought to resolve, specific internal community disputes. His radicality lay as much in his flexible organising and nurturing practice as it did in his ideas.

---

97   Bauckham 2000, p. 184. For an exploration of 'counterfactual' approaches to (the absence of) Paul's role in the development of the Jesus movement, see Gray 2016, pp. 157–70.
98   Both Badiou 2003 and Blanton 2014 suffer from this defect.
99   On this struggle, see Dunn 2009, pp. 133–494 and Evans 2014. From a postcolonial perspective, K. Jason Coker (2007; 2015) has compellingly argued that the author of the Letter of James sharply criticises 'Pauline hybridity' and defends a cultural and religious identity marked by 'purity' as a more effective way to contest Roman imperial rule. As Coker writes, 'James and Paul's argument can be seen … as an argument between nativist resistance to colonial power, which is characterized by reproducing colonial representations in order to resist colonial influence, and hybrid resistance, which is characterized by blurring the boundaries of colonizer/colonized in order to renegotiate a new set of power relations' (Coker 2007, p. 27). The point is not to endorse either anti-imperial strategy. Each failed; and for their efforts both Paul and James were killed.
100 On Apollos, see Hartin 2009.
101 Regarding other forms of 'missionary activity in New Testament Times', see Georgi 1986, pp. 83–228.
102 On the need for philosophical 'adjustment', see Althusser 2012, p. 103 and Althusser 2014a, pp. 339–40.
103 On women in the leadership of early assemblies of Jesus followers, see Osiek and MacDonald 2006.

In his conjuncture Paul strove to provide concrete analyses of concrete situations in a heroic effort to hold together fledging groups of Jesus followers struggling amid the clashing theological-political priorities and ideals of both First-Century Roman-imperial and Jewish cultures and traditions.

In this respect, the Jesus movement shaped Paul just as much as, if not more than, Paul shaped the Jesus movement.

CHAPTER 3

Paul's Gift Economy: Wages, Debt, and Debt Cancellation*

> Don't go along with the pattern of this age, but be transformed by the renewing of your mind.[1]

∴

Some scholars (in particular Scott Meikle)[2] have recognised the influence of Aristotle's economic thought on Marx, but relatively few have explored the relationship between biblical and socialist economic aims. For example, although Aristotle arguably provided the ancient world's best account of economic value, it was not he but key figures in the Biblical prophetic tradition who grasped the danger to social justice posed by mounting economic debt and who proclaimed the need periodically to cancel it.[3] As David Graeber has written in his book *Debt: The First Five Thousand Years*,

> ... we are long overdue for some kind of Biblical-style Jubilee: one that would affect both international debt and consumer debt. It would be salutary not just because it would relieve so much genuine human suffering, but also because it would be our way of reminding ourselves that money is not ineffable, that paying one's debts is not the essence of morality, that all these things are human arrangements and that if democracy is to mean anything, it is the ability to all agree to arrange things in a different way.[4]

With such a political vision in mind, my focus here is on the Biblical prophetic warning about, and solution to, severe debt injustice – whether individual

---

* This chapter has been previously published in *Continental Thought & Theory* 2, pp. 452–72.
1 Rom 12:2. I have followed Peter Oakes's translation to be found in Oakes 2009b, p. 99.
2 See Meikle 1985; 1995.
3 For introductions to Biblical views of money, possessions, debt, and debt cancellation, see Horsley 2009; Brueggemann 2016; and Gnuse 2011.
4 Graeber 2014, p. 390.

or collective. I seek to demonstrate the New Testament's continuity with the Jubilee theme of economic justice and debt cancellation laid out in the Hebrew Scriptures. In particular, I argue that Paul of Tarsus well understood the economic difficulties faced by wage labourers in the first-century Roman Empire and the all-too-real possibility of debt bondage, and – through his collection 'for the poor among the consecrated at Jerusalem'[5] – devised a creative means to reclaim the Biblical tradition of debt cancellation. In short, Paul envisioned what we could call a 'gift economy' based not only on mutuality but also, and especially, on addressing the needs of the weak, vulnerable, and poor.

Indeed, Larry Welborn has persuasively argued that in the historical context of the first-century ancient world Paul contributed 'to the tentative emergence of a new category of thought – the economic'.[6] In particular, Welborn argues, the 'novelty' of Paul's collection was its radical alternative to Greco-Roman models of patronage, namely, 'the equalization of resources between persons of different social classes through voluntary redistribution'.[7] Moreover, we see not only a local redistributive pattern of equality promoted by Paul but an unprecedented – and politically subversive – global form of economic redistribution from Jesus loyalists in assemblies scattered throughout the Roman Empire, but especially in strategic urban centres like Philippi, Ephesus, Corinth, and Rome.

Unfortunately, the driving force for such redistributive equality appears as a stumbling block to contemporary Christians and foolishness to Marxists:[8] divine grace, that is to say, an absent cause that initiates what the English sociologist (and socialist) Richard Titmuss called the 'gift relationship'.[9] One need not personify that cause as 'God' along the lines that Paul and other Jesus loyalists did in order to recognise that there must be such an absent cause to set into motion the double reciprocity involved, for example, between (a) individuals and the underlying economic structure of debt and (b) among the indebted individuals themselves.

---

5 Rom 15.26. I follow Gordon Zerbe, who translates the Greek word *hagioi*, which is standardly translated (for example, in the NSRV) as 'saints'. As Zerbe stresses, the term renders the Hebrew word *kadoš* and emphasises that the loyalty owed to Jesus by his followers – their 'fundamental identity' – took priority over competing loyalties that other theo-political forms of identity made upon them, e.g. their 'residential identity'. (See Zerbe 2016, pp. 44–5).
6 Welborn 2013, p. 88.
7 Welborn 2013, p. 89.
8 To update Paul's declaration in 1 Cor 1:23 that he preached 'a crucified Messiah', which was 'a stumbling block to Jews' and 'foolishness to the nations.'
9 Titmuss 1997. For Paul's conception of 'gift' (*charis*) in its first-century cultural setting, see Barclay 2015.

1   The Jesus Movement and Debt Cancellation

Paul, it should be well understood, became a follower – or *loyalist* – of Jesus[10] after having initially opposed the movement and helped to persecute its members. It is worth reflecting briefly on the nature of that movement during Jesus's lifetime and in the decades just after, when Paul would have encountered and ultimately embraced it.

The Jesus movement arose in the socio-historical context of – and as a bold critique of and stark alternative to – economic exploitation, indebtedness, and debt bondage.[11] Indeed, a generation after Jesus's state execution at the hands of the Roman imperial order, a social explosion occurred in Galilee and Judea that had at its core the demand for debt cancellation.

The defining feature of the movement, as Richard Horsley has emphasised, was 'covenant renewal', the appeal to ancient traditions of Israelites in order to address the economic woes of Galilean and Judean peasant, artisans, and their allies (few in number, to be sure, but hardly non-existent).

Against this historical backdrop, it is possible to see in a radically new way what have come to be known in Christian tradition as the 'Golden Rule'[12] and the 'Lord's Prayer'.[13] As opposed to the traditional interpretation of these texts as outlining the basis for individual piety, it becomes striking how Jesus's insistence on moral reciprocity entails the economic practice of mutual debt cancellation.[14] For example, in the early tradition conveyed by the author of the Gospel of Mark, Jesus sharply distinguishes between how he 'exercises lordship' and how it is practised by 'those recognized as rulers of the nations', in particular, how 'their great ones dominate them'. He cautions his disciples that whoever 'wishes to become great among you must be your servant, and whoever wishes to be first among you must be slave of all'. Jesus concludes his normative account of legitimate leadership by presenting himself as the embodiment of Debt Cancellation for All: 'For even the human one did not come to be served but to serve and to give his life as a payment for the deliverance (*lytron*) of many'.[15]

---

10   I owe the designation 'Jesus loyalist' to Zerbe 2012, pp. 26–46.
11   On exploitation, debt, and debt bondage in the ancient Greco-Roman world, see especially Ste. Croix 1981.
12   Matt 7:12; Lk 6:31.
13   Matt 6:9–13; Lk 11:2–4.
14   For a superb account of Jesus's project of debt cancellation, see Oakman 2014.
15   Mk 10:45. This early Christological formulation was retained in the Gospel of Matthew. Compare also Rom 3:24b–25a; Tim 2:6.

As Ched Myers has noted, the Greek word *lytron* (traditionally translated as 'ransom') 'referred to the price required to redeem captives or purchase freedom for indentured servants'.[16] Moreover, Richard Horsley observes that such a formulation can scarcely be construed as a 'proof text' for such later theories of divine atonement that have emphasised the 'vicarious death of Christ'.[17] Rather, it should be appreciated as a 'motivating sanction for the principle enunciated' in these verses. Significantly, Horsley adds, what is at stake is the 'covenantal mechanism' in Israelite tradition 'by which those who had fallen into debt-slavery could be ransomed and their land, which had come into another's control, could be redeemed ...'[18]

Jesus once even offered a compelling parable against the refusal to cancel debts. In the Gospel of Matthew, we find the following account of an unforgiving servant (or royal 'retainer'):[19]

> ... [T]he kingdom of heaven may be compared to a king who wished to settle accounts with his retainers. When he began the calculation, one who owed him ten thousand talents was brought to him; and, as he could not pay, his lord ordered him to be sold, together with his wife and children and all his possessions, and payment to be made. So the servant fell on his knees before him, saying, 'Have patience with me, and I will repay you everything'. And having been moved with compassion for him, the lord of that servant released him and cancelled his debt. But that same servant, as he went out, came upon one of his fellow servants who owed

---

16 Myers 2008, p. 279. On the broader topic of Roman practices of slavery, the manumission of slaves, and the stigma associated with freed slaves, see Knapp 2009, pp. 125–95.

17 Although I shall not do so here, one could well reflect on the ways in which the early Jesus movement articulated and advanced the interests of indebted Galilean and Judean peasants, artisans, and labourers and in which Paul later delineated the contours of a covenantal gift economy. Indeed, one could seek to construct a 'materialist theology' – to borrow David Horrell's term (see Horrell 1995) – of debt and debt cancellation. Such a theology would recover, rectify, and reorient Anselm's classic work *Cur Deus Homo* along the lines of a *Cur Deus Multitudo* that would not emphasise the substitutionary – and atoning – death of Jesus of Nazareth, a lone charismatic figure, but instead highlight the diverse egalitarian movement he boldly led – one that was subsequently embraced by Paul of Tarsus and redirected to a broader project, namely, 'grafting' non-Jews onto the 'olive branch' of Jewish tradition (the horticultural metaphor of Rom 11:17–25) – aiming at nothing less than a sweeping social-religious alternative to the Roman imperial order. At any rate, before this dissident movement was reabsorbed into, indeed, *baptized* by, that order (see Howard-Brook 2016).

18 Horsley 2009, p. 123. Horsley cites Lev 25:25–8, 47–55.

19 Herzog 1994, pp. 135–49. On this parable, see also Schottroff 2006.

him a hundred denarii; and choking him, he said, 'Pay what you owe'. Then his fellow servant fell down and pleaded with him, 'Have patience with me, and I will pay you'. But he refused; then he went and threw him into jail until he would pay the debt. When his fellow servant saw what had happened, they were greatly distressed, and they went and reported to their lord all that had taken place. Then his lord summoned him and said to him, 'You wicked servant! I forgave you all that debt because you pleaded with me. Should you not have had mercy on your fellow servant, as I had mercy on you?' And in anger his lord handed him over to the jailors until he would pay his entire debt. [So my heavenly Father will also do to every one of you, if you do not forgive your brother or sister from your heart.][20]

Taken at face value, the author of the Gospel of Matthew has framed this story as a normative counterexample – even proclaiming eschatological divine sanction – against one individual's refusal to cancel another's debts. Yet on closer examination, one can discern the forceful indictment of not only (a) an economic system rooted in debt, threats of enslavement, imprisonment, and violence but also (b) the illusion of debt cancellation from above by benevolent rulers.

This is a compelling example of what John Dominic Crossan has called a *challenge parable*, which has no clear resolution to the conflict depicted in the narrative and so forces the listener 'to think, to discuss, to argue, and to decide about meaning as present application. Here is its basic challenge. If tradition is changed, it *may* be destroyed. If tradition is not changed, it *will* be destroyed'.[21] Accordingly, it is not hard to grasp that the central challenge posed by Jesus in the Parable of the Unforgiving Servant is that, as William Herzog has argued, 'neither the messianic hope nor the tradition of popular kingship can resolve the people's dilemma. To reshape their world, the people of the land must look elsewhere. Just *where* is not the concern of this parable'.[22] Perhaps, though, the unspoken implication of Jesus's parable is that the people should look to themselves, to their own power of debt cancellation from below. Bearing in mind the importance of debt and debt cancellation in Jesus's mission

---

20 Matt 18:23–35. The last verse (as well as the opening verses 21–2 about the forgiveness of sins [cancellation of debts?]) is presumably an interpretative framing device added by the author of this Gospel. On the general tendency by the Gospel authors to allegorise Jesus's parables – and thereby 'domesticate' their radicality – see Levine 2014, pp. 1–23.
21 Crossan 2012, p. 47.
22 Herzog 1994, p. 149.

as it was remembered in the nascent Jesus movement,[23] let us turn now to the theological-economic contribution made by Paul of Tarsus.

2 Paul's Letter to the Romans

Although my interest in Paul lies in his broad contribution to the Jesus movement, I shall largely focus on his letter to the assemblies of Jesus loyalists in Rome, his so-called 'Letter to the Romans'. My overriding concern in providing a close reading of Paul's letter is to consider how participants in the Roman house assemblies would have reacted when they heard it read aloud and interpreted by Paul's co-worker Phoebe[24] – in other words, to overhear their concerns and conversations.

The vast majority of Paul's 'undisputed'[25] letters were addressed to assemblies of Jesus loyalists with whom Paul has already established a close personal relationship, a kind of partnership. Indeed, these letters generally functioned as 'problem-solving' interventions in which he tried to resolve a conflict, reiterate an important teaching or simply reassure other Jesus loyalists. By contrast, Paul's Letter to the Romans was written to a group of assemblies most of whose members he had never met. All Paul's letters typically rely on moral exhortation through paradigmatic example, but the Letter to the Romans is the most theologically – and politically – complex and is especially grounded in appeals to Jewish Scripture, in particular, the Torah and the Prophets.

Finally, in all his undisputed letters Paul confesses, in one way or another, his exclusive loyalty to Jesus as the Messiah, whose brutal death at the hands of Roman occupation forces he insists has been paradoxically vindicated as the inspiration for an alternative vision for building anti-imperial, egalitarian human communities that Jesus already proclaimed as the 'reign of God' and Paul calls 'assemblies' (*ekklēsiae*) that exemplify 'solidarity-partnership' (*koinō*-

---

23 Jesus was remembered by his followers not simply for what he did but for what he said – his ethical principles. Hence, the significance of Paul's willingness to 'remember the poor' as his mutual agreement with the 'pillars' of the Jerusalem community, namely, Peter, James, and John (see Gal 2:10).

24 In this respect I have been influenced by the methodological approach advanced by Reta Haltemann Finger and Peter Oakes; see Haltemann Finger 1993 and Oakes 2009, pp. 127–30.

25 Namely, 1Thessalonians, Galatians, Philippians, 1 and 2Corinthians, Philemon, and Romans. For an introduction to the scholarly discussion of the authenticity of letters attributed to Paul, see Puskas and Reasoner 2013.

nia).²⁶ Notwithstanding Nietzsche's uncomprehending complaint in *The Anti-Christ*,²⁷ Paul recognised that the transformative power of the Jesus movement lay precisely in its apparent *weakness* (from the hierarchical perspective of the established power of the Roman imperial order, at any rate).²⁸ This is the concrete sense of Jesus's resurrection as signifying what Alain Badiou has rightly called an Event that demands loyalty.²⁹

Consequently, it is hardly surprising that at the beginning and end of his Letter to the Romans, Paul clearly and directly confesses his loyalty as a follower of Jesus and thereby issues a challenge to 'the dominant politics of Rome and the Roman emperor'.³⁰ John Toews reminds modern readers of Paul's letters – who standardly fail to recognise the intertwining of the theological and political in the ancient world – of the implications that the audience to whom Paul wrote (dictated, actually)³¹ resided precisely in the capital of the Roman Empire:

> The center of the city had numerous temples to pagan gods and to the emperors of Rome. Every city block had an altar to the emperor at which people were expected to make confession or offer sacrifices. Every home was expected to have a cove with an image of the emperor.³²

Paul composed his letter shortly after the ascension of Nero in C.E. 54 to the emperorship. In this conjuncture, Paul's letter operated as 'a political theology, a *political* declaration of war on the Caesar'.³³ The basic message presented in this 'letter of resistance' was undoubtedly why Paul was killed by the regime.³⁴ Indeed, as Toews summarises,

---

26   On the Pauline *ekklēsiae*, see Banks 1994 and Thompson 2014, esp. pp. 28–33; on Paul's central organising norm of *koinōnia*, see Ogereau 2012; Thompson 2014, pp. 175–98; Zerbe 2016, pp. 69–70.
27   Nietzsche 2005, pp. 50–1.
28   On Paul's dialectical contrast between 'weak' and 'strong' throughout his letters, see Black 2012; on the 'power of weakness' in Paul's conception of apostleship, see Ehrensperger 2009, pp. 98–116; on his use in the Letter to the Romans in particular, see Reasoner 1999. See also Marcus 2006 and Longenecker 2015 on the disruptive ideological power of the cross in the early Jesus movement.
29   However, see the previous chapter for a complication of Badiou's point: the fervently anticipated 'return' of Jesus – in sharp contrast with imperial ceremonies of the 'arrival' of the Emperor or his appointees – served for Paul as a kind of Counter-Event.
30   Toews 2009.
31   On Paul's use of secretaries, see Richards 2004.
32   Toews 2009.
33   Taubes 2004, p. 16.
34   See Georgi 2005, pp. 147–60.

Paul's opening and concluding confessions in Romans are theological statements; he confesses that Jesus is the messianic fulfillment of the promises to David and the Jewish people. But every word in these confessions and in Paul's opening statement of his mission to the capital of the empire also are loaded with political meaning – gospel, son of God, Lord, rule the nations, hope for the nations, faith, father, salvation, righteousness are all understood in Rome as referents to Augustus, the emperor. The emperor is the son of God, lord, and father of the Roman people who rules the nations, who brings hope, salvation, and righteousness to all peoples of the world.

The confessions of Paul in Romans are theo-political assertions. They simultaneously outline Paul's understanding of the gospel and his counter-imperial claims about the politics of the gospel. Paul challenges what the people of Rome say about the Roman emperor. The Romans got it wrong, Paul says. Messiah Jesus is the son of God, the Lord, who brings hope, salvation and righteousness to all people and who will rule the nations in behalf of God the father.[35]

Toews argues persuasively that confessions of faith in Paul's letters serve as declarations of loyalty. However, it is hardly obvious that, as he goes on to argue, loyalty to Paul's (and Jesus's) inclusive, egalitarian vision of community – and concomitant disloyalty to Empire – requires retreat from politics and political struggles to build a more just world. Such retreat unjustifiably cedes ground to forms of class and state power and only makes more difficult the successful pursuit of one's presumed normative commitment to participate in the Jesus movement.

John Barclay has argued that to see Paul's declaration that 'Jesus is Lord' is not purely, simply, and narrowly a presumption that therefore 'The Emperor *is not* Lord'.[36] For Barclay, Paul's challenge is deeper and wider than a direct political challenge to the Roman imperial order. As he argues, in Paul's cosmic scheme of powers and principalities, the Roman Empire is relegated 'to the rank of a dependent and derivative entity, denied a distinguishable name or significant role in the story of the world'.[37] This is because, Barclay adds, Paul's

> systemic analysis of the world differs from ours: for him the 'political' is fused with other realities whose identity is clarified and named from the

---

35   Toews 2009.
36   Barclay 2016, pp. 363–87.
37   Barclay 2016, p. 384.

epistemological standpoint of the Christ-event. In this sense the Roman empire is not significant to Paul *qua the Roman empire*: it certainly features on his map, but under other auspices and as subservient to more significant powers.[38]

No doubt this is true – but neither should one argue that since Paul's theological vision was *more* than political his theological vision was thereby *less* than political. A material clash of systems, interests, and values remained.

As Mark Reasoner notes, it is clear that Paul's target was more broadly the 'polytheistic fabric' of the first-century Mediterranean world than it was the Roman imperial cult. And yet, Reasoner adds, somehow Paul – whether he intended it or not – posed a threat to the Roman imperial order. Otherwise, he wouldn't have fallen victim to it. Even if he was not 'intentionally subverting the Roman Empire in his letters', there existed 'a relationship of incompatibility' between 'Paul as the apostle to the nations and the Roman Empire'.[39]

3   Paul and Economic Mutualism

Paul's overall theological argument in the Letter to the Romans pivots on his drawing a line of demarcation between a conception of justice as retaliation and justice as restoration: Paul sets forth and defends the historical possibility of a transition between a 'regime of law' and a 'regime of generosity'.[40] Or, as Toews puts it, Paul is calling for the construction of 'a genuinely egalitarian worldview and value system'.[41]

Justin Meggitt has amply and ably demonstrated that in pursuit of such a worldview and value system Paul was committed to a form of economic 'mutualism' as a strategy for the survival of those living at a subsistence level in the first century world.[42] Meggitt defines 'mutualism' as 'the implicit or explicit

---

38   Barclay 2016, p. 385.
39   Reasoner 2013, p. 4.
40   Zerbe 2015.
41   Toews 2004, p. 309.
42   Not without sharp disagreement, however. Essentially, the complaint levelled against Meggitt's book has been that he has exaggerated the degree of homogeneity among the poor within the Roman Empire and thereby failed to provide nuance regarding social status vs. class in Pauline assemblies. (For an overview of this debate, see Friesen 2004.) But Meggitt is clear that he is exaggerating 'in order to bring out such an important and neglected aspect of the lives of Pauline Christians' (Meggitt 1998, p. 5). At any rate, I shall not enter into the controversy over what is the best historical-sociological method for

belief that individual and collective *well-being* is attainable above all by mutual interdependence'.[43] He insists that this is more than mere reciprocity. Consider an intriguing passage in which Paul observes that

> wages are not credited as a gift (*kata charin*) to a worker but as a debt owed (*kata opheilēma*). But to someone who doesn't work, trusting (*pisteuonti*) him who justifies (*dikaiounta*) the ungodly, his trust (*pistis*) is credited as righteousness (*eis dikaiosynēn*). So also David speaks of the blessedness of those to whom God credits righteousness apart from works (*logizetai dikaiousynēn chōris ergōn*): 'Blessed are those whose lawless deeds are forgiven, and whose errors are covered over; blessed is the one against whom the Lord will not credit error'.[44]

As Dieter Georgi comments, Paul demonstrates here a profound understanding of the relationship between wage labor and leisure. Georgi points out that

> whoever works for monetary gain counts on the fact that wages are not given as a favor, that is, in gracious condescension or with a similar attitude. Instead, it is expected and given according to the rate of indebtedness that accumulates according to time, energy, resources, and imagination invested and shown by the worker. This reference to wage as an indebtedness of the employer is an interesting one, certainly true today also, but not so often expressed in this kind of language. Employers on various levels have always tended to give their payments to employees a touch of grace. This is an attitude that Paul condemns outright, and Paul's opinion concerning the relationship of money and labor reflects that of contemporary society.[45]

Paul next considers an exemplary person of leisure: King David. Paul's point of contrast hinges on his use of the Greek words *pistis* (translated 'loyalty' or 'faithfulness') and *dikaiosynē* (conventionally translated as 'righteousness' but also having the societal connotation of 'justice'). In Paul's understanding of the Abraham story in the Hebrew Scriptures, Abraham is not 'justified' by a

---

'using economic evidence to read early Christian texts' (Oakes 2009a). My concern is primarily to note the external pressure of material necessities for most Jesus loyalists to adopt what Meggitt has called 'survival strategies' (Meggitt 1998, pp. 155–78).
43   Meggitt 1998, p. 158.
44   Rom 4:4–8.
45   Georgi 2005, p. 120.

set of abstract beliefs about God but rather by concretely expressing his *loyalty* to God through his actions. Paul does not understand human loyalty 'as a one-way concept, from the subject to the sovereign. It is a two-way affair, with the divine loyalty, in fact, preceding and causing human loyalty'.[46] Paul reiterates and condenses his point in the formulation: 'For the wages of sin is death, but the free gift (*charis*) of God is eternal life in our Lord Jesus the Messiah'.[47] Later on in the Letter to the Romans we also find Paul's commitment to mutualism:

> Do not become indebted to anyone, except to love one another; for one who unconditionally loves another has fulfilled the Torah. For 'You shall not commit adultery, You shall not murder, You shall not steal, You shall not covet', and, if there is any other commandment, it may be summed up in this expression: 'You shall love your neighbor as yourself'. Love for one's neighbor does not carry out evil; therefore, love is a fulfillment of the Torah.[48]

Paul sharply contrasts a negative requirement to avoid indebtedness with the positive requirement to love one's neighbour – here echoing the Torah and Jesus's 'Golden Rule'. What does the avoidance of debt have to do with fulfilment of the Torah? Paul appeals to a principle of economic reciprocity. Paul is sketching the outlines of an 'economy of the gift' or 'spiritual economy'[49] that would be based on what Peter Oakes has termed 'a new scale of value', in accordance with which 'Paul is not calling for realistic assessment of oneself on the usual scales of status and intellect. He does away with these scales of achievement and inherited qualities by putting in a scale based on unmerited gift'.[50] As a result, Paul seeks to undermine the very hierarchical structure of honour, status, and household that served as an ideological support for Greco-Roman societies; instead he proposes a new egalitarian model of community. Toward this end, Paul offers here – as well as elsewhere[51] – the metaphor of a body having many parts and functions, but each contributing to overall corporeal wellbeing: 'For just as in one body we have many parts, and not all the parts

---

46 Georgi 2005, p. 120.
47 Rom 6:23.
48 Rom 13:8–10.
49 See Blanton 2017.
50 Oakes 2009b, p. 100.
51 Most famously in his correspondence with Jesus loyalists in Corinth. On the political implications of Paul's metaphor of the body, see Kim 2008.

have the same function, just so, we who are many are one body in Christ and, individually, we are parts of each other'.[52] Moreover, within such an egalitarian economy, there exist diverse 'gifts' that 'are in line with the gift given to us'[53] and therefore should be shared.

Finally, though, the new system of value that Paul sketches, which reconfigures and exceeds the boundaries of the classical model of a household economy, recognises the hard work and suffering undergone by its members. It involves a commitment to sharing and hospitality with all, but with what could be called a preferential option for the poor: 'Be in agreement with one another. Don't be carried away to grandiose ideas but to lowly people'.[54] As Oakes comments, the Greek word used by Paul to characterise 'lowly people' is *tapeinos*, which has customarily been translated as 'humble'. However, the word conveys not a moral but a social category. Indeed, Oakes continues,

> Paul is probably not urging Christians to associate particularly with people who have the virtue of not thinking too highly of themselves. In this period, *tapeinos* was much more commonly used to denote the poor. It tended more towards being pejorative than complimentary.[55]

Undoubtedly the fullest expression of Paul's gift economy and his commitment to economic mutualism and debt cancellation as survival strategies was his project to collect contributions to assist the poor in Jerusalem and elsewhere. This was no charitable project, as some have claimed.[56] Rather, as Gordon Zerbe has argued, Paul's collection was to serve as

> a relief fund for his fellow Messianic compatriots of Judea, impoverished by food shortages caused by both famine and the Roman empire's tributary system of economic extraction from conquered territories. But Paul does not promote just charity and benevolence; rather, in this project he champions in concrete terms the goal of mutualism, partnership, and equality with the lowly and poor.[57]

---

52 Rom 12:4–5.
53 Rom 12:6.
54 Rom 12:16.
55 Oakes 2009b, p. 121.
56 This is the limitation of the interpretative framework of the otherwise excellent Nickle 2009. Even Alain Badiou has recently fallen victim to this traditional misunderstanding; see Badiou 2003, pp. 28–9.
57 Zerbe 2012, p. 76.

Indeed, increasing numbers of New Testament scholars have proposed that this collection served as a material way to demonstrate concrete commitment to 'solidarity-partnership' (*koinōnia*) not only among Jesus followers but also with all those who had been 'humiliated'[58] by Roman political domination and economic exploitation.[59] For example, Ross and Gloria Kinsler have argued that Paul's collection served as his concrete enactment of the ancient Israelite 'jubilee tradition' – as renewed by the Jesus movement – of debt cancellation and economic redistribution.[60]

4 A Cosmic Jubilee

Finally, Paul bears witness to the stark reality of debt bondage – and the hope of deliverance from it – even at the level of the natural world. As Paul reminds his fellow Jesus loyalists,

> I consider that the sufferings of this present time (*tou nyn kairou*) are not worth comparing with the glory about to be revealed (*apokalyphthēnai*) to us. For the creation waits with eager expectation for the revealing of the children of God; for the creation was subjected (*hypetagē*) to futility, not of its own will but by the will of the one who subjected it, in hope that the creation itself will be released from its servitude of destruction into the freedom of the glory of the children of God. We know that the whole creation has groaned and agonized until now; and not only the creation, but we ourselves, who have the first fruits of the Spirit, groan while we wait for divine adoption, the deliverance (*apolytrōsin*) of our bodies. For in hope we were saved. Now hope that is seen is not hope. For who hopes for what is seen? But if we hope for what we do not see, we wait for it with endurance (*di hypomonēs*).[61]

What is striking in this passage is the metaphor by which Paul identifies how the Roman Empire not only has enslaved human beings but also has under-

---

58 For an eloquent discussion of the significance of such solidarity in Jewish and early Christian traditions, see Wengst 1988.
59 Among the vast literature on Paul's collection, see especially Georgi 1992; Nickle 2009; Friesen 2010; Longenecker 2010; Ogereau 2012; Welborn 2013; Tucker 2014; and Downs 2016.
60 Kinsler and Kinsler 1999, pp. 146–9.
61 Rom 8:18–25.

mined and despoiled the created order of things. As Neil Elliott reminds us, 'creation is ... and has long been ... a *political* topic'.[62] Indeed, the 'manumission' that Paul expects is not just human but natural. Here I disagree with those who have argued that the 'groans' Paul evokes in this passage have to do primarily with the 'birth pangs' of a pregnant woman, essentially guided by the image of the imminent 'day of the Lord' (*hēmera kyriou*) that Paul offers.[63] Rather, it appears that the references in Romans 8.18–25 have to do as well with the physical and psychological torment brought about through enslavement. These are the sufferings 'of this present time', literally, 'of the now time' (*tou nyn kairou*). As I have argued elsewhere, during the course of his mission to the 'nations' (*ethnē*) subjected to Roman imperial order, and by means of his letter writing, Paul *intervenes* as a thinker of the conjuncture.[64]

But, remarkably, Paul envisions in these lines that even the ecological debt inflicted by empire[65] will ultimately be cancelled in a cosmic jubilee, indeed, through the divine declaration of what Elsa Tamez has called an 'amnesty of grace'.[66] This serves as the concrete basis for Paul's – and other Jesus loyalists' – hope. What will occur is not, as orthodox Christian theology would have us believe, the *redemption* of souls, but instead the *deliverance* of bodies. Here is Paul at his most materialist, identifying not only the domination inflected by Rome – its *imperium* – but also the glorious overcoming of that domination.

Just as in his earliest use of such emancipatory imagery, though, in this passage Paul is not interested in specifying precisely when such deliverance will occur; it is enough for Jesus loyalists to wait for it 'with endurance'.[67] Yet in a real sense, emancipation has already begun, since the Jesus loyalists are the 'first fruits of the Spirit', who an alternative way of sharing in a new egalitarian and inclusive life together, bound by the mutuality of gift exchange and not by the rational calculation of self-interest.

---

62 Elliott 2013, p. 137.
63 1 Thess 5.1–4. For the 'birth pangs' interpretation, see Jewett 2004, pp. 41–2; and Elliott 2013, pp. 153–4. Obviously, both possible readings are overdetermined by the recurrent Roman imperial artistic rendering of domination as a subjected woman; on which see Lopez 2008.
64 See the previous chapter.
65 On Roman imperial devastation of the landscape through such practices as copper mining and metallurgy, see Mattingly 2011, esp. 167–99.
66 Tamez 1993.
67 As Peter Oakes has noted, 'endurance' (*hypomonē*) serves as a 'surprisingly persistent minor motif' in Paul's letter (Oakes 2009b, p. 138). Compare Rom 2:7, 5:2–5, 12:12, 15:1–2, 15:4–5.

For contemporary Christians and Marxists alike, this emancipatory hope in the 'already-not yet'[68] remains a declaration of Good News. It is true that Karl Marx considered not Paul but Spartacus to be 'the most capital fellow in the whole history of antiquity and a REAL REPRESENTATIVE of the proletariat of ancient times'.[69] *But Spartacus was defeated.*[70]

Although Paul's project came to an equally bitter end, his materialist theology continues to have practical effects; and it retains a greater affinity with the socialist project of constructing an economic system based on solidarity and allocation based on human need. It is true enough that 'Paul's exhortations, while having a sharp, socially radical edge, fall short of calling for structural social change'.[71] Nonetheless, as Peter Oakes reminds us, 'for suffering people ... the gospel validates their suffering and encourages them in their day-to-day endurance. Hope can itself have a transforming effect on day-to-day experience'.[72] On this basis we might even glimpse the contours of what could be called 'Pauline Marxism'.[73]

---

68 Compare Paul's formulation in Phil 1.6 of this 'eschatological tension' of history understood as a decisive event in the past, an ongoing process in the present, into which the future unexpectedly breaks. See especially Dunn 1998, pp. 461–98.
69 Marx letter dated February 27, 1861 to Engels (in Marx and Engels 1985, p. 265).
70 For a fine recent introduction to Spartacus's historical aims, see Strauss 2009.
71 Oakes 2009b, p. 140.
72 Oakes 2009b, p. 140.
73 In this respect, Marxists could reclaim Richard Titmuss's work on the 'gift relationship' not only as a way to specify the damage wrought on individuals by market societies but as an invitation for Christians to reclaim Paul's own conception of a 'gift economy'. In his extraordinary *Paul and the Gift* John Barclay briefly acknowledges Titmuss's book but then criticises the latter's emphasis on gifts (such as blood donation) that are 'anonymous, unreciprocated and disinterested, where no return is possible or expected' (Barclay 2015, p. 60). By contrast, Barclay argues that Paul's own conception of grace/gift demands such reciprocity as the basis for robust forms of social solidarity.

CHAPTER 4

Althusser and the Problem of Historical Individuality*

> We are discussing living water which has not yet flowed away.[1]
> – LOUIS ALTHUSSER

∴

Louis Althusser's well-known formulation that 'ideology interpellates individuals as subjects'[2] has long concealed a key problem that Althusser himself once posed but quickly dropped and never resolved: What is an individual? An answer to this simple – but exceedingly difficult – question would go a long way to explain not only the limits of the interpellation of subjects *as individuals* but also how resistance to oppressive social structures and institutions is possible. As a point of departure for our investigation, let us first consider two brief references by Althusser to this problem in texts from 1965–6.

1   The Historical Forms of the Existence of Individuality

In *Reading Capital* Althusser addresses the question of individuality in the context of his outline of a Marxist 'concept of historical time', which he opposes to a 'Hegelian concept of history' that has two 'essential characteristics': 'homogeneous continuity' and 'contemporaneity'.[3] For Althusser this Hegelian approach allows for

---

* This chapter has been previously published in *Crisis & Critique* 2.2, 2015, pp. 195–214.
1   Althusser et al. 2015, p. 30. Althusser doubtless alludes here to a passage in the Gospel of John, in which Jesus cries out in the Jerusalem temple courtyard, 'Let anyone who believes in me drink. As the scripture has said, "Out of the believer's heart shall flow rivers of living water"' (Jn 7.37–8).
2   Althusser 2014b, pp. 188–94, 261–6.
3   Althusser et al. 2015, p. 240.

an *'essential section'* (*coupe d'essence*), i.e. an intellectual operation in which a *vertical break* is made at any moment in historical time, a break in the present such that all the elements of the whole revealed by this section are in an immediate relationship with one another, a relationship that immediately expresses their internal essence.[4]

According to this 'ideological' and 'empiricist' approach to historical time, we may envisage history as a linear sequence of homogeneous stages or 'moments', any one of which could easily be segmented from the rest (as indicated below):

... / PAST / ... / PRESENT / ... / FUTURE / ...

Althusser argues that this conception is inadequate to the task of accounting for the complex unity of different rates and rhythms by which the historical process unfolds. It also gives rise to a number of 'conceptual confusions and false problems', of which Althusser discusses three: 'the classical oppositions: essence/phenomena, necessity/contingency, and the "problem" of the action of the individual in history'.[5] Allow me to bypass the first two problems in order to focus on the third.

Althusser notes that the so-called 'problem' of the 'role of the individual in history'[6] is

> a tragic argument which consists of a comparison between the theoretical part or knowledge of a determinate object (e.g., the economy) which represents the essence of which the other objects (the political, the ideological, etc.) are regarded as the phenomena – and that fiendishly important (politically!) empirical reality, individual action.[7]

For Althusser, this is more than a 'tragic problem'; it is a *false* problem, because it is 'unbalanced, theoretically "hybrid", since it compares the theory of one object with the empirical existence of another'. In other words, the problem of the 'role of the individual in history' commits a serious category mistake by confusing two distinct theoretical levels of analysis. Yet Althusser readily admits that

---

4 Althusser et al., p. 241.
5 Althusser et al. 2015, p. 259.
6 Althusser is referring here to the title of a famous essay published in 1898 by the Russian Marxist Georgi Pekhanov; see Plekhanov 1969, pp. 139–77.
7 Althusser et al. 2015, p. 260.

this false problem of the 'role of the individual in history' is nevertheless an index to a true problem, one which arises by right in the theory of history: the problem of the concept of *the historical forms of existence of individuality*.[8]

What is more, it is precisely *Capital* that allows this problem to be properly posed. This is because Marx's text

> defines for the capitalist mode of production the different forms of individuality required and produced by that mode according to functions, of which the individuals are 'supports' (*Träger*), in the division of labour, in the different 'levels' of the structure.[9]

Yet caution is in order, for we should be careful not to align or match individuals as they are theoretically construed with individuals as they are empirically encountered and described. This is because

> the mode of historical existence of individuality in a given mode of production is not legible to the naked eye in 'history'; its concept, too, must therefore be *constructed*, and like every concept it contains a number of surprises, the most striking of which is the fact that it is nothing like the false obviousnesses of the 'given' – which is merely the mask of the current ideology.[10]

Althusser concludes with a scathing joke:

> So long as the real theoretical problem has not been posed (the problem of the forms of historical existence of individuality), we shall be beating about in the dark – like Plekhanov, who ransacked Louis XV's bed to prove that the secrets of the fall of the *Ancien Régime* were not hidden there. As a general rule, concepts are not hidden in beds.[11]

Althusser's jest about Plekhanov's theoretical naiveté arguably overlooks what is really at stake in the latter's essay, namely, the usefulness of counterfac-

---

8   Althusser et al. 2015, p. 260.
9   Althusser et al. 2015, p. 260.
10 Althusser et al. 2015, p. 260.
11 Althusser et al. 2015, p. 260.

tual statements and arguments in historical explanation.[12] But I set this matter aside.[13]

∴

Althusser returns to the question of 'forms of historical existence of individuality' in a lecture he delivered at the École normale supérieure in the early summer of 1966, which serves as an occasion for him to reflect on the 'philosophical conjuncture'.[14] After addressing such matters as how a *philosophical* differs from a *political* conjuncture and distinguishing the internally uneven and combined elements of the former, Althusser launches into an analysis of the three 'sedimented historical layers or elements' – what Althusser (and Pierre Macherey) would later call philosophical 'tendencies'[15] – in the history of French philosophy: the 'religious-spiritualist', the 'rationalist-idealist', and the 'rationalist-empiricist'. Althusser further proposes that the intervention of Marxists into contemporary French philosophy should operate on 'two fronts': first, against the spiritualism of Maurice Merleau-Ponty, Paul Ricoeur, and phenomenology; second, against the critical, rationalist idealism of Jean-Paul Sartre, Martial Guéroult, Claude Lévi-Strauss, and structuralism.

The first task of Marxists in philosophy is to define Marxist theory itself and to distinguish the theoretical status of historical materialism as a science from dialectical materialism as a philosophy. Then arises a series of key 'strategic questions' in both dialectical and historical materialism. My concern is with the last three (out of seven) strategic questions that, according to Althusser, have to be addressed in the field of dialectical materialism, namely, to develop theories of the following: ideology, the subject or 'subjectivity-effect', and the 'historical forms of individuality (including the social formation)'. As is well known, Althusser's famous essay 'Ideology and Ideological State Apparatuses', which was published in 1970 as an extract from a much longer 1969 manuscript

---

12 By a 'counterfactual' argument, I mean wondering whether or not, by imaginatively altering the actual historical conditions, an event (e.g., the American, French, or Russian Revolutions) would have turned out the way it did, or at all. An example of a counterfactual statement is: 'If Lenin had not been allowed to travel from Zurich through Germany to Russia on a sealed train in the spring of 1917, then the October Revolution would not have occurred'.

13 For a fine introduction to the problem of 'historical counterfactuals', see Evans 2013 (on pp. 40, 43 there is even a brief discussion of Plekhanov).

14 'The Philosophical Conjuncture and Marxist Theoretical Research', in Althusser 2003, pp. 1–18.

15 See Chapter 1.

'On the Reproduction of Capitalism', brings together the first two strategic questions and formulates both a Marxist ideology of ideology and of subjectivity.[16] However, as I have already suggested, in those texts, and subsequently, Althusser never fully worked out his theory of individuality.

2   Sève's Critique

Yet in the late 1960s Lucien Sève (a fellow philosopher and member of the French Communist Party) also proposed that a non-reductive version of historical materialism would require a theory of historical forms of individuality. The fruit of Sève's theoretical activity during that period was published as *Marxisme et théorie de la personnalité*.[17] Recently, he has summarised his lifelong research into this problem:

> Historical materialism is not ... as a mutilated Marxism has dramatically believed, the key to understanding human *societies* alone but is also inseparably the key to understanding *individualities*. After having created its own foundations, every social formation includes a related 'individual formation'; this is indeed why communism could not be the emancipation of the human species without ensuring the free development of all individuals. Marxist anthropology thus gives the lie to a double illusion: substantialist ('humans' *have a nature*) and existentialist ('humans' *have no essence*). In so far as they are socially evolved beings, human individuals have neither a nature nor a metaphysical essence, but indeed always concrete *historical presuppositions* from which we can make abstraction only in the imagination.[18]

Sève continues to agree with Althusser's 'theoretical anti-humanism' to the extent that 'humanism' is rooted in a commitment to some conception of 'the human'. However, Sève stresses that theoretical anti-humanism is merely the 'critical preamble for a *materialist anthropology* that for "the human" would substitute the dialectic of the human individual and human species that has at long last been untangled'.[19] To reject entirely such an anthropological dimension to historical materialism would be to lose sight of Marx's ultimate aim of

---

16   Both the manuscript and the excerpt are available in Althusser 2014b.
17   Sève 1981, available in translation as Sève 1978.
18   Sève 2015, pp. 72–3.
19   Sève 2015, p. 72.

social emancipation, namely, to expand and enrich human capabilities by surpassing capitalism and by realising a less oppressive, exploitative, and alienated society.[20]

Although this is not the place to develop at length a much-needed appreciation of Sève's work and its critical relationship to Althusser, it is worth noting that Sève himself has acknowledged the influence of Althusser's passing remarks in *Reading Capital* on 'the historical forms of existence of individuality'.[21] However, Sève has offered a compelling criticism of Althusser's non-dialectical approach to individuality. In Sève's view, Althusser has in mind

> the *general figures of individuality* that underpin a social formation of a given type and of which singular individuals become *supports* – for example, the capitalist and wage laborer in the capitalist mode of production.[22]

As a result, Althusser fails to capture the 'immense variety of the *constitutive relations of individuality in detail*, in historical forms of *individuation* in all their diversity'.[23] Speaking in general terms of the Capitalist and the Worker as representative figures of modern individuality falls far short of the fine-grained, concrete analysis that is required in order to show how a given mode of production appropriates human mental and physical capabilities, for instance, by constraining free time or stunting personal development.[24]

Sève has found his inspiration for his conception of historical forms of individuality especially in two sources:[25] Marx's Sixth Thesis on Feuerbach (on which there also exist brief commentaries by Althusser)[26] and a letter written by Marx in 1846 to his Russian acquaintance Pavel Vasilyevich Annenkov. In the first text, Marx observes that the German materialist philosopher Ludwig Feuerbach had rightly resolved 'the religious essence into the human essence'. However, as Marx insisted, 'the human essence is no abstraction inherent in each single individual. In its effective reality (*Wirklichkeit*) it is the ensemble (*das Ensemble*) of the social relations'.[27] In the second text, Marx argues that

---

20   See Sève 2012.
21   Sève 2008, pp. 118–21.
22   Sève 2008, p. 119.
23   Sève 2008, p. 120.
24   Seve 2008, p. 120.
25   See Sève 1981, pp. 97–106 n. 1 (Sève 1978, pp. 161–7 n. 27); 2008, pp. 63–8; 2015, pp. 70–3.
26   See especially Althusser 2003, pp. 253–6; Althusser 2005, pp. 242–3.
27   Marx 2000, p. 172. Translation slightly modified.

the social history of men is never anything but the history of their individual development, whether they are conscious of it or not. Their material relations are the basis of all their relations. These material relations are only the necessary forms in which their material and individual activity is realized.[28]

In each of these texts, Marx is at pains to emphasise the dialectical interaction of individuals and external social relations. As Sève has argued – employing Spinozist terminology[29] – we should distinguish between:
- The *forming form* of individuality (or 'matrix') that occurs outside of human beings as the 'ensemble' of material and social relations; and
- The *formed form* of individuality (or 'figure') that is the historical product of this complex process in its 'effective reality'.[30]

Consequently, Sève argues, by regarding individuals merely as social 'supports' (*Träger*), Althusser fails to address the 'historical substance'[31] of how individuation *actually* unfolds and so implies that such support is merely passive.[32] Yet such a perspective turns out to be non-dialectical, for individuals are both '*supports* for structural relations that dominate them and *actors* of social dynamics that make them move'.[33] One might add to Sève's objection that individuation results from more than an internalised ensemble of – or 'support' for – an external ensemble of relations; it requires an *active* unification of experience that is a precondition for understanding, acting in, and transforming the world.

---

28   Marx 2000, pp. 209–10.
29   Spinoza famously used 'naturing Nature' (*natura naturans*) and 'natured Nature' (*natura naturata*) to express the distinction between God (or substance) in its absolutely infinite *internal* productivity and the *external* infinity of finite modes that follow from that productivity; see E1p29s. However, Sève has carried out a materialist reversal of the distinction, since for Marx the ensemble of *external* material and social relations has always already existed prior to, and independent of, human beings, whose individuality only subsequently becomes effectively realised *internally*. With Gilles Deleuze, we could even speak of this external ensemble of relations becoming *folded* to form individuals; see Deleuze 1993, especially pp. 3–13.
30   Sève 2008, pp. 112–13.
31   Sève 2008, p. 120.
32   Sève 2008, pp. 120–1.
33   Sève 2008, p. 121.

3   Individuals and Subjects

There is much to commend in Sève's nuanced theory of the historical forms of individuality and his criticisms of Althusser. However, what I would like now to suggest is that his approach lends additional support for Althusser's materialist position in *Reading Capital* that a real object exists prior to, and independent of, thought about it. For Althusser,

> while the production process of a given real object, a given real-concrete totality (e.g., a given historical nation) takes place entirely in the real and is carried out according to the real order of *real* genesis (the order of succession of the moments of *historical* genesis), the production process of the object of knowledge takes place entirely in knowledge and is carried out according to *a different order*, in which the thought categories which 'reproduce' the real categories do *not* occupy *the same* place as they do in the order of real historical genesis, but quite different places assigned them by their function in the production process of the object of knowledge.[34]

Let me propose, then, that there exists a counterpart to Althusser's distinction between the *real object* and the *object in thought*, namely, a distinction between the *concrete individual* and the *subjected individual*. Indeed, each has its own 'genesis'. Although Althusser himself does not indicate as much (nor, for that matter, does Sève), we should equally insist on the materialist position that every concrete individual is prior to, and independent of, the same individual who has undergone interpellation as a subject. It may well be true, as Althusser insists, that even a newborn always already undergoes interpellation through the expectations of others regarding the infant's name, gender, future social position, and so forth.[35] Nevertheless, every individual-in-process is born at a precise conjuncture of world history, enjoying specific opportunities and confronted by specific material and ideological obstacles. As human beings in our individual composition, each of us strives to persist in our being

---

34   Althusser p. 44.
35   Althusser 2014b, pp. 192–3. As we shall see below, there is a serious problem regarding personal names. Althusser is rightly concerned with the ideological implications of assuming one's 'father's name'. However, personal names also denote reference to *this*, as opposed to some other, individual who has been, or is about to be, born. The dual nature of personal names registers a deeper division between historical forms of individuality and interpellation of such individuals as subjects.

and to increase our capacities to flourish. As a result, each of us in our own singularity always threatens to act as what could be called a 'counter friction' to disrupt the smooth operation of the interpellative machine.[36] Again using Spinozist language, Sève envisions constructing a 'science of the singular' that would help one to identify and open up an emancipatory path along which all of humanity may journey together.[37]

4 An Example from Christian Religious Ideology: Simon Peter

In order to appreciate how tension can arise between historical forms of individuality and the process of subjective interpellation, consider the following historical-theological case. In his chapter on ideology in *The Reproduction of Capitalism*, Althusser proposes that

> Christian religious ideology ... says: I address myself to you, a human individual called Peter (every individual is *called* by his name, in the passive sense, it is never the individual who gives *himself* his own name), in order to tell you that God exists and that you are answerable to Him. It adds: it is God who is addressing you through my voice (since Scripture has collected the Word of God, tradition has transmitted it, and papal infallibility has fixed it for ever on 'ticklish' points, such as Mary's virginity or ... papal infallibility itself). It says: This is who you are; you are Peter! This is your origin: you were created by God from all eternity, although you were born in 1928 Anno Domini! This is your place in the world! This is what you must do! In exchange, if you observe the 'law of love', you will be saved, you, Peter, and will become part of the Glorious Body of Christ! And so on ...[38]

As Judith Butler and Jacques Bidet have cautioned, religious ideology may not be the most useful illustration of the everyday operation of interpellation.[39] Nonetheless, it remains, as I hope to demonstrate, an interesting example in its

---

36   See Thoreau 1996b, p. 9.
37   Sève 1987, pp. 244–6. For Spinoza's famous distinction among three kinds of knowledge – (1) from 'random experience', hearsay, opinion, or imagination (2) by reasoning based on 'common notions', and (3) by 'intuition' of a singular thing in itself – see E2p40s.
38   Althusser 2014b, p. 194. This passage also appeared in Althusser's extracted essay 'Ideology and Ideological State Apparatuses' (p. 266).
39   Butler 1997, pp. 109–12; Bidet 2015, p. 81.

own right. In addition, although Althusser is clearly not discussing 'the historical Simon Peter', for purpose of illustration, it is worth considering the latter's concrete existence as an *individual* prior to, and independent of, becoming a subject.

According to the Gospel according to Mark, shortly after the arrest of John the Baptizer by order of Herod Antipas (the Roman-appointed 'tetrarch' of Galilee and Perea), Jesus announces his own mission based on 'good news' to the poor, journeys to the fishing village of Capernaum, and at some later point 'hails' two fisherman, Simon (Hebrew: *Shimon*), and his brother Andrew, to leave behind the tools of their trade and become disciples in order to 'fish for people'.[40] Simon is soon given the nickname 'Peter' (Greek: *Petros*) and becomes Jesus' leading disciple.[41] However, in keeping with the narrative's recurrent reversals of expectations,[42] Simon Peter's persistent failure to understand – and act in accordance with – Jesus' messianic mission of sacrifice for the wellbeing of others appears to be all the more tragic. Indeed, at a pivotal moment in the trajectory of Mark's story, Jesus rebukes Simon Peter for his misunderstanding: 'Get behind me, Satan!'[43] A dramatic interpellative reversal has occurred: Simon Peter's previous hailing of Jesus – 'You are the "Messiah"'[44] – has turned out to be a *misrecognition*, for it incorrectly presumed a conventional hierarchical model of power. Simon Peter, according to Jesus, has wrongly set 'his mind not on divine things but on human things'.[45] As a result, by means of a corrective *counter-interpellation*, Jesus rejects this model – and presumably so should listeners/readers of the gospel.[46]

---

40   Mk 1.16. Luke's retelling of this episode (5.1–10) adds a parabolic flourish: Peter and his companions, upon Jesus's directive, are able to catch so many fish that their nets cannot contain them!
41   Mk 3.16. Simon's nickname in Aramaic is *Kēphā*, which means 'the Rock'. Jesus also gives nicknames to – in effect, *interpellates* – two other fishermen who along with Simon became leading disciples: John and James, the sons of Zebedee, were called in Aramaic *Boanerges*, which has been badly transliterated into Greek and is then translated by Mark as 'Sons of Thunder' (Aramaic: *benē re'em* → Greek: *huioi brontēs*); see Mk 3.17. For a discussion of the complexities involved in understanding the meaning of such Aramaic nicknames, see Casey 2010, pp. 186–92.
42   Here I follow especially Myers 2002; 2008.
43   Mk 8.33.
44   Mk 8.30.
45   Mk 8.33.
46   In the Gospel according to Mark, the only genuine interpellations of Jesus as a messiah who will be killed for his egalitarian vision of the 'reign of God' turn out to be Bartimaeus ('son of Timaeus'), a blind beggar, who calls out to Jesus from the roadside during the latter's march to Jerusalem (10.46–52), and an unnamed woman in Bethany, who anoints

Yet apart from this orally transmitted and then narratively embedded remembrance, Simon Peter was a complex embodied individual who lived in a specific region of the world during a precise conjuncture: at the height of Roman Imperial power,[47] he was probably an illiterate (or marginally literate)[48] peasant fisherman, the son of Yonah,[49] grew up in Bethsaida[50] and later moved to Capernaum on the eastern periphery of the Empire,[51] eked out a living from the Sea of Galilee, and spoke a local dialect.[52] Simon Peter encountered Jesus and decided to follow him not simply as a result of Jesus's charismatic presence but was probably inspired by the latter's message of 'theological-economic' hope of debt forgiveness in a restored nation of Israel.[53] He evidently betrayed Jesus after the latter's arrest[54] and returned – or fled – to Galilee for a time.[55] Eventually he returned to Jerusalem and served as one of the three main leaders or 'pillars' (*styloi*) in the assembly of Jesus followers located there.[56]

One of the most moving episodes in the New Testament is a post-resurrection dialogue between Jesus and Peter that occurs in the Gospel according to John. Peter and several other disciples have gone fishing in the Sea of Tiberias in Galilee (another name for the Sea of Galilee), but they have returned to shore with an empty net. Just after daybreak Jesus appears on the beach as a stranger

---

Jesus with oil to affirm his messianic status – but as a prelude to his death and burial (Mk 14.3–9).

[47] For an introduction to the dynamics of First-Century Roman imperial power, see Carter 2006.

[48] In Acts 4.13 Simon Peter is described as 'illiterate' (*agrammatos*) and 'unsophisticated' (*idiōtēs*).

[49] See Mt 16.17.

[50] Only John's gospel provides this biographical information (see Jn 1.44). On First-Century Bethsaida, see Strickert 2011; Evans 2015, pp. 5–17; and Freyne 2015.

[51] An inference based on Mk 1.21, 29.

[52] Presumably, this is how, after Jesus's arrest, bystanders in the courtyard of the high priest are able to identify Simon Peter's accent when he denies that he is a follower of Jesus (Mk 14.71; Lk 22.59).

[53] On Jesus's central economic teaching debt-forgiveness (and tax-resistance), see Oakman 2014.

[54] Mk 14.66–72; Mt 26.69–75; Lk 22.54–62; Jn 18.25–7.

[55] Peter's return to Galilee is assumed by the two earliest Gospels, Mark and Matthew (Mk 14.28–9,16.7; Mt 26.32–3, 28.10, 16). The Galilean setting for post-Resurrection appearances is not shared by Luke-Acts, for which Jerusalem provides the hub of activity of an (improbably) unbroken and continuous Jesus movement. John 21 also provides a post-crucifixion Galilean context for Simon Peter, who has evidently returned to his previous life as a fisherman.

[56] At any rate, this is indicated in the opening sections of the Book of the Acts of the Apostles and is confirmed by Paul's letters.

and directs them to cast their net to the right side of the boat – with miraculous success. Subsequently, they all sit down to cook and eat a breakfast of fish and bread.

> When they had finished breakfast, Jesus said to Simon Peter, 'Simon son of John, do you love me more than these?' He said to him, 'Yes, Lord; you know that I love you'. Jesus said to him, 'Feed my lambs'. A second time he said to him, 'Simon son of John, do you love me?' He said to him, 'Yes, Lord; you know that I love you'. Jesus said to him, 'Tend my sheep'. He said to him the third time, 'Simon son of John, do you love me?' Peter felt hurt because he said to him the third time, 'Do you love me?' And he said to him, 'Lord, you know everything; you know that I love you'. Jesus said to him, 'Feed my sheep. Very truly, I tell you, when you were younger, you used to fasten your own belt and to go wherever you wished. But when you grow old, you will stretch out your hands, and someone else will fasten a belt around you and take you where you do not wish to go'. (He said this to indicate the kind of death by which he would glorify God.) After this he said to him, 'Follow me'.[57]

What exactly is going on in this mutually interpellative question-and-response between Master and student, between absent/present Shepherd and caretaker shepherd?[58]

At first glance, Simon Peter seems to have redeemed himself. After having previously denied Jesus three times in the aftermath of his arrest, and returned to his ordinary life as a Galilean fisherman, in this exchange Simon Peter three times expresses his trust in, and devotion to, Jesus and his cause. This trust and devotion will, Jesus forewarns, result in Simon Peter's own arrest and death; for genuine love for Jesus requires action, namely, to 'feed his lambs' and 'tend his sheep'. Yet such action is fraught with risk – *to be taken where you do not wish to go*. Has Simon Peter understood, and committed himself to, the demands of radical discipleship? Listeners/readers of John's narrative would doubtless have already known about Simon Peter's ultimate fate, which is not explicitly mentioned anywhere else in the New Testament but to which the narrator parenthetically refers here: he was probably executed (along with Paul and other Jesus followers) in Rome as a victim of the persecution initiated by the Emperor Nero following the fire that broke out in Rome in 64.[59] Simon Peter appears,

---

57 John 21.15–19.
58 My reading is indebted to Howard-Brook 2003, pp. 475–9.
59 See Dunn 2009, pp. 1071–4. For a compelling scholarly reconstruction of Peter's death in

then, to become a model disciple who will comply with Jesus's request to 'follow me', no matter the risk.

Yet several ambiguities destabilise the dialogue. First of all, when Jesus asks, 'Do you love me more than these?' it is unclear where in the sentence the emphasis (in English or Greek) lies. Two readings are possible:[60]
– Do *you* [Simon Peter] love me more than these [other disciples do]?
– Do you love me more than [you love] *these* [other disciples]?

Simon Peter's reply is not to the first question (for how could he know the answer?) but to the second question. Thus, Simon Peter assures Jesus that, yes, he loves *him* more than he loves the other disciples. Yet the listener/reader cannot simply evade the first question, which hauntingly concerns the depth of one's commitment to Jesus and his cause.

Thus, another ambiguity arises: the first two times that Jesus asks Simon Peter 'Do you love me?' he uses the Greek verb *agapao*, which connotes unconditional 'fidelity'. However, when Simon Peter responds each time 'You know that I love you', he uses the weaker Greek verb *phileo*, which connotes conditional 'fondness or friendship'. On the third questioning, Jesus deliberately switches to *phileo*, as if to meet Simon Peter on his own terms. Again, the listener/reader is invited to reflect on whether or not his or her loyalty to Jesus and his cause is conditional or unconditional.

As a final ambiguity, note that, according to Jesus, Simon Peter will be taken *where he does not wish to go*; in other words, *unwillingly*. Yet early in John's narrative, Jesus has already announced that he is the 'good shepherd ... who lays down his life for the sheep' (10:11). In other word, the model life of an Authentic Shepherd requires that one sacrifice, and even be willing to die, *willingly* out of unconditional love for others. By contrast, Simon Peter's death will indeed 'glorify God', but he will prove to be a reluctant martyr and a less-than-authentic shepherd.

Over generations, from conjuncture to conjuncture, of course, the degree of such loyalty fluctuated. It is worth noting that there are two letters in the New Testament attributed to Simon Peter – 1 and 2 Peter – that indicate waning commitment by Jesus followers to Jesus's egalitarian vision. Both letters express a second-century perspective of Jesus followers who looked back to Simon Peter's life as exemplary and formed a kind of 'Petrine circle'.[61]

Rome – likely by being burned alive wrapped in animal skins and not, as later tradition has it, by crucifixion – see Barnes 2015.

60 Actually, a third reading is conceivable: Jesus is asking Peter, 'Do you love me more than you love *these* [his fishing equipment]'; see Thompson 2015, p. 441 n. 79.

61 Elliott 2005. For a commentary on both of these so-called 'Catholic Epistles', see Nienhuis and Wall 2013, pp. 95–156.

In particular, the earlier 1 Peter retains a powerful ethos of solidarity to include and care for those who had been rendered homeless and marginalised by Roman imperial rule; and such an ethical commitment can be traced back to the historical figures of Jesus and Simon Peter. Yet 1 Peter contains passages that are sharply at odds with the practice of Jesus and the earliest Jesus followers. Indeed, these passages indicate a new conjuncture of increasing accommodation to Roman imperial norms ('Honor the emperor'),[62] to slavery ('Slaves, accept the authority of your masters ...'),[63] and to unequal gender roles ('Wives, in the same way, accept the authority of your husbands ...').[64] Simon Peter's authority as a disciple is being used to encourage conformity to the status quo instead of supporting critical inquiry into the continuing demands of radical discipleship.

5   From Naming-Using Practices to Social Emancipation

What should we conclude from this thumbnail sketch of Simon Peter's historical individuality – of his biographical life? First of all, we should insist on the extent to which richness of his ordinary Galilean life exceeds our contemporary ability fully to reconstruct through even the best textual, anthropological, folkloric, sociological, and archaeological evidence.[65] Let us, for the sake of argument, though, suggest that the name *Shimon bar Yonah* rigidly designates this concrete individual.[66] By contrast, let us reserve *Petros* (or *Kēphā*) for the subsequent linguistic, cultural, theological, indeed, the *interpellative*, shifts in how this individual was remembered and venerated over the decades following his death and the subsequent stages of a movement to whose founding he had vitally contributed.[67]

---

62   1 Peter 2.17.
63   1 Peter 2.18.
64   1 Peter 3.1.
65   For overviews of the 'historical Galilee', see Horsley 1995 and Freyne 2014, pp. 13–51.
66   Saul Kripke has famously defined something as a rigid designator 'if in every possible world it designates the same object' (Kripke 1980, p. 48). In other words, a rigid designator picks out the singularity of an individual as compared with others. Moreover, according to Kripke, a (personal) name can best be understood to function as a rigid designator and not as a more-or-less comprehensive collection of definite descriptions of an individual.
67   Although Slavoj Žižek has used Kripke's theory of names to understand the nature of ideology (Žižek 2008, pp. 95–144), he too sharply distinguishes between *descriptivist* (e.g. Russell and Searle) and *antidescriptivist* theories of names (e.g., Kripke), and so fails to appreciate the need for what amounts, in Gregory McCulloch's words, to adopting a 'mixed strategy' (McCulloch 1989, p. 308) that incorporates both *descriptivist* and *antidescriptivist*

In this respect, I disagree with Markus Brockmuehl, who has contended that

> history's Simon Peter, like history's Jesus of Nazereth, is from the start always already embedded in communal memory and interpretation of one kind or another. This apostle, in other words, is always *somebody's* Peter, whether friend or opponent – rather than a neutrally or objectively recoverable figure.[68]

The chief problem with Brockmuehl's historical methodology is that while seeking to reconstruct the transmission of collective memories of an individual – Simon Peter in this case[69] – he fails to distinguish between a memory and the individual of whom there is a more-or-less reliable recollection. A memory is always a memory *of* something or someone; no memory is an entirely autonomous and purely idiosyncratic fiction. In this respect, memories operate, for better or worse, as *intentional* acts of transmission.

Furthermore, we must take care to distinguish between the *production* of a personal name and subsequent name-using practices associated with the *consumption* of that name.[70] *Producers* of personal names are those who have had dealings with an individual x and are in a position to recognise *that* individual as having been assigned a name, whether through formal 'baptism'[71] or some informal means, and to correct inaccurate information about him or her. By contrast, *consumers* of personal names are not acquainted with the individual – indeed he or she may now be long dead – but have been introduced into a relevant name-using practice by means of which meaningfully to refer to that individual.[72]

---

elements, much as I am suggesting that an adequate theory of ideology grounded in 'the interpellation of individuals as subjects' has to emphasise the irreducible tension between subjects and (named) individuals.

68 Brockmuehl 2012, p. xv.
69 Strictly speaking, 'Simon Peter' is what we ought to call a *hybrid* personal name that combines features designating (a) the historical individual 'Shimon bar Yonah' and (b) that individual as interpellated by Jesus and the tradition subsequently associated with him, namely, *Kēphā → Petros →* 'The Rock'. On the difficult question of 'Petrine nomenclature', see Williams 2015.
70 In this paragraph I follow Gareth Evans's discussion of proper names in Evans 1982, pp. 373–404.
71 On 'baptism' as the means by which name-using practices are customarily initiated, Kripke writes: 'Someone, let's say a baby, is born; his parents call him by a certain name. They talk about him to their friends. Other people meet him. Through various sorts of talk the name is spread from link to link as if by a chain' (Kripke 1980, p. 91).
72 This process is already at work during Paul's missionary activity in Corinth, where he con-

We can make a further distinction between *active* and *passive* consumers.[73] Passive consumers of personal names act as mere 'mouthpieces' of the name-using practice; they simply 'parrot sentences' and pass along the information to which they have been exposed about how to use the name in question.[74] Active consumers, by contrast, take a genuine interest in acquiring new knowledge and so strive to keep 'the light burning' in the name-using practice.[75] For instance, to the extent that they operate as active consumers, biblical scholars may acquire new facts and draw insightful conclusions about Simon Peter that are lacking to ordinary consumers of the name 'Simon Peter'. In this respect, their knowledge of the historical individual may rival that of the producers of that personal name – those individuals such as his family, Jesus, the other disciples, and other 'eyewitnesses' to the events narrated in the gospels.[76]

Once all name-producers have become unavailable or have died, of course, only name-consumers remain. At this point, in the 'last phase' of a name-using

---

fronts a variety of factions in the assembly of Jesus followers who identify as 'belonging' to Paul, Apollos (about whose life and teachings relatively little is known), Christ, or Cephas. See 1 Cor 1.10–17.

73 McCulloch 1989, pp. 281–4.
74 McCulloch, pp. 268–72, 283.
75 McCulloch, p. 282.
76 Richard Bauckham has argued persuasively that the four gospels are ancient 'biographies' that can be presumed to rely on eyewitness testimony to the life and times of Jesus. Obviously, there is also creative license involved in the oral transmission and writing of those gospels. But there is equally a more-or-less reliable historical core of information about Jesus and the First-Century movement he led that rivals information about any other ancient figure, for example, Socrates or Julius Caesar. Interestingly, much of Bauckham's argument hinges on the use of personal names, especially for minor characters, in the gospels as rigid designators (not his term) for historical referents, who themselves likely provided eyewitness testimony to help establish either the oral tradition or written narratives. See Bauckham 2006 on names in the gospel traditions (pp. 39–66). For dissenting views, see Patterson 2008; Weeden 2008; for Bauckham's reply, see Bauckham 2008. Bart Ehrman has recently dismissed Bauckham for advocating a 'conservative evangelical' position that would ignore the unreliability of the testimony of eyewitnesses (Ehrman 2016, pp. 100–1). Yet a more charitable response to Bauckham would note that these eyewitnesses were not *authors of* but merely important *sources for* Jesus traditions that eventually became the Gospels. Undoubtedly the Gospels – indeed the entire New Testament and other noncanonical Christian materials – were and remain history *as remembered* and from a (shifting) perspective of faith. But the key question is not whether or not events happened to named historical individuals precisely as depicted but *whether or not they happened at all*. This remains as true of Jesus as of Socrates (whose life, personality, and teachings were recounted differently by Aristophanes, Xenophon, and Plato), Octavian (who was born 'Gaius Octavius' but became 'Caesar Augustus'), or Siddhartha Gautama (who later had various titles bestowed upon him: 'The Buddha', 'Shakyamuni' and 'Tathagata').

practice, it could turn out that everything associated with that personal name is false, because there are no longer name-producers able to correct the inaccuracies.[77] However, such widespread misinformation does not affect the personal name's referent, which continues to be the original individual x.[78] At any rate, the accumulation of falsehoods in the transmission of a personal name can eventually be identified, challenged, and corrected by active consumers of that name.

Let me reiterate, then: theological reassessment of the historical individual Shimon bar Yonah doubtless occurred during the first generations of the Jesus movement, but this does not mean that there never existed an individual *by that name* who underwent subsequent processes of interpellation by those who in various ways modified the name-using practice. Nor does it imply that there is no good reason today to try to reconstruct the life of that individual within his historical conjuncture in as objective and thorough a manner as possible.

Secondly, although individuals are always already interpellated as subjects (even before they are born, as Althusser suggests), it is equally true that naming and reclaiming a concrete individual – Shimon bar Yonah, for instance – can serve to disrupt an interpellated subject – *Petros/Kēphā* for instance – as much any counter-interpellation has or could. In this sense, although some names are 'unnameable' they must nonetheless be said.[79]

---

[77] Evans 1982, pp. 393–6. In New Testament studies, this would constitute the extreme scepticism of what is commonly called the 'mythicist' position. For strong criticisms of such skepticism as unwarranted, see Ehrman 2012 and Casey 2014.

[78] Evans 1982, p. 395. The presence of an Aramaic nickname *Kēphā* as preserved in Mark's gospel and Paul's letters helps to provide a basis for reasonable confidence not only in the historical Jesus but also in the historical Simon Peter. At the very least, it would suggest a pre-Greek Aramaic background to the traditions associated with the early Jesus movement.

[79] On 'unnameable names', see Lazarus 2015, pp. 115–66. Like Althusser, though, Lazarus has pitched his analysis at the general level of collective names like 'worker', whereas there exists a grave political need to name specific individuals in order to address specific injustices. Consider the case of Sandra Bland, an African-American woman who was en route from Naperville, Illinois to a new job at Prairie View A&M University in Texas. Bland was beaten and arrested in Prairie View for a minor traffic infraction on 10 July 2015. She then died under suspicious circumstances in a Waller County, Texas jail on 13 July. A key slogan of the Black Lives Matter solidarity movement that has arisen and drawn attention to police misconduct in her – and numerous other cases – is precisely 'Say her name!' The slogan contains a double emphasis: not only 'Say her *name*!' but also 'Say *her* name!' Institutional racism remains unnameable within the confines of the dominant racial ideology – and yet it must be named by anti-racist activists each and every time it occurs. On Sandra Bland's activist life and her death in police custody, see Nathan 2016.

Continuing struggle over how the historical Simon Peter has been remembered and venerated has profound theological and practical impact on the lives of contemporary Catholics in specific (the doctrine of papal infallibility, for instance)[80] and all Christians in general (the egalitarian practice of the Jesus movement).[81] But it equally provides a basis for Christians and non-Christians to agree on the vital role that this individual played in history and may continue to play through solidarity grounded in positive identification and emulation.

If Althusser is right that 'concepts are not hidden in beds', it is equally true that they are not hidden in Galilean fishermen's boats. And yet there is a world of difference between 'ransacking Louis XV's bed' and carefully reconstructing a vessel used by Galilean peasants as an artifact in order to provide insight into an ancient subsistence fishing economy[82] – this between the decadent reality of social domination from above and the hardscrabble prospect of social emancipation from below.

---

[80] The great value of Oscar Cullmann's classic book on Peter (2011) was its theological intervention – originally, in the aftermath of World War II, but then, in the second edition, the reforms associated with Vatican II – on the question of possible ecclesiological common ground between Catholics and Protestants; on Cullmann's book as a theological-ecclesiological intervention, see Hurtado 2015, pp. 2–7.

[81] On the egalitarianism of the Jesus movement, see Horsley 2013.

[82] See Wachsmann 2009.

CHAPTER 5

'The Roaring of the Sea': Hobbes on the Madness of the Multitude*

In *Leviathan* Thomas Hobbes offers a remarkable account of madness.[1] Hobbes's interest in the phenomenon of madness was not a mere historical curiosity or theoretical embarrassment, though, something on a par with Hegel's later fascination with physiognomy and phrenology.[2] On the contrary, as we shall see, madness figured prominently in Hobbes's political philosophy as he attempts to theorise – and ward off the dangers inherent in – mass protest and social upheaval. Madness for Hobbes concerned the passionate excess not just of individuals but, even more importantly, of the *multitude*. Yet Hobbes grounded his political philosophy in his 'first philosophy'.[3]

As a result, in order to understand how he conceived of the specifically political dimension of madness, we must first situate it within his general theory of the passions.

Hobbes's analysis of the passions relies on his well-known materialist metaphysics of bodily motions. Hobbes initially distinguishes between two kinds of motion characteristic of animals: 'vital' motion and 'animal', or, more specifically, 'voluntary' motion. The former begins 'in generation' and continues 'without interruption' until death. Examples of such vital motion are 'the *course* of the *blood*, the *pulse*, the *breathing*, the *concoction, nutrition, excretion* ...' (L 6.1). Hobbes maintains that such motions have no need of the imagination.

Voluntary motion, on the other hand, involves bodily movement or speech 'in such a manner as is first fancied in our minds' (L 6.1). Hobbes has already argued in the first two chapters of *Leviathan* (a) that sense results from internal bodily motion caused by the actions or pressures of external physical objects and (b) that 'fancy' is nothing but the remnant or 'decaying' of the movements

---

* This chapter has been previously published as "'Il mugghiare del mare": Hobbes e la follia della moltitudine', in *Quaderni Materialisti* Vol. 3–4, 2005, pp. 127–46.
1 Hobbes also takes up the issue of madness in the *Elements of Law* (1640). It is worth noting that Hobbes does not explicitly mention madness either in *De Cive* (1642, later revised in 1647, anonymously translated into English and published in 1651 as *Philosophical Rudiments Concerning Government and Society*) or in *De Homine* (1658).
2 See Hegel 1977, pp. 185–210.
3 This approach to the relationship between Hobbes's metaphysics and his politics has been most thoroughly and convincingly defended by Zarka 1999.

underlying sense. It is also clear (c) that either bodily movement or speech requires a 'precedent thought of *whither, which way,* and *what*' (L 6.1). As a result, Hobbes concludes (d) that the imagination is the 'first internal beginning of all voluntary motion' (L 6.1). He insists that such voluntary motion at its origin must be neither visible nor sensible:

> For let a space be never so little, that which is moved over a greater space, whereof that little one is part, must first be moved over that. These small beginnings of motion, within the body of man, before they appear in walking, speaking, striking, and other visible actions, are commonly called ENDEAVOUR (L 6.1).

'Endeavour'[4] can be distinguished according to whether it is directed toward or away from a given object. In the former case, endeavour is termed 'desire' (in a general sense) or 'appetite' (in a restricted sense to cover such desires as hunger or thirst). In the latter case, endeavour is termed 'aversion'. Hobbes suggests that another way to frame such a distinction between types of endeavour is to speak of 'love' and 'hate'. However, a qualification is in order here: desire and aversion pertain to the *absence* of a certain object, whereas love and hate imply the object's *presence*.

Although human beings are born having a minimum of innate desires (and aversions), these seem to involve general, not particular, objects. Desires for 'particular things … proceed from experience and trial of their effects upon themselves or other men' (L 6.4). Desire, then, involves a process of trial-and-error; whatever we have never experienced we can know nothing about, we can form no beliefs with respect to, and, hence, we can have no basis to desire: we can only 'taste and try'. Aversion, on the other hand, can result both from what we have already experienced and from what we have yet to experience. In other words, aversion can be a shrinking away in the face of the unknown.

Finally, Hobbes argues that no two individuals – nor even the same individual over the course of time – can share the same desires or aversions:

> … [B]ecause the constitution of a man's body is in continual movement, it is impossible that all the same things should always cause in him the same appetites, and aversions; much less can all men consent in the desire of almost any one and the same object (L 6.6).

---

4 For a full discussion of Hobbes's use of the concept of 'endeavour' (*conatus*), see Barnouw 1992, pp. 103–24.

As Hobbes insists in his introduction to *Leviathan*, there is a 'similitude' of passions from one person to another, even though the objects of passions differ (L intro.3). These objects vary according to the peculiarities of

> the constitution individual and particular education ... and they are so easy to be kept from our knowledge, that the characters of man's heart, blotted and confounded as they are with dissembling, lying, counterfeiting, and erroneous doctrines, are legible only to him that searcheth hearts (L intro.3).

As a result, it is crucial for philosophers to compare others' actions with their own in order to avoid biases of either 'too much trust' or 'too much diffidence' (L intro.3).

It is worth emphasising at this point that Hobbes does not believe that anyone ever consciously experiences the internal motions that underlie the passions:

> As in sense that which is really within us is ... only motion caused by the action of external objects (but in appearance, to the sight, light and colour, to the ear, sound, to the nostril, odour, &c.), so when the action of the same object is continued from the eyes, ears, and other organs to the heart, the real effect there is nothing but motion or endeavour, which consisteth in appetite or aversion, to or from the object moving. But the appearance, or sense of that motion, is that we either call DELIGHT, or TROUBLE OF MIND (L 6.9).

Each of us is usually no more aware of such motions than we are aware of, say, the circulation of blood or the release of hormones. Just as Hobbes has argued earlier in his discussion of the imagination that appearance or 'fancy' is only an indirect experience of the external motions of physical objects in the world that impact on the sense organs and thereby constitute the internal motions of sense proper; so too does he argue now that delight (or pleasure) is simply the appearance of the internal motion of desire. By the same reasoning, pain is none other than the appearance of the internal motion of aversion.

Hobbes proceeds to distinguish between two kinds of pleasures (and pains). 'Pleasures of the senses' concern 'all onerations and exonerations of the body, as also all that is pleasant in the *sight, hearing, smell, taste, or touch*' (L 6.12). 'Pleasures of the mind', on the other hand, 'arise from the expectation that proceeds from foresight of the end or consequence of things, whether those things in the sense please or displease' (ibid.). As Yves-Charles Zarka has commented,

Hobbes regards sensual pleasures as common to both humans and animals but mental pleasures as unique to humans.[5] This is because animals experience the world in ways almost exclusively tied to *present* sensations, whereas humans enjoy a greater capacity to extend the horizon of experience to include retrospection on past sensation and anticipation of future sensation. Thus mental pleasures and pains, e.g., aesthetic pleasures and pains, exceed the temporal constraints of sensual pleasure and provide the basis for the uniquely human passions of 'joy' and 'grief'.

At this point Hobbes seeks to demonstrate how the various 'simple' passions we have encountered so far – appetite, desire, love, aversion, hate, joy, and grief – become ramified according to an intricate taxonomy of various 'compound'[6] passions. Without examining this taxonomy at length, let us at least note that Hobbes's list of simple passions in *Leviathan* differs considerably from what we find in the earlier *Elements of Law* and the later *De Homine*. As Arrigo Pacchi has suggested, Hobbes, on the one hand, in the *Elements of Law* tries to derive every passion from the single primary passion of 'glory'; and, on the other hand, in *De Homine* abandons any attempt to establish a pattern among the simple passions.[7]

In *Leviathan*, however, Hobbes appears to be concerned precisely with both the irreducibility and interrelationship of six[8] (rather than one) primary passions.[9] According to Zarka, we can arrange these simple passions into three pairs:
– desire / aversion;
– love / hate;
– joy / grief.[10]

There is a powerful rationale for this arrangement in pairs. Desire and aversion refer to whether there is an endeavour toward or away from a given object. Love and hate refer to whether an object is present or absent. Finally, joy and grief refer to mental – as distinct from sensual – pleasure derived from experience with an object.

---

5 Zarka 1999, pp. 259–61.
6 Although Hobbes does not use the adjective 'compound', it would seem that he has in mind an analogy with simple and compound imagination (see ii, 4).
7 Pacchi 1998. See also Zarka 1999, pp. 255–71 for a careful treatment of Hobbes's classification of the passions.
8 Since in *Leviathan* Hobbes uses 'appetite' and 'desire' (despite their nominal difference) pretty much interchangeably, it is helpful to think in terms of only *six* simple passions.
9 For Hobbes's debt to (and implicit critique of) Descartes's catalogue of the passions in *The Passions of the Soul*, see Pacchi 1998, pp. 84–7; and Herbert 1989, pp. 100–12.
10 Zarka 1999, pp. 255–6.

Furthermore, Zarka argues, simple passions differ from compound[11] passions to the extent that the former are characteristic of more-or-less isolated individuals, whereas the latter require the mediation of other persons. Beyond the emergence of compound passions, of course, we find ourselves in the midst of the conflicts between passions that typify Hobbes's 'state of nature', and lead to Hobbes's arguments in favour of the social contract and absolute sovereignty. However, our concern here is with neither social contract nor absolute sovereignty but with the forms of passionate excess (madness) that endanger the realisation of both. It is no accident that when in Chapter 26 Hobbes specifies who can and cannot enter into a contract to constitute a commonwealth, he observes the following:

> Over natural fools, children, or madmen there is no law, no more than over brute beasts; nor are they capable of the title of just or unjust, because they had never power to make any covenant or to understand the consequences thereof, and consequently, never took upon them to authorize the actions of any sovereign, as they must do that make to themselves a commonwealth (L 22.12).

Among the compound passions only 'glory' (and 'vain-glory') have an immediate bearing on the topic of madness. So let us now consider the former within the framework of a more detailed investigation of the latter.

1   The Varieties of Madness

Hobbes's view of madness has two distinctive general features: first, it is a naturalistic account that excludes supernatural explanations of madness as involving possession by spirits (e.g., demonic forces);[12] second, it is an account that presents madness on a continuum with other ordinary passions whose excessive expression it would be. Historically, Hobbes maintains, there have

---

11   Zarka calls them 'complex' passions.
12   In this sense Hobbes's perspective on madness is analogous to his perspective on witchcraft and religious superstition. His materialist metaphysics also rules out any possible supernatural explanation in these cases. However, he argues that witches should still be punished! – not because they have any real power but 'for the false belief they have that they can do such mischief, joined with their purpose to do it if they can, their trade being nearer to a new religion than to a craft or science' (L 2.8). For Hobbes's metaphysical (and political) critique of religious superstition and magic, see Johnston 1986, pp. 101–6, 134–63.

been two competing views regarding the cause of madness: one view has accounted for madness in terms of the passions gone awry, whereas the other view has contended that madness is attributable to the adverse influence of demons, spirits, etc. Hobbes rejects the latter as a credible explanation. Those who are mad are not possessed by malign entities; they are not demoniacs. On the contrary, as we shall see, they are more like drunken individuals. In order to defend his materialist approach to madness, Hobbes considers a number of ancient (Greek and Biblical) accounts of madness as supernatural occurrences of spirit- or demon-possession and argues that we can better grasp their significance as instances of unregulated passionate outbursts.

In Chapter Eight Hobbes situates his discussion of madness within the broader context of the intellectual virtues. As a result, madness for Hobbes can best be appreciated as a kind of intellectual 'defect'. But in order to grasp what an intellectual defect is, we must first consider what Hobbes means by the intellectual virtues.

Intellectual virtues are 'abilities of mind' that are highly esteemed and comparative in nature. In common parlance, notes Hobbes, an individual displaying such abilities is said to possess a 'good wit' (L 8.1). There are two kinds of intellectual virtue: 'natural' and 'acquired'. Let us consider them in order.

Natural intellectual virtue, interestingly enough, does *not* mean innate intellectual virtue, since at birth human beings only exemplify certain sensory capacities. In this respect Hobbes is quick to insist on a natural equality among human beings (and even, in this specific instance, between humans and higher mammals). 'Natural', then, simply characterises 'that *wit* which is gotten by use only, and experience, without method, culture, or instruction' (L 8.2).

We can distinguish two aspects of natural wit: firstly, what Hobbes calls 'celerity of imagining'; secondly, the ability to maintain 'steady direction' to some approved end (ibid.). As a result, a natural intellectual *defect* would involve mental slowness, stupidity, or 'dullness'. Whether a person is more or less quick or slow depends on the state of his or her passions. By the same token, another defect would take the form of a lack of mental steadiness and direction to some desired end. Hobbes suggests that too great a fancy should be construed as a kind of madness in which an individual is subject to eclecticism, distraction, or digressions.

It is important to distinguish at this point between 'fancy' and 'judgment'. Hobbes sets forth a number of general rules by which to ascertain the relative importance to be assigned to either fancy or judgment in specific instances (L 8.3–10). In the writing of poetry, fancy should predominate, whereas in the writing of history judgment should predominate. Likewise, in orations of both praise and invective, fancy should predominate; whereas in hortatory speeches and pleadings, the predominance of one over the other should depend on whether truth or disguise is being served. Finally, in reasoning itself, fancy (and its associated metaphors) should be rigorously excluded. To violate these general rules is to foster a defect in what Hobbes calls 'discretion'.

Discretion is a virtue that involves good judgment in 'matter of conversation and business, wherein times, places, and persons are to be discerned' (L 8.3). Hobbes proposes that it is worse for a person to lack discretion than to lack fancy:

> ... [I]n any discourse whatsoever, if the defect of discretion be apparent, how extravagant soever the fancy be, the whole discourse will be taken for a sign of want of wit; and so will it never when the discretion is manifest, though the fancy be never so ordinary (L 8.9)

Hobbes provides two striking, even amusing, examples in which individuals may be said to lack discretion. The indiscretion in each case seems to hinge on the inappropriate public display of private thoughts or desires:

> An anatomist or a physician may speak or write his judgment of unclean things, because it is not to please, but profit; but for another man to write his extravagant and pleasant fancies of the same is as if a man, from being tumbled into dirt, should come and present himself before good company. And it is the want of discretion that makes the difference. Again, in professed remissness of mind and familiar company, a man may play with the sounds and equivocal significances of words; and that many times with encounters of extraordinary fancy; but in a sermon, or in public, or before persons unknown, or whom we ought to reverence, there is no jingling of words that will not be accounted folly; and the difference is only in the want of discretion (L 8.10).

Let us turn now to examine wit 'acquired by method and instruction' (L 8.13). Such acquired wit is none other than reason itself, which is 'grounded on the right use of speech, and produceth the sciences' (L 8.13). At this point Hobbes advances an important argument. He wants to demonstrate that the cause of the differences in wit among individuals has to do with differences in their respective passions. But the differences in passions among individuals cannot be explained solely in terms of natural (e.g., bodily) variation. If it were the case that people's physical constitutions varied greatly, then one could expect equally great variation in their senses of sight, hearing, and so forth. But this is not the case. Therefore, we must conclude that differences in passions (and hence in mental abilities) derive from *artificial* differences in customs and education as well.

Hobbes seeks to explain which passions serve as causes of fluctuation in mental abilities:

> The passions that most of all cause the difference of wit are principally: the more or less desire of power, of riches, of knowledge, and of honour. All which may be reduced to the first, that is, desire of power. For riches, knowledge, and honour are but several sorts of power (L 8.15).

This is not the place to enter into an extended discussion of Hobbes's conception of power,[13] except to note that he holds that 'the power *of a man* (to take it universally) is his present means to obtain some future apparent good, and is either *original* or *instrumental*' (L 10.1).[14] Consequently, an individual who has no great conscious interest in acquiring riches, knowledge, honour, or, ultimately, power must wind up lacking as well good fancy or judgment. As Hobbes suggests with a vivid metaphor, 'the thoughts are to the desires as scouts and spies, to range abroad and find the way to the things desired' (L 8.16). But weak passions induce mental dullness, and indifferent passions induce giddiness and distraction. Finally, we learn, 'stronger and more vehement passions for anything than is ordinarily seen in others is that which men call MADNESS' (L 8.16).

Although Hobbes proposes that there are almost as many kinds of madness as there are passions, he seems to think that the two crucial passions between whose poles madness oscillates are great 'vain-glory' and great 'dejection'. As we have already seen in his approach to the passions themselves, Hobbes thinks that madness can sometimes be caused by an 'evil constitution of the organs of the body or harm done them' (L 8.17); but this cannot be the sole explanation.

It is crucial not to confuse 'vain-glory' with 'glory'.[15] The latter is a perfectly ordinary 'exultation of the mind' that arises from the 'imagination of a man's own power and ability' (L 6.39). As long as this commonplace passion is grounded in the individual's own experience, it is a legitimate form of self-confidence. However, when self-regard is based on the flattery of others or is only a product of one's own imagination, it assumes the aberrant form of 'vain-glory'. This excessive passion often afflicts young men, Hobbes observes, and may be corrected by 'age and employment' (L 8.41).

---

13 On which see Benn 1972, pp. 184–212; and Hindess 1996, pp. 23–46.
14 Here again by 'original' Hobbes means 'natural' as opposed to 'acquired' (by education, training, etc.).
15 For a detailed presentation of Hobbes's views on glory, see Slomp 2000; 2007.

'Dejection', the polar opposite of vain-glory, is a passion of grief 'from opinion of want of power' (L 6.40). Thus it appears that Hobbes's view of madness fluctuates between two extremes in which the proper moderate passions associated with the self are upset. Madness can be considered in terms of a self that is based on either too great or too little an estimation of its actual ability or, in Hobbes's terminology, its *power*.[16]

To be more specific, the madness of rage and fury results from vain-glory, and the madness of melancholy results from dejection. It is important to see that Hobbes does not conceive of madness as discontinuous with ordinary experience. Madness is an intensification and exaggeration of otherwise commonplace passional activity. Hobbes provides an example that clearly places his analysis of madness within a naturalistic setting: drunkenness.[17]

According to Hobbes, someone who is drunk resembles someone who is mad to the extent that each exemplifies excessive passionate behaviour without the discretion that the sober or sane maintain. Both drunkenness and madness undermine the virtue of discretion insofar as they remove the 'dissimulation' that ordinarily keeps the passions under control. As Hobbes contends,

> the most sober men, when they walk alone without care and employment of the mind, would be unwilling the vanity and extravagance of their thoughts at that time should be publicly seen; which is a confession that passions unguided are for the most part mere madness (L 8.23).

Perhaps the most interesting example of all, though, is Hobbes's specific attempt to explain social upheaval as a kind of affective contagion, a madness of the 'multitude'.[18] As Hobbes observes,

> though the effect of folly, in them that are possessed of an opinion of being inspired be not visible always in one man by any very extravagant

---

16   Here emerges a sharp contrast between Hobbes's conception of the self and Descartes's *cogito*. Hobbes conceives of the self as inherently unstable because it is riven by the fluctuations of various passions. In the Cartesian account of the *cogito*, however, we discover an essentially stable, unchanging, *substantial* self rooted in reason. It appears that for Descartes madness is strictly external to reason and, although dangerous, can be kept at a safe distance through a transcendent guarantee that Hobbes regards as impossible.

17   This example is similar to the one concerning the significance of dreams (L 2.5–6).

18   As Susan James has observed, the metaphor of uncontrolled passions as rebels against the order of reason was widespread among early-modern philosophers; see James 1997, pp. 11–12.

action that proceedeth from such passion, yet when many of them conspire together, the rage of the whole multitude is visible enough. For what argument of madness can there be greater than to clamour, strike, and throw stones at our best friends? Yet this is somewhat less than such a multitude will do. For they will clamour, fight against, and destroy those by whom all their lifetime before, they have been protected and secured from injury. And if this be madness in the multitude, it is the same in every particular man. For as in the midst of the sea, though a man perceive no sound of that part of the water next to him, yet he is well assured that part contributes as much to the roaring of the sea as any other part of the same quantity, so also, though we perceive no great unquietness in one or two men, yet may we be well assured that their singular passions are parts of the seditious roaring of a troubled nation. And if there were nothing else that bewrayed their madness, yet that very arrogating such inspiration to themselves is argument enough. If some man in Bedlam should entertain you with sober discourse, and you desire in taking leave to know what he were, that you might another time requite his civility, and he should tell you he were God the Father, I think you need expect no extravagant action for argument of his madness (L 8.21).

In this passage Hobbes dramatically shifts from his preceding examination of madness that occurs in individuals (presumably having organic defects) to consider forms of madness that are supposed to afflict groups or even entire societies. If one were to proceed no further than an analytic reconstruction of Hobbes's argument here, it would seem that Hobbes has committed logical fallacies both of division and of composition. That is, just because a group manifests behaviour that we would call 'mad', there is no reason to conclude that each of the individuals in the group is (equally) mad. Likewise, the individual forms of madness expressed by a great number of persons need not coalesce into a common madness. If madness in individuals sometimes arises, as Hobbes argues, from 'the evil constitution of the organs of the body or harm done them' (L 8.17), then it is hard to understand how – at least in these cases – the onset of collective madness could be caused by the accumulation of individual organic deformations. Although Hobbes frequently uses organic metaphors in *Leviathan* to describe the structure of a commonwealth,[19] surely even a metaphor is inappropriate here.

---

19 Most thoroughly in Chapter 24, in which he considers 'those things that weaken or tend to the dissolution of a commonwealth'.

As we have already seen, Hobbes allows that madness in individuals sometimes has a non-organic aetiology; in such cases the excessive passions themselves are the cause of any subsequent organic damage. Unfortunately, Hobbes does not mention what these non-organic causes might be. But whatever the causes of madness in individuals – whether organic or not – why should such individual passionate excesses necessarily lead to collective passionate excess? In other words, must many cases of, say, individual vain-glory, add up to a kind of collective vain-glory?[20] Such a situation is not beyond the realm of possibility, but isn't it just as likely that the summation of *varied* individual forms of madness would counteract or even cancel out each other?

It would appear that Hobbes never accounts for how the excessive passion of vain-glory can in fact cascade from one person to another – 'transindividually', we might say[21] – and thereby intensify its collective effect. At best Hobbes can explain cumulative 'imitation of the affects'[22] in terms of a series of analogical inferences drawn in turn by each member of the multitude. As he observes in the Introduction to *Leviathan*,

> for the similitude of the thoughts and passions of one man to the thoughts and passions of another, whosoever looketh into himself and considereth what he doth, when he does *think, opine, reason, hope, fear*, &c; and upon what grounds, he shall thereby read and know, what are the thoughts and passions of all other men upon the like occasions (L intro.3).

Yet even if passions were universalised in this way by each member of the multitude, such inferences would explain nothing; on the contrary, they would *presuppose* an already operative transindividual relay of passions from one to another.[23]

For example, Hobbes clearly applies his theory of the 'similitude of passions' based on drawing analogical inferences between oneself and others in his analysis of pity. In Chapter Six he proposes that

> *Grief* for the calamity of another is PITY, and ariseth from the imagination that the like calamity may befall himself; and therefore is called also

---

20   By the same token, must many individual cases of dejection amount to collective dejection?
21   On the concept of 'transindividuality', see Balibar 1997 and Read 2015.
22   The concept of 'imitation of the affects' (*imitatio affectuum*) is, of course, introduced by Spinoza in Part Three, Proposition 27 of the *Ethics*.
23   See Zarka 1999, pp. 277–8.

COMPASSION, and in the phrase of this present time a FELLOW-FEELING; and therefore for calamity arriving from great wickedness, the best men have the least pity; and for the same calamity, those have least pity that think themselves least obnoxious to the same (L 6.46).

No doubt one's pity for another's misfortune could arise in this way, but why couldn't it just as easily result from a direct *identification* with the plight of another person? In short, Hobbes conflates compassion with pity: although pity implies a rift between one's own and another's interests, compassion (literally, in Latin, to 'suffer with') allows for the possibility of bridging those interests.

Something else is peculiar about Hobbes's discussion of the madness of the multitude. In Chapter Eight of *Leviathan* Hobbes is purportedly describing the vicissitudes of human beings in the state of nature *prior to* the emergence of the order and stability that is above all else the aim of a centralised sovereign power. Yet the scenario he actually depicts much more resembles one in which a previously law-abiding people has degenerated into what in Chapter 22 he terms an unlawful 'tumultuous assembly' (L 22.33.33).[24] As Hobbes explains in this later chapter, 'it is not a set number that makes the assembly unlawful, but such a number as the present officers are not able to suppress and bring to justice' (L 22.33). Although Hobbes does not explicitly characterise situations of 'unlawful tumult' (L 22.34) as manifestations of collective madness, the implication is there. The upshot of this theoretical 'discrepancy'[25] is that in Chapter Eight Hobbes has already provided an example of pre-political collective madness that would be much more appropriate for characterising the post-political multitude in revolt against an *already-existing* sovereign power.

---

24 Although the distinction between a tumultuous assembly (or 'multitude') and 'people' is implicitly operative in *Leviathan*, Hobbes's only explicit acknowledgement of it occurs in his lengthy footnote to *De Cive* 6.1. For a full consideration of this and other relevant passages in Hobbes's writings, see the following: Chanteur 1969; Yves-Charles Zarka 1999, pp. 329–30; Wood and Wood 1997, pp. 94–111; Montag 1999, pp. 90–103.

25 Louis Althusser used the term 'discrepancy' (*décalage*) to indicate the tendency especially among classical social contract theorists surreptitiously to introduce examples into their accounts of the state of nature that more properly belong to civic life (often as limit cases); see Althusser 1977.

2 Madness in the English Revolution

It would be a mistake to see Hobbes's fallacies, appeal to analogy, and reliance on a discrepant example either as lapses in his reasoning to be corrected or hastily passed over in embarrassment or as cases of intellectual dishonesty. On the contrary, they signify his earnest attempt to understand how mass social upheaval can arise. Nor was this attempt limited to Hobbes among his contemporaries. As Michael Heyd has compellingly argued, the critique of 'enthusiasm' was 'one of the recurring themes of seventeenth-century discourse'.[26] Heyd documents not only the wide variety of meanings that enthusiasm could take – religious, philosophical, scientific, and rhetorical – but also that these meanings all had social and political connotations. Indeed, Heyd has proposed that

> the phenomenon of enthusiasm was closely linked with a crisis of authority in the seventeenth century, and it is within this context that it gains its historical specificity ... Furthermore ... the critique of enthusiasm, that which sought to defend the social and intellectual order, itself underwent a certain crisis in the seventeenth century. Indeed, it may be suggested that the 'general crisis of the seventeenth century' was primarily a crisis in the ideological and cultural basis of the social order. Up to the middle of the seventeenth century, the critique of enthusiasm in Protestant societies was based on the traditional foundations of the religious and intellectual order, namely scripture, humanistic learning, Aristotelian scholasticism and Galenic medicine ... By the second half of the seventeenth century, however, it was becoming increasingly clear that these traditional bulwarks ... no longer provided a firm enough basis for the social and cultural order. Indeed, these were precisely the traditions attacked by the so-called 'enthusiasts'. Vis-à-vis such attacks, those who wished to defend the social, religious and cultural order could do so either by resorting repeatedly to the traditional arguments, or by searching for new responses.[27]

Hobbes offered one such response. First of all, as we have seen, he reinterpreted religious enthusiasm no longer as supernatural inspiration or divine possession but in terms of a scientific account of the passions – and their excessive mani-

---

26   Heyd 1995, p. 2.
27   Heyd 1995, pp. 8–9.

festation. This is none other than what Heyd means by the 'medicalisation' of the critique of enthusiasm:

> In designating religious eccentrics and non-conformists as 'mentally sick', the critics of enthusiasm imperceptibly redefined religious orthodoxy in medical terms of health and mental balance, rather than, or at least, side by side with, theological terms of correct faith.[28]

As we have just seen, too, Hobbes especially worried about the threat to the dominant social order presented by unbridled mass enthusiasm set into motion. His lurid portrayal of the crazed multitude roaring like the sea is emblematic of a much broader elite discourse about how best to hold on to power. Moreover, it serves as Hobbes's pointed – one could even say *panic-stricken* – response to the popular discourse of those contemporaries who praised exactly what he condemned.

For as Christopher Hill has argued in his magisterial exploration of 'radical ideas during the English revolution', throughout English society in the seventeenth century opposition to monarchy often assumed the form of a privileging of madness.[29] Although a wide variety of such opponents in seventeenth-century England appealed to visions, prophecy, and divine inspiration to make their cases, it is worth focusing on Gerrard Winstanley, who was a leader of the proto-communist True Levellers or Diggers and especially during 1649–52 wrote and acted as a kind of 'anti-Hobbes'.[30] In January 1649 Winstanley had a religious vision and proclaimed that a new

> law of righteousness shall rise out of the dust, out of the poor people that are trod underfoot: For, as the declaration of the Son of man was first declared by Fishermen, and men that the learned, covetous Scholars despised: so the declaration of the righteous law shall spring up from the poor, the base and despised ones, and fools of the world.[31]

In June of that year, two months after he and other Diggers had begun to plough up and plant on waste land located at St. George's Hill, just outside of London, Winstanley wrote a letter to Lord Thomas Fairfax, Commander-in-Chief

---

28   Heyd 1995, p. 10.
29   Hill 1972, esp. pp. 223–30.
30   Hill sharply contrasts Winstanley with Hobbes on pp. 313–19.
31   Winstanley 1965, p. 205. I have slightly modernised Winstanley's spelling in this and the next quotation.

of Parliament's recently victorious New Model Army. At the end of this letter Winstanley entreats Fairfax

> to consider ... this business of public community, which I am carried forth in the power of love, and clear light of universal righteousness, to advance as much as I can; and I can do no other, the Law of love in my heart does so constrain me, by reason whereof I am called fool, mad man, and have many slanderous reports cast upon me, and meet with much fury from some covetous people, under which my spirit is made patient, and is guarded with joy and peace. I hate none, I love all, I delight to see every one live comfortably. I would have none live in poverty, straits or sorrows.[32]

What is striking about Winstanley's writings was his keen awareness of just how bitterly the English nobility would resist the labouring poor in pursuit of their own political, economic, and religious interests. Men like Hobbes, Winstanley realised, could no longer ignore such 'base and despised ones' and so had to dismiss them as foolish or mad.

In historical retrospect, though, how might we comprehend these seventeenth-century outbreaks of passionate excess and disdain for earthly authority evident in the words and deeds of Winstanley and the English multitude at large? Hill offers three explanations. First of all, it is often the case historically that 'mental breakdown' serves as a form of 'social protest, or at least a reaction to intolerable social conditions: those who break down may be the truly sane ones'.[33] Secondly, such extremes in belief and behaviour could have been 'deliberate forms of advertisement, whether self-advertisement or advertisement for the cause, in so far as these could be distinguished'.[34] Hill suggests that 'many radicals recognized ... that their views were so extreme that they must appear mad to normal members of the ruling class'.[35] One of the few ways for the poor and disenfranchised to attract attention to their views would have been to feign madness. Thirdly, such praise of fools and their madness were a means by which social critics could disguise their ideas, 'allowing themselves to express dangerous thoughts under cover of insanity or delusions, from which one could retreat afterwards'.[36]

---

32   Winstanley 1965, p. 291.
33   Hill 1972, p. 224.
34   Hill 1972, p. 291.
35   Hill 1972, p. 225.
36   Hill 1972, p. 227.

There remains, however, a fourth possible explanation that Hill does not explicitly discuss. Mass movements typically release pent-up ideas and emotions that have been dismissed or repressed for years within a given society; they invariably arouse feelings of euphoria through the establishment of intense affective bonds of solidarity.

But whatever the best explanation for the countless seventeenth-century celebrations of madness, we find in *Leviathan* that Hobbes wants nothing to do with them. He expresses a 'fear of the masses'[37] that can only envision social protest as the dangerous result of passionate excess, as rampant vain-glory culminating in a generalised madness. Thus, it is not surprising, as David Johnston and Quentin Skinner have argued,[38] that Hobbes should write *Leviathan* precisely as a lengthy exercise of philosophical rhetoric that might help stem – or at least redirect – the tide of passionate excess that was then engulfing English society.[39] Hobbes thought that a new philosophical rhetoric was needed because his philosophical predecessors had been part of the problem. Philosophy itself – especially in its scholastic guise – all too often had evidenced a species of madness arguably more dangerous than either individual or collective follies, precisely because the former madness prepares the way for the latter.

In his discussion of reason and science in Chapter Five of *Leviathan*, Hobbes had already observed that among living creatures only humans are capable of error or 'absurdity', because they alone can use – and abuse – language. Philosophers have especially contributed to the generation of errors and absurdities in reasoning, chiefly because they have failed (until Hobbes) to make use of a proper method, for

---

37 Étienne Balibar uses this phrase to designate Spinoza's ambivalence about, as opposed to Hobbes's antipathy to, social movements; see Balibar 1994, pp. 3–37.
38 Johnston 1986 and Skinner 1996.
39 For a confirmation of Hobbes's alarm, especially in *Leviathan*, over the madness of the multitude, we might contrast his treatment of madness there with his earlier analysis in the *Elements of Law* (EL). By 1640 Hobbes had already come to understand madness in much the same terms as eleven years later in *Leviathan*. For example, he characterises madness as a 'principal defect of the mind' that is 'some imagination of such predominance above all the rest, that we have no passion but from it' and results from either (a) excessive vain-glory or (b) excessive vain dejection (EL 51). What is interesting about the several examples of madness provided by Hobbes is that they all pertain to individuals and not to groups. Hobbes was already convinced that religious belief could assume undesirable forms of enthusiasm. But the specifically political expression of madness had not yet dawned on him. That realisation was to await the social upheaval accompanying the English Revolution.

there is not one of them that begins his ratiocination from the definitions, or explications of the names they are to use; which is a method that hath been used only in geometry, whose conclusions have thereby been made indisputable (L 5.7).

Without proper method, philosophy risks falling into a form of madness analogous to the madness that individuals or groups suffer by virtue of 'passions unguided' (L 8.23). Hobbes sees the stability of the commonwealth as linked to the psychic stability of individuals; philosophy has a crucial role to play in assuring the regulation of individual and collective passions.[40] As Albert Hirschman has argued, Hobbes adopts a general strategy of pitting passion against passion – the 'tamers' vs. the 'wild ones' to be tamed.[41] The ultimate aim of such a 'countervailing strategy' is to strengthen the passions that incline persons to obedience and peace instead of disobedience and war.

In the final analysis, of course, Hobbes does not regard the practice of philosophy alone as sufficient to insure that the danger posed by the release of excessive passions be forestalled. Only the sovereign can serve as a common power adequate to the task of holding both individuals and groups in awe; only the sovereign can effect a mediation of fear designed to maintain the stability of a commonwealth. Yet there is no guarantee of such stability, since every commonwealth is capable of being undermined. Hobbes worries that 'though sovereignty, in the intention of them that make it, be immortal, yet is it in its own nature, not only subject to violent death by foreign war, but also through the ignorance and passions of men it hath in it, from the very institution, many seeds of a natural mortality by intestine discord' (L 21.21).[42] As a result, even the sovereign's power of physical force has an ongoing need for the philosopher's power of verbal persuasion.

3   Conclusion

Since the cogency of Hobbes's analysis of madness ultimately rests on the cogency of his theory of the passions, any problems with the latter cannot help but be problems with the former. Yet there are most assuredly serious deficien-

---

40   Hobbes likewise devotes all of Chapter 46 to the need to avoid the absurdities to which philosophers are prone – absurdities with dire social consequences.
41   See Hirschman 1997, p. 31.
42   The whole of Chapter 29 is also crucial in this regard.

cies in Hobbes's treatment of the passions. Tom Sorell has well identified some of the main weaknesses, and it is worth quoting him at length:

> The trouble with this highly individualistic account is that it does not seem to fit the case of creatures whose passions Hobbes is most concerned to catalogue, namely creatures like us. He usually neglects the ways in which appetites and aversions are formed by training or conditioning; consequently, he seems to leave out of account the ways in which patterns of training can enforce a single pattern of values that prevails in a wider community. Hobbes does of course admit that it is possible to have one's passions influenced by the eloquence of others ... and by the teaching of others ... but he typically regards this as only one influence among others when it can plausibly be claimed to be pre-eminent. He is typically over-individualistic in his account of how people develop their systems of valuation. In his attempt to tie together the effects of sense with the first beginnings of voluntary motion, he seems to look for causes mostly inside the agent and not around him.[43]

One way or another, then, we must come to terms with the problem of Hobbes's commitment to both individualism and materialism. On the one hand, he is caught in a dilemma similar to the one Marx and Engels identified in Feuerbach:[44] to the extent that Hobbes is a materialist he avoids history, and to the extent that he considers history he is not a materialist. He simply cannot explain adequately the historical dimension of human emotional life. On the other hand, Hobbes's individualism prevents him from fully grasping the mass political significance of the tumultuous events unfolding around him, their properly transindividual dynamic. As we have seen, his theory of the 'similitude of passions' inadequately accounts for full-fledged cases of affective identification and thereby reduces the complex psychology of collective struggle to the simple sum of individual emotional aberrations.

What does all this have to do with Hobbes's theory of madness? As Michel Foucault has compellingly argued,[45] the history of madness can best be appreciated as the history of how madness has been socially and discursively *constructed*. Madness cannot be explained solely in terms of organic dysfunction but should equally be viewed as the product of one among many means by which social elites have historically sought to regulate forms of beliefs and

---

43   Sorell 1986, p. 92.
44   Marx and Engels 1970, p. 64.
45   See Foucault 2006. See also Scull 2015.

modes of behaviour by distinguishing between what is to be deemed appropriate or inappropriate, normal or pathological. Hobbes proves no exception to this practice. Despite his radically materialist account of the passions and his rejection of supernatural accounts of madness, Hobbes ultimately winds up in the service of political reaction – an unwelcome service, to be sure, since his relentless materialism terrified his royalist contemporaries and continues to disturb liberal pieties about the nature and purpose of the state.

Yet, ironically, as we have seen, Hobbes himself recoiled before an unruly multitude that appeared to him to be the decomposition of what could, under favourable circumstances, become a more-or-less orderly (and submissive) people. By analysing his own fear we can, perhaps, draw a philosophical lesson of immense importance even, or especially, today: at its height mass struggle always threatens to burst the individualistic constraints of legitimacy implicit within any conception of social contract. Such would be a constituent power to contest the constituted power of both sovereigns and their philosophers.[46]

---

46   On the distinction between 'constituent' and 'constituted' forms of political power, see Negri 1999, esp. pp. 1–35.

CHAPTER 6

Spinoza's Three Modes of Rebellion: Indignant, Glorious, and Serene*

In the Preface to his *Tractatus Theologico-Politicus* (TTP) Spinoza famously raised an unsettling question. How was it possible, he wondered, that human beings could ever come 'to fight for their servitude as if for salvation, and count it no shame, but the highest honor, to spend their blood and lives for the vanity of one man'? This was for Spinoza 'the greatest secret of monarchical government and its main interest'. As Gilles Deleuze and Félix Guattari once remarked, in this passage Spinoza had posed 'the fundamental problem of political philosophy'.[1] Yet this would seem to be only *half* of the problem. The other half, equally important for both Spinoza and political philosophers today, is to know how it becomes possible for human beings to fight for their freedom, to revolt against oppression, and to establish what Spinoza called a 'free republic'. In this chapter, then, I want to consider not an individual's obligation to obey legitimate political authority but instead what can trigger his or her desire to resist illegitimate political authority.

This is a very different question than asking what might form the basis of one's *right* to resist. According to Spinoza's well-known formula: 'the natural right of each person extends as far as his or her desire and power'.[2] The radical implication of this formula is that we always have the right to resist oppression as long as we have the power and the desire to do so.[3] But what is the motivation

---

* This chapter has been previously published as 'Le tre forme della ribellione secondo Spinoza: indignata, gloriosa et soddisfatta', in *Storia politica della moltitudine: Spinoza et la modernità*, edited by Flippo Del Lucchese, pp. 150–69, Roma: Derive Approdi, 2009; and 'Spinoza on the Glory of Politics', in *Spinoza: individuo e moltitudine*, pp. 327–39, Cesena: Società Editrice 'Il Ponte Vecchio', 2007.
1 Deleuze and Guattari 1983, p. 29.
2 TTP Pref. 13. Spinoza presents his argument to this conclusion in TTP 16.1–4 and in TP 2.4. On Spinoza's conception of right, see Alexandre Matheron, 'Le droit du plus fort: Hobbes contre Spinoza', *Revue philosophique* 1985/2, pp. 149–76; and Lazzeri 1998.
3 On Spinoza's view of the political right to resistance, see Bove 1996, pp. 241–301 and Lazzeri 2001, pp. 173–90. Charles Ramond (2016, pp. 325–41) has dissented and insisted that Spinoza was fundamentally opposed to acts of 'sedition' (*seditio*), 'rebellion' (*rebellion*), and 'insubmission' (*contumacia*) because they result from 'the hysterical, unconscious, blind, manipulated, inconstant, and furious crowd (*vulgus*)' (p. 331) and are always related 'to superstitious hatred, never to noble or generous sentiments, still less to the general interest or the "public welfare"'

for such resistance? Perhaps even more importantly, what best *sustains* resistance over the long run? These are fundamental questions that I shall address below.

To do so requires that I examine three key affects in Spinoza's political lexicon that have seldom received the careful treatment they deserve: 'indignation' (*indignatio*), 'glory' (*gloria*), and 'serenity' (*acquiescentia*). Indeed, I shall argue that to each of these 'affects of resistance'[4] corresponds a distinctive mode of political rebellion, namely, *indignant* rebellion, *glorious* rebellion, and *serene* rebellion.[5]

1   The Logic of Indignation

Let us begin with the affect of indignation and investigate how it can trigger rebellion against perceived injustice. Spinoza defines indignation as 'a hatred toward someone who has harmed another (*alteri malefecit*)' (def aff 20) and refers the reader back to E3p27c1, by means of which it is clear that indignation is an imitation of the victim's affects.[6] The intensity with which I experience such affective imitation depends on the degree to which the victim resembles me. From E3p22, it follows that my reaction will be even stronger if the victim is someone whom I have previously loved.[7]

Indignation in Spinoza's account, then, is a three-part relation among oppressor, victim, and bystander, which I diagram in figure 1 below.

Spinoza's most complete treatment of the political logic of indignation occurs in TP 3/9, in which he argues that

---

(p. 340). At most, Ramond concludes, Spinoza will allow for resistance in the sense of individual freedom of conscience, especially by 'philosophers' against overtly tyrannical regimes (pp. 339–40). In my view, however, Ramond unduly takes Spinoza at his word and so fails to allow for a more plausible Spinozist distinction between actions by, on the one hand, what we could call the *vulgar* multitude – whose members are largely swayed by negative passive affects like fear and hatred – and, on the other hand, actions by a *reasonable* multitude – whose members have managed to cultivate and reinforce not only such active passive affects as hope and love but also active affects like courage and generosity, in short, *fortitude* (as we shall discuss in the next chapter). If Spinoza is not exactly Lenin, neither is he Camus!

4   I borrow the term 'affects of resistance' from Bove 1996, pp. 291–5. However, Bove identifies and discusses only two such affects, namely, indignation and 'benevolence' (*benevolentia*), which Spinoza defines as 'the desire to benefit one whom we pity' (def aff 35).

5   For a useful classification of the variety of Latin words Spinoza uses for political rebellion, see Ramond 2007, pp. 154–68.

6   For detailed treatments of Spinoza's view of indignation, see the following: Matheron 2011, pp. 219–29; Bove 1996, pp. 291–5; and Filippo Del Lucchese 2009, pp. 60–3.

7   Matheron 2011, p. 222.

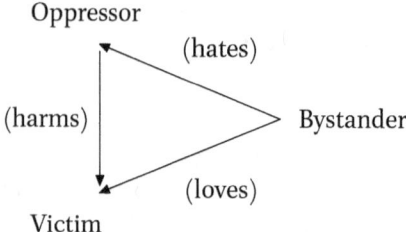

FIGURE 1   The Structure of Indignation

commands that arouse the indignation (*indignatio*) of many persons hardly belong to the right of the commonwealth. For it is certain that under the guidance of Nature human beings conspire together, either because of common fear, or desire to avenge (*ulciscendi*) some common injury; and since the right of a commonwealth is defined by the common power of the multitude (*jus civitatis communi multitudinis potentia definitur*), it is certain that the power of the commonwealth, and its right, are diminished insofar as it offers causes for more human beings to conspire together. Certainly, a commonwealth has dangers to fear, and what is true of each citizen, that is, a human being in a natural state, is also true of a commonwealth; the greater the cause for fear a commonwealth has, the less it is possessed of its own right (*sic civitas eo minus sui juris est, quo majorem timendi causam habet*).

The upshot of this passage is that since the right of a state is defined by the collective power of the multitude, every state's power – and thus its right – decreases as the number of rebellious individuals increases. As a result, and in keeping with his thoroughgoing political realism, Spinoza concludes that it is strictly contrary to the right of a state to do anything that might incite general indignation. At the end of TP 4.4 Spinoza provides further details of such a connection between excesses committed by a regime and the likelihood that the multitude will cease to be in awe, become indignant, and threaten to topple it. For example, if a ruler were to 'run drunk or naked through the streets with prostitutes, act on stage, openly break laws or hold them in contempt … slaughter or plunder subjects, abduct young women, and so forth', then the multitude's fear would 'turn into indignation', and, as a result, the 'civil state' (*status civilis*) would become a 'state of war' (*status hostilitatis*).[8]

---

[8] This description echoes Tacitus's account in *Annals* 13–16 of the deranged Roman Emperor Nero's abuses of power.

Consider now how subjects' fear of a tyrant can undergo a reversal to become indignation and then proceed to destabilise an oppressive regime. Tyrants govern principally by means of instilling fear in their subjects. Because fear is a form of sadness (E3p18s2) and hate is 'sadness with the accompanying idea of an external cause' (E3p13s), tyrants invariably incur their subjects' wrath. But, of course, if these subjects were only to remain afraid as isolated individuals, lest their loyalty be detected and punished, the tyrant would remain secure in power. Also, such isolated individuals' hatred would be 'episodic',[9] since no tyrant can simultaneously oppress every subject. As a result, as Spinoza remarks in TP 6.4 regarding his paradigmatic case of 'Turkish despotism', subjects who live under tyranny exist in an artificially induced condition of 'solitude' that is, contrary to Hobbes's position, itself the most glaring example of a 'state of nature' (*status naturalis*). Such a society approaches a kind of civic death in which people have lost all hope and become utterly apathetic.[10]

At some point, though, even the most cunning tyrant's excesses become too great to remain hidden. When his subjects become aware of these misdeeds and speak out against them, indignation erupts, and will result in a radical transformation of the situation as soon as each person knows that others are indignant too. We have a situation in which indignation 'catalyses' fear and generates a kind of affective 'contagion'.[11] Each subject's externally imposed solitude shatters and opens up the possibility of a collective rebellion against oppressive rule. There are, of course, two possible outcomes to any such rebellion.[12]

The tyrant could well come to his senses, realise the danger, appease his irate subjects, and so retain power – at least until he again oversteps his authority, oppresses his subjects, who eventually rebel, and so forth. Or, confronted with an indignant populace, a tyrant could remain obstinate and thus pave the way to insurrection. If an insurrection were to succeed in removing the tyrant but then devolve into civil war – Spinoza's favourite example here is the English multitude's overthrow of Charles I[13] – and from civil war into a myriad of local conflicts, there would occur a hypothetical limit-case in which all social relations would dissolve. Such a fictional scenario is precisely what Spinoza, like Hobbes before him, intends by the term 'state of nature'.

---

9   Matheron 2011, p. 222.
10 Matheron 1988, pp. 418–20.
11 Rizk 1995, pp. 117–18; and Rizk 2012, p. 217.
12 Matheron 2011, pp. 222–3.
13 See Spinoza's analysis in TTP 18.8 of the vicissitudes of the English Civil War.

But this would hardly be the end of the story, for Spinoza insists in TP 6.1 that socio-political life must re-emerge from such a state of nature:

> since human beings ... are led more by affect than reason (*magis affectu quam ratione ducuntur*), it follows that the multitude, led not by reason by some common affect (*non ex rationis ductu sed ex communi aliquo affectu*), naturally agrees and wants to be led as if by one mind (*veluti mente duci velle*), that is (as we said in 3.9), either by common hope, fear, or common desire to avenge (*ulciscendi*) some common harm. However, since fear of solitude belongs to all human beings, because no one in solitude has forces to defend himself and bring together those things which are necessary for life; it follows that human beings by nature desire the civil state (*statum civilem homines natura appetere*), nor can it happen that they ever entirely dissolve it.

The point of Spinoza's reference to TP 3.9 in this passage is that the way political authority reappears is analogous to the way it has dissolved. In other words, indignation is responsible for *both* the fall *and* the rise of states.

In Spinoza's view, such oscillations between oppression and resistance insure a dynamic equilibrium of socio-political life. Indeed, as Laurent Bove has proposed, indignation is 'a remedy that the collective body produces and applies to itself. It is the very process of a self-defense and a self-management'.[14] Filippo Del Lucchese has likewise argued that indignation represents 'the real, actual gap that exists between the power and the right of the commonwealth – the sovereign power – and the power and the right of the multitude'. Since these rights and powers 'may not correspond', general indignation is always possible.[15] As a result, even when subjects' indignation against a tyrant does not lead to the successful overthrow of an existing regime, it nonetheless plays a *regulative* role in socio-political life by forcing rulers to seek more securely to reestablish their power.

Alexandre Matheron has argued that the regulative and the constitutive functions of indignation are distinct but inseparable, since no independently existing, more-or-less stable state of nature could ever exist from which a transition to political authority would later arise.[16] On the contrary, the state of nature is highly unstable and is simply the ontological obverse of socio-political life, indeed, its irreducible materialist presupposition.

---

14   Bove 1996, p. 301.
15   Del Lucchese 2009, p. 61.
16   Matheron 1994, p. 226.

More precisely, for Spinoza the state of nature is but one moment during the continuous process through which every state produces, reproduces, and strives to regulate itself – an effort that Matheron has designated as a kind of collective *conatus*. It indicates an extreme situation when socio-political imbalance results from generalised indignation and leads to the possible dissolution of an existing regime. Yet such dissolution will immediately undergo an affective recomposition, and again through generalised indignation a more-or-less altered form of state will reemerge.

Yet there is a problem with indignation and the mode of rebellion with which it is associated: indignation is a 'necessarily bad' passion (E4P51S). Although, as Spinoza proposes in E4p54s, some passions can be intrinsically bad but instrumentally good – e.g., 'humility' (*humilitas*), 'repentance' (*paenitentia*), and 'reverence' (*reverentia*) – indignation is not one of them. Indignation is both intrinsically and instrumentally bad, because it is a form of interpersonal hate, and such forms of hate encourage us to 'strive to destroy' the person we hate (E4P45). Yet this destructive impulse is, as Spinoza writes in E4p37, contrary to reason's urging that we desire for others the good we desire for ourselves. As a result, we cannot distinguish good and bad forms of indignation. Even if indignation were collectively 'good' for the society as a whole (e.g., resistance to an especially oppressive regime), it would still be bad for those individuals experiencing it, and in turn bad for the larger society composed of those individuals.[17]

A final implication of Spinoza's analysis of indignation concerns not the repressive nature of the state but the political implications of the affects. Is every passive political affect sad? Not at all. Although monarchies – especially in their degenerate tyrannical forms – tend to rely on such sad passions as fear and shame in order to keep their subjects in thrall, democracies instead strive to cultivate in their citizens such joyous passions as hope and glory.

But a deeper question arises at this point: Must all sad passive political affects remain instrumentally bad? No doubt the sad passion of indignation is a natural and unavoidable response by individuals and the multitude to oppression. Nonetheless, Spinoza offers a form of *transition* from instrumentally bad to instrumentally good passions.[18] Let us call this *an affective transition of the first kind*. Surprisingly, perhaps, it is prophets who lead the way.

---

17   Matheron 2011, pp. 227–8.
18   For a systematic account of the importance of such transitions for Spinoza, see Tosel 2008, pp. 173–209. Following Martha Nussbaum's recent classification (Nussbaum 2016), we could say that Spinoza defends a 'transitional' theory of the affects, in this case, the species of anger we could call 'transition-indignation'.

2 Prophets and the Multitude

In E4p54s, echoing the Roman historian Tacitus, Spinoza famously observes that 'the vulgar terrify, if they are unafraid' (*terret vulgus, nisi metuat*). But it is less often recalled that he immediately provides a biblical qualification:

> and therefore it is not surprising that the prophets, who considered what is useful not just to a few but to all, so strongly recommended humility, repentance, and reverence (*prophetae, qui non paucorum, sed communi utilitari consuluerunt, tantopere humilitatem, poenitentiam, et reverentiam commendaverint*). And, in truth, those who are subject to these affects (*qui hisce affectibus sunt obnoxii*) can be induced much more easily than others to live at last under the guidance of reason, that is, to become free, and to enjoy the life of the blessed.

Not only does this passage contain the only occurrence of the word 'prophet' (*propheta*) in the entire *Ethics*, the prophet's vocation in this case would appear to be not so much to serve as an intermediary between God and humanity – the object of Spinoza's analysis in first two chapters of the TTP – but to perform a properly transindividual service: namely, to help a passive multitude under the influence of sad passions (in other words, the *vulgar* multitude) to become a more active multitude by controlling and redirecting its passions. Such an affective transition would be simultaneously theological and political; indeed, it would be properly *theological-political*.

As Henri Laux has exhaustively and persuasively argued, for Spinoza prophecy is not an exclusively religious phenomenon but equally concerns how best to achieve and maintain well-ordered societies.[19] Seen in this light, E4P54 has to do less with some esoteric prophetic knowledge that would be inaccessible to ordinary men and women than with 'an analysis of the affects ... applied to social cohesion'.[20]

Consider the three affects to which, according to Spinoza, the Biblical prophets sought to subject the vulgar: 'humility' (*humilitas*), 'repentance' (*poenitentia*), and 'respect' (*reverentia*). Spinoza defines 'humility' as 'a sadness born of the fact that a man considers his own lack of power, or weakness' (def aff 26); it is opposed to 'assurance in oneself' (*acquiescentia in se ipso*), which is defined as 'a joy arising born of the fact that we consider our power of acting' (exp def

---

19 Laux 1993.
20 Laux 1993, pp. 44–5.

aff 26). Spinoza further argues in Part Four that humility 'is not a virtue, or does not arise from reason' (E4p53).

Assurance in oneself is also opposed to 'repentance', which is 'a sadness accompanied by the idea of some deed we believe ourselves to have done from a free decision of the mind' (def aff 27). In the very proposition to which he adds the note regarding the vulgar's capacity to terrify, Spinoza argues that repentance 'is not a virtue, or does not arise from reason; instead, he who repents for what he has done is twice wretched, or lacking in power' (E4p54).

Finally, the term 'respect' appears in the *Ethics* only in this passage. In the *Tractatus Politicus*, however, we find two references regarding respect for – and fear of – laws.[21] It is precisely the lack of respect for the laws that can convert fear into indignation and social upheaval. For example, as Spinoza vividly observes in TP 4/4,

> there are certain conditions that, if operative, entail that subjects will respect and fear their commonwealth, while the absence of these conditions entails the annulment of that fear and respect and altogether with this, the destruction of the commonwealth. Thus, in order that a commonwealth should be in control of its own right, it must preserve the causes that foster fear and respect; otherwise it ceases to be a commonwealth. For if the rulers or the ruler of the state were to run drunk or naked through the streets with prostitutes, act on stage, openly break laws or hold them in contempt that he himself has enacted, it is no more possible for him to preserve the dignity of sovereignty than for something to be and not be at the same time. Then again, to slaughter or plunder subjects, to abduct young women and so forth turns fear into indignation, and consequently the civil state into a state of war.

What is fascinating about E4p54s is the political vocation it suggests for prophets, whether in ancient Israel or thereafter. But why does Spinoza use the term 'vulgar' (*vulgus*) instead of 'multitude' (*multitudo*) in this passage?

To answer this question we must understand who were the individuals that Spinoza regarded as the 'vulgar' in Holland during the 1670s. One could have the misimpression that he had in mind all of the common people or *plebs*.[22] However, it seems more likely that he was singling out Calvinist theocrats,

---

21　TP 4.4–5.
22　Almost invariably *vulgus* is rendered as 'common people' in Anglophone scholarship. Indeed, this dubious translation mars the otherwise outstanding Israel and Silverstone 2007.

Orangist royalists, and their supporters. From Spinoza's perspective, those were especially vulgar who had overturned the Dutch republic and re-established the monarchy.[23] It is no accident, I think, that in TP 4.4 Spinoza offers Nero as a kind of anti-type of those rulers who subvert the laws of their country and provoke popular opposition – to the point of open rebellion and civil war.

In short, a prophet's vocation is not to chastise the multitude as a whole but only those elements – indeed, let us call them the *vulgar* – that lack humility, repentance, and respect for the law. Accordingly, prophets side with the rest of the multitude in defence of the republic against those who would subvert it through corruption, appeals to superstition, and the like.

Later we shall consider other ways to control and redirect such negative political passions as indignation. But first let us consider the possibility that resistance to oppression may arise not by means of indignation but instead through a positive mode of rebellion triggered by the pursuit of *glory*.

3   The Drama of Glory

In Part Three of the *Ethics* Spinoza defines the affect 'glory' (*gloria*) as 'a joy, accompanied by the idea of some action of ours that we imagine that others praise' (def aff 30) and contrasts glory with the affect 'shame' (*pudor*), defined as 'a sadness, accompanied by the idea of some action of ours that we imagine that others blame' (def aff 31). At this initial stage in Spinoza's analysis, both glory and shame function as passive affects, glory being a joyous and shame a sad passion.

Moreover, Spinoza considers glory to be an affect whose field of force radiates beyond the individual. As Spinoza insists at the beginning of Chapter Three of the TTP,

> everyone's true happiness and blessedness consist solely in the enjoyment of the good, and not in the glory that he alone is enjoying that good to the exclusion of others. For one who regards himself as more blessed because things are going well for himself alone and not for others, or because he is more blessed and fortunate than others, is ignorant of true happiness and blessedness; and the joy he feels, if it is not childish, arises from nothing other than envy and malice (III.1).

---

23   On the nature and extent of the Orangist partial restoration of the monarchy, see Israel 1995, pp. 807–62.

In this respect Spinoza offers a striking contrast with Thomas Hobbes, according to whom glory is, and should remain, an individual affair.[24] In *De Cive* (Chapter I, Section 2), for example, Hobbes proposed that

> all society ... exists for the sake either of advantage or of glory, i.e. it is a product of love of self, not of love of friends. However, no large or lasting society can be based upon the passion for glory. The reason is that glorying, like honour, is nothing if everybody has it, since it consists in comparison and preeminence; nor does association ... with others increase one's reason for glorying in oneself, since a man is worth as much as he can do without relying on anyone else.[25]

What is even worse, Hobbes argued, and as we saw above in Chapter 5, is that collective action to realise glory quickly becomes a dangerous instance of vainglory, potentially erupting into a 'madness of the multitude'.

Finally, it is worth noting that Spinoza sought to extricate the concept of glory from its historical associations with 'the art of war' and instead to defend glory achieved through 'peace and freedom' (TTP Pref. 7, 18.5). Here Spinoza parts company with certain biblical and republican themes, for he no longer regards military prowess or triumph as the measure of a man or nation.[26]

∴

No doubt, as Pierre Macherey has observed, the very word 'glory' has become 'culturally devalued'.[27] But this is not surprising. As Albert Hirschman has powerfully argued,[28] during the rise of capitalism the rhetoric of glory yielded to that of interest and interest-based politics.

---

24 On Hobbes's conception of glory, see Slomp 2000; 2007.
25 Hobbes 1998, p. 24.
26 For example, on the concept of divine 'glory' in the Hebrew Bible (the customary translation of the Hebrew word *kābôd*, literally, 'heaviness') and its frequent association of God's power to lead the Israelites to success on the battlefield, see Brueggemann 2002, pp. 87–9. On the association of glory and waging war in Florentine Renaissance thought in general and Machiavelli's writings in particular, see Hörnqvist 2004. Spinoza's own conception of glory was arguably influenced by a different biblical tradition – running from the Hebrew Scriptures to the New Testament – that understood *kābôd* in terms of God's presence in the world. See, for example, Bauckham 2015, pp. 43–62 for an overview of John's usage of the Greek word *doxa* in his 'gospel of glory'.
27 Macherey 2003.
28 Hirschman 1997, pp. 9–12.

Following Quentin Skinner's lead, one could also chart the ideological displacement of 'glory' by 'interest' from the decline of classical republicanism to the emergence of modern liberalism. As Skinner notes, 'according to the ancient Roman writers and their disciples in the Renaissance, the most important benefit of living in a *civitas libera* is that such communities are especially well adapted to attaining glory and greatness'.[29] Spinoza's own politics lies at what one could call the seventeenth-century Anglo-Dutch crossroads of that displacement.[30]

Although this is not the place, one could even try to reconstruct the semantic field of 'glory' in seventeenth-century political theory and practice.[31] To give just a hint of what would be the value of such a historical reconstruction, consider that, as Peter Linebaugh and Marcus Rediker have argued, during the English Civil War 'glory signified ... not a passive waiting for a future in heaven but actions, to be taken by the dispossessed, to create Heaven here on earth ... Glorying symbolized historical agency'.[32] For example, in 1649, at the height of the English Civil War, Gerrard Winstanley, a leader of the radical Digger movement, proclaimed a new 'law of righteousness' according to which Christ was already

> arising and spreading himself again in the earth: And when he hath spread himself abroad amongst his Sons and daughters, the members of his mystical body, then this community of love and righteousness, making all to use the blessings of the earth as a common Treasury amongst them, shall break forth again in his glory, and fill the earth, and shall be no more suppressed: And none shall say, this is mine, but everyone shall preserve each other in love.[33]

Other such passages that could be culled from the radical literature of this period would indicate a complex interweaving of biblical and republican conceptions of glory that have striking affinities with Spinoza's own views. Notwithstanding the slightly archaic and obscure aspect of the concept of glory, then, it is well worth considering its role in Spinoza's political thought.

---

29   Skinner 1998, p. 61.
30   See especially Prokhovnik 2004.
31   Such a reconstruction would need to build on and extend another century Carlo Varotti's indispensable work on the meaning of glory during the Italian Renaissance; see Varotti 1998.
32   Linebaugh and Rediker 2000, pp. 83–4. See also Illuminati 2009, pp. 29–47.
33   Winstanley 1965, p. 205. I have slightly modernised Winstanley's spelling.

Macherey has argued that there is something highly 'theatrical' about Spinoza's account of glory and shame:

> to know the feelings released in us by the opinions that we attribute to others in what concerns ourselves and our actions, that is, of very personal emotions, having ourselves for objects, felt in the presence and under the gaze of others, in conditions that appear to make of our existence a theater in which we are permanently in representation: and it is doubtless no accident if the classical theater particularly cultivated the staging of these passions which are essentially theatrical.[34]

The dramatic quality of glory is not surprising, given Spinoza's well-attested love of theatre and, in particular, the Roman comedies of Terence.[35] Perhaps this accounts as well for Spinoza's positive reference to Cicero's view of glory: in Part III of the *Ethics* (exp def aff 44) Spinoza quotes from Cicero's famous speech in defence of the Syrian-born poet Archias (*Pro Archia* 26), whose status as a full-fledged Roman citizen was in dispute: 'The best persons are the ones most led by glory (*maxime gloria ducitur*). Even the philosophers who write books condemning glory inscribe their own names'.

For Cicero not only did glory serve as a kind of secular immortality, in particular through his attempt to secure his standing among the great Roman literary and political figures; but the very speech from which Spinoza quotes[36] has, as do most of Cicero's speeches, a highly charged dramatic quality. In this instance, the theatre was the Roman open-air forum where trials customarily took place.[37]

In the TTP Spinoza even offers the disturbing image of the scaffold as a perverse kind of theatre in which glory is sometimes displayed in extremis. In Chapter 20 of that work Spinoza famously defends freedom of thought and expression and opposes laws that would seek to prescribe 'what everyone must believe' and to prohibit 'speaking or writing against this or that opinion'. For Spinoza such laws would be more than useless (*inutiles*); they would only invite

---

34   Macherey 2003.
35   On Spinoza's love of classical theater, presumably cultivated in the school of Franciscus Van den Enden, see Nadler 1999, pp. 109–11.
36   See Cicero 2000, pp. 110–21.
37   On Roman courts' function as a kind of theatre, and with particular reference to Cicero's pursuit of glory as an orator, see Holland 2005, pp. 122–33.

violation by those who 'love the virtues and the arts' (*virtutes et artes amant*). At this point he wonders

> what greater misfortune for a republic can be conceived than for honorable men to be exiled as rebels because they think differently and cannot dissimulate? What, I say, can be more pernicious than to see human beings who have committed no crime or misdeed regarded as enemies and put to death, simply because they have a liberal temperament? That the scaffold, the terror of evildoers, should, by a remarkable abuse of majesty, become a most beautiful theater for showing the highest example of tolerance and virtue? For those who know that they are just do not fear the death of a criminal, and shrink from no punishment; their minds are not distraught with remorse for any shameful act: on the contrary, they think that to die for a good cause is no punishment, but an honor, and that to die for freedom is glorious (TTP 20.12–13).

∴

As a point of departure, let us diagram glory as a two-part relation between two individuals X and Y in which X performs some action and then imagines that Y praises it:

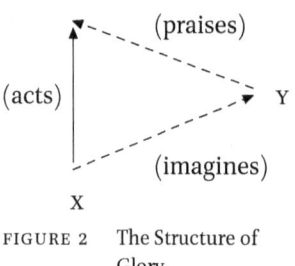

FIGURE 2 The Structure of Glory

Note that the structure of this two-part relation allows both for X wrongly (through over- or under-estimation) to imagine Y's praise and for Y falsely (through over- or under-appraisal or even deception) to praise X's action. One could then generalise this analysis in order to conceive of the 'glory of the multitude' as a complex set of transindividual affective relations that emerge from (a) how each individual imagines his or her actions to be praised by others and (b) the sum of how all individuals imagine their collective actions to be praised by others.

However, precisely because of its theatrical nature, glory is liable to degenerate into mere grandstanding. Accordingly, Spinoza defines 'ambition' (*ambitio*) as an 'excessive desire for glory' (def aff 44) and cautions against what, following Hobbes, he calls 'vainglory' (*gloria vana*):

> Vainglory is a self-contentment (*acquiescentia in se ipso*) that is fostered solely by the opinion of the vulgar. When that ceases, so does the contentment, that is (bypP52s), the highest good that each one loves. That is why one who glories in the esteem of the vulgar is made anxious daily, strives, acts, and schemes, in order to preserve his fame. For the vulgar are variable and inconstant; fame, unless it is preserved, is quickly destroyed. Indeed, because everyone desires to gain the applause of the vulgar, each one willingly plays down the fame of another. And since the struggle is over a good thought to be the highest, there this gives rise to a monstrous lust of each to crush the other in any way possible. The one who at last emerges as victor glories more in having harmed the other than in having benefited himself. This glory, *or* this contentment, then, is really vain; because it is nothing (E4p58s).

Just as vainglorious actors wind up playing to the 'applause of the vulgar', so too the multitude that revels in having overthrown an oppressive regime can lapse into a false sense of accomplishment. To see how, consider Spinoza's summary of the political lessons to be drawn from studying the rise and fall of ancient Israelite society or what Spinoza terms – anachronistically, to be sure, but doubtless intended for rhetorical effect on his Dutch readers[38] – the 'Hebrew republic'.

In Chapter Eighteen of the TTP Spinoza offers four general observations based on his detailed case study of the Hebrew republic – a case study intended to contribute to an understanding of 'what sovereign powers must principally concede to subjects in order to increase the security and prosperity of the state' (TTP 17.3). First of all, it is 'disastrous' (*pernicosum*) for both religion and the republic to allow religious leaders to make decrees or handle affairs of state. Everything would be 'more stable' (*constantius*) if such leaders were not allowed to respond to anything unless asked and to teach and practice only received ideas and customary beliefs.

Secondly, it is 'dangerous' (*periculosum*) to apply divine right to merely speculative matters and to establish laws concerning opinions about which citizens

---

38 On the relevance of ancient Israel for understanding the cultural dimension of the Dutch republic, see Schama 1987, esp. pp. 93–125.

typically or even can have disagreements. The most violent regimes arise when opinions to which everyone has a right are regarded as illegal. In fact, Spinoza warns, whenever opinions are criminalised, as a general rule (*solet*) 'the anger of the common people (*plebis ira*) will reign supreme'. Some Anglophone translators[39] have distorted Spinoza's point here, which is not that the greatest tyrant of all is mass rage and violence, but instead that tyrannies themselves breed mass rage and violence. Spinoza suggests that such evils can be avoided if 'piety' (*pietas*) and 'religious worship' (*religionis cultus*) become nothing but a matter of 'works' (*operes*) and individual freedom of judgment is left alone.

Spinoza's third generalisation is that both the republic and religion must grant to the sovereign power the right to decide what is 'right and wrong' (*fas nefasque*) – a theme Spinoza returns to at length in Chapter Nineteen.

In his fourth and final generalisation based on the experience of the ancient Israelites, Spinoza contends two things: (a) it is 'harmful' (*exitiale*) for a people not used to living under kings to establish a monarchy and (b) it is no less dangerous for a king to be deposed, even if he is obviously a tyrant.

Let us take a close look at Spinoza's twofold argument in these closing paragraphs of Chapter Eighteen. First, why does he think it would be potentially 'harmful' for a people unaccustomed to living under kings to establish a monarchy? The short answer is that the king and the people will ceaselessly be at odds with each other. The people will not 'tolerate' (*sustinere*) a monarchical state; and the monarch will not 'endure' (*pati*) the laws and rights of the people established by a lesser authority, much less defend these laws and rights, especially since they were established not with the idea of maintaining monarchical rule but the rule of the people or an assembly. As a result, if the king were in fact to defend the 'ancient rights of the people' (*jura populi antiqua*), he would seem to be more the people's 'servant' (*servus*) than its 'master' (dominus). And thus a new king strives to establish new laws and to change the rights the state holds 'for his own benefit' (*in suum usum*) and to 'subdue' (*redigere*) the people 'so that they cannot as easily remove kings as install them'.

What, on the other hand, is the danger arising from a people's attempt to depose even a tyrant? A people 'accustomed' (*assuetus*) to kings will tend to ridicule lesser authority. Consequently, if they remove one king, they will have

---

39 For example, Wernham misleadingly translates *plebis ira ... maxime regnare solet* as 'the supreme tyrant is usually the anger of the mob'; see Spinoza 1958, p. 199. Likewise, Shirley badly translates *plebis ira ... maxime regnare solet* as 'the anger of the mob is usually the greatest tyrant of all'; see Spinoza 2001, p. 208.

to replace him with another – but this second one will become a tyrant 'not voluntarily but out of necessity' (*non sponte sed necessario*) because (a) he will fear the very people who have overthrown his predecessor, (b) he will have to take measures to ensure his unquestioned rule, and (c) he will 'consequently follow in the footsteps of the previous tyrant'. Spinoza observes, then, that although peoples have been able to 'change' (*mutare*) tyrants, they have not been able to 'abolish' (*tollere*) them, nor have they been able to change a monarchical state into another 'form' (*forma*). Perhaps more disturbing, though, they even misrecognise what they have accomplished and wind up confusing defeat with victory, 'glorying in parricide as if there were something to celebrate' (*parricidio, tanquam re bene gesta, gloriari*).

Let us take stock of just what Spinoza is saying. He is not arguing that a people should not (in the sense of a moral imperative) try to change the form of their state; but instead that doing so is a risky undertaking and potentially harmful. (Spinoza's motto was *caute* for good political as well as personal reasons!)

Perhaps this is easier to see in the extended 'fatal example' (*fatale exemplum*) Spinoza offers of the danger inherent in regicide: a case he takes from recent English history. Spinoza observes that

> the English people (*populus Anglicanus*) ... sought causes, with the appearance of right (*specie juris*), for deposing the monarch. However, after he had been removed, they were utterly unable to change the form of state (*imperium*). But after much bloodshed they only brought it about that a new monarch was called by a different name (as if the whole question was only of the name). This new monarch could only persist by completely destroying the royal family, by killing the king's friends or those suspected of friendship, and by disturbing with war the ease of peace apt to generate rumors, so that the common people (*plebs*), preoccupied with and intent on new things, might be diverted from thinking about the king's murder. At last, therefore, the people realized that they had done nothing for the welfare of the country other than violate the right of the lawful king and change everything into a worse state (*in prejorem statum mutare*). They therefore decided to retrace their steps when it was possible, and they did not rest until they saw everything restored to its former state (*in pristinum suum statum restaurata*) (TTP 18.8).

What should we make of this strenuous critique of the course of the English Civil War from the execution of Charles I in 1649, through Oliver Cromwell's Protectorate, to the restoration of Charles II in 1660? Here is Spinoza's conclusion: '[I]t is clear that the form of every state (*uniuscuiusque imperii forma*) must be retained, and it cannot be changed without danger of its complete downfall'.

Some commentators would have us believe that such a passage indicates Spinoza's political 'conservatism',[40] but this claim appears to me unfounded for four reasons. First of all, in political terms, Spinoza's position on the English Civil War bears a striking resemblance to those advanced at various times by such radicals as Levellers, Diggers, and Ranters after Oliver Cromwell had begun to consolidate power as Lord Protector of the newly instituted Commonwealth. These political currents had come under increasing harassment, persecution, and, finally, violent repression during Cromwell's tenure because of their desire to broaden the franchise and their willingness to challenge the sanctity of private property rights. For example, consider a December 1649 appeal by the Digger leader Gerrard Winstanley – what he called his 'New Year's Gift' – to Parliament and the revolutionary New Model Army that had defeated and executed King Charles I. Winstanley commends these two forces for assisting the common people 'to cast out the head of oppression which was kingly power seated in one man's hand'. However, he immediately adds that 'kingly power is like a great spread tree, if you lop off the head or top bough, and let the other branches and root stand, it will grow again and recover fresher strength'.[41]

Secondly, on a more general theoretical level, recall that for Spinoza right is always coextensive with power: as he argues in Chapter Sixteen of the TTP, 'each individual thing has the sovereign right to do all that it can do, that is, the right of each thing extends as far as its determinate power does' (TTP 16.2). Thus, to criticizse the English people – or at any rate their parliamentary and military leadership – is to say that they did not go far enough, that they did not in fact change the form of the English state – despite the surface change in name from kingdom to commonwealth. In other words, Spinoza's objection could just as easily be regarded as to an incomplete or unfinished revolution than to revolution *tout court*. Such an interpretation finds further support in Chapter 17, when Spinoza makes essentially the same point regarding the prophets' attempt to rid the Israelite theocracy of corruption. Even though the prophets 'deposed a tyrant, the causes of tyranny nonetheless remained; and so they merely succeeded in purchasing a new tyrant at the cost of much citizen blood. There was no end, then, to discord and civil wars, but the causes that led to the violation

---

40   Perhaps most illustrative of this perspective is Feuer 1980.
41   Winstanley 1983, pp. 161–2. Thanks to Herb Patterson for this reference to Winstanley's critique of 'kingly power'.

of divine right were always the same and could be destroyed only along with the entire state (*imperium*)'.

Moreover, in the *Tractatus Politicus* Spinoza returns to this theme of the dangers involved in changing the form of a state, but now enlists 'the most acute' (*acutissimus*) Machiavelli in his defence. According to Spinoza, Machiavelli had shown 'with how little foresight have been many attempts to remove a tyrant, while yet the causes that have made the prince a tyrant have not been removed. On the contrary, they become much more firmly established as the prince is given more cause to fear, which happens when the multitude has made an example of its prince and glories in the parricide as if there were something to celebrate (*parricidio, quasi re bene gesta, gloriatur*)' (TP 5.7). Spinoza's reference, as editors have regularly noted, is undoubtedly to Machiavelli's *Discourses* (e.g., 1.1 and 1.26).[42] Yet Machiavelli's perspective throughout that work is arguably not on the impossibility of removing tyrants from power but simply on the difficulty of doing so.[43]

Thirdly, it is crucial to note the political conjuncture in which Spinoza was writing: in 1670 the Dutch republic was in grave danger. Despite his opposition to the republic's aristocratic distortions, Spinoza did not want to shrink from its defence in the face of Orangist reaction; indeed, he wanted to do his part to help consolidate and reinforce republican rule along more democratic lines. Moreover, he was well aware that the Orangists had no such democratic aspirations; on the contrary, they sought to re-establish monarchy and clamp down on freedom of religion, thought, and speech. As Gilles Deleuze once insightfully observed,

> the Dutch republic remained a republic by surprise and by accident, more for the lack of a king than by preference, and poorly accepted by the people. When Spinoza speaks of the harmfulness of revolutions, one must not forget that revolution is thought of in terms of the disappointment that Cromwell's revolution inspired, or the anxieties caused by a possible coup d'état by the House of Orange. During this period 'revolutionary' ideology is permeated with theology and is often, as with the Calvinist party, in the service of a politics of reaction.[44]

With this in mind, it would be more accurate to say that Spinoza primarily feared not a democratic revolution but a monarchical counter-revolution.

---

42   Machiavelli 1996.
43   See, for example, 1.17, 1.55, and 3.3.
44   Deleuze 1988, p. 9 (translation slightly modified).

Unfortunately, though, just such a counter-revolution was to occur in 1672, a mere two years after the publication of the *TTP*.[45]

Fourthly, let me return to, and re-emphasise, the drama of the triumphant multitude that Spinoza tries to capture by means of an apparently innocuous qualifying Latin phrase: *tanquam re bene gesta* ('as if there were something to celebrate'). This phrase occurs in TP 5.7 as *quasi re bene gesta*, but both passages echo line 775 of Terence's play Adelphi ('The Brothers'): *quasi re bene gesta*.[46] If Spinoza is indeed quoting Terence – several of whose works he had probably memorised as a young man[47] – much is explained: the plot of Adelphi involves a complex series of humorous reversals in fortune and the moral lessons to be learned from them. Near the end of that play, a Roman master uses the phrase *quasi re bene gesta* in order to chastise his drunken slave. Consequently, Spinoza's use of this qualifying phrase would again seem to indicate that he regards the multitude's glorying in regicide as misguided, or at least premature.

Thus far we have considered the collective expression of glory as a *passion*. Yet Spinoza interestingly proposes in E4p58 that glory can take the form of not only a passive but also an active affect, for, as he says, glory 'is not repugnant to reason but can arise from it'. As transmitted *between and among* individuals, active glory generates what one could call *common* glory, through which the multitude actively rejoices in its own creative powers. If there is a theatre in this limit-case of political action, it is perhaps the theatre of the entire world, since Spinoza's conception of the multitude exceeds, and cuts across, national boundaries. Common glory would no longer be confined to a particular place but would radiate outward to include as many human beings as possible, in the direction of what Linebaugh and Rediker have memorably called an 'internationale of glory'.[48]

In sum, the glory of politics is none other than the glory of the multitude in action as it imagines itself and its activities, and rejoices in its own collective powers on the stage of what Maurizio Viroli has called 'the great theater of politics'.[49] Yet a final question remains: Is there a mode of rebellion in accordance with which one could harness, redirect, and sustain not only such passions

---

45 On the nature and extent of the Orangist partial restoration of the monarchy, see Israel 1995, pp. 807–62.
46 Terence 2001. John Barsby translates *quasi re bene gesta* as 'as if to celebrate some great achievement' (p. 341).
47 See Nadler 1999, p. 110.
48 Linebaugh and Rediker 2000, p. 86.
49 Viroli uses this phrase as the title of Chapter Seven of his recent biography of Machiavelli (Viroli 2000).

as indignation and passive glory but also – or especially – active glory? In this case, it is not prophetic imagination but ethical meditation that comes to the fore.

4 A Political Therapy of the Affects

In Part Five of the *Ethics* Spinoza famously proposes a kind of cognitive therapy by means of which human passional servitude can partially be overcome by the power of reason to redirect bad affects.[50] Let us follow closely and carefully Spinoza's detailed discussion of such *an affective transition of the second kind* in E5p10s.

Spinoza begins with the general claim that human beings have the ability to order and connect bodily affections and thereby to reduce the influence of bad affects. Since we lack a complete knowledge of our affects, however, the way to carry out this task is to

> conceive a correct rule of living, that is, sure principles of life (*rectam vivendi rationem, seu certa vitae dogmata concipere*), to commit them to memory, and to apply them constantly to the particular things frequently encountered in life. In this way our imagination will be largely affected by these principles, and we shall always have them ready.

Spinoza has in mind what we could call *common ethical notions* by which we can guide our daily conduct. Through imaginative exercises involving these rules, he argues, we can overcome such negative affects as hate, fear, and anger.

Consider first how we might reduce the power of hatred. For Spinoza the best way to proceed would be to repay hatred not with hate but with love in the form of 'generosity' (*generositas*). This is easier said than done. Spinoza goes on to suggest that

> in order that we may always have this prescription of reason (*rationis praescriptum*) ready when it is needed, we ought to think about and meditate often on the common injuries of humanity (*communes hominum injuriae*), and how they may be warded off best by generosity. For if we join the image of an injury to the imagination of this principle, it will always be ready for us (by 3p18) when an injury is done to us.

---

50 Here I am indebted to Pierre Macherey's masterful account in Macherey 1994.

Another way to overcome hatred is to rely on

> the principle of our own true usefulness (*utilitas*), and also of the good that follows from mutual friendship and common society, and keep in mind, moreover, that the highest serenity of spirit (*summa animi acquiescentia*) arises from the correct rule of living (by 4p52), and that human beings, like others, act from the necessity of nature, then the injury, that is, the hate usually arising from it, will occupy a minimal part of the imagination, and will easily be overcome.

Spinoza next turns to anger, which he argues that we can also control, at least in part. He maintains that

> if the anger that usually arises from the greatest injuries is not so easily overcome, it will still be overcome, though not without some fluctuation of spirit (*quamvis non sine animi fluctuatione*). And it will be overcome in far less time than if we had not meditated on these things beforehand in this way.

Finally, Spinoza contends that we can minimise fear by strengthening the active affect of 'courage' (*animositas*). In other words, he suggests that we should 'enumerate and often imagine the common dangers of life, and how they can best be avoided and overcome by the presence of spirit and fortitude (*quomodo animi praesentia, et fortitudine optime vitari, et superari possunt*)'.

Yet another means by which Spinoza thinks that we can reduce the influence of bad affects is to

> pay attention to what good there is in each thing, so that in this way we are always determined to act from an affect of joy (*ut sic semper ex laetitiae affectu ad agendum determinemur*).

He then offers an example to which we shall return shortly:

> [I]f someone sees that he pursues glory too much, he should think of its correct use, the end of which it ought to be pursued, and by what means it can be acquired, not of its abuse and vanity, and the inconstancy of human beings, or other things of this kind, about which no one thinks unless out of a sick spirit (*nisi ex animi aegritudine*). For it is by such thoughts that those who are most ambitious are most upset when they despair of attaining the honor they seek; and then they vomit forth anger,

wanting to seem wise (*sapientes videri volunt*). It is certain that those who most desire glory are those who cry out most against its abuse and the vanity of the world.

After having identified other cases of ethical *ressentiment* that arise among those 'whose fortune is adverse and whose spirit is weak' (namely, the resentful poor and scorned lovers), Spinoza concludes this extraordinary scholium by proposing that

> one who seeks to moderate his affects and appetites from the love of freedom alone (*ex solo libertatis amore*) will strive, as much as he can (*quantum potest*), to know the virtues and their causes, and to fill his mind with the gladness of spirit (*animum gaudio*) that arises from their true knowledge, and as little as possible to contemplate human vices, to denigrate human beings, and to enjoy a false appearance of freedom (*falsa libertatis specie gaudere*). And one who diligently observes these things – for they are not difficult – and practices them, will in a short span of time be able to direct most of one's actions under the command of reason (*spatio actions suas ex rationes imperio plurumque dirigere poterit*).

Let us take stock of Spinoza's therapy of the affects by considering how he might advise that we overcome the bad affects of indignation and vainglory. We should not try directly to suppress or purge either affect but should instead try to reconstruct their complex underlying causes in as precise and complete a manner as possible.

Since indignation is complex kind of hatred, it is necessary to counter its effect by strengthening the affect of generosity by reflecting on the usefulness of social solidarity. Consider the case of a tyrannical ruler. The point of Spinoza's imaginative exercise would not be to alter our beliefs in such a way that we could somehow come to regard a tyrant as in fact a just ruler (or just misunderstood?), but to comprehend how and why the ruler governs in such an oppressive manner – the better to find an alternative to blind, incapacitating, and ineffective rage. As Laux has noted, by strengthening the active affect of fortitude (of which tenacity and generosity are the two varieties), we can strive to counteract passionate fluctuations.[51]

The affect of glory especially fluctuates between active and passive forms; in the worst cases, as we have seen, glory degenerates into outright ambition and

---

51   Laux 1993, pp. 223–6.

vainglory. At the level of the individual, this would be bad enough, although perhaps merely amusing or pathetic. However, when a process of affective imitation has led the pursuit of political glory to seize the imagination of the multitude, the results of such fluctuation could well prove to be 'fatal' (*fatalis*), as Spinoza believed had occurred during the English Civil War when the multitude 'gloried' in its achievement of removing Charles I but stopped short of uprooting all vestiges of monarchy and failed to establish a durable republic. How is it possible to avoid such a danger?

Recall that Spinoza urges us to 'pay attention to what good there is in each thing, so that in this way we are always determined to act from an affect of joy'. As a result, he cautions that we should think about the 'correct use' of glory, 'the end of which it ought to be pursued, and by what means it can be acquired'. Above all, as Spinoza reminds us, it is 'certain that those who most desire glory are those who cry out most against its abuse and the vanity of the world'. Again, this doesn't mean that, for example, the English multitude should not have risen up against the abuses of King Charles I, but a certain political humility could have helped premature glorying over incomplete results.

The multitude's pursuit of glory is not the problem. On the contrary, Spinoza warns only against the false allure of ambition and vainglory and so advocates a historical modesty about goals, means, and accomplishments. This is most assuredly not, as certain commentators would have it, an instance of Spinoza's political conservatism.[52] It is simply an indication of his high regard for the virtue of prudence.[53]

5 Serenity at Last

Beyond the therapeutic operation of reason to redirect and control the passions in general and indignation and glory in particular, we can glimpse *an affective transition of the third kind* leading toward the philosophical cultivation and expansion of 'wise persons' (*sapientes*) among the multitude. At the intellectual core of such a political project would be a greater and greater desire to understand more and more of reality, what Spinoza regards as the fullest realisation of reason in its effort to attain an 'intuitive science' or 'knowledge of the third kind'. As Pierre Macherey explains, such knowledge constitutes 'the supreme good and supreme virtue' for human beings and is accompanied by

---

[52] At most we could speak of Spinoza's 'paradoxical conservatism', on which see Zourabichvili 2002.
[53] See Matheron 2011, pp. 635–50.

'indestructible certainty ... through which the soul attains the summit of its power and of the exercise of its power, in complete tranquility, therefore, calm and serene'.[54]

How then would a wise person react to tyrannical rule or some other form of oppression? Beyond the affective fluctuations of indignation and the pursuit of glory lies the prospect of a rebellious 'serenity' (*acquiescentia*).[55] For Spinoza serenity implies neither passivity nor ascetic retreat from political engagement. As Macherey again puts it well,

> the sage ... is one who adopts an essentially active attitude regarding all of life's problems. He doesn't allow himself to be carried along by the flow of events, as if the latter constituted a blind fatality: but, from the fact that he manages to understand the necessity of these events, by considering them according to their actual causal genesis, he accepts them as they are produced – to the extent that they don't depend on his own good will – without allowing himself to be dominated by them.[56]

In short, serenity is an *essentially active* joyous affect in contrast both to indignation, which is a passive sad affect, and to glory, which is a joyous affect but one that fluctuates between passive and active forms.

In E5p27d Spinoza offers a dense, chain argument for the experience of the greatest 'serenity of the soul' (*mentis acquiescentia*) that arises from knowledge of the third kind. Because of its compactness, allow me to reconstruct Spinoza's demonstration with the detail it deserves. Here is the full argument in standard form, with an implicit premise provided in brackets:

1. The greatest virtue of the soul is to know God (E4p28).
2. But knowing God is the same as knowledge of the third kind (E5p25).
3. Therefore, the greatest virtue of the soul is knowledge of the third kind.
4. The more the soul knows by the third kind, the greater its virtue (E5p24).
5. Therefore, anyone who knows by the third kind undergoes a transition to the greatest human perfection.
6. Joy is a human being's transition from a lesser to a greater perfection (def aff 2).
7. Therefore, anyone who knows by the third kind experiences the greatest joy.

---

54 Macherey 1994, p. 140.
55 For an overview of the nuances of this term, see Totaro 1994, pp. 65–79.
56 Macherey 1994, pp. 197–8.

8. Whoever has a true idea at the same time knows that he or she has a true idea, and cannot doubt the truth of the thing (E2P43).
9. Therefore, this greatest joy is accompanied by the idea of oneself and one's virtue.
10. [A human being's virtue is the same as his or her power of acting (E2p43).]
11. Assurance in oneself (*acquiescentia in se ipso*) is the joy that arises from the fact that a human being considers himself or herself and his or her own power of acting (def aff 25)
12. Therefore, the greatest serenity (*summa acquiescentia*) there can be arises from knowledge of the third kind.

However much Spinoza may emphasise the power of reason to restrain and moderate the passions and convert them into active affects, his argument does not entail that such power is unlimited. On the contrary, in his preface to Part Five of the *Ethics* he takes his distance from what he regards as Stoic and Cartesian exaggerated claims about the ability of the mind to 'acquire an absolute command (*imperium absolutum*) over our passions' through force of will alone.

Nonetheless, as Spinoza argues in E5p42s, the wise person is undoubtedly capable of doing more and is 'much more powerful than one who is ignorant and is agitated only by lust (*qui sola libidine agitur*)'. Indeed, an ignorant person is 'agitated in many ways by external causes, and unable ever to possess true serenity of spirit (*vera animi acquiescentia*) ... [and] lives as if he knew neither himself, nor God, nor things; and as soon as he ceases to be acted on, he ceases to be'. In striking contrast, a wise person 'insofar as he is considered as such (*quatenus ut talis consideratur*), is hardly troubled in spirit, but being, by a certain eternal necessity, conscious of himself, and of God, and of things, he never ceases to be, but always possesses true serenity of spirit (*vera animi acquiescentia*)'. It is worth highlighting Spinoza's qualifying phrase 'insofar as he is considered as such' (*quatenus ut talis consideratur*), which reminds us that no human being can attain a condition of self-mastery in accordance with which he or she could establish a personal *imperium in imperio*, and permanently restrain the power of fortune from disrupting the stability of his or her life. All human beings remain a part of nature, and are to a greater or lesser extent acted on by forces beyond their control – forces that give rise, in turn, to the fluctuation of affections and affects. In short, wisdom must forever remain a matter of degree not of kind.

Although a wise person would experience less mental agitation and greater calm, Spinoza does not envision that he or she would or could pursue a contemplative retreat far from the madding crowd. As Del Lucchese has compellingly argued, serenity has nothing to do with mysticism, contemplation, or isolation but instead implies a continued active engagement in the passionate life of human beings.[57]

For Spinoza politics rooted in knowledge of the third kind would not be abstract and formal but would be qualitative, concrete, and would concern the order of everyday existence. As a result, persons who cultivated the affect of serenity would strive to extricate themselves from fear of failure and death and to understand that freedom is a constant struggle whose path is arduous: along the way victories are invariably mixed with defeats. A serene individual would not only persist in his or her desire for socio-political transformation over the long run, but in the very midst of social upheaval he or she would also seek to adopt, and sustain, what Spinoza memorably called the 'perspective of eternity' (*species aeternitatis*).

In a surprising, even startling, allusion to Spinoza, John Rawls once remarked that

> the perspective of eternity is not a perspective from a certain place beyond the world, nor the point of view of a transcendent being; rather it is a certain form of thought and feeling that rational persons can adopt within the world ... Purity of heart, if one could attain it, would be to see clearly and to act with grace and self-command from this point of view.[58]

As far apart as a Spinozist philosophical orientation may otherwise be from a Rawlsian one,[59] Rawls's conception of 'purity of heart' clearly echoes what Spinoza intended by 'serenity', once we grasp the latter not as a devotional exercise but as a distinctive form of political engagement.

6   Conclusion

Spinoza sought neither to praise nor to condemn resistance to oppressive regimes but instead to understand why political rebellion occurs and how it can all too easily fall short of its objective, namely, to change the form of state. The main problem with which Spinoza was concerned was not strategic but affective: how to transform a vulgar multitude dominated by sad passions into a more active multitude dominated not only by joyous passions but also, and espe-

---

57   Del Lucchese 2009, pp. 164–6.
58   Rawls 1999b, p. 514.
59   But perhaps not *so far* apart: see, for example, Jacques Bidet's recent attempt along these lines in Bidet 1999, pp. 336–43.

cially, such active affects as fortitude, generosity, tenacity, and glory. However, as we have seen, this problem is not easily solved; its difficulty endures.

And yet – beyond fear and even hope – remains the prospect of an active multitude whose constituent power would be capable of achieving freedom from domination.[60] Spinoza's conception of democracy as both process and goal endures. But there is no other way for philosophers to lend assistance to democratic processes and goals than by conceptual – and even physical! – labouring within, among, and through the multitude.[61] Each of the three affective transitions we have considered – prophetic imagination, ethical meditation, and the perspective of eternity – presumes that there is, and can be, no privileged position outside of the multitude from which to operate. Such a place was, and remains, merely a fantasy of elites – apologists for absolutist regimes in Spinoza's day[62] and their modern counterparts.

---

[60] Antonio Negri's witness to the diverse manifestations of the multitude's constituent power is one of his greatest legacies to the history of political thought. See, in particular, Negri 1999.

[61] Both senses of 'labouring' run through Aristides Baltas's investigation of the logic of immanence in Spinoza and Wittgenstein; see Baltas 2012.

[62] For François Zourabichvili's profound diagnosis of this absolutist, ultimately infantile, disorder, see Zourabichvili 2002, pp. 213–44.

CHAPTER 7

Alexandre Matheron on Militant Reason and the Intellectual Love of God*

> The contemporary proletariat is Spinoza's only genuine heir.
> – A.M. DEBORIN

In the introductory remarks to what he had intended in 1972 to be a course on 'Spinoza's conception of right and politics', Louis Althusser apologised and announced that he would lecture instead on Jean-Jacques Rousseau. This was because, Althusser explained, Alexandre Matheron's book *Individu et communauté chez Spinoza* [Individual and Community in Spinoza] had been recently published (in 1969), and he could hardly add anything to what Matheron had already written.[1] Yet over forty years later, Anglophone Marxists have scarcely engaged with Matheron or his major work, which is widely regarded as one of the landmarks of Spinoza scholarship.

Such neglect has doubtless largely persisted because Matheron's massive book (647 pages in French) remains to be translated into English.[2] Although the book continues to be duly – but selectively – referenced by Spinoza scholars, it has yet to be studied carefully and fully appreciated as a sustained Marxist intervention into the history of philosophy. To be precise, Matheron was deeply influenced by the early Marx and sought to apply Marx's concepts of alienation and ideology in order to understand Spinoza. Moreover, he reconstructed Spinoza's political thought along lines that owed much to Jean-Paul Sartre's account of collective action in the *Critique of Dialectical Reason*.[3] For example, he proposed an analogy 'between the Sartrean problematic of the passage from series to group and the classical problematic of the passage from the state of nature to the civil state'.[4]

---

* This chapter has been previously published in *Crisis and Critique* 2.1, 2015, pp. 153–69.
1 Althusser 2012, p. 45.
2 An equally massive (741 pages) collection of his articles on Spinoza and seventeenth-century philosophy has subsequently appeared. See Matheron 2011.
3 Sartre 2004a.
4 Matheron 1988, p. 201 n. 385. See also Matheron 1971, pp. 24–5 for a brief but intriguing application of Sartre's concept of 'fraternity-terror' in order to characterise the affective dynamics of ancient Israelite theocracy. For more on the affinities between Spinoza and Sartre, see Rizk 1996.

But for Antonio Negri, such influences were highly problematic. In *The Savage Anomaly*, his own great book on Spinoza, Negri observed that Matheron had introduced into the study of Spinoza 'dialectical or paradialectical schemes, characteristics of the existentialist Marxism of the 1960s' but then complained that Matheron had substituted for Spinoza's 'constructive continuity' a 'determinate dynamism fueled by a process of alienation and recomposition'.[5] Let us take Negri's complaint as a provocation and point of departure for engaging in a close reading of *Individu et communauté chez Spinoza* and reassessing the value of Matheron's project for contemporary Marxist theory and practice.

∴

Matheron's approach to the history of philosophy has not been narrowly historicist. For example, although Matheron has carefully considered the historical background to Spinoza's philosophy, he has chiefly reconstructed the development of Spinoza's philosophy in its own terms as a complex system of thought and has rarely quoted directly from Spinoza's writings or situated his own interpretation in relation to other commentators.[6] Ariel Suhamy offers a striking analogy: just as Lucretius sought to convey the essence of Epicurus' philosophy in poetic form, so too has Matheron sought to read Spinoza so meticulously that even if the latter's works 'were to disappear from the Earth', his argumentative reconstruction could nonetheless replace them![7]

But what is the value for Marxists in encountering Matheron's reconstruction of Spinoza's philosophical system? It is not to envision Spinoza as a kind of 'precursor' to Marx but to approach Marx himself as a 'successor' to problems that were already raised by Spinoza.[8] Indeed, Pierre-François Moreau observes that Matheron has been interested less in formulating a 'Marxist explanation of Spinozism' than in 'posing to Spinoza the questions that Marx posed to himself', for example, 'how do individuals enter into relations among themselves – and at what cost?' This latter question, Moreau observes, demanded in the seventeenth-century that a philosopher defend a 'theory of the passions'.[9]

---

5 Negri 1991.
6 In these respects, Matheron has made common cause with Martial Gueroult and Gilles Deleuze, whose own important books on Spinoza appeared at nearly the same time as Matheron's. See Suhamy 2011 and Vinciguerra 2009.
7 Suhamy 2011.
8 Matheron 2000, p. 176.
9 Matheron 2011, p. 7.

What I would like to do in this chapter is to contribute to a Marxist theory of the passions by exploring the question of the transindividual pursuit of collective action – but perhaps in an unexpected way for Marxists.

I shall focus on Matheron's warm embrace of Spinoza's conceptions of eternity and the 'Intellectual Love of God' as laid out in Part Five of the *Ethics*, that part which especially Anglophone Spinoza commentators have ignored, ridiculed, or quickly passed over in embarrassment along the way to their own reconstructions or evaluations of Spinoza's political thought.[10] For his part, Matheron has admitted that he once had a tendency to think that 'Spinozist eternity prefigured the life of a militant, which seemed … to be the best example of the adequation of our existence to our essence'.[11] I share that tendency, even though obviously Spinoza himself never said anything explicitly along these lines.[12] Yet – as successors to Spinoza – Marxists today can and should consider Part Five of the *Ethics* to culminate the adventure of 'militant reason'[13] recounted in the *Ethics*: from the very constitution and composition of individuals to their being estranged from their own mental powers to understand and physical powers to act through the impact of such reactive forces as superstition and sad passions, to the countervailing influence of active affects, to the precarious enlargement of reason; from the level of duration to the level of eternity; from individual liberation to the prospect of collective emancipation.

1   Spinoza on Love

Part Five of the *Ethics* consists of two main sections or argumentative 'movements': Propositions 1–20 and Propositions 21–40.[14] The first movement concerns the attempt to discover 'remedies for the affects' (*affectuum remedia*)[15] and culminates (in Propositions 14–20) with a discussion of 'love toward God'

---

10   See Jonathan Bennett's cavalier dismissal of what he calls Spinoza's 'unmitigated and seemingly unmotivated disaster' in his discussion of eternity (Bennett 1984, p. 357).

11   Matheron 2000, p. 175. Matheron suggests that his perspective was only a passing phase of youthful enthusiasm, whereas I take up the challenge to make good on an unfulfilled promise.

12   But, as Matheron frequently notes, 'he could have'. See Vinciguerra 2009, p. 435 n. 32.

13   Pautrat 2013, p. 22.

14   Moreau 1994b, p. 55. Propositions 41–2 return to what Pierre Macherey has called 'an ethics of everyday life' through which, in the face of actually existing non-perfected societies, one might nonetheless strive to lead an honest and generous life and thereby help to eradicate the causes of human servitude (see Macherey 1994, pp. 192–204).

15   E5p20.

(*amor erga Deum*). The second movement concerns the pursuit of the highest human happiness and culminates (in Propositions 32–7) with an account of the 'intellectual love of God' (*amor intellectualis Dei*). Spinoza's distinction between these two kinds of love not only lies at the heart of Part Five but also serves as the highest expression of the emancipatory project detailed in the *Ethics* as a whole. However, before launching into a full investigation of the political stakes involved in this distinction, we should briefly consider the nature and dynamics of each kind of love.

This requires that we return for a moment to Spinoza's treatment of love in Part 3, in which love is defined as 'joy accompanied by the idea of an external cause'.[16] Here, of course, Spinoza is concerned with love for a finite object or person. Such passional love has at least three distinctive features. First of all, it can become partially contaminated with hatred[17] or even fully replaced by hatred.[18] Secondly, it requires some degree of reciprocity by others;[19] in fact, too little reciprocity will typically unleash the pathology of jealousy and result in loathing for what was previously loved.[20] Finally, love for a finite object or person can be destroyed by a contrary and more powerful affect.[21] Yet this does not mean that one's body itself will be destroyed, for the same individual can 'successively pass through several contrary passions', and from one moment to the next 'the most powerful or the most lively' passion will replace the previously dominant passion.[22] In summary, we can say that the love of finite objects is 'precarious': it is both highly variable and inconstant.[23]

By way of contrast, love toward God manifests the highest degree of constancy possible under duration. Feature by feature, we can distinguish between love having a finite external cause and love having an (absolutely) infinite external cause. Firstly, love toward God cannot turn into hatred, since this would require that one both know something and be passive, and thus feel not joy but 'sadness accompanied by the idea of God'.[24] Secondly, there can be no

---

16   E3p13s, def aff 6.
17   E3p17.
18   E3p38.
19   E3p33.
20   One can see this process at work politically in Spinoza's analysis of the multitude's 'indignation' against corrupt rulers (Matheron 2011, pp. 219–29), the desire for private property (Matheron 2011, pp. 253–66), and the rationale for excluding servants and women from citizenship (Matheron 2011, pp. 267–304).
21   E4a1.
22   Moreau 1994b, p. 56.
23   Moreau 1994b, p. 56.
24   E5p18, c.

question of reciprocity in such love, since God cannot be affected by anything human beings do.[25] For this reason, Spinoza argues, 'neither envy nor jealousy can taint this love toward God; instead, the more human beings we imagine to be joined to God by the same bond of love, the more it is encouraged'. Finally, love toward God cannot be destroyed by a contrary or more powerful affect but can only cease when the body dies. As Spinoza summarizes, 'there is no affect that is directly contrary to this love and by which it can be destroyed. So we can conclude that this love is the most constant of all the affects, and insofar as it is related to the body (*quatenus ad corpus refertur*), cannot be destroyed, unless it is destroyed with the body itself'.[26]

In the second half of Part 5 Spinoza shifts direction to consider 'those things which pertain to the mind's duration without relation to the body (*sine relatione ad corporis*)'.[27] He sets forth and defends a conception of the intellectual love of God that goes beyond the constancy evident in love toward God. This is because, as we have just seen, love toward God still occurs on the level of duration and involves conceiving of God as the causal principle of bodily affections of images or things.[28] The intellectual love of God, by contrast, requires that one develop the so-called 'third kind of knowledge' (*tertium cognitionis genus*) and, through a process of abstraction, focus exclusively on what constitutes the 'eternal part' of love toward God.[29] Consequently, God is no longer conceived as the causal principle of the images of things affecting one's body but has become the orienting principle of how one can come to know the body and mind 'from the perspective of eternity' (*sub specie aeternitatis*).[30]

Two of the three chief features of love toward God are 'extended' by the intellectual love of God.[31] As was true of love toward God, the intellectual love of God cannot be tainted or undermined by hatred. More strikingly, though, the intellectual love of God cannot even be destroyed by the death of one's body.

Yet there is a crucial difference between these two kinds of love. Whereas love toward God is not reciprocal, the intellectual love of God is indeed reciprocal – albeit in a way unlike love for finite things. That is to say, God is capable of an intellectual love of both human beings and himself.[32] As I shall argue below, it is precisely the return of such reciprocity of love – no longer at the

---

25 E5p17c.
26 E5p20s.
27 E5p20s.
28 See E5pp14–15.
29 See Matheron 2011, pp. 707–25.
30 E5p30.
31 Moreau 1994b, p. 58.
32 E5pp35–6.

level of duration but at the level of eternity – that allows for the possibility of collective life beyond the need for an *imperium* (Spinoza's term for 'state' or 'state apparatus').³³

∴

Consider now a 1664 letter in which Spinoza consoled his distraught friend Pieter Balling on the recent illness and death of the latter's young son.³⁴ Spinoza's letter largely concerns the extent to which the imagination can in a confused way generate an omen of a future event – in this case Balling's premonition of his child's death. However, toward the end of the letter Spinoza also discusses the question of the extent to which one's love for another can bind two individuals:

> To take an example like yours, a father so loves his son that he and his beloved son are, as it were, one and the same. According to what I have demonstrated on another occasion, there must be in thought an idea of the son's essence, its affections, and its consequences. Because of this, and because the father, by the union he has with his son, is part of the said son, the father's mind must necessarily participate in the son's ideal essence, its affections, and consequences.

Spinoza contends that, as a result of his love for his son, a father can in some sense become part of his son, as his mind comes to 'participate' in the latter's 'ideal essence, its affections, and consequences'. To say the least, it is not clear what Spinoza means by such 'participation' of the father's mind in his son's essence. Balling or any other father could hardly have what Spinoza calls knowledge of the third kind of his son's essence. It would seem that at most one's love for another could be based on either knowledge of the first or second kind. But neither can Spinoza mean the affective imitation associated with love he discusses in Part Three of the *Ethics*,³⁵ since affective imitation allows separation between two persons to persist. On the level of duration, the father's mind only perceives his son through the ideas of the affections the latter has generated in his body. Spinoza possibly intends something intermediary between these two

---

33 See Moreau 1985.
34 Ep 17. See Matheron 1988, pp. 599–600. On Spinoza's relationship with Balling, and on this personal tragedy (the result of an outbreak of the plague in Amsterdam during the years 1663–4), see Nadler 1999, pp. 169, 212–13.
35 See E3pp19–26.

kinds of identification, which would permit an eventual transition from one to the other. This possibility cannot be ruled out, since Spinoza writes a few lines earlier in his letter that the mind 'can confusedly be aware, beforehand, of something that is future'.

For Spinoza passional joys have as their 'eternal condition of possibility' an 'unconscious', or 'barely conscious', beatitude.[36] Likewise, one's passional identification with others has as its eternal condition of possibility an implicit intellectual communion among the eternal parts of all our minds. Thus, the intellectual communion established by the third kind of knowledge only makes explicit the eternal foundation already implicit in every form of interpersonal love.[37] We might say that access to eternal life realises for human beings that toward which they have never ceased to strive. Throughout passional individual and collective life (whose travails Spinoza recounts in parts three and four of the *Ethics*) human beings endeavour as much as possible to agree with other human beings, not out of mere pursuit of self-interest but in order to rejoice in others' love and thereby to love themselves better. Next, at the level of reasonable individual and collective life, human beings come to desire to communicate their knowledge with other human beings in order to share their joy in knowing. But this is still only an abstract truth. They have to grasp that this activity leads them toward an interpenetration of individual minds through the mediation of God's love. Lastly, Matheron notes,

> after having moved from the level of duration to eternity itself, we assimilate ourselves to other human beings regarding what is singular in us: without ceasing to be ourselves, we coincide with them; their beatitude *is* ours. This would result in a complete transparency that, while suppressing alterity without abolishing *ipseity*, offers us at last, in its finished form, the glory to which we have always aspired.[38]

On the level of duration my love toward God will indeed cease when I die and my body decomposes.[39] However, not even death can destroy my intellectual love of God,[40] for it belongs to the nature of my mind insofar as the latter is

---

36   Matheron 1988, p. 600.
37   In this sense, too, as Gilles Deleuze once observed, 'Book V must be conceived as coextensive with all the others; we have the impression of arriving at it, but it was there all the time, for all time' (Deleuze 1998, p. 30).
38   Matheron 1988, p. 601.
39   E5p20s.
40   E5p37.

the eternally true idea of the singular essence of my body. For Spinoza no true idea can ever become false; its truth persists within God's eternal and infinite Intellect.

2   Collective Eternal Life

Finally, let us consider the nature of what Matheron has termed 'collective eternal life'. In a note to E5p40 Spinoza concludes his discussion of the intellectual love of God by alluding to the interpersonal relations that are now possible between a 'wise person' and other human beings. He writes that

> These are the things I have decided to show concerning the mind, insofar as it is considered without relation to the body's existence. From then ... it is clear that our mind, insofar as it understands, is an eternal mode of thinking, which is determined by another eternal mode of thinking, and this again by another, and so on, to infinity; so that together, they all constitute God's eternal and infinite Intellect.[41]

As Matheron has argued, Spinoza makes three claims in this note.[42] First of all, he argues that the mind, insofar as it understands, is an eternal mode of thought. This is another way of saying that to the extent that one has clear and distinct ideas, one's mind coincides with the eternal idea by which God, as manifested through the attribute of thought, conceives of the essence of one's body from the perspective of eternity.

Spinoza's second claim, however, is that this eternal mode cannot be actualised by itself. Its eternity follows from the fact that it exists simply because God exists, independent of every influence of fortune. But, as E1p21 shows, to which Spinoza refers here, the existence of this eternal mode does not derive from the absolute nature of God; otherwise, it would be infinite. If God – simply because of God's existence – forms the idea of the eternal essence of my body, it is because at the same time God forms eternal ideas of the essences of others' bodies. As a result, each finite eternal mode can exist only in relation to other finite modes.

Spinoza's third claim is that the horizontal order of causal interaction among modes is grounded in a vertical order of divine causal determination. Just as all

---

41   E5p40s.
42   Matheron 1988, pp. 609–10.

corporeal essences are logically realisable combinations of motion and rest, so too are the ideas of these essences actually realised consequences of the eternal Idea by means of which God thinks himself.[43] This is why every idea can be said to incorporate all others, since they derive from the same principle that permits them to communicate with the eternal Idea of God.

The ontological interconnection of these ideas, then, does not exclude their logical independence but, on the contrary, presupposes it. God directly conceives of every singular essence without the mediation of other singular essences. But insofar as God's knowledge of each singular essence refers to the knowledge of their common foundation – which itself refers to the knowledge of all other singular essences – God cannot conceive of a given singular essence without immediately conceiving of all other singular essences. It is because God conceives of all singular essences collectively that at the same time God conceives of the horizontal order according to which they are mutually determined to exist and operate. Thus, the eternal finite modes of the attribute of thought interpenetrate but do not become identical. They mutually imply one another through the mediation of their unique source in God, mutually condition each other through the mediation of this mutual implication, and together wind up forming a single Idea: God's eternal and infinite Intellect. However, contrary to what Spinoza's detractors often assume, this does not mean that in Part 5 he is advocating a kind of mysticism.[44] At most we should say that he engages in a non-mystical use of certain mystical intellectual influences.[45]

Essentially, Spinoza is arguing for an indefinite enlargement of collective beatitude or what we could call a 'politics of the third kind'. A wise person is able to form a 'community of minds' not only with a small number of privileged individuals but potentially with all of humanity. Indeed, such a community of all minds has always already existed *in itself*; this community-to-come only needs to be revealed to each of its members and thereby to be realised *for itself*. This requires the recomposition of finite modes and the establishment

---

43   E3p3.
44   Moreau 1994a, 287–93 offers a compelling argument that for Spinoza the experience of eternity is not mystical. For a contrary assessment, see Wetlesen 1977; 1979.
45   One might identify at least three such mystical influences: (a) the Kabbalistic school of Isaac Luria, to which Spinoza's Hebrew teacher Menasseh ben Israel belonged; (b) the esoteric writings of Giordano Bruno, with which Spinoza's Latin tutor Franciscus van den Enden was probably familiar; (c) the ideas of the radical collegiant communities with whose members Spinoza associated from the time of his banishment from the Amsterdam synagogue until the end of his life.

of enhanced communication among individuals.[46] It is worth noting that for Spinoza a community of wise persons would not be 'simpler' than societies with *imperia* but would embody complex social-political institutions and would promote robust democratic debate.

Perhaps such a community-to-come will never be fully realised, but for the wise person it nonetheless serves as an immanent norm or what Matheron has called 'a regulative Idea in the Kantian sense'.[47] To the extent that human minds know themselves to be identical to the ideas through which God conceives of their respective bodies, they can acquire at least a partial awareness of their union within the eternal and infinite Intellect. Consequently, as Matheron writes, a wise person strives as much as possible to enlighten other human beings; his or her objective is to insure that 'as many minds as possible eternalize themselves as much as possible by enlightening themselves as much as possible'.[48] Just as a wise person seeks to increase indefinitely the eternal part of his or her mind, so too should he or she seek to increase indefinitely the eternal part of everyone else's mind. Of course, the success of this project requires that certain external conditions continue to be satisfied.[49] As Spinoza writes in E4p40, 'things that are conducive to the common society of human beings, that is, bring it about that human beings live harmoniously, are useful; those, on the other hand, are evil that bring discord to the commonwealth'.

---

46   On the importance of communication in Spinoza's philosophy and political thought, see Balibar 1989, esp. pp. 18–19, 41–2; 2008, pp. 113–18; and Suhamy 2010.

47   Matheron 1988, p. 612 n. 95. Here Negri's anti-Kantian emphasis on 'constitution' in Spinoza's philosophy is well taken. As Negri puts it, 'The world is clay in the hands of the potter. On the metaphysical terrain of surfaces the modality is constructive. The order of the construction is within constitution. Necessity is within freedom. Politics is the fabric on which constitutive human activity principally unfolds' (Negri 1991, p. 186). Since human bodies and minds are capable of acting and perceiving the world in 'a great many ways' (E2p14,d), we must avoid speculating in advance about what a given 'concatenation' (E5p10) of human bodies and minds could or could not do. Indeed, it remains an ontologically – and so politically – open question whether or not such a 'multitude' could construct and preserve an egalitarian community of freely associated individuals.

   Although he is an unlikely bedfellow of either Spinoza or Negri, on this point Slavoj Žižek would seem to agree. Reclaiming Marx and Engels' perspective in the *German Ideology*, Žižek insists that communism is not a Kantian 'regulative Idea' establishing an a priori ideal, norm, or boundary; rather, communism signifies 'a movement which reacts to actual social antagonisms' and then surpasses them (Žižek 2010, p. 211).

48   Matheron 1988, p. 611.

49   For example, famine, epidemic, war, technological collapse, or ecological disaster would, to varying degrees, obstruct the realisation of Spinoza's political project and place it historically off the agenda.

Consequently, a wise person would extend around himself or herself a realm of social peace and friendship, in compliance with Spinoza's recommendations at the end of Part Four concerning the free human being's temperament and way of life: avoiding unnecessary dangers,[50] declining others' favours,[51] showing gratitude,[52] acting honestly,[53] and obeying (legitimate) civil laws.[54] In sum, a wise person would strive as much as possible 'to act well and rejoice'.[55]

Yet Spinoza does not claim that the power of militant reason to restrain and moderate the passions and convert them into active affects is unlimited. On the contrary, in his preface to Part 5 he distances himself from Stoic and Cartesian exaggerated claims about the ability of the mind to 'acquire an absolute command (*imperium absolutum*) over our passions' through force of will alone. At any rate, as Spinoza argues in E5p42s, a wise person is undoubtedly capable of doing more and is 'much more powerful than one who is ignorant and is agitated only by lust (*qui sola libidine agitur*)'. Indeed, an ignorant person is 'agitated in many ways by external causes, and unable ever to possess true serenity of spirit (*vera animi acquiescentia*)', whereas a wise person 'insofar as [he or she] is considered as such (*quatenus ut talis consideratur*), [is] hardly troubled in spirit ... but always possesses true serenity of spirit (*vera animi acquiescentia*)'. It is worth highlighting Spinoza's qualifying phrase 'insofar as [he or she is] considered as such' (*quatenus ut talis consideratur*), which reminds us that no human being can attain a condition of self-mastery in accordance with which he or she could establish a personal *imperium in imperio*, and permanently restrain the power of fortune from disrupting the stability of his or her life. All human beings remain a part of nature, and to a greater or lesser extent are acted on by forces beyond their control – forces that give rise, in turn, to the fluctuation of affections and affects. Wisdom only exists as a matter of degree.

Although a wise person would experience less mental agitation and greater calm than an ignorant person, Spinoza does not envision that he or she would or could pursue a quiet retreat 'far from the madding crowd'. Serenity has nothing to do with contemplation or isolation but instead implies a continued act-

---

50   E4p69.
51   E4p70.
52   E4P71.
53   E4P72.
54   E4P73. No doubt the legitimacy of specific civil laws has historically always been contested; but arguably there is a greater likelihood that laws fashioned by and within a well-ordered democratic republic are *more likely* to be obeyed. Oppressive regimes, by contrast, tend to generate what Spinoza calls the passion of 'indignation' (on the logic of which see Matheron 2011, pp. 219–29 and the previous chapter).
55   E4P73s.

ive engagement in the passionate life of human beings.[56] Although, as Roger-Pol Droit observes, to a certain extent Spinoza revives here an ancient figure of the 'sage', his perspective is solidly grounded in modernity; for he envisioned 'no renunciation of the world, no separation from life, the body, or matter'. On the contrary: sages would live in 'the fullness of the world'.[57]

As a result, politics rooted in knowledge of the third kind would not be abstract and formal but would be qualitative, concrete, and concern the order of everyday existence. As a result, persons who had cultivated the affect of serenity would strive to extricate themselves from fear of failure and death and to understand that freedom is a constant struggle whose path is arduous: along the way victories are invariably mixed with defeats. A serene militant would not only persist in his or her desire for socio-political transformation over the long run but in the very midst of social upheaval would also seek to adopt, and sustain, a perspective of eternity.

However, as Matheron contends, a wise person is involved in a 'much vaster meta-historical venture'[58] than even a free human being living under the external authority of an *imperium*. Beyond the various kinds and forms of *imperium*, beyond the transitional stage of an external collective life based on reason, a wise person does all that he or she can to establish an internal 'communism of minds', to deepen and enrich the struggle for, and transition to, an egalitarian society of freely associated individuals.[59] Indeed, for Matheron Spinoza's ethical-political project has as its ultimate goal

> to enable all of Humanity to exist as a totality conscious of itself, a microcosm of the infinite Understanding, in the heart of which every soul, although remaining itself, would at the same time become all the others. This is an eschatological perspective, which would be somewhat analog-

---

56 Del Lucchese 2009, p. 164.
57 Droit 2009, pp. 120–1.
58 Matheron 1988, p. 612.
59 'Freely associated' does not mean a fleeting convergence of individual interests or affective ties but instead a nexus of non-coercive relations among maximally reasoning individuals. For Spinoza every human being is free only insofar as he or she 'has the power to exist and operate in accordance with the laws of human nature (*postestam habet existendi et operandi secundum humanae naturae leges*)'. Moreover, to the extent that a human being 'exists from the necessity of his or her own nature, so too he or she acts from the necessity of his or her own nature; that is, he or she acts absolutely freely (*libere absolute agit*)' (TP 2.7). Finally, if a multitude of human beings were indeed to exercise absolute political freedom, then each individual would no longer be subject to another's power and would be able to live 'absolutely, insofar as one can live in accordance with his or her own complexion (*absolute quatenus ex suo ingenio vivere potest*)' (TP 2.9).

ous to certain Kabbalists, if the final outcome were not in Spinoza pushed back to infinity: this result will never actually be attained; but at least we can always approach it. Thus we shall wind up at a partial solution to the ontological drama at the origin of the human drama: infinite Understanding, separated from itself by the necessity in which it finds itself to think the modes of Extension in their existence *hic et nunc* [here and now], will all the better overcome this separation as Humanity more and more reconciles itself with itself.[60]

What is more, Matheron cites the Soviet philosopher A.M. Deborin, who insisted early in the twentieth century that a 'communism of minds' implies a 'communism of goods'.[61] Indeed, Spinoza envisioned a

> complete satisfaction to our individual and interhuman conatuses: surpassing all alienations and divergences; an actualization of the I in the most complete lucidity, an actualization of the We in the most complete of communions.[62]

The result would be a 'complete and definitive individual liberation in a community without restriction'.[63] Moreover, such a community would have no need of juridical laws or institutional constraints based on violence; the *imperium* would 'wither away' after having fulfilled the conditions of its own usefulness.[64]

∴

Let us conclude this estimation of the theological-political value of Matheron's scholarship on Spinoza for contemporary Marxist theory and practice. Laurent

---

60   Matheron 1988, pp. 612–13.
61   Deborin 1952, pp. 115–16.
62   Matheron 1988, p. 613.
63   Matheron 1988, p. 613.
64   Compare Spinoza's similar speculation in Chapter Five of his *Tractatus Theologico-Politicus* (Spinoza 2007). Joseph Almog rightly characterises Spinoza's position that human social-political organisations arise not by accident or through contracts 'against Nature' but simply as a result of 'Nature taking its course' (Almog 2014, pp. 63–87). However, he wrongly describes such organisations as so many variations on the 'state'. For Spinoza, it is possible to envision – but admittedly difficult to realise in practice – a 'non-state' (or 'post-state') that would require not the return to a simpler, pre-social 'state of nature' but instead arduous political struggles and the construction of a more complex – and hence more powerful (E4pp35–37; TP 2.13) – form of social-political organisation.

Bove has noted that between Matheron and Spinoza 'something happens'.[65] Not least of what happens, we have seen, is a revitalisation of the ethical-political immanent norm of a classless society, a compelling exemplar[66] of the serene militant, and a stark reminder of the rare, difficult, but excellent path ahead.[67] Perhaps more than ever, that path beckons.

---

65   Bove 2011.
66   See E4pref for Spinoza's conception of exemplars in general and human exemplars in specific.
67   As Spinoza concludes the *Ethics*, 'If the way I have shown to lead to these things now seems very hard, still, it can be found. And of course, what is found so rarely must be hard. For if salvation were at hand, and could be found without great effort, how could nearly everyone neglect it? But all things excellent are as difficult as they are rare' (E5p42s).

INTERLUDE

An Ethics for Marxism: Spinoza on Fortitude*

> [T]he question ... of courage and resolve ... is not a personal matter, but a question of which *class* is capable of manifesting courage and resolve. The only class capable of this is the proletariat.
> – V.I. LENIN ('One of the Fundamental Questions of the Revolution', September 1917)

∴

In interviews with Fernanda Navarro that took place in the early 1980s – at the depth of his personal and political misfortune – Louis Althusser proposed a 'new task', namely, 'to seek what kind of philosophy corresponds best to what Marx wrote in *Capital*'. He added that whatever such a philosophy turns out to be,

> it will not be a 'Marxist philosophy'. It will simply be a philosophy that takes its place in the history of philosophy. It will be capable of accounting for the conceptual discoveries that Marx put to work in *Capital*, but it will not be a Marxist philosophy: it will be a philosophy *for Marxism*.[1]

As a way to test Althusser's proposal, let us explore how the seventeenth-century philosopher Baruch de Spinoza offers not only a philosophy for Marxism but also a distinctive way for Marxists to persevere as socialists. What is more, as we shall see, Spinoza's philosophy provides the basis for developing a distinctively normative outlook or *ethics* for Marxism.

Warren Montag is correct that Spinoza described a world 'without transcendence'.[2] Spinoza's philosophy allows for no Divine Lawgiver or Transcendent Guarantor of moral values or rules. But even an entirely immanent world has room for – and need of – norms of belief and conduct, provided that, as Montag notes, there exists no norm 'external to that which exists, providing the

---

* This chapter has been previously published in *Rethinking MARXISM* 26.4, 2014, pp. 561–80.
1 Athusser 2006, p. 258.
2 Montag 1989.

standard against which a thing might be judged perfect or imperfect, adequate or inadequate'.[3] Norms continue to serve as objective criteria by which to distinguish whether or not an individual's encounters with the external world go well or badly, agree or disagree with one's nature, increase or decrease one's ability to act in the world, or foster greater or lesser degrees of wellbeing. In short, Spinoza was neither a moral relativist nor a subjectivist.[4]

As a result, I part company with Althusser's position that 'moral ideology' operates as a mere supplement to law – a matter of fact but not of value.[5] As Yvon Quiniou has shrewdly observed, moral inquiry is unavoidable and essential to the Marxist critique of capitalism:

> Marx ... tells us that communism must arrive historically on the basis of a necessity that is immanent to history. 'So what?' one can object to us. 'Why should this be good for humanity?' Or again, to speak of the present: 'You maintain', an imaginary interlocutor tells me, 'that capitalism rests on the exploitation of human labor. That is true, but why should I find that bad?' 'Exploitation', he will perhaps add in a provocative manner, 'contributes positively to the production of wealth and therefore to material progress. Why should I condemn it?'[6]

Nor, Quiniou observes, does it suffice to reiterate Marx and Engels' famous lines in the *German Ideology* that 'communism is for us not a *state of affairs* still to be established, not an *ideal* to which reality [will] have to adjust' but is instead 'the *real* movement which abolishes the actual state of affairs'.[7] Not only is this formulation of communism amoralistic, it is unacceptably *teleological*; indeed, it presumes without argument that such 'real movement' entails an *a priori* emancipatory orientation and would objectively lead on its own to the abolition of the actual unjust state of affairs without any need, as Quiniou puts it, to 'mobilize moral subjects'.[8] Yet without moral subjects – however conceptualised[9] – it is difficult to imagine how a socialist alternative to capitalism could ever be realised.

---

3   Montag 1989, p. 94.
4   For a persuasive account of Spinoza's defence of ethical objectivity in Propositions 29–38 of the Fourth Part of the *Ethics*, see Collin 2011, pp. 261–8.
5   See Althusser 1995, pp. 97–100.
6   Quiniou 2013, pp. 161–2.
7   Marx 1997, p. 426.
8   Quiniou 2013, p. 164.
9   This is not the place to address the vexed problem of how best to theorise moral subjectivity and political agency. An excellent point of departure for an empirically well-supported

At any rate, it is high time to abandon the notion that Marx was hostile to all normative discourse as being little more than pernicious moralism.[10] Roland Boer has rightly observed that ethics is a hotly contested terrain for the left today, but it simply won't do to claim, as he does, that Marx saw ethics as 'a mystifying ideology that justifies the status quo and keeps the ruling class in position'.[11] On the contrary, over the course of his intellectual and political activism, Marx consistently argued and acted on the basis of what early in his life he had designated as 'the *categorical imperative to overthrow all conditions* in which man is a debased, enslaved, neglected and contemptible being ...'[12]

Indeed, the mature author of *Capital* indicted not just the economic inefficiency of capitalism but also its structural violence. For example, in Chapter 15 of *Capital* ('Machinery and Large-Scale Industry')[13] Marx exhaustively describes and fiercely denounces the 'moral degradation'[14] resulting from 'the organized system of machinery in the factory'.[15] Marx returns to this theme in Chapter 25 ('The General Law of Capitalist Accumulation') when he argues that

> within the capitalist system all methods for raising the social productivity of labour are put into effect at the cost of the individual worker ... all

---

Spinozist perspective, however, would be Ravven 2013. Also valuable are Read's (2012) framing of Spinoza, Hegel, and Marx as philosophers of 'transindividuality' and Williams's (2012) discussion of Spinoza, Hegel, and the 'space of subjectivity'.

10 As Terry Eagleton makes the distinction, 'moralism abstracts something called "moral values" from the whole historical context in which they are set, and then generally proceeds to hand down absolute moral judgements. A truly moral inquiry, by contrast, is one which investigates all the aspects of a human situation. It refuses to divorce human values, behavior, relationships and qualities of character from the social and historical forces which shape them. It thus escapes the false distinction between moral judgement on the one hand and scientific analysis on the other' (Eagleton 2011, pp. 158–9). For more on the distinction between moralism and authentic moral inquiry, see Taylor 2011.

11 Boer 2013b, p. 38. Boer does not embrace an 'amoral position, beyond ethics' but instead insists that ethics always involves a 'taking of sides'. I agree with him that Marxists should embrace 'what is disruptive, unwelcome, what shakes up the customary and comfortable social order' (50). Yet it does not follow that this disruption requires 'an act of subverting the very discourse of ethics and its class associations', let alone an 'unethical and unmoral politics' (50). Following Althusser 1976, pp. 142–50, Macherey 1999, and Montag 2013, we should instead conceive of moral philosophy as an interminable 'struggle of tendencies'.

12 Marx 1992, p. 251.
13 Marx 1990, pp. 492–639.
14 Marx 1990, pp. 522–3, 593.
15 Marx 1990, p. 517.

means for the development of production undergo a dialectical inversion so that they become means of domination and exploitation of the producers; they distort the worker into a fragment of a man, they degrade him to the level of an appendage of a machine, they destroy the actual content of his labour by turning it into a torment; they alienate ... from him the intellectual potentialities of the labor process in the same proportion as science is incorporated in it as an independent power; they deform the conditions under which he works, subject him during the labour process to a despotism the more hateful for its meanness; they transform his lifetime into working-time, and drag his wife and child beneath the wheels of the juggernaut of capital.

Marx concludes this remarkable passage by insisting that 'accumulation of wealth at one pole is, therefore, at the same time accumulation of misery, the torment of labour, slavery, ignorance, brutalization and moral degradation at the opposite pole, i.e. on the side of the class that produces its own product as capital'.[16]

Note that Marx is addressing here only ordinary accumulation of capital at the point of production. Perhaps an even stronger case for Marx as an impassioned moral critic of capitalism can be made based on his account in Part 8 of the 'So-Called Primitive Accumulation', during which the peasantry was driven off the land, commons were expropriated, and colonies established. Such was, for Marx, a history 'written in the annals of mankind in letters of blood and fire'[17] and during which 'conquest, enslavement, robbery, murder, in short, force, play[ed] the greatest part'.[18]

In such passages of *Capital* it is hard not to see Marx engaged in strenuous moral criticism and justifying why the working class should build a movement to 'expropriate the expropriators'. But even if Marx had utterly rejected ethics as 'mystifying ideology' and sought to provide only a value-free scientific investigation of capitalism, why should this worry anyone today? Contemporary Marxists ought to develop their research programme beyond what Marx himself happened to say or do. So I shall proceed with my own exercise in normative Marxism.

Yet a qualification is in order. I am not going to provide a general survey of Marxism and the demands of morality. Here Kant or Rawls would perhaps be

---

16   Marx 1990, p. 799.
17   Marx 1990, p. 875.
18   Marx 1990, p. 874.

more useful conversation partners than Spinoza.[19] My concern, instead, will be with ethics in a restricted sense.

Gilles Deleuze famously draws attention to what he called Spinoza's 'ethical vision of the world'.[20] Whereas morality appeals to transcendent rights and duties, ethics engages in the concrete analysis of immanent 'norms of life, relating to the soul's "strength" and its power of action'. Deleuze grants that for Spinoza

> such norms [can] coincide with the laws of ordinary morality; but such coincidences are on the one hand not particularly numerous; and on the other, when reason enjoins or denounces something analogous to what morality orders or prohibits, it is always for reasons very different from those of morality. The *Ethics* judges feelings, conduct and intentions by relating them, not to transcendent values, but to modes of existence they presuppose or imply: there are things one cannot do or even say, believe, feel, think, unless one is weak, enslaved, impotent; and other things one cannot do, feel and so on, unless one is free or strong. *A method of explanation by immanent modes of existence* thus replaces the recourse to transcendent values. The question is in each case: Does, say, this feeling, increase our power of action or not? Does it help us come into full possession of that power?

In a word, he concludes, 'our ethical task properly so called' is simply 'to do all we can'.[21]

Yet Deleuze exaggerates and makes too sharp a distinction between ethics and morality, privileging the former's emphasis on singularity at the expense of the latter's universalizing perspective.[22] Ethics and morality are better conceived as existing within a creative dialectical tension of mutual interaction, or what Jean-Paul Sartre once called a 'singular universal'.[23] In other words, what enables flourishing for each individual has a bearing on what might enable all members of society to flourish; likewise, morally legitimate social institutions

---

19 For outstanding Kantian approaches, see van der Linden 1988 and Quiniou 2010. For Marxist engagements with Rawls, see Peffer 1990 and Cohen 2008.
20 Deleuze 1990a, pp. 255–72.
21 Deleuze 1990a, pp. 268–9.
22 Comte-Sponville 2015 criticises Deleuze's excessively 'Nietzschean' reading of Spinoza, which would unjustifiably implicate Spinoza in the rejection of all forms of moral evaluation. For more on the distinction between ethics and morality, and stress on the political urgency for Marxists of the latter's universal orientation, see Collin 2003 and Quiniou 2010.
23 See Sartre 2013.

that function as freely as possible from domination, oppression, exploitation, and ecological destruction tend to open up a space for individuals to lead less alienated lives[24] and more fully to exercise their concrete human capacities and capabilities.[25] Denis Collin has observed that

> if freedom is not capital that one puts to work as a sensible capitalist but is fundamentally a dynamic of life, an effort to liberate oneself from the multiple alienations within which the individual continually loses himself or herself; then it is a matter of constructing an ethics that can be shared by the greatest number. The details of such an ethics are laid out with the greatest clarity in Spinoza's work.[26]

Since there is already an impressive body of scholarly work on the topic of 'Marxism and morality',[27] let us shall restrict the scope of our discussion here to the importance of Spinoza's ethics for Marxism with respect to the concept of *fortitude*.[28] I do so with apprehension. As Louis Althusser once pointed out regarding his own debt to Spinoza, there is nothing riskier for Marxists than to borrow concepts from another theoretical problematic: one way or another, he insisted, you have to 'pay for it'.[29] So let us proceed with caution and hope that the theoretical risk we are going to incur will be worth the practical benefit.

1 The Education of Socialist Desire

First of all, let us pose a practical question for Marxists who embrace what Hal Draper called 'socialism from below'.[30] How do socialists *remain* socialists

---

24 For a compelling reaffirmation of why the Marxist understanding of human alienation remains crucial for developing a theory of collective emancipation, see Sève 2012.
25 For a stirring defense of socialism as the realisation of human capacities and capabilities, see Lebowitz 2010.
26 Collin 2013, p. 220.
27 On the moral foundations and implications of Marxism, see Lukes 1985, Martin 2008, Blackledge 2012, Dussel 2013, and Thompson 2015.
28 Fortitude is not the only ethical concept to which socialists should attend. Strong cases could equally be made for the significance of such political virtues as engaging in fearless and frank truth-telling (see Foucault 2010; 2011) or in maintaining pledges of loyalty to causes, movements, and groups (see Sartre 2004a, pp. 417–28).
29 Althusser 1976, p. 141.
30 See Draper 1992. There are Marxists, of course, who continue to prefer 'communism' to 'socialism' as a way to identify their political project (see Douzinas and Žižek 2010 and Žižek 2013). Yet I have been persuaded by Lebowitz 2010, who contends that twentieth-

over the course of their lives and continue to enlarge and deepen their beliefs, practices, and virtues (viz., by embracing a more thoroughly and consistently egalitarian ethos along feminist, anti-racist, and ecological lines)? Posing such a question for socialists is also intended to spur them to reflect concretely on why it is not enough simply to make a general 'case for socialism'.[31] No doubt, as most Marxists have espoused, elementary facts and sound arguments about the varied ills of capitalism have played – and should continue to play – a key role in persuading people to become socialists. However, facts and arguments do not stand on their own but are always infused with emotive force.

For example, many readers of the first volume of Marx's *Capital* have been as shocked by that book's graphic depiction of nineteenth-century English factory life as they have been impressed by its intricate analysis of circuits of capital. Likewise, artists, musicians, writers, and filmmakers today can convey through their various media something about the horrors of global capitalism that the most exhaustive empirical research and the most rigorous argumentation cannot.[32]

Yet there is the danger that too much reliance on emotion can degenerate into haranguing. For example, venting one's anger at injustice does not necessarily diminish the anger.[33] Moreover, as Erik Olin Wright observes, it is not enough 'to create an inspiring vision of a desirable alternative, grounded in anger at the injustices of the world in which we live and infused with hope and passion about human possibilities'. Wright acknowledges that 'at times, such charismatic wishful thinking has been a powerful force, contributing to the mobilization of people for struggle and sacrifice'. However, he cautions,

> it is unlikely to form an adequate basis for transforming the world in ways that actually produce a sustainable emancipatory alternative. The history of human struggles for radical social change is filled with heroic victories over existing structures of oppression followed by the tragic construction of new forms of domination, oppression, and inequality.[34]

---

century Stalinist authoritarianism has largely discredited communism in the popular imagination – or at least for the time being in North America. Lebowitz admits that in the twenty-first century 'socialism' as a socio-economic system must be reinvented in order to name 'the vision of a society in which the alienation of human beings from their activity, their lives, other human beings and nature has come to an end' (110).

31 For an admirably clear example, see Maass 2010.
32 See Reed 2005 and Duncombe 2007 on the political power of artistic imagination.
33 Not only is this Spinoza's considered philosophical judgment, Tavris 1989 offers substantial empirical support for it from the perspective of social psychology.
34 Wright 2010, p. 24.

Here we should emphasise the need to adopt, in Jacques Bidet's words, a kind of revolutionary 'prudence' to guide socialists in their political action that would be 'neither resigned nor impatient' but rather would inspire 'the multiform and plural association of the exploited and oppressed, the movement of their emancipation'.[35] As we shall soon see, Spinoza's ethics provides a basis for a kind of prudence or practical reasoning that Marxists would do well to incorporate into their theoretical framework.

But who ever becomes a socialist – and why? First and foremost, one might suggest, nascent socialists reject what Herbert Marcuse termed the sheer 'obscenity' of capitalist society. According to Marcuse's stinging indictment,

> This society is obscene in producing and indecently exposing a stifling abundance of wares while depriving its victims abroad of the necessities of life; obscene in stuffing itself and its garbage cans while poisoning and burning the scarce foodstuffs in the fields of its aggression; obscene in the words and smiles of its politicians and entertainers; in its prayers, in its ignorance, and in the wisdom of its kept intellectuals.[36]

Along similar lines – but more systematically than Marcuse – the anthropologist James Scott has identified moral outrage against perceived social indignities as the basis of resistance.[37] Scott provides ample comparative evidence to illustrate that resistance 'originates not simply from material appropriation but from the pattern of personal humiliations that characterize that exploitation'. This is not to 'ignore appropriation' but to 'enlarge the field of our vision' by providing greater cultural specificity and nuance. As Scott puts it,

> just as traditional Marxist analysis might be said to privilege the appropriation of surplus value as the social site of exploitation and resistance, our analysis ... privileges the social experience of indignities, control, submission, humiliation, forced deference, and punishment. The choice of emphasis is not to gainsay the importance of material appropriation in class relations. Appropriation is, after all, largely the purpose of domination. The very process of appropriation, however, unavoidably entails systematic social relations of subordination that impose indignities of

---

35 Bidet 1999, p. 342.
36 Marcuse 1969, pp. 7–8.
37 Scott 1990. Scott builds on such previous research as Moore 1978.

one kind or another on the weak. These indignities are the seedbed of ... anger, indignation, frustration, and swallowed bile ...[38]

Likewise, the historian T.H. Breen has recently urged 'a greater appreciation of the kinds of passions that have energized insurgencies throughout world history' and recommended that 'our revolutionary lexicon' should 'include popular anger and rage, a desire for revenge, and a feeling of betrayal – harsh concepts, perhaps, but ones that better reflect the actual revolutionary process than do those encountered in abstract histories of political thought'.[39]

In this spirit, properly philosophical claims arise. For example, Simon Critchley has proposed that anger is the 'first political emotion'. According to Critchley, 'it is often anger that moves the subject to action. Anger is the emotion that produces motion, the mood that moves the subject. But such anger at the multiple injustices and wrongs of the present provokes an ethical response'.[40] Similarly, while drawing up a 'genealogy of rebellion', and following Spinoza's own terminology, Antonio Negri and Michael Hardt have argued that indignation 'is the ground zero, the basic material from which moments of revolt and rebellion develop'.[41]

Let us identify indignation against oppression, then, as the first affective moment of resistance. Yet an initial burst of outrage at social injustice may not last long, for anger is an unstable and unreliable emotion.[42] Faced with the prospect of prolonged and seemingly intractable institutional obstruction to social change, one's indignation could well collapse into despair or resignation.

As a result, we should speak of the need for a second, more affirmative, moment of radicalisation: a 'utopian' – or perhaps 'romantic'[43] – desire for a profoundly different world. Eric Hobsbawm once explained the emergence of political radicalisation along such lines:

> Why do men and women become revolutionaries? In the first instance mostly because they believe that what they want subjectively from life cannot be got without a fundamental change in all society. There is of course that permanent substratum of idealism, or if we prefer the term, utopianism, which is part of all human life and it can become the domin-

---

38   Scott 1990, pp. pp. 111–12.
39   Breen 2010, pp. 10–11.
40   Critchley 2007, p. 130.
41   Hardt and Negri 2009, p. 235.
42   Again, for empirical support, see Tavris 1989.
43   On the revolutionary possibilities inherent within the romantic tradition, see Blechman 1999 and Löwy and Sayre 2001.

ant part for individuals at certain times, as during adolescent and romantic love, and for societies at the occasional historical moments which correspond to falling and being in love, namely the great moments of liberation and revolution. All men, however cynical, can conceive of a personal life or society which would not be imperfect. All would agree that this would be wonderful. Most men at some time of their lives think that such a life and society are *possible*, and quite a number think that we ought to bring them about. During the great liberations and revolutions most men actually think, briefly or only momentarily, that perfection is being achieved, that the New Jerusalem is being built, the earthly paradise within reach.[44]

Hobsbawm immediately qualifies his observation with a recognition that 'most people for most of their adult lives, and most social groups for most of their history, live at a less exalted level of expectation'.[45] Moreover, not all nascent revolutionaries are even initially attracted to socialism. For these reasons, he suggests, 'the function of a revolutionary ideology such as socialism in mass movements is to liberate their members from dependence on … fluctuations in their personal expectations'.[46]

Hobsbawm wonders not just how raw anti-capitalist desire arises; he poses E.P. Thompson's crucial question of how, and to what degree, such a desire can be 'educated'.[47] In other words, is it possible to modulate, reinforce, and refine a critical commitment to socialism over the course of one's life? In terms of a remixed slogan, how might socialists 'Keep Calm and Stay Radical'?[48]

This is where Spinoza enters the picture.

2 Affects of Resistance

Consider Spinoza's well-known formula: 'the natural right of each person extends as far as his or her desire and power'. The radical implication of this

---

44 Hobsbawm 2001, pp. 294–5.
45 Hobsbawm 2001, p. 295.
46 Hobsbawm 2001, p. 295 n. 3.
47 Here he echoes E.P. Thompson's view that the education of utopian desire is one of the highest aims of socialist theory and practice. See Thompson 2011, p. 791.
48 The original slogan, of course, was 'Keep Calm and Carry On', which appeared on a 1939 poster produced by the British government at the beginning of WWII. The poster was intended for public display in case of a German invasion, but it was never distributed. See Rall 2013.

formula is that we always have the right to resist oppression as long as we have the power and the desire to do so.[49] But what for Spinoza underlies such resistance? Perhaps even more importantly, what does he think best *sustains* resistance over the long run? The two main affective sources for resistance we find in Spinoza's writings are indignation and the pursuit of glory. Following Laurent Bove, we could call these 'affects of resistance', of which indignation is a negative source and glory a positive source to confront oppression.[50] However, Spinoza argues that both affects have disadvantages: indignation is a sad passion, and glory fluctuates between being a joyous passion and an active affect.[51] In short, they are unstable and unreliable affective means to the end of liberation. The question then becomes how to reorient and stabilise resistance to oppression in terms of what Spinoza calls the joyous 'active affects' of fortitude, courage, and generosity.

In the *Ethics* Spinoza defines 'fortitude' (*fortitudo*) as 'all actions that follow from affects related to the soul insofar as it understands'. In Pierre Macherey's succinct and elegant expression, fortitude is none other than our human 'internal power'.[52] After having defined fortitude, Spinoza next identifies its constituent affective parts: courage and generosity. He characterises 'courage' (*animositas*) as 'the desire by which each one strives, solely from the guidance of reason, to preserve one's being'. 'Generosity' (*generositas*) is the name he gives to 'the desire by which each one strives, solely from the guidance of reason, to aid other human beings and join them in friendship'.[53]

It is hardly surprising that Spinoza introduces the concept of fortitude at the end of the third part of the *Ethics*, for here he concludes his treatment of the precarious situation of human beings under the influence of passions and

---

49   Spinoza presents his argument to this conclusion in Chapter 16 of his *Theological-Political Treatise* and in Chapter Two of his *Political Treatise*. See Spinoza 2007 and Spinoza 2000. On Spinoza's conception of right, see Matheron 1985 and Lazzeri 1998. In a strict sense, then, as Lordon 2013, pp. 123–68 has compellingly argued, for Spinoza the classical problem of political legitimacy simply does not arise.

50   Bove 1996, pp. 291–5. Bove himself, though, identifies as 'affects of resistance' only indignation and 'benevolence' (*benevolentia*), which Spinoza defined as 'the desire to benefit one whom we pity' (def aff 35). Interestingly, van der Linden 1988, pp. 53–65 likewise identifies the 'negative' moral feeling of indignation and two 'positive' moral feelings of enthusiasm and solidarity in his Kantian account of resistance to oppression.

51   For detailed treatments of Spinoza's concept of indignation, see Matheron 1994; Bove 1996, pp. 291–5; and Del Lucchese 2009. On Spinoza's concept of glory, see Stolze 2007 and Illuminati 2009.

52   Macherey 1995, p. 386.

53   E3p59s. For a superb commentary on Spinoza's analysis of the virtues of fortitude, courage, and generosity, see Jaquet 2005.

begins to anticipate the means by which they can at least partially free themselves from passional servitude. As Henri Laux has argued, Spinoza identifies an alternative between 'fluctuation' (*fluctatio*) of the passions and 'fortitude' (*fortitudo*); for these are two 'antagonistic systems, whose distance composes the ethical field of the individual and societies. The opposition is that of weakness and force, inconstancy and stability, powerlessness and power, passion and action'. In other words, Laux proposes,

> the logic of *fortitudo* is opposed to that of *fluctatio*; not only in a restrictive way, in the sense that reason and passion are contrary, but in the sense that the former can realize fully the power that only remains approached in the composition of the latter – thus, of its proper usefulness.[54]

We can observe this fluctuation especially well in the affects of fear and hope, which for Spinoza are not good in themselves but are associated with sadness. This is because both fear and hope show a defect of knowledge and a lack of power in the soul. For this reason also confidence and despair, gladness and remorse are signs of a soul lacking in power. For though confidence and gladness are affects of joy, they still presuppose that sadness has preceded them, namely, hope and fear. Therefore, the more we strive to live according to the guidance of reason, the more we strive to depend less on hope, to free ourselves from fear, to conquer fortune as much as we can, and to direct our actions by the certain cause of reason.[55] Human beings acting under the guidance of reason strive to preserve their being as much as they can, and this desire is precisely what Spinoza means by courage.

Spinoza subdivides courage into three types: 'moderation' (*temperantia*), 'sobriety' (*sobrietas*), and 'presence of spirit in dangerous situations' (*animi in periculis praesentia*), each of which, as an active affect, can be distinguished, just like passive affects, by the function of its objects and relations. Finally, Spinoza is careful not to confuse courage with rashness. He allows that 'in a free human being, a timely flight testifies to as much courage as fighting: in other words, a free human being demonstrates the same courage, that is, presence of spirit, in choosing to flee as in choosing to struggle'.[56]

By contrast to the inward orientation of courage, generosity radiates outward and has to do with willing the joy and power of others; it is the desire by

---

54   Laux 1993, p. 224.
55   E4P47S.
56   E4P69C.

which individuals tend 'to join others to themselves in friendship'.[57] Spinoza further divides generosity into 'modesty' (*modestia*)[58] and 'clemency' (*clementia*). Generosity poses, in Laux's words, 'the conditions of the reality of the social bond' and 'stabilizes interpersonal relations by accentuating their respective powers, not by a neutralization of passions'.[59] Such bonds of friendship form the basis not just of morality but also of religion and the state.[60]

Let me conclude this sketch of fortitude by pointing out that there is nothing sentimental about Spinoza's ethics. Despite his insistence that 'one who lives according to the guidance of reason strives, as far as possible, to repay the other's hatred, anger, and contempt toward him, with love, that is, with generosity',[61] Spinoza famously criticises expressions of pity. A person 'who lives according to the dictates of reason', namely someone with fortitude, will strive not to be 'touched by pity', since he or she knows that 'all things follow from the necessity of the divine nature, and happen according to the eternal laws and rules of Nature'.[62] Indeed, pity represents a serious form of affective weakness, for it falsely implies inferiority on the part of a victim of misfortune and superiority on the part of one who pities. Consider a case of suffering due to social injustice. The preferable – but still problematic – emotional response would not be pity but indignation: love for the victim and hatred for the oppressor – and a determined effort to free the victim from this unjust situation. In the last instance, then, fortitude has to do with what Spinoza calls 'true human freedom'. For example, Spinoza writes that he does not seek

> to demonstrate separately all the properties of fortitude, much less that a person with fortitude hates no one, is angry with no one, and is not at all proud ... [and] above all considers that all things follow from the necessity of the divine nature, and hence, that whatever he thinks is troublesome and evil, and moreover, whatever seems immoral, dreadful, unjust, and dishonest, arises from the fact that he conceives the things themselves in a way which is disordered, mutilated, and confused. For this reason,

---

57 E4P37S1. Here Spinoza calls the affect 'honesty' (*honestas*).
58 In Def Aff 43 Spinoza also refers to this form of generosity as 'humanity' (*humanitas*), which he defines as 'the desire to do what pleases other persons and to abstain from what displeases them'.
59 Laux 1993, p. 225.
60 In E5P41 Spinoza explicitly links morality and religion to courage and generosity. Indeed, Negri (1991, pp. 165–6) has proposed that Spinoza lays out a materialist 'morality of generosity'.
61 E4P46.
62 E4P50C.

he strives most of all to conceive things as they are in themselves, and to remove the obstacles to true knowledge, like hatred, anger, envy, mockery, pride, and the rest of the things we have noted in the preceding pages. And so ... he strives, as far as he can, to act well and rejoice.[63]

'To act well and to rejoice' is not simply a private affair but has political implications. It is no accident that Spinoza's discussion of the relationship between fortitude and freedom occurs in a note to a proposition in which he is arguing that 'a person who is guided by reason is freer in a state, where he or she lives according to a common decision, than in solitude, where he or she obeys only himself or herself'.[64]

What then is the relevance of Spinoza's analysis of fortitude for radical political theory and practice? First of all, courage and generosity can emotionally bind persons together in pursuit of a collective project. As Macherey has argued, courage is a 'force of character' that is mutually reinforced and strengthened by generosity.[65] Moreover, since fortitude, courage, and generosity are active and joyous affects, their cultivation and stabilisation can help groups avoid the pitfalls of passive and sad affects, namely, such passions as fear and hope. They can bolster what Hasana Sharp has termed Spinoza's strategy of 'anti-fear'.[66] Finally, although Spinoza does not explicitly say as much, these affects can be, and are, imitated: those who find themselves in the company of courageous or generous persons are frequently led as well to take on these qualities.

But the question remains: Given the human tendency to affective fluctuation and weakness, wherein lies the source of our internal power? As Spinoza famously observes in his preface to the Fourth Part of the *Ethics*,

> human powerlessness to regulate and control the affects I call servitude. For persons who are subject to the affects are under the control, not of themselves, but of fortune, in whose power they so greatly are that often, though they see the better for themselves, they are still forced to follow the worse.

In a subsequent proposition, Spinoza offers a more precise and complete formulation of this ethical problem: 'I see and approve the better, but I follow the

---

63 E4P73S.
64 E4P73.
65 Macherey 1995, p. 386.
66 Sharp 2005.

worse (*video meliora, proboque, deteriora sequor*)'.[67] Scholars have traced this quote to the Roman poet Ovid, one of Spinoza's favourite classical authors,[68] but the underlying issue goes back even further to the philosophers Epictetus[69] and especially Aristotle,[70] namely, a contradiction in practical reasoning that arises in the case of a person who apparently knows what is in his or her best interest but nonetheless fails to act accordingly.[71] This is *akrasia*, or what philosophers have traditionally called incontinence or 'weakness of the will'.[72]

In the Marxist tradition, scant attention has been paid to the problem not of the ideological obscuring of what is in one's class interest, but why *even if one does know, one might still fail to act upon this interest*.[73] It is true enough that class interests often conflict with those based, for example, on race, gender, and nationality; but a deeper analysis of human moral psychology suggests that there is an affective undercurrent to political decision-making and acting. And this undercurrent is difficult to navigate successfully.

In light of Spinoza's rejection of 'absolute or free will',[74] the solution to the problem of ethical weakness cannot be found in simply consciously vowing to maintain sound judgment now and in the future. What is needed is more akin to the concrete exercises that Spinoza designated as 'remedies' (*remedia*) for the affects.[75] It is to these remedies that I now turn.

---

67 E4P17S.
68 In *Metamorphoses* VII, 20–1, Medea, the niece of the goddess Circe and granddaughter of the sun god Helios, cannot decide between obedience to her father, King Aeëtes of Colchis, and her love for the hero Jason (whom she will eventually marry).
69 See *Discourses* 2.26.4 (Epictetus 2014, p. 140).
70 See *Nicomachean Ethics*, Book 7. For Spinoza's critical relationship to Aristotle, see Manzini 2009.
71 Arguably, Spinoza also had in mind the following line in Paul's *Letter to the Romans* 7:19: 'For I do not do the good that I want, but the bad that I do not want – this I practice'.
72 Whether or not *akrasia* and weakness of will designate the same experience is a matter of a significant contemporary philosophical debate on which I take no position here. For introductions to the debate, however, see Holton 2009 and Mele 2012. For Spinoza's position on *akrasia*, see the following: Gagnon 2002, Lin 2006, Nadler 2006, pp. 223–5, and Manzini 2009, 92–4. For Spinoza's general conception of practical reasoning or prudence, see Matheron 1995 and Jaquet 1997.
73 Notable exceptions are Meyerson 1991 and Žižek 2008.
74 See his famous discussion in E2PP48–9. Steven Nadler provides a helpful commentary on Spinoza's rejection of freedom as understood in terms of volition or will; see Nadler 2006, pp. 185–9. See also Macherey 1997, pp. 367–407.
75 In his search for 'remedies' for excessive or misdirected expression of the affects, Spinoza takes his place in a longstanding tradition of philosophy as a practical pursuit embodying a distinctive way of life. See Hadot 1995.

3   Remedies for the Affects

In the Fifth Part of the *Ethics* Spinoza famously describes the means by which human passional servitude can partially be overcome by the power of reason to redirect bad affects.[76] As Bernard Vandewalle has compellingly argued, Spinoza conceived of philosophical activity as a kind of 'therapeutics of the body and mind' in both individual and transindividual respects.[77] Let us follow closely and carefully Spinoza's detailed discussion of this affective transition in his note to Proposition 10.[78]

Spinoza begins with the general claim that human beings have the ability to order and connect bodily affections and thereby to reduce the influence of bad affects. Since we lack a complete knowledge of our affects, however, the way to carry out this task is to

> conceive a correct rule of living, that is, sure principles of life, to commit them to memory, and to apply them constantly to the particular things frequently encountered in life. In this way our imagination will be largely affected by these principles, and we shall always have them ready.

Spinoza has in mind what we could call *common ethical notions* by which we can guide our daily conduct. Through imaginative exercises involving these rules, he argues, we can overcome such negative affects as hatred, fear, and anger. Essentially, we should engage in ethical *rehearsals* prior to acting in order to maintain our resolutions to carry out what we intend to do by resisting, and thereby avoid succumbing to, countervailing inclinations or temptations that weaken our capacity for effective practical reasoning.[79]

Consider first how we might resist and so weaken the power of hatred. For Spinoza the best way to proceed would be to repay hatred not with hatred but with generosity. This is easier said than done. Spinoza goes on to suggest that

---

76   See Pierre Macherey's masterful account in Macherey 1994.
77   Vandewalle 2011. Although Antonio Negri (1991, p. 262 n. 8) has been troubled that such talk of 'therapeutics' miscasts Spinoza as an individualist under the influence of late Renaissance, neo-Stoic, or Cartesian ideas, I agree with Vandewalle's response that there is a political dimension in Spinoza's philosophy specifically arising from 'medical or physiological inspiration' (Vandewalle [2011, 15 n. 1, 145–66]).
78   What follows is a detailed reconstruction of Spinoza's argument in E5P10S. For a commentary on this scholium, see Israel 2001, pp. 177–97.
79   The concept of 'rehearsal' is borrowed from Holton's (2009, pp. 123–5) account of how to strengthen one's willpower.

in order that we may always have this prescription of reason ready when it is needed, we ought to think about and meditate often on the common injuries of humanity, and how they may be warded off best by generosity. For if we join the image of an injury to the imagination of this principle, it will always be ready for us ... when an injury is done to us.

Another way to overcome hatred is to rely on 'the principle of our own true usefulness, and also of the good that follows from mutual friendship and common society, and keep in mind, moreover, that the highest serenity of spirit (*summa animi acquiescentia*) arises from the correct rule of living ... and that human beings, like others, act from the necessity of nature, then the injury, that is, the hatred usually arising from it, will occupy a minimal part of the imagination, and will easily be overcome'.

Spinoza next turns to anger, which he argues we can also control, at least in part. He maintains that 'if the anger that usually arises from the greatest injuries is not so easily overcome, it will still be overcome, though not without some fluctuation of spirit. And it will be overcome in far less time than if we had not meditated on these things beforehand in this way'.

Finally, Spinoza contends that we can minimise fear by strengthening the active affect of courage. In other words, he suggests that we should 'enumerate and often imagine the common dangers of life, and how they can best be avoided and overcome by the presence of spirit and fortitude'.

Yet another means by which Spinoza thinks that we can reduce the influence of bad affects is to 'pay attention to what good there is in each thing, so that in this way we are always determined to act from an affect of joy'. He then offers an example to which we shall return shortly:

> [I]f someone sees that he pursues glory too much, he should think of its correct use, the end of which it ought to be pursued, and by what means it can be acquired, not of its abuse and vanity, and the inconstancy of human beings, or other things of this kind, about which no one thinks unless out of a sick spirit. For it is by such thoughts that those who are most ambitious are most upset when they despair of attaining the honor they seek; and then they vomit forth anger, wanting to seem wise. It is certain that those who most desire glory are those who cry out most against its abuse and the vanity of the world.

After having identified other cases of ethical resentment that arise among those 'whose fortune is adverse and whose spirit is weak' (namely, the resentful poor and scorned lovers), Spinoza concludes this extraordinary passage by proposing that

> one who seeks to moderate his affects and appetites from the love of freedom alone will strive, as much as he can, to know the virtues and their causes, and to fill his mind with the gladness of spirit that arises from their true knowledge, and as little as possible to contemplate human vices, to denigrate human beings, and to enjoy a false appearance of freedom. And one who diligently observes these things – for they are not difficult – and practices them, will in a short span of time be able to direct most of one's actions under the command of reason.

Let us take stock of Spinoza's remedies for sad and passive affects by considering how he might advise that we overcome indignation and vainglory. We should not try directly to suppress or purge either affect but should instead try to reconstruct their complex underlying causes in as precise and complete a manner as possible.

Since indignation is a complex kind of hatred, it is necessary to counter its effect by strengthening the affect of generosity through reflection on the usefulness of social solidarity. Consider the case of a tyrannical ruler. The point of Spinoza's imaginative exercise would not be to alter our beliefs in such a way that we could somehow come to regard a tyrant as in fact a just ruler (or just misunderstood?), but to comprehend how and why the ruler governs in such an oppressive manner – the better to find an alternative to blind, incapacitating, and ineffective rage. As Laux has noted, by strengthening the active affect of fortitude (of which courage and generosity are the two varieties) we can stabilise and redirect passionate fluctuations.[80]

The affect of glory especially fluctuates between active and passive forms; in the worst cases, as we have seen, glory degenerates into outright ambition and vainglory. At the level of the individual, this would be bad enough, although perhaps merely amusing or pathetic. However, as we saw in the previous chapter, when a process of affective imitation has led the pursuit of political glory to seize the imagination of the multitude, the results of such fluctuation could well prove to be fatal, as Spinoza believed was the case during the mid-seventeenth-century English Civil War when the multitude 'gloried' in its achievement of removing Charles I but stopped short of uprooting all vestiges of monarchy and failed to establish a durable republic. How is it possible to avoid such a danger?

---

80   Laux 1993, pp. 223–26.

Recall that Spinoza urges us to 'pay attention to what good there is in each thing, so that in this way we are always determined to act from an affect of joy'. As a result, he cautions that we should think about the 'correct use' of glory, 'the end of which it ought to be pursued, and by what means it can be acquired'. Above all, as Spinoza reminds us, it is 'certain that those who most desire glory are those who cry out most against its abuse and the vanity of the world'. This doesn't imply, then, that the English multitude should not have risen up against the abuses of King Charles I. The multitude's pursuit of glory is not the problem. On the contrary, Spinoza warns only against the false allure of ambition and vainglory and so advocates a historical modesty about goals, means, and accomplishments. This is most assuredly not, as many commentators would have it, an example of Spinoza's political conservatism.[81] It is simply an indication of his desire to shore up and strengthen the faulty exercise of practical reasoning.

4 Conclusion

There remains an ideological struggle over Spinoza's possible political legacies for the twenty-first century. For example, Stephen Smith has also highlighted Spinoza's concept of fortitude. Smith argues that

> the willingness to view the human situation without recourse to either metaphysical comfort or to despair constitutes a new kind of bravery, what Spinoza calls *fortitudo* or strength of character ... Above all, *fortitudo* is the virtue of the free individual, someone who certainly understands the causal context of his or her situation but who uses this know-

---

81 At most we could speak of what Zourabichvili 2002 has called Spinoza's 'paradoxical conservatism', for it is crucial to note the political conjuncture in which Spinoza was writing. In 1670 the Dutch republic was in grave danger. Despite his opposition to the republic's aristocratic distortions, Spinoza did not want to shrink from its defence in the face of reaction arising from the House of Orange; indeed, he wanted to do his part to help consolidate and reinforce republican rule along more democratic lines. Moreover, he was well aware that the Orangists had no such democratic aspirations; on the contrary, they sought to reestablish monarchy and clamp down on freedom of religion, thought, and speech. With this in mind, it would be more accurate to say that Spinoza primarily feared not a democratic revolution but a monarchical *counter-revolution*. Unfortunately, though, just such a counter-revolution was to occur in 1672. *The moral*: even the best practical reasoning may confront a hostile balance of political forces. On the nature and extent of the Orangist partial restoration of the monarchy, see Israel 1995, pp. 807–62.

ledge to act resolutely and responsibly. Spinoza underscores especially the inner quality of this virtue. It is not dependent on the recognition or good opinion of others, but derives from the good opinion we have of ourselves. It could be called self-esteem properly understood. This is the first virtue of the new democratic individual.[82]

Smith certainly is right to emphasise the political relevance of fortitude for Spinoza. Nonetheless, he unjustifiably restricts the horizon of possible futures to liberal democracy. What I have tried to do is instead realign Spinoza with revolutionary Marxism. Spinoza would readily agree with the latter that individuals must continue to lack complete freedom apart from their collective emancipation.[83] But what Spinoza adds to this perspective is crucial: there can be no successful collective emancipation without the widespread participation of courageous and generous individuals.

In this light, it is worth recalling the 'Provisional Rules' drafted by Marx himself and that would be formally adopted in 1866 by the International Working Men's Association or 'First International'. We can clearly see in this document that the defining feature of Marx's mature politics was 'that the emancipation of the working classes must be conquered by the working classes themselves; that the struggle for the emancipation of the working classes means not a struggle for class privileges and monopolies, but for equal rights and duties, and the abolition of all class rule'.[84] Étienne Balibar has built on Marx's all-too-often forgotten 'principle of self-emancipation',[85] and insisted that not only does everyone in society have a fundamental 'right to politics', but also that no

---

[82] Smith 2003, pp. 200–1.
[83] I endorse Matheron's contention (1988, p. 613) that Spinoza sought a 'complete and definitive individual liberation in a community without restriction' and Montag's thesis (1999, p. xxi) that for Spinoza 'there can be no liberation of the individual without collective liberation'. See also André Tosel's insistence that emancipation is 'both collective and individual, since everyone takes up his or her responsibility by emancipating himself or herself from any authority that is not justifiable from the standpoint of the postulate of equal freedom'. In short, emancipation is 'both ethical and political, the reciprocity clause uniting ethics and politics' (Tosel 2016, p. 10).
[84] Marx (1974, p. 82). The best introductions to the First International and to Marx's (and less so Engels's) leadership role in building it as a democratic institution are Collins and Abramsky 1965; Nimtz 2000, pp. 169–251; and Léonard 2011.
[85] The idea of a 'principle of self-emancipation' is borrowed from Hal Draper's unrivalled studies; see Draper 1977–90 and Draper 1992, pp. 243–71. On the politics of self-emancipation, see also Löwy 2005 and Wood 2016, pp. 264–83. In Chapter 15 I shall return to, and consider at greater length, the topic of political self-emancipation.

one 'can be properly emancipated from outside or from above, but only by his or her own (collective) activity'.[86]

Self-emancipation is a laudable ideal; indeed, it provides a normative foundation for Marxist politics. But let me return one last time to the ethical question I have raised: what 'internal power' enables socialists and other activists to overthrow oppressive conditions by fostering working class self-emancipation? How can they overcome their various affective forms of internal weakness? How can they *be strong*? Spinoza's concept of fortitude offers no simple answer to these questions but only indicates the need to supplement concrete political analysis and strategic assessment of the balance of class forces with ethical practice. For, as the Marxist sociologist and Spinoza scholar Georges Friedmann once proposed in a journal entry dating from the period of the French Resistance to German occupation,

> this effort upon oneself is necessary; this ambition – just. Many are those who are completely absorbed in militant politics, preparation for the social Revolution. Rare, very rare, are those who, to prepare for the Revolution, want to make themselves worthy of it.[87]

In the last instance, of course, socialist transition 'is not a personal matter, but a question of which *class* is capable of manifesting courage and resolve'. Moreover, Lenin advanced a hypothesis: 'The only class capable of this is the proletariat'.

Capable, yes, one can agree with Lenin – but not without internal struggle by each for the external liberation of all.

---

86   Balibar 2002, p. 167.
87   Friedmann 1970, pp. 359–60. Friedmann's conception of politically engaged spiritual practices is dear to Pierre Hadot: see especially Hadot 1995, pp. 70, 81–2, 108 and Hadot 2002, pp. 276–7. It is worth noting that Friedmann's outstanding book on Spinoza and Leibniz (Friedmann 1974) was dedicated to the memory of Marc Bloch and Jean Cavaillès, both of whom were killed during the Resistance.

PART 2

Marxism and Contemporary Philosophy

∵

CHAPTER 8

Death and Life in Marx's *Capital*: an Ethical Investigation

> [W]e suffer not only from the living, but from the dead. Le mort saisit le vif!
> — KARL MARX[1]

⋮

> Unlike humanity which, according to Marx, poses only the problems which it can solve, life multiplies beforehand the solutions to problems of adaptation which could present themselves.
> — GEORGES CANGUILHEM[2]

⋮

In this chapter I would like to consider a missed encounter between Karl Marx and his French contemporary, Claude Bernard, the leading physiologist of the nineteenth century and the discoverer of the key biological concept of what has come to be known as 'homeostasis'.[3] Bernard was also arguably the first 'systems biologist'.[4] I also seek to build on recent research into Marx's ecological thinking undertaken by John Bellamy Foster, Paul Burkett, Ian Angus, and now Kohei Saito.[5] However, these ecosocialists have stressed the importance of Marx's own concept of metabolism in order to reconstruct and defend a Marxist theory of value and to better explain capitalist crisis in terms of metabolic rift; whereas in what follows I want to extend Marx's accounts of human alienation and exploitation biologically in terms of what I shall call

---

1 Marx 1990, p. 91.
2 Canguilhem 1991, p. 265.
3 Bernard himself did not coin the term; it first appeared in a 1926 article by the American physiologist Walter Bradford Cannon, on whom more at the end of this chapter.
4 Noble 2008.
5 See especially Foster, Clark, and York 2010; Burkett 2014;

the *homeostatic disruption* of living labour. Rather than pursue Marx's economic analysis and critique of capitalism, then, I am going to undertake a narrower and specifically *ethical* investigation of life and death in Volume I of *Capital*.

In this respect I strongly take exception to Saito's contention that those who 'emphasize the necessity of a normative critique of capitalism … miss Marx's point'. For Saito, after 1845 Marx was solely concerned to demonstrate that capitalism is 'not sustainable due to its destruction of the labor force and nature' and only aimed to understand 'the social and material relations of capitalism that structurally produce the misery of workers and exhaustion of natural resources'.[6] But there is no need for such a stark counter-position of theoretical objectives. Why not allow that the 'task of theory', to use Saito's terminology, is both to understand capitalism – its historical emergence, laws of development, and tendency to periodic crises – but also to evaluate its rightness or wrongness in terms of whether it enhances or frustrates human self-development and exercise of their capabilities? Even if Marx did not engage in such normative theory – although that is subject to debate – there is no reason why contemporary Marxists should shy away from it. The very terms that Saito uses – 'sustainable', 'destruction', 'misery', and 'exhaustion' – can and should be regarded from both descriptive and prescriptive sides. It is not enough to explain how capitalism functions; the very 'necessity' to criticise it arises from deep-seated moral intuition that (a) all is not well with capitalism and (b) there must be an alternative way to organise human productive capacities and resources under the 'conscious and planned control' of what Marx, using indisputably normative terminology, called 'freely associated men'.[7] At any rate, my investigation today remains ethical, even though it draws upon empirical support – not only from Saito but also from classical and contemporary biology and physiology.

1 Claude Bernard and Vitalism

Neither Marx nor Engels refers to Claude Bernard, at least as far as I have able to determine. This is surprising, given the former's extensive interest in science

---

6 Saito 2017, p. 271 n. 8. Saito identifies Axel Honneth and David Brudney but does not engage with Norman Geras, whose treatment of Marx on norms such as 'justice' and 'injustice' remains, in my view, unrivalled. See, for example, Geras 2017, pp. 3–57.
7 Marx 1990, pp. 172–3.

and Bernard's reputation as one of the greatest scientists of their historical conjuncture. Indeed, the contemporary American physiologist J. Scott Turner has recently argued that Bernard should be assigned a status coequal to Darwin.[8] Only indirectly has Bernard had an influence on Marxist thought – via the research of Georges Canguilhem, the twentieth-century French philosopher and historian of the life sciences who had a significant impact on Michel Foucault, Louis Althusser, Dominque Lecourt, and Pierre Macherey.[9] Canguilhem was an especially careful reader of Bernard and published several studies of the latter's thought.[10] For Canguilhem, Bernard was an exemplary 'philosophical physiologist'[11] who first introduced the term 'mechanism' into the language of scientists and philosophers but was not a 'mechanist'[12] nor, I would add, what Marxists would call a 'vulgar materialist'. As Canguilhem explains,

> Before Claude Bernard, biologists were forced to choose between identifying biology with physics, in the manner of the materialists and mechanists, or radically distinguishing between the two, in the manner of the French rationalists and German nature philosophers. The Newton of the living organism was Claude Bernard, in the sense that it was he who realized that living things provide the key to deciphering their own structures and functions. Rejecting both mechanism and vitalism, Bernard was able to develop techniques of biological experimentation suited to the specific nature of study.[13]

So, according to Canguilhem, Bernard was also not a 'vitalist' in the pejorative sense of someone who claims that there exists a mysterious cosmic force that infuses and distinguishes life from non-life. On the contrary: Bernard provided a scientific framework and research programme for understanding life in terms of organisms that are not fully explicable in terms of their physical-chemical constituent elements. In other words, we might say that Bernard was not a speculative vulgar vitalist but instead a working scientist whose research programme was to identify and carefully demarcate the 'external environment' (*milieu exterieur*) from what he called the 'internal environment' (*milieu*

---

8   Turner 2017, p. 25.
9   For Canguilhem's influence on Foucault and Althusser, see especially Roudinesco 2008, pp. 1–32. See also Lecourt 1975, pp. 162–86 and Macherey 1998, pp. 108, 161–87.
10 Canguilhem 2002, pp. 127–71; partially translated in Canguilhem 1994, pp. 261–82.
11 Canguilhem 1994, p. 261.
12 Canguilhem 1994, p. 272.
13 Canguilhem 1994, p. 267.

interieur).[14] Indeed, as Roy Porter has noted, 'it is through these equilibrating mechanisms ... that higher organisms achieved some autonomy within the law-governed determinism of the natural order'.[15]

As Turner explains, metabolism as a concept well designates the exchange between an organism and its external environment. But only homeostasis properly designates the complex self-regulation of an organism's internal environment.[16] For example, Bernard writes in his 1872 collection of lectures on 'general physiology' that

> life can only be conceived of by means of the conflict between the physical-chemical processes of the external environment and the vital properties of the organism reacting on each other. It is necessarily the concourse of these two factors; for, if one suppresses or modifies either the environment or the organism, life ceases or is altered right away. General physiology can be solidly established only on the condition of resting on this double basis; it must simultaneously consider in the organism the vital or physiological properties of living tissues and the physical-chemical properties of the environments under the influence of which the vitality of tissues becomes apparent. If physiologists remain too exclusively anatomists, physicians, or chemists, and rely only on an order of the form of knowledge we have indicated, or if they grant them too large a role, they necessarily make a false path, and are exposed in advance, regarding the phenomena of life, to erroneous or incomplete explanations. In a word, it would always be necessary to take account of two orders of conditions: firstly, the anatomical conditions of the organized matter given by the nature or form of physiological phenomena; secondly, the surrounding physical-chemical conditions that determine and govern vital manifestations.[17]

If vitalism seems an odd, even dangerous, physiological detour for Marxist philosophy to take, it is worth recalling Dominique Lecourt's insistence that for Canguilhem, one can see in vitalism 'the real and specific philosophy animating the progressive investigations in the biological sciences'. Vitalism, Lecourt continues, is

---

14   Canguilhem 1994, p. 268. On the influence of Bernard's notion of the internal environment, see Gross 1998.
15   Porter 2003, p. 83.
16   Turner 2017, pp. 11–23.
17   Bernard 1872, pp. 7–8. My translation.

a philosophy which works in the scientific practice and whose categories, far from being – or calling themselves – eternal, are constantly enriched by re-adjusting themselves to their 'object'.[18]

2 Metabolism and Homeostasis

Let us now see if Bernard's reworking of vitalism through his emphasis on the relative autonomy of an organism's internal environment can be used to clarify Marx's discussion in *Capital* of the dynamics of living labour. As William Clare Roberts has proposed, a mortal dialectic between living and dead labour unfolds in, and is fundamental to, Volume I:

> When capital employs labor, rather than ... natural life overflowing and enlivening the dead factors of production, the dead seizes hold of the living, reanimating itself to the detriment of the source of its animation. This is why Marx sees capital as a vampire.[19]

Moreover, early on in *Capital* Marx proposes that '... the present society is no solid crystal, but an organism capable of change, and constantly engaged in a process of change'.[20] But the change undergone by any living organism consists of two distinct processes: metabolism and homeostasis.

Turner distinguishes between metabolism, on the one hand, as 'order-generating chemistry' and, on the other, homeostasis as 'highly ordered, reliable, and reproducible'. He adds that 'bringing this orderliness reliably into being requires a high degree of specification, which must somehow be inherent in any presumptive living system'.[21] We might say, then, that these are *nested* concepts; in other words, metabolism is the condition of possibility for homeostasis to arise, but homeostasis is neither wholly explicable in terms of nor reducible to metabolism. Physical-chemical processes establish an external environment for organisms, but they do not determine the internal environment of biological processes of a given organism. In short, the latter processes are emergent and, as such, unfold in a relatively autonomous manner from the former processes.[22]

---

18 Lecourt 1975, pp. 179–80.
19 Roberts 2017, p. 137.
20 Marx 1990, p. 93.
21 Turner 2017, pp. 228–9.
22 For further discussion of the 'strange order' associated with homeostasis, see Damasio 2018.

In this regard, it is worth noting that although Saito provides a wealth of information regarding Marx's encounter with the research of his German contemporary, the chemist Justus von Liebig, he does not adequately discuss the latter's conception of the human body. As Roy Porter has summarised, for Liebig

> the body ... was an ensemble of chemical systems. Respiration brought oxygen into the body, where it mixed with starches to liberate energy, carbon dioxide and water. Nitrogenous matter was absorbed into muscle tissues; urine was the ultimate waste product, together with phosphates and assorted other chemical by-products. Chemical analysis of blood, sweat, tears and urine were undertaken, so as to quantify the equations in living organisms between food and oxygen consumption and energy production. Launching systematic investigation of nutrition and metabolism, Liebig and his school thus inaugurated what was to be called biochemistry.[23]

In other words, Liebig emphasised well what we have called an organism's *external* environment. However, he failed to address what Bernard would later call the *internal* environment. For the question is not just the metabolic one of what fuels the human body (and what wind up as its waste products) but the homeostatic one of *what holds it together as a body*.

3   Stresses on Living Labour

Saito has provided an invaluable road map from the early Marx to the later Marx, from a critique of capitalism based on the general notion of alienation to one based on the specific concept of metabolic rift. But even the concept of metabolic rift remains too broad and requires further specification. Metabolism and metabolic rift remain crucial aspects of an ecosocialist critique of capitalism and capitalist crises that damage the external conditions required for free human development on Earth. However, the toll taken on concrete human beings – what Marx poignantly calls their 'moral degradation'[24] – especially occurs in the production process, as the homeostasis of human organisms is disrupted through the varied stresses of physical, intellectual, and affective labour. For, on the one hand, as Marx argues, living human labour is

---

23   Porter 2003, pp. 79–80.
24   Marx 1990, p. 522.

the creator of use-values ... [and] ... is a condition of human existence which is independent of all forms of society; it is an eternal natural necessity which mediates the metabolism between man and nature, and therefore human life itself.[25]

Moreover, labour is

> a process between man and nature, a process by which man, through his own actions, mediates, regulates and controls the metabolism between himself and nature. He confronts the materials of nature as a force of nature. He sets in motion the natural forces which belong to his own body, his arms, legs, head and hands, in order to appropriate the materials of nature in a form adapted to his own needs. Through this movement he acts upon external nature and changes it, and in this way he simultaneously changes his own nature. He develops the potentialities slumbering within nature, and subjects the play of its forces to his own sovereign power.[26]

On the other hand, and in sharp contradiction, Marx scathingly observes that unless checked by workers' struggles and organisations,

> in its blind and measureless drive, its insatiable appetite for surplus labour, capital oversteps not only the moral but even the merely physical limits of the working day. It usurps the time for growth, development and healthy maintenance of the body. It steals the time required for the consumption of fresh air and sunlight. It haggles over the meal-times, where possible incorporating them into the production process itself, so that food is added to the worker as to a mere means of production, as coal is supplied to the boiler, and grease and oil to the machinery. It reduces the sound sleep needed for the restoration, renewal and refreshment of the vital forces to the exact amount of torpor essential to the revival of an absolutely exhausted organism. It is not the normal maintenance of labour-power which determines the limits of the working day here, but rather the greatest possible daily expenditure of labour-power, no matter how diseased, compulsory and painful it may be, which determines the limits of the workers' period of rest. Capital asks no questions about the

---

25   Marx 1990, p. 133.
26   Marx 1990, p. 283.

length of life of labour-power. What interests it is purely and simply the maximum of labour-power that can be set in motion in a working day. It attains this objective by shortening the life of labour-power, in the same way as a greedy farmer snatches more produce from the soil by robbing it of its fertility.[27]

To reestablish the dignity of freely associated labour, then, would require not only healing the metabolic rift between humanity and nature and the social metabolic rift among persons but also restoring human homeostasis in order to insure fair opportunity for the fulfilment of human 'purpose and desire'[28] in the workplace and throughout the larger society.

Yet the growing threat to human homeostasis has arisen not only directly at the point of production – whether it be a factory, office, field, or mine – as the result of stress and exposure to toxic materials. Indirectly, climate change poses the prospect of deadly heat that exceeds human thermoregulatory capacity. According to a new systematic review of medical literature by researchers at the University of Hawai'i at Manoa, there are at least 27 different 'physiological pathways' in which a heat wave can kill a human being, and by 2100 three-quarters of humanity will be exposed to this risk.[29] The authors conclude that 'only the rapid reduction of greenhouse gases paired with large economic investment in adaptation will help us to escape the health risks of heat waves'.[30] The moral is that effective ecosocialist critique of fossil capitalism must focus on the disruption to individual and collective homeostasis as well to the rift in social and natural metabolisms.

4   Conclusion: Reclaiming the Body's Wisdom

Let me conclude with another reference to physiology, this time to the great American scientist Walter Bradford Cannon. In 1932, at the onset of the US Depression, Cannon published a remarkable book: *The Wisdom of the Body*.[31] He expanded on Bernard's and others' research to identify in detail 'the ability of living beings to maintain their own constancy'.[32] As Cannon argued

---

27 Marx 1990, pp. 375–7.
28 To echo the title of Turner 2017.
29 Mora et al. 2017b. See also Mora et al. 2017a.
30 Mora et al. 2017b, p. 1.
31 Cannon 1927.
32 Cannon 1927, p. 20.

the coordinated physiological processes which maintain most of the steady states in the organism are so complex and so peculiar to living beings ... that I have suggested a special designation for these states, homeostasis. The word does not imply something set and immobile, a stagnation. It means a condition – a condition which may vary, but which is relatively constant.[33]

For my purposes here, what is most compelling about *The Wisdom of the Body* is its epilogue, which considers 'Relations of Biological and Social Homeostasis'. It turns out that Cannon was a 'socialist and militant antifascist'[34] who insisted that

just as in the body physiologic, so in the body politic, the whole and its parts are mutually dependent; the welfare of the large community and the welfare of its individual members are reciprocal.[35]

It is worth noting that although Cannon was a close friend of, and benefactor to, Ivan Pavlov,[36] such a dialectical formulation is utterly foreign to the latter's mechanistic research, which regarded both non-humans and humans as automata, whose actions, in Evald Ilyenkov's helpful summary,

were determined in advance by ready-made structures, internally inherent to it, and by the distribution of the organs located within its body. These actions, therefore, could and had to be completely explained by the following scheme: external effect → movement of the inner parts of the body → external reaction.[37]

Yet, Ilyenkov continues,

this scheme is not applicable to man because in him ... there is a supplementary link in the chain of events ... that powerfully interferes with it, forces its way into it, breaking the ready-made chain and then joining its disconnected ends together in a new way, each time in a different way, each time in accordance with new conditions and circumstances in

---

33   Cannon 1927, p. 24.
34   Kuznick 1988.
35   Cannon 1967, p. 310.
36   On Cannon's personal and scientific relationship with Pavlov, see Todes 2014, *passim*.
37   Ilyenkov 2009, p. 26.

the external action not previously foreseen by any prepared scheme and this supplementary link is 'reflection' or 'consideration'. But a 'reflection' is that activity (in no way outwardly expressed) which directs *reconstruction of the very schemes of the transformation* of the initial effect into response. *Here the body itself is the object of its own activity.*[38]

Deploying his own distinctive physiological idiom, Cannon envisioned a self-governing social order yet to be constructed:

> The main service of social homeostasis would be to support bodily homeostasis. It would therefore release the highest activities of the nervous system for adventure and achievement. With essential needs assured, the priceless unessentials could be freely sought.[39]

In response to the objection that 'social stabilisation would tend toward dull monotony, that the excitements of uncertainty would be lacking', Cannon emphasised that

> just as social stabilization would foster the stability, both physical and mental, of the members of the social organism, so likewise it would foster their higher freedom, giving them serenity and leisure, which are the primary conditions for wholesome recreation, for the discovery of a satisfactory and invigorating social milieu, and for the discipline and enjoyment of individual aptitudes.[40]

This is a striking illustration of physiology in the service of Marx's fundamental normative principle that the 'free development of each is the condition for the free development of all'. As a result, ecosocialists today should embrace Cannon's 'biopolitical'[41] vision and advocate not only a healing of the metabolic rift but a restoration of disrupted homeostasis through self-emancipatory collective action.

---

38 Ilyenkov 2009, p. 27.
39 Cannon 1927, p. 323.
40 Cannon 1927, p. 324.
41 See Bidet 2016 on the importance of Marx's biopolitical conception of the body in *Capital*.

CHAPTER 9

Hegel or Spinoza: Substance, Subject, and Critical Marxism*

Slavoj Žižek has wondered if it is possible *not* to love Spinoza. Indeed, he asks, 'Who can be against a lone Jew who, on top of it, was excommunicated by the "official" Jewish community itself? One of the most touching expressions of this love is how one often attributes to him almost divine capacities – like Pierre Macherey, who, in his otherwise admirable *Hegel ou Spinoza* (arguing against the Hegelian critique of Spinoza), claims that one cannot avoid the impression that Spinoza had already read Hegel and, in advance, answered his reproaches'.[1] Although Žižek is badly mistaken about Macherey's objective in his book and related articles,[2] one cannot avoid the impression that a century ago Lenin had already read Žižek and, in advance, answered the latter's numerous reproaches against the contemporary Marxist turn to Spinoza.

Buried in Lenin's *Philosophical Notebooks* are his excerpts from Vladimir Mikhailovich Shulyatikov's 1908 book, *The Justification of Capitalism in Western European Philosophy*.[3] In what evidently passed at the time for a serious Marxist history of philosophy, Shulyatikov had contended that

> [W]hen Spinoza died, as is well known, *the fine fleur of the Dutch bourgeoisie with great pomp accompanied* the hearse that carried his remains. And if we become more closely acquainted *with his circle of **acquaintances and correspondents***, we again meet with the fine fleur of the bourgeoisie – and not only of Holland but of the entire world ... *The bourgeoisie revered Spinoza*, their bard. Spinoza's conception of the world is the *song of triumphant capital, of all-consuming, all-centralising capital*. There is no being, there are no things, apart from the single substance; there can be no existence for producers apart from the large-scale manufacturing enterprise ...

---

* This chapter has been previously published in *Crisis & Critique* 1.3, 2014, pp. 355–69.
1 Žižek 2004, p. 33.
2 See Macherey 1992 and 1998.
3 Lenin 1972, pp. 486–502.

To Shulyavtivich's self-assured conclusion that 'Spinoza's conception of the world is the *song of triumphant capital, of all-consuming, all-centralising capital*', Lenin caustically replied with a single word in the margin of his notebook: 'infantile'.[4] It was as if Lenin were rebuking in advance Žižek's crass remark that Spinoza embodies 'the ideology of late capitalism'![5] How can Marxists avoid the false dilemma of either loving Spinoza, or hating him? Perhaps by trying to understand Spinoza, by reading him carefully and responsibly – and by critically appropriating some of his concepts.

1   Žižek and Badiou against Spinoza

In several dense pages of his monumental book *Less than Nothing: Hegel and the Shadow of Dialectical Materialism*,[6] Žižek has refined his earlier criticisms of the Marxist appropriation of Spinoza by seeking to identify the 'precise point' at which he thinks 'the contrast between Hegel and Spinoza appears at its "purest"'. Žižek begins with his own Lacanian variation on Hegel's famous complaint: 'Spinoza's Absolute is a Substance which "expresses" itself in its attributes and modes without the subjectivizing *point de capiton* [quilting point]'.[7] Žižek then addresses the limitations of what he takes to be Spinoza's 'famous proposition' that *omnis determinatio est negatio* ('all determination is negation'), which 'may sound Hegelian' but is in fact 'anti-Hegelian', despite two possible ways to understand what is negated, and how. If, on the one hand, negation

> refers to the Absolute itself, it makes a negative-theological point: every positive determination of the Absolute, every predicate we attribute to it, is inadequate, fails to grasp its essence and thus already negates it.

If, on the other hand,

> it refers to particular empirical things, it makes a point about their transient nature: every entity delimited from others by a particular determination will sooner or later join the chaotic abyss out of which it arose, for every particular determination is a negation not only in the sense that

---

4   Lenin 1972, p. 493. For a brief commentary, see Kline 1952, p. 21.
5   Žižek 1993, pp. 216–19.
6   Žižek 2012.
7   Žižek 2012, p. 367.

it will involve the negation of other particular determinations ... but in a more radical sense that it refers to its long-term instability.[8]

Žižek reconstructs a Hegelian criticism of these two possible interpretations of negation as follows:

> the Absolute is not a positive entity persisting in its impermeable identity beyond the transient world of finite things; the only true Absolute is nothing but this very process of the rising and passing away of all particular things.

But, Žižek continues, this would mean that, according to Hegel, Spinoza's philosophy resembles

> a pseudo-Oriental Heraclitean wisdom concerning the eternal flow of the generation and corruption of all things under the sun – in more philosophical terms, such a vision relies on the univocity of being.[9]

Žižek allows that one could defend Spinoza along the lines of what Althusser called 'aleatory materialism' by claiming that Substance

> is not simply the eternal generative process which continues without any interruption or cut, but that it is, on the contrary, the universalization of a cut or fall (*clinamen*): Substance is nothing but the constant process of 'falling' (into determinate/particular entities); everything there is, is a fall ... There is no Substance which falls, curves, interrupts the flow, etc.; substance simply *is* the infinitely productive capacity of such falls/cuts/interruptions, they are its only reality.

According to such an aleatory materialist defence of Spinoza, 'Substance and *clinamen* (the curvature of the Substance which generates determinate entities)' would 'directly coincide; in this ultimate speculative identity, Substance is nothing but the process of its own "fall", the negativity that pushes towards productive determination ...'[10]

Not surprisingly, Žižek rejects this move because, he contends, it would simply 'renormalize' the *clinamen* and, as a result, turn it 'into its opposite', for

---

8   Žižek 2012, pp. 367–8.
9   Žižek 2012, p. 368.
10 Žižek 2012, p. 368.

if all that there is are interruptions or falls, then the key aspect of surprise, of the intrusion of an unexpected contingency, is lost, and we find ourselves in a boring, flat universe whose contingency is totally predictable and necessary.[11]

Žižek seeks, then, not to 'radicalise' Spinoza by conceiving of substance as 'nothing but the process of *clinamen*', for in such a case, he contends, 'Substance remains One, a Cause immanent to its effects'. Instead, along Hegelian-Lacanian lines he seeks to 'take a step further' and 'reverse the relationship: there is no Substance, only the Real as the absolute gap, non-identity, and particular phenomena (modes) are Ones, so many attempts to stabilize this gap'.[12]

Žižek then sums up what he regards as the stark contrast between Spinoza and Hegel:

> In contrast to Spinoza, for whom there is no Master-Signifier enacting a cut, marking a conclusion, 'dotting the i', but just a continuous chain of causes, the Hegelian dialectical process involves cuts, sudden interruption of the continuous flow, reversals which retroactively restructure the entire field. In order to properly understand this relationship between a continual process and its cuts or ends, we should ignore the stupid notion of a 'contradiction' in Hegel's thought between method (endless process) and system (end); it is also not sufficient to conceive cuts as moment within an encompassing process, internal differences which arise and disappear.[13]

Žižek concludes with 'a parallel with the flow of speech'. Just as 'the flow of speech cannot go on indefinitely', there has to be something like 'the point that concludes a sentence', for 'it is only the dot at the end that retroactively fixes or determines the meaning of the sentence'. And yet, he adds, this dot cannot be 'a simple fixation which removes all risk, abolishing all ambiguity and openness'. Rather,

> the dotting itself, its cut ... releases – sets free – meaning and interpretation: the dot always occurs contingently, as a surprise, it generates a surplus – why *here?* What does this mean?[14]

---

11   Žižek 2012, pp. 368–9.
12   Žižek 2012, p. 377.
13   Žižek 2012, pp. 369.
14   Žižek 2012, p. 369.

How should one respond to Žižek's identification of the 'precise point' at which Hegel's philosophy diverges from Spinoza's? To begin with, it is astonishing that in Žižek's 1000-page work on Hegel there is not a single reference to Macherey. Although as of 2004 Žižek had clearly read *Hegel ou Spinoza*[15] (when *Organs without Bodies* was published),[16] his engagement with Macherey's book had lapsed by 2012.

As a result, Žižek's treatment of Spinoza's phrase *omnis determinatio est negatio* turns out to be irrelevant, since, as Macherey already ably demonstrated in *Hegel or Spinoza*, not only did Spinoza never use this exact phrase, but Hegel misquoted him, took the sentence Spinoza did use *once* in a letter – not a published work – out of context, and then seriously misconstrued its meaning.[17] Let us focus instead on Žižek's contention that, unlike Hegel, Spinoza's philosophy offers no way to grasp substance as subjectivity and so alternates between either 'a pseudo-Oriental Heraclitean wisdom concerning the eternal flow of the generation and corruption of all things under the sun' or 'a boring, flat universe whose contingency is totally predictable and necessary'. Neither is an appealing option, to say the least.

But Žižek is not alone in pitting Hegel against Spinoza with respect to the problem of substance that has not yet become subject. In *Logics of Worlds* Alain Badiou has likewise argued that Hegel's great philosophical insight can be summed up in three principles:
– The only truth is that of the Whole.
– The Whole is a self-unfolding, and not an absolute-unity external to the subject.
– The Whole is the immanent arrival of its own concept.
This means, for Badiou,

> that the thought of the Whole is the effectuation of the Whole itself. Consequently, what displays the Whole within thought is nothing other than the path of thinking, that is its method. Hegel is the methodical thinker of the Whole.[18]

By contrast, Badiou contends,

> Spinoza saw perfectly that every thought must presuppose the Whole as containing determinations in itself, by self-negation. But he failed to grasp

---

15   Now available in English translation as Macherey 2011b.
16   Žižek 2004.
17   Macherey 2011b, pp. 113–213. See also Melamed 2012.
18   Badiou 2009, p. 142.

the *subjective* absoluteness of the Whole, which alone guarantees integral immanence.[19]

Badiou's own Hegelian accusation that Spinoza 'failed to grasp the *subjective* absoluteness of the Whole' misses the mark, though. Spinoza called his major work *Ethics* for good reason: his overriding objective was how to understand and show how to attain individual and collective freedom and happiness – not to grasp the 'subjective absoluteness of the Whole'. Indeed, in the opening lines of Part 2 of the *Ethics* Spinoza warned that he was concerned not with the 'infinitely many things' that necessarily follow 'in infinitely many ways' from his conception of God as 'eternal and infinite being' but only with what 'can lead us as if by the hand to knowledge of the human mind and its highest blessedness'. As a result, Spinoza's 'metaphysics in the service of ethics'[20] was less concerned with mereology – the study of parts and wholes[21] – than, as Bernard Vandewalle has compellingly argued, with refashioning philosophical activity as a kind of 'therapeutics of the body and mind' in both individual and transindividual respects.[22]

To claim, then, as Badiou and Žižek have, that Spinoza failed to address the problem of subjectivity is to ignore the last four parts of the *Ethics* that concern the human mind, its relationship to the body and the external world, the nature of affects and their power, and the extent to which reason can moderate, stabilise, redirect, or transform passive into active affects in pursuit of individual and collective freedom. Since Žižek and Badiou offer only the barest of textual

---

19 Badiou 2009, p. 142.
20 To use A.W. Moore's felicitous designation. See Moore 2012, pp. 44–66.
21 It is worth noting, however, that Spinoza did address the parts/whole relation in a letter to Henry Oldenberg, dated 20 November 1665, in which he proposed a famous and striking analogy between human beings 'living in our part of nature' and a 'tiny worm living in the blood'. Just as such a worm 'would regard each individual particle of the blood as a whole, not a part ... and ... would have no idea as to how all the parts are controlled by the overall nature of the blood', so too do human beings fail to grasp that 'every body, in so far as it exists as modified in a definite way, must be considered as a part of the whole universe'. Moreover, just as the motion of blood itself is affected by external forces, and is only a part of a larger whole, so too the nature of the universe is 'absolutely infinite' and 'its parts are controlled by the nature of this infinite power [*potentia*] in infinite ways and are compelled to undergo infinite variations' (Ep 32).
22 Vandewalle 2011. Although Antonio Negri (1991, p. 262 n. 8) has been troubled that such talk of 'therapeutics' miscasts Spinoza as an individualist under the influence of late Renaissance, neo-Stoic, or Cartesian ideas, I agree with Vandewalle's response that there is a political dimension in Spinoza's philosophy specifically arising from 'medical or physiological inspiration' (Vandewalle 2011, pp. 15 n. 1, 145–66).

support for their criticisms of Spinoza, we should examine what the latter actually wrote about the nature of the self and consider what has caused Žižek and Badiou to miss, evade, or distort something important.

As Macherey has maintained, Hegel's philosophical problematic hindered him from grasping what Spinoza actually wrote; for Hegel, Spinoza's philosophy played 'the role of an indicator or a mirror, on whose surface conceptions which are apparently the most foreign to his own by contrast trace their contours'.[23] It would appear that Spinoza's philosophy continues to serve as a distorting mirror for Badiou and Žižek, who have engaged less frequently and less carefully with Spinoza's text than did Hegel. But in order to see how this distortion has occurred, allow me to make a brief detour via two tantalising references by Michel Foucault to Spinoza's early work, the *Treatise on the Emendation of the Intellect*.

2   Hegelian Subject or Spinozist Self?

In his *History of Madness* Foucault characterises Spinoza's project in the *Treatise* as

> a sort of ethical wager, which is won when it is discovered that the exercise of freedom is accomplished in the concrete fullness of reason, which, by its union with nature taken in its totality, is access to a higher form of nature … The freedom of the wager culminates in a unity where it disappears as a choice to reappear as a necessity of reason.[24]

Commenting on Foucault, Macherey has observed that Spinoza develops 'the idea according to which the individual has in itself no other reality than that communicated through its relation to the totality to which one can also say that it "belongs", a relation that governs its ethical destination'. Foucault clearly didn't embrace Spinoza's naturalism but set forth instead an idea of 'historical belonging' that would be 'irreducible to the universal laws of a nature considered in general'. Yet, according to Macherey, Foucault's reading of Spinoza enables us to ponder the meaning of Spinoza's 'naturalism'. By 'eternity of substance', Spinoza does not have in mind

---

23   Macherey 1998, p. 25.
24   Foucault 2006, p. 140.

the permanence of a nature already given in itself, in an abstract and static manner, according to the idea of 'substance which has not yet become subject' developed by Hegel regarding Spinoza; but, to the extent that this substance is inseparable from its productivity, that it manifests itself nowhere else than in the totality of its modal realizations, in which it is absolutely immanent, it is a nature that is itself produced in a history, and under conditions that the latter necessarily attaches to it. Thus for the soul to attain the understanding of its union with the whole of nature is also to recognize historically what confers on it its own identity, and it is in a certain way, then, to respond to the question 'Who am I now?'[25]

Foucault equally allows us to see that Spinoza advocates an 'ethics of freedom' that would not be 'enclosed within the framework and categories of a moral speculation, itself developed in terms of subjection to a law, whether the latter acts from inside or outside the individual it directs'.[26]

In one of his last series of lectures – those concerning the 'Hermeneutics of the Subject' – Foucault returns to Spinoza's *Treatise* and argues that

> in formulating the problem of access to the truth Spinoza linked the problem to a series of requirements concerning the subject's very being: In what aspects and how must I transform my being as subject? What conditions must I impose on my being as subject so as to have access to the truth, and to what extent will this access to the truth give me what I seek, that is to say the highest good, the sovereign good?[27]

Although Foucault rightly draws attention to Spinoza's distinctive 'practice of the self', one must admit that this self is a peculiar one – at least from the standpoint of Hegel's account of subjectivity – for after insisting that 'true knowledge proceeds from cause to effect', Spinoza notes that 'this is the same as what the ancients said ... except that so far as I know they never conceived the soul ... as acting according to certain laws, like a spiritual automaton'.[28]

Although Spinoza's metaphor of a *spiritual automaton* might be philosophically unsettling, there need be nothing reductive or mechanistic about a com-

---

25   Macherey 1998, p. 134.
26   Macherey 1998, p. 133.
27   Foucault 2005, p. 27. Foucault is concerned explicitly only with the first nine paragraphs of the *Treatise*, but I believe his observation applies equally to Spinoza's project in the *Ethics*.
28   TdIE 85.

posite self without a unified subject.[29] As Macherey has ably demonstrated, Spinoza's point was simply that the 'movement of thought proceeds from the same necessity as all reality', and so the 'absolutely natural character of the process must be mastered according to its own laws'.[30] Indeed, in this respect Spinoza anticipated Hegel, for 'in establishing a necessary relationship between knowledge ... and the process of its production, he permits it to grasp itself as absolute and thus to grasp the absolute. Taken outside this objective development, knowledge is nothing more than the formal representation of a reality for which it can provide only an abstract illusion'.[31] Yet Spinoza's position should not be confused with Hegel's. By making thought an attribute of substance, Spinoza construed knowledge as an absolutely objective process without a subject and freed its internal causal movement from any teleological presupposition.[32]

In sum, the soul operates as a *spiritual automaton* because it is 'not subjugated to the free will of a subject whose autonomy would be to all extents and purposes fictive'.[33] Moreover, ideas are not images or passive representations of an external reality that they would more or less resemble. As Macherey compellingly argues, Spinoza rejected the Cartesian conception of ideas as 'mute paintings on canvas'[34] and defended the perspective that all ideas are *acts* that

> always affirm something in themselves, according to a modality that returns to their cause, that is, in the last instance the substance that expresses itself in them in the form of one of their attributes, thought.[35]

The upshot is that 'there is no subject of knowledge, not even of truth beneath these truths, that prepares its form in advance, because the idea is true in itself – singularly, actively, affirmatively, in the absence of all extrinsic determinations that submit it to an order of things or the decrees of the creator'.[36]

Not surprisingly, Spinoza's perspective was unpalatable to Hegel, who cautioned in his *Lectures on the History of Philosophy* that

---

29   Indeed, Spinoza's conception of the self anticipates the empirical results of contemporary neuroscience. See Hood 2012.
30   Macherey 2011b, p. 59.
31   Macherey 2011b, p. 59.
32   Macherey 2011b, p. 59.
33   Macherey 2011b, p. 63.
34   E2p43s.
35   Macherey 2011b, p. 63.
36   Macherey 2011b, p. 63.

if thinking stops with ... substance, there is then no development, no life, no spirituality or activity. So we can say that with Spinozism everything goes into the abyss but nothing emerges from it.[37]

Hegel likewise writes in Part Three of the *Encyclopedia of the Philosophical Sciences* that

> as regards *Spinozism*, it is to be noted against it that in the judgement by which the mind constitutes itself as *I*, as free subjectivity in contrast to determinacy, the mind emerges from substance, and philosophy, when it makes this judgement the absolute determination of mind, emerges from Spinozism.[38]

Hegel's point is that Spinoza could not adequately account for what is distinctive about subjectivity, namely, its full-fledged *emergence* from substance. As Terry Pinkard puts it,

> the revolution in modern science was an essential part of the modern revolution in 'spirit', in our grasp of what it means to be human, just as the revolution in spirit's grasp of itself correspondingly called for a revolution in our theoretical stance to nature.

As a result, then, 'to grasp the revolution in spirit requires, so Hegel thinks, grasping just what nature was so that it would become intelligible how it could be that spirit had to define itself as a self-instituted liberation from nature'.[39] From Hegel's perspective, Spinoza's conception of the mind remains mired in substance and could not attain genuinely free self-development. But what is the theoretical price to be paid for Hegel's extrication of subjectivity from substance?

Arguably, Hegel's conception of subjectivity in its autonomous unfolding winds up losing its moorings in the body and the external world. Spinoza's conception of selfhood as inextricably caught up in causal relations, by contrast, provides the basis for an *ecologically embedded* perspective that continues to be both more plausible and useful for political theory and practice.[40] Moreover, Spinoza better describes and analyses the affective complexities of our indi-

---

37 Hegel 2009, p. 122.
38 EL 415; see Hegel 2007, p. 156.
39 Pinkard 2005, p. 30.
40 See Sharp 2011.

vidual and collective lives, in particular, the drama of what he called the 'imitation of the affects'.[41]

Žižek wrongly characterises Spinoza's conception of substance as a mere 'container' for the multiple identities that comprise our selves.[42] Or if we grant Žižek his metaphor, then substance serves at most as a very porous and leaky vessel that we would have to describe as an *affectively permeable* container. Although Žižek rightly cautions us not to play the speculative game of 'Spinoza anticipated such and such',[43] there remains a striking affinity between Spinoza's treatment in Part 2 of the *Ethics* of the composition of hard, soft, and fluid bodies and contemporary scientific research into 'sensitive matter' and the remarkable dual-affinity properties of such items as gels, foams, liquid crystals, and cell membranes.[44] Following Spinoza, perhaps Marxists today should seek to discern the contours of an 'amphiphilic'[45] self that lies between substance and subject – a *sensitive* materialist dialectic, if you will.

3 Conclusion: Hegel's Logic and Spinoza's Ethics

There can be no question of forcing contemporary Marxists to choose between Hegel and Spinoza.[46] His critics notwithstanding, Macherey has never opposed a 'good' Spinoza to a 'bad' Hegel but has instead tried to 'show how an insurmountable philosophical divergence' arose between them that generated misunderstanding when their two philosophies confronted each other.[47] Indeed, the very reason that Hegel failed to comprehend Spinoza was because the latter's philosophy was at work in his own and posed an internal threat that continually had to be warded off or conceptually contained.[48]

---

41 For an overview of Spinoza's concept of affective imitation, see Macherey 1995, pp. 183–262.
42 Žižek 2012, p. 381.
43 See his well-directed criticism in this regard of such prominent neuroscientists as Antonio Damasio (Žižek 2012, p. 717 n. 4).
44 See Mitov 2012.
45 Mitov's term for matter composed of dual-affinity molecules, for example, the lecithin in egg yolks without whose mediation between water and oil mayonnaise would not be stable (Mitov 2012, pp. 5–11).
46 Didn't Žižek (2000) himself once respond to the false alternative between postmodernism and Marxism with an insistent 'Yes, please!'
47 Macherey 1998, p. 25.
48 For a penetrating account of how 'Spinoza's philosophy is already realized in Hegel as the true other which he has already become', see Montag 2012.

Nonetheless, there remains a question of emphasis. Hegelian grandiosity needs to be tempered with Spinozist modesty. It is well and good to lay claim to a broad vision of the historical process, and strongly to believe that we are oriented in a rational direction: towards ever-greater freedom for all humanity. But actual historical transformation on the ground looks very different – messy, uneven, often boring, frustratingly slow – and then at other times so accelerated and intense that one may suffer from disorientation or even lapse into what Spinoza termed 'vain glory'.[49] How is it possible to cultivate and sustain such virtues as fidelity, courage, hope, and endurance in the face of the personal risks arising from activism? To answer such questions we must look to Spinoza not Hegel.

Žižek has argued that Marxists should 'proceed like Lenin in 1915 when, to ground anew revolutionary practice, he returned to Hegel – not to his directly political writings, but, primarily, to his *Logic*'.[50] One shouldn't disparage Lenin for his preferred choice of reading material when he retreated momentarily to reflect on the betrayal by so many socialist leaders of their presumed internationalist ideals and their political capitulation at the onset of a barbarous World War I. Moreover, Lenin was making an important philosophical intervention against the prevailing neo-Kantianism of the Second International.[51] But perhaps – just perhaps – he should also have taken the time to read Spinoza's *Ethics*. If he had done so, in the margin opposite his famous note 'Leaps! Leaps! Leaps!' he might have added Spinoza's Latin motto: '*Caute! Caute! Caute!*'[52]

---

49 In E4p58s.
50 Žižek 2004, p. 32.
51 See Anderson 2007 and Kouvelakis 2007.
52 See Lenin 1972, p. 123. For a discussion of the importance of the Hegelian idea of 'leaps', see Bensaid 2007. A literal translation of '*Caute!*' is 'Be careful!' but a looser 'Watch your step!' would probably be more appropriate.

CHAPTER 10

Contradictions of Hyperreality: Baudrillard, Žižek, and Virtual Dialectics*

> I see where [Žižek is] coming from, his vision of things, a particular kind of perception. I share the *'feeling'* of what he writes, whilst not agreeing with him at all. You can question it all: he wants to keep a sort of dialectic, there's still Marxism in there somewhere. He works with Jameson and people like him, with American neo-Marxists. Not forgetting the form of Lacanian real he uses. All of that is mixed in together, and there are all sorts of strange complexities. I don't know whether you can separate it all out, but it's very interesting – being very much in phase and also totally out of phase.
> ∴ — JEAN BAUDRILLARD[1]

∴

In Section Eight of his *Discourse on Metaphysics*[2] G.W. Leibniz asserts that

> all true predication has some basis in the nature of things and that, when a proposition is not an identity, that is, when the predicate is not explicitly contained in the subject, it must be contained in it virtually (*virtuellement*). That is what the philosophers call *in-esse*, when they say that the predicate is in the subject. Thus the subject term must always contain the predicate term, so that one who understands perfectly the notion of the subject would also know that the predicate belongs to it.[3]

Several sections later Leibniz specifies that

---

* This chapter has been previously published in *The International Journal of Žižek Studies* 10.1, 2016, pp. 88–100.
1 Hegarty 2004, p. 140.
2 Citations from *Discourse on Metaphysics* (DM) are based on Leibniz 1991. I have also consulted the superb French critical edition edited by Michel Fichant; see Leibniz 2004.
3 Leibniz 1991, p. 8. See also DM 13, 26 on 'virtual containment'.

everything that happens to a person is already contained virtually (*virtuellement*) in his nature or not, just as the properties of a circle are contained in its definition.[4]

In other words, using the classical logic available to Leibniz,[5] we may formalise the logic of predication as consisting of statements having the following structure:

S is P.

(Here 'S' stands for a given subject and 'P' stands for a given predicate.) Using a modern example, one could note that

1. Dr. Martin Luther King, Jr. was murdered on April 4, 1968.

From a Leibnizian perspective, the fact of King's assassination was 'virtually contained' in his soul from the beginning of time and space. Indeed, ontologically speaking, for Leibniz whatever is actual is only the realisation of virtual possibilities that have always existed in the mind of God. In this sense, we can say Leibniz held a position that the actual arises from, and is dependent on, the virtual. Let us call this *the hyporeality thesis*.[6]

By contrast, as Ernst Bloch argues in *The Principle of Hope*, the underlying structure of hope is not 'S is P' (nor 'S is not P') but 'S is not yet P'.[7] For Bloch, 'S is not yet P' is a properly dialectical assertion – not an *in*-esse but a *trans-esse* – in which a given predicate (P) is not already virtually contained in the subject (S) of a proposition but opens up in a forward direction that may in fact never be actualised, and that even God could not know in advance of its actualisation.[8] To give a variation on the example above that conveys the sense of 'S is not yet P' as the propositional structure of hope, we might propose that

---

4 DM 13; Leibniz 1991, pp. 12–13.
5 On Leibniz's place within the history of logic, see Jolley 2005, pp. 46–55; and Shenefelt and White 2013, p. 210.
6 I use the term 'hyporeality' in order to emphasise Leibniz's anti-materialism, according to which the virtual exists prior to, and independent of, the actual.
7 Indeed, Bloch once remarked to his friend Adolph Lowe that 'S is not yet P' served as a kind of one-sentence summary of his entire philosophy; see Cox 1970, p. 9.
8 Interestingly, in his famous 1963 'Letter from Birmingham Jail' King himself upheld such 'open theism' when he observed that 'human progress never rolls in on wheels of inevitability; it comes through the tireless efforts and persistent work of men willing to be coworkers with God, and without this hard work, time itself becomes an ally of the forces of social stagnation' (King 2015, p. 136).

2. Dr. Martin Luther King, Jr.'s vision of economic justice has not yet been realised in the United States.

As opposed to Leibniz, Bloch argues that

> knowledge itself becomes transformative only in ... a dialectics of events, which are not contemplated, not enclosed within contemplated history. It is not applied merely to the knowable past, but to a real becoming, to that which is occurring and not yet finished, to a knowable and pursuable future content. S is not yet P, the proletariat has not yet been sublated (*aufgehoben*), nature is not yet a home, the real is not yet articulated reality: this Not Yet is in process, indeed it has attained or is beginning to carve out its skyline here and there.[9]

Bloch sets forth a perspective that, ontologically speaking, holds that the virtual is what emerges from, and exceeds, a singular arrangement of actually existing tendencies in the objective 'world-process'. In other words, he defends a position that the virtual arises from, and is dependent on, the actual. Let us call this *the surreality thesis*.[10] Bloch observes that for Leibniz

> the choice between infinitely numerous logical possibilities is ... left spread out before his God (as realizer). Even inside the existing world, as one which is realized by its creator out of infinitely many possible ones, Leibniz still recognizes possibility as propensity, even though as one which cannot develop anything that is in reality new either, i.e. anything not contained in the whole of the previous world. And even if Leibniz, the only great philosopher of the Possible since Aristotle, also gives space to an infinite number of other possible world-contexts, these 'primae possibilitates' once again only live in the reason of the creator and not as possibilities still capable of realization projecting into this world now realized for once.[11]

In light of the respective theses of Leibniz and Bloch, I would like to situate and make sense of Jean Baudrillard's writings regarding *hyperreality* and then

---

9   Bloch 1976, p. 8.
10 I use the term 'surreality' in order to echo what Dominique Lecourt (1981, pp. 211–18) has called 'surmaterialism' and to signify the irreducible ontological excess of the actual over the virtual.
11 Bloch 1986b, Vol. 1, pp. 243–4.

to consider Slavoj Žižek's insistence on the 'reality of the virtual' as opposed to 'virtual reality'. As I shall argue below, Baudrillard has offered a contemporary, *inverted* variation on Leibniz's classical idealist position (*hyporeality* having become *hyperreality*),[12] whereas Žižek has followed the dialectical materialist course charted by Bloch.

1   Baudrillard on Hyperreality

Baudrillard's most fully elaborated account of hyperreality may be found in his essay 'The Precession of Simulacra'.[13] Baudrillard writes that

> Today abstraction is no longer that of the map, the double, the mirror, or the concept. Simulation is no longer that of a territory, a referential being, or a substance. It is the generation by models of a real without origin or reality: a hyperreal. The territory no longer precedes the map, nor does it survive it. It is nevertheless the map that precedes the territory – precession of simulacra – that engenders the territory, and if one must return to the fable, today it is the territory whose shreds slowly rot across the extent of the map. It is the real, and not the map, whose vestiges persist here and there in the deserts that are no longer those of the Empire, but ours. The desert of the real itself …
>
> It is all of metaphysics that is lost. No more mirror of being and appearances, of the real and its concept. No more imaginary coextensivity: it is genetic miniaturization that is the dimension of simulation. The real is produced from miniaturized cells, matrices, and memory banks, models of control – and it can be reproduced an indefinite number of times from these. It no longer needs to be rational, because it no longer measures itself against either an ideal or negative instance. It is no longer anything but operational. In fact, it is no longer really the real, because no imaginary envelops it anymore. It is a hyperreal, produced from a radiating synthesis of combinatory models in a hyperspace without atmosphere.[14]

---

12   Baudrillard's attempted inversion of Leibniz is clear in Baudrillard 2009, p. 63. As we know from Althusser, however, an inversion of another theoretical problematic fails to surpass it; what is still required is a displacement – which is what Bloch and Žižek achieve.
13   Baudrillard 1994, pp. 1–42.
14   Baudrillard 1994, pp. 1–2.

In order to explain what he means by hyperreality, Baudrillard also offers an image of the hologram:

> A segment has no need of imaginary mediation in order to reproduce itself, any more than the earthworm needs earth: each segment of the worm is directly reproduced as a whole worm, just as each cell of the American CEO can produce a new CEO. Just as each fragment of a hologram can again become the matrix of the complete hologram: the information remains whole, with perhaps somewhat less definition, in each of the dispersed fragments of the hologram.[15]

Moreover, Baudrillard contends,

> holographic reproduction, like all fantasies of the exact synthesis or resurrection of the real (this also goes for scientific experimentation), is already no longer real, is already *hyperreal*. Not an exact, but a transgressive truth, that is to say already on the other side of the truth. What happens on the other side of the truth, not in what would be false, but in what is more true than the true, more real than he real?[16]

Baudrillard has effectively *inverted* Leibniz by proposing that the latter's question 'Why is there something instead of nothing?' has become 'Why is there nothing instead of something?'[17] Moreover, Baudrillard has cut loose Leibniz's hyporeality thesis from its mooring in God's necessary existence. Indeed, as the real has disappeared, all that remains is contingent hyperreality. Moreover, hyperreality has somehow escaped or exceeded negation and contradiction:

> Thus, the modern world foreseen by Marx, driven on by the work of the negative, by the engine of contradiction, became, by the very excess of its fulfillment, another world in which things no longer even need their opposites in order to exist, in which light no longer needs shade, the fem-

---

15   Baudrillard 1994, p. 97.
16   Baudrillard 1994, p. 108.
17   See Leibniz's formulation in his implicitly anti-Epicurean 1697 essay 'On the Ultimate Origination of Things' (*De Rerum origination radicali*), see Leibniz 2006, pp/ 31–8. For Baudrillard's implicit reversal of Leibniz, see Baudrillard 2011, p. 63. In his foreword to Baudrillard 2011, François L'Yvonnet explicitly characterises Baudrillard's position as 'Leibniz's question, exactly reversed' and proposes that 'it is a radical way of taking one's leave of metaphysics' (p. 3). However, the question remains whether it is possible to 'take one's leave' of metaphysics through a process of reversal (or inversion) alone.

inine no longer needs the masculine (or vice versa?), good no longer needs evil – and the world no longer needs us.[18]

For Baudrillard this is a world from which human beings have – tendentially, at least – *disappeared* and in which there has occurred a 'dissolution of values, of the real, of ideologies, of ultimate ends'.[19] Yet not everything vanishes at once; traces remain; there is a 'clandestine existence ... [that] ... exert[s] an occult influence';[20] indeed, there remains an 'artificial survival', a 'prolongation to perpetuity of something that has disappeared, but just keeps on and on disappearing'. Consequently, what remains requires a 'whole art ... to know how to disappear before dying and instead of dying'.[21] At this point Baudrillard evokes the trace of God as akin to the frightening smile left over from Lewis Carroll's vanished Cheshire Cat: 'And God's judgment is terrifying in itself, but the judgment of God without God ...'[22] Baudrillard describes this as 'an overall hegemonic process' in which there is a

> reabsorption of any negativity in human affairs, the reduction to the simplest unitary formula, the formula to which there is no alternative, 0/1 – pure difference of potential, into which the aim is to have all conflicts vanish digitally.[23]

Not only the world is disappearing but the subject, too, 'as agency of will, of freedom, of knowledge, of history'.[24] Only the subject's 'ghost' or 'narcissistic double' is left behind by this process of disappearance:

> The subject disappears, gives way to a diffuse, floating, insubstantial subjectivity, an ectoplasm that envelopes everything and transforms everything into an immense sounding board for a disembodied, empty consciousness – all things radiating out from a subjectivity without object; each monad, each molecule caught in the toils of a definitive narcissism, a perpetual image-playback. This is the image of an end-of-world subjectivity, a subjectivity for an end of the world from which the subject as such

---

18   Baudrillard 2011, p. 16.
19   Baudrillard 2011, p. 21.
20   Baudrillard 2011, p. 26.
21   Baudrillard 2011, p. 25.
22   Baudrillard 2011, pp. 25–6.
23   Baudrillard 2011, pp. 44–5.
24   Baudrillard 2011, p. 27.

has disappeared, no longer having anything left to grapple with. The subject is the victim of this fateful turn of events, and, in a sense, it no longer has anything standing over against it – neither objects, nor the real, nor the Other.[25]

Digitalisation of images in turn leads to a disappearance of 'the entire symbolic articulation of language and thought':

> Soon there will no longer be any thought-sensitive surface of confrontation, any suspension of thought between illusion and reality. There will be no blanks any more, no silences, no contradiction – just a single continuous flow, a single integrated circuit.[26]

It would be difficult to find a more revealing account of Baudrillard's inverted Leibnizianism: the reassertion of windowless monads, the invocation of a holographic universe in which each individual expresses the totality of all individuals but only from within – the outside has effectively dissolved. External relations between and among individuals have folded into, been exhausted by, internal relations alone. In short, as Warren Montag has perceptively noted, 'Baudrillard celebrates a silent world, a world that has rid itself of every hint of conflict or contradiction'.[27]

2   A Žižekian Response to Baudrillard

What should one make of Baudrillard's account of the self-emptying of the real, its mundane *kēnosis*? It would be inadequate to say it is mistaken, just an exaggeration of a contemporary tendency toward dematerialisation. What is required is an immanent critique by which to restore the materialist lines of demarcation that might push Baudrillard's thought beyond itself without simply rejecting it *in toto*. In effect, what is needed is not only an *inversion* of Leibniz but also a *displacement*.

Here then arises, as Žižek has suggested, a new opportunity for materialism to assert itself at the ground zero of the real and subjectivity that Baudrillard has identified. We must begin anew with 'less than nothing' and nonetheless

---

25   Baudrillard 2011, p. 27.
26   Baudrillard 2011, p. 40.
27   Montag 1988, p. 101. My only qualification to Montag's observation would be that in his last work Baudrillard's tone is not celebratory but mournful; see Baudrillard 2011.

insist, as Galileo allegedly said of the earth, that *eppur si muove* ('and yet it moves').[28] Indeed, there remain contradictions of hyperreality itself that constitute a domain of *virtual dialectics*.

Following the lead of Engels and Lenin, Žižek has compellingly argued that philosophers periodically have to rethink the meaning of materialism in light of new scientific, cultural, and political events – such 'breakthroughs' as relativity theory, quantum physics, Freudian psychoanalysis, and 'the failures of twentieth-century communism'.[29] Such is certainly the case with the emergence of the new electronic technologies that Baudrillard has rightly identified as fostering a 'hegemonic process' that tendentially gives rise to *hyperreality*.

Baudrillard seeks to reverse Leibniz's question, 'Why is there something rather than nothing?' by asking 'Why is there nothing rather than something?' Let us even grant Baudrillard's point about the contemporary tendency to dematerialisation, disappearance, indeed – to *nothing*. But, as G.W.F. Hegel contends at the beginning of his *Science of Logic*, 'nothing' is highly unstable.[30] It operates, we could say, as a dynamic void:

> *Nothing, pure nothingness*; it is simple equality with itself, complete emptiness, complete absence of determination and content; lack of all distinction within. – In so far as mention can be made here of intuiting and thinking, it makes a difference whether something or *nothing* is being intuited or thought. To intuit or to think nothing has therefore a meaning; the two are distinguished and so nothing *is* (concretely exists) in our intuiting or thinking; or rather it is the empty intuiting and thinking itself, like pure being. – Nothing is therefore the same determination or rather absence of determination, and thus altogether the same as what pure *being* is.[31]

By similar reasoning, Hegel also shows that 'Being, the indeterminate immediate is in fact *nothing*, and neither more nor less than nothing'. As a result, not only is there an irreducible void in the midst of Being, but also something incessantly arises in the midst of Nothingness. So the inherent instability of both pure Being and pure Nothingness 'pass over' to 'becoming' – and the dialectic is off and running.

---

28 See Žižek 2012, pp. 3–4.
29 Žižek 2014a.
30 Here I follow Žižek's compelling reading of Hegel; see Žižek 2014a, p. 385.
31 Hegel 2010, p. 59.

Another plausible way to respond to Baudrillard, though, would be to note a key contrast between Leibniz and his contemporary Baruch de Spinoza. As we have already seen, according to Leibniz, God's primal act in creating the world serves only to initiate a drawn-out process of actualising what was virtually contained in his mind from the beginning; this truly is an origination of 'something from nothing'. Spinoza, however, explains the relationship between God and the world in a way that anticipates Hegel – or rather can be retrospectively appreciated from a Hegelian vantage point. Spinoza argues that the world was not created once long ago but instead always already commences – and not from nothing but only through the *internal division* within God (or substance) between 'naturing Nature' (*natura naturans*) and 'natured Nature' (*natura naturata*).[32] In Leibniz's metaphysics virtual possibilities simply await their actualisation; in Spinoza's metaphysics, though, we discover something 'less than substance' that drives and incessantly reopens the ontological process by which both singular things (actualities) and accompanying new real-possibilities (virtualities) arise.

The upshot is that both Leibniz's and Baudrillard's positions are one-sided and effectively amount to holding the same position. As Althusser famously put it regarding Marx's own relationship to Hegel,

> it is clear that to turn an object right round changes neither its nature nor its content by virtue merely of a rotation! A man on his head is the same man when he is finally walking on his feet. And a philosophy inverted in this way cannot be regarded as *anything more* than the philosophy *reversed* except in theoretical metaphor: in fact, its structure, its problems and the meaning of these problems is still haunted by the *same problematic*.[33]

What is required, then, is a conceptual shift or displacement with respect to both Leibniz's and Baudrillard's questions and a transformation of the theoretical problematic itself. The truth is to be sought in the dynamic interaction between something and nothing, in what Bloch notably called the category of the '*Front* of the world-process ... the so little thought-out, foremost segment of Being of animated, utopian open matter'.[34] For Bloch the Front not only helps to ground 'militant optimism' but also serves as the leading edge of material

---

32 See especially the scholium to Proposition 29 of the *Ethics* (Spinoza 1996, pp. 20–1). For the distinction between 'origination' and 'commencement', I draw on Althusser 2014a, p. 67.
33 Althusser 2005, p. 73.
34 Bloch 1986b, Vol. 1, p. 200.

movement or 'forward matter'.³⁵ In this context, Bloch distinguishes his conception of the 'merely cognitively or objectively Possible and the Real-Possible':

> Objectively possible is everything whose entry, on the basis of a mere partial-cognition of its existing conditions, is scientifically to be expected, or at least cannot be discounted. Whereas really possible is everything whose conditions in the sphere of the object itself are not yet fully assembled; whether because they are still maturing, or above all because new conditions – though mediated with the existing ones – arise for the entry of a new Real.³⁶

Finally, Bloch stresses how real possibility compels us to conceive of matter as processual continually opening what has not-yet been realised in the world:

> Real possibility thus does not reside in any ready-made ontology of the being of That-Which-Is up to now, but in the ontology, which must constantly be grounded anew, of the being of That-Which-Is-Not-Yet, which discovers future even in the past and in the whole of nature. Its new space thus emphasizes itself in the old space in the most momentous manner: real possibility is the categorical In-Front-of-Itself of material movement considered as a process; it is the specific regional character of reality itself, on the Front of its occurrence. How else could we explain the future-laden properties of matter? – there is no true realism without the true dimension of this openness.³⁷

Žižek has noted that Bloch's position is not simply non-teleological but acknowledges the 'ontological incompleteness of reality itself'.³⁸ As a result, Bloch's conception of a radically 'open universe' is at odds with a widespread perspective that we live in – or at least will do so in the near future – a closed 'simulated universe'.³⁹

The proper way to frame the contemporary ontological question, then, is not in terms of *hyperreality* or virtual reality but in terms of the underlying *reality of the virtual*. As Žižek writes in his book on Deleuze,

---

35 Bloch 1986b, Vol. 1, p. 209.
36 Bloch 1986b, Vol. 1, p. 196.
37 Bloch 1986b, Vol. 1, p. 237.
38 The thesis of 'ontological incompleteness' (or the 'non-All') is one of the central themes of his two recent books on dialectical materialism; see Žižek 2012 and Žižek 2014a.
39 Žižek 2013, p. xviii.

Virtual Reality in itself is a rather miserable idea: that of imitating reality, of reproducing its experience in an artificial medium. The reality of the Virtual, on the other hand, stands for the reality of the Virtual as such, for its real effects and consequences.[40]

It is, of course, true that Baudrillard regards hyperreality not as a mirror of reality but as a detachment from reality and, as we have already seen, it generates a disappearance of the real.[41] However, the problem with this way of framing the issue is that this very disappearance occurs as *an effect* of the material world itself. Baudrillard himself proposes that this effect historically arose from modern scientific inquiry into the structure of the external world as well as its technological transformation; indeed, for him 'the real world begins, paradoxically, to disappear at the very time as it begins to exist'.[42] Consequently, it would be more accurate to say that the material world has not disappeared but has remained causally effective, however much it has become increasingly mediated through technological, cultural, and conceptual means. Moreover, the *disappearance-effect* associated with hyperreality is conditioned, and determined 'in the last instance', by material causal factors. Hyperreality remains only relatively autonomous from its underlying and causally efficacious material reality.

3   Conclusion

Let me conclude with an example. Consider a screen – whether a computer, cell phone, or tablet. Recent neuro-linguistic research has indicated that screen-based reading and writing significantly reduce memory retention and have proven to be less effective means of study than simply reading and writing on paper.[43] One is tempted, in fact, to say that an electronic screen embodies and yields *less* virtuality than does a newspaper, magazine, or book. As a result, the contemporary situation has turned out not to be the proliferation of hyperreality via new technologies; rather, it has become the impoverishment of human imaginative, empathic, and cognitive capacities.[44]

---

40   Žižek 2004, p. 3.
41   Baudrillard 2011, p. 33.
42   Baudrillard 2011, p. 11.
43   See, for example, Baron 2015 and Greenfield 2015.
44   See especially Lynch 2016.

Moreover, a screen is composed of material and is materially produced, its illumination and functionality is materially generated, its energy source is materially produced and conveyed; and it is eventually discarded as material electronic waste – or perhaps it is materially recycled. There exists, in other words, an entire material economic process – extraction, production, distribution, consumption, and disposal[45] – underlying whatever effect is associated with the screen to provide information or entertainment. It is true that this effect cannot wholly be subsumed into an overdetermination of material causes; but neither can it be entirely detached from them; not least because of the actually existing *scarcity* of the rare earth metals whose continued extraction and recycling are essential for the production of such technology.[46]

In sum, Baudrillard is doubtless correct to point out that screens and their images give rise to certain disappearance-effects. But there is a more plausible response to the pointed question expressed in the title of one of his last books: 'Why has the world not disappeared?' Answer: Because the world has always already existed prior to, and forever remains independent of, the very posing of the question.

---

45 For an introduction to these five moments of the 'materials economy', see Leonard 2010.
46 On the problems associated with extracting and recycling rare earth metals, see Veronese 2015.

CHAPTER 11

A Marxist Encounter with the Philosophy of Gilles Deleuze*

> I would say that Anti-Oedipus (may its authors forgive me) is a book of ethics, the first book of ethics to be written in France in a long time.
> – MICHEL FOUCAULT[1]

∴

At the outset let me describe what I mean by an 'encounter'. Gilles Deleuze proposes in his *Dialogues* with Claire Parnet that to encounter is to enter into a 'becoming' with forces outside of oneself in order to create a kind of 'asymmetrical block' or 'a-parallel evolution'.[2] Of course there can be both good and bad encounters. As Deleuze observes elsewhere, when we encounter forces that 'agree' with us, our 'power of acting' is 'increased' or 'enhanced', and we experience the passion of joy. On the other hand, when we encounter forces that don't agree with us, our power of acting is 'diminished' or 'blocked', and we experience the passion of sadness.[3]

For Marxists who are accustomed to thinking in terms of interventions, an encounter may seem to lack the supposed rigour of a dialectical methodology or science. Yet in the history of Marxism, such rigour has often amounted to little more than overt domination or covert manipulation of others within a given practical or theoretical field. There is no reason, of course, why we should adopt this particular conception of a more general concept of intervention – or to think that all Marxists have adopted it. For example, we only have to recall one of Louis Althusser's greatest achievements: theorising what Marxists mean when they conceive of, or seek to carry out, interventions. Althusser enables us to identify and reject the caricature that for decades had passed for Leninism but in reality was only Stalinist deformation.

---

* This chapter has been previously published in *Rethinking MARXISM* 3.3–4, 1990, pp. 287–96.
1 Foucault 2009, p. xiii.
2 Deleuze 1987, pp. 7–10.
3 Deleuze 1988c, pp. 27–8; see also Deleuze 1969, pp. 218–25.

So if I retain the concept of encounter, it isn't because I think that Marxists should give up the concept of intervention, but because I want us to envision intervention even more than Althusser does as an immanent, risk-laden engagement with forces that can either strengthen or weaken us, but that we seek to control unilaterally only at our peril. I want to provoke us to take Deleuze as much as possible on his own terms without preconceived notions of where his philosophy might lead.

If Althusser teaches us anything, it is that it is both possible and necessary to abandon the pursuit of a specifically Marxist philosophy without ceasing to advance the cause of Marxism *within* philosophy. But philosophy involves the creation of new concepts.[4] As a result, the time is long overdue for Marxists who work within philosophy to become philosophers *within Marxism*: to elaborate new concepts that might contribute to the revitalisation of our tradition, to encounter forces outside Marxism that might help us to regain some of the joy we have lost during our prolonged crisis.

How might Marxists encounter Deleuze's philosophy? Before answering this question, let me immediately suggest that it is badly posed, for any encounter between a Marxist and Deleuze must include an encounter with Félix Guattari as well.[5] Furthermore, we must consider not only Guattari's collaboration with Deleuze[6] but also his separate work in its mutual, even if asymmetrical, presupposition with Deleuze's own work.[7]

Let us consider, then, the following possible entry for Marxists into both Deleuze and Guattari's writings. Deleuze and Guattari are probably best known for their notion of molecular or 'micro' politics. What most commentators have failed to see, though, is the extent to which this micropolitics can best be understood as an attempt to develop an ethics intended to supplement Marxism.

In the rest of this chapter I first examine what Deleuze and Guattari mean by micropolitics and what limitation in Marxism it is intended to correct. Secondly, I argue that, although micropolitics understood as an ethics of desire differs from usual notions of 'morality', it retains a normative dimension that can help to expand and regenerate a revolutionary socialist project for our time.

---

4 Deleuze 1988d, p. 16.
5 Antonio Negri has rightly insisted on 'the productive place' that these 'two thinkers, so different from each other, travelled through together, coexisting and confronting each other' (Negri 2011, p. 156).
6 See Deleuze and Guattari 2009 [1972]; Deleuze and Guattari 1986 [1975]; Deleuze and Guattari 1987 [1980]; and Deleuze and Guattari 1994 [1991].
7 See Guattari 1995; 2000; 2011; 2013.

I concur with Antonio Negri, who has passionately argued that Deleuze and Guattari provided 'the fundamental elements of renewal of historical materialism'.[8]

1   The Three Political Lines and Their Dangers

One of the most important lines of demarcation drawn by Deleuze and Guattari in *Anti-Oedipus* was between what they called the 'molar' and 'molecular' levels of social reality. Although it would be easy to misconstrue such a distinction as a simple opposition of 'large' and 'small' or 'passive' and 'active',[9] Deleuze and Guattari have something quite different in mind.

'Molar' refers to the various kinds of unity or totality that are organised in a more or less hierarchical, stratified way. As a result, the description pertains as much to individual subjects and objects as it does to social classes, political parties, or the state. 'Molecular', on the other hand, refers to pre-individual, pre-personal singularities and lines of force that are 'assembled' according to their heterogeneous, mass consistency.

Hasty or careless readings of *Anti-Oedipus* have led many commentators to conclude that Deleuze and Guattari naively champion the molecular and embrace a kind of anarchism that celebrates the unleashing of irrational, natural, and spontaneous desire from the constraints of social repression.[10] In fact, nothing could be further from the truth.

As Deleuze explains at length to his interlocutor Claire Parnet in their *Dialogues*, his project with Guattari in *Anti-Oedipus* is to posit desire as always already 'assembled' and to analyse it as an immanent process that escapes the constraints of both subject and object. For them desire is as much artificial as natural; it does not exist in some spontaneous free form but must always be constructed on a 'plane of immanence'.[11] In this regard, Deleuze and Guattari argue that although psychoanalytic theory from Freud to Lacan has provided

---

8   Negri 2011, p. 165. Guillaume Sibertin-Blanc has likewise stressed that historical materialism is the theoretical horizon within which Deleuze and Guattari's project unfolded; see Sibertin-Blanc 2012; 2016.
9   Guattari 2011b, pp. 149–50.
10 Slavoj Žižek has erroneously argued that 'we should ... move beyond the Deleuzian opposition between molecular and molar, which ultimately reduces the molar level to a shadowy theatre of representations, in relation to a molecular level of actual productivity and life-experience' (Žižek 2015). Not only did Deleuze and Guattari establish no such opposition, but also there is no question for them of a reduction of the molar to the molecular level.
11 Deleuze 1987, p. 89.

important insights into the nature of unconscious drives, it has nonetheless retained an essentially *reactive* conception of desire that associates the latter with negativity and lack. They propose instead an *active* conception of desire as a fundamentally positive and productive flow into which lack arises only secondarily, for instance, as a result of a capitalist economy's molar organisation of false wants and needs.[12] Consequently, despite Deleuze and Guattari's obvious (and arguably exaggerated) debt to Nietzsche, it is equally appropriate to envision their project in *Anti-Oedipus* as an attempt to work out, in Deleuze's words, a 'Spinozism of the unconscious',[13] that is, a contemporary version of the *Ethics*.

In short, what Deleuze and Guattari set forth in *Anti-Oedipus* is not an uncritical celebration of the molecular but, on the contrary, a painstaking analysis or 'logic' of desire in its various assemblages.[14] Their position becomes much clearer in *A Thousand Plateaus*, in which they more carefully distinguish not just two but three kinds of 'line' that compose the assemblages of desire: molar and molecular lines, as before, but also what they call 'lines of flight'. More importantly, they also consider in detail the 'dangers' associated with each line.

'Micropolitics' is the name that Deleuze and Guattari assign to the analysis of these three lines and their interrelationship. Let us briefly consider the nature of each in turn, beginning with the molar lines.

Molar lines divide or 'segment' groups and individuals in three different ways. First of all, we are segmented according to such binary categories as class, race, and sex. Next, we are segmented by means of ever-increasing circles from self, to neighbourhood, to region, to nation or state, to the world as a whole – in other words, from private to public. Finally, we are segmented in a linear manner throughout the various episodes of our lives, for example, infancy ... childhood ... adolescence ... adulthood, or family ... school ... work ... retirement. Each form of molar segmentation – binary, circular, and linear – overlaps, intersects, and reinforces the other two.

Molecular lines are quite different from molar lines. The segmentation they produce is 'supple' compared with the 'hard' segmentation produced by molar lines. Each individual and group is criss-crossed by lines of supple segmentation that tend to undermine hard segmentation. For example, social classes

---

12   Deleuze and Guattari 2009, p. 28.
13   Deleuze 1988c, p. 21.
14   See Lapoujade 2014, p. 26. As Lapoujade notes, 'logic doesn't mean rational. We could even say that for Deleuze a movement is all the more logical the more it escapes any rationality. The more irrational, the more aberrant, and yet the more logical' (Lapoujade 2017, p. 27).

considered as a form of molar segmentation already imply masses that 'do not have the same movement, distribution, or objectives and do not wage the same kind of struggle'.[15] The intricate relationship between class and mass can be understood as a specific case of the 'reciprocal presupposition' that characterises in general the complex interplay of molar and molecular segmentation. Thus, social classes tend to 'crystallise' masses; masses, on the other hand, are 'constantly flowing or leaking from classes'.[16]

The third line has nothing to do with either hard or supple forms of segmentation. Deleuze and Guattari conceive of the 'line of flight' as a line of pure abstraction or creativity. Lines of flight effect minute crackings or ruptures between molar segments and lead even molecular segments into imperceptible becomings. For example, 1905 and 1917 in Russia, May 1968 in France, 1989 in Eastern Europe, or the Arab Spring of 2011 cannot be explained solely in terms of the dynamics of class struggle or even 'the forcible entrance of the masses into the realm of rulership over their own destiny'.[17] There is something unanticipated, unprecedented, previously unimaginable, about social explosions that escapes even the most sophisticated (historical materialist or otherwise) analysis.

Again, it is crucial to emphasise that Deleuze and Guattari have no wish to romanticise molecular lines or lines of flight: these lines have inherent dangers no less than the ones that molar lines present.[18] I won't say much here about molar dangers, since Deleuze and Guattari are simply directing our attention to the untold human misery historically wrought by class exploitation and racial, sexual, and other oppression. However, the dangers associated with the other two lines may be less obvious.

For example, dangers can arise when molar segmentation reappears along molecular lines and establishes miniaturised versions of binary opposition: what might be called the 'microfascisms' of those who proclaim themselves the

---

15   Deleuze and Guattari 1987, p. 213.
16   Deleuze and Guattari 1987, p. 213. Here one finds a striking affinity between Deleuze and Guattari's conception of 'molecular' politics and Rosa Luxemburg's analysis of 'mass strikes' (Luxemburg 2008, pp. 111–81) in terms of how specific social struggles can become generalised and intensified to the point that they take on a revolutionary momentum. Influenced by Luxemburg, late in 1969 Ernest Mandel observed that the preconditions for social transformation are 'gradual, molecular, nearly invisible processes of accumulating self-confidence, consciousness of the potential power of one's own class, [and] are ... of the utmost importance in preparing class explosions like May 1968 in France and the one which is now being prepared in Italy' (Mandel 1974, p. 35).
17   Trotsky 1977, p. 17.
18   Deleuze and Guattari 1987, pp. 227–31; Deleuze 1987, pp. 137–40.

'avant-garde', 'truly marginal', or 'politically correct'. Likewise, lines of flight can suddenly deteriorate from lines of creativity into lines of death and destruction leading to individual or collective suicide. To use Deleuze and Guattari's vivid expression, lines of flight can collapse into 'black holes'.[19]

The political implications of Deleuze and Guattari's micropolitical analysis for Marxists can hardly be reduced to Perry Anderson's clever but ill-informed dismissal of their 'dejected post-lapsarian anarchism'[20] or Peter Dews's absurd charge that they are precursors to the virulent anti-Marxism of the French 'new philosophers'.[21] I would argue instead that Deleuze and Guattari sought to theorise the relationship between class struggle and social movements. Obviously in the last few decades they were hardly alone in such an endeavour, but it is worth noting that they never discarded Marxism or abandoned revolutionary politics. They consistently condemned both capitalist and bureaucratic socialist forms of domination. They never developed any enthusiasm for private property or the market.

More importantly, there is a wealth of evidence to indicate that they never rejected basic Marxist tenets about the existence of antagonistic social classes, the repressive nature of the state, the failure of both social democracy and Stalinism, the need for revolutionary organisation, and so forth. For example, in a 1980 interview Guattari carefully explains that for Deleuze and him, molecular revolution isn't opposed to, but is a necessary 'complement' of, social revolution.[22] Micropolitics isn't intended to replace class struggle but to operate as a militant analysis (or an analysis *for militants*) that might help to prevent left organisations and mass movements from reproducing within their ranks precisely the same hierarchies, the same certitudes, the same oppressions that already exist in class society. In a 1972 conversation with Michel Foucault, Deleuze acutely poses the following challenge for revolutionary socialists:

> [E]ven Marxism, especially Marxism, has posed the problem [of power] in terms of interest (it is a ruling class, defined by its interests, that holds the power). Suddenly, we run smack into the question: how does it happen that those who have so little stake in power follow, narrowly espouse, or grab for some piece of power? Perhaps it has to do with *investments*, as much economic as unconscious: there exist investments of desire which

---

19   See Deleuze and Guattari 1987, pp. 214–15.
20   Anderson 1980, p. 161.
21   Dews 1985.
22   Guattari 1986, p. 162.

explain that one can if necessary desire not against one's interest, since interest always follows and appears wherever desire places it, but desire in a way that is deeper and more diffuse than one's interest ... it is precisely the nature of the investments of desire that explains why parties or unions, which would or should have revolutionary investments in the name of class interest, all too often have investments which are reformist or totally reactionary at the level of desire.[23]

Micropolitics does not bypass or replace the socialist project. On the contrary: Deleuze and Guattari's aim is to hasten capitalism's demise precisely by supplying a more nuanced analysis of capitalist relations of power and structures of domination.

2   A Micropolitical Ethics of Desire

Perhaps Marxists can best appreciate micropolitics as an ethics of desire. Let me immediately add that this 'ethics' is not the same as 'morality'. For example, in his reading of Spinoza, Deleuze argues that an ethical 'typology of immanent modes of existence' must not be confused with a moral 'system of judgment'. Morality has to do with judging Good and Evil as an 'opposition of transcendent values'. Ethics, on the other hand, has to do with evaluating good and bad encounters within a 'quantitative difference of modes of existence'.[24]

This metaethical distinction between morality and ethics has a number of normative implications, but one is especially important: a micropolitical ethics would entail, in Foucault's elegant phrase, new 'practices of the self'.[25]

In his homage to Foucault, Deleuze seeks to grasp the significance of May 1968 with respect to what Marxists have sometimes called the 'subjective factor':[26]

---

23   Deleuze and Foucault 2004, p. 212.
24   Deleuze 1988c, pp. 22–3; see also Deleuze 1969, pp. 234–51.
25   Foucault 1985, p. 28.
26   Mandel 1976, p. 84. Indeed, Deleuze (1988a, p. 150 n. 45) proposes a modern genealogy of radical conceptions of subjectivity that 'on the level of currents of thought ... go back to Lukács, whose *History and Class Consciousness* was already raising questions to do with a new subjectivity; then the Frankfurt school, Italian Marxism and the first signs of "autonomy" (Tronti); the reflection that revolved around Sartre on the question of the new working class (Gorz); the groups such as "Socialism or Barbarism", "Situationism", "the Communist Way" (especially Félix Guattari and the "micropolitics of desire")'.

What is our light and what is our language, that is to say, our 'truth' today? What powers must we confront, and what is our capacity for resistance, today when we can no longer be content to say that the old struggles are no longer worth anything? And do we not perhaps above all bear witness to and even participate in the 'production of a new subjectivity'? Do not the changes in capitalism find an unexpected 'encounter' in the slow emergence of a new Self as a center of resistance? Each time there is a social change, is there not a movement of subjective reconversion, with its ambiguities but also its potential?[27]

Toward the end of their lives, Deleuze and Guattari each exhibited, in affinity with the late Foucault, a renewed interest in the nature of the self.[28] This may come as a surprise to those casual readers of *Anti-Oedipus* who have thought that they advocate there and elsewhere a schizophrenic dissolution of the subject and reckless plunge into delirium. Yet the question of subjectivity was a recurrent theme throughout all of Deleuze and Guattari's work prior to and including their collaboration on the two volumes of *Capitalism and Schizophrenia*. Their overriding concern was not to demolish the unity of the self but to analyse types of individualisation that have nothing to do with persons or egos. In earlier texts, Deleuze uses the term 'singularity' to characterise the constituents of such individuation;[29] later, he and Guattari borrow from scholastic philosophy the concept of 'haecceity' to characterise such temporal forms of individuation as events, for example, '*a* life, *a* season, *a* wind, *a* battle, 5 o'clock in the evening'.[30] The point is that we must reject the false alternative of having to choose between either 'singularities already comprised in individuals and persons' or else an 'undifferentiated abyss'.[31]

As I have suggested, the elaboration of such new practices of the self constitutes an important part of what Deleuze and Guattari propose should be included within an ethics of desire. Once again, though, we should regard such an ethics as normative not in the sense of an obedience to transcendent rules but instead in the sense of an evaluation of immanent criteria. To return to Deleuze's explication of Spinoza: an ethics of desire can help us to distinguish between good and bad encounters. This is of vital importance, since when we

---

27   Deleuze 1988a, p. 115.
28   Deleuze 1988a; 1993; Guattari 1995, pp. 1–32; Guattari 2000.
29   Deleuze 1968, pp. 330–5; 1990, pp. 100–8.
30   Deleuze 2006, p. 351; see also Deleuze 1987, pp. 92, 151–2; Deleuze and Guattari 1987, pp. 260–5.
31   Deleuze 1990b, p. 103.

'organise encounters' in this way we are more likely to sustain and enhance the joys that arise from good encounters and thereby attain a more intense and productive life.[32] As Deleuze argues concerning the late Foucault,

> The struggle for a modern subjectivity passes through a resistance to the two present forms of subjection, the one consisting in individuating ourselves on the basis of constraints of power, the other of attracting each individual to a known and recognized identity, fixed once and for all. The struggle for subjectivity presents itself, therefore, as the right to difference, variation and metamorphosis.[33]

Thus, an ethics of desire is equally an ethics of freedom; for by exposing and transforming the sad passions (e.g., fear and resentment) that enslave individuals and give rise to collective forms of oppression, we can promote both personal and social emancipation. As a result, Marxism (and Marxists) can only benefit from an encounter with such an ethics that functions not as a distraction from anti-capitalist struggle but as a powerful means to enlarge that struggle to include within it the concerns of everyday life.

3   Conclusion: Becoming-Revolutionary

As I draw this encounter to a close, I would like to draw attention to one of the most beautiful and moving passages of Deleuze and Parnet's *Dialogues*, a passage that concerns revolutions betrayed and all those who have given up hope in the future of revolution. Although these words were originally directed in 1977 against the French 'new philosophers' who had suddenly 'discovered' Stalin's crimes, they could just as easily be directed today against the intellectual progeny of the new philosophers who have joined a chorus strung around the world to proclaim that 'Socialism is dead! Capitalism has won! There is no alternative!' Allow me to quote the passage in full:

> We are not here to keep the tally of the dead and the victims of history, the martyrdom of the Gulags, and to draw the conclusion that 'The revolution is impossible, but we thinkers must think the impossible since the impossible only exists in thought!' It seems to us that there never would

---

32   Deleuze 1990a, p. 261.
33   Deleuze 1988a, pp. 105–6.

have been the tiniest Gulag if the victims had kept up the same discourse as those who weep over them today. The victims would have had to think and live in a quite different way to give substance to those who weep in their name, and who think in their name, and who give lessons in their name. It was their life-force which impelled them, not their bitterness; their sobriety, not their ambition; their anorexia, not their huge appetites, as Zola would have said.[34]

In other words, the crisis of socialism can never be resolved as long as Marxists continue to mourn the dead; the time has come to move on, not by burying the socialist project but by breathing new life into it.

In one of his last interviews Deleuze considers an ever-popular accusation against the Left: revolutions turn out badly; they give birth to monsters who devour their children. But, as Deleuze responds, 'when you say that revolutions have a bad future, you have still said nothing about the becoming-revolutionary of people'.[35]

Even – or especially – Marxists have to enter into this 'becoming-revolutionary', because what is presently at stake is not simply a matter of politics but also of art, religion, science – in fact, all those sources of creativity that can help to reinstill in people (ourselves included) a spirit of militancy and a will to struggle. Marxist obsession with, or despair over, the future of revolution only impedes others' becoming-revolutionary. My hope is that an encounter with Deleuze (and Guattari) will help to counteract that obsession and lift that despair. For in the memorable words of *Anti-Oedipus*: 'Revolutionaries often forget, or do not like to recognize, that one wants and makes revolutions out of desire, not duty'.[36]

---

34 Deleuze 1987, pp. 144–5.
35 Deleuze 1988c, p. 24.
36 Deleuze and Guattari 2009, p. 344.

CHAPTER 12

Deleuze and Althusser: Flirting with Structuralism*

Neither Gilles Deleuze nor Louis Althusser was ever a structuralist. Nonetheless, in 1974 Althusser famously admitted in his *Elements of Self-Criticism* to a 'flirtation' with structuralism that he viewed as a kind of repetition or re-enactment of Marx's previous flirtation with Hegel.[1] Less famously, in 1973 there appeared a remarkable essay by Deleuze on the criteria by which one might 'recognise' structuralism.[2]

As is well known, Althusser contends in his self-criticism that what was really most important for him was not structuralism at all but Spinoza: 'If we never were structuralists, we can now explain why: why we seemed to be, even though we were not, why there came about this strange misunderstanding on the basis of which books were written. We were guilty of an equally powerful and uncompromising passion: *we were Spinozists*'.[3] What is scarcely known, though, is that Althusser's relationship to both structuralism and Spinoza involved yet a third philosophical relationship, this time with Deleuze. Although only in the posthumous writings do we find explicit references to Deleuze's writings. Althusser and his circle seem to have been quite favourably disposed toward certain of Deleuze's early works (such as his 1961 essay on Lucretius[4] and his book on Nietzsche published in 1962).[5] What remains virtually unknown, however, is Althusser's (and Pierre Macherey's) response to an early draft of Deleuze's essay on structuralism. A significant part of that response is now available in the Althusser Archive in the form of a letter. As a result, in this chapter my objective is simply to fill in some missing intellectual and textual history by tracing the revision of Deleuze's essay from first draft to final publication in light of Althusser's critical remarks on the first draft. In my view, the conscious attempt to link the respective theoretical labours of Deleuze and Althusser marks a crucial moment in the endless struggle to persevere as a Marxist in philosophy.

---

* This chapter has been previously published in *Rethinking MARXISM* 10.3, 1998, pp. 51–63.
1 Althusser 1976, pp. 126–31.
2 Deleuze 1973.
3 Althusser 1976, p. 132.
4 See Deleuze 1961 (later reprinted with modifications as an appendix to Deleuze 1969, translated into English as Deleuze 1990b). For an exacting commentary on Althusser's appreciation of Deleuze's work on Lucretius, see Montag 2013, pp. 96–100.
5 Deleuze 1962, subsequently translated into English as Deleuze 1983.

1   Deleuze's First Draft

The first draft of Deleuze's essay on structuralism was a transcription from a tape recording of a talk given 6 December 1967.[6] In February 1968 Deleuze sent a copy of this talk to Althusser to ask whether he thought it 'publishable'.[7]

In keeping with his general view of philosophical thought as a kind of conceptual creation,[8] Deleuze's interest in structuralism lay not in criticising its shortcomings but in discerning what 'new forms of thought' it made possible. Deleuze opens his presentation with the question 'What is structuralism?' as an echo of Sartre's question 'What is existentialism?' Despite the great diversity of authors, texts, and 'domanins', Deleuze contended that there was a 'certain analogy' or 'family resemblance' among them. Thus the question 'What is structuralism?' is better posed as 'Who is a structuralist?' or 'Who are the structuralist?' Deleuze included Louis Althusser, Michel Foucault, Jacques Lacan, Roman Jakobson, Claude Lévi-Strauss, Roland Barthes, and the *Tel Quel* novelists (e.g., Philippe Sollers) within the structuralist camp; indeed, the rest of his lecture cites them and certain of their texts as exemplary of the structuralist approach. I should emphasise at this point that my concern here is primarily with Deleuze's references to Althusser.

Deleuze again transforms the question 'Who are the structuralists?' into 'How are structuralists recognized?' and into 'What does the structuralist recognize?' This is because he wanted to establish a kind of 'nomenclature', namely, the 'criteria' by which structuralism and structuralist can be recognised just as 'one recognizes someone in the street'. To facilitate such recognition, Deleuze proposed, and discussed in order, five 'basic' criteria: a symbolic criterion, a topological criterion, a differential and singular criterion, a serial criterion, and a criterion involving the 'empty case'.

First of all, the symbolic criterion marks the structuralist 'refusal' to be confined to the historical alternative in Western classical thought between the 'categories' or 'orders' of the 'real' and the 'imaginary', as well as their 'dialectical interplay'. Deleuze maintains that structure is distinct from 'sensible forms', 'imaginary figures', and 'intelligible essences'; instead, it is beyond the real and the imaginary. In his view, 'every structure is, by definition, unconscious', whether one is talking about politics, psychoanalysis, or language. For

---

6   Deleuze 1967. All translations from French are my own.
7   Deleuze 1968. All subsequent citations in this section are from Deleuze's lecture (my translation).
8   Explicitly defended in Deleuze and Guattari 1994 but implicit as early as Deleuze's 1962 book on Nietzsche (translated as Deleuze 1983).

example, in Althusser's writings we find the desire to seek 'behind real human beings and ideologies ... something deeper that he calls the symbolic order'. Likewise, Lacan seeks behind the real father and father images a properly symbolic 'name of the father'. His analysis of psychoses reveals that whatever is not integrated into the symbolic order of a subject's unconscious may well reappear in the real in a hallucinatory form.

Now the elements of a structure – its 'symbolic elements' – refer neither to 'preexisting realities' nor to 'immanent imaginary content'. Rather, according to Deleuze, these elements have 'neither interiority nor exteriority; they are neither external designations nor do they have internal signification'. How then should these elements be defined? Deleuze's answer is that we should define them by their 'place' within a 'combinatory' or 'topological space' that is not a sensible, imaginary, or intelligible extension but a purely logical 'intensive *spatium*'. These places have priority over both the 'real objects and beings' that come to 'occupy' them as well as the 'imaginary roles' that these objects and beings will play once they have taken their places:

> For example, Althusser informs us that the true subjects of a society are not those who come to occupy the places, but the places themselves, in a structural space, in a social *spatium*, which defines the types of society. And this *spatium* finally refers to the Marxist notion of the 'relations of production'.

Deleuze goes on to note three implications or consequences of the symbolic and topological criteria of structure. First of all, meaning is always 'a product, a result of the combination of symbolic elements that themselves have no intrinsic signification'. In other words, meaning is simply a 'surface-effect'. There is an irreducible production, a proliferation of non-sense is the midst of what Althusser would call an 'overdetermination' of meaning. A second consequence is that structuralists have a 'taste' for certain games, game theory, art, or even theatre; in this regard Deleuze mentions Althusser's essay on Brecht in *For Marx*,[9] in which is analysed not a 'theater of realities or a theater of ideas ... but ... a theater of structural places'. A third and final consequence is that structuralism lays claim to a 'new materialism, a new atheism, a new anti-humanism'. Here Deleuze evokes Althusser's 'reinterpretation of dialectical materialism' as a denunciation of the ideology of humanism 'by virtue of the primacy of structural places over the real human beings who occupy them'.

---

9   Althusser 2005, pp. 129–51.

Deleuze now turns to the third basic criterion by which one might recognise structuralism: that of differentiation and singularity. He notes that in the domain of linguistics a phoneme is the smallest unit by means of which one can distinguish two words having different significations; an individual phoneme has no existence apart from its relation to another phoneme. Moreover, to every determination of differential relations of phonemes in a language correspond singularities that are the 'true centers of signification for the words differentiated by the phonemes'. More generally, though, Deleuze proposes that every structure is composed of symbolic elements, differential relations, and the corresponding singularities; every structure is a 'combinatory'.

Deleuze admits that such a general – even 'obscure' – presentation of the problem is inadequate: in a specific domain of investigation one has to ask in an eminently 'practical' way whether or not that domain is suitable for structural analysis. To 'extract' the structure of a given domain is precisely to isolate the symbolic elements, their differential relations, and their points of singularity. Here again, Deleuze considers the 'basis' of Althusser's Marxism to be the following:

> What Marx calls the 'relations of production' must not be understood as the real relations between real data but must be interpreted as differential relations between symbolic elements in such a way that to these relations correspond the singularities that constitute a type of production, for example, capitalism in a given society.

All this has only been a matter of preliminaries, representing the definition of just 'half' a structure. Deleuze contends that every system of symbolic elements and differential relations can be organised into at least two different series, for example, between signifiers and signifieds. Since structural analysis is not the 'application of ready-made formulae' and cannot be given in advance, in a specific domain it is a practical task to construct such a series. A striking example in anthropology is Lévi-Strauss's 1963 analysis of totemism, which involves the construction of an animal series and a series of social places or functions between individuals or social groups. Likewise, in psychoanalysis Lacan constructs such series to characterise the structure of Edgar Allan Poe's short story 'The Purloined Letter'[10] and Freud's case study of the 'Rat Man'.[11]

---

10   Lacan 2006, pp. 6–48.
11   Lacan 1979.

As if the first four criteria weren't already sufficiently obscure and abstract, Deleuze proposes yet another, fifth, criterion by which to recognise structuralism: between the two series in a structure there are 'inversions, reversals ... disguises, discrepancies ... in short, for all that, let us use a concept, that of *displacement*'. The two series in a given structure are displaced in relation to one another, and communication between the two takes place only as a result of their respective shifting or displacements. Here the 'principle of displacement and communication of series' is the presence of a paradoxical object, what Deleuze calls the 'object = x' or 'object x'.[12] Deleuze mentions Lewis Carroll's and James Joyce's use of 'esoteric' words as classic literary deployments of such paradoxical objects. This object x has the property of always being displaced, not only in relation to what animates it but in relation to itself. As opposed to a real object that is always in the place it happens to occupy, a symbolic object is 'never where one looks for it' and 'is found only where it is not'. In his seminar on Poe's 'Purloined Letter', Lacan offers the example of a book that has been mislaid in a library; although the book is actually in full view (let us say, on a nearby shelf), it nonetheless remains symbolically hidden. The paradoxical object x introduces into every structure what Deleuze calls an 'empty square':

> Everything happens, then, as if the two series converged toward a mysterious object that is always displaced in relation to itself, and it is in relation to it that the terms of the two series are defined in their respective situations and in their roles.

Deleuze concludes his talk by arguing that the famous structuralist critique of time is 'secondary' and follows from, instead of governing, the five criteria he has put forth. For Deleuze structuralism in 1967 was not just a 'reflection on ... language, social reality, the unconscious, literature'; rather, it 'strives to be a new language, a new literature, a new practice, in every sense of the word'. Indeed, Deleuze insists that given the role of the empty place that 'makes possible a structural mutation ... in this sense there is no structuralism without revolutionary practice'. It is hard not to see in Deleuze's description of the present (December 1967) a 'very rich and unstable' anticipation of the May–June 'events' that were shortly to rock France.

---

12   Here Deleuze has appropriated for his own philosophical ends the striking way in which Kant had indicated the unknowability of 'things in themselves'. This paradoxical or virtual object = x will later play a prominent role in *Difference and Repetition* and *The Logic of Sense*; see, for example, Deleuze 1994, pp. 122–4; 1990; pp. 66–73.

2   An Exchange of Letters

It seems clear that Althusser gave Pierre Macherey a copy of Deleuze's transcribed lecture for comments.[13] In a note to Althusser written sometime in February 1968, Macherey quite sharply remarked that Deleuze's talk on structuralism

> only presents in a more refined form the illusion that feeds all ordinary publications on structuralism ... The content remains the same: confusion and amalgamation.

Moreover, according to Macherey, Deleuze '*establishes a continuity where there is a real disorder*. It would be necessary to show that in fact the structuralist ideology is made up of pieces and fragments. This is entirely astonishing to Deleuze, who also tirelessly teaches us, in speaking of Nietzsche, that it is necessary to differentiate, to distinguish'.[14]

Althusser's letter to Deleuze (dated 29 February, 1968) incorporates some of Macherey's criticisms but presents them in a less confrontational manner. Althusser opens his letter with the following praise:[15]

> I have read your text with passionate attention, and I am indebted to you for having understood a number of decisive points whose importance I had not seen, and that I had not even known how to express, above all on Lacan, and also (which is only normal, for you know how I 'advance', if one can say it: in a kind of mist in which I discern only the presence of the masses, a little like radar in the night) on the pages we have published. Everything concerning the object x (value) in particular has profoundly struck and enlightened me (everything concerning it and everything due to it).[16]

---

13   According to Étienne Balibar (personal communication), Althusser regularly passed along such material for his 'students' to read and evaluate.
14   Macherey 1968 (my translation). In this regard Macherey also mentions Deleuze's 1967 book on *Masochism* (Deleuze 1989).
15   Étienne Balibar (personal communication) has recalled that such praise was a stylistic device, even a ploy, that Althusser regularly used to begin letters in which he intended a few paragraphs later to voice criticisms of an author's work.
16   Althusser 1968. All subsequent quotations in this section are from this letter (my translation).

Althusser goes on to offer two main criticisms of Deleuze's lecture. First of all, he reiterates Macherey's complaint that Deleuze's analysis of structuralism suffers from a kind of 'amalgamation' of authors and texts that are not easily unified; for Althusser, though, this objection is more a matter of 'prudence' that need not greatly affect the substance of Deleuze's text. His second and more extended criticism concerns Deleuze's use of the concept of the 'symbolic' and suggests that, when taken out of a Lacanian context, the concept of the symbolic involves 'equivocation and a kind of word play'; it has a 'double meaning'. The rest of Althusser's letter develops this point.

According to Althusser, structuralism can first of all be designated in terms of '*what it rejects*' – a break with the 'real' object, whether sensible, historical, or empirical, in order to constitute a distinct 'theoretical' object. This was, he says, already true of Marx's break with the real, historicist, and empiricist object of history that was in fact the 'ideological object of philosophies of history'. Marx constituted the theoretical object of history as a science. We can also discern such a break in Freud and Lacan with psychologism, biologism, and sociologism, and in linguistics in its break with 'the historicism and empiricism of classical philology'. Finally, though, in the domain of anthropology Althusser insists that one sees such a theoretical break 'only to a *certain* extent in Lévi-Strauss'. In short, Althusser contends that

> behind the claim of 'structuralism' [is] this simple fact: a certain number of disciplines of the Human Sciences have discovered, (more or less) blindly, that they could only exist as *sciences* provided that they break with historicism, that is, with the *empiricist* ideology of their 'object'. They have 'discovered' the necessity of *theory* as an absolute condition of their scientific existence. I say 'discovered' with quotation marks, and I say blindly, *for they really don't know it and don't say it*. The only one to know it is doubtless Lacan, who is not only a theorist of psychoanalysis but also an epistemologist and a philosopher. The others don't know it. When they talk about 'structure' and 'structuralism', they don't know that they are expressing the fact of *theory*. Not being informed of this fact, they 'interpret' what they say by *oscillating* between two tendencies, which naturally refer to one another in an endless interplay. On the one hand, they take this *theory* for a 'model' ... on the other hand, they take this theory for a 'reality' (a specific modality of the 'real', distinct from the real, but real insofar as a modality: for example, they say – and you follow them on this point – that structuralism is a matter of the *symbolic*).[17]

---

17   Althusser 1968.

The upshot is that most structuralists amalgamate and only think in a confused way a crucial distinction between the real object and the object of knowledge. Although the concept of the symbolic may be appropriate in the domains of psychoanalysis and linguistics, it is not appropriate in the domains of biology, mathematics, or Marxism when Marx 'analyzes the relations of production, the forces of production, and the effects of their structural relations'. In this regard, Althusser apologises for his terminology of real object and object of knowledge, but he suggests that 'between Spinozists we understand ourselves'.

Structuralists fail to distinguish adequately between the 'fact' of theory and the 'content' of scientific concepts. In the last analysis, structuralism is a 'spontaneous philosophy of the scientists', which in its confusion reestablishes empiricism as the '*theoreticity* of the concept is amalgamated with the scientific *content* of the concept'.[18] Althusser sets forth three possible variants of this confusion, present above all in Lévi-Strauss's writings: an 'idealist' variant invoking 'models', a 'realist or even materialist' variant invoking an unconscious reality hidden under appearances, deep or latent structures, and a 'formalist' variant invoking a 'combinatory' or 'order of orders'. With this final variant – one that Deleuze himself seemed to endorse – 'electronic machines' have been entrusted 'the role, formerly allotted to God, of thinking the *fait accompli*'.

Althusser proffers that one should 'clear the ground' occupied by the spontaneous philosophy of structuralism in order to see what different authors, texts, and domains have in common. Firstly, one has to 'sort out' and distinguish truly scientific concepts and second, one has to see '*how* their concepts function before deciding if they arise from *really common* philosophical categories'. In conclusion, his advice to Deleuze is to be 'extremely prudent', even though he agrees that there is indeed something in common between Marx and Lacan, which is why Deleuze's lecture 'speaks' to him. He ventures to Deleuze that 'it is Lacan who is at the center of your thought, Lacan to the extent that he "communicates" with Marx'. Althusser indicates that he 'feels most in agreement' with Deleuze's discussion of the empty case, which at the beginning of the letter he had already implied takes the form of value in Marxist theory.

---

18   One might usefully compare Althusser's remarks in this letter with the general critical assessment of the 'spontaneous philosophy of the scientists' to be found in his 1967 lectures (see Althusser 2011, pp. 69–165) and with the particularly sharp attack on Lévi-Strauss to be found in a text dating from 1966 but only posthumously published (see Althusser 2003, pp. 19–32).

What Althusser (by way of Macherey) seems to be most concerned about in his letter to Deleuze, then, is the latter's failure to grasp the unevenness of structuralism or to see the struggle of tendencies within such a heterogeneous movement of diverse authors, texts, and insights. There is a pressing theoretical need to distinguish between those features of structuralism that can lead to enriching Marxism and those features that must be kept at a distance. In a word, Deleuze's lecture inadequately sorts out the materialist and idealist elements at work within the structuralist ideology.

3   Deleuze's Revision

Let us turn to consider some of the most important changes that Deleuze made in the transcription of his 1967 lecture before his text appeared six years later under the same title, but in a substantially lengthened and modified version. In his second version, Deleuze sets forth not five but six criteria by which one might recognise structuralism. Also, he identified these criteria no longer as 'basic' but as 'formal'. The first, second, and third criteria are, as in the first version, the symbolic, the positional (or topological), and the differential and singular. Likewise, the fourth and fifth criteria of the initial version are identical to the fifth and sixth criteria of the revised version, namely, those involving the serial and the empty square. What is most striking about Deleuze's second version is his inclusion, and detailed discussion, of a new fourth criterion called that of differen*c*iation, with a '*c*' to distinguish it from the criterion of differentiation with a '*t*'.

Regarding differen*t*iation, Deleuze considers at greater length in his second version 'the interpretation of Marxism by Louis Althusser and his collaborators', for whom in *Reading Capital* especially

> the relations of production are determined as differential relations that are established, not between real men or concrete individuals, but between objects and agents which, first of all, have a symbolic value (object of production, instrument of production, labour force, immediate workers, immediate non-workers, such as they are held in relations of property and appropriation). Each mode of production is thus characterized by singularities corresponding to the values of the relations. And if it is obvious that concrete men come to occupy the places and carry forth the elements of the structure, this happens by fulfilling the role that the structural place assigns to them (for example, the 'capitalist'), and by serving as supports for the structural relations ... The true subject is the structure

itself: the differential and the singular, the differential relations and the singular points, the reciprocal determination and the complete determination.[19]

As a new criterion by which to recognize structuralism and structuralists, differenciation concerns and in turn raises different questions. Deleuze introduces the concept of 'virtuality',[20] which he uses to 'designate the mode of the structure or the object of theory'.[21] A structure is *'real without being actual, ideal without being abstract'*; consequently, to 'discern the structure of a domain is to determine an entire virtuality of coexistence which pre-exists the beings, objects and works of this domain'.[22] In Deleuze's view, every structure is 'a multiplicity of virtual coexistence'. Again, he appeals to the example of Althusser, who 'shows in this sense that Marx's originality (his anti-Hegelianism) resides in the way in which the social system is defined by a coexistence of economic elements and relations, without one being able to engender them successively according to the illusion of a false dialectic'.

The relation between differenciation and differentiation depends on how the virtual is actualised. Deleuze argues that

> there is no total society, but each social form embodies certain elements, relationships, and production values (for example 'capitalism'). We must therefore distinguish between the total structure of a domain as an ensemble of virtual coexistence, and the sub-structures that correspond to diverse actualizations in the domain. Of the structure as virtuality, we must say that it is still undifferentiated (c), even though it is totally and completely differential (t). Of structures which are embodied in a particular actual form (present or past), we must say that they are differentiated, and that for them to be actualized is precisely to be differentiated. The structure is inseparable from this double aspect, or from this complex that

---

19 Deleuze 2004b, p. 178.
20 Deleuze first used this important concept in his book on Henri Bergson, which appeared in 1966 (see Deleuze 1988, pp. 51–72 and, in commentary, Boundas 1996 and Alliez 1998). For Deleuze's later elaboration of the crucial distinction between actuality and virtuality, see his previously unpublished text included as an appendix to the second edition of his *Dialogues* with Claire Parnet (Deleuze 1996, pp. 177–85). Also, Deleuze concluded the last text published during his lifetime with a poetic recapitulation of the key role played by virtuality in the effort to construct a philosophy of immanence (see Deleuze 1995, pp. 6–7).
21 Deleuze 2004b, p. 178.
22 Deleuze 2004b, p. 179 (Deleuze's emphasis).

one could designate under the name of differential (t) /differentiation (c), where the t / c constitutes the universally determined phonemic relationship.[23]

The process of actualisation, according to Deleuze, always implies an internal temporality that varies depending on what is actualised. Deleuze thus returns to the problem of time for structuralism, a problem he had raised but immediately dropped at the end of his December 1967 lecture.

> Not only does each type of social production have a global internal temporality, but its organized parts have particular rhythms. As regards time, the position of structuralism is thus quite clear: time is always a time of actualization, according to which the elements of virtual coexistence are carried out at diverse rhythms. Time goes from the virtual to the actual, that is, from structure to its actualizations, and not from one actual form to another.[24]

Contrary, then, to a standard view and criticism of structural analysis, Deleuze maintains that

> one can no more oppose the genetic to the structural than time to structure. Genesis, like time, goes from the virtual to the actual, from the structure to its actualization; the two notions of multiple internal time and static ordinal genesis are in this sense inseparable from the play of structures.[25]

Here we should note a striking affinity between Deleuze's conception of time and the conception that Althusser and Balibar offer in *Reading Capital*.[26] To be precise, in an important chapter devoted to 'The Errors of Classical Economics: An Outline for a Concept of Historical Time', Althusser had famously proposed that every social formation consists of different 'levels', none of which has 'the same type of historical existence'.

---

23 Deleuze 2004b, p. 179.
24 Deleuze 2004b, p. 180.
25 Deleuze 2004b, p. 180.
26 For excellent overviews of Deleuze's view on the nature of time, see respectively, Zourabichvili 1996, pp. 71–94; and Williams 2011 (regrettably, neither addresses the connection to Althusser). On Althusser's concept of historical time, see Resch 1992, pp. 65–7 (who does not address the Deleuze connection).

> On the contrary, we have to assign to each level a *peculiar time*, relatively autonomous and hence relatively independent, even in its dependence, of the 'times' of the other levels. We can and must say: for each mode of production there is a peculiar time and history, punctuated in a specific way by the development of the productive forces; the relations of production have their peculiar time and history, punctuated in a specific way; the political superstructure has its own history ... philosophy has its own time and history ... aesthetic productions have their own time and history ... scientific formations have their own time and history, etc. Each of these peculiar histories is punctuated with peculiar rhythms and can only be known on condition that we have defined the *concept* of the specificity of its historical temporality and its punctuations (continuous development, revolutions, breaks, etc.) ... The specificity of these times and histories is therefore *differential*, since it is based on the differential relations between the different levels within the whole: the mode and degree of *independence* of each time and history is therefore necessarily determined by the mode and degree of *dependence* of each level within the set of articulations of the whole.[27]

Quite clearly, then, Deleuze has embraced Althusser's critique of the 'homogeneous continuity' and 'contemporaneity' at work in the Hegelian account of historical time.[28] He agrees that the 'differential histories' comprising a given social formation manifest their own distinctive rhythms and only exist in a complex state of interdependence. However, Deleuze has enriched Althusser's analysis by further demarcating the 'virtual coexistence' or 'differen*t*iation' of these histories from their 'actualisation' as particular material *effects* – that is, their 'differen*c*iation'.

Moving on to the criterion of the 'empty square' or 'object = x', we should notice in the second version Deleuze's now explicit identification of 'value' as Marxism's paradoxical object that is always 'displaced in relation to itself'. In a footnote Deleuze acknowledges the importance of Pierre Macherey's contribution to *Reading Capital*,[29] a contribution that shows that value 'is always staggered in relation to the exchange in which it appears'.[30] In Deleuze's view,

---

27 Althusser et al. 2015, pp. 110–11.
28 Althusser et al. 2015, p. 104.
29 This important text, entitled 'On the Process of Exposition of *Capital* (The Work of Concepts)', has at long last been translated into English; see Althusser et al. 2015, pp. 175–213.
30 Deleuze 2004b, p. 308 n. 56.

> It is obvious that the empty square of an economic structure, such as commodity exchange ... consists of 'something' which is reducible neither to the terms of the exchange, nor to the exchange relation itself, but that forms an eminently symbolic third term in perpetual displacement, and as a function of which the relational variations will be defined. Such is *value* as expression of a *'generalized* labor', beyond any empirically observable quality, a locus of the question that runs through or traverses through the economy as structure.[31]

A final difference between Deleuze's first and second versions lies in the more extensive conclusion to the second version in which Deleuze discusses other 'final' criteria concerning the 'subject' and 'practice'. He connects the ideas of the subject and the empty square in terms of what he calls a 'nomadic subject', a term of which he will make substantial use in later writings.[32] Deleuze also addresses the question of how contradictions arise within a structure; in his view, they are derived from the empty square and its 'becoming in the structure'; such contradictions must be understood as 'immanent tendencies'.[33] Once again, he refuses to see present structures as closed off from the prospect of mutation or transition to new structures:

> This mutation point precisely defines a praxis, or rather the very site where praxis must take hold. For structuralism is not only inseparable from the works that it creates, but also from a practice in relation to the products that it interprets. Whether this practice is therapeutic or political, it designates a point of permanent revolution, or of permanent transfer.[34]

No longer an anticipation but a reminder of 1968 this time.

4 Conclusion

I have not tried to establish that by itself Althusser's letter played a decisive role in Deleuze's reworking of a second version of his text, for as yet I do not

---

[31] Deleuze 2004b, p. 188.
[32] See especially Deleuze 1973.
[33] Deleuze 2004b, p. 191. Regarding 'contradiction' and 'tendency', Deleuze cites Balibar's contribution to *Reading Capital* (see Althusser et al. 2015, pp. 357–480).
[34] Deleuze 2004b, p. 191.

know of others to whom Deleuze sent the transcription of his lecture for their comments. Further, despite a number of important modifications to his first version, Deleuze does not depart in the second version from his basic contention that it is indeed possible to isolate certain criteria by means of which it is possible to recognise structuralism and structuralists. Nonetheless, it seems to me that Deleuze clearly valued Althusser's opinion and altered the second version at least in part as a response to certain of Althusser's (and Macherey's) objections. In fact, Deleuze's references to Althusser are much more extensive – and no less favourable – than in the first. Indeed, Deleuze remarks near the beginning of the second version that 'no one better than Louis Althusser has assigned the status of structure as identical to "Theory" itself – and the symbolic must be understood as the production of the original and specific theoretical object'.

As most, then, what I have sought to do in this chapter is to 'clear the ground' for future research regarding Althusser's and Deleuze's complicated and mutually implicated intellectual itineraries. Such research would necessitate a new evaluation and appreciation of Deleuze's two great works of 1968 and 1969 – *Difference and Repetition*[35] and *The Logic of Sense*,[36] respectively – as 'virtualisations' of structuralism and as vital resources for the 'actualisation' not so much of a Marxist philosophy as, instead, of a philosophy for Marxism.[37]

---

35   Deleuze 1994.
36   Deleuze 1990b.
37   For a brief but highly suggestive characterisation of Deleuze's method of reading other philosophers and philosophies both in order to 'virtualise' and to 'actualise' them, see Alliez 1996. In addition, Zourabouchvili 1998 has identified the political stakes involved in actualising the virtual.

CHAPTER 13

Marxist Wisdom: Antonio Negri on the Book of Job*

> The Enlightenment ... will be all the more radical when it does not pour equal scorn on the Bible's all-pervading, healthy insight into man. It is for this very reason (one not remote from the Enlightenment) that the Bible can speak to all men, and be understood across so many lands and right on through the ages.
> – ERNST BLOCH[1]

∴

Louis Althusser once insisted that 'we ... have no religion, not even the religion of our theory, still less that of the goals of history'.[2] By contrast, Antonio Negri has remarked that, for him at least, the problem is not religion but transcendence:

> I've never had anything against religion – I'm simply against transcendence. I absolutely reject all forms of transcendence. But certain aspects of religion, and above all certain religious experiences, truly have the capacity to construct, not only in a mystical way but also in an ascetic way. Asceticism has always fascinated me: it is an internalized construction of the object; whereas mysticism, by contrast, is a distancing from the object – a negative theology, a theory of the margins. Asceticism is a constituent state, a transformation of the senses and the imagination, of the body and reason. In order to live well and to construct the common, asceticism is always necessary.[3]

---

* This chapter has been previously published in *The Philosophy of Antonio Negri, Volume 2: Revolution in Theory*, edited by Timothy S. Murphy and Abdul-Karim Mustapha, pp. 129–40, Ann Arbor, MI: Pluto Press, 2007.
1 Bloch 2009, p. 10.
2 Althusser 1977, p. 9.
3 Negri 2004a, p. 158.

An excellent illustration of Negri's perspective on asceticism and the struggle to 'construct the common' may be found in his work on the Book of Job.[4] As Negri relates, he began to write the book in 1982 or 1983, the beginning of his fourth year of imprisonment. Negri was only the most famous (or in the official vilification of the time the most 'notorious') of thousands of Italian activists who at the end of the 1970s had run up against the brutal force of state repression for their participation in the decade's radical movements. During such a bleak personal and political period of his life, the relevance of the Book of Job for Negri lay not primarily in how to reconcile the reality of human suffering with the existence of a just God but instead how to *resist* suffering of a most terrestrial sort. As he explains,

> There were numerous interpretations of Job but none of them had been able to provide a theological explanation of evil. *Si Deus est, unde malum? Si malum est, cur Deus?* [If God exists, whence arises evil? If evil exists, why does God exist?] It was not a question merely of understanding. It was a case of discovering how one could set oneself on a path of liberation. It was a practical problem, not a theodicy.[5]

Negri notes that he was offering neither a detailed commentary on, nor an exhaustive interpretation of, the Book of Job but instead was engaging in an 'intervention'.[6] And what an extraordinary intervention! For Negri, like Ernst Bloch before him,[7] compellingly shows that the Bible is too important to be ignored by Marxists or left to believers alone.

1   An Overview of the Book of Job

Before considering Negri's intervention in detail, however, it is perhaps useful to provide a brief overview of the Book of Job.[8] This complex biblical text opens with a prologue written in prose that recounts a folktale about a prosperous

---

4   Negri 2009.
5   Negri 2009, p. xviii.
6   Negri 2009, p. 4.
7   See Bloch's *Atheism in Christianity* (Bloch 2009), a book to which Negri refers several times, and his masterpiece *The Principle of Hope* (Bloch 1986b, especially pp. 1183–1311).
8   Perhaps the most impressive works on the Book of Job published after Negri's book appeared are Newsom 1996; Newsom 2003; Schifferdecker 2008; and Hankins 2015. Those interested in the most authoritative, still-standard commentaries that Negri himself employed should consult the following: Pope 1965 and Habel 1985.

man, Job, who despite undergoing incredible personal adversity nonetheless remains loyal to Yahweh (the sacred name of God in the ancient Israelite tradition). Unbeknownst to Job, the cause of his adversity are two divine tests between the 'Prosecutor' (literally, in Hebrew, the *satan*) and Yahweh that if Job were, first, to lose his possessions and children, and, second, his physical wellbeing, then he would abandon his faith. Indeed, Job's wife from the start advises him to 'curse Elohim [God] and die', but he rejects this 'foolish' thought and accepts his complete reversal in fortune.[9] Three friends – Eliphaz, Bildad, and Zophar – come to comfort Job, who humbly and patiently accepts pain and suffering at Yahweh's hand (1.1–2:10).

The main part of the book (3.1–42:6), however, is written in poetry and depicts a strikingly different image of Job: not a man who patiently endures but one who adamantly protests against the unjust treatment he thinks he has received by divine sanction. This poetic part begins (Chapter 3) with the common biblical literary form of a lament in which Job curses the day of his birth and longs for some way to escape the misery of his life. His friends prove to be sorry comforters and offer mere theological platitudes as explanations of Job's predicament. Each of them understands God to exercise ethical control over the universe, by rewarding the just and punishing the wicked. Consequently, each argues that Job himself (or his children!) must be responsible for his present dire straights. Each friend in turn affirms the conventional wisdom of divine justice – a kind of theodicy, in other words – and urges Job to make peace with God.

Job responds to his friends' arguments, accusations, and pious advice with vociferous protests that he is indeed innocent of any wrongdoing. He decries the disorder evident in a world that seems to be governed more by evil than good, and he boldly challenges God to listen to his complaint, indeed, to meet him face-to-face. In effect, as commentators have pointed out, Job is pressing a lawsuit against God. A dramatic – and for Negri an ethico-political and even ontological – highpoint occurs in Chapter 19 when Job envisions an 'avenger' (*go'el*) who will someday come to deliver him from his present torments (19.25).

In the midst of this series of speeches and responses occurs the interlude of a lengthy, self-standing poetic meditation on the nature of wisdom (Chapter 28). Wisdom is declared in this poem to be divine and thus beyond the comprehension of human beings, unless they 'fear' God and 'avoid evil' (28:25).

---

9 For quotations from the Book of Job I have used Edwin M. Good's vivid translation included with his commentary; see Good 1990.

The next three chapters (29–31) are soliloquies in which Job recalls his previously happy circumstances and honourable position in society (29), contrasts this with his present 'miserable days' (30.16), and concludes with an oath in which he upholds his integrity and issues a direct challenge to God: 'Here is my mark: let Shaddai [the Almighty] answer me ...' (31.35).

At this point a fourth, younger man, Elihu, angered by what he has heard so far, also enters into debate with Job. Elihu presents four rambling speeches in which he tries to refute the notion that suffering is necessarily the consequence of wrongdoing and rejects Job's rebellious assertion that God is acting unjustly (Chapters 32–7). Elihu contends that God inflicts suffering only to chasten human beings. God speaks to human beings in dreams in order to warn them against pride; those who have gone astray may hope for an intercessor to vouch for them and evoke divine grace. In the last analysis, however, Elihu maintains that God's actions are simply beyond human comprehension.

The dramatic climax of the Book of Job is a theophany. God appears and answers Job 'from the whirlwind'. In two powerful speeches (38.1–40.2 and 40.6–41.26) God directly reveals to Job the glorious expanse of the universe but only indirectly answers Job's question about the reason for his misfortunes. In these speeches the implication seems clear enough, however. At the beginning of the world God brought order out of chaos – represented by the mythical beasts Behemoth and Leviathan – but ever since has struggled to preserve this order. Chaos continually threatens to undermine that cosmic order – indeed, it invariably partially succeeds in doing so.

After God's first speech Job concedes the point: 'Oh, I am small, what could I reply to you? I put my hand to my mouth' (40.3–4). Moreover, following the second speech Job makes a crucial distinction: whereas before he had heard of God only 'with ears hearing ... now my eye sees you' (42.5a). Finally, Job utters what was once taken by many commentators to be an expression of contrition, but is more likely to be an acknowledgement that his demand has been satisfied, the time for him to lament has passed: 'I despise and repent of dust and ashes' (42.5b).

The book closes with another prose section, an epilogue that picks up where the prologue had left off. At this conclusion of the earlier folktale the patient, humble Job prays for his friends, his former fortunes are restored – indeed, they are doubled (likely an oblique indication that he has in effect won his lawsuit against God!) – and he lives to a ripe old age (42.7–17). Especially noteworthy, however, is Yahweh's admission that Job was right all along to protest: 'He said to Eliphaz the Temanite, "I am very angry with you and your two friends, because you have not spoken truth of me, as has my servant Job"' (42.7).

2 A Theological Fable

For Negri the Book of Job functions as a 'theological fable' or 'parable'[10] that can help one to construct a 'genealogy' of the 'origin of value and of the dynamic of its system, that is, also of the value of labor and of its creative aspects'.[11] Indeed, as Negri explains further,

> the reality of our wretchedness is that of Job, the questions and answers that we pose to the world are the same as Job's. We express ourselves with the same desperation, uttering the same blasphemous phrases.[12]

Several themes stand out in Negri's proposed genealogy: the ethico-political significance of pain and suffering, the rejection of all forms of theodicy, and the radical openness, or *immeasurability*, of the future.

Consider, first of all, the extreme suffering and pain that Job undergoes as the result of the two divine tests mentioned above. In Negri's view, Job's experience teaches us that pain and suffering is the destiny of all human beings and can only be defined through compassion. But compassion is not simply an intellectual act; it is a concrete way to 'sympathise with' or to suffer-together with others.[13] Here Negri's reading of the Book of Job dovetails with that of the Peruvian liberation theologian Gustavo Gutiérrez, who has pointed out that Job's 'solitude' is hardly passive or reactive. On the contrary, Gutiérrez argues, it is an active and productive solitude, in the sense that Job increasingly comes to identify with, and protest against, the various forms of pain and suffering in the world, not the least of which are due to socio-economic oppression.[14] As Gutiérrez puts it, 'Job begins to free himself from an ethic centered on personal rewards and to pass to another focused on the needs of one's neighbor'.[15] Consider in this light, then, the moving words in Chapter 24 of the Book of Job in which Job denounces those who 'snatch away boundary markers, seize flocks and pasture them ... drive off orphans' asses, take a widow's ox for collateral, shove the poor off the road' and expresses his solidarity with 'the land's destitute' who 'huddle together in hiding' and lodge naked, 'without clothing,

---

10 Negri 2009, p. 14.
11 Negri, p. 15.
12 Negri 2009, p. 15.
13 Negri develops his philosophical analysis of pain at greater length in Negri 2004b.
14 Gutiérrez 1987, pp. 31–8.
15 Gutiérrez 1987, p. 31.

uncovered in the cold, wet with mountain rain, [and] without shelter ... hug the rock' (24.2–4, 7–8).

Negri concludes that one of the most profound lessons of the Book of Job is the following:

> It is not the recognition of a behavior of pain nor the communication of a pain that provides us with the constitutive process of the social – pain is this constitutive process, and only by undergoing it, suffering ... with the world, can we reconstruct the world from pain. Compassion goes beyond recognition, beyond the concept, beyond representation. I am unable to represent pain to myself except by undergoing it. I do not recognize the suffering other unless I feel compassion ... for him. But through this action of putting myself in this place via love, by feeling pity ... I proceed to construct the world. It is not the divinity, then, not a meaning that descends from above, but suffering and pain, which come from below, that construct the very being of the world.[16]

Yet none of this implies that human suffering and pain are ever theologically justifiable. For Negri the whole point of the Book of Job is not really to solve the problem of evil, rather it is to undermine the reader's confidence that there *is* any such solution and thereby repudiate every conceivable form of theodicy. The leading biblical scholar Walter Brueggemann has pointed out that nowhere in the Hebrew Bible can one find a definitive solution to the problem of evil.[17] In a real sense, then, the Book of Job only pushes an already – existing biblical train of thought to its explosive conclusion. It is indeed remarkable – or pathetic – to behold how each of Job's interlocutors in turn offers a well-worn justification for God's actions, while Job himself defiantly continues to affirm his innocence and occasionally even expresses 'a laughter ... that resembles sarcasm and that refuses any consolation or pacification'.[18]

It is precisely the failure of theological justification for human suffering and evil that makes both possible and necessary what Negri regards as a 'subterranean presence' in the Book of Job that only 'gradually becomes evident until the point when it explodes':[19] the Messiah. It is only a Messiah who can come to Job's defence insofar as God has come to operate less as an impartial judge and more as a malicious adversary. It is only a Messiah who can lead Job beyond his

---

16 Negri 2009, p. 93.
17 See his entries for 'Suffering' and 'Theodicy' in Brueggemann, pp. 200–4, 212–14.
18 Negri 2009, p. 60.
19 Negri 2009, p. 69.

present world of pain and suffering toward a future state of redemption. But caution is in order here.

Negri is not lapsing into yet another dubious retrospective Christian interpretation of the 'avenger' (*go'el*) to whom Job appeals.[20] Rather, again like Ernst Bloch before him,[21] he is trying to identify a powerfully materialist dimension of the Book of Job. For the kind of messianic deliverance that Job seeks can only be secured with respect to the *body*, indeed through, a 'resurrection of the flesh'.[22]

As Negri is well aware, the idea of resurrection is hardly popular today. Even in contemporary religious belief and practice, a 'materialist' theory of resurrection has largely been displaced by an 'idealist' theory of the immortality of the soul. Good atheist that he is, Negri is quick to add that he favours a 'secularisation' of this and other theological concepts (e.g., creation or redemption),

> but only on the condition that we do not lose, through this pseudorationalist conversion, the practical, ethical, and passionate content of religious truth. It is not mystery that interests us, but grace and charity.[23]

As a result, as Negri elsewhere admits, it is not only the eschatological aspect of the concept of bodily resurrection that intrigues him, but, more importantly, it is the 'rediscovery of a materialist religion'.[24]

3 From the Messiah to the Immeasurable

It is worth emphasising at this point that adopting a messianic outlook need not imply any teleology. On the contrary, it suggests the radical openness of the historical process. For Negri, at least, the Messiah 'is a surplus of being, of materiality, that is original and outside all finality, diffused everywhere in

---

20 On the temptation for Christians to engage in theological proof-texting of this passage, and thereby to interpret the 'avenger' as a 'redeemer' (as most English translations still indicate), see Newsom 1996, pp. 477–9.

21 See *Atheism in Christianity*, pp. 106–22.

22 Negri 2009, pp. 69–73. The relationship between messianic expectation and resurrection is a dominant motif in biblical apocalypticism. On the historical emergence and development of the apocalyptic worldview in the ancient Near East, see Collins 1998, Murphy 2012, and Portier-Young 2014.

23 Negri 2009, p. 77.

24 Negri 2004a, p. 180.

the world'.[25] This radical openness of the future is what Negri designates as its 'immeasurability'.[26] What is immeasurable is assuredly not an instance of the Burkean[27] or Kantian 'sublime',[28] for this would misconstrue the 'ontological realism' of Job's suffering and encounter with God as merely an extreme form of subjective experience.[29] As a result, and notwithstanding Hegel's insistence that 'mankind has revered measure as something inviolable and sacred',[30] Negri gestures toward what is objectively beyond the possibility of even being measured, indeed, toward what is *measureless*.[31]

Yet in Negri's opinion most interpreters of the Book of Job have tended to do exactly what Job's own interlocutors do, namely, 'confine to a given form and measure his experience within the dimensions of the theologically known'.[32] Although Negri only briefly suggests as much,[33] one could point to Hegel as an especially revealing case of how *not* to interpret the Book of Job. For example, in his *Lectures on the Philosophy of Religion* Hegel admits that 'Job is guiltless; he finds his misfortune unjustifiable and so is dissatisfied'.[34] However, for Hegel this implies that

> there is an antithesis within him, the consciousness of the justice or righteousness that is absolute and of the incongruity between his fate and this righteousness. He is dissatisfied precisely because he does not regard necessity as blind fate; it is known to be God's purpose to bring about good things for those who are good. The critical point, then, occurs when this dissatisfaction and despondency has to submit to absolute, pure confidence. This submission is the end point.[35]

---

25 Negri 2009, p. 102.
26 Negri 2009, pp. 5–9.
27 See Burke 1998, pp. 49–199. It is worth noting that Burke invokes the Book of Job as an illustration of what he means by the sublime (see pp. 106–11).
28 See Kant 2000. Kant discusses the Book of Job at some length in his essay 'On the Miscarriage of All Philosophical Trials in Theodicy' in Kant 1996, pp. 24–37.
29 Negri 2009, pp. 60–2.
30 Hegel 1976, p. 329.
31 One could easily make the general case that biblical (as opposed to ancient Greek) thinking about space and time especially allowed for a positive appreciation of what the Norwegian scholar Thorleif Boman once characterised as 'boundlessness'. See Boman 1970, pp. 123–83.
32 Negri 2009, p. 96.
33 Negri 2009, pp. 6–7.
34 Hegel 1988, p. 369.
35 Hegel 1988, pp. 369–70.

Job's submission is, for Hegel, ultimately an expression of his complete trust in a purposeful God, in the 'harmony of the power of God with the truth'.[36] Indeed, this is why Hegel thinks that at the end God restores Job to a position of good fortune. The Hegelian dialectical method at work here could not be clearer – or more mistaken in its ability to grasp what is really at stake in the Book of Job. Misfortune, submission, and restoration: Hegel has turned Job's passion into a devotional exercise.

For Job to have seen God directly means something quite different, though. According to Negri,

> He saw God, hence Job can speak of him, and he – Job himself – can in turn participate in divinity, in the function of redemption that man constructs within life – the instrument of the death of God that is human constitution and the creation of the world.[37]

The point here is not that an object or a being could be too large or ill-defined to be measurable. Immeasurability has nothing to do with a theoretical shortcoming in the face of immensity (e.g., as occurs, Burke argues, when one contemplates God's 'almighty power')[38] but instead concerns the limitless self-measurement that arises in human creative activity.

In light of this immeasurability of social practice, Negri concludes, the antagonism between life and death that runs throughout the Book of Job ultimately 'is resolved in favor of life. My life is the recognition of you – my eyes have seen you. I am. Man is'.[39] Although the ontological foundation of the world continues to be menaced by great forces of death and destruction (depicted as Behemoth and Leviathan), human beings can nonetheless come to resist this evil through their own acts of creation. Job's vision of God holds out the prospect of redemption, 'as the world is formed and reformed through the struggle against evil'.[40] In short, as Negri puts it,

> The struggle against monsters is the condition for the ordering of nature. The order of nature is the condition for the order of the world, and this is the condition of redemption. But these passages are neither linear nor

---

36 Hegel 1988, p. 370.
37 Negri 2009, pp. 96–7.
38 Burke 1998, p. 111.
39 Negri 2009, p. 97.
40 Negri 2009, p. 98.

continuous. There is no objective; there is struggle, invention, victory, *there is constitution*.⁴¹

4 The Political Lesson of Job

As one would expect from the complex library of ancient Israelite traditions that it is, the Hebrew Bible contains a wide variety of modes of discourse, e.g., laws, records, genealogies, liturgies, quasi-historical reports, love poems, prophetic injunctions, and wisdom.⁴² Scholars usually categorise the Book of Job as an important example of biblical wisdom literature.⁴³ But there remains a crucial difference between the Book of Job and other wisdom texts like Proverbs and Ecclesiastes (Qohelet). As Gustavo Gutiérrez has observed, there exists another 'dimension' in the Book of Job that has a great deal in common with such prophetic books as Amos, Hosea, Micah, and Isaiah. Moreover, Gutiérrez has insisted on the inseparability of these prophetic and sapiential dimensions within the Book of Job:

> Vision of God (final stage in Job's suit against God) and defense of the poor (a role he discovers for himself because of his own innocence) are ... combined in the experience of Job as a man of justice ...
> Without the prophetic dimension the language of contemplation is in danger of having no grip on the history in which God acts and in which we meet God. Without the mystical dimension the language of prophecy can narrow its vision and weaken its perception of the God who makes all things new ... Each undergoes a distortion that isolates it and renders it unauthentic.⁴⁴

Although Negri would take exception with Gutiérrez's characterisation of Job's vision of God as 'mystical',⁴⁵ he too has identified in the Book of Job a con-

---

41 Negri 2009, p. 98.
42 For introductions to the panoply of biblical literary forms, see Gabel et al. 2000 and Johnson 2002.
43 On the ancient Israelite wisdom tradition, and the place of the Book of Job within it, see Bergant 1997 and Crenshaw 2010.
44 Gutiérrez 1987, p. 96.
45 Indeed, Negri identifies a mystical trap laid by Job's friend Zophar (Negri 2009, pp. 39–40). In his autobiographical interview Negri likewise characterises mysticism as 'the worst thing there is, because there is a negative foundation that one thinks one is escaping, only to fall back into it' (Negri 2004a, p. 101).

cern not only for social justice but for something more: the immeasurable. As we have already seen, for Negri what is ontologically immeasurable is not exactly 'God' but instead the radical openness of the future, always-already made possible by the immanent human power to imagine and create a different world.[46] This is why I would like to argue that Negri has introduced into – or recognised as nascent within – Marxism something more than just the secularised prophetic dimension so often commented on[47] – and not always favorably, it should be said![48] To be precise, Negri has made a formidable contribution to what could be termed a distinctively Marxist wisdom tradition.[49]

By way of conclusion, let us turn again to Negri's motivation at the beginning of the 1980s for working on the Book of Job. The accumulated violence of the twentieth century had already posed as never before fundamental questions about the nature of human evil that echoed Job's own anguished lament. For Negri such questions include the following: *'How can one believe in reason after Auschwitz and Hiroshima? How can one continue to be a communist after Stalin?'*[50] Humanity had found itself faced with an unprecedented dilemma in which, Negri wonders,

> Why do we produce evil? How can we find our way in a world in which every dialectic has shown its revolting ineffectiveness – where murder and the destruction of values have reached the immeasurable and where

---

46 Negri does admit, however, that if he had to define 'God', it would be in terms of 'overabundance, excess, and joy' (Negri 2004b, p. 101).
47 For example, John Raines has proposed that 'like the Hebrew prophets of old, Marx knew that to speak of social justice we must become socially self-critical, and that means becoming critical of the ruling powers – whether they be kings or priests or investment bankers ... For Marx, all ideas are relative to the social location and interests of their production. And like the prophets before him, the most revealing perspective is not from the top down or the center outward, but the point of view of the exploited and the marginalized. Suffering can see through and unveil official explanations; it can cry out and protest against the arrogance of power' (Raines 2002, p. 5).
48 Negri himself has cautioned against 'false prophets [who] lead only to a sort of general nihilism, an annihilation that ends up causing them to be forgotten in their turn. To question the world is to invent it at each instant, but there is in this a constructive dimension that is quite the opposite of prophetic nihilism' (Negri 2004a, p. 236).
49 Others who might be included within a genealogy of Marxist wisdom are Walter Benjamin and Ernst Bloch. Perhaps, too, this is one of the most important contributions made to Marxism by contemporary liberation theology. For a fine survey of the movement in Latin America and its implications for socialist renewal, see Löwy 1996. See, too, a remarkable book by the German liberation theologian Dorothee Soelle: Soelle 2001.
50 Negri 2009, p. 8.

absolute non-being, that is, the nuclear, absolute destruction of what exists, is for the first time at the disposal of Power? And what is salvation?[51]

In short, Negri admits, 'all the certainties that we have inherited and the values for which we have fought are up for discussion'.[52] This was a generalized, but *negative*, crisis of measure.

In a rather different, more hopeful, and *positive* way, though, the year 1968 had also introduced a 'crisis of measure and of the laws that structured it', and a challenge to official Marxism as a 'culture of measure, a labor of measure, the measured passion of the *Raison d'État*'.[53] Indeed, by the end of the 1970s there had, according to Negri, occurred 'a transformation of work … rest[ing] upon the ruins of the measure of value'.[54] As a result, both (state) socialism[55] and capitalism had become impossible; and there was a pressing need to create something new.

Such a collapse of the measure of value was, in Negri's estimation, again analogous to Job's experience, for he had once been 'loyal to all the measures that regulated the world supported by God'.[56] But Job's singularity – and universality – was to have wound up protesting 'against measure', whether theological, ontological, ethical, or political in nature. So too, Negri proposed, must contemporary Marxist theory and practice 'move with joy beyond measure',[57] and

---

51   Negri 2009, p. 9.
52   Negri 2009, p. 9.
53   Negri 2009, p. xix.
54   Negri 2009, p. xix.
55   Throughout his *oeuvre* Negri consistently fails, I believe, to distinguish between the former Stalinist bureaucracies and the possibility of an authentic socialist democracy. As a result, he often seems to pose an all-or-nothing alternative between capitalism and communism and thereby fails to provide an adequate theory of how *transition* to a classless society might occur. I don't mean that Negri has nothing important to say about the politics of such a transition – far from it. However, even when he does discuss transitional politics (e.g., in such works from the late 70s as *Il Dominio e il Sabotaggio* [Negri 1978] or *Marx Oltre Marx* [Negri 1984]), it occurs at a level of abstraction that is not particularly useful for concrete struggles to win structural reforms that could in fact initiate a break with capitalist social relations.
56   Negri 2009, p. xx.
57   Negri 2009, p. xx. Constructing an 'immeasurable Marxism' would seem to be an important aspect of Negri's project (with Michael Hardt) in the trilogy *Empire* (Hardt and Negri 2000); *Multitude* (Hardt and Negri 2004); and *Commonwealth* (Hardt and Negri 2009). There is an explicit discussion of measure and immeasurability in Hardt and Negri 2000, pp. 354–9.

resume the process of 'self-valorization'.⁵⁸ For Negri this was the only way to imagine communism again.

Although there is, perhaps, an inadequate anti-capitalist political strategy laid out in his writings (a point made generously by Leo Panitch and Sam Gindin⁵⁹ and rather uncharitably by Alex Callinicos),⁶⁰ political strategy has never been Negri's main concern. He has always been much more interested in political *ontology*, in other words, the general conditions of possibility for envisioning any political strategy at all.⁶¹ Negri was only half joking, I suspect, when he quipped that 'my dream is one day to have a chair of ontology!'⁶²

Consider in this light, then, the simultaneously political and ontological significance for Marxism of the concept of the Messiah whose incipient formation Negri discerns in the Book of Job. Negri argues that

> for Marx the Messiah is defined, revealed, and put into motion by the same contradictions that have enabled the development of capitalism and unleashed its crisis. The process is materially determined and resolved for Marx. But what is the plot, the corporeality of the theoretical struggle promoted here? In my opinion, the acknowledgement of the scientificity of Marx's argument cannot remove the echo of the religious experience that underlies these pages and sets up the innovative, redemptive, and revolutionary event; we should, instead, insist upon it. Science takes away the mystery from the portentous event, but it cannot negate its passion; on the contrary, it must restore it to us.⁶³

In the last analysis, what is most impressive about Negri's intervention regarding the Book of Job is how powerfully it can help Marxists themselves to recover and sustain a passion not just to interpret but also to change the world.

---

58   'Self-valorisation' is a key concept in Negri's theoretical lexicon and refers to workers' positive capacity through their own organising to free themselves from capitalist exploitation and thereby transform work into freely associated production. See, for example, Negri's discussion in Negri 1984, esp. pp. 162–3, 185–6.
59   Panitch and Gindin 2002.
60   Callinicos 2001.
61   The mutual implication of politics and metaphysics is one of the overriding themes of his books on Descartes (Negri 2007), Spinoza (Negri 1991), and the history of 'constituent power' (Negri 1999).
62   Negri 2004a, p. 70.
63   Negri 2009, p. 78.

CHAPTER 14

A Displaced Transition: Habermas on the Public Sphere*

In order for a critical theory of society to be adequate, Jacques Bidet has contended, it must include at least three key components: a description of actually existing injustice, a normative ideal of justice, and a strategy for transition from unjust to just social orders.[1] Like most contemporary political philosophers, Jürgen Habermas has primarily focused on the first two components. In what follows, though, I want instead to draw attention to, and express reservations about, Habermas's scattered observations regarding how to a bring about a just society.

Although in the last twenty years Habermas has often used a general terminology of 'transition' (*Übergang*), the specific examples he has provided are *symptomatic* for what they obscure as much as they reveal. Habermas's recent writings bear witness to a proliferation of transitions during what he has called a 'time of transitions' (*Zeit der Übergänge*).[2] Habermas identifies transitions 'from morality to law';[3] 'from discourse to action';[4] 'from conceptual history to social and political history';[5] to modernity;[6] to a unified Germany ('A Berlin Republic');[7] to a European Union;[8] from 'negative' to 'positive' European integration,[9] to a 'postnational' democracy[10] or 'form of consciousness';[11] from the nation-states (or international law) to a cosmopolitan order;[12] and to a 'less

---

*   This chapter has been previously published in *Masses, Classes, and Ideas*, edited by Mike Hill and Warren Montag, pp. 146–57, New York, NY: Verso Books, 2000.
1   In this regard, Jacques Bidet has well identified he shortcomings of both John Rawls's theory of justice and Jürgen Habermas's discourse ethics. See Bidet 1995, pp. 93–105 and Bidet 1999, pp. 399–426.
2   Habermas 2006b.
3   Habermas 2012, p. 85; Habermas, p. 93.
4   Habermas 2008, p. 34.
5   Habermas 2012, p. 92.
6   Habermas 2006b, p. 150.
7   Habermas 2001, p. 26.
8   Habermas 2001, p. 100; Habermas 2006a, p. 65; Habermas 2006b, pp. 71–110.
9   Habermas 2006a, p. 50.
10 Habermas 2001, p. 103; Habermas 2006a, p. 115, 172.
11 Habermas 2006, p. 78.
12 Habermas 2001, p. 119; Habermas 2006a, pp. 5, 19, 87, 123, 132, 137; Habermas 2006b, p. 30; Habermas 2008, pp. 313–14, 317.

fragmented, more peaceful society'.[13] Indeed, it would appear that the only transition that remains inadmissible – even inconceivable – for him is a transition beyond capitalism itself! Consequently, I have restricted my attention in this chapter to Habermas's earlier arguments for ruling out of theoretical order a transition that especially matters for Marxists: the one from capitalism to socialism.[14]

1   The Socialist Project in Crisis

It is worth noting at the outset that Habermas has always been clear about the kind of political mobilisation that he rejects, namely, the classical Marxist project of contesting with the hope of supplanting state and class power by setting up alternative institutions of workers' and popular power – what Antonio Negri has strikingly called new forms of 'constituent power'.[15] In *The Structural Transformation of the Public Sphere*,[16] for example, early on in his philosophical development Habermas expresses a certain admiration for Marx's politics:

> Marx shared the perspective of the propertyless and uneducated masses who, without fulfilling the conditions for admission to the bourgeois public sphere, nonetheless made their way into it in order to translate economic conflicts into the only form holding any promise of success – that is, into political conflict. In Marx's opinion the masses would employ the platform of the public sphere, institutionalized in the constitutional state, not to destroy it but to make it into what, according to liberal pretense, it had always claimed to be.

Yet he immediately adds the following qualification:

---

13   Habermas 2001, p. 140.
14   It should go without saying that for critical Marxists today other transitions *within capitalism*, e.g., from more sexist to less sexist, more homophobic to less homophobic, more racist to less racist, more corrupt to less corrupt, more violent to less violent, more ecologically destructive to less ecologically destructive are desirable. The point is that these transitions still require broad-based, mass movements to achieve success. As I argue below in Chapter Fifteen, the struggle against capitalism – and the transition to socialist democracy – must strengthen, and proceed through, the intersection of these ongoing concrete struggles.
15   For Negri's brilliant rereading of Marx in terms of the concept of 'constituent power', see Negri 1999.
16   Habermas 1989c.

In reality, however, the occupation of the political public sphere by the unpropertied masses led to an interlocking of state and society which removed from the public sphere its former basis without supplying a new one. For the integration of the public and private realms entailed a corresponding disorganization of the public sphere that once was the go-between linking state and society.[17]

Indeed, one of the key themes of *The Structural Transformation of the Public Sphere* concerns the failure of working-class struggles to make good the promise of liberalism (represented by the rise, temporary flourishing, and fall of bourgeois literary and political public spheres). The revolutions of 1848 and the 1871 Paris Commune illustrate for Habermas not only a proletarian inability to bring actually existing capitalist social and political institutions into conformity with such professed bourgeois ideals as freedom, equality, and democracy but also the grave danger that mass movements – especially when successful – pose to the separation between civil society and the state.[18] Since the original publication of *The Structural Transformation of the Public Sphere* in German in 1961, Habermas has maintained this position with remarkable consistency. Consider the following recent examples.

After making his famous 'linguistic turn' and subsequently formulating a theory of 'communicative action'[19] in an article published in the early 1980s, Habermas discerns what he calls an 'exhaustion of utopian energies' associated with a 'shift of paradigm from a society based on social labor to a society based on communication'.[20] Especially in light of the failed hopes of the 1960s and 1970s, he concludes, the Left must henceforth abandon 'the methodological illusion that was concerned with projections of a concrete totality of future life possibilities'. Instead:

> the utopian content of a society based on communication is limited to the formal aspects of an undamaged intersubjectivity. To the extent to which it suggests a concrete form of life, even the expression 'the ideal speech

---

17 Habermas 1989c, p. 177.
18 Habermas makes his case largely on the basis of a reading of Marx's early philosophical writings, especially *On the Jewish Question*; arguably, he undervalues the richness and subtlety of such later historical works as *The Civil War in France*. See Habermas 1989, pp. 122–9, 139–40. Also, see the contemporaneous article 'Natural Law and Revolution' in Habermas 1973, especially pp. 109–13.
19 See Habermas 1984; 1987.
20 Habermas 1989a, p. 68.

situation' is misleading. What can be outlined normatively are the necessary but general conditions for the communicative practice of everyday life and for a procedure of discursive will-formation that would put participants themselves in a position to realize concrete possibilities for a better and less threatened life, on their own initiative and in accordance with their own needs and insights.[21]

Thus, according to Habermas, the traditional socialist project required significant modification, for the 'socialist containment of capitalism' had become more than a matter of 'simple recipes of workers' self-management'. Indeed, he argues that there is a pressing need for 'something new, namely a highly innovative combination of power and intelligent self-restraint'. This is because 'not only capitalism but the interventionist state itself' must be 'socially contained'. Moreover, the task has consequently become 'considerably more complicated', because 'that combination of power and intelligent self-restraint can no longer be entrusted to the state's planning capacity' but must emerge from the activity of 'autonomous, self-organized public spheres'.[22]

In an article published in the immediate aftermath of what he designated the 'rectifying revolution' of 1989, Habermas likewise insists that the 'non-communist Left has no reason to be downhearted'.[23] Indeed, it continues to have an important political role. In Habermas's view, the 'socialist Left ... can generate the ferment that produces the continuing process of political communication that prevents the institutional framework of a constitutional democracy from becoming desiccated'.[24] However, political aspirations must be constrained, as socialist ideas are transformed 'into the radically reformist self-criticism of a capitalist society, which, in the form of a constitutional democracy with universal suffrage and a welfare state, has developed not only weaknesses but also strengths'.[25] Habermas then offers, and elaborates on, a telling biblical metaphor:

> With the bankruptcy of state socialism, this is the eye of the needle through which everything must pass. This socialism will disappear only when it no longer has an object of criticism – perhaps at a point when the society in question has changed its identity so much that it allows

---

21 Habermas 1989a, p. 68.
22 Habermas 1989a, pp. 63–4.
23 Habermas 1990.
24 Habermas 1990, p. 21.
25 Habermas 1990, p. 21.

the full significance of everything that cannot be expressed as a price to be perceived and taken seriously. The hope that humanity can emancipate itself from self-imposed tutelage and degrading living conditions has not lost its power, but it is filtered by a falliblist consciousness, and an awareness of the historical lesson that one would already have achieved a considerable amount if the balance of a tolerable existence could be preserved for the fortunate few – and, most of all, if it could be established on the other, ravaged continents.[26]

Habermas tries, then, to preserve what he took to be an ethical socialism. Although a long-term utopian hope remains in order (Kant's regulative idea of humanity one day freed from its 'self-imposed tutelage'), the immediate task before the Left is modest: to help shore up, indeed to strive to *universalize* the welfare state.

In the preface to *Between Facts and Norms*,[27] Habermas returns to this theme and urges the Left – 'after the collapse of state socialism and the end of the "global civil war"' – to cease envisioning socialism as 'the design – and violent implementation – of a concrete form of life'. 'If, however', he adds, 'one conceives of "socialism" as the set of necessary conditions for emancipated forms of life about which the participants themselves must first reach an understanding, then one will recognize that the democratic self-organization of a legal community constitutes the normative core of this project as well'.[28] It is worth noting that here again Habermas intentionally retained the term 'self-organisation' but dismissed any notion of workers' 'self-management'.[29]

Indeed, in a 1993 'Conversation about Questions of Political Theory' Habermas insists that:

> [W]e have to let go of interpretations that have become dear to us, including the idea that radical democracy is a form of self-administering socialism. Only a democracy that is understood in terms of communications

---

26 Habermas 1990, p. 21.
27 Habermas 1996.
28 Habermas 1996, p. xli.
29 In this regard, also note an interview that Habermas gave in February 1997 to *L'Humanité*, the newspaper of the French Communist Party. He insists that 'autonomy and democracy ... are tied to the idea of "self-organization". I can give the example of the university, with the forms of research that currently exist to popularize knowledge. That has nothing to do with the self-management of companies in a market in which everything is decided in advance'.

theory is feasible under the conditions of complex societies. In this instance, the relationship of center and periphery must be reversed: in my model the forms of communication in a civil society, which grow out of an intact private sphere, along with the communicative stream of a vital public sphere embedded in a liberal political culture, are what chiefly bear the burden of normative expectations.[30]

2 Unsurpassable Capitalism: from Sieges to Sluices

What is the significance of these references? First of all, although Habermas has regularly called attention to the failures of advanced capitalist societies, he has equally insisted that capitalism itself cannot be superseded. In a word, the capitalist market and capitalist state are the unsurpassable horizons of political theory and practice. No doubt Habermas has on occasion granted that 'capitalism is just as insensitive to harming the moral equilibrium of society as technology is to the way it disturbs the ecological balance of nature'; and so 'there is a practical need for the economic system to be reined in by the welfare state and ecologically restructured'. Yet in customary fashion he quickly cautions that such reforms are

> easier said than done, because society is indebted for both its productivity and its permanent crisis to the uncoupling of self-directed systems from the life-world – the autonomizing of the rationalities of partial systems with regard to the imperatives of life-forms integrated by way of values, norms, and achievements of understanding is an ambiguous phenomenon.[31]

Habermas's desire to achieve a realistic social theory thus led him to stress not only the increasing complexity and functional differentiation of modern capitalist societies but also the inadequacies of previous socialist strategies of transition. In fact, if we can speak of a transition any longer, it is not in the sense of superseding the capitalist mode of production but merely of counteracting the worst effects – the 'insensitivities' – of market maldistribution and state bureaucratisation. Since the late 1980s Habermas began to scale back and reconfigure socialism in terms of 'radical democracy' and advanced two

---

30 Habermas 1997, p. 133.
31 Habermas 1997, p. 71.

'models' of how such radical democratisation might occur under conditions of advanced capitalism.

In a 1988 article on 'Popular Sovereignty as Procedure' (included as an appendix to *Between Facts and Norms*), Habermas proposes a 'siege' model for how citizens can criticise and influence the state without actually trying to supplant state power and thereby – at least according to this line of reasoning – undermine the very autonomous public spheres and communicative freedoms that serve as the conditions of possibility for such criticism and influence.[32] Habermas's overriding concern in this article is to develop a 'desubstantialized' idea of popular sovereignty. In other words, sovereignty should be located not in the people themselves but

> in those subjectless forms of communication that regulate the flow of discursive opinion and will-formation in such a way that their fallible outcomes have the presumption of practical reason on their side. Subjectless and anonymous, an intersubjectively dissolved popular sovereignty withdraws into democratic procedures and the demanding communicative presuppositions of their implementation. It is sublimated into the elusive interactions between culturally mobilized public spheres and a will-formation institutionalized according to the rule of law. Set communicatively aflow, sovereignty makes itself felt in the power of public discourses. Although such power originates in autonomous public spheres, it must take shape in the decisions of democratic institutions of opinion- and will-formation, inasmuch as the responsibility for momentous decisions demands clear institutional accountability. Communicative power is exercised in the manner of a siege. It influences the premises of judgments and decision making in the political system without intending to conquer the system itself. It thus aims to assert its imperatives in the only language the besieged fortress understands: it takes responsibility for the pool of reasons that administrative power can handle instrumentally but cannot ignore, given its juridical structure.[33]

Although the basic point is clear, there follows no detailed account of the means by which autonomous public spheres are supposed to hold state power in check and redirect its activities to serve the common good. Moreover, the

---

32   Kenneth Baynes has been one of the few commentators to draw attention to Habermas's use of the siege model, but he does not distinguish this model from the later sluice model. See Baynes 1992, p. 179; 1995, p. 217.
33   Habermas 1996, pp. 486–7.

type of siege to be conducted via the public sphere is a largely symbolic affair, a kind of communicative 'sublimation' of actually existing forms of social struggle. This is a most peculiar siege, too: it is permanent and yet must never succeed. If the siege were in fact ever to succeed by supplanting the market and state through the establishment of workers' or popular power, the siege would in fact already have failed, for the autonomy of the public sphere would supposedly collapse.

In the preface to a new printing of *The Structural Transformation of the Public Sphere* (published in Leipzig just prior to German reunification and doubtless intended for readers in the German Democratic Republic),[34] Habermas equally stresses the siege model, which he presented as a kind of 'democratic dam'. He reiterates, too, the 'implications for his concept of democarcy' advanced in *The Theory of Communicative Action*. As an implied self-criticism, Habermas indicates that he has come to consider the

> state apparatus and economy to be systematically integrated action fields that can no longer be transformed democratically from within, that is, switched over to a political mode of integration, without damage to their proper systemic logic and therewith their ability to function. The abysmal collapse of state socialism has only confirmed this. Instead, radical democratization now aims for a shifting of forces within a "separation of powers" that itself is to be maintained in principle. The new equilibrium to be attained is not one between state powers but between different resources for social integration. The goal is no longer to supersede an economic system having a capitalist life of its own but to erect a democratic dam against the colonializing *encroachment* of system imperatives on areas of the lifeworld. Therewith we have bid farewell to the notion of alienation and appropriation of objectified essentialist powers, whose place is in a philosophy of praxis. A radical-democratic change in the process of legitimation aims at a new balance between the forces of societal integration so that the social-integrative power of solidarity – the 'communicative force of production' – can prevail over the powers of the other two control resources, i.e., money and administrative power, and therewith successfully assert the practically oriented demands of the lifeworld.[35]

---

34   Habermas 1992.
35   Habermas 1992, p. 444.

With the publication of *Between Facts and Norms* in 1992, though, Habermas finds this 'image of a democratically "besieged" fortress of the state' to be 'misleading', since it fails to allow for the possibility of a 'democratisation' of the state that goes 'beyond special obligations to provide information' and could 'supplement parliamentary and judicial controls on administration from within'.[36] He also reflects that his

> purpose in proposing the image of a 'siege' of the bureaucratic power of public administrations by citizens making use of communicative power was to oppose the classic idea of revolution – the conquest and destruction of state power. The unfettered communicative freedoms of citizens are supposed to become effective through – as Rawls says with Kant – the 'public use of reason'. But the 'influence' of the opinions that compete in the public sphere, and communicative power formed by means of democratic procedures on the horizon of the public sphere, can become effective only if they affect administrative power – so as to program and control it – without intending to take it over.

However, the model of citizens forming autonomous public spheres of such size and strength that they can surround, besiege, and limit abuses generated by the administrative power of the state now seems inadequate to Habermas. He ultimately regards

> the siege model [as] too defeatist, at least if you understand the division of powers in such a way that administrative and judicial authorities employing the law are to have limited access to the grounds mobilized in their full scope by legislative authorities in justifying their decisions. Today, the matters that need regulation are often such that the political legislator is in no position sufficiently to regulate them in advance. In such cases, it is up to administrative and judicial authorities to give them concrete form and to continue their legal development, and these require discourses that have to do with grounding rather than with application. However, to be legitimate, this implicit subsidiary legislation ... also requires different forms of participation – a part of the democratic will-formation must make its way into the administration itself, and the judiciary that creates subsidiary laws must justify itself in the wider forum of a critique of law. In this respect the sluice model counts on a more far-reaching democratization than the siege model does.[37]

---

36 Habermas 1996, p. 440.
37 Habermas 1997, pp. 135–6.

It is indeed such a sluice model of democratisation that Habermas defends in Chapter Eight of *Between Facts and Norms*, a chapter devoted to the descriptive and normative aspects of civil society and the public sphere. Let us consider the sluice model in some detail. Habermas acknowledges his debt to the work of Bernard Peters and explains that he wants 'to give a more precise form to, and seek a tentative answer to, the question of whether and how a constitutionally regulated circulation of power might be established'.[38] Habermas proposes that

> processes of communication and decision making in constitutional systems display the following features: they lie along a center-periphery axis, they are structured by a system of 'sluices', and they involve two modes of problem solving. The core area of the political system is formed by the familiar institutional complexes of administration (including the incumbent Government), judicial system, and democratic opinion- and will-formation (which includes parliamentary bodies, political elections, and party competition). Hence this center, distinguished from the periphery in virtue of formal decision-making powers and actual prerogatives, is internally organized as a 'polyarchy'. Within the core area, to be sure, the 'capacity to act' varies with the 'density' of organizational complexity. The parliamentary complex is the most open for perceiving and thematizing social problems, but it pays for this sensitivity with a lesser capacity to deal with problems in comparison to the administrative complex. At the ends of the administration, a kind of inner periphery develops out of various institutions equipped with rights of self-governance or with other kinds of oversight and lawmaking functions delegated by the state (universities, charitable organizations, foundations, etc.). The core area as a whole has an outer periphery that, roughly speaking, branches into 'customers' and 'suppliers'.[39]

By 'customers' Habermas has in mind public agencies and such private organisations as business associations, labour unions, and interest groups that give rise to 'complex networks ... [that] fulfill certain coordination functions in more or less opaque social sectors'. 'Suppliers', by contrast, consist of those

> groups, associations, and organizations that, before parliaments and through the courts, give voice to social problems, make broad demands,

---

38   Habermas 1996, p. 354.
39   Habermas 1996, pp. 354–5.

articulate public interests or needs, and thus attempt to influence the political process more from normative points of view than from the standpoint of particular interests.[40]

The image evoked by the sluice model is straightforward enough: we are to envision a filtering process from social periphery to administrative centre. Public opinion is generated in a wide variety of informal ways and eventually washes through to influence formal decision-making processes. The upshot of this model is that binding decisions with a society can be legitimate only if they are

> steered by communication flows that start at the periphery and pass through the sluices of democratic and constitutional procedures situated at the entrance to the parliamentary complex or the courts (and, if necessary, at the exit of the implementing administration as well). That is the only way to exclude the possibility that the power of the administrative complex, on the one hand, or the social power of intermediate structures affecting the core area, on the other hand, become independent vis-à-vis a communicative power that develops in the parliamentary complex.[41]

Habermas is, of course, well aware that the institutions of actually existing capitalist democracies hardly operate in such a smooth, friction-free manner. The sluice model is equally intended to draw attention to the extent to which social crises can and do arise:

> In cases in which perceptions of problems and problem situations have taken a conflictual turn, the attention span of the citizenry enlarges, indeed in such a way that controversies in the broader public sphere primarily ignite around the normative aspects of the problems most at issue. The pressure of public opinion then necessitates an extraordinary mode of problem solving, which favors the constitutional channels for the circulation of power and thus actuates sensibilities for the constitutional allocation of *political responsibilities*.[42]

It would appear, then, that for Habermas a theoretical advantage of the sluice over the siege model is precisely that the former model better captures the

---

40   Habermas 1996, p. 355.
41   Habermas 1996, p. 356.
42   Habermas 1996, p. 357.

alternation between normal and extraordinary socio-political circumstances. In turn, the sluice model lends an important nuance to the concept of the public sphere. Henceforth, the public sphere should not be regarded as simply a

> sounding board for problems that must be processed by the political system because they cannot be solved elsewhere ... From the perspective of democratic theory, the public sphere must, in addition, amplify the pressure of problems, that is, not only detect and identify problems but also convincingly and *influentially* thematize them, furnish them with possible solutions, and dramatize them in such a way that they are taken up and dealt with by parliamentary procedures.[43]

However, despite any advance that the sluice model of democratisation might mark over the siege model, neither model is adequate. Both models of democratisation unduly restrict the scope of collective action. A striking illustration of this restriction can be found in the important distinction made in *Between Facts and Norms* between the specific forums organised around administrative bodies of the state and the more general forums constituted by the citizenry at large. Using language strikingly reminiscent of Karl Popper's writings on the philosophy of science, Habermas explains that the former are 'structured predominantly as a *context of justification*' and

> rely not only on the administration's preparatory work and further processing but also on the *context of discovery* provided by a procedurally unregulated public sphere that is borne by the general public of citizens.[44]

Appropriating a distinction first made by Nancy Fraser,[45] Habermas calls this general public sphere 'weak' inasmuch as it only forms opinions but, unlike a 'strong' public sphere, makes no decisions. It consists of an 'open and inclusive network of overlapping subcultural publics having fluid temporal, social, and substantive boundaries'. Habermas adds that

> on account of its anarchic structure, the general public sphere is, on the one hand, more vulnerable to the repressive and exclusionary effects of unequally distributed social power, structural violence, and systematically distorted communication than are institutionalized public spheres

---

43   Habermas 1996, p. 359.
44   Habermas 1996, p. 307.
45   On the distinction between 'strong' and 'weak' publics, see Fraser 1992, pp. 132–6.

of parliamentary bodies. On the other hand, it has the advantage of a medium of *unrestricted* communication. Here new problem situations can be perceived more sensitively, discourses aimed at achieving self-understanding can be conducted more widely and expressively, collective identities and need interpretations can be articulated with fewer compulsions than is the case in procedurally regulated public spheres. Democratically constituted opinion- and will-formation depends on the supply of informal public opinions that, ideally, develop in structures of an unsubverted public sphere. The informal public sphere must, for its part, enjoy the support of a societal basis in which equal rights of citizenship have become socially effective.[46]

Again we see that the chief function of the general public sphere is to mediate between social and administrative power. Yet Habermas's refinement of the concept of the public sphere through the introduction of a strong/weak nuance fails to resolve a fundamental problem in his account of democratic transition. Although Habermas explicitly permits citizens within 'weak' public spheres to discuss anything they like – presumably even the structural transformation of capitalist social relations – nonetheless his allowance for such freewheeling discussion has a political price to be paid. These opinions, no matter how urgently or persuasively expressed, remain mere opinions; and ultimately citizens must be content either symbolically to storm an administrative fortress (the siege model) or else generate certain messages from the periphery that at best will eventually filter across to be interpreted, and legitimated, by the administrative centre (the sluice model). Either way, their ability to carry out genuinely collective action has been seriously undercut. Despite his professed search for 'post-metaphysical' means to legitimise modern societies 'in which normative orders must be maintained without metasocial guarantees',[47] Habermas nonetheless retains what amounts to a transcendent moral barrier to prevent citizens – to say nothing of workers and oppressed groups – from exercising their immanent power to change the basic structure of their society. Here is a contradiction that cannot be resolved: it can only be displaced.

---

46 Habermas 1996, pp. 307–8.
47 Habermas 1996, p. 26.

PART 3

Self-Emancipation, Then and Now

CHAPTER 15

Self-Emancipation and Political Marxism

In this chapter I take as a philosophical point of departure my longstanding dismay at Richard Rorty's rejection of a 'bottom-up way of achieving utopia'. In his 1993 Oxford Amnesty Lecture[1] Rorty was at pains to insist that 'our only hope for a decent society consists in softening the self-satisfied hearts of a leisure class'.[2] Although once upon a time some may have hoped for 'moral progress to burst up from below', Rorty proposed that we must henceforth abandon such metaphysical dreams and accustom ourselves to wait 'patiently upon condescension from the top'.[3] What I find both revealing and disturbing about Rorty's lecture is his explicit coupling of socio-political reform based on a gradual 'progress of sentiments' with a rejection of what he considered to be the outdated quest for a universal foundation of human rights.

In what follows I shall argue in opposition to Rorty that what is universal about human rights is precisely that they can only reliably – and legitimately – be secured 'in a bottom-up way'. Thus has it been the case historically; thus will it be the case in the future.[4] In other words, I am going to argue that rights have justifiably emerged as claims by the oppressed while engaged in *struggle against* their oppressors. In Frederick Douglass's justifiably famous words, 'power concedes nothing without a demand'.[5]

The main difficulty with Rorty's argument in his Amnesty Lecture occurs when he sets up against his own position the false alternative of 'human rights foundationalism', a supposedly misguided search for 'what is essential to being human'.[6] According to Rorty, our contemporary 'human rights culture' would be better off if we abandoned foundationalism as an 'outmoded' project.[7] Indeed, he would have us accept the claim that 'nothing relevant to moral choice separates human beings from animals except historically contingent

---

1   Rorty 1993.
2   Rorty 1993, p. 130.
3   Rorty 1993, p. 130.
4   Support for this empirical claim may be found in the following studies: Burns and Burns 1991; George 1998; Harman 1999; and Brecher 2014.
5   Douglass 1999, p. 367. For a definitive history of abolitionism from below as a 'radical, interracial movement', at the heart of which was 'slave resistance, not bourgeois liberalism', see Sinha 2016.
6   Rorty 1993, p. 114.
7   Rorty 1993, p. 116.

facts of the world, cultural facts'.[8] Lest he be accused of endorsing 'cultural relativism', Rorty hastens to add that he considers 'our human rights culture, the culture with which we in this democracy identify ourselves' to be 'morally superior' to other cultures.[9] It is just that we would be better off if we were guided less by reason and more by sentiment. According to Rorty, moral progress in general, and the advancement of human rights in particular, requires not critical measurement against standards for justifiable action but a 'sentimental education'. A 'progress of sentiments' sustained by such an education would generate 'an increasing ability to see the similarities between ourselves and people very unlike us as outweighing the differences ... The relevant similarities are not a matter of sharing a deep true self which instantiates true humanity, but are such little, superficial, similarities as cherishing our parents and our children – similarities that do not interestingly distinguish us from many nonhuman animals'.[10]

Although Rorty rejects the 'cultural relativist' label, I agree with Norman Geras that it is difficult to know how else to characterise his opposition to universalism.[11] For instance, Rorty elsewhere quips that 'the rhetoric we Westerners use in trying to get everyone to be more like us would be improved if we were more frankly ethnocentric, and less professedly universalist'.[12] But whatever the best way to characterise Rorty's position – other than simply as 'Rorty's position' – it is clear what he rejected: any and all universalist attempts to ground human rights in an 'ahistorical human nature'.[13] Rorty considered such endeavours pragmatically speaking a waste of time and energy that could better be devoted to the task of trying to make the world a slightly less 'cruel' place in which to live.[14]

Here, then, was – and remains – Rorty's challenge: Must a universalist position on human rights be foundationalist, must it be based on some common human attribute such as rationality? In the rest of this chapter I want to take up Rorty's challenge and argue that indeed it is possible to defend a non-foundationalist universalism – a 'weak' universalism, if you will, but a universalism nonetheless.

---

8   Rorty 1993, p. 116.
9   Rorty 1993, p. 116.
10 Rorty 1993, p. 129.
11 See Geras's devastating criticism of Rorty in Geras 1995.
12 Rorty 1997, p. 19.
13 Rorty 1993, p. 119.
14 Rorty offered an extended treatment of the problem of cruelty and the prospects for human solidarity in Rorty 1989, pp. 141–98.

I shall base my case for weak universalism on certain theses defended by Étienne Balibar.[15] Before proceeding any further, I should emphasise that my concern here is not with the classification of kinds of human rights into so-called 'negative' civil and political rights, on the one hand, and 'positive' economic, social, and cultural rights, on the other hand.[16] Likewise, I am not interested in attempting to rank individual rights or entire categories of rights, for example, by granting priority to civil and political rights. As will become clear in what follows, I regard human rights as indivisible, incorporating both negative claims against arbitrary external interference and positive claims to assistance in the pursuit of wellbeing. To reiterate what I said above, my desire is to show that – Rorty's view notwithstanding – what is universal about human rights is that they have been, *and ought to be*, advanced through popular struggles from below.

1   The Ambiguities of Universalism

I turn now to an article by Balibar entitled 'Ambiguous Universality'.[17] In this dense text Balibar distinguishes three senses of what he suggests is an inherently 'equivocal' term: *real* universality, *fictive* universality, and *ideal* universality. He maintains that these three 'instances' of universality are 'never isolated, independent of one another, but they remain irreducible, and make sense in different realms'.[18] Allow me to characterise each instance in order.

Real universality refers to the actually existing interrelationships among the world's institutions, groups, and individuals, for example, 'the circulation of commodities and people, the political negotiations, the juridical contracts, the communication of news and cultural patterns ...'[19] Balibar contends that universality in this descriptive sense has been 'the "modern world"; therefore it has been the permanent background of what we call modernity'.[20] However, the present extension and intensification characteristic of contemporary 'globalisation' have both brought together and divided humanity in unprecedented ways:

---

15   See especially his collection of articles on citizenship, immigration, and the latest forms of European racism contained in Balibar 2002a.
16   For standard overviews of such classifications of human rights, see Nickel 2007 and Donnelly 2013.
17   Balibar 2002b, pp. 146–76.
18   Balibar 2002b, p. 170.
19   Balibar 2002b, p. 147.
20   Balibar 2002b, p. 148.

> Real universality is a stage in history where, for the first time, 'humankind' as a single web of interrelationships is no longer an ideal or utopian notion but an actual condition for every individual; nevertheless, far from representing a situation of mutual recognition, it actually coincides with a generalized pattern of conflicts, hierarchies and exclusions. It is not even a situation in which individuals communicate at least virtually with each other, but much more one where global communication networks provide every individual with a distorted image or a stereotype of all the others, either as 'kin' or as 'aliens', thus raising gigantic obstacles to any dialogue. 'Identities' are less isolated *and* more incompatible, less univocal *and* more antagonistic.[21]

At the beginning of the twenty-first century, then, the key political task before humanity is no longer to create a unified world but to transform its social and economic structures from within.

Fictive universality has more to do with what we have come to think of as the 'Enlightenment values' of freedom, equality, and democracy. Balibar, like Rorty, does not think that these values are grounded in a natural, objective realm but are wholly historical and cultural constructs. This poses no problem to the extent that dominated groups have sought to appropriate these values for their own purposes in their struggles to have their basic rights recognised, e.g., in efforts to expand the franchise. Historically, though, there has been a heavy price to pay for this recognition: what Balibar, no doubt following Michel Foucault, calls the forces of 'normalisation'.[22] To the extent that individuals have attained rights within a given nation, those very rights have invariably been constrained by new forms of domination. 'Normality', as Balibar conceives it, is not simply a matter 'of adopting customs and obeying rules or laws'. Rather, it involves

> internalizing representations of the 'human type' or the 'human subject' (not exactly an essence, but a norm and a standard way of behaving) in order to be recognized as a person in one's own right – to become *presentable* (fit to be seen) in order to be represented. To become *responsible* (fit to be answered) in order to be respected.[23]

---

21   Balibar 2002b, pp. 154–5.
22   Balibar 2002b, pp. 162–3.
23   Balibar 2002b, pp. 162–3.

Of course this does not mean that all forms of normalisation are equally undesirable. For instance, even a radically egalitarian society as envisaged by Balibar would require some institutional and symbolic means by which individuals could recognise themselves as having a personal stake in upholding and reproducing egalitarian social relations.[24] The main point, then, is that especially oppressive forms of normalisation cannot long exist without generating some form of resistance: not everybody is 'normal' in a 'normalised' society. Nonetheless, Balibar hastens to add, anyone who is unable or willing to conform can expect 'to be segregated or repressed or excluded, or to hide himself or herself, or to play a double game one way or another'.[25]

Finally, *ideal* universality signifies the historically creative opposition to the constraints implicit within fictitious universality. Much as Antonio Negri has analysed the dynamics of 'constituent power',[26] Balibar explores those insurrectionary moments during which individuals engage in collective action against established – what Negri has called 'constituted' – forms of power, especially but not limited to state power. Balibar proposes the term 'ideal' universality

> not only because it supports all the idealistic philosophies which view the course of history as a general process of emancipation, a realization of the idea of man (or the human essence, or the classless society, etc.), but because it introduces the notion of *the unconditional* into the realm of politics.[27]

For Balibar what is unconditional in politics is none other than the *inseparability* of the demands for freedom and equality in the midst of social and political upheaval. Here he returns to a term he had already coined in earlier articles concerning the history and present status of the 'Rights of Man'. By using the single word *equaliberty* Balibar rejects all attempts to provide a lexical ordering of freedom and equality and instead seeks to register linguistically their practical inseparability. Indeed, he insists that equaliberty is

---

24 Balibar insists that he is 'not taking a moral stance *pro* or *con* the existence of the normal subject' but is 'simply reiterating that normality is the standard price to be paid for the universalistic liberation of the individual from immediate subjection to primary communities' (Balibar 2002, p. 162).
25 Balibar 2002b, p. 163.
26 See Negri 1999.
27 Balibar 2002b, p. 165.

an all-or-nothing notion: it cannot be relativized, according to historical or cultural conditions, but it is there or it is not there, it is recognized or ignored (as a principle – or better, as a demand).[28]

From the inseparability of freedom and equality follows, in Balibar's view, the intersubjective or 'transindividual'[29] nature of ideal universality: 'Rights to equality and liberty are indeed *individual*: only individuals can claim and support them. But the abolition of both coercion and discrimination (which we may call emancipation) is always clearly a *collective process*, which can be achieved only if many individuals (virtually all of them) unite and join forces against oppression and social inequality'.[30] Balibar concludes that 'equaliberty is never something that can be *bestowed* or *distributed*, it has to be won'.[31]

Balibar originally proposed his concept of equaliberty in an article devoted to a close reading of the 1789 'Declaration of the Rights of Man and the Citizen' proclaimed during the height of the French Revolution when

> the revolutionaries ... were fighting against two adversaries and two principles *at once*: *absolutism*, which appears as the negation of freedom ... and *privileges*, which appear as the negation of equality ...[32]

Balibar's central claim in this article is that

> the proposition of equaliberty is ... an irreversible truth, discovered by and in the revolutionary struggle. It is precisely the universally true proposition upon which, at the decisive moment, the different 'forces' making up the revolutionary camp had to agree. In turn, the historical effects of this proposition, however contradictory they may be, can only be understood thus, as the effects of a truth or as truth-effects.[33]

One can imagine an immediate relativist – perhaps Rortyan – objection: 'Where is the proof?' Balibar's compelling response is worth quoting at length:

---

28 Balibar 2002b, p. 165.
29 Balibar's concept of transindividuality derives from his readings of Spinoza and Marx. See Balibar 1995, pp. 30–3; Balibar 1997; and Read 2015.
30 Balibar 2002b, p. 166.
31 Balibar 2002b, p. 166.
32 Balibar 1994, p. 47.
33 Balibar 1994, p. 48.

> Since it is an issue of a universal truth ... (an *a posteriori* universal, or better, a historical universal), the proof can only be *negative*, but it can be carried out at any moment, in situations as diverse as can be desired. If it is absolutely true that equality is *practically* identical with freedom, this means that they are necessarily always *contradicted together*. This thesis is to be interpreted 'in extension': equality and freedom are contradicted in exactly the same 'situations', because there is no example of conditions that suppress or repress freedom that do not suppress or limit – that is, do not abolish – equality, and vice versa. I have no fear of being contradicted here either by the history of capitalist exploitation, which by denying in practice the equality proclaimed by the labor contract ends up in the practical negation of the freedom of expression, or by the history of socialist regimes that, by suppressing public freedoms, end up constituting a society of privileges and reinforced inequalities. Clearly, the distinction between 'individual' and 'collective' freedoms, like that between 'formal' and 'real' equality, is meaningless here: what would instead be at issue would be the *degree* of equality necessary to the collectivization of individual freedoms, and the *degree* of freedom necessary to the collective equality of individuals, the answer being the same every time: *the maximum* in the given conditions.[34]

In this passage Balibar offers a quasi-transcendental argument regarding the historical conditions of possibility for human rights. It is, he contends, impossible to imagine either (a) a situation in which freedom could be fully realised without equality or (b) a situation in which equality could be fully realised without freedom. Of course he allows that there can be 'degrees' or 'secondary tensions' at any given historical moment, since rights cannot be realised instantaneously, once and for all. Nor is there any *a priori* reason to suppose that various rights-claims will nicely harmonise with one another. One must expect a certain amount of give-and-take, jostling for position, dashed hopes, delayed prospects; in short, conflicts arising both between struggles and within any particular struggle for rights. No list of human rights could ever be complete but must constantly be updated to take account of new social conditions, beliefs, and desires. In a strict and important sense, we should say that rights-claims are non-satisfiable demands.[35]

---

[34] Balibar 1994, p. 48.
[35] See also Balibar 1990, p. 213.

By the same token, as Balibar observes, there can be 'periods of unstable equilibrium, compromise situations in which exploitation and domination are not homogeneously distributed upon all individuals'.[36] As we have already seen, rights invariably become 'normalised' – rendered fictive to a greater or lesser extent. Nonetheless, Balibar's general point remains: there can be no 'restrictions or suppressions of freedoms without social inequalities, nor of inequalities without restrictions or suppressions of freedom'.[37] The demand for equaliberty is, in this sense, the deepest truth of politics.

2 Self-Emancipation and Political Marxism

Although earlier I quoted Frederick Douglass on the necessity of struggle for the attainment of rights, Balibar himself invokes the opening lines of the 'Provisional Rules' drafted by Karl Marx in 1864 and formally adopted in 1866 by the International Working Men's Association or 'First International'. The defining feature of Marx's mature politics was

> that the emancipation of the working classes must be conquered by the working classes themselves; that the struggle for the emancipation of the working classes means not a struggle for class privileges and monopolies, but for equal rights and duties, and the abolition of all class rule.[38]

---

36 Balibar 1994, p. 49.
37 Balibar 1994, p. 49.
38 Marx 2010, p. 82. The best introductions to the First International and to Marx's (and less so Engels's) leadership role in building it as a democratic institution are Collins and Abramsky 1965; Nimtz 2000, pp. 169–251; and Léonard 2011. Considering Marx and Engels's mature political activity – as these books do exceptionally well – is the best response to Rorty's disdain expressed for 'the Marxist cult of the proletariat, the belief that there is virtue only among the oppressed' (Rorty 1998, p. 65). For Marx and Engels were concerned not with moral virtue (or vice) but with political *strategy*. Moreover, Marx and Engels did not reject any and all reforms in favour of some abstract – even apocalyptic – commitment to revolution. On the contrary, the question for Marx and Engels was what *kinds* of reforms would actually promote, and deepen the institutionalisation of, the liberal values that Rorty himself espoused in all his political writings. Rorty's preference was for 'piecemeal reform within the framework of a market economy' (Rorty 1998, p. 105). By contrast, Marx and Engels envisioned that – especially if successful – such reforms would sooner or later raise the question of deeper 'structural reforms' leading beyond a *capitalist* market economy. At any rate, I would agree with Rorty that this is a pragmatic matter: which strategy has the best chance of succeeding at any given moment? In his 1993 Amnesty Lecture Rorty exclusively favoured 'top-down' initiatives and opposed 'bottom-up' initiatives. Five years later, he had changed his mind and come to favour a combination of both kinds

If we were to generalise Marx's all-too-often forgotten principle of self-emancipation,[39] not only would we have to say that everyone in society has a fundamental 'right to politics', but – notwithstanding Rorty's contention – no one 'can be properly emancipated from outside or from above, but only by his or her own (collective) activity'.[40] Although Balibar does not do so himself, one could go beyond a strategic assessment about how best to realise equaliberty and construct a specifically *normative* Principle of Self-Emancipation, which I formalise as follows:

> Actions undertaken to improve the wellbeing of the oppressed should be either led by the oppressed themselves or, to the extent that this is not feasible, at their behest and under their authority.

Several remarks on this normative principle are in order. First of all, by 'oppressed' I mean those who are subject to unreasonable structural or institutional constraint on self-development.[41] Or, in Jean-Paul Sartre's plain terms, oppression consists in 'treating the Other as an *animal*'.[42]

Secondly, following Roy Bhaskar, I use the stronger term 'emancipation' instead of 'liberation' in order to stress that what is at stake is not simply

---

of initiative – he granted that there have been both 'top-down' and 'bottom-up' initiatives in US history. All the more reason, he thought, though, 'to get rid of the Marxist idea that only bottom-up initiatives, conducted by workers and peasants who have somehow been so freed from resentment as to show no trace of prejudice, can achieve our country. The history of leftist politics in America is a story of how top-down initiatives and bottom-up initiatives have interlocked' (Rorty 1998, p. 53). To sum up: I cannot offer a conclusive positive case against Rorty; I have only the negative suspicion that such struggles will not in fact be successful in the long run unless they come from below (undoubtedly with assistance from other quarters). More importantly, though, and in keeping with a normative principle of self-emancipation, I argue below that such struggles *ought* to come from below.

39 I borrow the idea of a 'principle of self-emancipation' from Hal Draper's unrivalled studies (Draper 1977–90). For a summary presentation of Draper's views, see Draper 1992, pp. 243–71. Although in this chapter I only consider in passing nineteenth-century abolitionist affinities with Marx's mature politics, it would be well worth formulating a comparative 'grammar of emancipation' (Newman 2017). Such a philosophical-political project would build on the insights of such historical works as Levine 1992; Lynd 2009; Honeck 2011; Zimmerman 2015; and Manning 2016.

40 Balibar 2002b, p. 167.

41 For an extremely useful analysis of five 'faces' of oppression (viz., exploitation, marginalisation, powerlessness, cultural imperialism, and violence), see Young 1990, pp. 39–65. See also Haslanger 2012, pp. 311–38 for drawing a further distinction between 'structural' and 'agent' oppression.

42 Sartre 2004a, p. 110.

the 'amelioration of states of affairs' but the 'transformation of structures'. Moreover, as Bhaskar puts it in his own critique of Rorty's account of human freedom, self-emancipation depends as well on 'a conscious transformation in the transformative activity or praxis of the social agents concerned'.[43]

Thirdly, I have qualified this principle to allow the oppressed on prudential grounds – e.g., physical incapacity or external impediment – to solicit their emancipators from among the non-oppressed. Such solicitation, of course, need not in every case be the result of a formal election process but can be a matter of a general willingness to cooperate with actions undertaken on their behalf by emancipators.[44]

Fourthly, it follows that the appropriate role of activists is not to 'organise' the oppressed in pursuit of the latter's emancipation. As Staughton Lynd has eloquently argued, 'organising' connotes political knowledge to be conveyed by those who have it to those who lack it; it is, in other words, a *hierarchical* conception of political practice. By contrast, Lynd has proposed that activists ought to 'accompany' the oppressed by seeking 'with them ... appropriate means for social transformation'.[45] This would be not only a more respectful but also a more effective *horizontal* conception of political practice. Yet even horizonality should not be thought of as an end in itself. As Félix Guattari once warned,[46] there remains a danger that horizontality can generate individual conformity to an existing group and inhibit openness to, and capacity for, critical self-reflection. As a result, Guattari stressed the importance of preserving a group's *transversality*, which he characterised as

---

43   On Bhaskar's distinction between 'liberation' and 'emancipation', see Bhaskar 1991b, pp. 75–6. One could add that 'liberation' implies a 'once for all' occurrence, whereas 'emancipation' suggests that the way forward to freedom is varied, uneven, and with 'no sense of unifying themes, no foreknowledge of the coming twists and turns in the road' (Manning 2016, p. 40) – and precariously subject to reversals of fortune.

44   Although there have been relatively few cases of such 'surrogate emancipation', what I have in mind is classically illustrated by the actions of the nineteenth-century 'underground railroad' (see Bordewich 2005; Blackett 2013; and Foner 2015). One immediately thinks, too, of the volunteers who journeyed to Spain in order to aid the Spanish Republic during its 1936–9 civil war to oppose a fascist coup led by General Francisco Franco (see especially Hochschild 2016). Finally, a less well-known but extraordinary recent example would be the Cuban material and military assistance to freedom struggles of Southern Africa in the 1970s and 1980s (see Gleijeses 2013).

45   Lynd 1997, p. 7. Lynd has drawn his concept of 'accompaniment' from the practices of liberation theologians like Oscar Romero, the Archbishop of El Salvador who was assassinated in 1980, and from the experiences of Paul Farmer, the founder of Partners in Health. However, Lynd has extended the idea to make sense of successful efforts in the labour, civil rights, anti-war, and prisoner-rights movements. See Lynd 2013.

46   Guattari 2015, pp. 102–20.

a dimension that tries to overcome both the impasse of pure verticality and that of mere horizontality: it tends to be achieved when there is maximum communication among different levels and, above all, in different meanings. It is this that an independent group is working towards.[47]

Fifthly, the Principle of Self-Emancipation is not generally applicable as a comprehensive *moral* principle (given the problematic cases of children, the severely disabled, and non-humans); hence, following John Rawls's important distinction, I construe it in a restricted and specifically *political* way.[48] As an immediate implication of Rawls's distinction, then, I stipulate that my commitment is not to a metaphysical Marxism that applies to 'all subjects' and covers 'all values' but is to a self-standing, political Marxism that more narrowly focuses on *transforming*[49] the 'basic structure of a modern democratic society'.[50] Indeed, it is precisely in this restricted sense that I endorse Robin

---

47   Guattari 2015, p. 113. Drawing on Sartre's distinction between 'series' and 'group', Guattari and Gilles Deleuze used the concept of 'transversality' to distinguish between 'subjugated' groups (or series) with a minimal degree of transversality and 'subject' groups with a maximal degree of tranversality; see Deleuze and Guattari 2009, pp. 348–9.

48   For example, by bracketing, or suspending judgment about, general ideas of a good life or society based on religious or metaphysical worldviews. On the distinction between 'metaphysical' (or 'comprehensive') conceptions of justice and 'political' conceptions, see especially Rawls 1999a, pp. 388–414. Harry Brighouse persuaded me many years ago that such a distinction was important for Marxists to borrow (although he would doubtless not agree with my own appropriation). Paul Patton has likewise argued that for Deleuze and Foucault 'the appropriate form of justification for rights should not be moral but political in Rawls's sense of the term' (Patton 2014, p. 247). For a scathing assessment of Rawls's turn in *Political Liberalism* as the product of an 'amputation' and 'intellectual renunciation' of *A Theory of Justice* (Rawls 1999a), see Anderson 2005, pp. 103–12. By contrast, for more appreciative reconstructions and extensions of Rawls's reorientation, see Brooks and Nussbaum 2015 and Edmundson 2017.

49   It is worth stressing that the political Marxist desire is to transform the basic structure of society by initiating a break with capitalist democratic institutions and carrying out a *transition* to socialist democratic institutions. In sharp contrast, Rawls largely failed to consider such a transition. He allowed for 'civil disobedience' as a legitimate means to challenge unjust laws (see Rawls 1999a, pp. 176–89; 1999b, pp. 319–43), but he did not discuss 'this mode of protest, along with militant action and resistance, as a tactic for transforming or even overturning an unjust and corrupt system'; and he set aside 'other kinds of dissent or resistance' (Rawls 1999b, p. 319). For a careful examination of the inadequacy of Rawls's account of 'just political practice', see Bidet 1995, pp. 93–105.

50   Rawls 2001, p. 14. As should be clear from Chapter One, it is not that I find the materialism of the early Marx (or the later Engels) implausible or unappealing; it is just that I find such a worldview largely beside the point when considering a contemporary critique of capitalism and proposing a strategy for the transition to socialism. It should also be

Blackburn's classic formulation that Marx and Engels's major contribution in the field of politics was their 'theory of proletarian revolution'.[51]

What is more, one can find an especially good illustration of political Marxism in Marx's opposition to the Russian anarchist Mikhail Bakunin's efforts to make atheism a condition of membership in the International Working Men's Association. Although Marx himself, as is well known, was an atheist, he was equally pragmatic and feared a split in the International over 'the religious question' that would have resulted in the loss of most of the English members.[52] The point for Marx was not to fight over differing worldviews but to unite around concrete political programmes and strategies for achieving them.[53]

Note, finally, that there is an unavoidable gap between an ideal of self-emancipation and the non-ideal circumstances that arise in the world. No doubt in certain emergency situations, there is no possibility for consultation between oppressed and emancipators. Nonetheless, even in emergencies an emancipator ought (a) to act *as if* such consultation had occurred and (b) to be willing and able later to justify to the victim of oppression why she acted as she did. Let us call this a *Reasonableness Proviso* that should be invoked in order to ascertain the legitimacy of any contemplated or culminated emancipatory action.[54]

3 Defending Self-Emancipation

How might the Principle of Self-Emancipation be defended? As Ellen Meiksins Wood once argued, the key political message of E.P. Thompson's writings was the proposition that 'socialism can come only through the self-emancipation of the working class'. Wood elaborated as follows:

---

clear that my own conception of *political* Marxism should not be confused with how the term has arisen in association with the writings of, among others, Robert Brenner and Ellen Meiksins Wood. For an introduction to political Marxism in this other sense, see Blackledge 2009.

51 Blackburn 1978.
52 See Collins and Abramsky 1965, pp. 110–12, 120–1.
53 Arguably, this expresses the early Marx's view as well. On Marx's political attitude to religion – according to which philosophers (and activists) should reorient themselves from 'a criticism of religion' to 'a criticism of law'; and from 'a criticism of theology' to 'a criticism of politics' – see Bertrand 1979 and Boer 2013a.
54 Here I follow Rawls's stress on 'reasonableness' (see Rawls 2005, pp. 48–54) as a key factor in the use of public reason and extend it to the realm of political action, in this case, emancipatory action. For a sharply dissenting view on the usefulness of Rawls's account of reasonableness, see Finlayson 2015, pp. 37–63.

This proposition implies that the working class is the only social group possessing not only an immediate interest in resisting capitalist exploitation but also a collective power adequate to end it. The proposition also implies a scepticism about the authenticity – or, indeed, the likelihood – of emancipation not achieved by self-activity and struggle but won by proxy or conferred by benefaction. There are no guarantees here; but however difficult it may be to construct socialist practice out of popular consciousness, there is, according to this view, no other material out of which it can be constructed and no other socialism that is consistent with both political realism and democratic values. Perhaps the point is simply that socialism will come about either in this way or not at all.[55]

'Either in this way or not at all': this is no false dichotomy; rather, it is a stark reminder about the historical rise and fall of emancipatory movements. Moreover, it is a strategic prognosis and a normative claim about how and why emancipation would be worth the protracted fight to realise it. Emancipation is not a gift bestowed from on high; it is instead the fruit of the concerted and intergenerational efforts of millions of ordinary human beings to achieve a society worthy of their collective struggle. The main point is that self-emancipation preserves the autonomy of the victim and avoids paternalism.

Although bystanders may be in a position to know who is a victim and why, who other than victims themselves are in a position to express the *demand* that they be rescued, and in what manner? Victims are never merely victims; they are never simply objects to be manipulated. As Terrence Des Pres argued in *The Survivor*, his moving 'anatomy of life in the death camps', even under the most nightmarish circumstances victims of oppression remain persons who struggle to retain their dignity.[56] A victim's dignity must be respected by a would-be emancipator, no matter how admirable that emancipator's intentions otherwise are. We must beware of lapsing into what Alex Callinicos has termed 'moral imperialism',[57] by which self-serving emancipators wind up unilaterally *imposing* assistance on those deemed to be in need of deliverance from oppression.

Similarly, Michael Ignatieff has argued that

---

55 Wood 2016, p. 103.
56 Des Pres 1976. On the importance of human dignity as the 'first of the ordinary virtues', see also Todorov 1996, esp. pp. 59–70.
57 See Callinicos 2000, pp. 175–89.

if human rights principles exist to validate individual agency and collective rights of self-rule, then human rights practice is obliged to seek consent for its norms and to abstain from interference when consent is not freely given. Only in strictly defined cases of necessity – where human life is at risk – can coercive human rights interventions be justified.[58]

But this is precisely the point of the Principle of Self-Emancipation: rights should never be *imposed* from above but must always be *claimed* from below, either directly by victims of oppression themselves or, if this is not feasible, by those who indirectly seek to support the self-emancipation of such victims by acting *as if* the oppressed themselves were in charge.

Yet Samuel Moyn has rightly cautioned that by using the concept of 'dignity' one risks setting the normative bar too low. By seeking to avoid worst cases of human rights abuses, one may thereby undermine the pursuit of higher aspirations to human wellbeing on a national or global scale.[59] As Moyn has noted,

> a consensus about dignity may have become deep enough for us to insist the state not torture, but it has proved far less useful when some of us insist that our fellow human beings care about one another's broader welfare or collective emancipation. Isn't that undignified?[60]

Accordingly, I stipulate that by 'dignity' I intend something akin to Ernst Bloch's compelling image of the 'upright gait' (*aufrechter Gang*) – 'the proper stature' that human beings have 'not yet achieved'.[61] Bloch argues that human emancipation as envisioned by Marx would take place through a potent combination of two historical tendencies: social utopia and natural law. However, he stresses that

> the intended 'emancipation of men' takes far less from the philanthropic affect of social utopias than ... from the pride of natural law. Happiness and dignity, the concerns emphasized on the one hand by social utopias and on the other hand by doctrines of natural law, for so long marched separately and sadly never stuck together with the priority of human care and support, and the *primat* of human dignity: It is more than ever necessary that along with the concrete heritage of social utopian thought, an

---

58   Ignatieff 2001, p. 18.
59   See Moyn 2014, pp. 19–33.
60   Moyn 2014, p. 33.
61   Bloch 1971, p. 168.

equally concrete program of the *citoyen* be recognized. It is more necessary than ever before that even the differences in the intentional fields finally be recognized as functionally related and practically surmounted. This thanks to the certainty that there can be no human dignity without the end of misery and need, but also no human happiness without the end of old and new forms of servitude. The spotty aspect with which Marxism accords social utopias as its own forerunner is included as that respect which is *touched* by natural law. Both belong to the noble power of anticipation of something "better" than that which has "become" – in the one case the experimental material of its effort at the *humanum* is made of colorful, in the other, of more rigid stuff, but both issue from the empire of hope. The wish of natural law was and is *uprightness as a right*, so that it might be respected in *persons* and guaranteed in their *collective*. And if there were only one person to honor the dignity of humanity, then even this vast and all-encompassing dignity would be sufficient to form the quintessence of natural law. This is precisely what we find in socialism insofar as it simultaneously seeks to come to grips with the person and the collective, and to the extent that – far from the normalized masses of men, near to unalienated solidarity – it seeks to contain the one within the other.[62]

In short, for Bloch the heritage of bourgeois conceptions of natural law can be fully realised only through a revolutionary project that would feature dignity as 'the supreme human right'.[63] Just as for rights in general, so too for dignity in specific: what remains today is a struggle over, and reworking of, the concept itself. (Without any guarantee of success, of course.)[64] Bloch insists that

> it is not tenable to hold that man is free and equal from birth. There are no *innate* rights; they are all either acquired or must be acquired in battle. The upright path is inclined to be something that must be won; even the ostrich walks upright and yet sticks its head in the sand.[65]

With apologies to ostriches, the Principle of Self-Emancipation provides a reliable moral compass to orient social movements and political organisations so

---

62   Bloch 1986a, p. 208.
63   Bloch 1971, p. 170.
64   As Jan Robert Bloch has – perhaps too severely – judged in the case of his father's political commitments; see Bloch 1988.
65   Bloch 1986a, p. 188.

that they may steadily advance along this upright path. Assertion of one's and others' dignity serves as a principled means by which to challenge and reverse the indignity of oppression that has been experienced or witnessed. In this sense, it can be thought of as the conceptual counterpart to the affect of indignation that I discussed above (in Chapter Six and the interlude).[66]

In this light, it is not surprising that Norman Geras focuses on the *educative* nature of self-emancipation and characterises the multifaceted 'education of the proletariat' in terms of

> the throwing off of all habits of deference acquired by virtue of its subordinate position in capitalist society and reinforced by the dominant ideology of that society; liberation from all traces of that ideology, recognition of its real class interests and of the means necessary for the realization of those interests; the acquisition of confidence in its own ability to organize and rule, or experience in organization and in the making of political decisions – such confidence and experience being more or less denied to the proletariat by the political apparatus of the bourgeois state. In other words ... the education of the proletariat is simply the process by which it acquires an autonomous class consciousness and through which it forms autonomous class organizations up to and including the institutions of dual power and of the future proletarian state. And this education of the proletariat is part and parcel of the socialist revolution which would be unthinkable without it.[67]

Geras next raises the crucial political question, 'How is such education acquired?' He responds that

> the proletariat transforms and educates itself in the process of its revolutionary struggle to overthrow capitalist society. The education of the proletariat is essentially a *self*-education.[68]

However, Geras quickly adds that proletarian self-education neither amounts to political 'spontaneism' nor does it preclude the need for socialist organisation. For example, he observes that

---

66 For a fine Blochian defence of human rebellion and revolt against the 'negation of our dignity', see also Holloway 2016, pp. 4–11.
67 Geras 2017, p. 137.
68 Geras 2017, p. 137.

for Marx and Lenin, the party is nothing other than the instrument *of* the working class, its own organization for struggle; it is not, for them, yet another *external* agent of liberation above or superior to the masses ... [T]he party can only have an effective influence over the masses outside it, if these masses are themselves drawn in to political struggle and learn through their *own* experience the lessons conveyed to them in propaganda and agitation. And this is to say nothing of what the party itself must learn from them in order to demonstrate its capacity for successful leadership. In any case, the relationship is reciprocal and political rather than unilateral and pedagogic.[69]

By the same token, socialist intellectuals and leaders need not orginate from working-class backgrounds, provided that they recognise that Marxist theory does not arise from 'outside, or independently of, the working class movement' and cannot bring it to this movement 'in a unilateral way'.[70]

As a final normative argument in support of self-emancipation, I would like to emphasise its connection to civility. By 'civility' I mean, following Balibar, a social condition in which violence and cruelty have been reduced to a minimum. Balibar has explicitly defended a 'bottom-up' approach to civility by which

> 'multitudes' – 'ordinary' citizens, classes, 'mass' parties – have come together to force the state to *recognize* their dignity, and to introduce norms of civility into public service or the public sphere. They have done so precisely in so far as they have used the state and its institutions (schools, the legal and political systems) to civilize themselves – that is to say, in the first instance, to represent the world to themselves as a shared space in which they have their place.[71]

Indeed, the historical achievement of 'mutual recognition' would seem to require ongoing *asymmetrical* popular pressure on, democratisation of, and, ultimately, dismantling of the repressive state apparatus. As Balibar writes elsewhere, 'in the course of the class struggle itself' we can see a 'practical anticipation of a communist civility'.[72]

---

69 Geras 2017, pp. 138–9.
70 Geras 2017, p. 140.
71 Balibar 2002, p. 33. For reflections on strategies for reducing social violence in the name of 'civility', see Balibar 2015 and Balibar et al. 2015.
72 Balibar 1994, p. 123.

∴

Beyond the theoretical question of how best to respect the dignity of the oppressed, however, there is an eminently *practical* justification for self-emancipation. For I take it that the purpose of a social movement is not to go down fighting but ultimately to win![73] Yet, as Alan Gilbert has observed, if a movement to improve the wellbeing of the oppressed is indeed to be successful, it must stimulate internal discussion of central issues that arise before it.[74] Gilbert puts it well:

> To combat a centralized, brutal regime with an experienced network of activists, these movements need decisive leadership. They cannot expect to convene or even vote on every important issue. But to be democratic, that movement needs an understanding of political autonomy, of the Rousseauan and Rawlsian test that each participant can conceive of himself or herself as a member of an ideal sovereign, deliberating in favorable circumstances on the best policies for that movement and the best institutions for a new regime, and, even when disagreeing, can find the main decisions reasonable.[75]

Here is a key point, then: as a movement of the oppressed takes shape, to the greatest feasible extent the oppressed must be able to deliberate among themselves regarding *their own* interests and objectives in lessening or eliminating the oppression they experience.[76] As a result, third parties who want to support the cause of the oppressed must do so cautiously and with humility. No doubt, as Henry David Thoreau concisely suggested in his impassioned 'Plea for Captain John Brown', they should always be 'ready to step between the oppressor and the oppressed'.[77] Yet they should equally repudiate such political pater-

---

73 Here I echo the poignant words spoken by the character Esperanza (who is trying to calm her indignant husband and strike-leader Ramón) in the remarkable 1954 film about the self-emancipation of both Mexican-American zinc miners and women: *Salt of the Earth*. See Michael Wilson's screenplay and Deborah Silverton Rosenfelt's invaluable commentary in Wilson and Rosenfelt 1978. Esperanza's lines – 'You want to go down fighting, is that it? I don't want to go down fighting. I want to win' – appear on p. 81.
74 Gilbert 1991.
75 Gilbert 1991, pp. 190–1.
76 For a similar approach, see Young 2001.
77 Thoreau 1996a, p. 152. For example, Thoreau insisted that 'a man has a perfect right to interfere by force with the slaveholder, in order to rescue the slave' (p. 153). I set aside here the question of whether or not Brown (and his companions) consistently acted *as if* slaves

nalism as is evident, for example, in Rorty's advocacy of 'condescension from above'. With a striking analogy, Thoreau countered the complaint that John Brown and his companions had succumbed to riotous 'indignation' and should instead have more calmly pursued what Rorty has called a 'progress of sentiments'. Let us imagine that

> The slave-ship is on her way, crowded with its dying victims; new cargoes are being added in mid-ocean; a small crew of slaveholders, countenanced by a large body of passengers, is smothering four millions under the hatches, and yet the politician asserts that the only proper way by which deliverance is to be obtained, is by 'the quiet diffusion of the sentiments of humanity', without any 'outbreak'. As if the sentiments of humanity were ever found unaccompanied by its deeds, and you could disperse them, all finished to order, the pure article, as easily as water with a watering-pot, and so lay the dust. What is that that I hear cast overboard? The bodies of the dead that have found deliverance. That is the way we are 'diffusing' humanity, and its sentiments with it.[78]

Thoreau's point is not that reckless action fuelled by indignation is *always* preferable to contemplation aiming at sentimental education; instead, he stresses that *sometimes* indignant action is unavoidable, necessary, and even commendable: 'the same indignation that is said to have cleared the temple once will do it again'.[79] My disagreement with Thoreau, then, is simply that democratic collective action from below is preferable to directed action from above. The dispute is not over the desired goal of emancipation – freedom and equality – but over whether or not self-emancipation is a morally better means to realise this goal.

---

themselves were engaged in a process of self-emancipation. However, despite his clearly heroic leadership of daring emancipatory actions in Kansas in 1856, Missouri in 1858–9, and culminating in the disastrous raid at Harpers Ferry, Virginia in 1859, it seems clear that Brown regularly employed a top-down or 'substitutionist' command structure that eschewed shared leadership and compromise and relied instead on a combination of his own judgment and divine sanction (see Horwitz 2011, especially pp. 71, 78). Despite their diametrically opposed religious sensibilities, Brown arguably had more in common with Mikhail Bakunin than with Frederick Douglass – or Marx and Engels.

78   Thoreau 1996, p. 147.
79   Thoreau 1996, p. 153.

4   Objections to Self-Emancipation

Consider now three objections to the political ideal of self-emancipation.[80] First of all, it could be argued that instead of my 'weak' universalism I should seek a stronger basis for human rights more compatible with Marx's own theoretical commitment to the development and flourishing of human 'species-being'. In response to this objection, let me reiterate that my aim is not primarily to reject a foundationalist defence of human rights. Indeed, I personally find the 'capabilities' approach of Amartya Sen[81] and Martha Nussbaum[82] and the young Marx's concept of human 'species-being' to be extremely attractive ways to ground human-rights discourse in a comprehensive doctrine. My overriding concern lies elsewhere, though: what are the best *political* means by which to recognise and support human rights?

Here – despite my strong disagreement with him over the current direction of US foreign policy[83] – I again find myself in substantial agreement with Ignatieff when, echoing Rawls, he argues that the best way to defend human rights is not to rely on any especially controversial views regarding human nature but to identify their prudential, historical, and ultimately fragile foundation; in short, he advances a 'decidedly "thin" theory of what is right, a definition of the minimum conditions for any kind of life at all'.[84] Although Ignatieff himself appeals to protecting human agency,[85] Amy Gutmann shrewdly points out in her introduction to Ignatieff's book that there is no reason to think that agency is any less controversial a basis for human rights than dignity, respect, or equal creation.[86] And this is precisely why I have used the language of self-emancipation instead of the language of species-being.

By privileging the mature over the young Marx, I am doing my own part to reclaim a Marxism that is political not metaphysical. Moreover, a political Marxism need not offer a total explanation of the origin of *all* forms of oppres-

---

80   For these objections – and for bringing Michael Ignatieff's writings to my attention – I am grateful to Paul Hughes, who replied to an earlier version of this paper given at the 2002 Pacific Division meeting of the American Philosophical Association.
81   See Sen 2009.
82   See Nussbaum 2011.
83   See, for example, his preposterous claim that 'we would not have a global language of freedom without the ascendancy of the American empire' (quoted in Danny Postel, 'From Tragedy and Bloodshed, Michael Ignatieff Draws Human-Rights Ideals', *The Chronicle of Higher Education*, March 8, 2002, p. A15).
84   Ignatieff, p. 56. Ignatieff acknowledges his debt to Rawls in a footnote on p. 97.
85   Ignatieff 2001, p. 57.
86   Ignatieff 2001, pp. vii–xxviii.

sion; it need only contend that oppressions based on, or due to, gender, race, sexual orientation, ethnicity, nationality, or religion intersect with, and are powerfully shaped by, class exploitation.[87] Indeed, as Michael Hardt and Antonio Negri have argued, 'there are infinite paths of struggle and liberation', of which at any given time in a social formation we may happen to recognise only a limited number: 'the plurality and even the indefinite number is not the problem. Most important instead is how we articulate them along parallel lines in a common project'.[88]

An illustration of the contours of such a common project can be discerned in the self-emancipation of slaves[89] during and in the aftermath of the US Civil War. Building on the research of W.E.B. Du Bois's great work on *Black Reconstruction in America* – with its emphasis on the centrality of a 'general strike of the slaves'[90] – David Roediger has gone on to stress the tendency for one struggle to ramify and set others into motion as well, e.g., generating a 'hydra of liberation movements'[91] dealing not only with race but, in turn, with gender, class, and disability (wounded war veterans). Indeed, Roediger has identified the nineteenth-century vision of a *generalised freedom for all* that was to have a decisive impact not only on Karl Marx but on the First International's advocacy of workers' self-emancipation.[92]

---

87 For an introduction to the 'intersectionality' of forms of oppression and its relevance for Marxism, see Brenner 2000, pp. 293–324. From a different theoretical problematic (drawing especially on Spinoza and Althusser), Jaquet 2014 emphasises the role of a myriad of 'transclasses' not only in the reproduction of capitalism but also in the possibility for mobilising an alliance whose objective would be the 'non-reproduction' of capitalist social relations.

88 Hardt and Negri 2009, p. 343.

89 It is crucial to stress the process of slave *self-emancipation* as a direct challenge to the dominant tendency not only in popular culture but also among professional historians to regard emancipation as initiated from above through the noble efforts of abolitionists, radical Republicans, or even Abraham Lincoln himself. For an alternative conceptualisation and documentation of slave emancipatory initiative from below, see Williams 2014. Kerr-Ritchie 2013 also provides a detailed comparative analysis of slave self-emancipation in the nineteenth-century Atlantic Americas.

90 Du Bois 1995, pp. 55–83. See also Hahn 2009, pp. 55–114 for a compelling argument that the Civil War unleashed, and was in turn radicalised by, a great slave rebellion that for too many historians has been hidden in plain sight.

91 Roediger 2014, p. 14.

92 Roediger 2014, pp. 112–19. To this list could be added those Native Americans who 'seized on the war as an opportunity for advancing or protecting political agendas of their own, although ... those agendas varied from place to place and tribe to tribe' (Guelzo 2012, p. 387). A powerful instance of such indigenous self-emancipatory action would be the 1862 'Great Sioux Uprising' in Minnesota and its brutal suppression by Union soldiers;

A second objection to my construal of self-emancipation along normative lines is that throughout his writings Marx was hostile to 'rights talk'.[93] Yet early in his life Marx also spoke of 'the *categorical imperative to overthrow all conditions* in which man is a debased, enslaved, neglected and contemptible being ...'[94] It is true that in *On the Jewish Question*[95] Marx criticised merely formal rights in the name of substantive rights, but this scarcely means that he rejected the very idea of rights.[96] Moreover, as I have already indicated above in my interlude on an 'ethics for Marxism', a careful reader of *Capital* will find that Marx indicted not just the economic inefficiency of capitalism but also its structural injustice, above all in Chapter Ten on 'The Working Day' and in Part Eight on the 'So-Called Primitive Accumulation'.[97] Finally, in *The Civil War in France*, one of the highpoints of his politically engaged writing, Marx decried in the strongest possible moral terms the French ruling class's bloody suppression of the 1871 Paris Commune.[98] But even if Marx had advocated only the heartless scientific critique of capitalism that his detractors and even some of his supporters have claimed, why should this worry anyone? Surely Marxists today should continue to develop their research programme beyond what Marx himself said or did. Presumably the Marxist political objective is not to reject the language of rights altogether but to 'start from the real world'[99] and

---

on which see Berg 2012 and Niebuhr 2014. On the Civil War as it was waged West of the Mississippi River, and generally at the expense of the native populations (both Indigenous and Mexican), see Josephy 1991; Weeks 2001; Williams 2005; and Nichols 2012. On the history of Indigenous resistance to the emergence and expansion of the US 'settler-state', see Dunbar-Ortiz 2014; and on the theoretical question of how Marxism should construe and embrace the right of Indigenous peoples to resist 'settler-colonization', see Coulthard 2014.

93 For introductions to the complex debate regarding Marx, Marxism, and the status of rights, see Bartholomew 1990 and Teeple 2005.
94 Marx 1992, p. 251.
95 Marx 1992, pp. 211–41.
96 See, for example, Waldron 1987, pp. 119–36. It is worth noting that John Rawls especially well recognised the importance of Marx's distinction between formal and substantive rights. See Rawls 2001, pp. 176–7.
97 Marx 1990, pp. 340–416, 873–940.
98 Marx 2010, pp. 187–236. Marx concludes this extraordinary work of political analysis with unbridled fury: 'Working men's Paris, with its Commune, will be for ever celebrated as the glorious harbinger of a new society. Its martyrs are enshrined in the great heart of the working class. Its exterminators history has already nailed to that eternal pillory from which all the prayers of their priests will not avail to redeem them' (p. 233).
99 See Moyn 2014, p. 135. For Moyn's own recommendations about how to engage in this struggle – and even citing Engels on the need to be less 'utopian' and more 'scientific' – see especially Moyn 2014, pp. 142–6.

then engage in an ideological struggle to reshape and redirect that individualist language along more collectivist lines and embracing more welfarist aspirations.[100]

This leads to what is perhaps the strongest objection, namely, that advocacy of self-emancipation is *utopian* and suffers from romantic illusions about the capacities of ordinary men and women to free themselves from oppressive social structures and institutions. For example, James McPherson, an eminent US Civil War historian, has chastised other historians and activists for emphasising slave self-emancipation to the detriment of what he regards as President Abraham Lincoln's ultimately decisive role as commander in chief of the Union's victorious 'army of liberation'.[101] In a famous essay, 'Who Freed the Slaves?',[102] McPherson challenges what he calls the 'self-emancipation thesis' set forth by such scholar-activists as Vincent Harding and Barbara Fields.[103] McPherson emphasises the role of Lincoln as providing the 'sine qua non' of slave emancipation. He does not deny the active role of slaves in pressuring Lincoln and in supporting the war effort. Indeed, he agrees that 'a degree of self-emancipation did occur', for example, by means of slave flight to Union army lines.[104] Yet he insists that

> such emancipation was very different from *the abolition of the institution of slavery* ... Ending the institution of bondage required Union victory; it required Lincoln's reelection in 1864; it required the Thirteenth Amendment. Lincoln played a vital role, indeed the central role, in all these achievements.[105]

---

100   Moyn has emphasised that 'human rights in their specific contemporary connotations are an invention of recent date, which drew on prior languages and practices the way a chemical reaction depends on having elements around from different sources, some of them older than others' (Moyn 2014, p. 17). On the recent origin of the 'politics of human rights', see Moyn 2010. Notwithstanding his impressive critique of humanitarian human rights as a kind of 'anti-politics', Slavoj Žižek has largely failed to intervene in this conjunctural sense; see Žižek 2005; 2014c.

101   McPherson 1996, p. 207.

102   McPherson 1996, pp. 192–207.

103   McPherson singles out such works as Harding 1981 and Fields 1990; Mcpherson 2015, p. 102 adds Bennett 2000 to the list.

104   However, more slaves were emancipated as a result of Union military advances, and all slaves were emancipated only as a result of the Thirteenth Amendment, for whose passage Lincoln deserves *some* credit – but less so than McPherson assigns him. For less 'Lincoln-centric' histories of the legislative battle over passage of the Thirteenth Amendment, see Richards 2015 and Crofts 2016.

105   McPherson 1996, p. 207.

McPherson defends his position in terms of a complex historical counterfactual, which in standard argument form would look something like the following:

1. If (a) Lincoln had not been elected, or (b) Lincoln had not drafted the Emancipation Proclamation, or (c) Lincoln had not thereby become the commander-in-chief of an army of liberation, or (d) Lincoln had not been reelected, or (e) Lincoln had not supported the Thirteenth Amendment; then the slaves would not have been freed.[106]
2. But none of situations (a)–(e) occurred.
3. Therefore, Lincoln was the 'sine qua non' of slave emancipation.

In response to McPherson, Ira Berlin, a prestigious historian of US slavery, has conceded that slaves could not and did not free themselves by their desire alone; they acted within limits:

> They could not vote, pass laws, issue field orders, or promulgate great proclamations. That was the realm of citizens, legislators, military officers, and the president. However, the actions of the slaves made it possible and necessary for citizens, legislators, military officers, and the president to act.[107]

Nonetheless, Berlin insists that slaves 'did what was in their power to do with the weapons they had':

> Slaves could and they did put the issue of freedom on the wartime agenda; they could and they did make certain that the question of their liberation did not disappear in the complex welter of the war; they could and they did ensure that there was no retreat from the commitment to emancipation once the issue was drawn.[108]

In sum,

---

[106] One could add (f) Lincoln's death had not been widely mourned (on which see Hodes 2015). The antecedent of this conditional should be understood as an inclusive disjunction, in which *all* of the disjunctive statements comprising it could have been the case historically. But Mcpherson's point is that even if *only one* disjunct had occurred, then the entire antecedent would still be true, and the entire conditional would stand.

[107] Berlin 1997, p. 112. Another crucial limit for slaves who contemplated escape during the course of the Civil War itself was the proximity of the Union army lines; see Ash 1995. On the alliances forged between escaped slaves and the army in so-called 'contraband camps' that served as a bulwark for emancipation, see Manning 2016.

[108] Berlin 1997, p. 111.

> Slaves were the prime movers. Slaves set others in motion, including many who would never have moved if left to their own devices. How they did so is nothing less than the story of emancipation.[109]

Yet Berlin concedes too much to McPherson: by abandoning the self-emancipation thesis because of its supposed implication of 'singl[ing] out slaves or exclud[ing] Lincoln',[110] he evidently also disallows its use as a normative principle (as I seek to do). Against McPherson, Berlin wants to emphasise

> the force of contingency, the crooked course by which universal freedom arrived ... the ebb and flow of events ... the clash of wills that is the essence of politics, whether it involves enfranchised legislators or voteless slaves. Politics, perforce, necessitates an on-the-ground struggle among different interests, not the unfolding of a single idea or perspective, whether that of an individual or an age.[111]

So far, so good. However, Berlin's terminological concession also opens up a risk of moral obfuscation regarding human emancipation from oppression. If emancipation is indeed in the interest, and for the sake, of the oppressed, then to the extent that it is feasible, the oppressed themselves not only must guide the process but also retain the right to repudiate the unilateral efforts of condescending saviours. The rejection of political paternalism is precisely what I have sought to capture in the Principle of Self-Emancipation.

Another problem with McPherson's argument against self-emancipation is that there are serious problems with assessing historical counterfactual statements and arguments of the kind that he employs.[112] The issue is not narrowly a counterfactual historical argument about whether or not Lincoln was the 'sine qua non' of slave emancipation. The broader question concerns what we could call an *ethico-political counterfactual*, according to which leaders ought not to undermine self-emancipatory actions by the oppressed but should encourage and support them. In other words, consider an *Emancipatory Self-Restraint Proviso*:

---

109   Berlin 1997, p. 112.
110   Berlin 1997, p. 120.
111   Berlin 1997, p. 120.
112   For an introduction to the value of counterfactual statements in history inquiry, see Evans 2013.

Even if the non-oppressed could free the oppressed, then the non-oppressed should resist the temptation to do so.

A classic illustration of such restraint – not to be confused with a 'self-limiting revolution' that would seek to avoid a rupture with capitalism – may be found in the words of the leading US socialist Eugene Victor (Gene) Debs, who in a speech in Detroit on 11 January 1906 cautioned his audience:

> I don't want you to follow me, or anyone else. If you are looking for a Moses to lead you out of this capitalist wilderness, you will stay right where you are. I would not lead you into the promised land if I could, because if I could lead you in someone else could lead you out. You must use your heads as well as your hands, and get yourself out of your present condition.[113]

Debs's argument is that the only politically reliable basis for emancipation is self-initiative by the oppressed themselves. Although Debs is somewhat unclear on the matter, charitably his point is not that the oppressed should simply be left to their own capacities; rather, it is that the oppressed alone provide what we could call the moral 'sine qua non' for their own emancipation. Or, as Martin Luther King, Jr. (evoking Frederick Douglass's dictum) reminded those attending a mass rally in support of striking sanitation workers in Memphis, Tennessee on 18 March 1968:

> Never forget that freedom is not something that is voluntarily given by the oppressor. It is something that must be demanded by the oppressed. Freedom is not some lavish dish that the power structure and the white forces in policy-making positions will voluntarily hand down on a silver platter while the Negro merely furnishes the appetite ... If we are going to get equality, if we are going to get adequate wages, we are going to have to struggle for it.[114]

Finally, the Emancipatory Self-Restraint Proviso applies in force to those who seek to organise political parties that claim to represent the interests of the oppressed. As Ralph Miliband and Marcel Liebman warned, gone are the days when a single party can – or ought to – claim to be able to operate as a 'van-

---

113 Quoted in Ginger 2007, p. 244.
114 King 2011, pp. 177–8.

guard' or universalising catalyst of social struggles. Their words continue to ring true, even as some Left theorists have sought to reclaim the concept of The Party as a necessary response to the amorphousness of social movements and their seeming inability to change what Rawls called the 'basic structure of society'. Miliband and Leibman observed that

> ... [T]he notion of a tightly-organised, democratic-centralist organisation has proved to be a very good recipe for top-down and manipulative leadership, for undemocratic centralism and the stifling of genuine debate, sharp divisions and resort to expulsions, and a turnover of members so high as to make the organisation a transit camp from innocence and enthusiasm to disillusionment and bitterness. Only the leadership remains permanently entrenched, presiding year after year over a constantly renewed membership, and virtually irremovable save by internal upheavals, splits and excommunications. Parties and groupings such as this have shown very little capacity to think through the problems which the socialist project presents, and have tended instead to resort to incantation and sloganeering as a substitute. They have often included some very talented individuals, who have made important contributions to socialist thinking. But the groupings themselves have generated remarkably little that was fresh and innovative: the ardour and dedication of their members have more often than not been doomed to ineffectiveness because of the shortcomings of the organisations of which they were members and the distrust which these shortcomings engendered among socialist activists in the labour movement whom they needed to attract.
>
> Secondly, the very notion of a 'vanguard' party has acquired an arrogant and 'imperialistic' ring, quite unacceptable in labour movements with a long history and with many different and contradictory or at least disparate tendencies. Vanguard parties are by definition unique and dominant: there cannot be two or more such parties. But it is only by compulsion and coercion that one party can impose itself as the 'vanguard' or 'leading' party. In the circumstances of advanced capitalist societies, with a high density of different organisations, interests, purposes, tendencies and aspirations, a socialist party can only expect to be one element in a comradely alliance between different formations. It may hope, by virtue of its conduct, clear sightedness and support, to become a major reference point in that alliance, even a senior partner in it, but without any pretension to an arbitrary and stifling predominance.
>
> This is not only a matter of strategy in struggle. It raises larger issues concerning the political system appropriate to a socialist society. All the

available evidence suggests that the concept of 'the leading party' (in effect the monopolistic party) tends to produce authoritarianism and the suppression of dissent – indeed the construal of all dissent as counter-revolutionary and therefore unacceptable. There are no doubt circumstances of extreme peril where diversity, pluralism, and conflicting tendencies are very difficult to maintain: but failure to maintain them should be seen for what it is, namely a major retreat from socialist principles. What happened to the Bolshevik Party after the banning of 'factions' at the xth Party Congress in 1921 offers an instructive lesson of what such banning entails for the life of a revolutionary party.[115]

No doubt, as Jodi Dean has argued, the 'party form' can and does play an affectively vital role in bringing together and sustaining organisers in their diverse fields of struggle.[116] However, she remains curiously ambivalent about whether a unique party[117] is required, or else whether a *coalition*[118] of Left parties could accomplish the same end without succumbing to the authoritarian temptations identified by Miliband and Leibman.

In sum, emancipation involves the *dialectical* interplay of two forces: (a) the oppressed themselves seeking freedom from oppression and (b) third parties who respond – whether in a restricted or expansive manner – to demands and actions by the oppressed.[119] In accordance with the Principle of Self-Emancipation, over the course of this dialectics of struggle, the oppressed themselves retain a normative priority over those who sympathise with or purport to lead them to freedom.[120] Accordingly, not just Abraham Lincoln but *all*

---

115   Miliband and Liebman 1985, pp. 484–5.
116   See Dean 2016.
117   Despite the singular term 'party' in the book's title, she occasionally uses the indefinite term 'a party' or the plural term 'parties'.
118   On the strategic need for Left coalitions serving as an 'alliance of different forces, with negotiation and compromise between them as an essential condition of advance and success', see Miliband 1995, p. 141.
119   Of course, such demands need not be simple, direct, or instantaneous. For example, see Berlin 2015, pp. 165–70 on the protracted, indirect, and convoluted mediations of pressure from below (slaves themselves) to above (rank-and-file soldiers, officers, citizens, legislators, and finally Lincoln himself) during the US Civil War. As Berlin summarises, 'using the weapons they had, slaves drove the issue of emancipation to the top of the wartime agenda ... Slaves were not the only movers in the drama of emancipation, but their assertion of their rights and their willingness to die for them made them the prime movers in this final assault on slavery' (p. 165).
120   I disagree with John Holloway's view that emancipatory movements are always betrayed by third parties like parties or states who regard them as a They and not properly as a

leaders must be 'forced into glory'.[121] The only remaining question, then, is: *How much* force must be applied?[122]

∴

To conclude, it is worth emphasising that one of the great events[123] of Marx's mature years was the emancipation of African-American slaves, or what Du Bois movingly characterised as

> the finest effort to achieve democracy for the working millions which this world had ever seen. It was a tragedy that beggared the Greek; it was an upheaval of humanity like the Reformation and the French Revolution.[124]

Of course, this was no utopia; the realisation of freedom, equality, and self-government proved to be short-lived and partial.[125] Nonetheless, the historical process of slave emancipation signalled a previously unimaginable 'revolutionary time'[126] during which unfolded what Du Bois called 'the most magnificent

---

We (see Holloway 2016, *passim*). Holloway is quite correct to stress the *priority* of the oppressed as a We; however, this does not preclude the normative option that third parties may provide assistance to the oppressed as a They while nonetheless acting in accordance with the Principle of Self-Emancipation and the Emancipatory Restraint Proviso. Holloway's claim that parties and states invariably betray movements simply does not square, for instance, with the historical experience of Abolitionism (as exhaustively recounted in Sinha 2016), in which a dynamic multiracial alliance of oppressed and non-oppressed was, despite its vicissitudes, successful in the long run at overturning slavery throughout the Americas.

121 Bennett 2007. As Bennett summarises his thesis: 'Lincoln didn't make emancipation; emancipation, which he never understood or supported or approved, made Lincoln' (p. 58).

122 In the case of slave emancipation, the ultimate force required was military occupation – a case, as Gregory Downs has shown, of 'emancipation at gunpoint'. As Downs puts it, 'slavery needed to be killed because it had not died' (Downs 2015, p. 41).

123 Another significant event for the mature Marx was, of course, the 1871 Paris Commune; with regard to which, see McCarthy 2018, pp. 272–91.

124 Du Bois 1995, p. 727. For an overview of the impact of the Civil War and slave emancipation on Marx and subsequent US Marxists like Du Bois, see Zimmerman 2015 and McCarthy 2018, pp. 291–6.

125 On the eventual 'counter-revolution of property', see Du Bois 1995, pp. 580–636. See also Roediger, pp. 147–98 on how the collapse of the social movements arose from both repression and political misjudgments. Finally, see Downs 2015 on the breakdown of popular support among Northerners for a lengthy military occupation.

126 'Revolutionary time' is a term Roediger has borrowed from historical work on the French

drama in the last thousand years of human history'.[127] What is more pertinent to our discussion here, though, is that the transformation of the Civil War into a full-fledged social revolution *induced a progress of sentiments* in millions around the world.[128] In the United States, in particular, slave emancipation energised the campaign by the women's movement in pursuit of universal suffrage. Moreover, the 'collapse of the House of Dixie'[129] galvanized the nascent labour movement, which soon took up the campaign for an eight-hour workday.[130] Finally, by envisioning such positive rights as those to 'public amusement', slave emancipation 'transformed the human rights tradition inherited from the Age of Revolution'.[131]

It bears recalling that in 1869 Marx drafted and sent (in English), in the name of the General Council of the First International, an 'Address to the National Labor Union of the United States' in which he observed that the powerful effect of slave emancipation was the 'moral impetus it gave to your own class movement'. Marx concluded his address with a rousing call to action:

> On you, then, depends the glorious task to prove to the world that now at last the working classes are bestriding the scene of history no longer as servile retainers, but as independent actors, conscious of their own responsibility, and able to command peace where their would-be masters shout war.[132]

In a word: without political struggle from below, there can be no moral progress from above.[133]

Revolution and defined as 'a period in which the pace and the possibility of freedom accelerate[s] the very experience of time' (Roediger 2014, p. 9).

127 Du Bois 1995, p. 727.
128 On how the Civil War became 'the cause of all nations', see Doyle 2015.
129 See Levine 2013.
130 On the emergence of a distinctive form of 'labour republicanism', see especially Gourevitch 2015. Marx's radicalisation of the republican tradition has been explored with keen insight by Roberts 2017.
131 Stanley 2015.
132 Marx 1973b, p. 103.
133 Thanks to Darrel Moellendorf for his careful reading of an old draft of this chapter. Thanks as well to Carol Stanton of United Faculty and to John Hess and my union sisters and brothers in the California Faculty Association and the California Federation of Teachers who individually and collectively helped me to put the ideal of self-emancipation to the test of organising practice.

CHAPTER 16

Islamophobia and Self-Emancipation

In the aftermath of World War II, the French philosopher Jean-Paul Sartre published a remarkable work, *Réflexions sur la question juive* [*Reflections on the Jewish Question*], which was soon translated into English and published in 1948 as *Anti-Semite and Jew*.[1] Although in his book Sartre was above all concerned with assessing the French post-war situation, it is for this very reason – not in spite of it – that a return to his intervention can help us in understanding our post-9/11 U.S. and global situation. After all, wasn't it Sartre himself who proposed that insofar as someone writes for his or her 'age',[2] then he or she discloses something historically concrete that may prove to be useful to later generations?

What I seek to do below is to present Sartre's argument in this book (to which I shall henceforth refer as *Reflections on the Jewish Question*) and then extend it to conceptualise what has come to be called *Islamophobia*, namely, the fear that (a) the religion of Islam is somehow especially prone to intolerance, sexism, or violence and that, therefore, (b) Muslims pose a unique and grave danger to such key 'Western' or 'liberal' values as democracy, freedom, and equality. I readily admit that Sartre's diagnosis of anti-Semitism cannot be simply appropriated and redirected to make sense of the equally twisted logic of Islamophobia, since his historical situation and ours differ greatly. Nonetheless, we may be able to find in it some theoretical resources in order more effectively to advance the causes of human dignity and emancipation.

1   Sartre on Anti-Semitism

Sartre's book is divided into four parts. In Part One, which was originally published separately, Sartre provides a detailed inquiry – what elsewhere he famously termed 'existential psychoanalysis'[3] – into the nature of anti-Semitism. His topic in Part Two is the liberal-minded 'democrat' who favours a 'politics of assimilation' but turns out to be a 'feeble protector' of Jews. The longest

---

1 Sartre 1995; 2004b.
2 See Sartre's famous 1948 manifesto 'Writing for One's Age', in Sartre 1988, pp. 239–45.
3 Sartre 1984, pp. 712–34.

section of Sartre's book is his account in Part Three of the negative impact of anti-Semitism on Jews themselves, whose responses oscillate between inauthenticity and authenticity. Finally, in Part Four Sartre sketches a social goal and a political means to contest and one day to overturn anti-Semitism by offering a concrete emancipatory solution to the Jewish question.

Sartre observes that anti-Semitism is not merely an opinion or idea; it is a *passion* that is not attributable to either historical events or individual experiences. The overriding passion in question, of course, is *hatred*. Yet the peculiarity of anti-Semitic hatred is that it 'precedes the facts that are supposed to call it forth; it seeks them out to nourish itself upon them; it must even interpret them in a special way so that they may become truly offensive'.[4] For example, he relates that a young woman once related to him that she had had 'horrible experiences' with Jewish furriers, whom she accused of burning her furs. 'But why', wonders Sartre, 'did she choose to hate Jews instead of furriers? Why Jews or furriers rather than such and such a Jew or such and such a furrier? Because she had in her a predisposition toward anti-Semitism'.[5] Experience, Sartre reiterates, doesn't give rise to an idea of stereotypical Jewish attitudes, characteristics, or behaviour but is explained by them: 'If the Jew did not exist, the anti-Semite would invent him'.[6] In sum, no

> external factor can produce anti-Semitism in the anti-Semite. Anti-Semitism is a free and total choice of oneself, a comprehensive attitude that one adopts not only toward Jews but toward human beings in general, toward history and society; it is at one and the same time a passion and a conception of the world.[7]

Such a conception of the world can best be described as 'form of Manichaeism' that 'explains the course of the world by the struggle of the principle of Good with the principle of Evil. Between these two principles no reconciliation is conceivable; one of them must triumph and the other be annihilated'.[8] Such extreme dualism is precisely why Sartre condemns anti-Semitism: by devaluing words and reasons,[9] it 'favors laziness of mind'[10] and 'represents a basic

---

4   Sartre 1995, p. 17.
5   Sartre 1995, pp. 11–12.
6   Sartre 1995, p. 13.
7   Sartre 1995, p. 17; translation modified.
8   Sartre 1995, pp. 40–1.
9   Sartre 1995, p. 19.
10 Sartre 1995, p. 43.

sadism'.[11] Indeed, it is worth quoting at length Sartre's remarkable estimation of anti-Semitic unreason. According to Sartre, an anti-Semite

> is a man who is afraid. Not of the Jews, to be sure, but of himself, of his own consciousness, of his liberty, of his instincts, of his responsibilities, of solitariness, of change, of society, and of the world – of everything except the Jews. He is a coward who does not want to admit his cowardice to himself; a murderer who represses and censures his tendency to murder without being able to hold it back, yet who dares to kill only in effigy or protected by the anonymity of the mob; a malcontent who dares not revolt from fear of the consequences of his rebellion. In espousing anti-Semitism, he does not simply adopt an opinion, he chooses himself as a person. He chooses the permanence and impenetrability of stone, the total irresponsibility of the warrior who obeys his leaders – and he has no leader. He chooses to acquire nothing, to deserve nothing; he assumes that everything is given him as his birthright – and he is not noble. He chooses finally a Good that is fixed once and for all, beyond question, out of reach; he dares not examine it for fear of being led to challenge it and having to seek it in another form. The Jew only serves him as a pretext; elsewhere his counterpart will make use of the Negro or the man of yellow skin. The existence of the Jew merely permits the anti-Semite to stifle his anxieties at their inception by persuading himself that his place in the world has been marked out in advance, that it awaits him, and that tradition gives him the right to occupy it. Anti-Semitism, in short, is fear of the human condition. The anti-Semite is a man who wishes to be pitiless stone, a furious torrent, a devastating thunderbolt – anything except a man.[12]

Sartre next considers the timid defence of Jews by liberal democrats, whose solution envisions a 'politics of assimilation'. Although this approach is doubtless preferable to an overtly anti-Semitic 'politics of destruction', from Sartre's perspective it proves to be abstract and ineffective at dealing with the root cause of the problem – which is not Jewish behavior but anti-Semitic hatred and violence. Liberal democrats seek to 'separate the Jew from his religion, from his family, from his ethnic community, in order to plunge him into the democratic crucible whence he will emerge naked and alone, an individual and

---

11   Sartre 1995, p. 46.
12   Sartre 1995, pp. 53–4.

solitary particle like all the other particles'.[13] As Sartre puts it, although the anti-Semite certainly 'wishes to destroy him as a man and leave nothing in him but the Jew, the pariah, the untouchable', the liberal democrat 'wishes to destroy him as a Jew and leave nothing in him but the man, the abstract and universal subject of the rights of man and the rights of the citizen'.[14] As we shall see, Sartre does not reject liberal ideals together but seeks to ground them in a more robust conception of citizenship rights.

The longest section of *Reflections on the Jewish Question* is the third part, in which Sartre discusses the wide-ranging negative impact of anti-Semitism on Jewish life. Admittedly, Sartre's account is highly speculative and largely based on anecdotal accounts of Jewish acquaintances and friends, but it nonetheless offers a valuable philosophical framework for understanding how to respond most effectively to anti-Semitism. In keeping with his analysis of *bad faith* in his philosophical masterpiece *Being and Nothingness*, Sartre characterises Jewish people as caught between anti-Semitic threats and liberal democratic false hopes. They cannot simply deny that they are Jewish, strive to be 'good' Jews, or seek to assimilate. Such efforts only betray an *inauthentic* flight from their responsibilities and are ineffective. The only way out of the anti-Semitic trap is to engage in an *authentic* struggle for Jews to define themselves both as Jews and as human beings.

2   The Nature of Islamophobia

As Stephen Eric Bronner has observed, Sartre's analysis of anti-Semitism provided the basis not only for his (and Frantz Fanon's) later critical assessment of racism and colonialism[15] but also for Simone de Beauvoir's ground-breaking work on sexism;[16] indeed, Bronner himself has recently incorporated Sartre's

---

13   Sartre 1995, p. 57.
14   Sartre 1995, p. 57.
15   Sartre's first major engagement with racism may be found in his essay 'Black Orpheus', which is devoted to an appreciation of the 'Négritude' literary and cultural movement (Sartre 2013, pp. 149–86). On the development of Sartre's opposition to colonialism, see the writings collected as Sartre 2006 and, in commentary, Arthur 2010. Finally, on Fanon's critical appropriation and reworking of Sartre's analysis of anti-Semitism in order to understand the logic of colonialism and racism, see Fanon 2008 and, in commentary, Macherey 2012; 2014b, pp. 66–91.
16   Beauvoir applies the category of the 'Other' to the situation of women, blacks, and Jews but also argues that there exists 'deep analogies' between racism and sexism not shared with anti-Semitism. In her view, 'the Jewish problem is on the whole very different from

perspective into a general theory of bigotry.[17] My concern in this chapter is less ambitious than Bronner's theory, however. What I offer here are a few reflections of my own, philosophically inspired by Sartre, on the nature of Islamophobia, why it is both morally objectionable and politically disastrous, and how it might be confronted. First, however, let us briefly consider both the word and the associated concept of Islamophobia.

As Fernando Bravo López has demonstrated,[18] although contemporary usage of the word 'Islamophobia' arose in the United Kingdom in the 1980s and 1990s to designate anti-Muslim discrimination, its first use may be traced back as far as early twentieth-century French writers who criticised what they regarded as erroneous colonial and Christian missionary conceptions of, and hostile attitudes toward, Islam as essentially 'the eternal and implacable enemy of Christianity and Europe'.[19] But what *concept* does the word designate? López stresses that Islamophobia should properly be understood as a 'hostile attitude toward Islam and Muslims based on the image of Islam as an enemy, as a threat to "our" wellbeing and even to "our" survival'.[20] As a result, he contends that Islamophobia is not simply a matter of religious intolerance or racism, although in everyday life it can intersect with and strengthen these other forms of discrimination. Since, he goes on, 'Islamophobia can be shared by many people irrespective of ideology or religious beliefs ... being racist does not necessarily mean being Islamophobic, just as being Islamophobic does not necessarily imply being a racist'.[21]

In contrast to the hatred that, according to Sartre, drives anti-Semitism, the passion underlying Islamophobia appears to be a distinctive *social anxiety* regarding Islam and Muslims. As Peter Gottshalk and Gabriel Greenberg have noted,

> Instead of arising from traumatic personal experiences, like its more psychological cousins, this phobia results from distant social experiences

---

the two others: for the anti-Semite, the Jew is more an enemy than an inferior, and no place on this earth is recognized as his own; it would be preferable to see him annihilated' (Beauvoir 2010, p. 12).

17 Bronner 2014, pp. 37–40. For a detailed critical reconstruction of Sartre's evolution from *Reflections on the Jewish Question* to address other forms of oppression through a 'project of universal emancipation', see Judaken 2006, pp. 146–83.

18 López 2011.

19 López 2011, p. 15.

20 López 2011, p. 20.

21 López 2011, p. 20.

that mainstream American culture has perpetuated in popular memory, which are in turn buttressed by a similar understanding of current events. This anxiety relies on a sense of otherness, despite many common sources of thought.[22]

Moreover, following Deepa Kumar, we can identify at the heart of Islamophobia five longstanding and persistent but distorted narratives or myths about Muslims:[23]
– Islam is a monolithic religion;
– Islam is a uniquely sexist religion;
– The 'Muslim Mind' is incapable of reason and rationality;
– Islam is a uniquely violent religion;
– Muslims are incapable of democracy and self-rule.

My interest here is not to debunk these five myths (since Kumar has admirably done so herself).[24] Rather, my point is that in the United States we encounter them in one form or another every day – whether in personal life, the corporate media, social media, classrooms, or during elections and political debates over domestic and foreign policy. More seriously, Muslims in this country find themselves regularly subjected to these ideological distortions – whether as neighbours, students, employees, residents, citizens, civic leaders, or elected officials. Such ideological practices cannot simply be wished away; they must be directly challenged today and in the foreseeable future.

Moreover, even if Islamophobia does not always intersect with racism proper, it remains morally objectionable. First of all, just as Sartre charged anti-Semites with lazy thinking, Islamophobes fail to grasp the concreteness and uniqueness of each human being who happens to be a Muslim; instead, and without warrant, they hastily categorise all Muslims as a homogeneous group. Secondly, they wrongly attribute to this group negative features that are thought to deserve contempt or rejection – e.g., being dogmatic, intolerant, sexist, or violent. Thirdly, Islamophobes proceed to act upon these hastily drawn and inaccurate attributions in order to engage in a wide variety of discrimination, marginalisation, and verbal or physical abuse. Finally, and most alarmingly, Islamophobia that operates at the micro-level lends support to, and reinforces, at the macro-level such institutionalised forms of Islamophobia as

---

22 Gottshalk and Greenberg 2008, p. 5.
23 Kumar 2012.
24 See Kumar 2012, pp. 41–60.

media stereotyping,[25] profiling by law enforcement and immigration authorities,[26] and militaristic foreign policy objectives.[27]

3 The Charge of Moral Relativism

A common accusation made by those who criticise the term 'Islamophobia' is that its usage precludes any and all criticism of Islam as a belief system and set of practices and the conduct of Muslims who engage, for example, in *unjustifiable*[28] acts of violence. But such an accusation has little merit. It hastily, and unfairly, assumes that seeking to identify and oppose patterns and instances of Islamophobia lapses into a form of moral relativism (or subjectivism) that would thereby disallow criticism of the beliefs and conduct of groups (or individuals) in the name of 'tolerance'.

But those who make use of the term 'Islamophobia' can unproblematically admit that Islam as a tradition (and Muslims as its adherents, to use a narrow and potentially misleading classification)[29] has been as replete with immoral or unjust institutions and actions as any other tradition, including biblically rooted faiths[30] and liberalism.[31] No doubt such institutions and actions can and

---

25 See Gottschalk and Greenfield 2008.
26 See Kumar 2012, pp. 139–92; Kundnani 2015.
27 See Mamdani 2004; Kumar 2012, pp. 63–136.
28 I use 'unjustifiable' here to indicate that some so-called acts of *violence*, for example, property destruction, do not constitute violence per se; and some *acts* of violence (harm directed against human individuals or groups) may well be justifiable after all – for example, in individual or collective self-defence.
29 By 'Muslims' in the narrow sense, I mean those who in one way or another recognise the Qur'an as a divinely revealed and normative discourse and the prophet Muhammad as God's final and definitive messenger to humanity. In the broad sense, however, all human beings – or at any rate, all those who find peace by 'submitting' to God – are 'muslims', beginning with 'Adam' (as an historical or metaphorical way of indicating humanity from its emergence as a species). See Murata and Chittick 1994, pp. 3–7 for an account of this narrow/broad distinction. In the broad sense, then, Abraham, Moses, Isaiah, and Jesus were all muslims; and there is theological allowance for other prophetic figures or followers of revealed discourses to be regarded as muslims (for example, Hindus, Buddhists, Sikhs, Jains, Daoists, or Confucians). Obviously, the question remains whether or not 'animists', polytheists, skeptics, atheists, agnostics, or humanists who strive to lead morally upstanding lives may be so characterised. Even if not, Islam fares no worse on that count than historical Judaism or Christianity; and Islamophobes really ought to be considered 'Monotheophobes'.
30 On biblically sanctioned violence, see Jenkins 2012 and Creach 2013.
31 On the unacknowledged historical crimes of actually existing liberalism, see Losurdo 2011.

must be criticised. However, one needs to be scrupulously clear about whether or not criticism applies broadly to Islam itself or rather to the conduct of specific Muslim men, group leadership, or Muslim-majority states. Todd Green has provided three useful criteria for distinguishing legitimate criticisms of Islam and Muslims from Islamophobia proper. According to Green's normative criteria, criticisms of Islam

- Should be 'based on aspects of the religion that many Muslims recognize as part of their faith and should avoid guilt by association';
- Should not 'lapse into hate speech or otherwise endanger the safety of Muslim citizens';
- Should not be 'translated into actions undermining the freedom of religion or the equal opportunity for Muslims to practice their religion as other religious communities do'.[32]

Moreover, I would add, to avoid the charge of maintaining a moral double standard, non-Muslim critics of Islam should henceforth put their own ethical house in order as well as – or preferably before – making charges against others. Indeed, one must seek a common set of norms that applies to all individuals and cuts across cultures. Unfortunately, there does not – as yet – exist such a set of norms. One could provisionally ground such norms either in a concept of human dignity (as I have done in the previous chapter), or else in concepts of basic needs, interests, rights, capabilities, or flourishing. The difficulty for critics of those who continue to insist on using the term 'Islamophobia', then, lies in their hasty assumptions about what the adequate norms already are and in presuming that Islam lacks them. On the contrary: an urgent challenge for the world today lies precisely in engaging in the protracted, inclusive, and collaborative pursuit of the *construction* of such norms. Arguably, humanity's survival depends on it (as I argue in the next chapter).

4   Opposing Anti-Semitism and Islamophobia

Since I agree with Sartre that 'one does not redeem evil, one fights it',[33] how might we envision and support opposition to the evil embodied in Islamophobia? Just as Sartre insisted that Jews have been caught in the trap of anti-Semitism whether they admit it or not, so too are Muslims ensnared and must find their own authentic paths of escape. Anyone who is not a Muslim should nonetheless publicly oppose anyone who would hate, exclude, marginalise, or

---

32   Green 2015, pp. 21–2.
33   Sartre 1988, p. 240.

do violence to Muslims because of their religion, race, gender, ethnicity, culture, or national origin. Moreover, non-Muslims should seek to cultivate relationships with Muslims and to educate the broader public about not only the historical and contemporary diversity within Islam but also the common intellectual and moral ground that Islam shares with other traditions.[34]

Bearing in mind Stephen Eric Bronner's caveat that 'solidarity with one's own group is easy – solidarity with the Other is always more difficult',[35] my concern is not with how Muslims themselves act in a self-emancipatory manner but with how Muslims and non-Muslims can engage in a common struggle against Islamophobia. This is the question of how, to use Deleuzian terminology,[36] non-Muslims may enter into a *becoming-Muslim*[37] – a 'minoritarian' emancipatory process that can help to *dialecticise* the 'majoritarian' emancipatory process associated with class. As Balibar puts it, each process

> can justify itself by way of a critique of the other's shortcomings. Each endeavors to demonstrate the other's insufficiency as a means of containing or neutralizing extreme violence, or even its latent tendency to reproduce extreme violence.[38]

As I argued in the previous chapter, emancipation from social, political, cultural, and religious forms of oppression requires that all those who uphold the cause of the oppressed should act in accordance with both a Principle of Self-Emancipation and a Self-Emancipatory Self-Restraint Proviso. In short, opposing Islamophobia by 'becoming-Muslim' helps to broaden, deepen, and strengthen the cause of proletarian self-emancipation.

∴

In the final part of his *Reflections on the Jewish Question*, Sartre seeks to provide a broad political framework that will offer a way out of the anti-Semitic impasse that avoids the pitfalls associated with liberal democracy and an abstract and

---

34 Here I draw on Green 2015, pp. 311–35.
35 Bronner 2014, p. 66.
36 On the conception of 'becoming' as a form of solidarity with the oppressed, see Deleuze and Guattari, especially pp. 291–2.
37 A compelling example of such a 'becoming-Muslim' is found in journalist Carla Power's account of her year-long study of the Qur'an with the Islamic scholar Sheikh Mohammad Akram Nadwi – an intellectual and spiritual journey that does not avoid the difficult questions of violence, peace, and women's equality; see Power 2015.
38 Balibar 2015, p. 123.

ineffective 'politics of assimilation'. By contrast, Sartre proposes a 'concrete liberalism', in accordance with which 'all persons who through their work collaborate toward the greatness of a country have the full rights of citizens of that country'.[39] Moreover, it is revealing that he then identifies Jews, Blacks, and Arabs as those in French society who have been excluded from such citizenship rights.[40] As a result, Sartre's solution to what today could be called the 'Islamic Question' is to be found in daily individual and collective struggle against Islamophobia and by means of concrete steps taken to support the revitalisation of freedom, equality, and democracy in the United States and around the world.

It is vitally important *not* to respond to Islamophobia by slipping into 'culture talk' that would seek to distinguish 'good Muslims' from 'bad Muslims'.[41] Such a crude distinction fails, as Mahmood Mamdani has stressed, to recognise myriad variations among actually existing Muslims that arise from national, ethnic, and political differences. Muslims, like Jews, Christians, Hindus, Buddhists, and atheists are complex human beings whose identities are multiple and shifting. Just as anti-Semites have tried, Islamophobes would also have us believe that one's religious identity overrides or exhausts all others. As a result, resistance to anti-Semitism and to Islamophobia lies in reclaiming the concrete features of our human condition and in fashioning societies grounded in solidarity and justice for all.

Sartre closed *Reflections on the Jewish Question* with an urgent call to action: 'Not one Frenchman will be free as long as the Jews do not enjoy the fullness of their rights. Not one Frenchman will be secure as long as a single Jew – in France or *in the world at large* – can fear for his or her life'.[42] Of course Sartre was speaking from a post-war French perspective. How might we hail[43] others in the post-9/11 United States?

---

39 Sartre 1995, p. 146.
40 Sartre specifies that 'Jews – and likewise Arabs and Blacks – from the moment that they are participants in the national enterprise, have a right in that enterprise; they are citizens. But they have these rights *as* Jews, Blacks, or Arabs – that is, as concrete persons' (Sartre 1995, p. 146); translation modified.
41 Mamdani 2004, especially pp. 17–62.
42 Sartre 1995, p. 153; translation modified.
43 I use the term 'hail' to evoke Louis Althusser's conception of ideology as a form of intersubjective 'hailing' or 'interpellation' (see Althusser 2014, especially pp. 261–70) the objective of which is to transform potentially rebellious individuals into more-or-less docile subjects. However, the difficulty for those who oppose anti-Semitism, Islamophobia, or any other ideological practice is to construct a form of 'counter-interpellation' that does not simply mirror the practice being contested but finds a way to exit that practice altogether; see Pêcheux 1982, pp. 164–6.

If one were to apply Sartre's summons to the contemporary US situation, one might turn to the thesis advanced by historian Denise Spellberg in her recent book *Thomas Jefferson's Qur'an*. Spellberg has argued compellingly that during the eighteenth-century founding of the United States, Muslims 'symbolized the universality of religious inclusion and equality' and so 'any attack upon the rights of Muslim citizens should be recognized for what it remains: an assault upon the universal ideal of civil rights promised all believers at the country's founding'.[44] Following Spellberg's lead, and in the spirit of Sartre, here and now one might then pledge: 'Not one American will be free as long as Muslims do not enjoy the fullness of their rights. Not one American will be secure as long as a single Muslim – in the United States or *in the world at large* – can fear for his or her life'.

44 Spellberg 2013, p. 302.

CHAPTER 17

Climate Crisis, Ideology, and Collective Action*

According to new scientific research, there exist nine *planetary boundaries*, which are interlinked Earth-system processes and biophysical constraints: climate change, changes in biospheric integrity, biogeochemical flows, stratospheric ozone depletion, ocean acidification, freshwater use, land-system change, atmospheric aerosol loading, and the introduction of novel entities. Crossing even one of these boundaries would risk triggering abrupt or irreversible environmental changes that would be very damaging or even catastrophic for society. Furthermore, if any of these boundaries were crossed, then there would be a serious risk of crossing the others. However, as long as these boundaries are not crossed, 'humanity has the freedom to pursue long-term social and economic development'.[1]

Unfortunately, the following three boundaries have already been crossed: climate change, changes in biospheric integrity, and interference with biogeochemical flows. The threat that humanity has posed to the conditions of life for our own and other species has never been greater.[2] We face a planetary 'tipping point' by which 'what we like to think are gradual environmental changes in fact turn into sudden ones that we don't expect'.[3]

In response to this emergency, let us consider the following moral argument. Call it the *Urgency Argument*:

1. One should urgently act to halt any grave threat posing serious harm to others.
2. Crossing any of the nine planetary boundaries would be a grave threat posing serious harm to human development.

---

* This chapter has been previously published in *Crisis & Critique* 1.1, 2014, pp. 137–52.
1 Rockström et al. 2009; Rockström and Klum 2015; Steffen et al. 2015.
2 The planetary boundaries associated with stratospheric ozone depletion, ocean acidification, freshwater use, and land-system change have not yet been crossed; and those boundaries associated with atmospheric aerosol loading and the introduction of novel entities have yet to be quantified scientifically.
3 Barnosky and Hadly 2015, p. 6. Ian Angus provides a vivid analogy to distinguish planetary boundaries from tipping points: the former can 'be compared to guardrails on mountain roads, which are positioned to prevent drivers from reaching the edge, not on the edge itself' (Angus 2016, p. 74). Following Angus (2016, pp. 63–6), it is also worth noting that the concept of 'tipping point' provides the basis for a convergence between climate science and (a negative moment of) materialist dialectics.

3. Therefore, humanity should urgently act to avoid crossing these boundaries, or, if already crossed, to reverse course and resume social and economic development within them.
4. Dangerous climate change will result from crossing one of the nine planetary boundaries.
5. But dangerous climate change is caused by releasing excessive greenhouse gas emissions into the earth's atmosphere (>350 ppm CO_2).
6. Therefore, humanity should urgently act to reduce greenhouse gas emissions into the earth's atmosphere to a safe target (<350 ppm CO_2).[4]

But given the imminent prospect of severe climate disruption, why as yet has there occurred relatively little collective action in response? Psychologist Daniel Gilbert thought he had the answer. In an opinion piece provocatively titled 'If Only Gay Sex Caused Global Warming'[5] Gilbert argued[6] that the real psychological obstacle to effective action on climate change is that human brains have evolved to deal most effectively with threats that:

– are intentional and personal;
– violate our moral sensibilities;
– are a clear and present danger; and
– involve quick changes rather than gradual changes

Unfortunately, as Greg Craven has noted, climate change has none of these properties; '[i]t is impersonal, morally neutral, in the future, and gradual, and we're just not wired to watch out for stuff like that'.[7]

Lisa Bennett has offered additional neurological evidence: not only do humans initially assess risks not by means of rational analysis but through emotion, but we also depend heavily on our background worldview for interpreting information. For example, individuals with 'hierarchical' worldviews are likely to discount the need for political action on climate change, whereas individuals with 'egalitarian' worldviews are likely to be motivated to participate in a movement for climate justice.[8]

---

[4] Premise one is a moral presupposition that relies on broad intuitive appeal, whether from consequentialist, deontological, or virtue-based approaches. For evidence in support of premise two, see Wijkman and Rockström 2012, pp. 36–48; and Hansen 2016; in support of premise four, see Anderson 2012; and in support of premise five, see Hansen and Sato 2012. Berners-Lee and Clark 2013 provides an up-to-date, but non-technical, overview of climate science research and projections. From a frustratingly contrarian perspective, Mark Lynas well explains the concept of planetary boundaries but then chides Green activists for their 'pessimism' and insists – with scant argument – that there is no need for 'ditching capitalism, the profit principle, or the market' (Lynas 2011, p. 9).

[5] Gilbert 2006.
[6] See Greg Craven's (2009, pp. 72–3) careful reconstruction of Gilbert's argument.
[7] Craven 2009, p. 73.
[8] Bennett 2008.

What should we make of Gilbert's and Bennett's explanations? Let us be blunt. They are striking examples of what we could call ideological evasion by recourse to neuroscience. Essentially, they are claiming that the fault lies not in external social conditions but within us. Each of our individual brains has failed us; and this is why we haven't set about to do together what we must in order to mitigate climate change.

Yet, as neuroscientist Steven Rose has insisted, 'the mind is wider than the brain'.[9] Likewise is the reach of ideology.

Consider that denial about climate change is hardly new but only the latest in a long series of corporate and pseudo-scientific efforts to discredit evidence for, and undermine action on, such problems as acid rain, dangers of second-hand smoke, and ozone depletion.[10] Such efforts rely not on how the human brain is hardwired to distinguish between immediate and long-term risk but on what Naomi Oreskes and Erik Conway call a deliberate strategy of 'doubt-mongering'. In short, urgent action on climate change requires not a rewiring of our brains but a fundamental critique of, and struggle against, global capitalism. Organisers must take up the difficult issues of how best to challenge the dominant ideological structure of climate change denial and how most effectively to mobilise collective action in favour of radical social transformation.

No doubt such a perspective goes against the contemporary grain of organising efforts by otherwise admirable reform-oriented environmental organisations like 350.org.[11] Yet even a greener capitalism is scarcely plausible apart from the sustained pressure exerted by a deeper systemic challenge to the capitalist mode of production itself. Climate justice organisers simply must confront capitalism as a whole – above all with respect to its 'mental conception of the world'.[12] This is why Annie Leonard's challenge to mainstream environmentalists is refreshingly candid: 'Can we put capitalism on the table and talk about it with the same intellectual rigor that we welcome for other topics?'[13]

---

9   Rose 2005a, p. 88.
10   Oreskes and Conway 2010.
11   In his impressive recent book *Eaarth* (McKibben 2010), the co-founder of 350.org, Bill McKibben still fails to identify capitalism as the chief cause of the climate crisis.
12   See Marx's footnote on technology (1990, pp. 493–4 n. 4) and Harvey's commentary (2010a, pp. 189–201).
13   Leonard 2010, p. xxii.

1 Ecological Rift: a New Climate Case against Capitalism

Consider now a second moral argument, which we may call the *Unsustainability Argument*:[14]

1. The capitalist mode of production has already crossed, and will unavoidably continue to cross, one or more of the nine planetary boundaries.
2. A mode of production that unavoidably crosses even one of the nine planetary boundaries is ecologically unsustainable.
3. Therefore, the capitalist mode of production is ecologically unsustainable.
4. An ecologically unsustainable mode of production is a grave threat posing serious harm to human development.
5. Therefore, the capitalist mode of production is a grave threat posing serious harm to human development.

The first, and most important, premise of this argument can readily be justified. Without external constraints imposed by the state or by organised social forces, capitalism will have a strong tendency to exceed the nine planetary boundaries. There are three basic features of capitalism that account for this problem.[15] First of all, a relentless profit imperative underlies capitalist accumulation. Since capitalist firms face competitive pressure from other firms, there exists a strong motivation for them to externalise costs onto the natural world.

Secondly, the profit imperative inherent in capitalism results in an ever-expanding search for new markets or, as Marx strikingly put it in the *Grundrisse*,

---

14 For a complementary moral case against capitalism that appeals to the alarming increase of species extinction and loss of biodiversity, see Dawson 2016. In sharp contrast, Edward O. Wilson has implausibly claimed that the 'evolution of the free market system ... and the way it is increasingly shaped by high technology' will tend to favor 'both shrinkage of the ecological footprint and the resulting improvement of biodiversity conservation ... because of the acceleration of the replacement of extensive economic growth by intensive economic growth' (Wilson 2016, pp. 191–2). After powerfully documenting the dire threat to biodiversity posed by the 'Anthropocene' and advancing a bold project to dedicate half of the Earth's surface to natural preservation, Wilson timidly concludes his book by appealing to *economic* 'evolution' that minimises the global *socio-political* upheaval required to achieve what he calls a 'shift in worldview from wealth based on quantity to wealth based on quality, with the latter made permanent through ecological realism' (p. 193). Indeed, if the 'central idea is to view the entire planet as an ecosystem, to see Earth as it is and not as we wish it to be' (p. 193), then the basic structure of capitalist exploitation – whether extensive or intensive – remains the chief obstacle that must be dismantled and surpassed.

15 See Williams 2010, pp. 191–214; Derber 2010, pp. 105–15; and Baer 2012, pp. 57–116.

to regard natural 'boundaries' as mere 'barriers' to be overcome or simply shifted elsewhere[16] – with no less deleterious effects.[17]

Thirdly, capitalism emphasises short-term economic calculation to the detriment of long-term planning that is essential for sustainable human development. Even worse, 'capitalist time' invariably collides with, and disrupts, such natural rhythms, cycles, and temporalities as weather patterns,[18] the migration of species,[19] and seasonal adaptation.[20]

In sum, capitalism has tended 'to undermine the very process of interaction with nature on which it, like every other form of human society, depended'.[21] Indeed, as John Bellamy Foster, Brett Clark, and Richard York have powerfully argued, capitalism has introduced a profound 'ecological rift' into the relationship between humanity and the natural world, which has arisen from 'the conflicts and contradictions of the modern capitalist society' and has severely disrupted the essential metabolic interchange between human beings and nature. As they write,

> the planet is now dominated by a technologically potent but alienated humanity – alienated both from nature and itself; and hence ultimately destructive of everything around it. At issue is not just the sustainability of human society, but the diversity of life on Earth.[22]

And so, they continue,

> for a sustainable relation between humanity and the earth to be possible under modern conditions, the metabolic relation between human beings and nature needs to be rationally regulated by the associated producers in line with their needs *and* those of future generations. This means that the vital conditions of life and the energy involved in such processes need to be conserved.[23]

---

16   On this dialectical interplay between ecological 'rifts' and economic 'shifts', see Foster, Clark, and York 2010, pp. 73–87.
17   Marx 1973a, pp. 334–5. See the implicit disagreement between Harvey (2010b, pp. 70–84) and Foster, Clark, and York (2010, pp. 13–49, 275–87) on whether or not contemporary capitalism can in fact continue to turn the nine planetary boundaries into barriers.
18   See Cullen 2010.
19   See Wilcove 2007.
20   See Foster and Kreitzman 2009.
21   Harman 2010, p. 307.
22   Foster, Clark, and York 2010, p. 14.
23   Foster, Clark, and York 2010, p. 60.

But capitalism is incapable of reining in its relentless drive to expansion beyond what planetary boundaries can withstand. As a result, Foster, Clark, and York conclude, an 'ecological revolution' against global capitalism is not only desirable but is imperative.[24]

2   Some Difficulties for Collective Action

Building on the Unsustainability Argument, consider now the *Obstruction Argument*:

1. Humanity should urgently act to reduce greenhouse gas emissions into the earth's atmosphere to a safe target (<350 ppm CO_2).
2. But capitalism structurally obstructs individual actions to reduce greenhouse gas emissions to a safe target.
3. Therefore, collective action to reduce greenhouse gas emissions to a safe target is necessary.
4. But capitalism also obstructs collective action to reduce greenhouse gas emissions to a safe target.
5. If both individual and collective means of action to reduce greenhouse gas emissions to a safe target are obstructed, then the obstruction itself must be removed.
6. But capitalism cannot be removed through individual actions.
7. Therefore, capitalism must be removed through collective action.[25]

How might we justify the second and sixth premises of the Obstruction Argument? How exactly does capitalism obstruct individual actions to tackle the problem of climate change? In no small part this occurs by means of ideological practices and strategies.

If we consider what Raymond Geuss has called ideology in the 'pejorative sense',[26] we can see that the onset of climate change has generated an especially pernicious ideology, or rather an 'assemblage'[27] of ideological strategies and practices. In particular, ideology operates on, and distorts, people's historically contingent beliefs, desires, and intentions; and by so doing presents the latter as if they were universal, natural, and inevitable.[28]

---

24   See especially Foster, Clark, and York 2010, pp. 423–42.
25   Thanks to an anonymous reviewer for *Crisis & Critique* for noticing, and suggesting how to correct, a serious flaw in an earlier version of the Obstruction Argument.
26   Geuss 1981, pp. 4–22.
27   David Harvey (2010b, p. 128) has incorporated Deleuze and Guattari's concept of assemblage (see Deleuze and Guattari 1987, *passim*) into a new critical Marxist lexicon.
28   See Geuss's (2008, pp. 52–3) recent formulation.

The upshot is that ideology 'interpellates individuals as subjects'[29] not just with respect to such mental states as beliefs but also with respect to desires, intentions, and resolutions.[30] Following Terry Eagleton, let us note that ideology has a twofold nature: it operates at both cognitive and conative levels.[31] In the first instance, ideology channels or obscures what is known to people; in the second instance, ideology weakens or misdirects people's desires, intentions to act as they determine best and resolutions to resist countervailing temptations. With some notable exceptions,[32] Marxists have devoted more attention to the cognitive than to the conative side of ideology. Without denying the importance of that extensive, and impressively variegated, tradition, literature, and debate, in what follows let us aim to reset a theoretical imbalance.

There undoubtedly never exists a condition of perfect ideological dominance by one group over others, whether at the level of belief, desire, intention, or resolution. In the introduction to his trenchant critique of 'American ideology' Howard Zinn offered an especially lucid account of such ideological unevenness. In Zinn's view,

> the dominance of [an ideology] is not the product of a conspiratorial group that has devilishly plotted to implant on society a particular point of view. Nor is it an accident, an innocent result of people thinking freely. There is a process of natural (or, rather, *unnatural*) selection, in which certain orthodox ideas are encouraged, financed, and pushed forward by the most powerful mechanisms of our culture. These ideas are preferred because they are safe; they don't threaten established wealth or power.[33]

Since ideology cannot be restricted to ideas or beliefs alone, we should add to Zinn's account that person's basic desires, intentions, and resolutions equally become distorted, channelled, weakened, or misdirected as a result of ideological strategies serving powerful socio-economic interests.

∴

---

29 To use Louis Althusser's expression. See Althusser 2014b.
30 On the irreducibility of intentions and resolutions to beliefs and desires, see Holton 2009.
31 Eagleton 2007, p. 19. Eagleton himself distinguishes 'cognitive' from 'affective' aspects of ideology.
32 See especially Eagleton 2007, pp. 33–61 on 'ideological strategies'. See also Meyerson 1991.
33 Zinn 1990, p. 3.

Consider now the fourth premise of the Obstruction Argument: 'capitalism also obstructs collective action to reduce greenhouse gas emissions to a safe target'. By 'collective action' let us understand, following Alex Callinicos, 'any attempt by persons to co-ordinate their actions so as to achieve some goal or goals'.[34] Yet collective action is easier to envision and encourage than it is to carry out successfully. A number of difficulties arise along the way. Let us consider seven of these difficulties. Too many individuals

- may not know basic facts about the problem; or
- may not want to know basic facts about the problem; or
- may not know what to do about the problem; or
- may not want to know what to do about the problem; or
- may not intend to do anything about the problem; or
- may not resolve to act with others to solve the problem; or
- may fail to act with resolve with others to solve the problem.

At each step along the way to collective action, specific ideological strategies arise to delay, distort, obstruct, or misdirect individuals. The task for organisers in general – and for anti-capitalists specifically – is to intervene at each link in this sequence of practical reasoning about the desirability of collective action. How best can we help to educate, agitate, and organise an anti-capitalist movement for climate justice? Consider each step in order as it pertains to the problem of climate change.

If individuals do not know the basic facts about climate change, then the appropriate response is to demand better science education and to disseminate such information effectively through corporate or alternative media.[35]

However, *if individuals do not want to know basic facts about climate change*, we encounter not *ignorance* about a problem that can be relatively easily corrected but instead *stupidity* proper. In this case, what is required is a detailed account of the 'genesis of stupidity' along the lines of what Max Horkheimer and Theodor Adorno once attempted, namely, to examine stupidity as a 'scar' – a symptom of a damaged psychic life.[36]

But stupidity is only part of the problem. As James Rachels once observed, 'accepting a moral argument often means that we must change our behavior. People may not want to do that. So, not surprisingly, they will sometimes turn

---

34 Callinicos 2004, p. 153.
35 See, for example, the thoughtful proposals by Mooney and Kirshenbaum 2009; Olson 2009; and Gorman and Gorman 2017 for improving basic scientific literacy in the United States.
36 Horkheimer and Adorno 2002, pp. 213–14. Also see Pierce 2010.

a dear ear'.[37] Moreover, anxiety about an uncertain future is a key factor that inhibits willingness to accept risks involved in social transformation. Chris Hedges writes that

> our passivity is due, in part, to our inability to confront the awful fact of extinction, either our own inevitable mortality or that of the human species. The emotional cost of confronting death is painful. We prefer illusion.[38]

How should organisers respond to such flight from the painful truth of climate change? By instilling courage in others that radical change is necessary, that future delay will only make matters worse.

Simply acknowledging, and knowing in the abstract about, a collective problem takes us only so far along the way to collective action, however. The next three steps are crucial. Firstly, *individuals may not know what to do about climate change*. The appropriate response to such practical uncertainty would be to offer concrete tactics and strategies that are appealing. An exceptionally fine, detailed programme is the demand by the UK-based Campaign against Climate Change for the establishment of a National Climate Service and creation of 'one million, green climate jobs'.[39]

However, there is another aspect of this first obstacle: any serious solution to climate change must break with the 'productivist' and 'consumerist' logics of capitalism.[40] Yet, as Ozzie Zehner has argued, there exist widespread 'green illusions' that pursuing alternative technologies alone can provide a sure path to a sustainable future.[41] Even the vaunted pursuit of greater economic efficiency turns out, under scrutiny, to be a pernicious trap that will result in greater consumption, faster depletion of natural resources, more waste, and continued surpassing of planetary boundaries.[42] What is required, by contrast, is a rapid shift from production for profit to production for meeting human needs; and a profound transformation in individual and collective patterns of consumption, regardless of the technologies deployed.[43]

---

37 Rachels and Rachels 2009, p. 160.
38 Hedges 2010, pp. 198–9.
39 See the campaign's excellent pamphlet: Neale et al. 2014.
40 See especially Baer 2012 and Tanuro 2013.
41 Zehner 2012.
42 On the perils of the 'efficiency trap', see Hallett 2013.
43 For a set of concrete proposals on how this might occur, see especially Berners-Lee and Clark 2013.

Secondly, *individuals may not want to know what to do about climate change*. Here the problem is not ignorance, stupidity, or practical uncertainty, but a range of 'rogue desires',[44] ranging from disillusionment and despair to cynicism. Consider cynicism. Even if we allow for a distinction between official cynicism from above and populist *kynicism* from below,[45] not all ideology is an exercise of 'cynical reason'. For example, two of the main reasons in the United States for the lack of public demand for climate change policy have been the failure of basic science education in schools[46] and the failure of corporate media to provide accurate information about the gravity of the problem.[47]

Thirdly, *individuals may not intend to do anything about the problem*. Such paralysis above all afflicts academics whose fetish of deliberation reins in every decision about what to do for fear that it may be premature or ill-considered. In this case, a good Sartrean response would be to insist that failure, or refusal, to act, is by default still a form of action – but in bad faith.[48] The only way out of bad faith is to undergo what Simone de Beauvoir once called a radical 'conversion'.[49] As a result of such conversion, an individual would recognise that his or her concrete freedom is not separate from, but is interdependent with, the concrete freedoms of everyone else. However, de Beauvoir clearly rejected all 'utopian reveries' of voluntary conversion by oppressors to the cause of freedom; they must be forced to change through revolt by the oppressed themselves acting in concert.[50]

The final two links in the theoretical-practical chain bring us at last to the threshold of collective action. Consider, though, the following difficulty: *individuals may not resolve to act with others to solve the problem of climate change*. Here we encounter above all an ideological strategy that Andrew Szasz has brilliantly identified and critiqued: what he calls the 'inverted quarantine'.[51] Through illuminating case studies – from the 1961 US 'fallout shelter panic' to the current reliance on bottled drinking water – Szasz examines how indi-

---

44 On the concept of 'rogue desires' see Meyerson 1991, pp. 130–45.
45 See Žižek 2008, pp. 24–7.
46 On US teachers' 'insufficient grasp' of basic climate science, the limited class time they (are permitted to) devote to climate change, and their misguided efforts to address 'both sides' of the issue, see Plutzer et al. 2016.
47 Mooney and Kirshenbaum 2009.
48 On the connection between ideology and bad faith in Sartre, see Coombes 2008, especially pp. 89–116.
49 Beauvoir 1976, pp. 13–14, 66–7. On the concept of 'conversion' in Beauvoir's (and Sartre's) writings, see Deutscher 2008.
50 Beauvoir 1976, pp. 96–7.
51 Szasz 2007.

viduals have often responded to perceived social and environmental threats 'by *isolating themselves* ... by erecting some sort of barrier or enclosure and withdrawing behind it or inside it'. Instead of acting jointly with others to bring about structural change by 'making history', individuals opt to deal with collective problems on their own. This inverted quarantine strategy as a 'mass phenomenon' invariably leads to the displacement of politics through consumption as individuals seek to 'shop their way to safety'.[52]

The appropriate response to the perverse logic of 'inverted quarantine' is to construct means by which individuals can break out from such an 'I-mode' and adopt instead a 'we-mode' that embodies genuinely shared intentions, resolutions, and commitments.[53] Without such a shift in perspective, collective action regarding climate change is not possible. As John Holloway has elegantly written,

> More and more, the key figure is We. And if we ask who is We or, if we want to be a bit more grammatical, who are We, then we come quickly to the idea that We are a Question. We don't actually know very well. It's not a predefined question, it's an open We, it's a We that invites, that provokes. It's a We that asks: Who are We?[54]

Another relevant factor is the affective power of media images to redirect or channel collective action by decontextualising the problem. For example, Finis Dunaway has provided ample empirical evidence that

> media images do not simply illustrate environmental politics, but also shape the bounds of public debate by naturalizing particular meanings of environmentalism. As they draw a broader public of media consumers into popular environmentalism, images act as both revelations and veils, creating tensions between what they visualize and what they hide, which ideas they endorse and which they deny.[55]

In other words, such images are just as 'vital and contested'[56] as any philosophical concepts and arguments. In general, dominant images of thought

---

52   Szasz 2007, p. 5.
53   I borrow the distinction between 'I-perspective' and a 'we-perspective' from Tuomela 2007. On the nature of 'shared agency', see Bratman 2014.
54   Holloway 2016, p. 3.
55   Dunaway 2015, pp. 1–2.
56   Dunaway 2015, p. 7.

assert decontextualised, individual, short-term, and technological 'quick-fix' solutions to causally determinate, collective, long-term, structural problems. Moreover, such images tend to ignore 'the vastly unequal experience of environmental risk to promote a vision of universal vulnerability'.[57] As a result, climate justice organisers must continually seek not only to challenge the legitimacy of these dominant images but also to fabricate countervailing images as affective support for alternative political projects and collective courses of action.

Finally, *individuals may fail to act with resolve with others to solve the problem*. This is a political manifestation of what philosophers have traditionally called 'weakness of the will' but more simply could be termed *ethical weakness* (or *backsliding*).[58]

In the Marxist tradition, scant attention has been paid to the problem not of the ideological obscuring of what is in one's class interest but why *even if one does know, and resolve to act upon this interest, one may still fail to do so*.[59] It is true enough that class interests often conflict with those based, for example, on race, gender, and nationality; but a deeper analysis of human moral psychology suggests that there is an affective undercurrent to political decision-making and acting. And this undercurrent is difficult to navigate successfully.

The solution to the problem of ethical weakness cannot be found in simply consciously vowing to maintain sound judgment now and in the future. What is needed is more akin to cultivating what Spinoza called 'fortitude' or, more simply, ethical strength.[60] How is this possible? In Part 5 of the *Ethics* Spinoza recommended certain imaginative practices that inspired what the Marxist sociologist and Spinoza scholar Georges Friedmann called 'spiritual exercises'.[61] As Friedmann proposed in a journal entry dating from the French Resistance to German occupation, 'this effort upon oneself is necessary; this ambition – just. Many are those who are completely absorbed in militant politics, preparation for the social Revolution. Rare, very rare, are those who, to prepare for the Revolution, want to make themselves worthy of it'.[62]

---

57   Dunaway 2015, p. 46.
58   See Mele 2012.
59   A notable exception is Meyerson 1991, pp. 165–8.
60   As discussed in the interlude to this book, Spinoza classifies 'fortitude' (*fortitudo*) as a key 'active affect' in the *Ethics*; see the note to Proposition 59, Part Three, and the note to Proposition 73, Part four (Spinoza 1996, pp. 102–3, pp. 154–5). Holton 2009, pp. 112–36 uses the term 'strength of will', but he thereby presumes the existence of a 'will', which is an unnecessary postulate.
61   Friedmann 1970, p. 359.
62   Friedmann 1970, pp. 359–60.

Yet spiritual exercises are not the exclusive preserve of individuals. Ethical strength cannot be based on one's internal resources alone. On the contrary, the enduring Spinozist question is, 'How can we increase our individual powers to act by joining together with others?'[63] What we need above all to envision and put into practice is the common exercise of ethical strength made possible through collective action. In the face of threatened or actual state violence, the pressing question then becomes how to give each other courage in order to sustain what Jeremy Brecher has plainly called an *insurgency* oriented toward 'climate protection from below'.[64]

What has weakened this insurgency? Brecher admits that 'in the face of increasing scientific certainty and experience', overt and widespread denial about human-caused climate change has declined. However, he continues,

> the next big barrier to climate action is the argument that global warming is now inevitable and that there is nothing people can do to halt it. The climate insurgency needs to persuade the public that society can forestall climate change by transition from fossil fuels. To do so it needs Climate Action Plans that show this is possible. It needs examples showing that it can be done and how. And it needs exemplary action that demonstrates that the people can defeat the climate destroyers ... The main reason people don't act is probably that they doubt their action will be effective. Overcoming that doubt is a core objective of the climate insurgency.[65]

Thus arises the key question of how to mobilise effective collective action against the 'fossil capitalism'[66] that has given rise to, and continues to undergird, increasingly dangerous climate change.

3 From Weakness to Strength: Building an Anti-capitalist Movement for Climate Justice

Let us take stock. Thus far we have considered an Urgency Argument, an Unsustainability Argument, and an Obstruction Argument. Add finally a fourth argu-

---

63 See Spinoza's note to Proposition 18 in Part Four of the *Ethics* (Spinoza 1996, pp. 125–6).
64 I have borrowed the idea of 'climate protection from below' from Brecher 2016.
65 Brecher 2017, pp. 57, 59.
66 On the concept and historical development of fossil capitalism, see Malm 2016 and Angus 2016, especially pp. 107–88.

ment, which links the results of the previous three. Call it the *Removal Argument*:

1. The capitalist mode of production is a grave threat posing serious harm to human development.
2. Any mode of production that is a grave threat posing serious harm to human development should be removed.
3. But capitalism *must* be removed through collective action.
4. Therefore, capitalism *should* be removed through collective action.

Of course building a successful anti-capitalist movement for climate justice won't be easy. It will require no less than 'a world uprising transcending all geographical boundaries'.[67] Indeed, parents who gaze at their children in the early morning hours while the latter are fast asleep may worry that the prospects for success are not great. Yet honest despair or even rage is preferable to what Roger Hodge has aptly termed the 'mendacity of hope'.[68] As Thomas McGrath once put it so eloquently, '[A]nger sustains me – it is better than hope – /it is *not* better than/Love …/But it *will* keep warm in the cold of the wrong world'.[69]

There are anger and despair aplenty in Chris Hedges' recent work. Hedges has stared into the capitalist abyss and decried liberal complicity with a descent into barbarism. Hedges warns that

> corporate interests have seized all mechanisms of power, from government to mass propaganda. They will not be defeated through elections or influenced through popular movements. The working class has been wiped out. The economy is in ruins. The imperial expansion is teetering on collapse. The ecosystem is undergoing terrifying changes unseen in recorded human history. The death spiral, which will wipe out whole sections of the human race, demands a return to a radical militancy that asks the uncomfortable question of whether it is time to break laws that, if followed, ensure our annihilation.[70]

Yet in spite of the dismal state of the world Hedges discerns a glimmer of hope arising from such renewed militancy:

> The best opportunities for radical social change exist among the poor, the homeless, the working class, and the destitute. As the numbers of disen-

---

67 Foster, Clark, and York 2010, p. 440.
68 Hodge 2010.
69 McGrath 1997, p. 317.
70 Hedges 2010, pp. 194–5.

franchised dramatically increase, our only hope is to connect ourselves with the daily injustices visited upon the weak and the outcast. Out of this contact we can resurrect, from the ground up, a social ethic, a new movement.[71]

Hedges concedes that 'it is too late to prevent profound climate change'. But, he quickly adds, 'why allow our ruling elite, driven by the lust for profits, to accelerate the death spiral? Why continue to obey the laws and dictates of our executioners?'[72]

Although Hedges rightly stresses the imperative to resist the global capitalist order, he fails to provide a nuanced assessment of what is required for successful collective action against capitalism.

Hedges is profoundly correct to stress the *priority* of what he has termed the 'moral imperative to revolt',[73] but equally important, as I have tried to show in previous chapters, are (a) the need to orient such revolt according to the norm of self-emancipation, (b) to formulate a strategic anti-capitalist plan of action according to reasonable standards, and (c) to sustain political commitment affectively over the long haul, indeed, across generations. The cost of failure is simply too great for the global climate justice movement to rely principally on what Hedges has called the power of 'sublime madness' (a term borrowed from the theologian Reinhold Niebuhr).[74]

Here David Harvey has offered an invaluable strategic corrective to Hedges' undue reliance on impassioned appeals to rebellion. Harvey has identified 'seven distinctive "activity spheres" within the evolutionary trajectory of capitalism' and within which any anti-capitalist movement must intervene if it is to increase its strength and effectiveness. These activity spheres are:

> technologies and organizational forms; social relations; institutional and administrative arrangements; production and labour processes; relations to nature; the reproduction of daily life and of the species; and 'mental conceptions of the world'.[75]

For Harvey, a movement can begin in any of these activity spheres, but 'the trick is to keep the political movement moving from one sphere of activity to

---

71 Hedges 2010, p. 156.
72 Hedges 2010, p. 202.
73 Hedges 2015.
74 See Hedges 2015, especially pp. 201–26.
75 Harvey 2010b, p. 123.

another in mutually reinforcing ways'.[76] Such a 'co-revolutionary politics'[77] has the following implication:

> [W]e can start anywhere and everywhere as long as we do not stay where we start from! The revolution has to be a *movement* in every sense of the word. If it cannot move within, across and through the different spheres then it will ultimately go nowhere at all. Recognising this, it becomes imperative to envision alliances between a whole range of social forces configured around the different spheres. Those with deep knowledge of how the relation to nature works need to ally with those deeply familiar with how institutional and administrative arrangements function, how science and technology can be mobilised, how daily life and social relations can most easily be re-organised, how mental conceptions can be changed, and how production and the labour process can be reconfigured.[78]

It is striking that for Harvey a militant workers' movement will not necessarily be at the forefront of this 'broad alliance of the discontented, the alienated, the deprived and the dispossessed'.[79] On the contrary, he fully expects that a 'youthful, student-led revolutionary movement' will lead the way.[80] Whether Harvey is correct in his forecast, or whether, by contrast, Charles Derber is right to stress that 'the labor movement is at the intersection of the economic and environmental crises that make a green revolution possible'[81] cannot be decided *a priori* and apart from self-emancipatory efforts actually to build a movement that would formulate structural reforms leading beyond capitalism and toward ecosocialism.[82]

At any rate, a movement toward ecosocialism should strive to contest and delegitimise the ideological 'pillars of support' for fossil capitalism.[83] For example, participants in this movement could argue that 'government actions are illegal and unconstitutional' and that they are performing a vital duty to reclaim, renew, and defend the 'public trust'.[84] As Brecher writes,

---

76 Harvey 2010b, p. 228.
77 Harvey 2010b, p. 241.
78 Harvey 2010b, pp. 138–9.
79 Harvey 2010b, p. 240.
80 Harvey 2010b, p. 239.
81 Derber 2010, p. 209.
82 Excellent initial formulations of a 'transitional programme' for ecosocialists to rally around may be found in Baer 2012, pp. 213–44; and Löwy 2015.
83 Brecher 2017, p. 65.
84 Brecher 2017, p. 85.

> Constitutional and public trust principles make it possible for the climate insurgency to turn the tables on the governments that purport to represent the world's people and to have the authority to rule the world. They stand for the proposition that governments do not have the right to destroy the climate – and that the people have the right to stop them when they do so. Governments have no more right to authorize the emission of greenhouse gases that destroy the climate than the trust officers of a bank have to loot the assets placed under their care. The people of the world have a right to our common natural resources. And we have a right, if necessary, to protect our common assets against those who would destroy them.[85]

An ecosocialist movement could even help to set up 'climate justice tribunals' to make the case that

> the governments and corporations of the world are systematically violating human rights, international law, and their duty to protect the public trust by allowing greenhouse gas emissions that are destroying the earth's climate. Future climate tribunals could examine the evidence in greater detail. They could issue declaratory judgments and injunctions. They could also make findings on the rights and responsibilities of global citizens to enforce the law and their legal rights vis-à-vis governments that try to subdue them when they do so. Tribunals can be convened as part of the legitimation and public education activities of specific campaigns. Although they may be initiated by the insurgency, the validity of their judgments can be based on the fairness of their conclusions and the evidence and argument on which they are based. Some tribunals could become permanent institutions. In specific instances, people could apply to such tribunals for 'advisory opinions' on questions like the need to halt new fossil fuel infrastructure or the adequacy of Climate Action Plans. Tribunals could weigh the evidence and issue judgments. They could then negotiate consent decrees or issue advisory orders. The people could then attempt to impose or implement those orders by mass action.[86]

Such tribunals would operate as a form of 'dual power' aiming not just at ideological disruption but at the creation of a new world: an ecologically sustain-

---

85 Brecher 2017, p. 86.
86 Brecher 2017, p. 91.

able planet, a planet whose boundaries still allow for the flourishing of human beings and other species, a planet fit for our children and theirs.[87]

Yet for any or all of the seven difficulties considered in this chapter, the movement might founder or fail long before such advanced forms of struggle as climate dual power ever arise. As Ian Angus soberly reminds us,

> there are no guarantees. Marxism is not deterministic. An ecosocialist revolution is not inevitable. It will only happen if people consciously decide it is necessary, and take the steps needed to bring it about.[88]

Two starkly contrasting climate 'scenarios' loom before humanity: 'Doom' and 'Fossil Free'.[89] Accordingly, our personal and political choices have never mattered more than they do now. Without being able to forecast the future and without any assurance of divine protection or historical inevitability, let us then – in the spirit of revolutions past – mutually pledge our lives and our fortunes on resisting the former and securing the latter prospect.

---

87 On the impracticality, even the undesirability, of restoring nature to a pristine 'original baseline', however, see MacKinnon 2013.
88 Angus 2016, p. 222.
89 Brecher 2017, pp. 95–100.

CODA

Beatitude: Marx, Aristotle, Averroes, Spinoza*

> The knell of capitalist private property sounds. The expropriators are expropriated.[1]

∴

It has recently become commonplace to argue that both Spinoza and Marx should be appreciated philosophically as Epicureans, indeed, as key figures in a subterranean current of 'aleatory materialism'.[2] Although there is much to be said in favour of such an interpretation, I believe it is one-sided. Consequently, in this article I seek to show that an equally important conceptual influence on both Spinoza and Marx was neither Epicurus nor Lucretius but Aristotle, in particular with respect to what Aristotle called *eudaimonia*, Spinoza called *beatitudo*, and Marx called 'real' – as opposed to 'illusory' – happiness. I hope to supplement efforts by others to chart the 'Aristotelian lineage of Marx's eudaimonism'.[3] By reclaiming the normative materialist current that links Aristotle to Averroes to Spinoza to Marx, we can more effectively criticise capitalism, refashion a credible model of ecological sustainability, and make good on the Marxist promise of human emancipation. Let us begin with Marx, and then retrace our steps.

∴

---

* This chapter has been previously published in *Continental Thought & Theory* 4, 2017, pp. 527–65.
1 Marx 1990, p. 929.
2 See especially Althusser 2006, pp. 163–207; and, in commentary, Ibrahim 2012. See, too, Morfino 2014, esp. pp. 72–88.
3 Gilbert 1990, pp. 263–304. Other notable attempts to reclaim Marx's Aristotelian heritage are Depew 1981–2; Meikle 1985; 1991; Wilde 1998, pp. 1–50; Groff 2012; 2015; Wilde 2013, pp. 106–41; and McCarthy 2015; 2018. Although Scott Meikle has admitted that the Aristotelian tradition 'is not an unchanging monolith ... but a diversity with a unity and continuity given by shared metaphysical principles' (Meikle 1991, p. 296), none of these authors has demarcated the conflicting materialist and idealist tendencies in this tradition along the lines of Bloch 1972.

In 1843 Karl Marx famously wrote that 'the abolition of religion as the illusory happiness of the people is the demand for their real happiness' (*Die Aufhebung der Religion als des illusorischen Glücks des Volkes ist die Forderung seines wirklichen Glücks*).[4] In this single line Marx makes a twofold distinction. Firstly, he explicitly distinguishes between an imaginary resolution of human social ills through religious, or some other, ideology and the actual social-political transformation required in order to reduce human suffering to the greatest possible extent. This is why Marx envisions the *Aufhebung* of religion. This does not mean the 'abolition' of religion in the sense of its 'elimination' but of its 'supersession', that is to say, the incorporation of what has been historically valuable, but inadequate, about religion. Hence, we find Marx using the adjective *wirklich* to characterise the 'happiness' (*Glück*) for which there has arisen a 'demand' (*Forderung*). The connotation of *wirklich* here is not 'real' as opposed to 'unreal' but 'effective' as opposed to 'ineffective' means to bring about happiness. Secondly, though, Marx implicitly distinguishes between happiness conceived of as subjective pleasure, contentment, or fulfilment and happiness as an objective, all-around human flourishing. In this respect, as we shall see, Marx should be regarded as a theoretical ally of Aristotle.[5] Indeed, as Terry Eagleton has succinctly written, Marx

---

4   Marx 2000, p. 72. I have taken the German text from the following online source for the Marx-Engels *Werke*: http://www.mlwerke.de/me/me01/me01_378.htm; last accessed 30 October 2015.

5   *Contra* the sensationalist charge recently revived by the neo-conservative historian Arthur Herman that Marx should be understood as a kind of misguided utopian Platonist whose 'concept of history comes straight out of Book 8 of the *Republic* ... history as class struggle pure and simple, a ruthless cycle of "war and hatred" without end' (Herman 2014, p. 440). Herman acknowledges his debt to Karl Popper's Cold War indictment of Marx and Hegel's supposed 'historicism' (see pp. 537–42). *Contra*, too, the attempt by Frank Ruda to 'exorcise the last remaining bits of Aristotelianism from contemporary thought' (Ruda 2016, p. 3). Ruda's argument is that Aristotelianism misconceptualises freedom in terms of the capacity for making choices and winds up generating 'a gigantic production and administration of indifference' that tends to reduce human existence to 'being an animal' (pp. 3–4). According to Ruda, Spinoza was indeed an Aristotelian in this bad sense and erred in 'naturalizing our essence' as human beings (p. 69). Although this is not the place to provide the full argument, it seems clear to me that Aristotle understands human freedom not in terms of capacity but in terms of whether or not an individual justifiably experiences 'mastery' by others (Hampton 1997, pp. 13–21). This also seems to be the main thrust of Spinoza's position in Chapter 2 of the *Political Treatise* (especially Sections 9–11). The project for Marxists in philosophy, then, is hardly to 'exorcise' Aristotle's influence but to discern and prolong a 'materialist tendency' in his writings and thereby to 'radicalise' them. At any rate, this was Ernst Bloch's project, which I seek to extend.

belonged to the great Aristotelian tradition for which morality was not primarily a question of laws, obligations, codes and prohibitions, but a question of how to live in the freest, fullest, most self-fulfilling way. Morality for Marx was in the end all about enjoying yourself. But since nobody can live their lives in isolation, ethics had to involve politics as well. Aristotle thought just the same.[6]

Let us turn, then, briefly to consider Aristotle's ethics.

∴

Aristotle begins and ends his *Nicomachean Ethics* by trying to understand the nature of *eudaimonia*.[7] This widely used term in ancient Greek thought is best translated in Aristotle's writings not as 'happiness' but as 'flourishing', for it concerns not subjective pleasure as 'ordinary people, the most vulgar ones, suppose'[8] but instead the embodiment and realisation of an objective sense of life going as well as possible. By *eudaimonia* Aristotle seeks to identify the highest and most worthy life: for human beings, it is one grounded in rational activity. Of course, he does not claim that each of us should, or even could, experience precisely the same form of *eudaimonia*. What enables me to flourish does not necessarily enable a star athlete, accomplished musician, political activist, or you to flourish.[9] Yet each of us is a human being, and so my and your versions of flourishing remain variations on human flourishing. Similarly, we can conceive of universal as opposed to culturally relative flourishing and human flourishing as opposed to non-human animal flourishing.[10]

However, as commentators have noticed, in the *Nicomachean Ethics* there is a distinction, even a tension, between 'two sorts of *eudaimonia*'. Whereas in Book VI we encounter a practical orientation that aims to further *eudaimonia*, in Book X we find a theoretical orientation that sets forth contemplation as the model for 'complete *eudaimonia*'.[11] And for the latter there is a catch:

---

6   Eagleton 2011, p. 159.
7   Reeve 2014. For a more detailed account of happiness in Aristotle, see Reeve 2012, pp. 223–77.
8   NE I5 1095^b (Aristotle 2014, p. 5).
9   Aristotle's own example is Milo of Croton, who was a famous wrestler and supposedly ate an entire cow in a single day; see NE I16 1106^b (Aristotle 2014, pp. 28, 237).
10 On the cognitive abilities, emotional lives, and capacities for flourishing of non-human animals, see De Waal 2016.
11 Reeve 2014, pp. 29–32.

according to Aristotle, only gods are capable of complete *eudaimonia*, since by their very nature they want for nothing. Yet human beings require, but to varying degrees lack, external goods – not least of which is leisure time – in order to devote themselves to a life of contemplation. As a result, actually existing human beings in a world of relative scarcity must fall back on a 'second-best kind of *eudaimonia* that consists in activity in accord with practical wisdom and the virtues of character'.[12] I stress this tension between Aristotle's two models for the good life, because, as we shall soon see, it occurs as well for Spinoza and Marx. It is quite true that 'happiness for Marx, as for Aristotle, was a practical activity, not a state of mind'.[13]

∴

This practical dimension of *eudaimonia* is at issue in Volume I of Marx's *Capital*. Near the end of Chapter One on 'The Commodity', for example, Marx sketches the relationship between religion and the historical development of economic relations in societies. As he concludes,

> The religious reflections of the real world can ... vanish only when the practical relations of everyday life between man and man, and man and nature, generally present themselves to him in a transparent and rational form. The veil is not removed from the countenance of the social life-process, i.e. the process of material production, until it becomes production by freely associated men, and stands under their conscious and planned control. This, however, requires that society possess a material foundation, or a series of material conditions of existence, which in their turn are the natural and spontaneous product of a long and tormented historical development.[14]

But what would a society of 'freely associated' producers look like, and what would be its economic organisation that resulted from 'their conscious and planned control'? Marx offers the following thought experiment, which is a variation on classical economists' use of Daniel Defoe's tale of the shipwrecked Robinson Crusoe:

---

12   Reeve 2014, p. 32.
13   Eagleton 2011, p. 140.
14   Marx 1990, pp. 172–3.

> Let us ... imagine ... an association of free men, working with the means of production held in common, and expending their many different forms of labour-power in full self-awareness as one single social labour force. All the characteristics of Robinson's labour are repeated here, but with the difference that they are social instead of individual. All Robinson's products were exclusively the result of his own personal labour and they were therefore directly objects of utility for him personally. The total product of our imagined association is a social product. One part of this product serves as fresh means of production and remains social. But another part is consumed by the members of the association as means of subsistence. This part must therefore be divided amongst them. The way this division is made will vary with the particular kind of social organization of production and the corresponding level of social development attained by the producers.[15]

We could call this passage an *Aristotelian* moment in *Capital*. Why? Compare these passages with one that occurs much later in Chapter Fifteen on 'Machinery and Large-Scale Industry' and also involves a thought experiment – this time, though, explicitly attributed to Aristotle (in Book I, Chapter Four of the *Politics*):[16]

> 'If', dreamed Aristotle, the greatest thinker of antiquity, 'if every tool, when summoned, or even by intelligent anticipation, could do the work that befits it, just as the creations of Daedalus moved of themselves,[17] or the tripods of Hephaestus went of their own accord to their sacred work,[18] if the weavers' shuttles were to weave of themselves, then there would be no need either of apprentices for the master craftsmen, or of slaves for the lords' ... And Antipater, ... a Greek poet of the time of Cicero, hailed the waterwheel for grinding corn, that most basic form of all productive machinery, as the liberator of female slaves and the restorer of the golden age ... Oh those heathens! They understood nothing of political economy and Christianity, as the learned Bastiat discovered, and before

---

15   Marx 1990, pp. 171–2.
16   Pol. I 4 1253b (Aristotle 2017, p. 6).
17   Daedalus was a legendary Greek craftsman and inventor whose statues were supposedly self-moving. As Aristotle relates in *De Anima* (DA 406b8–20), Daedalus was supposed to have 'made his wooden Aphrodite move by pouring liquid silver into it'; see Aristotle 2016a, p. 10. For a superb commentary, see Mayor 2018, pp. 85–104.
18   Hephaestus was the Greek god of fire and metallurgy.

him the still wiser MacCulloch.[19] They did not, for example, comprehend that machinery is the surest means of lengthening the working day. They may perhaps have excused the slavery of one person as a means to the full human development of another. But they lacked the specifically Christian qualities which would have enabled them to preach the slavery of the masses in order that a few crude and half-educated parvenus might become 'eminent spinners', 'extensive sausage-makers' and 'influential shoe-black dealers'.[20]

What is Marx's point in this curious passage? In the chapter on 'The Commodity', Marx has already commended Aristotle's analysis of exchange-value (in the *Nicomachean Ethics*, Book v, Chapter Five) but noted that the latter failed to identify the 'homogeneous element, i.e. the common substance' that is human labor.[21] What historical-material obstruction accounted for Aristotle's theoretical blind spot regarding value? As Marx puts it, Aristotle could not see that

> in the form of commodity-values, all labour is expressed as equal human labour and therefore as labour of equal quality, by inspection from the form of value, because Greek society was founded on the labour of slaves, hence had as its natural basis the inequality of men and of their labour-powers. The secret of the expression of value, namely the equality and equivalence of all kinds of labour because and in so far as they are human labour in general, could not be deciphered until the concept of human equality had already acquired the permanence of a fixed popular opinion. This however becomes possible only in a society where the commodity-form is the universal form of the product of labour, hence the dominant social relation is the relation between men as possessors of commodities. Aristotle's genius is displayed precisely by his discovery of a relation of equality in the value-expression of commodities. Only the historical limitation inherent in the society in which he lived prevented

---

19 Frédéric Bastiat (1801–50) was a French economist and advocate of 'classical liberalism'. John Ramsay McCulloch (1789–1864) was a Scottish economist, leader of the 'Ricardian' school of economics, and was appointed the first professor of political economy at University College London in 1828. Both Bastiat and McCulloch were leading figures of what Marx sarcastically called 'vulgar political economy'.
20 Marx 1990, pp. 531–3.
21 Marx 1990, p. 151.

him from finding out what 'in reality' this relation of equality consisted of.[22]

David Harvey comments as follows:

> Of course, slavery varies a great deal in what it is about, but it is not about the production of value in the sense that Marx means it. It entails a different kind of labor process. There is no abstract labor in a pure slave system. This was why Aristotle could not formulate a labor theory of value – because this theory only works in the case of free labor. Remember, value for Marx is not universal but specific to wage labor within a capitalist mode of production.[23]

Or, more succinctly, in Louis Althusser's words, 'the present that enabled Aristotle to make this brilliant intuitive reading, simultaneously prevented him from solving the problem he had posed'.[24]

With Marx's critical assessment of Aristotle as an economic thinker in mind, we can better appreciate that in the passage cited above from the *Politics*, Aristotle falls short but in an interestingly different way: he poses a solution without providing a means of realising that solution. He evokes a remarkable 'dream of self-moving tools'.[25] And yet such a utopian future could scarcely be achieved under the technological conditions that prevailed in the ancient world. The reliance on slaves – and free persons – to move the tools was in that epoch unavoidable. However, the supersession of capitalist commodity production – and its reliance on 'enslaving' machinery in the production process – allows us in the twenty-first century to envision a 'full automation'[26] that would no longer require the 'moral degradation' of workers and their families.[27] On the contrary, humanity could aim at maximal leisure time through democratic control not just of technology but also of the larger economy. Indeed, such a future would be a socio-economic realisation of *eudaimonia* that would go well beyond Aristotelian limitations.

---

22   Marx 1990, p. 152.
23   Harvey 2010a, p. 127.
24   Althusser et al. 2015, p. 272.
25   Wending 2011, p. 25.
26   Srnicek and Williams 2016.
27   On the moral degradation especially resulting from machine production, see Marx 1990, pp. 517–26.

Precisely such a utopian vision – arising in particular from Marx's reference to the Greek poet Antipater – was to form the basis of William Morris's late nineteenth-century response to *Capital*. Morris once acknowledged in his article 'How I Became a Socialist' that 'although I had thoroughly enjoyed the historical part of *Capital*, I suffered agonies of confusion of the brain over reading the pure economics of the great work'.[28] Nonetheless, Morris's candid admission has been identified by S.S. Prawer as 'a welcome illustration of the way in which the quotations from literature introduced into *Capital* could bring home Marx's arguments to minds that did not respond naturally or easily to economic formulas or statistics'.[29] Morris himself notes that his

> study of history and … love and practice of art forced him into a hatred of the civilization which, if things were to stop as they are, would turn history into inconsequent nonsense, and make art a collection of the curiosities of the past, which would have no serious relation to the life of the present.[30]

In other words, Morris maintains, he 'fell into *practical* Socialism'.[31] Such an orientation is abundantly clear in a lecture he first delivered in 1883 (the year of Marx's death) entitled 'Art under Plutocracy'.[32] Midway through his lecture, Morris contends that

> something must be wrong … in art, or the happiness of life is sickening in the house of civilization. What has caused the sickness? Machine-labour will you say? Well, I have seen quoted a passage from one of the ancient Sicilian poets rejoicing in the fashioning of a water-mill, and exulting in labour being set free from the toil of the hand-quern in consequence; and that surely would be a type of man's natural hope when foreseeing the invention of labour-saving machinery as 'tis called; natural surely, since though I have said that the labour of which art can form a part should be accompanied by pleasure, so one could deny that there is some necessary labour even which is not pleasant in itself, and plenty of unnecessary labour which is merely painful. If machinery had been used for minimiz-

---

28   Morris 1979, p. 241.
29   Prawer 1978, p. 334.
30   Morris 1979, p. 244.
31   Morris 1979, p. 242. Emphasis in the original.
32   Morris 1979, pp. 57–85.

> ing such labour, the utmost ingenuity would scarcely have been wasted on it; but is that the case in any way? Look round the world, and you must agree with John Stuart Mill in his doubt whether all the machinery of modern times has lightened the daily work of one labourer. And why have our natural hopes been so disappointed? Surely because in these latter days, in which as a matter of fact machinery has been invented, it was by no means invented with the aim of saving the pain of labour. The phrase labour-saving machinery is elliptical, and means machinery which saves the cost of labour, not the labour itself, which will be expended when saved on tending other machines. For a doctrine which, as I have said, began to be accepted under the workshop-system, is now universally received, even though we are yet short of the complete development of the system of the Factory. Briefly, the doctrine is this, that the essential aim of manufacture is making a profit; that it is frivolous to consider whether the wares when made will be of more or less use to the world so long as any one can be found to buy them at a price which, when the workman engaged in making them has received of necessaries and comforts as little as he can be got to take, will leave something over as a reward to the capitalist who has employed him. This doctrine of the sole aim of manufacture (or indeed of life) being the profit of the capitalist and the occupation of the workman, is held, I say, by almost every one; its corollary is, that labour is necessarily unlimited, and that to attempt to limit it is not so much foolish as wicked, whatever misery may be caused to the community by the manufacture and sale of the wares made.[33]

Although Morris only obliquely refers here to Marx – 'I have seen quoted a passage from one of the ancient Sicilian poets rejoicing in the fashioning of a water-mill, and exulting in labour being set free from the toil of the hand-quern in consequence' – his source is unquestionably Chapter Fifteen of *Capital*.

Moreover, earlier in his lecture Morris envisions the substitution of association for competition 'in all that relates to the production and exchange of the means of life' and heralds a 'new birth of art, which is now being crushed to death by the money-bags of competitive commerce'.[34] Since, for Morris, 'art is

---

33 Morris 1979, pp. 72–3. For a discussion of Morris's socialist critique of the capitalist use of machinery, see Thompson 2011, pp. 649–54.
34 Morris 1979, p. 66.

man's expression of his joy in labour',[35] only a socialist society would be able to provide the expansion of free time that is the prerequisite for the attainment of human flourishing.

But now let us add Spinoza to the discussion to see how his writings help to enrich an account of the dialectically imbricated individual and collective aspects of human flourishing.

∴

In a letter sent to the Dutch jurist Hugo Boxel during the autumn of 1674, Spinoza once wrote that 'the authority of Plato, Aristotle and Socrates carries little weight with me'.[36] Spinoza's confession occurs in the last of several letters exchanged with Boxel, who had initially posed the question of whether or not Spinoza believed in ghosts.[37] Spinoza continued:

> I should have been surprised if you had produced Epicurus, Democritus, Lucretius or one of the Atomists or defenders of the atoms. It is not surprising that those who have thought up occult qualities, intentional species, substantial forms and a thousand more bits of nonsense should have devised spectres and ghosts, and given credence to old wives' tales with a view to disparaging the authority of Democritus, whose high reputation they so envied that they burned all the books which he had published amidst so much acclaim.[38]

As a result of this passage in particular, Spinoza has often been classified as a kind of Epicurean who rejected Aristotle.[39] But this draws a hasty conclusion. As Alain Billecoq has observed, it is true that in this passage Spinoza aligns himself with a materialist 'philosophical camp' associated with Epicurus, Democritus, and Lucretius.[40] However, classifying philosophers into oppos-

---

35 Morris 1979, p. 67.
36 Letter 56. Translations from Spinoza's letters are based on Samuel Shirley's in Spinoza 1995. For an excellent commentary on the broader philosophical implications of the Spinoza-Boxel correspondence, see Billecoq 1986.
37 Letter 51.
38 Letter 56.
39 This common claim fails to account for Spinoza's positive references to the Aristotelian view of human beings as 'social animals' (see Ep35 and TP 2.15) and does not acknowledge the epistemological and metaphysical debt Spinoza owes to Aristotle. Manzini 2009 is invaluable for having made the extent of this debt explicit.
40 Billecoq 1986, pp. 95–7. Billecoq borrows the term 'philosophical camp' from the Marxist philosopher Lucien Sève; see Sève 1980, pp. 258–61.

ing idealist/materialist camps is only a crude first approximation for a more nuanced investigation of idealist and materialist *tendencies* that traverse all philosophical texts and traditions.[41]

For example, following Ernst Bloch, one could speak of an 'Aristotelian Left'[42] and seek to identify materialist elements not only in Aristotle's *Nicomachean Ethics* but also in the writings of an Islamic thinker like Averroes,[43] whose work bears a striking affinity with Spinoza's regarding both the interpretation of Scripture[44] and the unity of the intellect.[45] Indeed, it is even possible to identify in Thomas Aquinas's *Summa Theologiae* and other texts a materialist tendency that would allow for a fruitful comparison of his conception of *beatitudo* with Spinoza's.[46] Thus it appears that in his final letter to Boxel Spinoza is primarily trying to undercut Boxel's appeal to authority by invoking a countervailing materialist 'camp'. In a seventeenth-century philosophical (and scientific) context, this is hardly surprising.[47]

---

41 For more on the history of philosophy as a struggle of tendencies, see Chapter 1 above.
42 Bloch 1972, pp. 479–546. Bloch includes Spinoza's 'philosophy of immanence' as continuous with the 'Aristotelian Left' (pp. 511–12), and he suggests that the argument of Spinoza's *Theological-Political Treatise* falls within this tradition's varied attempts to reduce religion to morality (p. 515).
43 I retain the Latinised name of the twelfth-century jurist-philosopher Abū al-Walīd Muḥammad ibn Aḥmad ibn Rushd to emphasise the 'universalisable nature' of his thought (Ricard 2015, p. 115) and his vital influence on the reception of Aristotle in the thirteenth-century European philosophical conjuncture that was structured in terms of three secondary tendencies regarding (a) the eternity of the world, (b) the unity of the intellect, and (c) the relationship between faith and reason. For a superb analysis of the sharply opposed positions taken by various Christian thinkers regarding these tendencies, see van Steenberghen 1980.
44 On Averroes's approach to reading the Qur'an, see his *Decisive Treatise* (Averroes 1976) and, in commentary, Ricard 2015. On a possible dialogue between Spinoza and Islamic philosophy, see Djedi 2010; and for specifically Averroistic sources of Spinoza's thinking about religion and philosophy, see Fraenkel 2011; 2012, pp. 202–12; 2013.
45 As we shall see below, Averroes's distinctive conception of the intellect arose from his radical interpretation of Aristotle's *De Anima* (Aristotle 2016a).
46 Briefly, for Aquinas beatitude is the highest form of human happiness; however, unlike for Spinoza, beatitude is transcendent and only fully achievable after one's death, since it requires union with God. Moreover, Aquinas's conception of beatitude lacks the collective dimension that can be found in Spinoza's writings. For Aquinas's conception of beatitude, see Davies 2014, pp. 154–8. For a persuasive attempt to reconstruct and reclaim Aquinas's own qualified 'materialism', see Turner 2013, pp. 47–69.
47 On the widespread strategic use of Epicurean materialism to bypass or undercut Scholastic appeals to 'the Philosopher' (as Aquinas called Aristotle), see especially Jones 1992 and Wootton 2015.

At any rate, Spinoza undoubtedly shares Epicurus's emphasis on the (moderate) pursuit of pleasure and avoidance of pain. But although such a perspective seems to make sense of the third and fourth parts of the *Ethics*, it fails to do justice to Part Five, in which Spinoza writes about *beatitudo*, which has regularly been translated into English as 'blessedness' (with its clearly religious connotation). However, as Frédéric Manzini has argued persuasively, when we track down the source of Spinoza's concept of *beatitudo*, we find not Epicurus but Aristotle, and, in particular, the *Nicomachean Ethics*, of which Spinoza owned a Latin translation (since he did not read Greek).[48]

Manzini has rigorously investigated how various terms were translated from Greek into Latin in the standard edition of Aristotle's writings that Spinoza possessed in his personal library.[49] For our purposes we can restrict ourselves to the single word in question, namely, *eudaimonia*, which we find translated into Latin as *beatitudo*. As a result, let us insist that Spinoza's concept must not be understood as pleasure, satisfaction, or contentment in a subjectivist sense; rather, it must be understood as a variant of objective 'flourishing'. Moreover, we find such an interpretation confirmed through an attentive reading of Spinoza's *Ethics*.[50]

For example, in the preface to the Second Part of the *Ethics*, Spinoza reminds his readers that he is going to discuss only those things that 'follow from the essence of God, or the infinite and eternal being ... that can lead us, as if by the hand, to knowledge of the human mind and its greatest beatitude (*ad mentis humanae, eiusque summae beatitudinis cognitionem*)'.[51] Moreover, in the extended note to E2p49, Spinoza writes that 'our greatest happiness, that is, our beatitude (*nostra summa felicitas sive beatitudo*), consists ... in the knowledge of God alone, by which we are led to do only those things which love and piety (*amor et pietas*) advise'.

In E4p21 Spinoza makes the additional claim: 'No one can desire to be blessed (*beatus esse*), to act well and to live well, unless at the same time he desires to be, to act, and to live, that is, actually to exist'. Here is his supporting argument:

---

48   Manzini 2009, pp. 9–15.
49   A 1548 edition of Aristotle's *Omnia Opera* published in Basel, which reprinted a 1542 edition.
50   For somewhat different reconstructions of Spinoza's conception of beatitude, which do not draw out its political implications as I do here, see Manzini 2014 and Ramond 2016, pp. 205–21.
51   Spinoza 1996, p. 67, translation slightly modified.

1. Desire is the very essence of human beings (def aff 1).
2. So it follows that the specific desire to live blessedly, or well, to act, and so on is also the very essence of human beings.
3. But the very essence of human beings is the striving (*conatus*) by which each one of us strives to preserve his or her own being (E3p7).
4. Therefore, the desire to live blessedly, to act well, and to live well, is the striving by which each one of us strives to preserve his or her being, that is, actually to exist.

At odds with the pervasive myth that Spinoza reserved the experience of beatitude for an apolitical pursuit of the 'intellectual love of God', in E4p54 we next find him arguing that if the multitude is led by the affects of humility, repentance, and reverence, then it 'may live from the guidance of reason, that is, may be free and enjoy the life of the blessed (*beatorum vita*)'. Indeed, for Spinoza 'the prophets' served historically as what we could call *affective-organic intellectuals*.[52]

However, in the transition from Part Four to Part Five of the *Ethics*, Spinoza apparently does make a turn inward when he proposes the following:

> In life ... it is especially useful to perfect, as far as we can, our intellect, or reason. In this one thing consists the greatest human happiness, or beatitude. Indeed, beatitude is nothing but that serenity of mind (*animi acquiescentia*) that stems from intuitive knowledge of God. But perfecting the intellect is nothing but understanding God, his attributes, and his actions, which follow from the necessity of his nature. So the ultimate end of the human being who is led by reason, that is, his highest desire, by which he strives to moderate all the others, is that by which he or she is led to conceive adequately both himself and all things which can fall under his understanding (E4app4).

But he quickly adds that the human power to moderate all desires and to conceive of oneself adequately is always limited, since we are 'part of Nature' (*pars naturae*). Consequently, we must be satisfied by, and remain serene in the face of, such constraint.

In Part Five Spinoza completes his earlier account of *beatitudo* in a way that certainly lends itself to a religious, even mystical or visionary, interpretation. For instance, we read in E5p33s that 'if joy ... consists in the transition to a greater perfection, beatitude must surely consist in the fact that the mind is

---

52 See my discussion of prophets and the multitude in Chapter Six above.

endowed with perfection itself' and in Ep36s that 'our salvation, or beatitude, or freedom ... consists in a constant and eternal love of God, or in God's love for human beings. And this love, or beatitude, is called glory in the Sacred Scriptures – not without reason'.

Yet there remains an important qualification of the prospect for beatitude that is comparable to Aristotle's realisation that in the world of actually existing human beings contemplation is beyond the reach of most, if not all, of us. Spinoza sombrely admits in Ep39s that

> we live in continuous change ... as we change for the better or worse, we are called happy or unhappy. For one who has passed from being an infant or a child to being a corpse is called unhappy. On the other hand, if we pass the whole length of our life with a sound mind in a sound body, that is considered happiness.

Even as we continually strive to increase the capabilities of our bodies and minds over the course of our lives, we unavoidably fall short of achieving what, echoing Aristotle, could be called *complete beatitude*.

Let me add in passing a few thoughts about how Spinoza's conception of beatitude fits into his larger project in the *Ethics*. The conventional – and perhaps the obvious – way to read Spinoza's *Ethics* is to begin with Part One and read sequentially through to Part Five: in other words, to proceed from abstract metaphysical discussions of God, substance, attributes, and modes; next to infinite and finite modes in general and human modal existence in particular; then to passions and actions, servitude and freedom; and finally to the highest manifestations of human happiness – the intellectual love of God and beatitude.

But there is a danger in this 'protocol of reading'[53] for the *Ethics*, namely, one of falling into what has been called *acosmism*, the philosophical position that denies the reality of the physical universe, which is considered to be illusory or lacking existence apart from God.[54] Beginning with the oneness of substance, as Spinoza apparently does, how could we ever arrive at the diversity of singular things in the material world? Finite modes might turn out to exist only in the human imagination. As the early modern German philosopher Salomon Maimon put it,

---

53 To borrow Althusser's terminology from *Reading Capital*; see Althusser et al. 2015, p. 218.
54 On the charge of 'acosmism' levelled against Spinoza by Maimon and Hegel, see Melamed 2010.

> In Spinoza's system the unity is real while the diversity is merely ideal. In the very nature of things, while the unity which one observes in the order and regularity of nature, is consequently only coincidental; through this unity we determine our arbitrary system for the sake of our knowledge. *It is inconceivable how one could turn the Spinozistic system into atheism since these two systems are the exact opposite of each other.* Atheism denies the existence of *God*, Spinozism denies the existence of the *world*. Rather, Spinozism should be called 'acosmism'.[55]

But what if we were to read Spinoza's *Ethics* not according to its order of presentation but instead according to its conceptual order? What if we were to carry out a *materialist reversal* and begin with finite modes, human in particular, seek what is common to all as we move ontologically outward, and come to appreciate how everything holds together as diversity in unity? Beginning with Part three, we would move in succession to Part Four, Part Two, Part One, and still wind up at Part Five – but with a new appreciation of what Spinoza means by substance and beatitude. Substance would then be seen as a point of arrival and not as a point of departure; and we would grow accustomed to calling metaphysics not first but *last* philosophy.

Beatitude would turn out to be not the solitary experience of a fortunate few but a common good to be experienced through sharing with others to the greatest degree conceivable, ultimately, with all of humanity and the entire world. In continuity with the Aristotelian Left, and in particular with his Islamic philosophical predecessor Averroes, Spinoza agrees that the human intellect is not privately and exclusively held by individuals but opens up to the entire cosmos.[56]

∴

---

[55] Translated by and quoted in Melamed 2010, p. 79.
[56] In a remarkable book Augusto Illuminati has linked Marx to Averroes regarding the concept of a 'public' or 'general' intellect; see Illuminati 1996. Robert Esposito has also proposed that Averroes sets into motion a 'philosophy of the impersonal' that 'entails a dislocation of the "place" of thought' – in other words has a 'tendency to externalize thought with respect to the interiority of consciousness' (Esposito 2015, pp. 9–10). Esposito fashions his own lineage of philosophers who have historically destabilised the coincidence of external, objective thought and subjective, internal consciousness: after Averroes, Bruno and Spinoza, and leading up to such modern figures as Schelling, Nietzsche, Bergson, and Deleuze (pp. 143–202).

Based on his reading of Aristotle's *De Anima*, Book III, Averroes argues in his *Epistle on the Possibility of Conjunction with the Active Intellect*[57] that the 'Active Intellect conjoins with us from the outset in a conjunction of inexistence, I mean, the conjunction of form with the bearer of the form'. As a result, every human being is internally divided: 'One part produces the intelligibles through cognition and opinion, in the same way as it makes something through its form into another thing'.[58] At this early stage of his philosophical development, Averroes simply distinguished between the innate human capacity for thought that he called the *receptive* intellect and the transcendent activity of what he called the *agent* intellect. Later on, though, especially in his great commentary on Aristotle's *De Anima*,[59] Averroes drew an additional line of demarcation between the material intellect – now conceived as 'a single, eternal, incorporeal substance' – and each individual's uniquely materially constituted *imaginative* intellect.[60]

It is not surprising and was no accident, then, that G.W. Leibniz – as a representative figure along with Thomas Aquinas[61] of what could be called the 'Aristotelian Right' – later associated his contemporary Spinoza with a 'disquieting' predecessor Averroes and condemned both as advocates of a philosophical position against which he recoiled, namely, that each individual's specific receptive intellect is but, in Leibniz's metaphor, 'a drop in the ocean' of the general agent intellect.[62] Indeed, Leibniz opens his *Essais de théodicée* (published in 1710)[63] with a 'Discourse on the Conformity of Reason and Faith', and in Sections Seven and Eight he attacks the 'Averroists' – disparagingly called a 'sect of philosophers' – who, by contrast, had relied on Aristotle in order to defend the superiority of reason over faith and bore responsibility for 'the great schism in the West that still endures'.[64] In Section Seven Leibniz

---

57   Averroes 1982.
58   Averroes 1982, p. 45.
59   Averroes 2009.
60   See Davidson 1992, pp. 220–356 for an unrivalled account of Averroes's philosophical development regarding the intellect.
61   The two polemical works by Thomas Aquinas that explicitly address, encroach on, and seek to counteract the Averroist materialist threat through an idealist rereading of Aristotle are *De unitate intellectus contra Averroistas* (On the Unity of the Intellect against the Averroists, 1270) and *De aeternitate mundi* (On the Eternity of the World, 1271); see Aquinas 1993; 1998, pp. 710–17.
62   See Brenet 2015, p. 115 n. 22. Leibniz's key text at stake here is his 1702 essay 'Considérations sur la doctrine d'un esprit universel unique' (Considerations on the Doctrine of a Unique Universal Mind); see Leibniz 1994, pp. 217–32; Leibniz 1989, pp. 554–60.
63   Leibniz 1969; see the somewhat dated English translation available in Leibniz 1985.
64   Leibniz 1969, p. 54.

seeks to reconstruct Averroes's argument against the immortality of individual souls:

> The human species is eternal, according to Aristotle; therefore, if particular souls don't perish, one must resort to the metempsychosis rejected by this philosopher. Or, if there are always new souls, one must admit the infinity of these souls preserved from all eternity; but actual infinity is impossible, according to the doctrine of the same Aristotle. Therefore, one must necessarily conclude that souls, that is, the forms of organic bodies, must perish with these bodies, or at least this must happen to the passive intellect that properly belongs to each one of them. Thus, there will only remain the agent intellect common to all human beings, which Aristotle said comes from outside, and which must work wherever the organs are arranged; just as the wind produces a kind of music when it is blown into properly adjusted organ pipes.[65]

In Section Eight Leibniz proceeds to object that 'nothing could be weaker than this would-be proof' and insists that 'it is not true that Aristotle refuted metempsychosis, or that he proved the eternity of the human kind; and after all, it is quite untrue that an actual infinity is impossible'. In sum, Leibniz denounces 'this bad doctrine [that] is very ancient and very capable of dazzling the vulgar (*capable d'éblouir le vulgaire*)'.[66]

But is Averroes's argument really as weak as Leibniz presents it? Is the interaction of the active and passive intellects – or their *conjunction*, to use Averroes's term – reducible to Leibniz's lively baroque analogy of 'the wind produc[ing] a kind of music when it is blown into properly adjusted organ pipes'?[67] It is doubtless true, as Peter Adamson has noted, that although the Averroist position on the 'unity of the intellect', namely, that 'all humans share only one intellect ... sounds scarcely credible', in his historical context Averroes's 'innov-

---

65 Leibniz 1969, p. 55.
66 Leibniz 1969, p. 55.
67 Leibniz tries out the core analogy of **wind : agent intellect :: organ pipes : receptive intellect** in his earlier unpublished 1702 'Considerations on the Doctrine of a Unique Universal Mind': 'just as the same breath of wind causes various pipes of an organ to sound differently' (*comme un même soufflé de vent fait sonner différemment divers tuyaux d'orgue*); see Leibniz 1994, p. 219. It is worth noting that a decade later Leibniz has modified the analogy by qualifying the organ pipes as ones that have been 'properly adjusted' (*bien ajustés*). At any rate, Leibniz's analogy fails to do justice to Averroes's threefold distinction of agent, receptive, and imaginative intellects.

ation was less shocking', for 'it was perfectly standard to posit a single *agent* intellect for all humankind'.[68] Averroes

> simply added that there is likewise only one *potential* or 'material' intellect for all humankind. And this makes a certain amount of sense. How, after all, can a single actual intellect be paired with an unlimited number of potentialities (one per human)? Furthermore ... intellection is meant to be universal. And there is only one set of universals to be known. Anything grasped by just one human to the exclusion of all others would be particular to that human, not universal. The unity of the intellect guarantees that when the teacher conveys some universal truth to a student, the teacher and student are literally thinking the same thing.[69]

Anthony Kenny has proposed his own interesting argument regarding the Averroist position: that, just as much as the agent intellect, the receptive material intellect 'is a single, eternal, incorporeal substance':

> Aristotle told us that the receptive intellect receives all material forms. But it cannot do this if in itself it possesses any material form. Accordingly it cannot be a body nor can it be in any way mixed with matter. Since it is immaterial, it must be indestructible, since matter is the basis of corruption, and it must be single and not multiple, since matter is the principle of multiplication. The receptive intellect is the lowest in the hierarchy of incorporeal intelligences, located one rung below the agent intellect. Paradoxically, though itself incorporeal, it is related to the incorporeal agent intellect in a manner similar to that in which the matter of a body is related to the form of a body; and so it can be called the material intellect.[70]

One could immediately object to this line of reasoning that my thoughts cannot really be *my* thoughts 'if they reside in a super-human intellect'. But, Kenny suggests, Averroes's reply would be that

---

[68] Adamson 2015, p. 88. See Davidson 1992 for an unrivalled account of how the agent intellect operated as a contested concept from Aristotle, through late Greek antiquity, to the rise of Arabic philosophy and such key figures as Alfarabi, Avicenna, and Averroes.

[69] Adamson 2015, pp. 88–9.

[70] Kenny 2005, p. 230.

thoughts belong to not one, but two subjects. The eternal receptive intellect is one subject: the other is my imagination. Each of us possesses our own individual, corporeal, imagination, and it is only because of the role played in our thinking by this individual imagination that you and I can claim any thoughts as our own.[71]

Finally, Kenny argues that Averroes's view is that 'there is not … any personal immortality for individual humans … [and so] after death, souls merge with each other'.[72] Kenny would have us imagine that

> Zaid and Amr are numerically different but identical in form. If, for example, the soul of Zaid were numerically different from the soul of Amr in the way Zaid is numerically different from Amr, the soul of Zaid and the soul of Amr would be numerically two, but one in their form, and the soul would possess another form. The necessary conclusion is therefore that the soul of Zaid and the soul of Amr are identical in their form. An identical form inheres in a numerical, i.e. a divisible multiplicity, only through the multiplicity of matter. If then the soul does not die when the body dies, or if it possesses an immortal element it must, when it has left the body, form a numerical unity.[73]

What, then, is beatitude for Averroes, and how may it be realised? Beatitude would consist of the blissful 'conjunction' (Latin: *coniunctio*; Arabic: *ittisal*) of the receptive intellect with the agent intellect.[74] In this elevated 'eudaimonic state',[75] as Averroes writes in his commentary on Aristotle's *Metaphysics*,

> human beings … are made like unto God in that he is all beings in a way and one who knows these in a way, for beings are nothing but his knowledge and the cause of beings is nothing but his knowledge. How marvelous is that order and how mysterious is that mode of being![76]

---

71   Kenny 2005, p. 230.
72   Kenny 2005, p. 231.
73   Kenny 2005, p. 231.
74   For an overview of Averroes's conception of beatitude and 'its echoes in the Latin West', see Spruit 2013. Esposito notes that for Averroes, as for Spinoza, beatitude 'consists of a process of deindividuation or desubjectification, which reassembles the unity of being beyond our imagination' (Esposito 2015, p. 165).
75   Davidson 1992, p. 4.
76   Averroes 1984, p. 399.

Or, to adopt a poetically charged image of lover and beloved:

> The active intellect, insofar as it is separate and principle for us, must move us in the same way as the beloved moves the lover and if every motion must be in contact with the thing which produces it as end, we must ultimately be in contact with this separate intellect, so that we depend on such a principle, on which the heaven depends, as Aristotle says, although this happens to us for but a short time.[77]

Although Leibniz polemicised against what he regarded as Averroes's (and Spinoza's) conception of a mystical union of individual souls with the divine intellect, Charles Genequand has pointed out that what Averroes is arguing in this passage is simply that the highest human happiness

> resides in the intellectual apprehension of the intelligible. This is God's permanent state, whereas we can only attain it for a short period because our intellect is still tied down to matter and potentiality. When we reach that state, however, we become like God in that we think ourselves, or our own essence ... but this 'like' indicates a mere comparison: there is no identification, no union.[78]

The implication of such a perspective, however, was – and remains – at odds with traditional monotheistic conceptions of individual survival after death. As Herbert Davidson comments,

> When Averroes ... recognizes the possibility of conjunction with the active intellect, whether or not he takes conjunction to be a complete union of the material intellect, he maintains that conjunction guarantees the survival of the material intellect ... The material intellect will be void of all scientific thoughts acquired during the human lifetime, seeing that those thoughts are successive levels of abstraction, all of them ultimately rooted in images presented by the imaginative faculty ... the state of conjunction with the active intellect ... is not just one further level of abstraction, but a leap beyond. In conjunction, the material intellect transcends discursive science. It catapults itself beyond thought rooted in the impermanent images presented by the imaginative faculty, to a condition wherein the

---

77   Averroes 1984, p. 157.
78   Averroes 1984, p. 51.

active intellect, an eternal being consisting in pure thought, is the direct object of thought ... Obviously, no shred of anything resembling a human personality remains.[79]

In a real sense, Leibniz was correct: Averroes *was* a scandalous philosopher. Moreover, the philosophical opprobrium directed against Averroes would later be used to stigmatise Spinoza. The dual offensive against Averroism-Spinozism arguably reached its zenith – or nadir – in the early eighteenth century in Pierre Bayle's multivolume *Dictionnaire historique et critique*.[80] Bayle declares in his entry on Averroes[81] that the latter was 'one of the most subtle philosophers who had appeared among the Arabs' and in his commentaries had 'perfectly understood Aristotle's thought'; nevertheless, he should be regarded as the 'inventor of a sentiment that is quite absurd and quite contrary to Christian orthodoxy'.[82] Bayle recoils in particular at Averroes's 'extension ... and development of the principles of Aristotle', namely, the 'hypothesis of this philosopher' that 'the multiplication of individuals can have no foundation other than matter, whence it follows that the intellect is unique, since, according to Aristotle, it is separate and distinct from matter'.[83] In other words, there exists a 'unity of the intellect for all human beings'.[84] Bayle also reports that, according to the Jesuits,

> [Michael] Scot[85] said that Averroes was worthy of being excommunicated by the human species, and others say that his doctrine is a monster so appalling that the forests of Arabia have never produced one greater.[86]

As 'appalling' as Averroes's doctrine is for Bayle, it finds its most 'monstrous' expression in Spinoza's philosophy.

In his entry on Spinoza[87] Bayle provides the fullest account of his effort to detect and combat a kind of 'eternal pan-Spinozism'[88] in the history of philo-

---

79   Davidson 1992, pp. 337–8.
80   Bayle 1740.
81   Bayle 1740, vol. 1, pp. 384–91.
82   Bayle 1740, vol. 1, pp. 384–5.
83   Bayle 1740, vol. 1, p. 386, Remark E.
84   Bayle 1740, vol. 1, p. 385, Remark E.
85   Scot (1175–c. 1232) was a noted translator from Arabic into Latin of Averroes's commentaries on two works by Aristotle: *De anima* (On the Soul) and *De caelo* (On the Heavens).
86   Bayle 1740, vol. 1, p. 386, Remark E.
87   Bayle 1740, vol. 4, pp. 253–71; Bayle 1965, pp. 288–338.
88   I borrow this term from Charles-Daubert and Moreau in their introduction to Bayle 1983,

sophy. Bayle begins his article by characterising Spinoza as a 'systematic atheist'[89] whose philosophical system 'is the most monstrous hypothesis that could be imagined, the most absurd, and the most diametrically opposed to the most evident notions of our mind'.[90] What is that 'monstrous hypothesis'? According to Bayle, it is

> that there is only one substance in nature, and that this unique substance is endowed with an infinity of attributes – thought and extension among others. In consequence of this, he asserts that all the bodies that exist in the universe are modifications of this substance in so far as it is extended, and so far as it is extended, and that, for example, the souls of men are modifications of this same substance in so far as it thinks; so that God, the necessary and infinitely perfect being, is indeed the cause of all things that exist, but he does not differ from them. There is only one being, and only one nature; and this nature produces in itself by an immanent action all that we call creatures. It is at the same time both agent and patient, efficient cause, and subject. It produces nothing that is not its own modification. There is a hypothesis that surpasses all the heap of all the extravagances that can be said.[91]

Bayle charges Spinoza with 'quietism' and compares him unfavourably with certain Chinese sages who sought contemplative lives.[92] According to Bayle, Chinese quietists

> say that all those who seek true beatitude must allow themselves to be so absorbed in profound meditations that they make no use of their intel-

---

p. 10. The term designates for Bayle precisely what in Chapter 1 above we called a philosophical (*secondary*) *tendency*. It connotes a danger not just in the Western world (from such ancient thinkers as Xenophon to medieval European pantheists like David of Dinant and Giordano Bruno); rather, Bayle sees evidence of it in India, China, and Japan as well.

89 Bayle 1740, vol. 4, p. 253; Bayle 1965, p. 288. It is true that in his 'clarification concerning atheists' (Bayle 1740, vol. 4, pp. 627–9; Bayle 1965, pp. 399–408) Bayle allows for the possibility of 'virtuous' atheists like Epicurus (Bayle 1740, vol. 4, p. 627; Bayle 1965, p. 401) and Spinoza (Bayle 1740, vol. 4, p. 629; Bayle 1965, p. 405). What it might mean to call Spinoza an 'atheist' and whether or not it correctly describes Spinoza's actual view of the interrelationship of God, religious belief and practice, and morality is carefully examined in Rosenthal 2012 and Billecoq 2016.
90 Bayle 1740, vol. 4, p. 259; Bayle 1965, pp. 296–7.
91 Bayle 1740, vol. 4, p. 259, Remark N; Bayle 1965, pp. 300–1, Remark N.
92 Bayle 1740, vol. 4, pp. 254–5, Remark B; Bayle 1965, pp. 288–93, Remark B.

lect, but, by a complete insensibility, sink into the rest and inaction of the first principle, which is the true means of perfectly resembling it and partaking of happiness. They assert also that after one has reached this state of quietude, he should follow the ordinary course of life outwardly and teach others the commonly received doctrine. It is only in private and for his internal use that it is necessary for one to practice the contemplative institute of beatific inaction.[93]

Beatific inaction: Bayle fully contributes here to fashioning a 'caricature'[94] of Spinoza as a philosopher-renunciant utterly disengaged from, and uninterested in, worldly affairs:

He felt such a strong passion to search for truth that to some extent be renounced the world to be better able to carry on that search. He was not content with having removed himself from all sorts of affairs; he also left Amsterdam because his friends' visits interrupted his speculations too much. He retired to the country, he meditated there at his leisure, and he worked on microscopes and telescopes there. He kept up this kind of life after he settled in The Hague; and he gained so much pleasure from meditating, from putting his meditations in order, and from communicating them to his friends, that he allowed very little time for mental recreation; and sometimes he let three whole months go by without setting foot outside his lodgings.[95]

---

93 Bayle 1740, vol. 4, p. 255; Bayle 1965, p. 291 (translation slightly modified).
94 Moreau 2003, p. 110. This caricature extends as well to Bayle's confusion of Spinoza's concepts of 'naturing Nature' (*natura naturans*) and 'natured Nature' (*natura naturata*). As a result, as Pierre-François Moreau puts it, for Bayle 'Spinozism appears as a gigantic fusion of God with the world, which makes contradictions in the world incomprehensible … the thought of one substance suppresses transcendence and illustrates the contradictions of a reason left to its own excesses without the restraint of dogma' (Moreau 2003, p. 110). More recently, Carolyn Merchant (2016, pp. 101–24) has also mistakenly equated *natura naturans* and *natura naturata* in Spinoza's thought and argued that the latter regarded the world as exhaustively describable in terms of physical laws. Yet this distinction marks an internal division within substance ('God') and signifies the infinite causal productivity of substance over its diverse modal effects. Since human beings, according to Spinoza, in fact perceive only two attributes of substance – mind and extension – they cannot in principle arrive at a complete account of the world (as it exists in itself with an infinity of attributes) prior to, and independent of, the operation of the intellect.
95 Bayle 1740, vol. 4, pp. 256–7; Bayle 1965, p. 294.

Yet, as we shall see in the next section, for a reason unimagined by Bayle, Spinoza's hypothesis is indeed monstrous – not for advocating individual retreat and quietism but for allowing one better to understand the nature of political engagement and collective action.

∴

If we consider Spinoza's philosophy in continuity with a 'Left Aristotelian' tradition, in particular, as that tradition was inflected through 'Averroism', we can better appreciate Spinoza's conception of the intellect, especially as presented in Part 2 of the *Ethics*, and its implications for politics and collective action. Let us focus on E2p45, in which Spinoza argues that whenever we form an idea of 'a singular thing that actually exists', our knowledge 'necessarily involves an eternal and infinite essence of God'. Here, in a nutshell, is Spinoza's dense chain argument to this conclusion (with missing premises supplied in brackets):

1. The idea of a singular thing that actually exists necessarily involves both the essence of the thing and its existence (E2p8c).
2. Singular things have God for a cause insofar as God is considered under the attribute of which things are modes (E2p6).
3. [Whatever is, is in God, and nothing can be or be conceived without God (E1p15)]
4. Therefore, singular things cannot be conceived without God.
5. [The knowledge of an effect depends on, and involves, the knowledge of its cause (E1a4).]
6. Therefore, the idea of each singular thing must involve the concept of its attribute.
7. [God is a being absolutely infinite, that is, a substance consisting of an infinity of attributes, of which each one expresses an eternal and infinite essence (E1d6).]
8. Therefore, the idea of each singular thing must involve an eternal and infinite essence of God.

Bearing in mind Spinoza's conception of God as an 'absolutely infinite being, that is to say, a substance consisting of an infinity of attributes, of which each one expresses an eternal and infinite essence', we can grasp the radicality of this argument for the purpose of understanding collective action. We can discern here in Spinoza's metaphysics of mental nonlocality[96] the operation of what

---

96 At the risk of historico-scientific anachronism, I use the term 'nonlocality' (drawn from

Roberto Esposito has called 'the principle of the impersonality of thought' – a profoundly subversive principle that

> calls into question ... the set of exclusionary thresholds that cut the human race into overlapping segments based on the amount of reason attributed to them – starting from the unbreakable line that separates the bearers of thought from those who are incapable of true speculative activity and therefore subjected to the control of those who are. To see intelligence not as a property of the few, to the detriment of others, but as a resource for all, through which one can pass without appropriating it for oneself, means to assign it a collective power that only the human species as a whole can fully actualize.[97]

Let us consider, then, a *historical conjuncture* to be a singular thing in Spinoza's sense. What Spinoza is arguing in E2p45 is that whenever one forms an idea of a given conjuncture, then one's finite individual intellect opens up to an infinite collective intellect as we undergo a transition from an understanding of the world *sub specie durationis* to an understanding of the world *sub specie aeternitatis*.[98] As Spinoza adds in a note to the proposition:

> By existence here I do not understand duration, that is, existence insofar as it is conceived abstractly, and as a certain species of quantity. For I am

---

quantum mechanics) to register that for Spinoza the intellect is not separate from the body; rather, the embodied mind is 'out of place': it is simultaneously located (as well as dislocated and relocated) at two different ontological levels: (a) among modes and (b) between finite modes and absolutely infinite substance.

97 Esposito 2015, p. 12. Esposito points out, however, that 'there is an important point which clearly differentiates the definition of thought in Spinoza from both the possible intellect and, all the more so, from the agent intellect that Averroes talks about, in part due to the lack of difference between potency and act: this is its separate dimension, at the heart of Averroes's theory. That thought is impersonal and does not belong to anyone, as both philosophers maintain, does not mean that it is necessarily separate' (Esposito 2015, p. 165). Esposito attributes Spinoza's 'leap forward' from Averroes's 'radical Aristotelianism' to the latter's effort to 'deconstruct the Christian or Platonic composite of mind and soul' (p. 166), whereas the former seeks to 'deconstruct' both the Cartesian duality between mind and body and the Hobbesian materialist reduction of mind to body. For Spinoza, as Esposito puts it, 'not only can a mind not exist outside the body, the body is actually the content of the mind' (p. 165).

98 Esposito rightly points out, however, that Averroes's conception of a common active intellect that is external to individual imaginative intellect remains anthropocentric in a way that Bruno and Spinoza will later reject (Esposito 2015, pp. 155, 165).

speaking of the very nature of existence, which is attributed to singular things because infinitely many things follow from the eternal necessity of God's nature in infinitely many modes ... I am speaking, I say, of the very existence of singular things insofar as they are in God. For even if each one is determined by another singular thing to exist in a certain way, still the force (*vis*) by which each one perseveres in existing follows from the eternal necessity of God's nature.[99]

If human beings are to transform social structures and institutions effectively and lastingly, then they must go beyond conceiving them abstractly and isolated from one another; instead, they must grasp how these structures and institutions fit concretely into a larger scheme (whether it is called 'divine' or 'natural' is moot, for these descriptions are functionally equivalent in Spinoza's metaphysics). Indeed, this realisation allows for the demarcation of an *eternal* dimension to political struggle that is not limited to merely episodic skirmishes. In order to overturn capitalism one must be able to step back and comprehend it from 'the perspective of eternity'[100] and thereby orient anti-capitalist strategy that could lead to a new mode of production under – as Marx put it in *Capital* – the 'conscious and planned control' of 'freely associated' men and women.[101] Let us call the anticipatory experience of this eternal dimension of political struggle by its Spinozist name, *beatitude*, for it points beyond the present conjuncture to how one day society could be reorganised in the common interest of all humanity, once the 'capitalist integument' binding production and dominating labour has at last been 'burst asunder' and 'the knell of capitalist private property [has] sound[ed]'.[102]

In sum, as Robert Misrahi has observed, for Spinoza 'beatitude is not a mystical experience but a human and existential plenitude ... it is the highest moment of a humanist ethics of freedom and joy'. As a result, 'far from being elitist, the ethics of beatitude is, on the contrary, a universalist doctrine ... simultaneously concerned about happiness and democracy'.[103] Unfortunately, though, we continue to live in societies that are far from democratic and not especially happy. Thus returns the demand for *real* happiness.

Interestingly, this demand has recently been made by a number of environmental theorists who have contended that the much used, and regularly

99 E2p45s.
100 See E2p44c2, d; E5p29.
101 Marx 1990, p. 173.
102 Marx 1990, p. 929.
103 Misrahi 2005, pp. 89–90.

abused, term 'sustainability' needs to be rethought.[104] Since none of us is – to use Spinoza's language – an *imperium in imperio*, or a 'state within a state', individual flourishing depends on the flourishing not only of other human beings but also of other forms of life on this planet. As Edward McCord puts it,[105] we must seek 'attributes of character that optimize a flourishing life':

> Focusing on your personal fulfillment in a flourishing life provides a more accurate perspective on your 'rational self-interest'. The values that you favor are not measured only by the commodities you buy with money but more fundamentally by the qualities of character that you allow to influence what you buy. In other words, to gain a true sense of your values, it would be misleading to focus only on the specific things you choose to do, for those choices may emanate from traits of your character that you would rather not have.
>
> Aristotle's civilization was different from ours, and it flourished a long time ago, but a striking measure of his timeless insight is that the evaluation of qualities of character remains pervasive and fundamental in our reflections about ourselves and one another. Such evaluation is readily prompted by our attitudes about other species.[106]

John Ehrenfeld has also offered a striking definition of ecological sustainability: 'the possibility that human and other life will flourish on this planet forever'.[107] One could quibble with Ehrenfeld's choice of words: to flourish *forever* is presumably not within our means. But to flourish *eternally*, that is, to consider sustainability as flourishing from the perspective of eternity, is an entirely different matter. Not only is this possible, it is necessary if we are to contest the ideological appropriation of 'sustainability'.[108]

In Chapter Twenty-Three of *Capital* Marx makes the following keen observation: 'The Roman slave was held by chains; the wage-labourer is bound to his owner by invisible threads. The appearance of independence is maintained by a constant change in the person of the employer, and by the legal fiction of a contract'.[109] If philosophy has any contemporary value for Marxism, it must be

---

104   The best critical introduction to the history and contemporary usage of the term 'sustainability' is Jacques 2015.
105   McCord 2012.
106   McCord 2012, pp. 119–20.
107   Ehrenfeld 2008, p. 6, emphasis removed. For more on sustainability as flourishing, see also Ehrenfeld and Hoffman 2013.
108   See Parr 2009 and Rogers 2013.
109   Marx 1990, p. 719.

to make visible and help to sever the invisible threads of capitalist exploitation, to serve the cause of an independent working class movement, and to plead the case for a truly sustainable economic system. But we need something more in the fierce urgency of the present conjuncture.[110]

We need a new materialist beatific vision, or what L.A. Paul has called a 'transformative experience',[111] which would motivate our actions today for a future about which we cannot be certain. If we were to succumb to the grim perspective that this is *the last generation*,[112] then we would indeed have reason for despair that there is no point in struggling to change the world. But if, on the other hand, as Naomi Klein has aptly put it, the climate crisis 'changes everything',[113] then we should act accordingly. In the spirit of previous freedom movements, we should take up a 'fight for each other',[114] restrain the worst features of the 'Anthropocene',[115] and thereby avoid collapse into the 'Eremocene', or 'Age of Loneliness', in which 'all that remains of global biodiversity is people ... our domesticated plants and animals, and our croplands all around the world as far as the eye can see'.[116] Beyond this, we should urgently build the fossil-fuel-free world that is a precondition for collective flourishing – for what Marx called *real* happiness.

Yet, as Leif Wenar cautions, the scope and difficulty of this struggle is historically unprecedented. For example, although it resembles the abolitionist cause,

> breaking the world's slave chains was a moral triumph; breaking the world's supply chains is not an option. Fighting these new crises means disciplining the creations of which we are so proud. Climate change is

---

110 Here I am deliberately mixing the language of Marxism and of Martin Luther King, Jr., who famously spoke in his 1963 'I Have a Dream' speech about the 'fierce urgency of now' (see Younge 2013, p. xii.).
111 Paul 2014.
112 An unsettling thought experiment devised by the philosopher Samuel Scheffler and developed in Scheffler 2013.
113 Klein 2014.
114 To adopt Wen Stephenson's formulation. Stephenson has especially well invoked the Abolitionist movement as a way to orient the next steps of the climate justice movement; see Stephenson 2015, especially pp. 23–45.
115 As Ian Angus has compellingly argued, although it is not possible to reverse the Anthropocene as a new geological epoch, it is both technologically feasible and morally imperative to transcend capitalism by constructing an ecosocialist alternative that would allow humanity and other species to remain within the planetary boundaries that provide a safe operating space for us and them. See Angus 2016.
116 Wilson 2016, p. 20.

a crisis of invention. So many more humans, living longer, eating better, traveling more to see the world and each other – how poignant to see that all of this avalanches into a mortal threat.

As a result, Wenar insists, 'both self-control and ingenuity will be needed to limit the threats that rise with our success'.[117] Let us expand on Wenar's two requirements in reverse order. 'Ingenuity' would seem to be a matter especially of technology, which as Marx insightfully wrote in a footnote in *Capital*, 'reveals the active relation of man to nature, the direct process of the production of his life, and thereby it also lays bare the process of the production of the social relations of his life, and of the mental conceptions that flow from those relations'.[118]

'Self-control', however, has to do with how human beings adjust the 'mental relations' that arise from a given socio-historical level of technology; it returns us to the realm of ethics in the precise sense that, following Gilles Deleuze's formulation, we should aspire 'to do all we can'[119] – this time by endeavouring to flourish within the contours set by what Earth System scientists have called 'planetary boundaries'.[120] In a word: there can be no beatitude without fortitude, but there is no need for fortitude apart from the struggle for a better world.[121]

∴

As a final point of orientation, let us note that in his *Theological-Political Treatise* Spinoza interprets Jesus'[122] second beatitude 'Blessed are those who mourn, for they shall be comforted' (Mt 5.4) by suggesting that 'those who mourn' refers only to 'those who mourn that the kingdom of God and justice are neglected by human beings; for only those can mourn this who love nothing but the kingdom of God and justice, and wholly despise all fortune besides'.[123] According to Spinoza, Jesus was not, however, 'laying down ordinances as a legislator' but

---

117   Wenar 2016, p. 339.
118   Marx 1990, p. 493. David Harvey has fully explored the multiple implications of Marx's footnote; see especially Harvey 2010a, pp. 189–212.
119   Deleuze 1990a, pp. 268–9.
120   For an overview of the science of planetary boundaries, see Angus 2016, pp. 59–77.
121   For Spinoza's concept of 'fortitude' and its application to an 'ethics for Marxism', see the 'Interlude' above.
122   Spinoza standardly uses in Latin not the personal name *Iesus* but instead the title *Christus* ('Annointed One' or 'Messiah').
123   TTP 7.7.

was 'offering doctrine as a teacher',[124] as a kind of people's philosopher who 'understood revealed things truly and adequately'.[125] Spinoza even ventures that Jesus spoke 'to people who were oppressed and living in a corrupt state where justice was completely neglected, and he saw that the ruin of that state was imminent'.[126]

This is the properly political meaning of beatitude – for then and now.[127]

---

124 TTP 7.7.
125 TTP 4.10.
126 TTP 7.7.
127 To be more precise: although the Latin Vulgate from which Spinoza quotes uses the plural *beati*, the underlying Greek text of the Gospel of Matthew has *makarioi*, which means the 'blessed', but with a distinctive religious and passive nuance that *eudaimonia* lacks. Yet when Jesus singles out peasants and artisans for 'blessing' and not socio-economic-religious elites, he upends passivity by the poor (generally maligned by Aristotle) to participate in a transformational movement for the renewal of Israel and to pursue an egalitarian kingdom of God that would be the antithesis of the existing Roman imperial order. At any rate, Spinoza clearly expresses here his sympathy for Jesus's radical 'doctrine'. For a fascinating commentary on the Sermon on the Mount in terms of Jesus's conception of human flourishing, see Pennington 2017.

Bibliography

Adams, Edward 2016, *The Earliest Christian Meeting Places: Almost Exclusively Houses?*, revised edition, New York, NY: Bloomsbury T&T Clark.

Adamson, Peter 2015, *Philosophy in the Islamic World: A Very Short Introduction*, New York, NY: Oxford University Press.

Aland, Kurt and Barbara et al. 1997, *Novum Testamentum Graece et Latine*, 27th edition, Stuttgart: Deutsche Bibelgesellschaft.

Alliez, Eric 1996, *Deleuze: Philosophie virtuelle*, Paris: Synthélabo Groupe.

Alliez, Eric 1998, 'Sur la bergonisme de Deleuze', in Gilles Deleuze: *Une vie philosophique*, edited by Eric Alliez, Paris: Institut Synthélabo, pp. 243–64.

Almog, Joseph 2014, *Everything in its Right Place: Spinoza and Life by the Light of Nature*, New York: Oxford University Press.

Althusser, Louis 1968, an unpublished typed letter to Gilles Deleuze dated 29 February, 1968, Paris: IMEC Archive.

Althusser, Louis 1976, *Essays in Self-Criticism*, translated by Grahame Lock, London: NLB.

Althusser, Louis, 'Introduction: Unfinished History', in Dominique Lecourt, *Proletarian Science? The Case of Lysenko*, translated by Grahame Lock, London: New Left Books, 1977.

Althusser, Louis 1977 [1972], 'Rousseau: The Social Contract (The Discrepancies)', in *Politics and History: Montesquieu, Rousseau, Hegel and Marx*, translated by Ben Brewster, London: NLB.

Althusser, Louis 1993, *The Future Lasts Forever: A Memoir*, edited by Olivier Corpet and Yann Moulier Boutang, translated by Richard Veasey, New York, NY: The New Press.

Althusser, Louis 1995, *Sur la reproduction*, Paris: Presses Universitaires de France.

Althusser, Louis 1998, *La Solitude de Machiavelli*, edited by Yves Sintomer, Paris: Presses Universitaires de France.

Althusser, Louis 2000 [1999], *Machiavelli and Us*, translated by Gregory Elliott, New York, NY: Verso.

Althusser, Louis 2001, *Lenin and Philosophy and Other Essays*, New York, NY: Verso.

Althusser, Louis 2003, *The Humanist Controversy and Other Writings*, edited by François Matheron, translated by G.M. Goshgarian, New York, NY: Verso.

Althusser, Louis 2005 [1969], *For Marx*, translated by Ben Brewster, New York, NY: Verso.

Althusser, Louis 2006, *Philosophy of the Encounter: Later Writings, 1978–1987*, edited by François Matheron and Oliver Corpet, translated by Geoff Goshgarian, New York, NY: Verso.

Althusser, Louis 2008 [1971], 'Ideology and Ideological State Apparatuses', in *On Ideology*, pp. 1–60, New York, NY: Verso.

Althusser, Louis 2011 [1990], *Philosophy and the Spontaneous Philosophy of the Scientists and Other Essays*, edited by Gregory Elliott, New York, NY: Verso.

Althusser, Louis 2012, *Cours sur Rousseau*, edited by Yves Vargas, Paris: Le Temps des Cerises.

Althusser, Louis 2014a, *Initiation à la philosophie pour les non-philosophes*, edited by G.M. Goshgarian, Paris: Presses Universitaires de France.

Althusser, Louis 2014b, *On the Reproduction of Capitalism: Ideology and Ideological State Apparatuses*, translated by G.M. Goshgarian, New York, NY: Verso.

Althusser, Louis et al. 2015, *Reading Capital: The Complete Edition*, translated by Ben Brewster and David Fernbach, New York, NY: Verso.

Anderson, Kevin B. 2007, 'The Rediscovery and Persistence of the Dialectic in Philosophy and in World Politics', in Budgen, Kouvelakis, and Zizek 2007, pp. 120–47.

Anderson, Kevin 2012, 'Climate Change Going Beyond Dangerous – Brutal Numbers and Tenuous Hope', *Development Dialogue*, 61, pp. 16–40.

Anderson, Perry 1980, *Arguments within English Marxism*, New York, NY: NLB.

Anderson, Perry 2005, *Spectrum: From Right to Left in the World of Ideas*, New York, NY: Verso.

Angus, Ian 2016, *Facing the Anthropocene: Fossil Capitalism and the Crisis of the Earth System*, New York, NY: Monthly Review Press.

Aquinas, Thomas 1993, *Aquinas against the Averroists: On There Being Only One Intellect*, translated and edited by Ralph McInerny, West Lafayette, IN: Purdue University Press.

Aquinas, Thomas 1998, *Selected Writings*, translated and edited by Ralph McInerny, New York, NY: Penguin Books.

Arendt, Hannah 1998 [1958], *The Human Condition*, 2nd edition, Chicago, IL: The University of Chicago Press.

Aristotle 2014, *Nicomachean Ethics*, translated by C.D.C. Reeve, Indianapolis, IN: Hackett Publishing Company, Inc.

Aristotle 2016a, *De Anima*, translated by Christopher Shields, New York, NY: Oxford University Press.

Aristotle 2016b, *Metaphysics*, translated by C.D.C. Reeve, Indianapolis, IN: Hackett Publishing Company, Inc.

Aristotle 2017, *Politics*, translated by C.D.C. Reeve, Indianapolis, IN: Hackett Publishing Company, Inc.

Arthur, Paige 2010, *Unfinished Projects: Decolonization and the Philosophy of Jean-Paul Sartre*, New York, NY: Verso.

Ash, Stephen 1995, *When the Yankees Came: Conflict and Chaos in the Occupied South, 1861–1865*, Chapel Hill, NC: The University of North Carolina Press.

Averroes 1976, *On the Harmony of Religion and Philosophy*, edited and translated by George Hourani, London: Luzac & Co.

Averroes 1982, *The Epistle on the Possibility of Conjunction with the Active Intellect by Ibn Rushd with the Commentary of Moses Narboni*, translated and edited by Kalman P. Bland, New York, NY: The Jewish Theological Seminary of America.

Averroes 1984, *Ibn Rushd's Metaphysics: A Translation with Introduction of Ibn Rushd's Commentary on Aristotle's Metaphysics, Book Lām*, translated and edited by Charles Genequand, Leiden: E.J. Brill.

Averroes 2009, *Long Commentary on the* De Anima *of Aristotle*, translated by Richard C. Taylor with Thérèse-Anne Druart, subeditor, New Haven, CT: Yale University Press.

Badiou, Alain 2003, *Saint Paul: The Foundation of Universalism*, translated by Ray Brassier, Palo Alto, CA: Stanford University Press.

Badiou, Alain 2009, *Logics of Worlds*, translated by Alberto Toscano, New York, NY: Continuum.

Baer, Hans 2012, *Global Capitalism and Climate Change: The Need for an Alternative World System*, Lanham, Maryland: AltaMira Press.

Bales, Kevin 2016, *Blood and Earth: Modern Slavery, Ecocide, and the Secret to Saving the World*, New York, NY: Spiegel & Grau.

Balibar, Étienne 1989, 'Spinoza, politique et communication', *Cahiers philosophiques*, 39, pp. 17–42.

Balibar, Étienne 1994, 'Spinoza, the Anti-Orwell: The Fear of the Masses', translated by Ted Stolze and revised by James Swenson and Étienne Balibar, in *Masses, Classes, Ideas*, New York: Routledge, 1994, pp. 3–37.

Balibar, Étienne 1995, *The Philosophy of Marx*, translated by Chris Turner, New York, NY: Verso.

Balibar, Étienne 1997, *Spinoza: From Individuality to Transindividuality*, Delft, The Netherlands: Eburon.

Balibar, Étienne 2002a, *Droit de cité*, 2nd edition, Paris: Presses Universitaires de France.

Balibar, Étienne 2002b, *Politics and the Other Scene*, New York, NY: Verso.

Balibar, Étienne 2008, *Spinoza and Politics*, translated by James Snowdon, New York, NY: Verso.

Balibar, Étienne 2015, *Violence and Civility: On the Limits of Political Philosophy*, translated by G.M. Goshgarian, New York, NY: Columbia University Press.

Balibar, Étienne et al. 2015, *Violence, civilité, revolution: Autour d'Étienne Balibar*, Paris: La Dispute.

Baltas, Aristides 2012, *Peeling Potatoes or Grinding Lenses: Spinoza and Young Wittgenstein Converse on Immanence and Its Logic*, Pittsburgh, PA: University of Pittsburgh Press.

Banks, Robert J., 1994, *Paul's Idea of Community: The Early House Churches in Their Cultural Setting*, Grand Rapids, MI: BakerAcademic.

Barclay, John M.G. 2015, *Paul and the Gift*, Grand Rapids, MI: William B. Eerdmans Publishing Company.

Barclay, John M.G. 2016, 'Why the Roman Empire Was Insignificant to Paul', in *Pauline Churches and Diaspora Jews*, pp. 363–87, Grand Rapids, MI: William B. Eerdmans Publishing Company.

Barnes, Timothy D. 2015, '"Another Shall Gird Thee": Probative Evidence for the Death of Peter', in Bond and Hurtado 2015, pp. 76–95.

Barnosky, Anthony D. and Elizabeth A. and Hadly 2015, *Tipping Point for Planet Earth: How Close Are We to the Edge?*, New York, NY: Thomas Dunne Books.

Barnouw, Jeffrey 1992, 'Le vocabulaire du *conatus*', in *Hobbes et son vocabulaire*, edited by Yves-Charles Zarka, pp. 103–24, Paris: J. Vrin, 1992.

Baron, Naomi S. 2015, *Words Onscreen: The Fate of Reading in a Digital World*, New York, NY: Oxford University Press.

Bartholomew, Amy 1990, 'Should a Marxist Believe in Marx on Rights?' *Socialist Register* 1990, pp. 244–264.

Baudrillard, Jean 1994, *Simulacra and Simulation*, translated by Sheila Faria Glaser, Ann Arbor, MI: The University of Michigan Press.

Baudrillard, Jean 2001, *Selected Writings*, 2nd edition, edited by Mark Poster, Palo Alto, CA: Stanford University Press.

Baudrillard, Jean 2009, *Why Hasn't Everything Already Disappeared?*, trans. by Chris Turner, New York, NY: Seagull Books.

Bauckham, Richard 2000, 'What if Paul had Travelled East Rather than West?', in *Virtual History and the Bible*, edited by J. Cheryl Exum, Leiden: Brill, pp. 171–84.

Bauckham, Richard 2006, *Jesus and the Eyewitnesses: The Gospels as Eyewitness Testimony*, Grand Rapids, MI: Eerdmans.

Bauckham, Richard 2008, 'In Response to My Respondents: *Jesus and the Eyewitnesses* in Review', *Journal for the Study of the Historical Jesus*, 6, 2, pp. 225–53.

Bauckham, Richard 2015, *Gospel of Glory: Major Themes in Johannine Theology*, Grand Rapids, MI: Baker Academic.

Bayle, Pierre 1740, *Dictionnaire historique et critique*, 5th Edition, Amsterdam, Leyde, La Haye, Utrecht; 4 vols. in-folio (available online at https://artfl-project.uchicago.edu/content/dictionnaire-de-bayle; last accessed February 22, 2016).

Bayle, Pierre 1965, *Historical and Critical Dictionary: Selections*, translated and edited by Richard H. Popkin with the assistance of Craig Brush, Indianapolis, IN: The Bobbs-Merrill Company Inc.

Bayle, Pierre 1983, *Écrits sur Spinoza*, edited by Françoise Charles-Daubert and Pierre François Moreau, Paris: Berg International Editeurs.

Baynes, Kenneth 1992, *The Normative Grounds of Social Criticism: Kant, Rawls, and Habermas*, Albany, NY: State University of New York Press.

Baynes, Kenneth 1995, 'Democracy and the *Rechtsstaat*: Habermas's *Faktizität und Geltung*', in *The Cambridge Companion to Habermas*, pp. 201–32, edited by Stephen K. White, New York, NY: Cambridge University Press.

Beauvoir, Simone de 1976 (1948), *The Ethics of Ambiguity*, translated by Bernard Frechtman, New York, NY: Citadel Press.
Beauvoir, Simone de 2010, *The Second Sex*, translated by Constance Borde and Sheila Malovany-Chevallier, New York, NY: Alfred A. Knopf.
Benn, S.I. 1972, 'Hobbes on Power', in *Hobbes and Rousseau: A Collection of Critical Essays*, edited by Maurice Cranston and Richard S. Peters Garden City, NY: Anchor Books.
Bennett, Jonathan 1984, *A Study of Spinoza's Ethics*, Indianapolis, IN: Hackett Publishing Company.
Bennett, Jr., Lerone 2007, *Forced into Glory: Abraham Lincoln's White Dream*, Chicago, IL: Johnson Publishing Company.
Bennett, Lisa 2008, 'The Hot Spot', *The Greater Good*, Fall, pp. 40–3.
Bensaid, Daniel 2007, 'Leaps! Leaps! Leaps!', in Budgen, Kouvelakis, and Zizek 2007, pp. 148–63.
Berg, Scott 2012, *38 Nooses: Lincoln, Little Crow, and the Beginning of the Frontier's End*, New York, NY: Vintage Books.
Bergant, Dianne 1997, *Israel's Wisdom Literature: A Liberation-Critical Reading*, Minneapolis, MN: Fortress Press.
Berlin, Ira 1997, 'Who Freed the Slaves? Emancipation and Its Meaning', in *Union and Emancipation: Essays on Politics and Race in the Civil War Era*, edited by David W. Blight and Brooks D. Simpson, pp. 105–21, Kent, Ohio: The Kent State University Press.
Berlin, Ira 2015, *The Long Emancipation: The Demise of Slavery in the United States*, Cambridge, MA: Harvard University Press.
Bernard, Calude 1872, *De la physiologie generale*, Paris: J.-B. Balliere.
Bernard, Claude 1957 [1927], *An Introduction to the Study of Experimental Medicine*, translated by Henry Copley Greene, New York, NY: Dover Publications Inc.
Berners-Lee, Mike and Duncan Clark 2013, *The Burning Question*, Vancouver/Berkeley: Greystone Books.
Berrigan, Daniel 1998, *And the Risen Bread: Selected Poems, 1957–1997*, New York, NY: Fordham University Press.
Bertrand, Michèle 1979, *Le statut de la religion chez Marx et Engels*, Paris: Éditions sociales.
Betz, Hans Dieter 1997, 'Jesus and the Purity of the Temple (Mark 11:15–18): A Comparative Religion Approach', *Journal of Biblical Literature*, 116, #3, pp. 455–72.
Bhaskar, Roy 1991a, 'Materialism', in *A Dictionary of Marxist Thought*, 2nd edition, edited by Tom Bottomore et al., Cambridge, MA: Blackwell, pp. 369–73.
Bhaskar, Roy 1991b, *Philosophy and the Idea of Freedom*, Cambridge, MA: Blackwell.
Bidet, Jacques 1990, *Théorie de la modernité*, Paris: Presses Universitaires de France.
Bidet, Jacques 1995, *John Rawls et la théorie de la justice*, Paris: Presses Universitaires de France.

Bidet, Jacques 1999, *Théorie générale*, Paris: Presses Universitaires de France.
Bidet, Jacques 2015, 'The Interpellated Subject: Beyond Althusser and Butler', translated by Ted Stolze, *Crisis & Critique*, 2, 2: pp. 62–85.
Bidet, Jacques 2016, *Marx et la loi travail: Le corps biopolitique du Capital*, Paris: Les éditions sociales.
Billecoq, Alain 1986, *Spinoza et les spectres: un essai sur l'ésprit philosophique*, Paris: Presses Universitaires de France.
Billecoq, Alain 2016, *Spinoza ou L''Athée vertueux'*, Paris: Le Temps des Cerises.
Black, David Alan 2012, *Paul, Apostle of Weakness: Astheneia and Its Cognates in the Pauline Literature*, revised edition, Eugene, OR: Pickwick Publications.
Blackburn, Robin 1978, 'Marxism: Theory of Proletarian Revolution', in *Revolution and Class Struggle: A Reader in Marxist Politics*, edited by Robin Blackburn, pp. 25–68, Atlantic Highlands, NJ: The Humanities Press.
Blackett, R.J.M. 2013, *Making Freedom: The Underground Railroad and the Politics of Slavery*, Chapel Hill, NC: The University of North Carolina Press.
Blackledge, Paul 2009, 'Political Marxism', in *Critical Companion to Contemporary Marxism*, edited by Jacques Bidet and Sathis Kouvelakis, pp. 267–84, Chicago, IL: Haymarket Books.
Blackledge, P. 2012. *Marxism and Ethics: Freedom, Desire, and Revolution*, Albany, NY: State University of New York Press.
Blanton, Ward 2007, *Displacing Christian Origins: Philosophy, Secularity, and the New Testament*, Chicago, IL: The University of Chicago Press.
Blanton, Ward 2014, *A Materialism for the Masses: Saint Paul and the Philosophy of Undying Life*, New York, NY: Columbia University Press.
Blanton, IV, Thomas R. 2017, *A Spiritual Economy: Gift-Exchange in the Letters of Paul of Tarsus*, New Haven, CT: Yale University Press.
Blechman, Max 1999, *Revolutionary Romanticism*, San Francisco: City Lights Books.
Bloch, Ernst 1971, *On Karl Marx*, translated by John Maxwell, New York: Herder and Herder.
Bloch, Ernst 1972, 'Avicenna und die Aristotelische Linke', in *Gesamtausgabe Band 7: Das Materialismusproblem, Seine Geaschichte und Substanz*, Frankfurt am Main: Suhkamp Verlag.
Bloch, Ernst 1976, 'Dialectics and Hope', translated by M. Ritter, *New German Critique* 9: 3–10.
Bloch, Ernst 1986a, *Natural Law and Human Dignity*, translated by Dennis J. Schmidt, Cambridge, MA: The MIT Press.
Bloch, Ernst 1986b, *The Principle of Hope*, three volumes, translated by Neville Plaice, Stephen Plaice, and Paul Knight, Cambridge, MA: The MIT Press.
Bloch, Ernst 2009, *Atheism in Christianity: The Religion of the Exodus and the Kingdom*, new edition, translated by J.T. Swann, New York, NY: Verso.

Bloch, Jan Robert 1988, 'How can We Understand the Bends in the Upright Gait?', *New German Critique*, 45, 9–39.

Bloch, Olivier 1995, *Le matérialisme*, deuxième edition corrigée, Paris: Presses Universitaires de France.

Bockmuehl, Markus 2012, *Simon Peter in Scripture and Memory: The New Testament Apostle in the Early Church*, Grand Rapids, MI: Baker Academic.

Boer, Roland 2013a, *Criticism of Earth: On Marx, Engels, and Theology*, Chicago, IL: Haymarket Books.

Boer, Roland 2013b, 'Toward Unethical Insurgency', *Rethinking MARXISM* 25(1): 38–51.

Boer, Roland and Christina Petterson 2014, *Idols of Nations: Biblical Myth at the Origin of Capitalism*, Minneapolis, MN: Fortress Press.

Boman, Thorleif 1970, *Hebrew Thought Compared with Greek*, translated by Jules T. Moreau, New York, NY: W.W. Norton.

Bond, Helen K. and Larry W. Hurtado 2015, *Peter in Early Christianity*, Grand Rapids, MI: William B. Eerdmanns Publishing Company.

Bordewich, Fergus G. 2005, *Bound for Canaan: The Epic Story of the Underground Railroad, America's First Civil Rights Movement*, New York, NY: Amistad.

Borg, Marcus and John Dominic Crossan 2009, *The First Paul: Reclaiming the radical Visionary Behind the Church's Conservative Icon*, New York, NY: HarperCollins Publishers.

Boundas, Constantin V. 1996, 'Deleuze-Bergson: An Ontology of the Virtual', in Paul Patton, *Deleuze: A Critical Reader* New York, NY: Blackwell, pp. 81–106.

Bove, L. 1996, *Stratégie du conatus: affirmation et résistance chez Spinoza*, Paris: Vrin.

Bove, Laurent 2011, '"Entre Matheron et Spinoza, il se passe quelque chose ..."', *Revue des livres*, 2, 53–7.

Bratman, Michael 2014, *Shared Agency: A Planning Theory of Acting Together*, New York, NY: Oxford University Press.

Brecher, Jeremy 2014, *Strike*, revised, expanded, and updated edition, Oakland, CA: PM Press.

Brecher, Jeremy 2016, *Climate Insurgency: A Strategy for Survival*, West Cornwall, CT: Stone Soup Books (available online at: http://www.jeremybrecher.org/download-climate-insurgency/; last accessed March 14, 2017).

Brecher, Jeremy 2017, *Against Doom: A Climate Insurgency Manual*, Oakland, CA: PM Press.

Breen, T.H. 2010, *American Insurgents, American Patriots: The Revolution of the People*, New York, NY: Hill and Wang.

Brenet, Jean-Baptiste 2105, *Averroès l'inquiétant*, Paris: Les Belles Lettres.

Brenner, Johanna 2000, *Women and the Politics of Class*, New York: Monthly Review Press.

Breton, Stanislas 2011, *A Radical Philosophy of Saint Paul*, translated by Joseph N. Ballan, New York, NY: Columbia University Press.

Breton, Stanislas 2016, 'Althusser and Religion', translated by Ted Stolze, *Althusser and Theology: Religion, Politics, and Philosophy*, edited by Agon Hamza, pp. 7–17, Boston, MA: Brill.

Bronner, Stephen Eric 2014, *The Bigot: Why Prejudice Persists*, New Haven, CT: Yale University Press.

Brooks, Thom and Martha Nussbaum 2015, *Rawls's Political Liberalism*, New York, NY: Columbia University Press.

Brown, Lesley 1998, 'Innovation and Continuity: The Battle of Gods and Giants, *Sophist* 245–249', in *Ancient Philosophy*, edited by Jyl Gentzler, Oxford: Clarendon Press, pp. 181–207.

Brueggemann, Walter 2002, 'Glory', in *Reverberations of Faith: A Theological Handbook of Old Testament Themes*, Louisville, KY: Westminster John Knox Press.

Brueggemann, Walter 2016, *Money and Possessions*, Louisville, KY: Westminster John Knox Press.

Burke, Edmund 1998, *A Philosophical Enquiry into the Sublime and Beautiful and Other Pre-Revolutionary Writings*, edited by David Womersley, New York, NY: Penguin.

Burkett, Paul 2014, *Marx and Nature: A Red and Green Perspective*, Chicago, IL: Haymarket Books.

Burns, James MacGregor and Stewart Burns, *A People's Charter: The Pursuit of Rights in America*, New York, NY: Vintage Books.

Butler, Judith 1997, *The Psychic Life of Power: Theories in Subjection*, New York, NY: Columbia University Press.

Calhoun, Craig (ed.) 1992, *Habermas and the Public Sphere*, Cambridge, MA: The MIT Press.

Callinicos, Alex, 2001, 'Toni Negri in Perspective', *International Socialism*, 92, pp. 33–61.

Calhoun, Craig (ed.) 1992, *Habermas and the Public Sphere*, Cambridge, MA: MIT Press.

Callinicos, Alex 2000, 'The Ideology of Humanitarian Intervention', in *Masters of the Universe: NATO's Balkan Crusade*, edited by Tariq Ali, New York, NY: Verso.

Callinicos, Alex 2004, *Making History: Agency, Structure, and Change in Social Theory*, Boston: Brill.

Canguilhem, Georges 1991, *The Normal and the Pathological*, translated by Carolyn R. Fawcett in collaboration with Robert S. Cohen, New York, NY: Zone Books.

Canguilhem, Georges 1994, *A Vital Rationalist: Selected Writings from Georges Canguilhem*, edited by François Delaporte, translated by Arthur Goldhammer, New York, NY: Zone Books.

Canguilhem, Georges 2002, *Études d'histoire et de philosophie des sciences concernant les vivants et la vie*, seventh expanded edition, Paris: Librairie Philosophique J. Vrin.

Cannon, James B. 1967 [1966; 1963; 1939; 1932], *The Wisdom of the Body*, New York, NY: W.W. Norton & Company.

Carnap, Rudolf 2003 [1967], *The Logical Structure of the World and Pseudo-Problems in Philosophy*, translated by Rolf A. George, Chicago and La Salle, IL: Open Court.

Carter, Warren 2006, *The Roman Empire and the New Testament: An Essential Guide*, Nashville, TN: Abingdon Press.

Carter, Warren 2010, 'Paul and the Roman Empire: Recent Perspectives', in Given 2010, pp. 7–26.

Carver, Terrell (ed.) 1991, *The Cambridge Companion to Marx*, New York, NY: Cambridge University Press.

Casey, Maurice 2010, *Jesus of Nazareth: An Independent Historian's Account of His Life and Teaching*, New York, NY: T&T Clark.

Casey, Maurice 2014, *Jesus: Evidence and Argument or Mythicist Myths?*, New York, NY: Bloomsbury.

Chandler, David 2002, *From Kosovo to Kabul: Human Rights and International Intervention*, Sterling, VA: Pluto Books.

Chanteur, Janine 1969, 'Note sur les notions de "people" et de "multitude" chez Hobbes', in *Hobbes-Forschungen*, edited by R. Koselleck and R. Schnur, Berlin: Dunker and Humblot.

Cicero 2000, *Defense Speeches*, translated by D.H. Berry, New York, NY: Oxford University Press.

Cohen, G.A. 2008, *Rescuing Justice and Equality*, Cambridge, MA: Harvard University Press.

Coker, K. Jason 2007, 'Nativism in James 2:14–26: A Post-Colonial Reading', in *Reading James with New Eyes: Methodological Reassessments of the Letter of James*, edited by Robert L. Webb and John S. Kloppenborg, New York, NY: T&T Clark International, pp. 27–48.

Coker, K. Jason 2015, *James in Postcolonial Perspective: The Letter as Nativist Discourse*, Minneapolis, MN: Fortress Press.

Collier, Andrew 1994, *Critical Realism: An Introduction to Roy Bhaskar's Philosophy*, New York, NY: Verso.

Collier, Andrew 2008 [2004], *Marx: A Beginner's Guide*, Oxford: Oneworld Publications.

Collin, Denis 2003, *Questions de morale*, Paris: Armand Colin.

Collin, Denis 2011, *La longueur de la chaîne: Essai sur la liberté*, Paris: Max Milo.

Collin, Denis 2013, *À dire vrai: incursions philosophiques*, Paris: Armand Colin.

Collins, Henry and Chimen Abramsky 1965, *Karl Marx and the British Labour Movement: Years of the First International*, New York, NY: St. Martin's Press.

Collins, John J. 1998, *The Apocalyptic Imagination: An Introduction to Jewish Apocalyptic Literature*, 2nd edition, Grand Rapids, MI: William B. Eerdmans Publishing Company.

Comte-Sponville, André 2015, 'Bien faire et se tenir en joie (La philosophie morale de Spinoza)', *Du tragique au matérialisme: Vingt-six etudes sur Montaigne, Pascal,*

Spinoza, Nietzsche et quelques autres, pp. 179–201, Paris: Pressues Universitaires de France.

Coogan, Michael et al, eds. 2010, *The New Oxford Annotated Bible*, 4th edition, New York, NY: Oxford University Press.

Coombes, Sam 2008, *The Early Sartre and Marxism*, New York, NY: Peter Lang.

Coulthard, Glen Sean 2014, *Red Skin, White Masks: Rejecting the Colonial Politics of Recognition*, Minneapolis, MN: University of Minnesota Press.

Cox, Harvey 1970, 'Foreward', in Ernst Bloch, *Man on His Own: Essays in the Philosophy of Religion*, translated by E.B. Ashton, New York: Herder and Herder.

Craven, Greg 2009, *What's the Worst that Could Happen? A Rational Response to the Climate Change Debate*, New York, NY: Penguin Books.

Creach, Jerome F.D. 2013, *Violence in Scripture*, Louisville, KY: Westminister John Knox Press.

Crenshaw, James L. 2010, *Old Testament Wisdom: An Introduction*, third edition, Louisville, KY: Westminster John Knox Press.

Critchley, Simon, 2007, *Infinitely Demanding: Ethics of Commitment, Politics of Resistance*, New York, NY: Verso.

Crofts, Daniel W. 2016, *Lincoln and the Politics of Slavery: The Other Thirteenth Amendment and the Struggle to Save the Union*, Chapel Hill, NC: The University of North Carolina Press.

Crossan, John Dominic 2012, *The Power of Parables: How Fiction by Jesus Became Fiction about Jesus*, New York, NY: HarperOne.

Crossan, John Dominic and Jonathan Reed 2004, *In Search of Paul: How Jesus's Apostle Opposed Rome's Empire with God's Kingdom*, New York, NY: HarperSanFrancisco.

Cullen, Heidi 2010, *The Weather of the Future: Heat Waves, Extreme Storms, and Other Scenes from a Climate-Changed Planet*, New York: Harper.

Cullmann, Oscar 2011, *Peter: Disciple, Apostle, Martyr*, Waco, TX: Baylor University Press.

Damasio, Antonio 2018, *The Strange Order of Things: Life, Feeling, and the Making of Cultures*, New York, NY: Pantheon Books.

Danker, Frederick William with Kathryn Krug 2009, *The Concise Greek-English Lexicon of the New Testament*, Chicago, IL: The University of Chicago Press.

Davidson, Herbert A. 1992, *Alfarabi, Avicenna, and Averroes on Intellect: Their Cosmologies, Theories of the Active Intellect, and Theories of Human Intellect*, New York, NY: Oxford University Press.

Davies, Brian 2014, *Thomas Aquinas's* Summa Theologiae: *A Guide and Commentary*, New York, NY: Oxford University Press.

Dawson, Ashley 2016, *Extinction: A Radical History*, New York, NY: OR Books.

Dean, Jodi 2016, *Crowds and Party*, New York, NY: Verso.

De Boer, Sander W. 2013, *The Science of the Soul: The Commentary Tradition on Aristotle's* De anima, *c. 1260–c. 1360*, Leuven: Leuven University Press.

Deborin, A.M. 1952 [1927], 'Spinoza's World-View', in *Spinoza and Soviet Philosophy*, edited by George Kline, pp. 90–119, London: Routledge and Kegan Paul.

Deleuze, Gilles 1961, 'Lucrèce et le naturalisme', *Etudes philosophique*, 16, 1, pp. 19–29.

Deleuze 1962, *Nietzsche et la philosophie*, Paris: Presses Universitaires de France.

Deleuze, Gilles 1967, unpublished manuscript dated 6 December, 1967, ALT2.A8–03.02, 'À quoi reconnait-on le structuralisme?', Paris: IMEC Archive.

Deleuze 1968, unpublished typed letter to Louis Althusser, dated February, 1968, Paris: IMEC Archive.

Deleuze, Gilles 1969, *Logique du sens*, Paris: Les Editions de Minuit.

Deleuze, Gilles 1983, *Nietzsche and Philosophy*, translated by Hugh Tomlinson, New York, NY: Columbia University Press.

Deleuze, Gilles 1988a, *Foucault*, translated and edited by Seán Hand, Minneapolis, MN: University of Minnesota Press.

Deleuze, Gilles 1988b, *Spinoza: Practical Philosophy*, translated by Robert Hurley, San Francisco, CA: City Lights Books.

Deleuze, Gilles 1998c, 'Signes et événements', *Magazine littéraire*, 257, pp. 16–25.

Deleuze, Gilles 1990a, *Expressionism in Philosophy: Spinoza*, translated by Martin Joughin. New York, NY: Zone Books.

Deleuze, Gilles 1990b, *The Logic of Sense*, edited by Constantin V. Boundas, translated by Mark Lester with Charles Stivale, New York, NY: Columbia University Press.

Deleuze, Gilles 1993, *The Fold: Leibniz and the Baroque*, translated by Tom Conley, Minneapolis, MN: University of Minnesota Press.

Deleuze, Gilles 1994, *Difference and Repetition*, translated by Paul Patton, New York, NY: Columbia University Press.

Deleuze, Gilles 1998, 'Spinoza and the Three "Ethics"', translated by Daniel W. Smith and Ariel Greco, in *The New Spinoza*, edited by Warren Montag and Ted Stolze, pp. 21–34, Minneapolis, MN: University of Minnesota Press.

Deleuze, Gilles 2004a, *Desert Islands and Other Texts, 1953–1974*, edited by David Lapoujade, translated by Michael Taormina, New York, NY: Semiotext(e).

Deleuze, Gilles 2004b, 'How Do We Recognize Structuralism?' in Deleuze 2004, pp. 170–92.

Deleuze, Gilles 2006, *Two Regimes of Madness: Texts and Interviews, 1975–1995*, edited by David Lapoujade, translated by Ames Hodges and Mike Taormina, New York, NY: Semiotext(e).

Deleuze, Gilles and Michel Foucault 2004, 'Intellectuals and Power', in Deleuze 2004, pp. 206–13.

Deleuze, Gilles and Félix Guattari 1986, *Kafka: Toward a Minor Literature*, translated by Dana Polan, Minneapolis, MN: University of Minnesota Press.

Deleuze, Gilles and Félix Guattari 1987, *A Thousand Plateaus*, translated by Brian Massumi, Minneapolis: The University of Minnesota Press.

Deleuze, Gilles and Félix Guattari 1994, *What is Philosophy?*, translated by Hugh Tomlinson and Graham Burchell, New York, NY: Columbia University Press.

Deleuze, Gilles and Felix Guattari 2009, *Anti-Oedipus*, translated by Robert Hurley, Mark Seem, and Helen R. Lane, New York, NY: Penguin Books.

Del Lucchese, Filippo 2009, *Conflict, Power, and Multitude in Machiavelli and Spinoza*, New York: Continuum.

Dennett, Daniel 1996 [1995], *Darwin's Dangerous Idea: Evolution and the Meaning of Life*, New York, NY: Touchstone.

Depew, David J. 1981–1982, 'Aristotle's *De Anima* and Marx's Theory of Man', *Graduate Faculty Philosophy Journal* 8.1–2, pp. 133–87.

Derber, Charles 2010, *Greed to Green: Solving Climate Change and Remaking the Economy*, Boulder, CO: Paradigm Publishers.

Desanti, Jean-Toussaint 1975, 'Matérialisme et épistémologie', in *La philosophie silencieuse, ou critique des philosophies de la science*, pp. 133–53, Paris: Éditions du Seuil.

Desanti, Jean-Toussaint 1994, *Introduction à la phénoménolgie*, nouvelle édition revue, Paris: Gallimard.

Desanti, Jean-Toussaint 2006 [1956], *Introduction à l'histoire de la philosophie*, Paris: Presses Universitaires de France.

Desanti, Jean-Toussaint 2008, *Une pensée captive: Articles de* La Nouvelle Critique *(1948–1956)*, Paris: Presses Universitaires de France.

Des Pres, Terrence 1976, *The Survivor: An Anatomy of Life in the Death Camps*, New York, NY: Oxford University Press.

Deutscher, Penelope 2008, *The Philosophy of Simone de Beauvoir: Ambiguity, Conversion, Resistance*, New York, NY: Cambridge University Press.

De Waal, Frans 2016, *Are We Smart Enough to Know How Smart Animals Are?*, New York, NY: W.W. Norton & Company.

Dewey, Arthur J. et al, eds. 2010, *The Authentic Letters of Paul: A New Reading of Paul's Rhetoric and Meaning*, Salem, OR: Polebridge Press.

Dews, Peter 1985, '"The New Philosophers" and the End of Leftism', *Radical Philosophy Reader*, pp. 361–84, New York, NY: Verso.

Diogenes Laertius 1925, *Lives of Eminent Philosophers*, volume 2, translated by R.D. Hicks, Cambridge, MA: Harvard University Press.

Djedi, Youcef 2010, 'Spinoza et Islam: un état des lieux', *Philosophiques*, 37, 2, pp. 275–98.

Donnelly, Jack 2013, *Universal Human Rights in Theory and Practice*, 3rd edition, Ithaca, NY: Cornell University Press.

Douglass, Frederick 1999, 'West India Emancipation', in *Selected Speeches and Writings*, edited by Philip S. Foner, abridged and adapted by Yuval Taylor, Chicago, IL: Lawrence Hill Books.

Douzinas Costas and Slavoj Žižek (eds.) 2010, *The Idea of Communism*, New York, NY: Verso.

Downs, David J. 2016, *Alms: Charity, Reward, and Atonement in Early Christianity*, Waco, TX: Baylor University Press.

Downs, David J. 2016 [2008], *The Offering of the Gentiles: Paul's Collection for Jerusalem in Its Chronological, Cultural, and Cultic Contexts*, Grand Rapids, MI: William B. Eerdmans Publishing Company.

Downs, Gregory P. 2015, *After Appomattox: Military Occupation and the Ends of War*, Cambridge, MA: Harvard University Press.

Downs, Gregory P. and Kate Masur 2015, *The World the Civil War Made*, Chapel Hill, NC: The University of North Carolina Press.

Doyle, Don H. 2015, *The Cause of All Nations: An International History of the American Civil War*, New York, NY: Basic Books.

Draper, Hal 1977–90, *Karl Marx's Theory of Revolution*, four volumes, New York, NY: Monthly Review Press.

Draper, Hal 1992, *Socialism from Below*, edited by Ernest Haberkern, Atlantic Highlands, NJ: Humanities Press, 1992.

Droit, Roger-Pol 2012 [2009], *Les Héros de la sagesse*, Paris: Flammarion.

DuBois, Page 2014, *A Million and One Gods: The Persistence of Polytheism*, Cambridge, MA: Harvard University Press.

Du Bois, W.E.B. 1995 [1992; 1935], *Black Reconstruction in America, 1860–1880*, New York, NY: Simon & Schuster.

Dunaway, Finis 2015, *Seeing Green: The Use and Abuse of American Environmental Images*, Chicago, IL: The University of Chicago Press.

Dunbar-Ortiz, Roxanne 2014, *An Indigenous Peoples' History of the United States*, Boston, MA: Beacon Press.

Duncombe, Stephen 2007, *Dream: Re-imagining Progressive Politics in an Age of Fantasy*, New York, NY: The New Press.

Dunham, Jeremy, Iain Hamilton Grant, and Sean Watson 2011, *Idealism: The History of a Philosophy*, Montreal: McGill-Queen's University Press.

Dunn, James D.G. 1998, *The Theology of the Apostle Paul*, Grand Rapids, MI: William B. Eerdmans Publishing Company.

Dunn, James 2009, *Christianity in the Making, Volume 2: Beginning from Jerusalem*, Grand Rapids, MI: Eerdmans.

Dussel, Enrique 2013, *Ethics of Liberation: In the Age of Globalization and Exclusion*, translated by Eduardo Mendieta et al. Durham, NC: Duke University Press.

Eagleton, Terry 2011, *Why Marx Was Right*, New Haven, CT: Yale University Press.

Edmundson, William A. 2017, *John Rawls: Reticent Socialist*, New York, NY: Cambridge University Press.

Ehrenfeld, John R. 2008, *Sustainability by Design: A Subversive Strategy for Transforming our Consumer Culture*, New Haven, CT: Yale University Press.

Ehrenfeld, John R. and Andrew Hoffman 2013, *Flourishing: A Frank Conversation about Sustainability*, Stanford, CA: Stanford University Press.

Ehrensperger, Kathy 2009 [2007], *Paul and the Dynamics of Power: Communication and Interaction in the Early Christ-Movement*, New York: T&T Clark.

Ehrman, Bart 2012, *Did Jesus Exist? The Historical Argument for Jesus of Nazareth*, New York, NY: HarperOne.

Ehrman, Bart 2016, *Jesus Before the Gospels: How the Earliest Christians Remembered, Changed, and Invented Their Stories of the Savior*, New York, NY: HarperOne.

Elliott, John H. 2005, *A Home for the Homeless: A Social-Scientific Criticism of 1 Peter, Its Situation and Strategy*, Eugene, OR: Wipf and Stock.

Elliott, Neil 2006, *Liberating Paul: The Justice of God and the Politics of the Apostle*, Minneapolis, MN: Fortress Press.

Elliott, Neil 2013, 'Creation, Cosmos, and Conflict in Romans 8–9', in *Apocalyptic Paul: Cosmos and Anthropos in Romans 5–8*, pp. 131–56, edited by Beverly Roberts Gaventa, Waco, TX: Baylor University Press.

Elliott, Neil 2015, 'The Question of Politics: Paul as a Diaspora Jew under Roman Rule', in *Paul within Judaism: Restoring the First-Century Context to the Apostle*, edited by Mark D. Nanos and Magnus Zetterholm, pp. 203–43, Minneapolis, MN: Fortress Press.

Elliott, Neil and Mark Reasoner (eds.) 2011, *Documents and Images for the Study of Paul*, Minneapolis, MN: Fortress Press.

Engels, Frederick 1990, 'Ludwig Feuerbach and the End of Classical German Philosophy', in Karl Marx and Frederick Engels, *Collected Works*, Volume 26, New York, NY: International Publishers, pp. 353–98.

Epictetus 2014, *Discourses, Fragments, Handbook*, translated by Robin Hard, New York, NY: Oxford University Press.

Esposito, Roberto 2015, *Two: The Machine of Political Theology and the Place of Thought*, translated by Zakiya Hanafi, New York, NY: Fordham University Press.

Evans, Craig A. 2014, *From Jesus to the Church: The First Christian Generation*, Louisville, KY: Westminster John Knox Press.

Evans, Craig A. 2015, *Jesus and the Remains of His Day: Studies in Jesus and the Evidence of Material Culture*, Peabody, MA: Hendrickson Publishers.

Evans, Gareth 1982, *The Varieties of Reference*, New York, NY: Oxford University Press.

Evans, Richard 2013, *Altered Pasts: Counterfactuals in History*, Waltham, MA: Brandeis University Press.

Fanon, Frantz, *Black Skin, White Masks*, translated by Richard Philcox, New York, NY: Grove Press.

Feuer, Lewis 1980, 'Spinoza's Political Philosophy: The Lessons and Problems of a Conservative Democrat', in *The Philosophy of Spinoza*, edited by Richard Kennington, Washington, D.C.: The Catholic University of America Press.

Fields, Barbara J. 1990, 'Who Freed the Slaves?' in Geoffrey C. Ward with Ric Burns and Ken Burns, *The Civil War: An Illustrated History*, New York, NY: American Documentaries, Inc.

Finger, Reta Halteman 2007, *Paul and the Roman House Churches: A Simulation*, 2nd edition, Scottdale, PA: Herald Press.

Finlayson, Lorna 2015, *The Political is Political: Conformity and the Illusion of Dissent in Contemporary Political Philosophy*, New York, NY: Rowman and Littlefield International, Ltd.

Flynn, Thomas R. 2014, *Sartre: A Philosophical Biography*, New York, NY: Cambridge University Press.

Foner, Eric 2015, *Gateway to Freedom: The Hidden History of the Underground Railroad*, New York, NY: W.W. Norton & Company Foster, John Bellamy, Brett Clark, and Richard York 2010, *The Ecological Rift: Capitalism's War on the Planet*, New York, NY: Monthly Review Press.

Foster, John Bellamy and Paul Burkett 2017, *Marx and the Earth: An Anti-Critique*, Chicago, IL: Haymarket Books.

Foster, Russell G. and Leon Kreitzman 2009, *Seasons of Life: The Biological Rhythms that Enable Living Things to Thrive and Survive*, New Haven, CT: Yale University Press.

Foucault, Michel 2009, 'Preface', in Deleuze and Guattari 2009, pp. xi–xiv.

Foucault, Michel 1985, *The Use of Pleasure*, translated by Robert Hurley, New York, NY: Pantheon Books.

Foucault, Michel 2005, *The Hermeneutics of the Subject: Lectures at the Collège de France 1981–1982*, edited by Frédéric Gros, translated by Graham Burchell, New York, NY: Picador.

Foucault, Michel 2006, *History of Madness*, edited by Jean Khalfa, translated by Jonathan Murphy and Jean Khalfa, New York, NY: Routledge.

Foucault, Michel 2010, *The Government of Self and Others: Lectures at the Collège de France, 1982–1983*, edited by Frédéric Gros, translated by Graham Burchell, New York, NY: Palgrave Macmillan.

Foucault, Michel 2011, *The Courage of Truth (The Government of Self and Others II): Lectures at the Collège de France, 1983–1984*, edited by Frédéric Gros, translated by Graham Burchell, New York, NY: Palgrave Macmillan.

Fraenkel, Carlos 2011, 'Spinoza on Philosophy and Religion: The Averroistic Sources', in *The Rationalists: Between Tradition and Innovation*, edited by Carlos Fraenkel et al., New York, NY: Springer Science+Business Media B.V.

Fraenkel, Carlos 2012, *Philosophical Religions from Plato to Spinoza: Reason, Religion, and Autonomy*, New York, NY: Cambridge University Press.

Fraenkel, Carlos 2013, 'Reconsidering the Case of Elijah Delmedigo's Averroism and Its Impact on Spinoza', in *Renaissance Averroism and its aftermath: Arabic Philosophy in Early Modern Europe*, Dordrecht: Springer Science+Business Media.

Fraser, Nancy 1992, 'Rethinking the Public Sphere: A Contribution to the Critique of Actually Existing Democracy', in Calhoun 1992.
Freyne, Sean 2014, *The Jesus Movement and Its Expansion: Meaning and Mission*, Grand Rapids, MI: William B. Eerdmans Publishing Company.
Freyne, Sean 2015, 'The Fisherman from Bethsaida', in Bond and Hurtado 2015, pp. 19–29.
Friedmann, Georges 1970, *La puissance et la sagesse*, Paris: Gallimard.
Friedmann, Georges 1974, *Leibniz et Spinoza*, 3rd edition, Paris: Gallimard.
Friesen, Steven J. 2004, 'Poverty in Pauline Studies: Beyond the So-called New Consensus', *Journal for the Study of the New Testament*, 26.3, pp. 323–61.
Friesen, Steven J. 2010, 'Paul and Economics: The Jerusalem Collection as an Alternative to Patronage', in *Paul Unbound: Other Perspectives on the Apostle*, edited by Mark D. Given, pp. 27–54, Peabody, MA: Hendrickson Publishers.
Gabel, John B. et al. 2000, *The Bible as Literature: An Introduction*, 4th edition, New York, NY: Oxford University Press.
Gabrielson, Jeremy 2013, *Paul's Non-Violent Gospel*, Eugene, OR: Pickwick Publications.
Gagnon, J.-H. 2002. 'Spinoza et le problem de l'*akrasia*: Un aspect negligee de l'*ordo geometricus*', *Philosophiques* 29, 1: 57–71.
George, Charles H., *Five Hundred Years of Revolution: European Radicals from Hus to Lenin*, Chicago, IL: Charles H. Kerr Publishing Company.
Georgi, Dieter 1986, *The Opponents of Paul in Second Corinthians*, Philadelphia, PA: Fortress Press.
Georgi, Dieter 1992, *Remembering the Poor: The History of Paul's Collection for Jerusalem*, Nashville, TN: Abingdon.
Georgi, Dieter 2005, *The City in the Valley: Biblical Interpretation and Urban Theology*, Atlanta, GA: Society of Biblical Literature.
Georgi, Dieter 2009 [1991], *Theocracy in Paul's Practice and Theology*, Minneapolis, MN: Fortress Press.
Geras, Norman 2017 [1986], *Literature of Revolution: Essays on Marxism*, pp. 133–41, New York, NY: Verso.
Geras, Norman 1990, *Discourses of Extremity: Radical Ethics and Post-Marxist Extravagances*, New York, NY: Verso.
Geras, Norman 1995, *Solidarity in the Conversation of Humankind: The Ungroundable Liberalism of Richard Rorty*, New York, NY: Verso.
Geuss, Raymond 2008, *Philosophy and Real Politics*, Princeton, NJ: Princeton University Press.
Gilbert, Alan 1990, *Democratic Individuality*, New York, NY: Cambridge University Press.
Gilbert, Alan 1991, 'Political Philosophy: Marx and Radical Democracy', in Carver 1991, pp. 168–95.
Gilbert, Daniel 2006, 'If Only Gay Sex Caused Global Warming', *L.A. Times*, 2 July, (http://articles.latimes.com/2006/jul/02/opinion/op-gilbert2; last accessed 26 April, 2016).

Ginger, Ray 2007 [1947], *The Bending Cross: A Biography of Eugene V. Debs*, Chicago, IL: Haymarket Books.

Glancy, Jennifer A. 2002, *Slavery in Early Christianity*, New York, NY: Oxford University Press.

Gleiser, Marcelo 2014, *The Island of Knowledge: The Limits of Science and the Search for Meaning*, New York, NY: Basic Books.

Gleijeses, Piero 2013, *Visions of Freedom: Havana, Washington, Pretoria, and Struggle for Southern Africa, 1976–1991*, Chapel Hill, NC: The University of North Carolina Press.

Gnuse, Robert 2011, *You Shall Not Steal: Community and Property in the Biblical Tradition*, Eugene, OR: Wipf and Stock Publishers.

Good, Edwin 1990, *In Turns of Tempest: A Reading of Job, with a translation*, Stanford, CA: Stanford University Press.

Goodman, Martin 2007, *Rome and Jerusalem: The Clash of Ancient Civilizations*, New York, NY: Alfred A. Knopf.

Gorman, Michael 2015, *Becoming the Gospel: Paul, Participation, and Mission*, Grand Rapids, MI: William B. Eerdmans Publishing Company.

Gorman, Sara E. and Jack M. 2017, *Denying to the Grave: Why WE Ignore the Facts that Will Save Us*, New York, NY: Oxford University Press.

Gottschalk, Peter and Gabriel Greenberg 2008, *Islamophobia: Making Muslims the Enemy*, Lanham, MD.

Gourevitch, Alex 2015, *From Slavery to the Cooperative Commonwealth: Labor and Republican Liberty in the Nineteenth Century*, New York, NY: Cambridge University Press.

Graeber, David 2014, *Debt: The First 5,000 Years*, updated and expanded edition, Brooklyn, NY: Melville House Publishing.

Gray, Patrick 2016, *Paul as a Problem in History and Culture*, Grand Rapids, MI: BakerAcademic.

Graziosi, Barbara 2014, *The Gods of Olympus: A History*, New York, NY: Metropolitan Books.

Green, Todd H. 2015, *Fear of Islam: An Introduction to Islamophobia in the West*, Minneapolis, MN: Fortress Press.

Greenfield, Susan 2015, *Mind Change: How Digital Technologies are Leaving Their Mark on Our Brains*, New York, NY: Random House.

Groff, Ruth 2012, 'Aristotelian Marxism/Marxist Aristotelianism: MacIntyre, Marx and the Analysis of Abstraction', *Philosophy and Social Criticism*, 38, 8: 775–92.

Groff, Ruth 2015, 'On the Ethical Contours of Thin Aristotelian Marxism', in Thompson 2015, pp. 313–35.

Gross, Charles G. 1998, 'Claude Bernard and the Constancy of the Internal Environment', *The Neuroscientist*, 4: 380–85.

Guattari, Félix 1995, *Chaosmosis*, translated by Paul Bains and Julian Pefanis, Bloomington, IN: Indiana University Press.

Guattari, Félix 2000, *The Three Ecologies*, translated by Ian Pindar and Paul Sutton, New Brunswick, NJ: The Athlone Press.

Guattari, Félix 1986, 'Petites et grandes machines à inventer la vie', in *Les Années d'hivers*, pp. 152–66, Paris: Bernard Barrault.

Guattari, Félix 2011a, *Lignes de Fuite: Pour un autre monde de possibles*, Paris: Éditions de l'Aube.

Guattari, Félix 2011b, *The Machinic Unconscious*, translated by Taylor Adkins, New York, NY: Semiotext(e), *Fateful Lightning: A New History of the Civil War and Reconstruction*, New York, NY: Oxford University Press.

Guattari, Félix 2013, *Schizoanalytic Cartographies*, translated by Andrew Goffey, New York, NY: Bloomsbury.

Guattari, Félix 2015, *Psychoanalysis and Transversality: Texts and Interviews 1955–1971*, translated by Ames Hodges, New York, NY: Semiotext(e).

Guelzo, Allen C. 2012, *Fateful Lightning: A New History of the Civil War and Reconstruction*, New York, NY: Oxford University Press.

Gutiérrez, Gustavo 1987, *On Job: God-Talk and the Suffering of the Innocent*, translated by Matthew J. O'Connell, Maryknoll, NY: Orbis Books.

Habel, Norman 1985, *The Book of Job: A Commentary*, New York, NY: Cambridge University Press.

Habermas, Jürgen 1971, *Knowledge and Human Interests*, translated by Jeremy J. Shapiro, Boston, MA: Beacon Press.

Habermas, Jürgen 1973, *Theory and Practice*, translated by John Viertel, Boston, MA: Beacon Press.

Habermas, Jürgen 1984, *The Theory of Communicative Action, Volume One: Reason and the Rationalization of Society*, translated by Thomas McCarthy, Boston, MA: Beacon Press.

Habermas, Jürgen 1987b, *The Theory of Communicative Action, Volume Two: Lifeworld and System: A Critique of Functionalist Reason*, translated by Thomas McCarthy, Boston, MA: Beacon Press.

Habermas, Jürgen 1989a, 'The New Obscurity: The Crisis of the Welfare State and the exhaustion of Utopian Energies', in *The New Conservatism: Cultural Criticism and the Historians' Debate*, edited and translated by Shierry Weber Nicholsen, Cambridge, MA: The MIT Press.

Habermas, Jürgen 1989b, 'The Public Sphere', translated by Shierry Weber Nicholsen, in *Habermas, Jürgen on Society and Politics: A Reader*, pp. 231–6, edited by Steve Seidman, Boston, MA: Beacon Press.

Habermas, Jürgen 1989c, *The Structural Transformation of the Public Sphere: An Inquiry into a Category of Bourgeois Society*, translated by Thomas Burger with the assistance of Frederick Lawrence, Cambridge, MA: The MIT Press.

Habermas, Jürgen 1990, *Moral Consciousness and Communicative Action*, translated by Christian Lenhardt and Shierry Weber Nicholsen, Cambridge, MA: The MIT Press.
Habermas, Jürgen 1992, 'Further Reflections on the Public Sphere', translated by Thomas McCarthy, in Calhoun 1992, pp. 421–61.
Habermas, Jürgen 1996, *Between Facts and Norms*, translated by William Rehg, Cambridge, MA: The MIT Press.
Habermas, Jürgen 1997, *A Berlin Republic: Writings on Germany*, translated by Steven Rendall, Lincoln, NE: University of Nebraska Press.
Habermas, Jürgen 2001, *The Postnational Constellation: Political Essays*, translated and edited by Max Pensky, Cambridge, MA: The MIT Press.
Habermas, Jürgen 2006a, *The Divided West*, edited and translated by Ciaran Cronin, Malden, MA: Polity Press.
Habermas, Jürgen 2006b, *Time of Transitions*, edited and translated by Ciaran Cronin and Max Pensky, Malden, MA: Polity Press.
Habermas 2008, *Between Naturalism and Religion: Philosophical Essays*, translated by Ciaran Cronin, Malden, MA: Polity Press.
Habermas, Jürgen 2012, *The Crisis of the European Union: A Response*, translated by Ciaran Cronin, Malden, MA: Polity Press.
Hadot, Pierre 1995. *Philosophy as a Way of Life*, edited by Arnold I. Davidson, translated by Michael Chase. Malden, MA: Blackwell Publishing.
Hadot, Pierre 2002, *What is Ancient Philosophy?*, translated by Michael Chase, Cambridge, MA: Harvard University Press.
Hahn, Steven 2009, *The Political Worlds of Slavery and Freedom*, Cambridge, MA: Harvard University Press.
Hall, Edith 2014, *Introducing the Ancient Greeks*, New York, NY: W.W. Norton and Company.
Hallett, Steve 2013, *The Efficiency Trap: Finding a Better Way to Achieve a Sustainable Energy Future*, Amherst, NY: Prometheus Books.
Hampton, Jean 1997, *Political Philosophy*, Boulder, CO: Westview Press.
Hankins, Davis 2015, *The Book of Job and the Immanent Genesis of Transcendence*, Evanston, IL: Northwestern University Press.
Hansen, James E. and Makiko Sato 2012, 'Paleoclimate Implications for Human-Caused Climate Change', *Climate Change: Inferences from Paleoclimate and Regional Aspects*, edited by André Berger et al., New York, NY: Springer-Verlag Wien.
Hansen, James E. et al. 2016, 'Ice melt, sea level rise and superstorms: evidence from paleoclimate data, climate modeling, and modern observations that 2°C global warming could be dangerous', *Atmos. Chem. Phys.* 16: 3761–3812.
Harding, Vincent 1981, *There is a River: The Black Struggle for Freedom in America*, New York, NY: Harcourt Brace Jovanovich.

Hardt, Michael and Antonio Negri 2004, *Empire*, Cambridge, MA: Harvard University Press.
Hardt, Michael and Antonio Negri 2002, *Multitude*, Cambridge, MA: Harvard University Press.
Hardt, Michael and Antonio Negri 2009, *Commonwealth*, Cambridge, MA: Harvard University Press.
Harman, Chris 1999, *A People's History of the World*, London: Bookmarks.
Harman, Chris 2010 [2009], *Zombie Capitalism: Global Crisis and the Relevance of Marx*, Chicago, IL: Haymarket Books.
Hartin, Patrick J. 2009, *Apollos: Paul's Partner or Rival?*, Collegeville, MN: Liturgical Press.
Harvey, David 2010a, *A Companion to Marx's Capital*, New York, NY: Verso.
Harvey, David 2010b, *The Enigma of Capital and the Crises of Capitalism*, New York, NY: Oxford University Press.
Haslanger, Sally 2012, *Resisting Reality: Social Construction and Social Critique*, New York, NY: Oxford University Press.
Hedges, Chris 2010, *Death of the Liberal Class*, New York, NY: Nation Books.
Hedges, Chris 2015, *Wages of Rebellion: The Moral Imperative of Revolt*, New York, NY: Nation Books.
Hegarty, Paul 2004, *Jean Baudrillard: Live Theory*, New York, NY: Continuum.
Hegel, Georg Wilhelm Friedrich 1976 [1969], *Science of Logic* 1976 [1969], translated by A.V. Miller, New York, NY: Humanities Press.
Hegel, Georg Wilhelm Friedrich 1977, *Phenomenology of Spirit*, translated by A.V. Miller, New York, NY: Oxford University Press.
Hegel, Georg Wilhelm Friedrich 1986, *Vorlesungen über die Philosophie der Geschichte* (*Werke*, vol. 12), edited by Eva Moldenhauer and Karl Markus Michel, Frankfurt am Main: Suhrkamp.
Hegel, Georg Wilhelm Friedrich Hegel 1988, *Lectures on the Philosophy of Religion, One Volume Edition: The Lectures of 1827*, translated by R.F. Brown et al., edited by Peter C. Hodgson, Berkeley, CA: University of California Press.
Hegel, Georg Wilhelm Friedrich 2011, *Lectures on the Philosophy of World History, Volume I: Manuscripts of the Introduction and the Lectures of 1822–3*, edited and translated by Robert F. Brown and Peter C. Hodgson, with the assistance of William G. Geuss, New York, NY: Oxford University Press.
Hegel, G.W. Friedrich 2007, *Philosophy of Mind*, translated by William Wallace and A.V. Miller, revised by Michael Inwood, New York, NY: Oxford University Press.
Hegel, Georg Wilhelm Friedrich 2009, *Lectures on the History of Philosophy 1825–6, Volume III: Medieval and Modern Philosophy*, revised edition, translated and edited by Robert F. Brown, New York, NY: Oxford University Press.
Hegel, Georg Wilhelm Friedrich 2010, *The Science of Logic*, translated by George Di Giovanni, New York, NY: Cambridge University Press.

Heidegger, Martin 2003 [1997], *Plato's Sophist*, translated by Richard Rojcewicz and André Schuwer, Bloomington, IN: Indiana University Press.

Herbert, Gary B. 1989, *Thomas Hobbes: The Unity of Scientific and Moral Wisdom*, Vancouver: University of British Columbia Press.

Herman, Arthur 2014 [2013], *The Cave and the Light: Plato Versus Aristotle, and the Struggle for the Soul of Western Civilization*, New York, NY: Random House.

Herzog II, William R. 1994, *Parables as Subversive Speech: Jesus as Pedagogue of the Oppressed*, Louisville, KY: Westminster/John Knox Press.

Heyd, Michael 1995, *'Be Sober and Reasonable': The Critique of Enthusiasm in the Seventeenth and Early Eighteenth Centuries*, New York, NY: E.J. Brill.

Hill, Christopher 1972, *The World Turned Upside Down: Radical Ideas During the English Revolution*, New York, NY: Penguin.

Hindess, Barry 1996, *Discourses of Power: From Hobbes to Foucault*, Malden, MA: Blackwell Publishers.

Hirschman, Albert 1997, *The Passions and the Interests: Political Arguments for Capitalism before Its Triumph*, twentieth anniversary edition, Princeton, NJ: Princeton University Press.

Hobbes, Thomas 1994, *Leviathan*, edited by Edwin Curley, Indianapolis, IN: Hackett Publishing Company.

Hobbes, Thomas 1998, *On the Citizen*, edited and translated by Richard Tuck and Michael Silverthorne, New York, NY: Cambridge University Press.

Hobsbawm, Eric 2001 [1973], *Revolutionaries*, New York, NY: The New Press.

Hochschild, Adam 2016, *Spain in Our Hearts: Americans in the Spanish Civil War*, New York, NY: Houghton Mifflin Harcourt Publishing Company.

Hock, Ronald 1987 [1980], *The Social Context of Paul's Ministry: Tentmaking and Apostleship*, Minneapolis, MN: Fortress Press.

Hodes, Martha 2015, *Mourning Lincoln*, New Haven, CT: Yale University Press.

Holland, Tom 2005 [2003], *Rubicon: The Last Years of the Roman Republic*, New York, NY: Anchor Books.

Holloway, John 2016, *In, Against, and Beyond Capitalism: The San Francisco Lectures*, Oakland, CA: PM Press.

Holton, R. 2009, *Willing, Wanting, Waiting*. New York, NY: Oxford University Press.

Honeck, Mischa 2011, *We Are the Revolutionists: German-Speaking Immigrants and American Abolitionists after 1848*, Athens, GA: The University of Georgia Press.

Hood, Bruce 2012, *The Self Illusion: How the Social Brain Creates Identity*, New York, NY: Oxford University Press.

Horkheimer, Max 1986 [1972], 'Materialism and Metaphysics', translated by Mathew J. O'Connell, *Critical Theory: Selected Essays*, New York, NY: Continuum, pp. 10–46.

Horkheimer, Max and Theodor W. Adorno 2002, *Dialectic of Enlightenment: Philosophical Fragments*, edited by Gunzelin Schmid Noerr, translated by Edmond Jephcott, Stanford, CA: Stanford University Press.

Hörnqvist, Mikael 2004, *Machiavelli and Empire*, New York, NY: Cambridge University Press.

Horrell, David G. 1995, 'Paul's Collection: Resources for a Materialist Theology', *Epworth Review* 22, 2: pp. 74–83.

Horsley, Richard 1995, *Galilee: History, Politics, People*, Valley Forge, PA: Trinity Press International.

Horsley, Richard A. (ed.) 1997, *Paul and Empire: Religion and Power in Roman Imperial Society*, Harrisburg, PA: Trinity Press International.

Horsley, Richard 2000, *Paul and Politics: Ekklesia, Israel, Interpretation*, Harrisburg, PA: Trinity Press International.

Horsley, Richard 2004, *Paul and the Roman Imperial Order*, Harrisburg, PA: Trinity Press International.

Horsley, Richard A. 2009, *Covenant Economics: A Biblical Vision of Justice for All*, Louisville, KY: Westminster John Knox Press.

Horsley, Richard 2013, *Jesus and the Politics of Roman Palestine*, Columbia, SC: The University of South Carolina Press.

Horsley, Richard A. and Neil Asher Silberman 1997, *The Message and the Kingdom: How Jesus and Paul Ignited a Revolution and Transformed the Ancient World*, New York, NY: Grosset/Putnam.

Horwitz, Tony 2011, *Midnight Rising: John Brown and the Raid that Sparked the Civil War*, New York, NY: Picador.

Howard-Brook 2003, *Becoming Children of God: John's Gospel and Radical Discipleship*, Eugene, OR: Wipf and Stock.

Howard-Brook, Wes 2016, *Empire Baptized: How the Church Embraced What Jesus Rejected (Second – Fifth Centuries)*, Maryknoll, NY: Orbis Books.

Hurtado, Larry 2015, 'The Apostle Peter in Protestant Scholarship', in Bond and Hurtado 2015, pp. 1–15.

Ibrahim, Annie 2013, *Autour d'Althusser: Penser un materialism aléatoire: problèmes et perspectives*, Paris: Le Temps des Cerises.

Ignatieff, Michael 2001, *Human Rights as Politics and Idolatry*, edited by Amy Gutmann, Princeton, NJ: Princeton University Press.

Illuminati, Augusto 1996, *Averroè e l'intelletto pubblico: antologia di scritti di Ibn Rushd sull'anima*, Rome: manifesto libri.

Illuminati, Augusto 2009, *Spinoza atlantico*, Milano: Edizioni Ghibli.

Ilyenkov, Evald Vasilyevich 2009, *The Ideal in Human Activity*, Pacifica, CA: Marxists Internet Archive.

Israel, Jonathan 1995. *The Dutch Republic: Its Rise, Greatness, and Fall, 1477–1806*. New York, NY: Oxford University Press.

Israel, Nicolas 2001, *Spinoza: le temps de la vigilance*, Paris: Éditions Payot & Rivages.

Jacques, Peter 2015, *Sustainability: The Basics*, New York, NY: Routledge.

James, Susan, *Passion and Action: The Emotions in Seventeenth-Century Philosophy*, New York, NY: Oxford University Press, 1997.
Jaquet, Chantal 1997, *Spinoza ou la prudence*, Paris: Éditions Quintette.
Jaquet, Chantal 2005. 'La fortitude cachée', *Les expressions de la puissance d'agir chez Spinoza*, pp. 293–304, Paris: Publications de la Sorbonne.
Jaquet, Chantal 2014, *Les transclasses ou la non-reproduction*, Paris: Presses Universitaires de France.
Jenkins, Philip 2012, *Laying Down the Sword: Why We Can't Ignore the Bible's Violent Verses*, New York, NY: HarperCollins Publishers.
Jewett, Robert 2004, 'The Corruption and Redemption of Creation: Reading Rom 8:18–23 within the Imperial Context', in *Paul and the Roman Imperial Order*, edited by Richard A. Horsley, pp. 25–46, Harrisburg, PA: Trinity Press International.
Johnston, David 1986, *The Rhetoric of Leviathan: Thomas Hobbes and the Politics of Cultural Transformation*, Princeton, NJ: Princeton University Press.
Johnson, Marshall D. 2002, *Making Sense of the Bible: Literary Type as an Approach to Understanding*, Grand Rapids, MI: William B. Eerdmans Publishing Company.
Jolley, Nicholas 2005, *Leibniz*, New York, NY: Routledge.
Jones, Howard 1992 [1989], *The Epicurean Tradition*, New York, NY: Routledge.
Josephy, Alvin 1991, *The Civil War in the American West*, New York, NY: Alfred A. Knopf, Inc.
Judaken, Jonathan 2006, *Jean-Paul Sartre and the Jewish Question: Anti-antisemitism and the Politics of the French Intellectual*, Lincoln, NE: University of Nebraska Press.
Kahl, Brigitte 2014, 'Justification and Justice: Reading Paul with the Economically Vanquished', *Journal of Religion & Society Supplement Series*, Supplement 10, edited by Ronald A. Simkins and Thomas M. Kelly, pp. 132–46.
Kalupahana, David J. 1992, *A History of Buddhist Philosophy: Continuities and Discontinuities*, Honolulu, HI: University of Hawaii Press.
Kalupahana, David J. 2001 [1991], 'Pratityasamutpada and the Renunciation of Mystery', *Buddhist Thought and Ritual*, edited by David J. Kalupahana, Delhi: Motilal Banarsidass, pp. 19–33.
Kant, Immanuel 1996, *Religion and Rational Theology*, translated and edited by Allen W. Wood and George di Giovanni, New York, NY: Cambridge University Press.
Kant, Immanuel 2000, *Critique of the Power of Judgment*, edited by Paul Guyer, translated by Paul Guyer and Eric Matthews, New York, NY: Cambridge University Press.
Karatani, Kōjin 2017, *Isonomia and the Origins of Philosophy*, translated by Joseph A. Murphy, Durham, NC: Duke University Press.
Keazirian, Edward M. 2014, *Peace and Peacemaking in Paul and the Greco-Roman World*, New York, NY: Peter Lang.
Kenny, Anthony 2005, *A New History of Western Philosophy, Volume 2: Medieval Philosophy*, New York, NY: Oxford University Press.

Kerr-Ritchie, Jeffrey R. 2013, *Freedom's Seekers: Essays on Comparative Emancipation*, Baton Rouge, LA: Louisiana State University Press.

Kim, Yung Suk 2008, *Christ's Body in Corinth: The Politics of a Metaphor*, Minneapolis, MN: Fortress Press.

King, Martin Luther, Jr. 2011, *'All Labor Has Dignity'*, edited by Michael K. Honey, Boston, MA: Beacon Press.

King, Martin Luther, Jr. 2015, *The Radical King*, edited by Cornel West, Boston, MA: Beacon Press.

Kinsler, Ross and Gloria 1999, *The Biblical Jubilee and the Struggle for Life*, Maryknoll, NY: Oribis Books.

Klauck, Hans-Josef 2003 [2000], *The Religious Context of Early Christianity: A Guide to Graeco-Roman Religions*, translated by Brian McNeil, Minneapolis, MN: Fortress Press.

Klein, Naomi 2014, *This Changes Everything: Capitalism vs. The Climate*, New York, NY: Simon & Schuster.

Kline, George L. 1952, *Spinoza in Soviet Philosophy*, London: Routledge and Kegan Paul.

Knapp, Robert 2011, *Invisible Romans*, Cambridge, MA: Harvard University Press.

Knox, John 1964, 'Romans 15:14–33 and Paul's Conception of his Apostolic Mission', *Journal of Biblical Literature*, 83, pp. 1–11.

Kouvelakis, Stathis 2007, 'Lenin as Reader of Hegel: Hypotheses for a Reading of Lenin's Notebooks on Hegel's *The Science of Logic*', in Budgen, Kouvelakis, and Zizek 2007, pp. 164–204.

Kumar, Deepa 2012, *Islamophobia and the Politics of Empire*, Chicago, IL: Haymarket Books.

Kundnani, Arun 2015 [2014], *The Muslims are Coming! Islamophobia, Extremism, and the Domestic War on Terror*, New York, NY: Verso.

Kripke, Saul 1980, *Naming and Necessity*, Cambridge, MA: Harvard University Press.

Kuznick, Peter J. 1988, 'The Birth of Scientific Activism', *Bulletin of the Atomic Scientists*, December 1988, pp. 39–43.

Lacan, Jacques 1979, 'The Neurotic's Individual Myth', translated by Martha Noel Evans, *The Psychoanalytic Quarterly*, 48:3, pp. 405–25.

Lacan, Jacques 2006, *Écrits*, translated by Bruce Fink, New York, NY: W.W. Norton.

Lapine 1960, 'La première critique approfondie de la philosophie de Hegel par Marx', *Recherches Internationales à la lumière du marxisme*, No. 19, pp. 53–71.

Lapoujade, David 2017, *Aberrant Movements: The Philosophy of Gilles Deleuze*, translated by Joshua David Jordan, South Pasadena, CA: Semiotext(e).

Laux, Henri 1993, *Imagination et religion chez Spinoza: La* potentia *dans l'histoire*. Paris: Vrin.

Lazarus, Sylvain 2015, *Anthropology of the Name*, translated by Gila Walker, New York, NY: Seagull Books.

Lazzeri, Christian 1998, *Droit, pouvoir, et liberté: Spinoza critique de Hobbes*, Paris: Presses Universitaires de France.

Lazzeri Christian 2001, *'In unum conspirare*: Principes de la rébellion et de la résistance dans la politique de Spinoza', in *Le Droit de résistance XIIe–XXe siécle*, edited by Jean-Claude Zancarini, Paris: ENS Éditions.

Lebowitz, Michael A. 2010, *The Socialist Alternative: Real Human Development*, New York, NY: Monthly Review Press.

Lecourt, Dominique 1973, *Une crise et son enjeu: essai sur la position de Lénine en philosophie*, Paris: François Maspero.

Lecourt, Dominique 1975, *Marxism and Epistemology: Bachelard, Canguilhem, and Foucault*, translated by Ben Brewster, London: NLB.

Lecourt, Dominique 1981, *L'Ordre et les jeux: le positivisme logique en question*, Paris: Bernard Grasset.

Leibniz, Gottfried Wilhelm 1969, *Essais de théodicée*, edited by J. Brunschwig, Paris: GF Flammarion.

Leibniz, G.W. 1985, *Theodicy: Essays on the Goodness of God, the Freedom of Man, and the Origin of Evil*, translated by E.M. Huggard, edited by Austin Farrer, La Salle, IL: Open Court Publishing Company.

Leibniz, Gottfried Wilhelm 1989 [1969], *Philosophical Papers and Letters*, 2nd edition, translated and edited by Leory E. Loemker, Boston, MA: Kluwer Academic Publishers.

Leibniz, G.W. 1991, *Discourse on Metaphysics and Other Essays*, translated by D. Garber and R. Ariew, Indianapolis, IN: Hackett Publishing Company.

Leibniz, G.W. 1994, *Système nouveau de la nature et de la communication des substances*, edited by Christiane Frémont, Paris: GF Flammarion.

Leibniz, G.W. 2004, *Discours de métaphysique suivi de Monadologie et autres textes*, edited by M. Fichant, Paris: Éditions Gallimard.

Leibniz, G.W. 2006, *The Shorter Leibniz Texts: A Collection of New Translations*, edited and translated by Lloyd Strickland, New York, NY: Continuum.

Lenin, V.I. 1972a, *Collected Works, Volume 38: Philosophical Notebooks*, Moscow: Progress Publishers.

Lenin, V.I. 1972, *Collected Works, Volume 38: Philosophical Notebooks*, Moscow: Progress Publishers.

Lenin, V.I. 1972b [1927], *Materialism and Empirio-Criticism: Critical Comments on a Reactionary Philosophy*, New York, NY: International Publishers.

Leonard, Annie 2010, *The Story of Stuff: How Our Obsession with Stuff is Trashing the Planet, Our Communities, and Our Health – And a Vision for Change*, New York: Free Press.

Léonard, Mathieu 2011, *L'émancipation des travailleurs: Une histoire de la Première Internationale*, Paris: La Fabrique éditions.

Levenson, Jon 1994 [1987], *Creation and the Persistence of Evil: The Jewish Drama of Divine Omnipotence*, Princeton, NJ: Princeton University Press.

Levine, Bruce 1992, *The Spirit of 1848: German Immigrants, Labor Conflict, and the Coming of the Civil War*, Urbana, IL: University of Illinois Press.

Levine, Bruce 2013, *The Fall of the House of Dixie: The Civil War and the Social Revolution that Transformed the South*, New York, NY: Random House.

Libera, Alain de 2014, *La philosophie médiévale*, 2nd edition, Paris: Presses Universitaires de France.

Lin, Martin 2006. 'Spinoza's Account of Akrasia', *Journal of the History of Philosophy* 44, 395–414.

Linebaugh, Peter and Marcus Rediker 2000, *The Many-Headed Hydra: Sailors, Slaves, Commoners, and the Hidden History of the Revolutionary Atlantic*, Boston, MA: Beacon Press.

Longenecker, Bruce W. 2010, *Remember the Poor: Paul, Poverty, and the Greco-Roman World*, Grand Rapids, MI: William B. Eerdmans Publishing Company.

Longenecker, Bruce W. 2015, *The Cross before Constantine: The Early Life of a Christian Symbol*, Minneapolis: Fortress Press.

Longenecker, Bruce W. and Todd D. Still 2014, *Thinking through Paul: A Survey of His Life, Letters, and Theology*, Grand Rapids, MI: Zondervan.

Lopez, Davina 2008, *Apostle to the Conquered: Reimagining Paul's Mission*, Minneapolis, MN: Fortress Press.

López, Fernando Bravo 2011, "Toward a Definition of Islamophobia: Approximations of the Early Twentieth Century" (https://www.academia.edu/2098927/Towards_a_definition_of_Islamophobia_approximations_of_the_early_twentieth_century.) (Published in *Ethnic and Racial Studies*, 34:4, pp. 556–73.)

Lordon, Frédéric 2013, *La société des affects: pour un structuralisme des passions*, Paris: Éditions du Seuil.

Losurdo, Domenico 2011, *Liberalism: A Counter-History*, translated by Gregory Elliott, New York, NY: Verso.

Löwy, Michael 1996, *The War of Gods: Religion and Politics in Latin America*, New York, NY: Verso.

Löwy, Michael 2005 [2003], *The Theory of Revolution in the Young Marx*, Chicago IL: Haymarket Books.

Löwy, Michael and Robert Sayre 2001, *Romanticism against the Tide of Modernity*, translated by Catherine Porter, Durham, NC: Duke University Press.

Löwy, Michael 2015, *Ecosocialism: A Radical Alternative to Capitalist Catastrophe*, Chicago, IL: Haymarket Books.

Lukes, Steven 1985, *Marxism and Morality*, New York, NY: Oxford University Press.

Luxemburg, Rosa 2008, *The Essential Rosa Luxemburg: Reform or Revolution and The Mass Strike*, edited by Helen Scott, Chicago, IL: Haymarket Books.

Lynas, Mark 2011, *The God Species: Saving the Planet in the Age of Humans*, Washington, D.C.: National Geographic.

Lynch, Michael Patrick 2016, *The Internet of Us: Knowing More and Understanding Less in the Age of Big Data*, New York, NY: Liveright Publishing Corporation.

Lynd, Staughton 1997, *Living Inside Our Hope: A Steadfast Radical's Thoughts on Rebuilding the Movement*, Ithaca, NY: Cornell University Press.

Lynd, Staughton 2009 [1968], *The Intellectual Origins of American Radicalism*, new edition, New York, NY: Cambridge University Press.

Lynd, Staughton 2013 [2012], *Accompanying: Pathways to Social Change*, Oakland: PM Press.

Maass, Alan 2010, *The Case for Socialism*, Chicago, IL: Haymarket Books.

MacKinnon, J.B. 2013, *The Once and Future World: Nature as It Was, As It Is, As It Could Be*, New York, NY: Houghton Mifflin Harcourt.

McKibben, Bill 2010, *Eaarth*, New York, NY: Times Books.

Macherey, Pierre 1968, undated handwritten letter to Louis Althusser, Paris: IMEC Archive.

Macherey, Pierre 1983, 'In a materialist way', translated by Lorna Scott Fox, in *Philosophy in France Today*, edited by Alan Montefiore, pp. 136–54.

Macherey, Pierre 1992, 'Le Spinoza idéaliste de Hegel', in *Avec Spinoza: Études sur la doctrine et l'histoire du spinozisme*, pp. 187–97, Paris: Presses Universitaires de France.

Macherey, Pierre 1994, *Introduction à l'Ethique de Spinoza. La cinquième partie: Les voies de la libération*, Paris: Presses Universitaires de France.

Macherey, Pierre 1995, *Introduction à l'Ethique de Spinoza, La troisième partie: La vie affective*, Paris: Presses Universitaires de France.

Macherey, Pierre 1995, *The Object of Literature*, translated by David Macey, New York, NY: Cambridge University Press.

Macherey, Pierre 1997, *Introduction à l'Ethique de Spinoza: La seconde partie, La réalité mentale*, Paris: Presses Universitaires de France.

Macherey, Pierre 1998, *In a Materialist Way*, edited by Warren Montag, translated by Ted Stolze, New York, NY: Verso.

Macherey, Pierre 1999, *Histoires de dinosaure: Faire de la philosophie, 1965–1997*, Paris: Presses Universitaires de France.

Macherey 2003, 'Le couple catégoriel *Gloria*/pudor (gloire/honte) chez Descartes et Spinoza' (http://stl.recherche.univ-lille3.fr/sitespersonnels/macherey/accueilmacherey.html; last accessed June 5, 2015).

Macherey, Pierre 2006 [1978], *A Theory of Literary Production*, translated by Geoffrey Wall, New York, NY: Routledge.

Macherey, Pierre 2009, *Petits riens: ornières et derives du quotidian*, Paris: Éditions le Bord de L'Eau.

Macherey, Pierre 2011a, *De L'utopie!*, Paris: De L'Incidence Editeur.

Macherey, Pierre 2011b, *Hegel or Spinoza*, translated by Sue Ruddick, Minneapolis, MN: University of Minnesota Press.

Macherey, Pierre 2012, 'Figures of Interpellation in Althusser and Fanon', *Radical Philosophy*, 173, pp. 9–20.

Macherey, Pierre 2013a, *Études de philosophie 'française': De Sieyès à Barni*, Paris: Publications de la Sorbonne.

Macherey, Pierre 2013b [1990], *Philosopher avec la literature: Exercises de philosophie littéraire*, Paris: Hermann.

Macherey, Pierre 2014a, *Querelles cartésiennes*, Paris: Septentrion Presses Universitaires.

Macherey, Pierre, 2014b, *Le sujet des norms*, Brezje, Slovenia: Éditions Amsterdam.

Macherey, Pierre 2015, "The Productive Subject," *Viewpoint Magazine*, 5.

Machiavelli, Niccolò 1996, *Discourses on Machiavelli*, translated by Harvey C. Mansfield and Nathan Tarcov, Chicago, IL: The University of Chicago Press.

Magda, Ksenija 2008, 'Unity as a Prerequisite for a Christian Mission: A Missional Reading of Rom 15:1–12', *Kairos – Evangelical Journal of Theology*, II, 1, pp. 39–52.

Malherbe, Abraham J. 2006 [1989], *Paul and the Popular Philosophers*, Minneapolis, MN: Fortress Press.

Malina, Bruce J. and John J. Pilch 2008, *Science-Science Commentary on the Book of Acts*, Minneapolis, MN: Fortress Press.

Malm, Andreas 2016, *Fossil Capital: The Rise of Steam Power and the Roots of Global Warming*, New York, NY: Verso.

Mamdani, Mahmood 2004, *Good Muslim, Bad Muslim: America, the Cold War, and the Roots of Terror*, New York, NY: Pantheon Books.

Mandel, Ernest 1974, 'Revolutionary Strategy in the Imperialist Countries', in Ernest Mandel and George Novack, *The Revolutionary Potential of the Working Class*, pp. 29–39, New York, NY: Pathfinder Press.

Mandel, Ernest 1976, 'Introduction', in Marx 1990, pp. 11–86.

Manning, Chandra 2016, *Troubled Refuge: Struggling for Freedom in the Civil War*, New York, NY: Alfred A. Knopf.

Manzini, Fréderic 2009, *Spinoza: une lecture d'Aristote*. Paris: Presses Universitaires de France.

Manzini, Frédéric 2014, 'La Valeur de Joie chez Spinoza', *Les Études philosophiques*, 109, pp. 237–51.

Marcus, Joel 2006, 'Crucifixion as Parodic Exaltation', *Journal of Biblical Literature* 125, 1: pp. 73–87.

Marcuse, H. 1969. *An Essay on Liberation*, Boston, MA: Beacon Press.

Marot, John Eric 2012, *The October Revolution in Prospect and Retrospect: Interventions in Russian and Soviet History*, Leiden: Brill.

Marquis, Timothy Luckritz 2013, *Transient Apostle: Paul, Travel, and the Rhetoric of Empire*, New Haven, CT: Yale University Press.

Martin, Randy, 1998–9, 'Rereading Marx: A Critique of Recent Criticisms', *Science and Society*, 62, 4: 513–36.

Martin, Bill 2008, *Ethical Marxism: The Categorical Imperative of Liberation*, Chicago, IL: Open Court Publishing Company.

Marx, Karl and Friedrich Engels 1970, *The German Ideology*, edited by C.J. Arthur, NY: International Publishers.

Marx, Karl 1973a, *Grundrisse*, translated by Martin Nicolaus, New York, NY: Penguin Books.

Marx, Karl 1973b, *The Karl Marx Library, Volume III: On the First International*, edited By Saul K. Padover, New York, NY: McGraw-Hill Book Company.

Marx, Karl 1990 [1976], *Capital*, Volume I, translated by Ben Fowkes, New York, NY: Penguin Books.

Marx, Karl 1992 [1975], *Early Writings*, translated by Rodney Livingstone and Gregor Benton, New York, NY: Penguin Books.

Marx, Karl 1997 [1967], *Writings of the Young Marx on Philosophy and Society*, edited and translated by L.D. Easton and K.H. Guddat, Indianapolis, IN: Hackett Publishing Company.

Marx, Karl 2000, *Selected Writings*, 2nd edition, edited by David McLellan, New York, NY: Oxford University Press.

Marx, Karl 2010 [1974], *Political Writings, Volume III: The First International and After*, edited by David Fernbach, New York, NY: Vintage Books.

Marx, Karl and Frederick Engels 1985, *Collected Works*, Volume 41: Letters, 1860–4, New York: Lawrence and Wishart.

Marx, Karl and Friedrich Engels 2015 [1996, 1848], 'Manifesto of the Communist Party', translated by Terrell Carver, pp. 237–60, in *The Cambridge Guide to The Communist Manifesto*, edited by Terrell Carver and James Farr, pp. 237–60, New York, NY: Cambridge University Press.

Mason, Steve 2016, *A History of the Jewish War A.D. 66–74*, New York, NY: Cambridge University Press.

Matheron, Alexandre 1971, *Le Christ et le salut des ignorants chez Spinoza*, Paris: Aubier Philosophie.

Matheron, Alexandre 1985, 'Le droit du plus fort: Hobbes contre Spinoza', *Revue philosophique* 2: 149–76.

Matheron, Alexandre 1988, *Individu et communauté chez Spinoza*, nouvelle edition, Paris: Minuit.

Matheron, Alexandre 1995, 'Y a-t-il une Théorie Spinoziste de la Prudence?', *De la prudence des anciens comparée à celle des modernes*, 129–47, Paris: Annales Littéraires de l'Université de Bensançon.

Matheron, Alexandre 2000, 'Entretien avec Alexandre Matheron: A propos de Spinoza', *multitudes* 3: 169–200.

Matheron, Alexandre 2011, *Études sur Spinoza et les philosophies de l'âge classique*, Paris: ENS Éditions.

Matheron, François 2012, 'Louis Althusser et le "groupe Spinoza"', *Lectures contemporaines de Spinoza*, edited by Pierre-François Moreau et al., Paris: Presses de l'Université Paris-Sorbonne, pp. 77–93.

Mattingly, David J. 2011, *Imperialism, Power, and Identity: Experiencing the Roman Empire*, Princeton, NJ: Princeton University Press.

Mayor, Adrienne 2018, *Gods and Roberts: Myths, Machines, and Ancient Dreams of Technology*, Princeton, NJ: Princeton University Press.

McCarthy, George E. 2015, 'Last of the Schoolmen: Natural Law and Social Justice in Karl Marx', in Thompson 2015, pp. 192–232.

McCarthy, George E. 2018, *Marx and Social Justice: Ethics and Natural Law in the Critique of Political Economy*, Boston: Brill.

McCord, Edward L. 2012, *The Value of Species*, New Haven, CT: Yale University Press.

McCulloch, Gregory 1989, *The Game of the Name: Introducing Logic, Language, and Mind*, New York, NY: Oxford University Press.

McGrath, Thomas 1997, *Letter to an Imaginary Friend*, Port Townsend, WA: Copper Canyon Press.

McPherson, James 1996, 'Who Freed the Slaves?', in *Drawn with the Sword: Reflections on the American Civil War*, New York: Oxford University Press.

McPherson, James 2015, *The War that Forged a Nation: Why the Civil War Still Matters*, New York, NY: Oxford University Press.

Meggitt, Justin J. 1998, *Paul, Poverty, and Survival*, Edinburgh: T&T Clark.

Meikle, Scott 1985, *Essentialism in the Thought of Karl Marx*, Chicago, IL: Open Court Publishing.

Meikle, Scott 1991, 'History of Philosophy: The Metaphysics of Substance in Marx', in Carver 1991, pp. 296–319.

Meikle, Scott 1995, *Aristotle's Economic Thought*, New York, NY: Oxford University Press.

Mele, Alfred R. 2012, *Backsliding: Understanding Weakness of Will*, New York, NY: Oxford University Press.

Melamed, Yitzhak Y. 2010, 'Acosmism or Weak Individuals? Hegel, Spinoza, and the Reality of the Finite', *Journal of the History of Philosophy*, 48, 1: 77–92.

Melamed, Yitzhak Y. 2012, '"*Omnis determinatio est negatio*": determination, negation and self-negation in Spinoza, Kant, and Hegel', in *Spinoza and German Idealism*, edited by Eckart Förster and Yitzhak Y. Melamed, pp. 175–96, New York, NY: Cambridge University Press.

Merchant, Carolyn 2016, *Autonomous Nature: Problems of Prediction and Control from Ancient Times to the Scientific Revolution*, New York, NY: Routledge.

Meyerson, Diane 1991, *False Consciousness*, New York, NY: Oxford University Press.

Míguez, Néstor O. 2012, *The Practice of Hope: Ideology and Intention in 1 Thessalonians*, Minneapolis, MN: Fortress Press.

Miliband, Ralph 1995, *Socialism for a Skeptical Age*, New York, NY: Verso.

Miliband, Ralph and Marcel Liebman 1985, 'Beyond Social Democracy', in *The Socialist Register*, 22: 476–89.

Misrahi, Robert 2005, *100 mots sur l'Éthique de Spinoza*, Paris: Les Empêcheurs de penser en rond.

Mitov, Michel 2012, *Sensitive Matter: Foams, Gels, Liquid Crystals, and Other Miracles*, translated by Giselle Weiss, Cambridge, MA: Harvard University Press.

Molyneux, John 2012, *The Point is to Change It! An Introduction to Marxist Philosophy*, London: Bookmarks Publications.

Montag, Warren 1988, 'What is at Stake in the Debate on Postmodernism?', in *Postmodernism and Its Discontents: Theories, Practices*, edited by E.A. Kaplan, New York, NY: Verso.

Montag, Warren 1989, 'Spinoza: Politics in a World without Transcendence', *Rethinking MARXISM*, 2, 3, pp. 89–103.

Montag, Warren 1999. *Bodies, Masses, Power: Spinoza and His Contemporaries*, New York, NY: Verso.

Montag, Warren 2012, 'Pierre Macherey: Between the Quotidian and Utopia', *Décalages* 1, 3 (http://scholar.oxy.edu/decalages/Vol1/iss10; last accessed April 21, 2016).

Montag, Warren 2012, 'Hegel, *sive* Spinoza: Hegel as His Own True Other', in *Between Hegel and Spinoza*, edited by Hasana Sharp and Jason E. Smith, pp. 83–97, New York, NY: Bloomsbury.

Montag, Warren 2013, *Althusser and His Contemporaries: Philosophy's Perpetual War*, Durham, NC: Duke University Press.

Mooney, Chris and Sheril Kirshenbaum, 2009, *Unscientific America: How Scientific Illiteracy Threatens our Future*, New York, NY: Basic Books.

Moore, A.W. 2012, *The Evolution of Modern Metaphysics: Making Sense of Things*, New York, NY: Cambridge University Press.

Moore, Jr., Barrington, 1978, *Injustice: The Social Bases of Obedience and Revolt*, White Plains, NY: M.E. Sharpe.

Mora, Camilo et al. 2017a, 'Global Risk of Deadly Heat', *Nature Climate Change* 7: 501–6; DOI: 10.1038/nclimate3322.

Mora, Camilo et al. 2017b, 'Twenty-Seven Ways a Heat Wave Can Kill You: Deadly Heat in the Era of Climate Change', *Circulation: Cardiovascular Quality and Outcomes* 10: e004233; DOI: 10.1161/CIRCOUTCOMES.117.004233.

Moreau, Pierre-François 1985, 'La Notion d'*Imperium* dans le *Traité politique*', *Proceedings of the First Italian International Conference on Spinoza*, edited by Emilia Giancotti, Naples: Bibliopolis, pp. 355–66.

Moreau, Pierre-François 1994a, *Spinoza: L'éxperience et l'éternité*, Paris: Presses Universitaires de France.

Moreau, Pierre-François 1994b, 'Métaphysique de la gloire. La scholie de la proposition 36 et le "tourant" du livre V', *Revue philosophique* 1, pp. 55–64.

Moreau, Pierre-François 2003, *Spinoza et le spinozisme*, Paris: Presses Universitaires de France.

Morfino, Vittorio 2015 [2014], *Plural Temporality: Transindividuality and the Aleatory Between Spinoza and Althusser*, Chicago, IL: Haymarket Books.

Morley, Neville 2010, *The Roman Empire: Roots of Imperialism*, New York, NY: Pluto Press.

Morris, William 1979, *Political Writings*, edited by A.L. Morton, London: Lawrence and Wishart.

Moyn, Samuel 2010, *The Last Utopia: Human Rights in History*, Cambridge, MA: Harvard University Press.

Moyn, Samuel 2014, *Human Rights and the Uses of History*, New York, NY: Verso.

Murata, Sachiko and William C. Chittick 1994, *The Vision of Islam*, St. Paul, MN: Paragon House.

Murphy, Frederick J. Murphy 2002, *Early Judaism: The Exile to the Time of Jesus*, Peabody, MA: Hendrickson Publishers, Inc.

Murphy, Frederick 2012, *Apocalypticism in the Bible and Its World: A Comprehensive Introduction*, Grand Rapids, MI: Baker Academic.

Murphy-O'Connor, Jerome 1997 [1996], *Paul: A Critical Life*, New York, NY: Oxford University Press.

Myers, Ched 2008, *Binding the Strong Man: A Political Reading of Mark's Story of Jesus*, twentieth anniversary edition, Maryknoll, NY: Orbis Books.

Myers, Ched 2002, 'Mark's Gospel: Invitation to Discipleship', in *The New Testament – Introducing the Way of Discipleship*, edited by Wes Howard-Brook and Sharon H. Ringe, pp. 40–61, Maryknoll, NY: Orbis Books.

Nadler, Steven 1999, *Spinoza: A Life*, New York: Cambridge University Press.

Nadler, S. 2006, *Spinoza's Ethics: An Introduction*. New York, NY: Cambridge University Press.

Nasser, Alan 2012, 'What the Market Does to Our Souls: Revisiting Richard Titmuss's *The Gift Relationship*', *Counterpunch* (http://www.counterpunch.org/2012/06/28/what-the-market-does-to-our-souls/; last accessed October 22, 2016).

Nathan, Debbie 2016, 'What Happened to Sandra Bland?', *The Nation*, May 9–16 (http://www.thenation.com/article/what-happened-to-sandra-bland/; last accessed 21 April, 2016).

Neale, Jonathan et al. 2014, *One Million Climate Jobs: Tackling the Environmental and Economic Crises*, 3rd edition, London: The Campaign against Climate Change.

Negri, Antonio 1984, *Marx Beyond Marx: Lessons on the* Grundrisse, translated by Harry Cleaver, Michel Ryan, and Maurizio Viano, South Hadley, MA: Bergin & Garvey.

Negri, Antonio 1991, *The Savage Anomaly: The Power of Spinoza's Metaphysics*, translated by Michael Hardt, Minneapolis, MN: The University of Minnesota Press.

Negri, Antonio 1999, *Insurgencies: Constituent Power and the Modern State*, translated by Maurizia Boscaglia, Minneapolis, MN: University of Minnesota Press.

Negri, Antonio 2003, *Time for Revolution*, translated by Matteo Mandarini, New York, NY: Continuum.

Negri, Antonio with Anne Dufourmantelle 2004a, *Negri on Negri*, translated by M.B. DeBevoise, New York, NY: Routledge.

Negri, Antonio 2004b, 'Wittgenstein and Pain: Sociological Consequences', translated by Timothy S. Murphy, *Genre*, 37, 3–4, pp. 353–67.

Negri, Antonio 2007, *Political Descartes: Reason, Ideology, and the Bourgeois Project*, translated by Matteo Mandarini and Alberto Toscano, New York, NY: Verso.

Negri, Antonio 2009, *The Labor of Job: The Biblical Text as a Parable of Human Labor*, translated by Matteo Mandarini, Durham, NC: Duke University Press.

Negri, Antonio 2011, 'Gilles-felix', translated by Shane Lillis and revised by Andrew Goffey, in *The Guattari Effect*, edited Éric Alliez and Andrew Goffey, pp. 156–71, New York, NY: Continuum Books.

Negri, Antonio 2014, *Factory of Strategy: Thirty-Three Lessons on Lenin*, translated by Arianna Bove, New York, NY: Columbia University Press.

Newman, Richard 2017, 'The Grammar of Emancipation: Putting Final Freedom in Context', in *Beyond Freedom: Disrupting the History of Emancipation*, edited by David W. Blight and Jim Downs, pp. 11–25, Athens, GA: The University of Georgia Press.

Newsom, Carol A. 1996, 'The Book of Job', in *The New Interpreter's Bible*, volume IV, pp. 319–637, Nashville, TN: Abingdon Press.

Newsom, Carol A. 2003, *The Book of Job: A Context of Moral Imaginations*, New York, NY: Oxford University Press.

Nichols, David A. 2012, *Lincoln and the Indians: Civil War Policy and Politics*, St. Paul, MN: Minnesota Historical Society Press.

Nickel, James 2007, *Making Sense of Human Rights*, 2nd edition, Malden, MA: Blackwell Publishing.

Nickle, Keith F. 2009 [1966], *The Collection: A Study in Paul's Strategy*, Eugene, OR: Wipf and Stock Publishers.

Niebuhr, Gustav 2014, *Lincoln's Bishop: A President, A Priest, and the Fate of Dakota Sioux Warriors*, New York, NY: HarperOne.

Nienhuis, David R. and Robert W. Wall 2013, *Reading the Epistles of James, Peter, John, and Jude as Scripture: The Shaping and Shape of a Canonical Collection*, Grand Rapids, MI: William B. Eerdmans Publishing Company.

Nietzsche, Friedrich 2005, *The Anti-Christ, Ecce Homo, Twilight of the Idols, and Other Writings*, translated by Judith Norman, edited by Aaron Ridley and Judith Norman, New York, NY: Cambridge University Press.

Nimtz, Jr., August H. 2000. *Marx and Engels: Their Contribution to the Democratic Breakthrough*, Albany, NY: State University of New York Press.

Noble, Denis 2008, 'Claude Bernard, the first systems biologist, and the future of physiology', *Experimental Physiology*, 93, 1: 16–26.

Noonan, Jeff 2012, *Materialist Ethics and Life-Value*, Montreal: McGill-Queen's University Press.

Novenson, Matthew V. 2012, *Christ among the Messiahs*, New York, NY: Oxford University Press.

Nussbaum, Martha 2011, *Creating Capabilities: The Human Development Approach*, Cambridge, MA: Harvard University Press.

Nussbaum, Martha 2016, *Anger and Forgiveness: Resentment, Generosity, Justice*, New York, NY: Oxford University Press.

Oakes, Peter 2005, 'Re-mapping the Universe: Paul and the Emperor in 1 Thessalonians and Philippians', *The Journal for the Study of the New Testament* 27: 301–22.

Oakes, Peter 2009a, 'Methodological Issues in Using Economic Evidence in Interpretation of Early Christian Texts', in *Engaging Economics: New Testament Scenarios and Early Christian Reception*, pp. 9–34, edited by Bruce W. Longenecker and Kelly D. Liebengood, Grand Rapids, MI: William B. Eerdmans Publishing Company.

Oakes, Peter 2009b, *Reading Romans in Pompeii: Paul's Letter at Ground Level*, Minneapolis, MN: Fortress Press.

Oakman, Douglas E. 2014, *Jesus, Debt, and the Lord's Prayer: First-Century Debt and Jesus' Intentions*, Eugene, OR: Cascade Books.

Ogereau, Julien M. 2012, 'The Jerusalem Collection as Κοινωνια: Paul's Global Politics of Socio-Economic Equality and Solidarity', *New Testament Studies*, 58, 3: 360–78.

Olson, Randy 2009, *Don't Be Such a Scientist: Talking Substance in an Age of Style*, Washington, DC: Island Press.

Oreskes, Naomi and Erik M. Conway 2010, *Merchants of Doubt: How a Handful of Scientists Obscured the Truth on Issues from Tobacco Smoke to Global Warming*, New York, NY: Bloomsbury Press.

Osiek, Carolyn, Margaret Y. MacDonald; with Janet Tulloch 2006, *A Woman's Place: House Churches in Earliest Christianity*, Minneapolis, MN: Augsburg Fortress Press.

Pacchi, Arrigo 1998, 'Hobbes and the Passions', *Scritti Hobbesiani*, pp. 79–95, Milano: FrancoAngeli.

Panitch, Leo and Sam Gindin 2002, 'Gems and Baubles in *Empire*', *Historical Materialism*, 10, 2: 17–43.

Parr, Adrian 2009, *Hijacking Sustainability*, Cambridge, MA: The MIT Press.

Patterson, Stephen J. 2008, 'Can You Trust a Gospel? A Review of Richard Bauckham's *Jesus and the Eyewitnesses*', *Journal for the Study of the Historical Jesus*, 6, 2: 194–210.

Patton, Paul 2014, 'History, Normativity, and Rights', in *The Meanings of Rights: The Philosophy and Social Theory of Human Rights*, edited by Costas Douzinas and Conor Gearty, pp. 233–50, New York, NY: Cambridge University Press.

Paul, L.A. 2014, *Transformative Experience*, New York, NY: Oxford University Press.

Pautrat, Bernard 2013, 'Pourquoi retraduire le *Tractatus Politicus*?', in Baruch Spinoza, *Traité politique*, pp. 7–22, Paris: Éditions Allia.

Pêcheux, Michel 1982, *Language, Semantics, and Ideology*, translated by Harbans Nagpal, New York, NY: St. Martin's Press.

Peden, Knox 2014, *Spinoza Contra Phenomenology: French Rationalism from Cavaillès to Deleuze*, Stanford, CA: Stanford University Press.

Peffer, Rodney 1990, *Marxism, Morality, and Social Justice*, Princeton, NJ: Princeton University Press.

Pennington, Jonathan T. 2017, *The Sermon on the Mount and Human Flourishing*, Grand Rapids, MI: Baker Academic.

Peters, Shawn Francis 2012, *The Catonsville Nine: A Story of Faith and Resistance in the Vietnam Era*, New York, NY: Oxford University Press.

Phillips, Thomas E. 2009, *Paul, His Letters, and Acts*, Peabody, MA: Hendrickson Publishers.

Pierce, Charles P., 2010, *Idiot America: How Stupidity Became a Virtue in the Land of the Free*, New York, NY: Anchor Books.

Pinkard, Terry 2005, 'Speculative *Naturphilosophie* and the Development of the Empirical Sciences: Hegel's Perspective', in *Continental Philosophy of Science*, edited by Gary Gutting, Malden, MA: Blackwell Publishing.

Plato 1993, *Sophist*, translated by Nicholas P. White, Indianapolis, IN: Hackett Publishing Company.

Plekhanov, George V. 1969, *Fundamental Problems of Marxism*, New York, NY: International Publishers.

Plutzer, Eric et al. 2016, 'Climate confusion among U.S. teachers', *Science*, 351: 6274, pp. 664–5.

Pope, Marvin 1965, *The Anchor Bible: Job*, New York, NY: Doubleday.

Porter, Roy 2003 [2002], *Blood and Guts: A Short History of Medicine*, London: Penguin Books.

Portier-Young 2014, *Apocalypse against Empire: Theologies of Resistance in Early Judaism*, Grand Rapids, MI: Eerdmans Publishing Company.

Power, Carla 2015, *If the Oceans Were Ink: An Unlikely Friendship and a Journey to the Heart of the Qur'an*, New York, NY: Henry Holt and Company.

Prawer, S.S. 1978, *Karl Marx and World Literature*, New York, NY: Oxford University Press.

Prigogine, Ilya (in collaboration with Isabelle Stengers) 1997, *The End of Certainty: Time, Chaos, and the New Laws of Nature*, New York, NY: The New Press.

Prokhovnik, Raia 2004, *Spinoza and Republicanism*, New York, NY: Palgrave Macmillan.

Punt, Jeremy 2012, 'Postcolonial Approaches: Negotiating Empires, Then and Now', in *Studying Paul's Letters: Contemporary Perspectives and Methods*, edited by Joseph A. Marchal, Minneapolis, MN: Fortress Press.

Puskas, Charles B. and Mark Reasoner 2013, *The Letters of Paul: An Introduction*, 2nd edition, Collegeville, MN: Liturgical Press.

Quiniou, Yvon 2010, *L'ambition morale de la politique*, Paris: L'Harmattan.
Quiniou, Yvon 2013, *Retour à Marx: pour une société post-capitaliste*, Paris: Buchet Chastel.
Rachels, James and Stuart Rachels 2009, *Problems from Philosophy*, 2nd edition, New York, NY: McGraw-Hill.
Raines, John 2002, *Marx and Religion*, Philadelphia, PA: Temple University Press.
Rall, Ted 2013, 'Why Are Americans So Passive? Get Pissed Off and Break Things', June 22, 2013 (http://www.commondreams.org/view/2013/06/22-1; last accessed 26 June, 2013).
Ramond, Charles 2007, *Dictionnaire Spinoza*, Paris: Ellipses, 2007.
Ramond, Charles 2016, *Spinoza contemporain: philosophie, éthique, politique*, Paris: L'Harmattan.
Ravven, Heidi 2013, *The Self Beyond Itself: An Alternative History of Ethics, the New Brain Sciences, and the Myth of Free Will*, New York, NY: The New Press.
Rawls, John 1999a, *Collected Papers*, edited by Samuel Freeman, Cambridge, MA: Harvard University Press.
Rawls, John 1999b, *A Theory of Justice*, revised edition, Cambridge, MA: Harvard University Press.
Rawls, John 2001, *Justice as Fairness: A Restatement*, Cambridge, MA: Harvard University Press.
Rawls, John 2005, *Political Liberalism*, expanded edition, New York, NY: Columbia University Press.
Rawls, John 2007, *Lectures on the History of Moral Philosophy*, edited by Samuel Freeman, Cambridge, MA: Harvard University Press.
Raymond, Pierre 1973, *Le passage au materialisme*, Paris: François Maspero.
Raymond, Pierre 1977, *Matérialisme dialectique et logique*, Paris: François Maspero.
Raymond, Pierre 1982, *La resistible fatalité de l'histoire*, Paris: J.E. Hallier-Albin Michel.
Raymond, Pierre 2015 [1997], 'Althusser's Materialism', translated by Ted Stolze, *Historical Materialism*, 23, 2: 176–88.
Read, Jason 2012, '"Desire is Man's Very Essence": Spinoza and Hegel as Philosophers of Transindividuality', in *Between Hegel and Spinoza: A Volume of Critical Essays*, pp. 42–60, edited by Hasana Sharp and Jason E. Smith, New York: Bloomsbury.
Read, Jason 2015, *The Politics of Transindividuality*, Leiden: Brill.
Reasoner, Mark 1999, *The Strong and the Weak: Romans 14.1–15.13 in Context*, New York, NY: Cambridge University Press.
Reasoner, Mark 2013, *Roman Imperial Texts: A Sourcebook*, Minneapolis, MN: Fortress Press.
Reed, T.V. 2005, *The Art of Protest: Culture and Activism from the Civil Rights Movement to the Streets of Seattle*, Minneapolis, MN: University of Minnesota Press.
Reeve, C.D.C. 2012, *Action, Contemplation, and Happiness: An Essay on Aristotle*, Cambridge, MA: Harvard University Press.

Reeve, C.D.C. 2014, 'Beginning and Ending with *Eudaimonia*', in *The Cambridge Companion to Aristotle's Nicomachean Ethics*, edited by Ronald Polansky, pp. 14–33, New York, NY: Cambridge University Press.
Resch, Robert Paul 1992, *Althusser and the Renewal of Marxist Social Theory*, Berkeley, CA: University of California Press.
Ricard, Hubert 2015, 'Pour illustrer le rationalisme d'Averroès: Le savoir et le sujet', in *De Spinoza à Lacan: Autre Chose et la mystique*, pp. 115–40, Paris: EME.
Richards, E. Randolph 2004, *Paul and First-Century Letter Writings: Secretaries, Composition and Collection*, Downers Grove, IL: IVP Academic.
Richards, Leonard L. 2015, *Who Freed the Slaves? The Fight over the Thirteenth Amendment*, Chivago, IL: The University of Chicago Press.
Ricoeur, Paul 1986, *Lectures on Ideology and Utopia*, edited by George H. Taylor, New York, NY: Columbia University Press.
Rizk, Hadi 1995, 'Les affects du pouvoir', *Rue Descartes* 12, 3.
Rizk, Hadi 1996, *La Constitution de l'être social: le statut ontologique du collectif dans La Critique de la raison dialectique*, Paris: Éditions Kimé.
Rizk, Hadi 2012, Spinoza: L'expérience et l'infini, Paris: Armand Colin.
Roberts, William Clare 2017, *Marx's Inferno: The Political Theory of Capital*, Princeton, NJ: Princeton University Press.
Rockmore, Tom 2007, *Kant and Idealism*, New Haven, CT: Yale University Press.
Rockström, Johan et al. 2009, 'A Safe Operating Space for Humanity', *Nature*, 461: 472–5.
Rockström, Johan and Mattias Klum, with Peter Miller 2015, *Big World, Small Planet: Abundance within Planetary Boundaries*, New Haven, CT: Yale University Press.
Roediger, David 2014, *Seizing Freedom: Slave Emancipation and Liberty for All*, New York, NY: Verso.
Rogers, Guy MacLean 2012, *The Mysteries of Artemis of Ephesos: Cult, Polis, and Change in the Greco-Roman World*, New Haven, CT: Yale University Press.
Rogers, Heather 2013, *Green Gone Wrong: How Our Economy is Undermining the Environmental Revolution*, New York, NY: Verso.
Rorty, Richard 1989, *Contingency, Irony, and Solidarity*, New York, NY: Cambridge University Press.
Rorty, Richard 1993, 'Human Rights, Rationality, and Sentimentality', in *On Human Rights: The Oxford Amnesty Lectures 1993*, edited by Stephen Shute and Susan Hurley, New York, NY: Basic Books.
Rorty, Richard 1997, 'Justice as a Larger Loyalty', in *Justice and Democracy: Cross-Cultural Perspectives*, edited by Ron Bontekoe and Marietta Stepaniants, Honolulu: University of Hawai'i Press.
Rorty, Richard 1998, *Achieving Our Country: Leftist Thought in Twentieth-Century America*, Cambridge, MA: Harvard University Press.
Rose, Steven 2005a, *The Future of the Brain: The Promise and Perils of Tomorrow's Neuroscience*, New York, NY: Oxford University Press.

Rose, Steven 2005b, *Lifelines: Life Beyond the Gene*, revised edition, London: Vintage.

Rosenthal, Michael 2012, 'Why Spinoza is Intolerant of Atheists: God and the Limits of Early Modern Liberalism', *Review of Metaphysics*, 65, 4: 813–39.

Rosner, Brian 2007, *Greed as Idolatry: The Origin and Meaning of a Pauline Metaphor*, Grand Rapids, MI: Eerdmans.

Roudinesco, Elisabeth 2008, *Philosophy in Turbulent Times: Canguilhem, Sartre, Foucault, Althusser, Deleuze, Derrida*, translated by William McCuaig, New York, NY: Columbia University Press.

Rovelli, Carlo 2011, *The First Scientist: Anaximander and His Legacy*, translated by Marion Lignana Rosenberg, Yardley, PA: Westholme Publishing.

Rowe, C. Kavin 2009, *World Upside Down: Reading Acts in the Graeco-Roman World*, New York, NY: Oxford University Press.

Ruda, Frank 2014, 'Idealism without Idealism: Badiou's Materialist Renaissance', *Angelaki*, 19, 1: 85–98.

Ruda, Frank 2016, *Abolishing Freedom: A Plea for a Contemporary Use of Fatalism*, Lincoln, NE: University of Nebraska Press.

Ruden, Sarah 2010, *Paul Among the People: The Apostle Reinterpreted and Reimagined in His Own Time*, New York, NY: Pantheon Books.

Saito, Kohei 2017, *Karl Marx's Ecosocialism: Capital, Nature, and the Unfinished Critique of Political Economy*, New York, NY: Monthly Review Press.

Sartre, Jean-Paul 1984 [1956], *Being and Nothingness*, translated by Hazel E. Barnes, New York, NY: Washington Square Press.

Sartre, Jean-Paul 1988, *'What is Literature?' and Other Essays*, Cambridge, MA: Harvard University Press.

Sartre, Jean-Paul 1995 [1948], *Anti-Semite and Jew*, New York, NY: Schocken Books.

Sartre, Jean-Paul 2004a [1960], *Critique of Dialectical Reason, Volume 1: Theory of Practical Ensembles*, new and corrected edition, translated by Alan Sheridan-Smith, edited by Jonathan Rée, New York, NY: Verso.

Sartre, Jean-Paul 2004b [1946], *Réflexions sur la question juive*, Paris: Éditions Gallimard.

Sartre, Jean-Paul 2007, *Existentialism Is a Humanism*, translated by Carol Macomber, edited by John Kulka, New Haven, CT: Yale University Press.

Sartre, Jean-Paul 2013, 'Kierkegaard: The Singular Universal', translated by John Matthews, *We Have Only This Life to Live: The Selected Essays of Jean-Paul Sartre, 1939–1975*, pp. 403–32, edited by Ronald Aronson and Adrian van den Hoven, New York, NY: New York Review Books.

Sartre, Jean-Paul 2013, *We Have Only This Life to Live: The Selected Essays of Jean-Paul Sartre*, edited by Ronald Aronson and Adrian van den Hoven, New York, NY: New York Review Books.

Schama, Simon 1987, *The Embarrassment of Riches: An Interpretation of Dutch Culture in the Golden Age*, New York, NY: Random House.

Scheffler, Samuel 2013, *Death and the Afterlife*, New York: Oxford University Press.
Schifferdecker, Kathryn 2008, *Out of the Whirlwind: Creation Theology in the Book of Job*, Cambridge, MA: Harvard University Press.
Schwartz, Seth 2014, *The Ancient Jews from Alexander to Muhammad*, New York, NY: Cambridge University Press.
Schottroff, Luise 2006, The Parables of Jesus, translated by Linda M. Maloney, Minneapolis, MN: Fortress Press.
Scott, James C. 1990, *Domination and the Arts of Resistance: Hidden Transcripts*, New Haven, CT: Yale University Press.
Scull, Andrew 2015, *Madness in Civilization: A Cultural History of Insanity, from the Bible to Freud, from the Madhouse to Modern Medicine*, Princeton, NJ: Princeton University Press.
Schüssler Fiorenza, Elisabeth 2000, 'Paul and the Politics of Interpretation', in Horsley 2000, pp. 40–57.
Seaford, Richard 2004, *Money and the Early Greek Mind: Homer, Philosophy, Tragedy*, New York, NY: Cambridge University Press.
Seaford, Richard 2013, 'Coinage and Early Greek Thought', *Radical Anthropology*, 7: 1–5.
Seaford, Richard, ed. 2017, *Universe and Inner Self in Early Indian and Early Greek Thought*, Edinburgh: Edinburgh University Press.
Sellars, Kirsten 2002, *The Rise and Rise of Human Rights*, London: Sutton.
Sen, Amartya 2009, *The Idea of Justice*, Cambridge, MA: Harvard University Press.
Sève, Lucien 1978, *Man in Marxist Theory and the Psychology of Personality*, translated by John McGreal, Atlantic Highlands, NJ: Humanities Press.
Sève, Lucien 1980, *Une introduction à la philosophie marxiste*, Paris: Terrains/Éditions Sociales.
Sève, Lucien 1981, *Marxisme et théorie de la personnalité*, fifth edition, Paris: Terrains/Éditions Sociales.
Sève, Lucien 1987, 'La personnalité en question', in *Je: sur la individualité*, pp. 209–49, Paris: Messidor/Éditions sociales.
Sève, Lucien 2004, *Penser avec Marx aujourd'hui, Tome 2: 'L'homme'?*, Paris: La Dispute.
Sève, Lucien 2012, *Aliénation et emancipation*, Clamecy: La Dispute.
Sève, Lucien 2015, *Pour une science de la bibliographie*, Paris: les editions sociales.
Shantz, Colleen 2009, *Paul in Ecstasy: The Neurobiology of the Apostle's Life and Thought*, New York, NY: Cambridge University Press.
Sharp, Hasana 2005, 'Why Spinoza Today? Or, "A Strategy of Anti-Fear"', *Rethinking Marxism*, 17, 4: 591–608.
Sharp, Hasana 2011, *Spinoza and the Politics of Renaturalization*, Chicago, IL: The University of Chicago Press.
Shenefelt, Michael and Heidi White 2013, *If A then B: How the World Discovered Logic*, New York, NY: Columbia University Press.

Sibertin-Blanc, Guillaume 2012 [2010], *Deleuze et l'anti-Oedipe: La production du désir*, Paris: Presses Universitaires de France.

Sibertin-Blanc, Guillaume 2016, *State and Politics: Deleuze and Guattari on Marx*, translated by Ames Hodges, South Pasadena, CA: Semiotext(e).

Sinha, Manisha 2016, *The Slave's Cause: A History of Abolition*, New Haven, CT: Yale University Press.

Skinner, Quentin 1996, *Reason and Rhetoric in the Philosophy of Hobbes*, New York, NY: Cambridge University Press.

Skinner, Quentin 1998, *Liberty Before Liberalism*, New York, NY: Cambridge University Press.

Slomp, Gabriella 2000, *Thomas Hobbes and the Political Philosophy of Glory*, New York, NY: St. Martin's Press.

Slomp, Gabriella 2007, 'Hobbes on Glory and Civil Strife', in *The Cambridge Companion to Hobbes's* Leviathan, edited by Patricia Springborg, pp. 181–96, New York, NY: Cambridge University Press.

Smith, Dennis E. and Joseph B. Tyson (eds.) 2013, *Acts and Christian Beginnings: The Acts Seminar Report*, Salem, OR: Polebridge Press.

Smith, Justin 2016, *The Philosopher: A History in Six Types*, Princeton, NJ: Princeton University Press.

Smith, Steven B. 2003. *Spinoza's Book of Life: Freedom and Redemption in the* Ethics, New Haven, CT: Yale University Press.

Smolin, Lee 2014 [2013], *Time Reborn: From the Crisis in Physics to the Future of the of the Universe*, New York, NY: Mariner Books.

Soelle, Dorothee 2001, *The Silent Cry: Mysticism and Resistance*, translated by Barbara and Martin Rumscheidt, Minneapolis, MN: Fortress Press.

Sohn-Rethel, Alfred 1978, *Intellectual and Manual Labour: A Critique of Epistemology*, London: Macmillan.

Sorrell, Tom 1986, *Hobbes*, New York, NY: Routledge and Kegan Paul.

Spellberg, Denise A. 2013, *Jefferson's Qur'an: Islam and the Founders*, New York, NY: Alfred A. Knopf.

Spinoza, Benedictus de 1925 [1677], *Opera*, volume II, edited by Carl Gebhardt, Heidelberg: Carl Winter.

Spinoza, Benedict de 1958, *The Political Works*, translated by A.G. Wernham, London: Oxford University Press.

Spinoza, Baruch 1995, *The Letters*, translated by Samuel Shirley, Indianapolis, IN: Hackett Publishing Company, Inc.

Spinoza, Baruch 1996 [1677], *Ethics*, translated by Edwin Curley, New York, NY: Penguin Books.

Spinoza, Baruch 1999, *Oeuvres, III: Tractatus Theologico-Politicus/Traité Théologico-Politique*, edited by Pierre-François Moreau, text established by Fokke Akkerman, translated by Jacqueline Lagrée and Pierre-François Moreau, Paris: Presses Universitaires de France.

Spinoza, Baruch 2001 [1677], *The Political Treatise*, 2nd edition, translated by Samuel Shirley, Indianapolis, IN: Hackett Publishing Company.

Spinoza, Baruch 2002, *Complete Works*, translated by Samuel Shirley and others, edited by Michael L. Morgan, Indianapolis, IN: Hackett Publishing Company.

Spinoza, Baruch 2005, *Oeuvres, V: Tractatus Politicus/Traité Politique*, edited by Pierre-François Moreau, text established by Omero Proietti, translated by Charles Ramond, Paris: Presses Universitaires de France.

Spinoza, Baruch 2007 [1670], *Theological-Political Treatise*, edited by Jonathan Israel, translated by Jonathan Israel and Michael Silverthorne, New York, NY: Cambridge University Press.

Spruit, Leen 2013, 'Intellectual Beatitude in the Averroist Tradition: The Case of Agostino Nifo', in *Renaissance Averroism and Its Aftermath: Arabic Philosophy in Early Modern Europe*, edited by Anna Akasoy and Guido Giglioni, Dordrecht: Springer Science+Business Media.

Srnicek, Nick and Alex Williams 2016, *Inventing the Future: Postcapitalism and a World Without Work*, revised and updated edition, New York: Verso.

Stanley, Amy Dru 2015, 'Slave Emancipation and the Revolutionizing of Human Rights', in Downs and Masur 2015, pp. 269–303.

Ste. Croix, G.E.M. de 1981, *The Class Struggle in the Ancient Greek World: From the Archaic Age to the Arab Conquests*, Ithaca, NY: Cornell University Press.

Steenberghen, Fernand van 1980, *Thomas Aquinas and Radical Aristotelianism*, Washington, D.C.: The Catholic University of America Press.

Steffen, Will et al. 2015, 'Planetary Boundaries: Guiding human development on a changing planet', *Sciencexpress*, January 15, pp. 1–17.

Stegemann, Ekkehard W. and Wolfgang Stegemann 1999, *The Jesus Movement: A Social History of Its First Century*, translated by O.C. Dean, Jr., Minneapolis, MN: Fortress Press.

Stendahl, Krister 1976, *Paul Among Jews and Gentiles and Other Essays*, Philadelphia, PA: Fortress Press.

Stephenson, Wen 2015, *What We're Fighting for Now is Each Other: Dispatches from the Front Lines of Climate Justice*, Boston, MA: Beacon Press.

Stolze, Ted 2007, 'Spinoza on the Glory of Politics', in *Spinoza: individuo e moltitudine*, edited by Riccardo Caporali, Vittorio Morfino, and Stefano Visentin, pp. 327–39, Cesena: Società Editrice 'Il Ponte Vecchio'.

Stoops, Jr., Robert F., 'Riot and Assembly: The Social Context of Acts 19: 23–41', *The Journal of Biblical Literature*, 108, 1: 73–91.

Strauss, Barry 2009, *The Spartacus War*, New York, NY: Simon and Schuster.

Strickert, Fred 2011, *Philip's City: From Bethsaida to Julias*, Collegeville, MN: Liturgical Press.

Suchting, Wal 1986, *Marx and Philosophy*, New York, NY: New York University Press.

Suhamy, Ariel 2010, *La Communication du bien chez Spinoza*, Paris: Éditions Classiques Garnier.

Suhmay, Ariel 2011, 'L'historien de la vérité. Alexandre Matheron ou la maturation des idées', *La Vie des idées* (http://www.laviedesidees.fr/L-historien-de-la-verite.html; last accessed August 2, 2013).

Swartley, Willard M. 2006, *Covenant of Peace: The Missing Peace in New Testament Theology and Ethics*, Grand Rapids, MI: William B. Eerdmans Publishing Company.

Szasz, Andrew 2008, *Shopping Our Way to Safety: How We Changed from Protecting the Environment to Protecting Ourselves*, Minneapolis, MN: University of Minnesota Press.

Tamez, Elsa 1993, *The Amnesty of Grace*, translated by Sharon H. Ringe, Nashville, TN: Abingdon Press.

Tanuro, Daniel 2013, *Green Capitalism: Why It Can't Work*, translated by Jane Ennis, London: Merlin Press.

Taubes, Jacob 2004, *The Political Theology of Paul*, translated by Dana Hollander, Palo Alto, CA: Stanford University Press.

Tavris, C. 1989, *Anger: The Misunderstood Emotion*, revised edition, New York, NY: Simon and Schuster.

Taylor, Craig 2011, *Moralism: A Study of a Vice*, Montreal: McGill-Queens University Press.

Teeple, Gary 2005, *The Riddle of Human Rights*, Amherst, NY: Humanity Books.

Terence 2001, *Phormio, The Mother-in-Law, The Brothers*, edited and translated by John Barsby, Cambridge, MA: Harvard University Press.

Thao, Trinh Van 1999 [1982], 'Conjoncture', *Dictionnaire critique du marxisme*, edited by Gérard Bensussan and Georges Labica, Paris: Presses Universitaires de France, pp. 220–5.

Thomson, George 1977 [1972], *Studies in Ancient Greek Society: The First Philosophers*, 2nd edition, London: Lawrence and Wishart.

Thompson, E.P. 2011 [1976, 1955], *William Morris: Romantic to Revolutionary*. Oakland, CA: PM Press.

Thompson, James W. 2014, *The Church according to Paul: Rediscovering the Community Conformed to Christ*, Garnd Rapids, MI: BakerAcademic.

Thompson, Marianne Meye 2015, *John: A Commentary*, Louisville, KY: Westminster John Knox Press.

Thompson, Michael J. (ed.) 2015 [2014], *Constructing Marxist Ethics: Critique, Normativity, Praxis*, Chicago, IL: Haymarket Books.

Thoreau, Henry David 1996a [1860], 'A Plea for Captain John Brown', in *Political Writings*, edited by Nancy L. Rosenblum, pp. 137–57, New York, NY: Cambridge University Press.

Thoreau, Henry David 1996b, 'Resistance to Civil Government', in *Political Writings*, edited by Nancy L. Rosenblum, pp. 1–21, New York, NY: Cambridge University Press.

Titmuss, Richard 1997 [1970], *The Gift Relationship: From Human Blood to Social Policy*, expanded and updated edition, New York, NY: The New Press.

Todes, Daniel P. 2014, *Ivan Pavlov: A Russian Life in Science*, New York, NY: Oxford University Press.

Tzvetan Todorov 1996, *Facing the Extreme: Moral Life in the Concentration Camps*, translated by Arthur Denner and Abigail Pollak, New York: Henry Holt and Company.

Toews, John E. 2004, *Romans (Believers Church Commentary)*, Scottdale, PA: Herald Press.

Toews, John E. 2009, 'The Politics of Confession', *Directions*, 38, 1: 5–16; (http://www.directionjournal.org/38/1/politics-of-confession.html; last accessed November 4, 2016).

Trebilco, Paul 2004, *The Early Christians in Ephesus from Paul to Ignatius*, Grand Rapids, MI: William B. Eerdmans Publishing Company.

Trebilco, Paul 2012, *Self-Designation and Group Identity in the New Testament*, New York, NY: Cambridge University Press.

Toscano, Alberto 2009, 'Partisan Thought', *Historical Materialism*, 17: 175–91.

Tosel, André 1992, 'Champ et dialectique des logiques de l'agir', in *Les logiques de l'agir dans la Modernité*, Paris: Les Belles Lettres.

Tosel, André 1993, 'Quelle pensée de l'action aujourd'hui?', *Actuel Marx*, 13: 16–39.

Tosel, André 1996, 'Vers une théorie néo-marxienne de l'action', *Actuel Marx*, 19: 129–39.

Tosel, André, 1992, 'Champ et dialectique des logiques de l'agir', in *Les logiques de l'agir dans la Modernité*, 40, Paris: Les Belles Lettres.

Tosel, André 1995, *Démocratie et libéralismes*, Paris: Editions Kimé.

Tosel, André 1996, *Etudes sur Marx (et Engels): vers un communisme de la Finitude*, Paris: Editions Kimé.

Tosel, André 2008, *Spinoza ou l'autre (in)finitude*, Paris: L'Harmattan.

Tosel, André 2013, 'Matérialisme de la rencontre et pensée de l'événement-miracle', in Ibrahim 2013, pp. 19–53.

Tosel, André 2016, *Émancipations aujourd'hui? Pour une reprise critique*, Paris: Éditions du Croquant.

Totaro, Giuseppina 1994, '"Acquiescentia" dans la cinquième partie de l'"Ethique" de Spinoza', *Revue de la France et de l'Étranger*, 184.

Trotsky, Leon 1977, *The History of the Russian Revolution*, translated by Max Eastman, London: Pluto Books.

Tucker, J. Brian 2014, 'The Jerusalem Collection, Economic Equality, and Human Flourishing: Is Paul's Concern the Redistribution of Wealth, or a Relationship of Mutuality (or Both)?', *Canadian Theological Review*, 3, 3: 52–70.

Tuomela, Raimo 2007, *The Philosophy of Sociality: The Shared Point of View*, New York, NY: Oxford University Press.

Turner, Denys 2013, *Aquinas: A Portrait*, New Haven, CT: Yale University Press.

Turner, J. Scott 2017, *Purpose and Desire: What Makes Something 'Alive' and Why Modern Darwinism Has Failed to Explain It*, New York, NY: HarperOne.

Unger, Roberto Mangabeira 2007, *The Self Awakened: Pragmatism Unbound*, Cambridge, MA: Harvard University Press.

Unger, Roberto and Lee Smolin 2015, *The Singular Universe and the Reality of Time*, New York, NY: Cambridge University Press.

Van der Linden, Harry 1988, *Kantian Ethics and Socialism*, Indianapolis, IN: Hackett Publishing Company.

Vandewalle, Bernard 2011, *Spinoza et la médecine: éthique et thérapeutique*, Paris: L'Harmattan.

Van Norden, Bryan W. 2017, *Taking Back Philosophy: A Multicultural Manifesto*, New York, NY: Columbia University Press.

Varotti, Carlo 1998, *Gloria e ambizione politica nei Rinascimento. Da Petrarca a Machiavelli*, Milan: Bruno Mondadori.

Veronese, Keith 2015, *Rare: The High-Stakes Race to Satisfy Our Need for the Scarcest Metals on Earth*, Amherst, NY: Prometheus Books.

Vinciguerra, Lorenzo 2009, 'Spinoza in French Philosophy Today', *Philosophy Today* 53, 4: 422–37.

Viroli, Maurizio 2000, *Niccolò's Smile*, New York, NY: Farrar, Straus and Giroux.

Wachsmann, Shelley 2009, *The Sea of Galilee Boat*, College Station, TX: Texas A&M University Press.

Waldron, Jeremy 1987, *Nonsense upon Stilts: Bentham, Burke and Marx on the Right*.

Weeden, Theodore J. 2008, 'Polemics as a Case for Dissent: A Response to Richard Bauckham's *Jesus and the Eyewitnesses*', *Journal for the Study of the Historical Jesus*, 6, 2: 211–24.

Weeks, Philip 2001, *Farewell, My Nation: The American Indian and the United States in the Nineteenth Century*, 2nd edition, Wheeling, IL: Harlan Davidson.

Welborn, L.L. 2012, review of Bruce W. Longenecker, *Remember the Poor: Paul, Poverty, and the Greco-Roman World*, *Review of Biblical Literature* [http://www.bookreviews.org].

Welborn, L.L. 2013, '"That There May Be Equality": The Contexts and Consequences of a Pauline Ideal', *New Testament Studies*, 59, 1, pp. 73–90.

Wenar, Leif 2016, *Blood Oil: Tyrants, Violence, and the Rules that Run the World*, New York, NY: Oxford University Press.

Wendling, Amy E. 2011, *Karl Marx on Technology and Alienation*, New York, NY: Palgrave Macmillan.

Wengst, Klaus 1987, *Pax Romana and the Peace of Jesus Christ*, translated by John Bowden, London: SCM Press Ltd.

Wengst, Klaus 1988, *Humility: Solidarity of the Humiliated*, translated by John Bowden, Philadelphia, PA: Fortress Press.

Wetlesen, Jon 1977, 'Body awareness as a gateway to eternity: a note on the mysticism of Spinoza and its affinity to Buddhist meditation', in *Speculum Spinozanum*, edited by Siegfried Hessing, pp. 479–94, Boston, MA: Routledge and Kegan Paul.
Wetlesen, Jon 1979, *The Sage and the Way: Spinoza's Ethics of Freedom*, Assen, The Netherlands: Van Gorcum.
Wilcove, David S. 2007, *No Way Home: The Decline of the World's Great Animal Migrations*, Washington, D.C.: Island Press.
Wilde, Lawrence 1998, *Ethical Marxism and its Radical Critics*, Basingstoke: Macmillan.
Wilde, Lawrence 2013, *Global Solidarity*, Edinburgh: Edinburgh University Press Ltd.
Wilde, Lawrence 2015, 'The Marxian Roots of Radical Humanism', in Thompson 2015, pp. 32.
Wijkman, Anders and Johan Rockström 2012, *Bankrupting Nature: Denying Our Planetary Boundaries*, revised edition, New York, NY: Routledge.
Williams, Caroline 2012, 'Thinking the Space of the Subject *between* Hegel and Marx', in *Between Hegel and Spinoza: A Volume of Critical Essays*, pp. 170–85, edited by Hasana Sharp and Jason E. Smith, New York, NY: Bloomsbury.
Williams, David 2005, *A People's History of the Civil War*, New York, NY: The New Press.
Williams, David 2014, *I Freed Myself: African American Self-Emancipation in the Civil War Era*, New York, NY: Cambridge University Press.
Williams, James 2011, *Gilles Deleuze's Philosophy of Time: A Critical Introduction and Guide*, Edinburgh: Edinburgh University Press.
Williams, Margaret H. 2015, 'From Shimon to Petros – Petrine Nomenclature in the Light of Contemporary Onomastic Practices', in Bond and Hurtado 2015, pp. 30–45.
Wilson, Edward O. 2016, *Half-Earth: Our Planet's Fight for Life*, New York, NY: Liveright.
Wilson, Michael and Deborah Rosenfelt 1978, *Salt of the Earth*, New York: The Feminist Press at CUNY.
Winstanley, Gerrard 1965 [1941], *The Works of Gerrard Winstanley*, edited by George Sabine, NY: Russell & Russell.
Winstanley, Gerrard 1983 [1973], *The Law of Freedom and Other Writings*, edited by Christopher Hill, Cambridge: Cambridge University Press.
Wolfe Charles T. 2016, *Materialism: A Historico-Philosophical Introduction*, Heidelberg: Springer.
Wood, Ellen Meiksins 2016 [1995], *Democracy Against Capitalism: Renewing Historical Materialism*, New York, NY: Verso.
Wood, Ellen Meiksins and Neal Wood 1997, *A Trumpet of Sedition: Political Theory and the Rise of Capitalism, 1509–1688*, Washington Square, NY: New York University Press.
Wootton, David 2015, *The Invention of Science: A New History of the Scientific Revolution*, London: Allen Lane.
Wright, Eric Olin 2010, *Envisioning Real Utopias*, New York, NY: Verso.
Young, Iris Marion 1990, *Justice and the Politics of Difference*, Princeton, NJ: Princeton University Press.

Young, Iris Marion 2001, 'Activist Challenges to Deliberative Democracy', *Political Theory*, 29, 5: 670–90.
Younge, Gary 2013, *The Speech: The Story behind Dr. Martin Luther King Jr.'s Dream*, Chicago, IL: Haymarket Books.
Zarka, Yves-Charles 1999, *La decision métaphysique de Hobbes: Conditions de la politique*, deuxième edition augmentée, Paris: Vrin, 1999.
Zehner, Ozzie 2012, *Green Illusions: The Dirty Secrets of Clean Energy and the Future of Environmentalism*, Lincoln: University of Nebraska Press.
Zerbe, Gordon Mark 2012, *Citizenship: Paul on Peace and Politics*, Winnipeg, Manitoba, CMU Press.
Zerbe, Gordon Mark 2015, 'From Retributive to Distributive Justice in Romans', *Direction*, 44, 1: 43–58; (http://www.directionjournal.org/44/1/from-retributive-to-restorative-justice.html; last accessed October 28, 2016).
Zerbe, Gordon Mark 2016, *Philippians (Believers Church Commentary)*, Harrisonburg, VA: Herald Press.
Zevit, Ziony 2013, *What Really Happened in the Garden of Eden?*, New Haven, CT: Yale University Press.
Zimmerman, Andrew 2015, 'From the Second American Revolution to the First International and Back Again', in Downs and Masur, pp. 304–36.
Zinn, Howard 1990, *Declarations of Independence: Cross-Examining American Ideology*, New York, NY: HarperCollins.
Žižek, Slavoj 1993, *Tarrying with the Negative: Kant, Hegel, and the Critique of Ideology*, Durham, NC: Duke University Press.
Žižek, Slavoj 2000, 'Class Struggle or Postmodernism? Yes, please!' in Judith Butler, Ernesto Laclau, and Slavoj Zizek, *Contingency, Hegemony, Universality: Contemporary Dialogues on the Left*, pp. 90–135, New York, NY: Verso.
Žižek, Slavoj 2004, *Organs without Bodies: On Deleuze and Consequences*, New York, NY: Routledge.
Žižek, Slavoj 2005, 'Against Human Rights', *New Left Review*, 34: 115–31.
Žižek, Slavoj 2008 [1989], *The Sublime Object of Ideology*, 2nd edition, New York, NY: Verso.
Žižek, Slavoj 2010, 'How to Begin from the Beginning', in *The Idea of Communism*, edited by Costas Douzinas and Slavoj Žižek, New York, NY: Verso, pp. 209–26.
Žižek, Slavoj 2012, *Less Than Nothing: Hegel and the Shadow of Dialectical Materialism*, New York, NY: Verso.
Žižek, Slavoj (ed.) 2013, *The Idea of Communism 2: The New York Conference*, New York, NY: Verso.
Žižek, Slavoj 2013, 'Preface', in *The Privatization of Hope*, edited by Peter Thompson and Slavoj Žižek, Durham, NC: Duke University Press.
Žižek, Slavoj 2014a, *Absolute Recoil: Towards a New Foundation for Dialectical Materialism*, New York, NY: Verso.

Žižek, Slavoj 2014b, *Event: A Philosophical Journey through a Concept*, Brooklyn, NY: Melville House.

Žižek, Slavoj 2015, 'Ecology against Mother Nature: Slavoj Žižek on *Molecular Red*' (http://www.versobooks.com/blogs/2007-ecology-against-mother-nature-slavoj-zizek-on-molecular-red; last accessed 31 May, 2015).

Zourabichvili, François 1996, *Deleuze: Une philosophie de l'événement*, 2nd edition, Paris: Presses Universitaires de France.

Zourabichvili, François 1998, 'Deleuze et le possible (de l'involontarisme en politique)', in *Gilles Deleuze: Une vie philosophique*, pp. 335–57, Paris: Institut Synthélabo.

Zourabichvili, François 2002, *Le conservatisme paradoxal de Spinoza: Enfance et royauté*, Paris: Presses Universitaires de France.

Index

Abramsky, Chimen   172n84, 270n38, 274n52
Action
   Marxist theory of   32–4
   Collective   309–16
Adams, Edward   55–6n86
Adamson, Peter   338–9
Adorno, Theodor   311
Adjustment, Philosophical   10–1, 58n102
Affects
   of resistance   163
   Remedies for   168–71
Alliez, Eric   230n20
Almog, Joseph   151n64
Alquié, Ferdinand   22
Althusser, Louis   xiv, 3, 9–16, 28–9, 36–7, 40, 48–9, 75–92, 104n25, 153, 158, 179, 202n12, 207, 221–35, 302, 322n2, 328, 335n53
   Theory of ideology   40, 45–8, 82–3, 302n54, 309–10
Anderson, Kevin   305n4
Anderson, Kevin B.   198n51
Anderson, Perry   216, 273n48
Anger/Indignation   113–7, 159–61
Angus, Ian   177, 304n3, 316, 321, 349n115, 350n120
Anselm   63n17
Antipater   329
Anti-Semitism
   Sartre on   293–6
Aquinas, Thomas   332, 337n61
Aristotle   35n158, 60, 167, 322–28, 351n127
Ash, Stephen   286n107
Averroes   28n122, 322, 332, 336–43, 345, 346n97

Badiou, Alain   xiii, 44, 48, 50–2, 55, 57, 58n98, 66, 71n56, 191–3
Baer, Hans   307n15, 312n40
Bakunin, Mikhail   274, 281n77
Balibar, Etienne   103n21, 108n37, 148n46, 172–3, 226n13,15, 265–70, 271, 279, 301
Balling, Pieter   144
Baltas, Aristides   138n61
Banks, Robert   66n26

Barclay, John   61n9, 67–8, 74n73
Barnes, Timothy   86–87n59
Barnosky, Anthony D.   304n3
Barnouw, Jeffrey   94n4
Baron, Naomi S.   209n43
Bartholomew, Amy   284n93
Bastiat, Frédéric   327n19
Bauckham, Richard   57–8, 80n76, 121n26
Baudrillard, Jean   199–210
Bayle, Pierre   342–5
Baynes, Kenneth   254
Beauvoir, Simone de   296, 313
Becoming
   Marxist   xix
   Muslim   301
   Revolutionary   219–20
Benjamin, Walter   245n49
Benn, Stanley   100n13
Bennett, Jonathan   141n10
Bennett, Jr., Lerone   285n103, 291n121
Bennett, Lisa   305–6
Bensaid, Daniel   198n52
Berg, Scott   284n92
Bergant, Dianne   244n43
Bergson, Henri   230n20
Berlin, Ira   286–287, 290n119
Bernard, Claude   177–81
Berners-Lee, Mike   305n4, 312n43
Berrigan, Daniel   xiv
Bertrand, Michèle   274n53
Betz, Hans-Dieter   43n29
Bhaskar, Roy   27–8, 271–2
Bidet, Jacques   83, 137n59, 160, 186n40, 248n1
Billecoq, Alain   331, 343n89
Black, David Alan   66n28
Blackburn, Robin   274
Blackett, R.J.M.   272n44
Blackledge, Paul   158n27, 274n50
Bland, Sandra   91n79
Blanton, Ward   45n36, 57n93, 58n98, 70n49
Blechman Max   161n43
Bloch, Ernst   20, 200–1, 207–8, 235–6, 241, 245n49, 276–7, 322n3, 323n5, 332n42
Bloch, Jan Robert   277n64
Bloch, Marc   173n87

INDEX

Boer, Roland   155, 274n53
Boman, Thorleif   242n31
Bordewich, Fergus G.   272n44
Borg, Marcus   48n50
Boundas, Constantin V.   230n20
Bove, Laurent   112n3, 113n4, 6, 151–2, 163
Boxel, Hugo   331
Bratman, Michael   314n53
Brecher, Jeremy   263n4, 316, 319–21
Breen, T.H.   161
Brenet, Jean-Baptiste   337n62
Brenner, Johanna   283n87
Brenner, Robert   274n50
Breton, Stanislas   48n51, 50
Brighouse, Harry   273n48
Brockmuehl, Markus   89
Bronner, Stephen Eric   296–7, 301
Brooks, Thom   273n48
Brown, John   280–1
Brudney, David   178
Brueggemann, Walter   60n3, 121n26, 240
Bruno, Giordano   147n45
Burke, Edmund   242n27, 243
Burkett, Paul   177
Burnes, James MacGregor   263n4
Burns, Stewart   263n4
Butler, Judith   83

Callinicos, Alex   247, 275, 311
Camus, Albert   113n3
Canguilhem, Georges   177, 179–80
Cannon, Walter Bradford   177, 184–6
Capitalism   35n157, 80, 121, 154–6, 159, 178, 182, 217, 219, 246, 249n14, 251, 253–4, 273n50, 283n87, 284, 288, 306–9, 312, 316–9, 322, 347
Carnap, Rudolf   24–26
Carter, Warren   46n40, 47, 85n47
Casey, Maurice   84n41
Cavaillès, Jean   173n87
Chanteur, Janine   104n24
Chittick, William C.   299n29
Cicero   123
Civility   279
Clark, Brett   308–9
Clark, Duncan   305n4, 312n43
Climate Change   305–6, 309, 311–2, 318, 349
Cohen, G.A.   157n19

Coker, K. Jason   58n99
Collier, Andrew   27–8, 31
Collin, Denis   154n4, 157n23, 158
Collins, Henry   172n84, 270n38, 274n52
Collins, John J.   241n22
Communism
  Marx and Engels on   35n157, 148n47
  Spinoza on the 'communism of minds (and bodies)'   148n47, 150–1
  Tosel on   34
Comte-Sponville, André   157
Conjuncture
  Philosophical   xiii, 12, 22, 36–38, 45, 78, 82, 85, 87–8, 91, 129, 171n81, 332n43, 346, 349
  Elements of Paul's   38–49, 59, 66, 73
Conversion   313
Conway, Erik   306
Coombes, Sam   313n48
Coulthard, Glen Sean   284n92
Courage
  Spinoza on   113n3, 132, 153, 163–6, 169–70, 172–3, 198, 312, 316
  See also fortitude; generosity
Cox, Harvey   200n7
Craven, Greg   305
Creach, Jerome F.D.   299n30
Crenshaw, James L.   244n43
Critchley, Simon   161
Crofts, Daniel W.   285n104
Cromwell, Oliver   127–8
Crossan, John Dominic   37n6, 45, 48n50, 64
Cullen, Heidi   308n18
Cullmann, Oscar   92n80

Daedalus   326n17
Damasio, Antonio   181n22, 197n43
Darwin, Charles   179
Davidson, Herbert A.   337n60, 339n69, 341–2
Davies, Brian   332n46
Dean, Jodi   290
Deborin, A.M.   151
Debs, Eugene Victor   288
Debt and debt cancellation   60–74
Deleuze, Gilles   xi, xiii, 20, 81n29, 112, 129, 140n6, 145n37, 157, 211–34, 301, 309n27, 350
Del Lucchese, Filippo   113n6, 136–7, 163n51

Demetrius of Ephesus   40–4
Democritus   331
Dennett, Daniel   3
Depew, David J.   322n3
Derber, Charles   307n15, 319
Derrida, Jacques   22
Desanti, Jean-Toussaint   3, 7–9, 26
Descartes, René   20, 22, 96n9, 101n16
Des Pres, Terrence   275
Deutscher, Penelope   313n49
De Waal, Frans   324n10
Dews, Peter   216
Dignity   275–8
Djedi, Youcef   332n44
Donnelly, Jack   265n16
Douglass, Frederick   263, 270, 281n77, 288
Downs, David   72n59
Downs, Gregory P.   291n122, 125
Doyle, Don H.   292n128
Draper, Hal   xiin1, 158, 172n85, 271n39
Droit, Roger-Pol   150
DuBois, Page   40n19
Du Bois, W.E.B   283, 291, 292n127
Dunaway, Finis   314–5
Dunbar-Ortiz, Roxanne   284n92
Duncombe, Stephen   159n32
Dunn, James A.   51n68, 58n99, 74n68, 86n59
Dussel, Enrique   158n27

Eagleton, Terry   155n10, 310, 323–4, 325n13
Ecological Rift   307–9
Ecosocialism   177, 182, 184, 186, 319–21, 349n115
Edmundson, William A.   273n48
Ehrenfeld, John   348
Ehrensperger, Kathy   66n28
Elliott, John H.   87n61
Elliott, Neil   44–5n32, 48n52, 73
Emancipation
  Paul on   73
  vs. liberation   28, 141, 271–2
Encounter, philosophical
  vs. intervention   211–2
Encroachment, philosophical   14, 12, 26, 337n61
  See also reversal, philosophical; tendency, philosophical
Engels, Friedrich   7n23, 284n99

Enthusiasm   105–6
Environment
  External vs. internal   179–80, 182
  See also homeostasis; metabolism
Epictetus   167
Epicurus   12–3, 322, 331
Esposito, Roberto   336n56, 340n74, 346
Eternity   13, 28n122, 39n13, 70, 83, 126–38, 141, 143–8, 150, 165, 181, 183, 189, 191–3, 284n98, 297, 332n43, 333, 335, 337–40, 342, 345–48
  See also time
Ethics
  for Marxism   153–8, 178
  vs. Morality   157–8, 217
  of desire   217–9
Evans, Craig A.   58n99, 85n50
Evans, Gareth   89n89
Evans, Richard   78n13, 287n112
Event and counter-event   44–8, 66
  See also kairos; time

Fanon, Frantz   296
Fear
  Hobbes on   108, 109, 111
  Sartre on   293, 295, 302–3
  Spinoza on   113n3, 114–7, 119, 124, 127, 129, 131–2, 137–8, 150, 158n28, 164, 166, 168–169, 171n81
  See also hope
Feuer, Lewis   128n40
Feuerbach, Ludwig   110
Fields, Barbara J.   285
Finger, Reta Halteman   38, 65n24
Finlayson, Lorna   274n54
Foner, Eric   272n44
Fortitude
  Spinoza's conception of   153–73, 315
  See also courage; generosity
Foster, John Bellamy   177, 308–9
Foster, Russell G.   320n20
Foucault, Michel   22, 110, 158n28, 179, 193–4, 211, 217, 219
Fraenkel, Carlo   332n44
Fraser, Nancy   259
'Freely associated producers', society of   33, 148n47, 150, 178, 184, 186, 247, 325, 347
  See also communism

Freyne, Sean   85n50, 88n65
Friedmann, Georges   173, 315
Friesen, Steven J.   53n76, 68n42, 72n59

Gabel, John B.   244n42
Gabrielson, Jeremy   47n45
Gagnon, J.-H.   167n72
Generosity
    Spinoza on   68, 112–113n3, 123n3, 131, 133, 138, 141n114, 163–6, 168, 170, 172
    See also courage; fortitude
George, Charles H.   263n4
Georgi, Dieter   43, 46, 48–9, 53, 58n101, 66n34, 69–70, 72n59
Geras, Norman   178, 264, 278–9
Geuss, Raymond   309
Gift and gift Economy
    Paul on   60–74
Gilbert, Alan   322n3
Gilbert, Daniel   305–6
Gindin, Sam   247
Gleiser, Marcelo   29n128
Gleijeses, Piero   272n44
Glory
    Hobbes on   100, 121
    Machiavelli on   121n26, 129–30
    Spinoza on   120–31, 133–4
    Vainglory   100–1, 125, 133–4, 170–1, 198
    See also shame
Good, Edwin M.   237n9
Goodman, Martin   50n65
Gorman, Jack M.   311n35
Gorman, Michael   49n57
Gorman, Sarah E.   311n35
Gourevitch, Alex   292n130
Gnuse, Robert   60n3
Gottshalk, Peter   297–9
Graeber, David   60
Gratton, Peter   29n131
Gray, Patrick   58n97
Graziosi, Barbara   39–40
Green, Todd   300, 301n34
Greenberg, Gabriel   297–299
Greenfield, Susan   209n43
Groff, Ruth   322n3
Gross, Charles G.   180n14
Guattari, Félix   xii, 112, 211–20, 272–3, 301n36, 309n27
Guelzo, Allen C.   283n92

Gueroult, Martial   22
Gutiérrez, Gustavo   239, 244
Guttman, Amy   282

Habel, Norman   236n8
Habermas, Jürgen   xiii, 248–60
Hadly, Elizabeth A.   304n3
Hadot, Pierre   167n75, 173n87
Hahn, Steven   283n90
Hall, Edith   41n22, 42n25
Hallett, Steve   312n42
Hankins, Davis   236n8
Hansen, James E.   305n4
Happiness
    Aristotle on *eudaimonia* ('flourishing')   324–5
    Jesus's beatitudes   350–1
    Aquinas on beatitude   332n46
    Averroes on beatitude   340–2
    Marx on illusory vs. real happiness   323–4, 349
    Marx on flourishing   325–8
    Morris on utopia   329–31
    Spinoza on beatitude   331–6, 347
    Sustainability as ecological flourishing   347–9
Harding, Vincent   285
Hardt, Michael   161, 246n57, 283
Harman, Chris   263n4, 308n21
Hartin, Patrick J.   58n100
Harvey, David   306n12, 308n17, 309n27, 318–9, 328, 350n118
Haslanger, Sally   271n41
Hatred
    Sartre on   294–5, 297
    Spinoza on   112–113n3, 131–3, 142–3, 165–6, 168–70
    See also love
Hedges, Chris   312, 317–8
Hegel, Georg Friedrich Wilhelm   6, 21, 93, 187–8, 206, 242–3, 335n54
Heidegger, Martin   23
Hephaestus   326n18
Herbert, Gary   96n9
Herman, Arthur   323n5
Herzog II, William R.   63n19, 64
Heyd, Michael   105–6
Hill, Christopher   106–8
Hindess, Barry   100n13

Hirschmann, Albert O.   109, 121
Historical Counterfactual   78n12, 286–7
Hobbes, Thomas   93–111, 115, 121, 125
Hobsbawm, Eric   161–2
Hochschild, Adam   272n44
Hock, Ronald   56
Hodes, Martha   286n106
Hodge, Roger   317
Holland, Tom   123n37
Holloway, John   278n66, 290–291n120, 314
Holton, Richard   167n72, 168n79, 310n30, 315n60
Homeostasis   181–6
   See also metabolism
Homeostatic disruption   178, 182, 184, 186
Honeck, Mischa   271n39
Honneth, Axel   178
Hood, Bruce   195
Hope   45–6, 52, 64, 67, 72–4, 85, 219, 249–50, 252, 263, 269, 296, 317, 329–30
   Bloch on   200
   Spinoza on   113, 115–7, 138, 159, 164, 166, 198
   See also fear
Horkheimer, Max   32, 311n36
Hörnqvist, Mikael   121n26
Horrell, David   63n17
Horsley, Richard   37n6, 50n60, 60n3, 63, 88n65, 92n81
Horwitz, Tony   281n77
Howard-Brook, Wes   63n17, 86n58
Hughes, Paul   282n80
Hurtado, Larry   92n80
Hyperreality
   Baudrillard on   202–5
Hyporeality
   Leibniz on   199–200

Ibrahim, Annie   322n2
Idealism, Philosophical   5, 19, 24, 27–8, 30–1
   See also philosophical; materialism, philosophical; tendency, philosophical
Ideology   309–10
   See also Althusser, theory of ideology
Ignatieff, Michael   275–6, 282
Ilyenkov, Ivan Vasilyevich   185–6
Illuminati, Augusto   122n32, 163n51, 336n56
Immeasurable/Immeasurability   239, 241–4
Indignation/Anger   113–7, 133, 159–61, 281

Individuality, Historical   75–92
Interpellation and counter-interpellation   46–8, 82–4, 88, 91, 302n43, 310
   See also ideology
Intervention
   Philosophical   3
   vs. Encounter   211–2
Islamophobia   293–303
Israel, Jonathan   130n45, 171n81
Israel, Menasseh ben   147n45

Jacques, Peter   348n104
James, Susan   101n18
Jaquet, Chantal   163n53, 167n72, 283n87
Jenkins, Philip   299n30
Jesus of Nazareth   43n29, 45, 49, 51, 54, 62, 63n17, 64, 65n23, 66–7, 70, 75n1, 84–91, 299n29, 350–1
   Jesus followers/loyalists/movement   xiii, 38, 40n21, 43, 44n32, 45–7, 50–5, 57–9, 61–67, 69–70, 72–3, 85–8, 90–2
Jewett, Robert   73n63
Job, Book of   235–47
Johnson, Marshall D.   244n42
Johnston, David   97n12, 108
Jolley, Nicholas   200n5
Jones, Howard   332n47
Josephy, Alvin   284n92
Jubilee   53, 60–1, 72–4
Judaken, Jonathan   297n17

Kahl, Brigette   52n75
Kairos ('now time' or 'transitional moment')   45, 52
   See also eternity; event; time
Kalupahana, David   26–27n119
Kant, Immanuel   7n22, 11, 20, 156, 163n50, 225n12, 242n28
Keazirian, Edward M.   47n45
Kenny, Anthony   339–40
Kerr-Ritchie, Jeffrey R.   283n89
Kim, Jung Suk   70n51
King, Jr., Martin Luther   200n8, 288, 349n110
Kinsler, Gloria and Ross   53n77, 72n60
Kirschenbaum, Sheril   311n35, 313n47
Klauck, Hans-Josef   43
Klein, Naomi   349
Kline, George L.   188n4
Knapp, Robert   42, 63n16

Knox, Robert   52n72
Kouvelakis, Stathis   198
Kreitzman, Leon   308n20
Kripke, Saul   88n66, 89n71
Kumar, Deepa   298–9
Kundnani, Arun   299n26
Kuznick, Peter J.   185

Lacan, Jacques   223–5, 227–8
Lapine, Nikolai   9, 19
Lapoujade, David   214n14
Laux, Henri   118, 133, 164–5, 170
Lazarus, Sylvain   91n79
Lazzeri, Christian   112n2–3, 163n49
Lebowitz, Michael   158n25, 158–159n30
Lecourt, Dominique   179–181, 201
Leibniz, Gottfried Wilhelm   199–203, 205, 207, 337–8
Lenin, V.I.   3–7, 30, 113n3, 173, 187–8, 198
Leonard, Annie   210n45, 306
Léonard, Mathieu   172n84, 270n38
Lévi-Strauss, Claude   224, 227–8
Levine, Bruce   271n39, 292n129
Liebig, Justus von   182
Liebman, Marcel   288–90
Lin, Martin   167n72
Lincoln, Abraham   283n89, 285–7, 290n119
Linebaugh, Peter   122, 130
Longenecker, Bruce   53, 66n28, 72n59
Lopez, Davina   51n66, 73n63
López, Fernando Bravo   297
Lordon, Frédéric   163n49
Losurdo, Domenico   299n31
Love
   Spinoza's theory of   141–6
   See also hatred
Lowe, Alfred   200n7
Löwy, Michael   161, 172n85, 245n49
Lucretius   13, 221n4, 322, 331
Lukes, Steven   158n27
Luria, Isaac   147n45
Luxemburg, Rosa   215n16
Lynas, Mark   305n4
Lynch, Michael Patrick   209n44
Lynd, Staughton   271n39, 272
L'Yvonnet, François   203n17

Maass, Alan   159n31
MacDonald, Margaret   58n103

Mach, Ernst   6
Macherey, Pierre   3, 4–24, 30, 32, 121, 123, 134–5, 141n14, 155n11, 166, 167n74, 168n76, 179, 187, 191, 193–5, 221, 296n15
Machiavelli, Niccolò   37, 129
MacKinnon, J.B.   321n87
Madness
   Hobbes on   93–111
Magda, Ksenija   52n72
Maimon, Salomon   335–336
Malherbe, Abraham   45n37, 46n40
Malm, Andreas   316n66
Mamdani, Mahmood   299n27, 302n41
Mandel, Ernest   215n16, 217n26
Manning, Chandra   271n39, 286n107
Manzini, Frédéric   167n70, 72, 333
Marcus, Joel   66n28
Marcuse, Herbert   160
Marquis, Timothy Luckritz   52n72
Martin, Bill   158n27
Marx, Karl   xii, 7, 12, 74, 79–81, 110, 154–6, 177–8, 181–4, 250n18, 270–4, 282–5, 292, 306n12, 307–8, 322–4, 347–50
Marxism/Marxist   xi, xiii, 3–4, 7–12, 16, 18, 23–4, 26–9, 32, 34–6, 61, 74–5, 78–9, 139–41, 151, 153–4, 155n11, 156, 158, 160, 167, 172–3, 177–80, 187, 188, 197–8, 211–2, 216–7, 219–21, 224, 228–9, 232, 234, 236, 245–7, 249, 270n38, 271n38, 273, 274n50, 279, 282, 283n87, 284, 309n27, 310, 315, 321–2, 323n5, 348
   Metaphysical vs. Political   273–4
Materialism, philosophical
   vs. idealism   4–7
   Aleatory   11–2, 322
   Averroist   27–28n122
   See also idealism, philosophical; tendency, philosophical
Matheron, Alexandre   7, 112n2, 113n6–7, 134, 139–52, 163n51, 167n72, 172n83
Mattingly, David J.   73n65
Mayor, Adrienne   326n17
McCarthy, George E.   291n123–124, 322n3
McCord, Edward L.   348
McCulloch, Gregory   88–89n67
McCulloch, John Ramsey   327n19
McGrath, Thomas   317
McKibben, Bill   306n11

McPherson, James 285–7
Meggitt, Justin 68–9
Meikle, Scott 60, 322n3
Mele, Alfred R. 167n72, 315n58, 322n3
Melamed, Yitzhak Y. 191n17, 335n54, 336n55
Merchant, Carolyn 344n94
Metabolic rift 177, 182, 184, 186
Metabolism 177, 180–2
    See also homeostasis
Meyerson, Diane 167n73, 310n32, 313n44, 315n59
Míguez, Néstor O. 46n42, 49
Miliband, Ralph 288–90
Militant Philosopher xiii–xiv
Misrahi, Robert 347
Mitov, Michel 197n44–45
Molar vs. molecular politics 212–7
Molyneux, John 3
Montag, Warren 12, 19–20, 49, 104n24, 153, 155n11, 172n83, 197n48, 205n27, 221n4
Mooney, Chris 311n35, 313n47
Moore, A.W. 192n20
Moore, Jr., Barrington 160n37
Mora, Camilo 184n28–29
Moreau, Pierre-François 140, 141n14, 344n94
Morfino, Vittorio 322n2
Morley, Neville 46n40
Morris, William 329–31
Moyn, Samuel 276, 284n99, 285n100
Multitude
    Hobbes on 93, 101–4, 106–7, 108n39, 111
    Spinoza on 113–21, 125, 130, 134, 137–8, 142n20, 148n47, 150n59, 170–1, 334
    vs. people 104
    Passive vs. active 118
    Vulgar vs. reasonable 113n3
Murata, Sachiko 299n29
Murphy, Frederick 50n65, 241n22
Murphy-O'Connor, Jerome 38
Myers, Ched 63

Nadler, Steven 123n35, 130n47, 144n34, 167n72, 74
Names and name-using practices 82n35, 88–92
Nathan, Debbie 91n79

Navarro, Fernanda 12, 153
Neale, Jonathan 312n39
Negri, Antonio 6, 111n46, 138n60, 140, 148n47, 161, 165n60, 168n77, 212n5, 213, 235–47, 249, 267, 283
Nero 114n8, 120
Nested concepts 181
Newman, Richard 271n39
Newsom, Carol A. 236n8, 241n20
Nichols, David A. 284n92
Nickel, James 265n16
Nickle, Keith F. 71n56, 72n59
Niebuhr, Gustav 284n92
Niebuhr, Reinhold 318
Nienhuis, David R. 87n61
Nietzsche, Friedrich 12, 66
Nimtz, Jr., August H. 172n84, 270n38
Noble, Denis 177
Nonlocality, Mental 345–346n96
Noonan, Jeffrey 30n134, 35n159
Novenson, Matthew 45n32
Nussbaum, Martha 117n18, 273n48, 282

Oakes, Peter 46n44, 55n86, 65n24, 69n42, 70–1, 73n67, 74
Oakman, Douglas 62n14, 85n53
Ogereau, Julien M. 53n76, 66n26, 72n59
Olson, Randy 311n35
Oreskes, Naomi 306
Osiek, Cynthia 58n103
Ovid 167

Pacchi, Arrigo 96
Panitch, Leo 247
Parnet, Claire 211, 213, 219, 230n20
Parousia ('return', 'arrival', 'appearance') 45
Parr, Adrian 348n108
Partisanship, philosophical 4–7
Passions
    Hobbes on 93–7
Patterson, Herb 128
Patterson, Stephen J. 90n76
Patton, Paul 273n48
Paul of Tarsus xiii, 36–74, 89–90n72, 167n71
Paul, L.A. 349
Pautrat, Bernard 141n13
Pavlov, Ivan 185
Pêcheux, Michel 31, 47n46, 48n48, 302n43
Peffer, Rodney 157n19

INDEX

Pennington, Jonathan T.   351n127
Peters, Shawn Francis   xivn9
Phillips, Thomas E.   38n9
Pierce, Charles P.   311n36
Pinkard, Terry   196
Planetary boundaries   304–5, 308, 350
Plato   23
Plekhanov, Georgi   76n6, 77, 78n13
Pliny the Younger   43–4
Politics of the third kind   136–7, 146–51
  See also eternity
Pope, Marvin   236n8
Popper, Karl   259
Porter, Roy   180, 182
Portier-Young, Anathea E.   241n22
Postel, Danny   282n83
Power, Carla   301n37
Practice
  Paul's   48–57
  Primacy of   25, 31–2
Prawer, S.S.   329
Prigogine, Ilya   29
Prophets   118–20
Public sphere
  Weak vs. strong   259
Punt, Jeremy   47n47
Puskas, Charles B.   65n25

Quiniou, Yvon   154, 157n19, 22

Rachels, James   311–2
Raines, John   245n47
Rall, Ted   162n48
Raven, Heidi   154–155n9
Rawls, John   137, 156, 248n1, 273, 274n54, 282, 284n96
Ramond, Charles   112–113n3, 113n5, 333n50
Raymond, Pierre   3, 12, 30
Read, Jason   103n21, 268n29
Realism, philosophical   5, 28–9
  See also idealism; philosophical; materialism, philosophical
Reasoner, Mark   65n25, 66n28, 68
Rebellion
  Spinoza on   112–38
Rediker, Marcus   122, 130
Reed, Jonathan   37n6, 45
Reed, T.V.   159n32
Reeve, C.D.C.   324n7,11, 325n12

Resch, Robert Paul   231n26
Resistance   15, 33, 49, 58n99, 66, 75, 85n53, 112n3, 113, 116–7, 120, 137, 160–1, 163, 173, 218–9, 263n5, 267, 273n49, 284n92, 302
Reversal, philosophical   12, 14, 24, 46–7, 81n29, 84, 203n17, 336
  See also encroachment, philosophical; tendency, philosophical
Ricard, Hubert   332n43–44
Richards, E. Randolph   66n31
Richards, Leonard L.   285n104
Ricoeur, Paul   5, 28–9
Rizk, Hadi   139n4
Roberts, William Clare   181, 292n130
Rockström, Johan   304n1, 305n4
Roediger, David   283, 29–292n125–126
Rogers, Heather   348n108
Rorty, Richard   263–5, 270n38, 271, 281
Rose, Steven   306
Rosenfelt, Deborah Silverton   280n73
Rosenthal, Michael   343n89
Rosner, Brian   43n27
Roudinesco, Elisabeth   179n9
Rovelli, Carlo   26
Rowe, C. Kavin   44n31
Ruda, Frank   7n22, 323n5
Ruben, David-Hillel   6
Ruden, Sarah   49n54

Saito, Kohei   177–8
Sartre, Jean-Paul   29n129, 139, 157, 158n28, 293–303, 271, 273n47
Soto, Makiko   305n4
Sayre, Robert   161
Schama, Simon   125
Scheffler, Samuel   349n112
Schifferdecker, Kathryn   236n8
Schottroff, Luise   63n19
Schwartz, Seth   50–51n65
Scot, Michael   342n85
Scott, James C.   160–1
Scull, Andrew   110n45
Schüssler Fiorenza, Elisabeth   47n47
Seaford, Richard   27n130
Self-Education, proletarian   278–9
Self-Emancipation   32, 80, 172–3, 270–292, 301, 318
  See also emancipation

Sen, Amartya 282
Serenity
  Spinoza on 134–7, 149–50
Sève, Lucien 79–83, 158n24, 331n40
Shantz, Colleen 48n50
Shame
  Spinoza on 112, 117, 120, 123–4
  See also glory
Sharp, Hasana 166, 196
Shenefelt, Michael 200n5
Shulyatikov, Vladimir Mikhailovich 187–8
Silberman, Neil 50n60
Silbertin-Blanc, Guillaume 213n8
Simon Peter 83–8
Sinha, Manisha 263n5
Skinner, Quentin 108
Slomp, Gabriela 100n152, 121n24
Smith, Dennis E. 38n9
Smith, Justin xiii
Smith, Stephen 171–2
Smolin, Lee 29–30
Socialism 60–1, 74, 153–4, 158–60, 162, 173, 212, 217, 219–20, 246n55, 249, 249n14, 251–53, 268, 273n49–50, 274, 278–9, 329, 330n33, 331
Soelle, Dorothee 245n49
Sohn-Rethel, Alfred 27n130
Sorell, Tom 110
Sotiris, Panagiotis 26n118
Spartacus 74
Spellberg, Denise 303n44
Spinoza, Baruch de 8, 12, 81n29, 83n37, 112–73, 187–98, 207, 315–6, 323n5, 350–1
Spruit, Leon 340n74
Srnicek, Nick 328n26
Stanley, Amy Dru 292n131
State of Nature
  Myth of 14–5
Ste. Croix, G.E.M. 62n11
Steenberghen, Fernand van 332n43
Steffen, Will 304n1
Stendhal, Krister 57
Stephenson, Wes 349
Still, Todd 53
Stolze, Ted 163n51
Stoops, Robert 40–41n21
Strategy
  Anti-capitalist/socialist 248, 270n38, 273n50, 289, 347

Hobbes on pitting 'passion against passion' 109
'Inverted quarantine' 313–4
Negri on 247
Paul's missionary 36, 46, 49–53, 58n99, 68
Spinoza on 'anti-fear' 166
See also self-emancipation; socialism
Strauss, Barry 74n70
Strength, Ethical 173, 316
Strickert, Fred 85n50
Structuralism
  Deleuze on 221–34
Subjectivity/self
  Hegel vs. Spinoza 192–7
Suchting, Wal 5
Suhamy, Ariel 140n6, 148n46
Surreality 201
Sustainability, Ecological 348
Swartley, Willard M. 47n45
Szasz, Andrew 313–4

Tacitus 114n8
Tamez, Elsa 66, 73
Tanuro, Daniel 312n40
Taubes, Jacob 53n76, 66n33
Tavris, Carol 159n33, 161n42
Teeple, Gary 284n93
Tendency, philosophical 3–35, 78, 331–2, 343n88
Terence 123, 130
Thao, Trinh Van 36n2
Thomas, Peter 41n22
Thompson, E.P. 274, 330
Thompson, James W. 66n26
Thompson, Marianne Meye 87n60
Thompson, Michael J. 159n27
Thoreau, Henry David 83n36, 280–281
Time
  Historical 75–6, 231–2
  Materialist 29
  Revolutionary 291–2
  See also eternity; event; kairos
Titmuss, Richard 61, 74n73
Todes, Daniel P. 185n35
Todorov, Tzvetan 275n56
Toews, John 66–67
Toscano, Alberto 4
Tosel, André 32–4, 117n18, 172n83

Transformation
  Social-political   xiv, 7n22, 28, 33, 115, 137, 198, 215n16, 272, 292, 312, 323, 351n127
  'Transformative experience'   349
  See also conversion
Transindividuality   103, 268
Transition
  Habermas on   248–60
  Paul on   68
  to (Eco)Socialism   173, 246n55, 273n49, 273n50, 319n82
  Spinoza on   145, 150, 334, 346
  Three kinds of affective   117–8, 131, 134–5, 138
  See also self-emancipation; strategy
Transversality   272–3
Trebilco, Paul   42n24, 50n60
Trotsky, Leon   215n17
Tucker, J. Brian   72n59
Tuomela, Raimo   314n53
Turner, Denys   332n46
Turner, J. Scott   179–81, 184n27
Tyson, Joseph B.   38n9

Unger, Roberto   29
Universalism   265–70
Utopian Desire   161–2

Van den Enden, Franciscus   147n45
Van der Linden, Harry   157n19, 163n50
Vandewalle, Bernard   168, 192
Varotti, Carlo   122n31
Veronese, Keith   210n46
Vinciguerra, Lorenzo   140n6, 141n12, 141n12
Viroli, Maurizio   130n49
Virtual vs. Actual   230–1, 207–209, 230, 234n37
Vitalism   178–81

Waldron, Jeremy   284n96
Wall, Robert W.   87n61
Waschmann, Shelley   92

Weakness, Ethical   167, 315
Weeden, Theodore J.   90n90
Weeks, Philip   284n92
Welborn, Laurence   51–2, 53n76, 53n80, 61, 72n59
Wenar, Leif   349
Wendling, Amy E.   328n25
Wengst, Klaus   47n45, 52n74, 72n58
Wetlesen, Jon   147n44
White, Heidi   200n5
Wijkman, Anders   305n4
Wilcove, David S.   308n19
Wilde, Lawrence   322n3
Williams, Alex   328n26
Williams, Chris   307n15
Williams, David   283n89, 284n92
Williams, James   231n26
Wilson, Edward O.   307n14, 349n116
Wilson, Michael   280n73
Winstanley, Gerard   106–7, 122, 128
Wolfe, Charles T.   27n122
Wood, Ellen Meiksins   104n24, 172n85, 274–5
Wood, Neal   104n24
Wootton, David   332n47
Wright, Erik Olin   159n34

York, Richard   308–9
Young, Iris Marion   271n41, 280n76
Younge, Gary   349n110

Zarka, Yves-Charles   93n3, 96–7
Zehner, Ozzie   312
Zerbe, Gordon   47n45, 50n62, 54n82, 61n5, 62n10, 66n26, 68n40, 71
Zimmerman, Andrew   27n9, 291n124
Zinn, Howard   310
Žižek, Slavoj   3, 30n138, 48, 88n67, 148n47, 187–98, 213n10, 285n100, 313n45
Zourabichvili, François   134, 138n62, 171n81, 231n26, 234n37

www.ingramcontent.com/pod-product-compliance
Lightning Source LLC
Chambersburg PA
CBHW071145070526
44584CB00019B/2662